THE GREAT LEGAL PHILOSOPHERS

THE GREAT LEGAL PHILOSOPHERS

PHILOSOPHERS

Selected Readings in Jurisprudence

edited by

CLARENCE MORRIS

PROFESSOR OF LAW
UNIVERSITY OF PENNSYLVANIA

PHILADELPHIA
UNIVERSITY OF PENNSYLVANIA PRESS

ISBN: 0-8122-1008-5 (Paper)
ISBN: 0-8122-7050-9 (Cloth)

PRINTED IN THE UNITED STATES OF AMERICA

For
My Mother

"The great jurists who have been actively engaged in the development of the law are always numbered among the greatest men of the human race. Their names are being mentioned and their works are being read centuries after they have departed this life."

—EUGEN EHRLICH, *Fundamental Principles of the Sociology of Law*
(Moll trans.), p. 355

"One man cannot make another a philosopher, however much learning he may impart, though he may help him to become one; for it is only by the exercise of his own reason, by thinking for himself, that one becomes a philosopher.

". . . Whoever wants to become a philosopher must view all systems of philosophy as merely a history of the use of reason and as material on which to exercise his philosophic talent."

—J. H. W. STUCKENBERG, *Life of Immanuel Kant*, pp. 74–75

Preface

This compendium is an attempt to give readers in one volume a speaking acquaintance with the great legal philosophers of the ages. It is large—a little too heavy for comfortable reading. Yet each chapter is a lean abridgment. Perhaps I could have squeezed out a few more pages, but expunging the unnecessary engaged me past the point of diminishing returns.

My selection is more intuitive than reasoned. Some of my omissions do not lend themselves to closely reasoned defense. Inclusions are more easily justified.

One Greek seemed to be about all I could afford, and the choice seemed clearly to be Aristotle—the most influential, the most representative. Rome abounded in important lawyers, but few legal philosophers. Marcus Tullius Cicero (often cited as "Tully" by Thomas Aquinas) seemed the clear choice here. Aquinas towered in influence in the Middle Ages—in fact, his influence is lively today. Hugo Grotius is an important link between ancient legal philosophy and modern jurisprudential thought. These four were all the earlier thinkers that could be included without making the work too antiquarian.

Hobbes, Locke, Montesquieu, Hume, and Rousseau were the giants of legal philosophy in the times of burgeoning nationalism. They represent many directions taken by jurisprudential thought when first freed from feudalism and theology and reacting to science.

Kant and Hegel illustrate jurisprudential flights into metaphysics and influenced, directly or indirectly, the great legal philosophy that followed.

Little-known Savigny, representative of the important Historical school, seemed a better choice than the more obscure Puchta.

Though Bentham, Austin, and Mill all call themselves Utilitarians and purport to start from the same premises, their differences are striking. Bentham's advocacy of legislative law making, Austin's talent for close analysis, and Mill's humanitarianism and concern for civil liberty give each an important, unshared place.

Holmes, Dewey, and von Ihering represent three widely differing views of modern pragmatic or instrumental approaches to law. Ehrlich's "sociology of law" has a broader societal base than Pound's more pragmatic "social engineering." Jean Dabin is a fine representative of current neo-Thomism. Many-sided Cardozo, with his ability to draw on ideas of the ages, was an obvious candidate.

Omissions that were hardest to make were, for the most part, contemporaries—Thurman Arnold, Edmund Cahn, Jerome Frank, Max Weber, Morris R. Cohen, Hans Kelsen, and others. They may come to have much greater influence than some of the writers included. A collector who leaves out Plato has at least put other omitted great legal philosophers in fine company. Morris R. Cohen himself once said at close of a too-short essay, "But the limitations of space, like death, are not conducive to a rational development and ending." Perhaps another time a publisher may be willing to print a compendium of 20th century abridgments for me.

My biographical notes are based on secondary sources. I lay no claim to skill in historiography and have done no research in original materials. Philosophers' writings have more interest for me when focused against their lives and times, and I have tried to instill the same interest in readers by doing quick amateur profiles. These biographical notes may be a little like Montesquieu's reports on folkways; he seems to give easy credence to all bizarre tales about faraway practices; I tend to report all colorful anecdotes about my subjects (though I finally did bring myself to delete a tale about one philosopher whiling away time by tossing peanuts in the air and catching them in his mouth).

No bibliography of commentaries on the works abridged is offered, for two reasons: (1) I have not tried, extensively, to read the secondary material and have not done the work on which such a bibliography must be based. (2) By and large I recommend extended study of legal philosophers rather than study of commentaries on them. At times, however, orientation and explanation make the study of legal philosophers more rewarding. Two reference books have proved especially valuable to me: Patterson's *Jurisprudence, Men and Ideas of the Law,* in which all twenty-two philosophers are discussed, and Sabine's *History of Political Theory,* which is especially valuable for an understanding of philosophies as abstruse as, for example, Hegel. But one who must ration his time and read either about the great legal philosophers or their own works will usually be wiser to stick to the latter, even if the return is slow and comes only after re-readings.

Though I hope this book proves interesting to lawyers and other post-graduate readers, my main goal was development of a course-book for law students. I have taught courses and seminars in jurisprudence for several years; they seem more effective when focused on a few great thinkers, than when organized more topically—as are such fine collections as Hall's *Readings in Jurisprudence,* and Simpson and Stone's *Law and Society.* These books give me too little of each writer, too scant a chance to think about each philosopher's integrated system. I prefer to sacrifice breadth of such books for a little more depth on the work of fewer philosophers. Still this compendium covers much ground and, therefore, does not cut very deep; it, too, is a survey—but my transit focuses widely on each corner and gives a graphic view of some important landmarks.

I ask my students to read comparatively. After we have studied, say, Aristotle for two class hours, we read Cicero to find out how he differs from, or agrees with, Aristotle. Then we compare Aquinas with the earlier two. Later, we try to compare Mill with the dozen philosophers already read, and still later we try to compare Cardozo with a score of other thinkers. Of course, in a two semester hour course, detailed comparison of each philosopher with every other is impossible, but significant resemblances and differences make for lively discussion. My lesson plans have changed radically each time I teach these materials; when they stabilize, the course should be assigned to another teacher.

Twenty-two philosophers are a few too many for a two-hour course. Only the most apt students can cover nineteen or twenty. Perhaps the course would be better if still fewer philosophers were studied. My own candidates for omission (assignments vary from year to year) are Cicero, Grotius, Hegel (because he is too hard, and in spite of his importance), Ihering, and Pound. Perhaps some years I may bring myself to omitting Montesquieu, or Austin, or Dewey—but I'll do so only with a tear. I have cut down coverage by assigning only one of the two works of Mill, Dewey, and Holmes.

The index, which has not yet been made as I write this preface, will be an exhaustive, topical one. It will be valuable to me for spotting points of comparison. Perhaps other teachers and students may get some help from it.

Legal philosophy has never been my full-time vocation. While this compendium has been in the making I taught, wrote, and thought in other fields. These words are not by way of apology, but by way of encouragement. Part-time legal philosophy can satisfyingly put in perspective the lives of us who work in the law.

CLARENCE MORRIS

*University of Pennsylvania Law School
Summer, 1957*

Contents

Contents

1

Aristotle

384–322 B.C.

In a little Greek colonial town, Stagira, on the shore of the Aegean sea, Aristotle's father practiced medicine—after better days as court physician to Amyntas II, king of Macedonia. Here Aristotle was born and grew up on the rim of the Greek world. At seventeen he left home to study at the hub of Greek culture—the Academy at Athens. There he became a favorite disciple of aging Plato, and studied, researched, and taught for twenty years. Plato was sixty-one when Aristotle arrived at the Academy; he was engaged in fine embroidery on his philosophic system, the main lines of which had become set. Plato was a beloved master who, as head of the Academy, presided over a circle of intellectual friends. Aristotle fitted comfortably into these surroundings; though his interests differed from his master's the two had no disturbing disagreements. Plato's death at eighty-one was a bitter loss to Aristotle.

Speusippis, Plato's nephew, inherited headship of the Academy. Several of Plato's disciples, including Aristotle, would not serve under him. Aristotle went to Assus, where a group of Platonists gathered around Hermias—a tycoon-eunuch with scholarly pretensions. Here Aristotle set up a school and taught for three years, and in middle age married Hermias' adopted daughter.

Shortly after his marriage he moved to the Island of Lesbos where he spent the next two years in studious quietude. This idyl ended when he accepted a call to the court of Macedonia to tutor crown-prince Alexander who later became world-conquering Alexander the Great. He taught Alexander for seven years. When Alexander became king, Aristotle quit wandering and returned to Athens, which was still the favorite gathering place of Greek intellectuals.

Aristotle did not rejoin the Academy. Instead he set up his own school in the Lyceum, a grove out of the city, decorated with colonnades and shrines sacred to Apollo and the Muses. Here Aristotle devised a scholarly way of life for students and teachers; he established a library and a museum; he attracted many disciples. He liked to teach informally on walks through Lyceum gardens; because of his walking-talking method his school was called Peripatetic. In this school Aristotle's writings were reorganized, developed, and edited. His learning expanded to include and order virtually all the knowledge of his time.

When Aristotle reached sixty-one, his world fell apart. Political forces that had favored him waned. He was looked on with suspicion and accused (as was Socrates before him) of impiety. Unlike Socrates he was not philosophic enough to await hemlock; he fled to his mother's home in Chalcis. Though he eluded his enemies, he did not escape from death—he died of disease within a year.

It is said that Aristotle spoke with a lisp, was foppishly careful of his appearance, had great affection for and took loving care of his family and dependents. One clause in his will emancipated some of his favorite slaves.

Perhaps no scholar has been more influential than Aristotle. His work was eclipsed for a few hundred years after his death, but in the last 700 years nearly all well-educated men in the Western world (and many in the Near East) have studied and respected his works—works that are characterized by a feeling for dynamics of life. Not only Christian Schoolmen, but also many important Moslem and Jewish divines sought to square their faiths with works of Aristotle. His inquiries were beginnings or milestones in diverse disciplines such as Logic, Biology, Psychology, Aesthetics, Politics, and Ethics. He was the first to identify, separate, and classify these disciplines and to recognize that each has its own appropriate methods and techniques. His civilization, simple in social organization, presented few problems resembling those plaguing law and the social sciences of today. The Greek city states were small and rural, perhaps easily ordered. Nevertheless radical legal and ethical problems were of concern even in Aristotle's world.

The excerpts that follow are from two of his treatises, the Nicomachean Ethics and the Politics. There are two Aristotelean Ethics— The Nicomachean (named after and edited by his son) and the Eudemian (named after one of Aristotle's pupils). The former, thought to be more mature, develops a theory of justice not touched on by the latter. What appears hereafter is a major part of Book V, one of the ten books of the Nicomachean Ethics. Aristotle's Politics is divided into eight books; the second set of excerpts is from only the first two of these; the last six books are more political than legal philosophy.

NICOMACHEAN ETHICS *

Book V

In regard to Justice and Injustice, we have to enquire what sort of actions precisely they are concerned with, in what sense Justice is the observance of a mean, and what are the extremes between which that which is just is a mean. . . .

* Translated by H. Rackham, in the Loeb Classical Library. Reprinted by permission of the Harvard University Press.

Now we observe that everybody means by Justice that moral disposition which renders men apt to do just things, and which causes them to act justly and to wish what is just; and similarly by Injustice that disposition which makes men act unjustly and wish what is unjust. Let us then assume this definition to start with as broadly correct . . .

. . . The terms Justice and Injustice are used in several senses, but as their equivocal uses are closely connected, the equivocation is not detected. . . .

Let us then ascertain in how many senses a man is said to be "unjust." Now the term "unjust" is held to apply both to the man who breaks the law and the man who takes more than his due, the unfair man. Hence it is clear that the law-abiding man and the fair man will both be just. "The just" therefore means that which is lawful and that which is equal or fair, and "the unjust" means that which is illegal and that which is unequal or unfair.

Again, as the unjust man is one who takes the larger share, he will be unjust in respect of good things; not all good things, but those on which good and bad fortune depend. These though always good in the absolute sense, are not always good for a particular person. Yet these are the goods men pray for and pursue, although they ought not to do so; they ought, while choosing the things that are good for them, to pray that what is good absolutely may also be good for them.

The unjust man does not however always choose the larger share: of things that, speaking absolutely, are bad he chooses the smaller share; but nevertheless he is thought to take more than his due, because the lesser of two evils seems in a sense to be a good, and taking more than one's due means taking more than one's due of good. Let us call him "unfair," for that is a comprehensive term, and includes both taking too much of good things and too little of bad things.

Again, we saw that the law-breaker is unjust and the law-abiding man just. It is therefore clear that all lawful things are just in one sense of the word, for what is lawful is decided by legislature, and the several decisions of the legislature we call rules of justice. Now all the various pronouncements of the law aim either at the common interest of all, or at the interest of a ruling class determined either by excellence or in some other similar way; so that in one of its senses the term "just" is applied to anything that produces and preserves the happiness, or the component parts of the happiness, of the political community.

And the law prescribes certain conduct; the conduct of a brave man, for example not to desert one's post, not to run away, not to throw down one's arms; that of a temperate man, for example not to commit adultery or outrage; that of a gentle man, for example not to strike, not to speak evil; and so with actions exemplifying the rest of the virtues and vices, commanding these and forbidding those—rightly if the law has been rightly enacted, not so well if it has been made at random.

Justice then in this sense is perfect Virtue, though with a qualification, namely that it is displayed towards others. This is why Justice is often thought to be the chief of the virtues, and more sublime "or than the evening or the morning star"; and we have the proverb—

In Justice is all Virtue found in sum.

And Justice is perfect virtue because it is the practice of perfect virtue; and perfect in a special degree, because its possessor can practise his virtue towards others and not merely by himself; for there are many who can practise virtue in their own private affairs but cannot do so in their relations with another. This is why we approve the saying of Bias, "Office will show a man"; for in office one is brought into relation with others and becomes a member of a community.

The same reason, namely that it involves relationship with someone else, accounts for the view that Justice alone of the virtues is "the good of others," because it does what is for the advantage of another, either a ruler or an associate. As then the worst man is he

who practises vice towards his friends as well as in regard to himself, so the best is not he who practises virtue in regard to himself but he who practises it towards others; for that is a difficult task. . . .

Now we have distinguished two meanings of "the unjust," namely the unlawful and the unequal or unfair, and two meanings of "the just," namely the lawful and the equal or fair. Injustice then, in the sense previously mentioned, corresponds to the meaning "unlawful"; but since the unfair is not the same as the unlawful, but different from it, and related to it as part to whole (for not everything unlawful is unfair, though everything unfair is unlawful), so also the unjust and Injustice in the particular sense are not the same as the unjust and Injustice in the universal sense, but different from them, and related to them as part to whole; for Injustice in this sense is a part of universal Injustice, and similarly the Justice we are now considering is a part of universal Justice. We have therefore to discuss Justice and Injustice, and the just and unjust, in the particular sense.

We may then set aside that Justice which is coextensive with virtue in general, being the practice of virtue in general towards someone else, and that Injustice which is the practice of vice in general towards someone else. It is also clear how we should define what is just and unjust in the corresponding senses. For the actions that spring from virtue in general are in the main identical with the actions that are according to law, since the law enjoins conduct displaying the various particular virtues and forbids conduct displaying the various particular vices. . . .

Particular Justice on the other hand, and that which is just in the sense corresponding to it, is divided into two kinds. One kind is exercised in the distribution of honour, wealth, and the other divisible assets of the community, which may be allotted among its members in equal or unequal shares. The other kind is that which supplies a corrective principle in private transactions. This Corrective Justice again has two sub-divisions, corresponding to the two classes of private transactions, those which are voluntary and those which are involuntary. Examples of voluntary transactions are selling, buying, lending at interest, pledging, lending without interest, depositing, letting for hire; these transactions being termed voluntary because they are voluntarily entered upon. Of involuntary transactions some are furtive, for instance, theft, adultery, poisoning, procuring, enticement of slaves, assassination, false witness; others are violent, for instance, assault, imprisonment, murder, robbery with violence, maiming, abusive language, contumelious treatment.

Now since an unjust man is one who is unfair, and the unjust is the unequal, it is clear that corresponding to the unequal there is a mean, namely that which is equal; for every action admitting of more and less admits of the equal also. If then the unjust is the unequal, the just is the equal—a view that commends itself to all without proof; and since the equal is a mean, the just will be a sort of mean too. Again, equality involves two terms at least. It accordingly follows not only that (a) the just is a mean and equal [and relative to something and just for certain persons], but also (b) that, as a mean, it implies certain extremes between which it lies, namely the more and the less; (c) that, as equal, it implies two shares that are equal; and (d) that, as just, it implies certain persons for whom it is just. It follows therefore that justice involves at least four terms, namely, two persons for whom it is just and two shares which are just. And there will be the same equality between the shares as between the persons, since the ratio between the shares will be equal to the ratio between the persons; for if the persons are not equal, they will not have equal shares; it is when equals possess or are allotted unequal shares, or persons not equal, equal shares, that quarrels and complaints arise.

This is also clear from the principle of 'assignment by desert.' All are agreed that justice in distributions must be based on desert of some sort, although they do not all mean the same sort of desert; democrats

make the criterion free birth; those of oligarchical sympathies, wealth, or in other cases birth; upholders of aristocracy make it virtue. Justice is therefore a sort of proportion; for proportion is not a property of numerical quantity only, but of quantity in general, proportion being equality of ratios, and involving four terms at least. . . .

The just in this sense is therefore the proportionate, and the unjust is that which violates proportion. The unjust may therefore be either too much or too little; and this is what we find in fact, for when injustice is done, the doer has too much and the sufferer too little of the good in question; though *vice versa* in the case of an evil, because a lesser evil in comparison with a greater counts as a good, since the lesser of two evils is more desirable than the greater, but what is desirable is good, and the more desirable it is, the greater good it is.

This then is one kind of Justice.

The remaining kind is Corrective Justice, which operates in private transactions, both voluntary and involuntary. This justice is of a different sort from the preceding. For justice in distributing common property always conforms with the proportion we have described (since when a distribution is made from the common stock, it will follow the same ratio as that between the amounts which the several persons have contributed to the common stock); and the injustice opposed to justice of this kind is a violation of this proportion. But the just in private transactions, although it is the equal in a sense (and the unjust the unequal), is not the equal according to geometrical, but according to arithmetical proportion. For it makes no difference whether a good man has defrauded a bad man or a bad one a good one, nor whether it is a good or a bad man that has committed adultery; the law looks only at the nature of the damage, treating the parties as equal, and merely asking whether one has done and the other suffered injustice, whether one inflicted and the other has sustained damage. Hence the unjust being here the unequal, the judge endeavours to equalize it: inasmuch as when one man has received and the other has inflicted a blow, or one has killed and the other been killed, the line representing the suffering and doing of the deed is divided into unequal parts, but the judge endeavours to make them equal by the penalty or loss he imposes, taking away the gain. (For the term "gain" is used in a general way to apply to such cases, even though it is not strictly appropriate to some of them, for example to a person who strikes another, nor is "loss" appropriate to the victim in this case; but at all events the results are called "loss" and "gain" respectively when the amount of the damage sustained comes to be estimated.) Thus, while the equal is a mean between more and less, gain and loss are at once both more and less in contrary ways, more good and less evil being gain and more evil and less good loss; and as the equal, which we pronounce to be just, is, as we said, a mean between them, it follows that Justice in Rectification will be the mean between loss and gain.

This is why when disputes occur men have recourse to a judge. To go to a judge is to go to justice, for the ideal judge is so to speak justice personified. Also, men require a judge to be a middle term or *medium*—indeed in some places judges are called *mediators*—, for they think that if they get the mean they will get what is just. Thus, the just is a sort of mean, inasmuch as the judge is a medium between the litigants.

Now the judge restores equality. . . .

The terms "loss" and "gain" in these cases are borrowed from the operations of voluntary exchange. There, to have more than one's own is called gaining, and to have less than one had at the outset is called losing, as for instance in buying and selling, and all other transactions sanctioned by law; while if the result of the transaction is neither an increase nor a decrease, but exactly what the parties had of themselves, they say they "have their own" and have neither lost nor gained. Hence Justice in involuntary transactions is a mean between gain and loss in a sense: it is to have after the transaction an amount equal to the amount one had before it.

The view is also held by some that simple Reciprocity is Justice. This was the doctrine of the Pythagoreans, who defined the just simply as "suffering reciprocally with another."

Reciprocity however does not coincide either with Distributive or with Corrective Justice (although people mean to identify it with the latter when they quote the rule of Rhadamanthys—

> An a man suffer even that which he did,
> Right justice will be done).

For in many cases Reciprocity is at variance with Justice: for example, if an officer strikes a man, it is wrong for the man to strike him back; and if a man strikes an officer, it is not enough for the officer to strike him, but he ought to be punished as well. Again, it makes a great difference whether an act was done with or without the consent of the other party. But in the interchange of services Justice in the form of Reciprocity is the bond that maintains the association: reciprocity, that is, on the basis of proportion, not on the basis of equality. The very existence of the state depends on proportionate reciprocity; for men demand that they shall be able to requite evil with evil—if they cannot, they feel they are in the position of slaves—and to repay good with good—failing which, no exchange takes place, and it is exchange that binds them together. This is why we set up a shrine of the Graces in a public place, to remind men to return a kindness; for that is a special characteristic of grace, since it is a duty not only to repay a service done one, but another time to take the initiative in doing a service oneself.

Now proportionate requital is effected by diagonal conjunction. For example, let A be a builder, B a shoemaker, C a house, and D a shoe. It is required that the builder shall receive from the shoemaker a portion of the product of his labour, and give him a portion of the product of his own. Now if proportionate equality between the products be first established, and then reciprocation take place, the requirement indicated will have been achieved; but if this is not done, the bargain is not equal, and intercourse does not continue. For it may happen that the product of one of the parties is worth more than that of the other, and in that case therefore they have to be equalized. This holds good with the other arts as well; for they would have passed out of existence if the active element did not produce, and did not receive the equivalent in quantity and quality of what the passive element receives. For an association for interchange of services is not formed between two physicians, but between a physician and a farmer, and generally between persons who are different, and who may be unequal, though in that case they have to be equalized. Hence all commodities exchanged must be able to be compared in some way. It is to meet this requirement that men have introduced money; money constitutes in a manner a middle term, for it is a measure of all things, and so of their superior or inferior value, that is to say, how many shoes are equivalent to a house or to a given quantity of food. As therefore a builder is to a shoemaker, so must such and such a number of shoes be to a house [or to a given quantity of food]; for without this reciprocal proportion, there can be no exchange and no association; and it cannot be secured unless the commodities in question be equal in a sense.

It is therefore necessary that all commodities shall be measured by some one standard, as was said before. And this standard is in reality demand, which is what holds everything together, since if men cease to have wants or if their wants alter, exchange will go on no longer, or will be on different lines. But demand has come to be conventionally represented by money. . . .

Now money serves us as a guarantee of exchange in the future: supposing we need nothing at the moment, it ensures that exchange shall be possible when a need arises, for it meets the requirement of something we can produce in payment so as to obtain the thing we need. . . . Though therefore

it is impossible for things so different to become commensurable in the strict sense, our demand furnishes a sufficiently accurate common measure for practical purposes. . . .

We have now stated what Justice and Injustice are in principle. From the definition given, it is plain that just conduct is a mean between doing and suffering injustice, for the former is to have too much and the latter to have too little. And Justice is a mode of observing the mean, though not in the same way as the other virtues are, but because it is related to a mean, while Injustice is related to the extremes. Also, Justice is that quality in virtue of which a man is said to be disposed to do by deliberate choice that which is just, and, when distributing things between himself and another, or between two others, not to give too much to himself and too little to his neighbour of what is desirable, and too little to himself and too much to his neighbour of what is harmful, but to each what is proportionately equal; and similarly when he is distributing between two other persons. Injustice on the contrary is similarly related to that which is unjust, which is a disproportionate excess or deficiency of something beneficial or harmful. Hence Injustice is excess and defect, in the sense that it results in excess and defect: namely, in the offender's own case, an excess of anything that is generally speaking beneficial and a deficiency of anything harmful, and in the case of others, though the result as a whole is the same, the deviation from proportion may be in either direction as the case may be.

Of the injustice done, the smaller part is the suffering and the larger part the doing of injustice.

So much may be said about the nature of Justice and Injustice, and of the Just and the Unjust regarded universally.

But seeing that a man may commit injustice without actually being unjust, what is it that distinguishes those unjust acts the commission of which renders a man actually unjust under one of the various forms of injustice, for example, a thief or an adulterer or a brigand? Or shall we rather say that the distinction does not lie in the quality of the act? For a man may have intercourse with a woman knowing who she is, yet not from the motive of deliberate choice, but under the influence of passion; in such a case, though he has committed injustice, he is not an unjust man: for instance, he is not a thief, though guilty of theft, not an adulterer, though he has committed adultery, and so forth.

The relation of Reciprocity to Justice has been stated already.

But we must not forget that the subject of our investigation is at once Justice in the absolute sense and Political Justice. Political Justice means justice as between free and (actually or proportionately) equal persons, living a common life for the purpose of satisfying their needs. Hence between people not free and equal political justice cannot exist, but only a sort of justice in a metaphorical sense. For justice can only exist between those whose mutual relations are regulated by law, and law exists among those between whom there is a possibility of injustice, for the administration of the law means the discrimination of what is just and what is unjust. Persons therefore between whom injustice can exist, can act unjustly towards each other (although unjust action does not necessarily involve injustice): to act unjustly meaning to assign oneself too large a share of things generally good and too small a share of things generally evil. This is why we do not permit a man to rule, but the law, because a man rules in his own interest, and becomes a tyrant; but the function of a ruler is to be the guardian of justice, and if of justice, then of equality. A just ruler seems to make nothing out of his office; for he does not allot to himself a larger share of things generally good, unless it be proportionate to his merits; so that he labours for others, which accounts for the saying mentioned above, that "Justice is the good of others." Consequently some recompense has to be given him, in the shape of honour and dignity. It is those whom such rewards do not satisfy who make themselves tyrants.

Justice between master and slave and between father and child is not the same as absolute and political justice, but only analogous to them. For there is no such thing as injustice in the absolute sense towards what is one's own; and a chattel, or a child till it reaches a certain age and becomes independent, is, as it were, a part of oneself, and no one chooses to harm himself; hence there can be no injustice towards them, and therefore nothing just or unjust in the political sense. For these, as we saw, are embodied in law, and exist between persons whose relations are naturally regulated by law, that is, persons who share equally in ruling and being ruled. Hence Justice exists in a fuller degree between husband and wife than between father and children; or master and slaves; in fact, justice between husband and wife is Domestic Justice in the real sense, though this too is different from Political Justice.

Political Justice is of two kinds, one natural, the other conventional. A rule of justice is natural that has the same validity everywhere, and does not depend on our accepting it or not. A rule is conventional that in the first instance may be settled in one way or the other indifferently, though having once been settled it is not indifferent: for example, that the ransom for a prisoner shall be a mina, that a sacrifice shall consist of a goat and not of two sheep. . . . Some people think that all rules of justice are merely conventional, because whereas a law of nature is immutable and has the same validity everywhere, as fire burns both here and in Persia, rules of justice are seen to vary. That rules of justice vary is not absolutely true, but only with qualifications. Among the gods indeed it is perhaps not true at all; but in our world, although there is such a thing as Natural Justice, all rules of justice are variable. But nevertheless there is such a thing as Natural Justice as well as justice not ordained by nature; and it is easy to see which rules of justice, though not absolute, are natural, and which are not natural but legal and conventional, both sorts alike being variable. The same distinction will hold good in all other matters; for instance, the right hand is naturally stronger than the left, yet it is possible for any man to make himself ambidextrous.

The rules of justice based on convention and expediency are like standard measures. Corn and wine measures are not equal in all places, but are larger in wholesale and smaller in retail markets. Similarly the rules of justice ordained not by nature but by man are not the same in all places, since forms of government are not the same, though in all places there is only one form of government that is natural, namely, the best form.

The several rules of justice and of law are related to the actions conforming with them as universals to particulars, for the actions done are many, while each rule or law is one, being universal.

There is a difference between "that which is unjust" and "unjust conduct," and between "that which is just" and "just conduct." Nature or ordinance pronounces a thing unjust: when that thing is done, it is "unjust conduct"; till it is done, it is only "unjust"! . . .

Such being an account of just and unjust actions, it is their voluntary performance that constitutes just and unjust conduct. If a man does them involuntarily, he cannot be said to act justly, or unjustly, except incidentally, in the sense that he does an act which happens to be just or unjust. Whether therefore an action is or is not an act of injustice, or of justice, depends on its voluntary or involuntary character. When it is voluntary, the agent is blamed, and only in that case is the action an act of injustice; so that it is possible for an act to be unjust without being an act of injustice, if the qualification of voluntariness be absent. By a voluntary action . . . I mean any action within the agent's own control which he performs knowingly, that is, without being in ignorance of the person affected, the instrument employed, and the result (for example, he must know whom he strikes, and

with what weapon, and the effect of the blow); and in each of these respects both accident and compulsion must be excluded. For instance, if A took hold of B's hand and with it struck C, B would not be a voluntary agent, since the act would not be in his own control. Or again, a man may strike his father without knowing that it is his father, though aware that he is striking some person, and perhaps that it is one or other of the persons present; and ignorance may be similarly defined with reference to the result, and to the circumstances of the action generally. An involuntary act is therefore an act done in ignorance, or else one that though not done in ignorance is not in the agent's control, or is done under compulsion; since there are many natural processes too that we perform or undergo knowingly, though none of them is either voluntary or involuntary; for example, growing old, and dying.

Also an act may be either just or unjust incidentally. A man may restore a deposit unwillingly and from fear of consequences, and we must not then say that he does a just act, nor that he acts justly, except incidentally; and similarly a man who under compulsion and against his will fails to restore a deposit can only be said to act unjustly or do what is unjust incidentally.

Again voluntary acts are divided into acts done by choice and those done not by choice, the former being those done after deliberation and the latter those done without previous deliberation.

There are then three ways in which a man may injure his fellow. An injury done in ignorance is an error, the person affected or the act or the instrument or the result being other than the agent supposed; for example, he did not think to hit, or not with this missile, or not this person, or not with this result, but it happened that either the result was other than he expected (for instance he did not mean to inflict a wound but only a prick), or the person, or the missile. When then the injury happens contrary to reasonable expectation, it is (1) a misadventure. When, though not contrary to reasonable expectation, it is done without evil intent, it is (2) a culpable error; for an error is culpable when the cause of one's ignorance lies in oneself, but only a misadventure when the cause lies outside oneself. When an injury is done knowingly but not deliberately, it is (3) an act of injustice or wrong; such, for instance, are injuries done through anger, or any other unavoidable or natural passion to which men are liable; since in committing these injuries and errors a man acts unjustly, and his action is an act of injustice, but he is not *ipso facto* unjust or wicked, for the injury was not done out of wickedness. When however an injury is done from choice, the doer is unjust and wicked. Hence acts due to sudden anger are rightly held not to be done of malice aforethought, for it is the man who gave the provocation that began it, not he who does the deed in a fit of passion. And moreover the issue is not one of fact, but of justification (since it is apparent injustice that arouses anger); the fact of the injury is not disputed (as it is in cases of contract, where one or the other of the parties must be a knave, unless they dispute the facts out of forgetfulness). They agree as to the facts but dispute on which side justice lies; so that one thinks he has been unjustly treated and the other does not. On the other hand, one who does an injury intentionally is not acting in ignorance; but if a man does an injury of set purpose, he is guilty of injustice, and injustice of the sort that renders the doer an unjust man, if it be an act that violates proportion or equality. Similarly one who acts justly on purpose is a just man; but he acts justly only if he acts voluntarily.

Of involuntary actions some are pardonable and some are not. Errors not merely committed in ignorance but caused by ignorance are pardonable; those committed in ignorance, but caused not by that ignorance but by unnatural or inhuman passion, are unpardonable.

But it may perhaps be doubted whether our discussion of suffering and doing injustice has been sufficiently definite; and in the first place, whether the matter really is as Euripides has put it in the strange lines—

I killed my mother—that's the tale in brief!
Were you both willing, or unwilling both?

Is it really possible to suffer injustice voluntarily, or on the contrary is suffering injustice always involuntary, just as acting unjustly is always voluntary? And again, is suffering injustice always voluntary, or always involuntary, or sometimes one and sometimes the other? And similarly with being treated justly (acting justly being always voluntary). Thus it would be reasonable to suppose that both being treated unjustly and being treated justly are similarly opposed to acting unjustly and acting justly respectively: that either both are voluntary or both involuntary. But it would seem paradoxical to assert that even being treated justly is always voluntary; for people are sometimes treated justly against their will. The fact is that the further question might be raised, must a man who has had an unjust thing done to him always be said to have been treated unjustly, or does the same thing hold good of suffering as of doing something unjust? One may be a party to a just act, whether as its agent or its object, incidentally. And the same clearly is true of an unjust act: doing what is unjust is not identical with acting unjustly, nor yet is suffering what is unjust identical with being treated unjustly, and the same is true of acting and being treated justly; for it is impossible to be treated unjustly unless the other acts unjustly, or to be treated justly unless he acts justly.

But if to act unjustly is simply to do harm to someone voluntarily, and voluntarily means knowing the person affected, the instrument, and the manner of injury, it will follow both that the man of defective self-restraint, inasmuch as he voluntarily harms himself, voluntarily suffers injustice, and also that it is possible for a man to act unjustly towards himself (for the possibility of this is also a debated question). Moreover, lack of self-restraint may make a person voluntarily submit to being harmed by another;

which again would prove that it is possible to suffer injustice voluntarily. But perhaps this definition of acting unjustly is incorrect, and we should add to the words "to do harm knowing the person affected, the instrument and the manner," the further qualification "against that person's wish." If so, though a man can he harmed and can have an unjust thing done to him voluntarily, no one can suffer injustice voluntarily, because no one can wish to be harmed: even the unrestrained man does not, but acts contrary to his wish, since no one wishes for a thing that he does not think to be good, and the unrestrained man does what he thinks he ought not to do. One who gives away what is his own—as Homer says that Glaucus gave to Diomede

> golden arms for bronze,
> An hundred beeves' worth for the
> worth of nine—

cannot be said to suffer injustice; for giving rests with oneself, suffering injustice does not—there has to be another person who acts unjustly.

It is clear then that it is not possible to suffer injustice voluntarily.

There still remain two of the questions that we proposed to discuss: (1) Is it ever he who gives the unduly large share, or is it always he who receives it, that is guilty of the injustice? and (2) Can one act unjustly towards oneself?

If the former alternative is possible, that is, if it may be the giver and not the receiver of too large a share who acts unjustly, then when a man knowingly and voluntarily assigns a larger share to another than to himself—as modest people are thought to do, for an equitable man is apt to take less than his due—this is a case of acting unjustly towards oneself. But perhaps this also requires qualification. For the man who gave himself the smaller share may possibly have got a larger share of some other good thing, for instance glory, or intrinsic moral nobility. Also the inference may be refuted by referring to our definition of acting unjustly: in the case supposed, the distributor has

nothing done to him against his wish; therefore he does not suffer injustice merely because he gets the smaller share: at most he only suffers damage.

And it is clear that the giver as well as the receiver of an undue share may be acting unjustly, and that the receiver is not doing so in all cases. For the charge of injustice attaches, not to a man of whom it can be said that he does what is unjust, but to one of whom it can be said that he does this voluntarily, that is to say one from whom the action originates; and the origin of the act in this case lies in the giver and not in the receiver of the share.

Again, "to do a thing" has more than one meaning. In a certain sense a murder is done by the inanimate instrument, or by the murderer's hand, or by a slave acting under orders. But though these do what is unjust, they cannot be said to act unjustly.

Again, although if a judge has given an unfair judgement in ignorance, he is not guilty of injustice, nor is the judgement unjust, in the legal sense of justice (though the judgement is unjust in one sense, for legal justice is different from justice in the primary sense), yet if he knowingly gives an unjust judgment, he is himself taking more than his share, either of favour or of vengeance. Hence a judge who gives an unjust judgement for these motives takes more than his due just as much as if he shared the proceeds of the injustice; for even a judge who assigns a piece of land on that condition does not receive land but money.

Men think that it is in their power to act unjustly, and therefore that it is easy to be just. But really this is not so. It is easy to lie with one's neighbour's wife or strike a bystander or slip some money into a man's hand, and it is in one's power to do these things or not; but to do them as a result of a certain disposition of mind is not easy, and is not in one's power. Similarly men suppose it requires no special wisdom to know what is just and what is unjust, because it is not difficult to understand the things about which the law pronounces. But the actions prescribed by law are only accidentally just actions. *How* an action must be performed, *how* a distribution must be made to be a just action or a just distribution—to know this is a harder task than to know what medical treatment will produce health. Even in medicine, though it is easy to know what honey, wine and hellebore, cautery and surgery are, to know how and to whom and when to apply them so as to effect a cure is no less an undertaking than to be a physician. And for this very reason men think that the just man may act unjustly no less than justly, because the just man is not less but rather more able than another to do any particular unjust thing: for example, he *can* lie with a woman, or strike a blow, and a brave man *can* throw away his shield, and *can* wheel to the right or left and run away. But to be a coward and to be guilty of injustice consists not in doing these things (except accidentally), but in doing them from a certain disposition of mind; just as to be a physician and cure one's patients is not a matter of employing or not employing surgery or drugs, but of doing so in a certain manner.

Claims of justice exist between persons who share in things generally speaking good, and who can have too large a share or too small a share of them. There are persons who cannot have too large a share of these goods: doubtless, for example, the gods. And there are those who can derive no benefit from any share of them: namely, the incurably vicious; to them all the things generally good are harmful. But for others they are beneficial within limits; and this is the case with ordinary mortals.

We have next to speak of Equity and the equitable, and of their relation to Justice and to what is just respectively. For upon examination it appears that Justice and Equity are neither absolutely identical nor generically different. Sometimes, it is true, we praise equity and the equitable man, so much so that we even apply the word "equitable" as a term of approval to other things besides what is just, and use it as the equivalent of "good," denoting by "more equitable" merely that a thing is better. Yet at other times, when we think the matter out, it seems strange that the equitable should be praiseworthy if it is something other than the just. If they are different, either the just or the equitable is not good; if both are good, they are the same thing.

These then are the considerations, more or less, from which the difficulty as to the equitable arises. Yet they are all in a manner correct, and not really inconsistent. For equity, while superior to one sort of justice, is itself just: it is not superior to justice as being generically different from it. Justice and equity are therefore the same thing, and both are good, though equity is the better.

The source of the difficulty is that equity, though just, is not legal justice, but a rectification of legal justice. The reason for this is that law is always a general statement, yet there are cases which it is not possible to cover in a general statement. In matters therefore where, while it is necessary to speak in general terms, it is not possible to do so correctly, the law takes into consideration the majority of cases, although it is not unaware of the error this involves. And this does not make it a wrong law; for the error is not in the law nor in the lawgiver, but in the nature of the case: the material of conduct is essentially irregular. When therefore the law lays down a general rule, and thereafter a case arises which is an exception to the rule, it is then right, where the lawgiver's pronouncement because of its absoluteness is defective and erroneous, to rectify the defect by deciding as the lawgiver would himself decide if he were present on the occasion, and would have enacted if he had been cognizant of the case in question. Hence, while the equitable is just, and is superior to one sort of justice, it is not superior to absolute justice, but only to the error due to its absolute statement. This is the essential nature of the equitable: it is a rectification of law where law is defective because of its generality. In fact this is the reason why things are not all determined by law: it is because there are some cases for which it is impossible to lay down a law, so that a special ordinance becomes necessary. For what is itself indefinite can only be measured by an indefinite standard, like the leaden rule used by Lesbian builders; just as that rule is not rigid but can be bent to the shape of the stone, so a special ordinance is made to fit the circumstances of the case.

It is now plain what the equitable is, and that it is just, and that it is superior to one sort of justice. And from this it is clear what the equitable man is: he is one who by choice and habit does what is equitable, and who does not stand on his rights unduly, but is content to receive a smaller share although he has the law on his side. And the disposition described is Equity; it is a special kind of Justice, not a different quality altogether.

The foregoing discussion has indicated the answer to the question, Is it possible or not for a man to commit injustice against himself? (1) One class of just actions consists of those acts, in accordance with any virtue, which are ordained by law. For instance, the law does not sanction suicide (and what it does not expressly sanction, it forbids). Further, when a man voluntarily (which means with knowledge of the person affected and the instrument employed) does an injury (not in retaliation) that is against the law, he commits injustice. But he who kills himself in a fit of passion, voluntarily does an injury (against the right principle) which the law does not allow. Therefore the suicide commits injustice; but against whom? It seems to be against the state rather than against himself; for he suffers voluntarily, and nobody suffers injustice voluntarily. This is why the state exacts a penalty; suicide is punished by certain marks of dishonor, as being an offence against the state. . . .

In a metaphorical and analogical sense however there is such a thing as justice, not towards oneself but between different parts of one's nature; not, it is true, justice in the full sense of the term, but such justice as subsists between master and slave, or between the head of a household and his wife and children. For in the discourses on this question a distinction is set up between the rational and irrational parts of the soul; and this is what leads people to suppose that there is such a thing as injustice towards oneself, because these parts of the self may be thwarted in their respective desires, so that there may be a sort of justice between them, such as exists between ruler and subject.

So much may be said in description of Justice and of the other Moral Virtues.

THE POLITICS *

Book I

Every state is a community of some kind, and every community is established with a view to some good; for mankind always act in order to obtain that which they think good. But, if all communities aim at some good, the state or political community, which is the highest of all, and which embraces all the rest, aims, and in a greater degree than any other, at the highest good.

Now there is an erroneous opinion that a statesman, king, householder, and master are the same, and that they differ, not in kind, but only in the number of their subjects. For example, the ruler over a few is called a master; over more, the manager of a household; over a still larger number, a statesman or king, as if there were no difference between a great household and a small state. The distinction which is made between the king and the statesman is as follows: When the government is personal, the ruler is a king; when, according to the principles of the political science, the citizens rule and are ruled in turn, then he is called a statesman.

But all this is a mistake; for governments differ in kind, as will be evident to any one who considers the matter according to the method which has hitherto guided us. As in other departments of science, so in politics, the compound should always be resolved into the simple elements or least parts

* Translated by Benjamin Jowett. Published with the permission of the Oxford University Press.

of the whole. We must therefore look at the elements of which the state is composed, in order that we may see in what they differ from one another, and whether any scientific distinction can be drawn between the different kinds of rule.

He who thus considers things in their first growth and origin, whether a state or anything else, will obtain the clearest view of them. In the first place (1) there must be a union of those who cannot exist without each other; for example, of male and female, that the race may continue; and this is a union which is formed, not of deliberate purpose, but because, in common with other animals and with plants, mankind have a natural desire to leave behind them an image of themselves. And (2) there must be a union of natural ruler and subject, that both may be preserved. For he who can foresee with his mind is by nature intended to be lord and master, and he who can work with his body is a subject, and by nature a slave; hence master and slave have the same interest. Nature, however, has distinguished between the female and the slave. For she is not niggardly, like the smith who fashions the Delphian knife for many uses; she makes each thing for a single use, and every instrument is best made when intended for one and not for many uses. . . .

Out of these two relationships between man and woman, master and slave, the family first arises, and Hesiod is right when he says,—

'First house and wife and an ox for the plough',

for the ox is the poor man's slave. The family is the association established by nature for the supply of men's every-day wants . . . But when several families are united, and the association aims at something more than the supply of daily needs, then comes into existence the village. And the most natural form of the village appears to be that of a colony from the family, composed of the children and grandchildren, who are said to be 'suckled with the same milk.' And this is the reason why Hellenic states were orig-inally governed by kings; because the Hellenes were under royal rule before they came together, as the barbarians still are. Every family is ruled by the eldest, and therefore in the colonies of the family the kingly form of government prevailed because they were of the same blood. As Homer says [of the Cyclopes]:—

Each one gives law to his children and to his wives . . .

When several villages are united in a single community, perfect and large enough to be nearly or quite self-sufficing, the state comes into existence, originating in the bare needs of life, and continuing in existence for the sake of a good life. And therefore, if the earlier forms of society are natural, so is the state, for it is the end of them, and the [completed] nature is the end. For what each thing is when fully developed, we call its nature, whether we are speaking of a man, a horse, or a family. Besides, the final cause and end of a thing is the best, and to be self-sufficing is the end and the best.

Hence it is evident that the state is a creation of nature, and that man is by nature a political animal. And he who by nature and not by mere accident is without a state, is either above humanity, or below it; he is the

Tribeless, lawless, heartless one,

whom Homer denounces—the outcast who is a lover of war; he may be compared to an unprotected piece in the game of draughts.

Now the reason why man is more of a political animal than bees or any other gregarious animals is evident. Nature, as we often say, makes nothing in vain, and man is the only animal whom she has endowed with the gift of speech. And whereas mere sound is but an indication of pleasure or pain, and is therefore found in other animals . . . the power of speech is intended to set forth the expedient and inexpedient, and likewise the just and the unjust. And it is a characteristic of man that he alone has any sense of good and evil, of just and unjust, and the association of living beings who have this sense makes a family and a state.

Thus the state is by nature clearly prior to the family and to the individual, since the whole is of necessity prior to the part; for example, if the whole body be destroyed, there will be no foot or hand, except in an equivocal sense, as we might speak of a stone hand; for when destroyed the hand will be no better. But things are defined by their working and power; and we ought not to say that they are the same when they are no longer the same, but only that they have the same name. The proof that the state is a creation of nature and prior to the individual is that the individual, when isolated, is not self-sufficing; and therefore he is like a part in relation to the whole. But he who is unable to live in society, or who has no need because he is sufficient for himself, must be either a beast or a god: he is no part of a state. A social instinct is implanted in all men by nature, and yet he who first founded the state was the greatest of benefactors. For man, when perfected, is the best of animals, but, when separated from law and justice, he is the worst of all; since armed injustice is the more dangerous, and he is equipped at birth with the arms of intelligence and with moral qualities which he may use for the worst ends. Wherefore, if he have not virtue, he is the most unholy and the most savage of animals, and the most full of lust and gluttony. But justice is the bond of men in states, and the administration of justice, which is the determination of what is just, is the principle of order in political society. . . .

Let us first speak of master and slave, looking to the needs of practical life and also seeking to attain some better theory of their relation than exists at present. For some are of opinion that the rule of a master is a science, and that the management of a household, and the mastership of slaves, and the political and royal rule, as I was saying at the outset, are all the same. Others affirm that the rule of a master over slaves is contrary to nature, and that the distinction between slave and freeman exists by law only, and not by nature; and being an interference with nature is therefore unjust.

Property is a part of the household, and therefore the art of acquiring property is a part of the art of managing the household; for no man can live well, or indeed live at all, unless he be provided with necessaries. And as in the arts which have a definite sphere the workers must have their own proper instruments for the accomplishment of their work, so it is in the management of a household. Now, instruments are of various sorts; some are living, others lifeless; in the rudder, the pilot of a ship has a lifeless, in the lookout man, a living instrument; for in the arts the servant is a kind of instrument. Thus, too, a possession is an instrument for maintaining life. And so, in the arrangement of the family, a slave is a living possession, and property a number of such instruments; and the servant is himself an instrument, which takes precedence of all other instruments . . . A possession is spoken of as a part is spoken of; for the part is not only a part of something else, but wholly belongs to it; and this is also true of a possession. The master is only the master of the slave; he does not belong to him, whereas the slave is not only the slave of his master, but wholly belongs to him. Hence we see what is the nature and office of a slave; he who is by nature not his own but another's and yet a man, is by nature a slave; and he may be said to belong to another who, being a human being, is also a possession. And a possession may be defined as an instrument of action, separable from the possessor.

But is there any one thus intended by nature to be a slave, and for whom such a condition is expedient and right, or rather is not all slavery a violation of nature?

There is no difficulty in answering this question, on grounds both of reason and of fact. For that some should rule and others be ruled is a thing, not only necessary, but expedient; from the hour of their birth, some are marked out for subjection, others for rule . . . .

But that those who take the opposite view have in a certain way right on their side, may be easily seen. For the words slavery and slave are used in two senses. There is a slave or slavery by law as well as by nature. The law of which I speak is a sort of convention, according to which whatever is taken in war is supposed to belong to the victors. But this right many jurists impeach, as they would an orator who brought forward an unconstitutional measure: they detest the notion that, because one man has the power of doing violence and is superior in brute strength, another shall be his slave and subject. Even among philosophers there is a difference of opinion. The origin of the dispute, and the reason why the arguments cross, is as follows: Virtue, when furnished with means, may be deemed to have the greatest power of doing violence: and as superior power is only found where there is superior excellence of some kind, power is thought to imply virtue. But does it likewise imply justice?—that is the question. And, in order to make a distinction between them, some assert that justice is benevolence: to which others reply that justice is nothing more than the rule of a superior. If the two views are regarded as antagonistic and exclusive [i.e. if the notion that justice is benevolence excludes the idea of a just rule of a superior], the alternative [viz. that no one should rule over others] has no force or plausibility, because it implies that not even the superior in virtue ought to rule, or be master. Some, clinging, as they think, to a principle of justice (for law and custom are a sort of justice), assume that slavery in war is justified by law, but they are not consistent. For what if the cause of the war be unjust? No one would ever say that he is a slave who is unworthy to be a slave. Were this the case, men of the highest rank would be slaves and the children of slaves if they or their parents chance to have been taken captive and sold. Wherefore Hellenes do not like to call themselves slaves, but confine the term to barbarians. Yet, in using this language, they really mean the natural slave of whom we spoke at first; for it must be admitted that some are slaves everywhere, others nowhere. The same principle applies to nobility. Hellenes regard themselves as noble everywhere, and not only in their own country, but they deem the barbarians noble only when at home, thereby implying that there are two sorts of nobility and freedom, the one absolute, the other relative. The Helen of Theodectes says:—

'Who would presume to call me servant who am on both sides sprung from the stem of the Gods?'

What does this mean but that they distinguish freedom and slavery, noble and humble birth, by the two principles of good and evil? They think that as men and animals beget men and animals, so from good men a good man springs. But this is what nature, though she may intend it, often fails to accomplish.

We see then that there is some foundation for this difference of opinion, and that some actual slaves and freemen are not so by nature, and also that there is in some cases a marked distinction between the two classes, rendering it expedient and right for the one to be slaves and the others to be masters: the one practising obedience; the others exercising the authority which nature intended them to have. The abuse of this authority is injurious to both; for the interests of part and whole, of body and soul, are the same, and the slave is a part of the master, a living but separated part of his bodily frame. Where the relation between them is natural they are friends and have a common interest, but where it rests merely on law and force the reverse is true.

The previous remarks are quite enough to show that the rule of a master is not a constitutional rule, and therefore that all the different kinds of rule are not, as some affirm, the same with each other. For there is one rule exercised over subjects who are by nature free, another over subjects who are by nature slaves. The rule of a household is a monarchy, for every house is under one head: whereas constitutional rule is a government of freemen and equals. . . .

. . . Now if nature makes nothing incomplete, and nothing in vain, the inference must be that she has made all animals and plants for the sake of man. And so, in one point of view, the art of war is a natural art of acquisition, for it includes hunting, an art which we ought to practise against wild beasts, and against men who, though intended by nature to be governed, will not submit; for war of such a kind is naturally just.

Of the art of acquisition then there is one kind which is natural and is a part of the management of a household. Either we must suppose the necessaries of life to exist previously, or the art of household management must provide a store of them for the common use of the family or state. They are the elements of true wealth; for the amount of property which is needed for a good life is not unlimited, although Solon in one of his poems says that,

'No bound to riches has been fixed for man.'

But there is a boundary fixed, just as there is in the arts; for the instruments of any art are never unlimited, either in number or size, and wealth may be defined as a number of instruments to be used in a household or in a state. And so we see that there is a natural art of acquisition which is practised by managers of households and by statesmen, and what is the reason of this.

There is another variety of the art of acquisition which is commonly and rightly called the art of making money, and has in fact suggested the notion that wealth and property have no limit. Being nearly connected with the preceding, it is often identified with it. But though they are not very different, neither are they the same. The kind already described is given by nature, the other is gained by experience and art.

Let us begin our discussion of the question with the following considerations:—

Of everything which we possess there are two uses: both belong to the thing as such, but not in the same manner, for one is the proper, and the other the improper or secondary use of it. For example, a shoe is used for wear, and is used for exchange; both are uses of the shoe. He who gives a shoe in exchange for money or food to him who wants one, does indeed use the shoe as a shoe, but this is not its proper or primary purpose, for a shoe is not made to be an object of barter. The same may be said of all possessions, for the art of exchange extends to all of them, and it arises at first in a natural manner from the circumstance that some have too little, others too much. Hence we may infer that retail trade is not a natural part of the art of money-making; had it been so, men would have ceased to exchange when they had enough. And in the first community, which is the family, this art is obviously of no use, but only begins to be useful when the society increases. For the members of the family originally had all things in common; in a more divided state of society they still shared in many things, but they were different things which they had to give in exchange for what they wanted, a kind of barter which is still practised among barbarous nations who exchange with one another the necessaries of life and nothing more; giving and receiving wine, for example, in exchange for corn and the like. This sort of barter is not part of the money-making art and is not contrary to nature, but is needed for the satisfaction of men's natural wants. The other or more complex form of exchange grew out of the simpler. When the inhabitants of one country became more dependent on those of another, and they imported what they needed, and exported the surplus, money necessarily came into use. For the various necessaries of life are not easily carried about, and hence men agreed to employ in their dealings with each other something which was intrinsically useful and easily applicable to the purposes of life, for example, iron, silver, and the like. Of this the value was at first measured by size and weight, but in process of time they put a stamp upon it, to save the trouble of weighing and to mark the value.

When the use of coin had once been discovered, out of the barter of necessary articles arose the other art of money-making, namely, retail trade; which was at first probably a simple matter, but became more complicated as soon as men learned by experience whence and by what exchanges the greatest profit might be made. Originating in the use of coin, the art of money-making is generally thought to be chiefly concerned with it, and to be the art which produces wealth and money; having to consider how they may be accumulated. Indeed, wealth is assumed by many to be only a quantity of coin, because the art of money-making and retail trade are concerned with coin. Others maintain that coined money is a mere sham, a thing not natural, but conventional only, which would have no value or use for any of the purposes of daily life if another commodity were substituted by the users. And, indeed, he who is rich in coin may often be in want of necessary food. But how can that be wealth of which a man may have a great abundance and yet perish with hunger, like Midas in the fable, whose insatiable prayer turned everything that was set before him into gold?

Men seek after a better notion of wealth and of the art of making money than the mere acquisition of coin, and they are right. For natural wealth and the natural art of money-making are a different thing . . . The quality of courage, for example, is not intended to make money, but to inspire confidence; neither is this the aim of the general's or of the physician's art; but the one aims at victory and the other at health. Nevertheless, some men turn every quality or art into a means of making money; this they conceive to be the end, and to the promotion of the end all things must contribute.

Thus, then, we have considered the art of money-making, which is unnecessary, and why men want it; and also the necessary art of money-making, which we have seen to be different from the other, and to be a natural part of the art of managing a household, concerned with the provision of food, not, however, like the former kind, unlimited, but having a limit.

And we have found the answer to our original question, Whether the art of money-making is the business of the manager of a household and of the statesman or not their business?—viz. that it is an art which is presupposed by them. For political science does not make men, but takes them from nature

and uses them; and nature provides them with food from the element of earth, air, or sea. At this stage begins the duty of the manager of a household, who has to order the things which nature supplies;—he may be compared to the weaver who has not to make but to use wool, and to know what sort of wool is good and serviceable or bad and unserviceable. Were this otherwise, it would be difficult to see why the art of money-making is a part of the management of a household and the art of medicine not; for surely the members of a household must have health just as they must have life or any other necessary. And as from one point of view the master of the house and the ruler of the state have to consider about health, from another point of view not they but the physician; so in one way the art of household management, in another way the subordinate art, has to consider about money. But, strictly speaking, as I have already said, the means of life must be provided beforehand by nature; for the business of nature is to furnish food to that which is born, and the food of the offspring always remains over in the parent. Wherefore the art of making money out of fruits and animals is always natural.

Of the two sorts of money-making one, as I have just said, is a part of household management, the other is retail trade: the former necessary and honorable, the latter a kind of exchange which is justly censured; for it is unnatural, and a mode by which men gain from one another. The most hated sort, and with the greatest reason, is usury, which makes a gain out of money itself, and not from the natural use of it. For money was intended to be used in exchange, but not to increase at interest. . . .

. . . It would be well also to collect the scattered stories of the ways in which individuals have succeeded in amassing a fortune; for all this is useful to persons who value the art of making money. There is the anecdote of Thales the Milesian and his financial device, which involves a principle of universal application, but is attributed to him on account of his reputation for wisdom.

He was reproached for his poverty, which was supposed to show that philosophy was of no use. According to the story, he knew by his skill in the stars while it was yet winter that there would be a great harvest of olives in the coming year; so, having a little capital, he gave earnest-money for the use of all the olive-presses in Chios and Miletus, which he hired at a low price because no one bid against him. When the harvest-time came, and many wanted them all at once and of a sudden, he let them out at any rate which he pleased, and made a quantity of money. Thus he showed the world that philosophers can easily be rich if they like, but that their ambition is of another sort. He is supposed to have given a striking proof of his wisdom, but, as I was saying, his device for getting money is of universal application, and is nothing but the creation of a monopoly. It is an art often practised by cities when they are in want of money; they make a monopoly of provisions. . . .

. . . Statesmen ought to know these things; for a state is often as much in want of money and of such devices for obtaining it as a household, or even more so; hence some public men devote themselves entirely to finance.

Of household management we have seen that there are three parts—one is the rule of a master over slaves, which has been discussed already, another of a father, and the third of a husband. A husband and father rules over wife and children, both free, but the rule differs, the rule over his children being a royal, over his wife a constitutional rule. For although there may be exceptions to the order of nature, the male is by nature fitter for command than the female, just as the elder and full-grown is superior to the younger and more immature. But in most constitutional states the citizens rule and are ruled by turns, for the idea of a constitutional state implies that the natures of the citizens are equal, and do not differ at all. Nevertheless, when one rules and the other is ruled we endeavour to create a difference of outward forms and modes of address and titles of respect, which may be illustrated by the saying of Amasis about his foot-pan. The relation of the male to the female is of this kind, but there the inequality is permanent. The rule of a father over his children is royal, for he receives both love and the respect due to age, exercising a kind of royal power. And therefore, Homer has appropriately called Zeus 'father of Gods and men,' because he is the king of them all. For a king is the natural superior of his subjects, but he should be of the same kin or kind with them, and such is the relation of elder and younger, of father and son. . . .

. . . In general we may ask about the natural ruler, and the natural subject, whether they have the same or indifferent virtues. For a noble nature is equally required in both, but if so, why should one of them always rule, and the other always be ruled? Nor can we say that this is a question of degree, for the difference between ruler and subject is a difference of kind, and therefore not of degree; yet how strange is the supposition that the one ought, and that the other ought not, to have virtue! For if the ruler is intemperate and unjust, how can he rule well? if the subject, how can he obey well? If he be licentious and cowardly, he will certainly not do his duty. It is evident, therefore, that both of them must have a share of virtue, but varying according to their various natures . . . almost all things rule and are ruled according to nature. But the kind of rule differs;—the freeman rules over the slave after another manner from that in which the male rules over the female, or the man over the child; although the parts of the soul are present in all of them, they are present in different degrees. For the slave has no deliberative faculty at all; the woman has, but it is without authority, and the child has, but it is immature. So it must necessarily be with the moral virtues also; all may be supposed to partake of them, but only in such manner and degree as is required by each for the fulfilment of his duty. Hence the ruler ought to have moral virtue in perfection, for his duty is entirely that of a master artificer, and the master artificer is reason; the subjects, on the other hand, require only that measure of virtue which is proper to each of them. Clearly, then, moral virtue belongs to all of them; but the temperance of a man and of a woman, or the courage and justice of a man and of a woman, are not, as Socrates maintained, the same; the courage of a man is shown in commanding, of a woman in obeying. And this holds of all other virtues, as will be more clearly seen if we look at them in detail, for those who say generally that virtue consists in a good disposition of the soul, or in doing rightly, or the like, only deceive themselves. Far better than such definitions is their mode of speaking, who, like Georgias, enumerate the virtues. All classes must be deemed to have their special attributes; as the poet says of women,

> Silence is a woman's glory,

but this not equally the glory of man. The child is imperfect, and therefore obviously his virtue is not relative to himself alone, but to the perfect man and to his teacher, and in like manner the virtue of the slave is relative to a master. Now we determined that a slave is useful for the wants of life, and therefore he will obviously require only so much virtue as will prevent him from failing in his duty through cowardice and intemperance. . . .

Book II

Our purpose is to consider what form of political community is best of all for those who are most able to realize their ideal of life. . . .

We will begin with the natural beginning of the subject. Three alternatives are conceivable: The members of a state must either have (1) all things or (2) nothing in common, or (3) some things in common and some not. That they should have nothing in common is clearly impossible, for the state is a community, and must at any rate have a common place—one city will be in one place, and the citizens are those who share in that one city. But should a well-ordered state have all

things, as far as may be, in common, or some only and not others? For the citizens might conceivably have wives and children and property in common, as Socrates proposes in the Republic of Plato. Which is better, our present condition, or the proposed new order of society?

There are many difficulties in the community of women. The principle on which Socrates rests the necessity of such an institution does not appear to be established by his arguments; and then again as a means to the end which he ascribes to the state, taken literally, it is impossible, and how we are to limit and qualify it is nowhere precisely stated. I am speaking of the premiss from which the argument of Socrates proceeds, "that the greater the unity of the state the better." Is it not obvious that a state may at length attain such a degree of unity as to be no longer a state?—since the nature of a state is to be a plurality, and in tending to greater unity, from being a state, it becomes a family, and from being a family, an individual; for the family may be said to be more one than the state, and the individual than the family. So that we ought not to attain this greatest unity even if we could, for it would be the destruction of the state. Again, a state is not made up only of so many men, but of different kinds of men; for similars do not constitute a state. It is not like a military alliance, of which the usefulness depends upon its quantity even where there is no difference in quality. For in that mutual protection is the end aimed at; and the question is the same as about the scales of a balance: which is the heavier? . . .

. . . Extreme unification of the state is clearly not good; for a family is more self-sufficing than an individual, and a city than a family, and a city only comes into being when the community is large enough to be self-sufficing. If then self-sufficiency is to be desired, the lesser degree of unity is more desirable than the greater.

But, even supposing that it were best for the community to have the greatest degree of unity, this unity is by no means indicated by the fact "of all men saying 'mine' and 'not mine' at the same instant of time," which, according to Socrates, is the sign of perfect unity in a state . . . For that which is common to the greatest number has the least care bestowed upon it. Every one thinks chiefly of his own, hardly at all of the common interest; and only when he is himself concerned as an individual. For besides other considerations, everybody is more inclined to neglect the duty which he expects another to fulfil; as in families many attendants are often less useful than a few. Each citizen will have a thousand sons who will not be his sons individually, but anybody will be equally the son of anybody, and will therefore be neglected by all alike . . . Nor is there any way of preventing brothers and children and fathers and mothers from sometimes recognizing one another; for children are born like their parents, and they will necessarily be finding indications of their relationship to one another. Geographers declare such to be the fact; they say that in Upper Libya, where the women are common, nevertheless the children who are born are assigned to their respective fathers on the ground of their likeness. And some women, like the females of other animals—for example mares and cows—have a strong tendency to produce offspring resembling their parents, as was the case with the Pharsalian mare called Dicaea (the Just).

Other evils, against which it is not easy for the authors of such a community to guard, will be assaults and homicides, voluntary as well as involuntary, quarrels and slanders, all which are most unholy acts when committed against fathers and mothers and near relations, but not equally unholy when there is no relationship. Moreover, they are much more likely to occur if the relationship is unknown, and, when they have occurred, the customary expiations of them cannot be made. . . .

. . . In a word, the result of such a law would be just the opposite of that which good laws ought to have, and the intention of Socrates in making these regulations about women and children would defeat itself. For friendship we believe to be the greatest good

of states and the preservative of them against revolutions; neither is there anything which Socrates so greatly lauds as the unity of the state which he and all the world declare to be created by friendship. But the unity which he commends would be like that of the lovers in the Symposium, who, as Aristophanes says, desire to grow together in the excess of their affection, and from being two to become one, in which case one or both would certainly perish. Whereas [the very opposite will really happen;] in a state having women and children common, love will be watery; and the father will certainly not say "my son," or the son "my father." As a little sweet wine mingled with a great deal of water is imperceptible in the mixture, so, in this sort of community, the idea of relationship which is based upon these names will be lost; there is no reason why the so-called father should care about the son, or the son about the father, or brothers about one another. Of the two qualities which chiefly inspire regard and affection—that a thing is your own and that you love it—neither can exist in such a state as this . . . .

Next let us consider what should be our arrangements about property: should the citizens of the perfect state have their possessions in common or not? . . .

. . . If they do not share equally in enjoyments and toils, those who labour much and get little will necessarily complain of those who labour little and receive or consume much. There is always a difficulty in men living together and having things in common, but especially in their having common property. The partnerships of fellow-travellers are an example to the point; for they generally fall out by the way and quarrel about any trifle which turns up. So with servants: we are most liable to take offence at those with whom we most frequently come into contact in daily life.

These are only some of the disadvantages which attend the community of property; the present arrangement, if improved as it might be by good customs and laws, would be far better, and would have the advantages of both systems. Property should be in a certain sense common, but, as a general rule, private; for, when every one has a distinct interest, men will not complain of one another, and they will make more progress, because every one will be attending to his own business. And yet among the good, and in respect of use, "Friends," as the proverb says, "will have all things common." Even now there are traces of such a principle, showing that it is not impracticable, but, in well-ordered states, exists already to a certain extent and may be carried further. For, although every man has his own property, some things he will place at the disposal of his friends, while of others he shares the use with them. The Lacedaemonians, for example, use one another's slaves, and horses and dogs, as if they were their own; and when they happen to be in the country, they appropriate in the fields whatever provisions they want. It is clearly better that property should be private, but the use of it common; and the special business of the legislator is to create in men this benevolent disposition. Again, how immeasurably greater is the pleasure, when a man feels a thing to be his own; for the love of self is a feeling implanted by nature and not given in vain, although selfishness is rightly censured; this, however, is not the mere love of self, but the love of self in excess, like the miser's love of money; for all, or almost all, men love money, and other such objects in a measure. And further, there is the greatest pleasure in doing a kindness or service to friends or guests or companions, which can only be rendered when a man has private property. The advantage is lost by the excessive unification of the state. Two virtues are annihilated in such a state: first, temperance towards women (for it is an honourable action to abstain from another's wife for temperance sake); secondly, liberality in the matter of property. No one, when men have all things in common, will any longer set an example of liberality or do any liberal action; for liberality consists in the use which is made of property.

Such legislation may have a specious appearance of benevolence; men readily listen to it, and are easily induced to believe that in some wonderful manner everybody will become everybody's friend, especially when some one is heard denouncing the evils now existing in states, suits about contracts, convictions for perjury, flatteries of rich men and the like, which are said to arise out of the possession of private property. These evils, however, are due to a very different cause—the wickedness of human nature. Indeed, we see that there is much more quarrelling among those who have all things in common, though there are not many of them when compared with the vast numbers who have private property. . . .

. . . The error of Socrates must be attributed to the false notion of unity from which he starts. Unity there should be, both of the family and of the state, but in some respects only. For there is a point at which a state may attain such a degree of unity as to be no longer a state, or at which, without actually ceasing to exist, it will become an inferior state, like harmony passing into unison, or rhythm which has been reduced to a single foot. The state, as I was saying, is a plurality, which should be united and made into a community by education; and it is strange that the author of a system of education, which he thinks will make the state virtuous, should expect to improve his citizens by regulations of this sort, and not by philosophy or by customs and laws, like those which prevail at Sparta and Crete respecting common meals, whereby the legislator has [to a certain degree] made property common. Let us remember that we should not disregard the experience of ages; in the multitude of years these things, if they were good, would certainly not have been unknown; for almost everything has been found out, although sometimes they are not put together; in other cases men do not use the knowledge which they have. . . .

Plato in the *Laws* was of opinion that, to a certain extent, accumulation should be allowed, forbidding, as I have already observed, any citizen to possess more than five times the minimum qualification. But those who make such laws should remember what they are apt to forget—that the legislator who fixes the amount of property should also fix the number of children; for, if the children are too many for the property, the law must be broken. And, besides the violation of the law, it is a bad thing that many from being rich should become poor; for men of ruined fortunes are sure to stir up revolutions. That the equalization of property exercises an influence on political society was clearly understood even by some of the old legislators. Laws were made by Solon and others prohibiting an individual from possessing as much land as he pleased; and there are other laws in states which forbid the sale of property: among the Locrians, for example, there is a law that a man is not to sell his property unless he can prove unmistakably that some misfortune has befallen him. Again, there have been laws which enjoin the preservation of the original lots. Such a law existed in the island of Leucas, and the abrogation of it made the constitution too democratic, for the rulers no longer had the prescribed qualification. Again, where there is equality of property, the amount may be either too large or too small, and the possessor may be living either in luxury or penury. Clearly, then, the legislator ought not only to aim at the equalization of properties, but at moderation in their amount. And yet, if he prescribe this moderate amount equally to all, he will be no nearer the mark; for it is not the possessions but the desires of mankind which require to be equalized, and this is impossible, unless a sufficient education is provided by the state. But Phaleas will probably reply that this is precisely what he means; and that, in his opinion, there ought to be in states, not only equal property, but equal education. Still he should tell us what will be the character of his education; there is no use in having one and the same for all, if it is of a sort that predisposes men to avarice, or ambition, or both. Moreover, civil troubles arise, not only out of the inequality of property, but out of the inequality of honour, though in opposite ways. For the common people quarrel about the in-

equality of property, the higher class about the equality of honour; as the poet says—

The bad and good alike in honour share.

There are crimes of which the motive is want; and for these Phaleas expects to find a cure in the equalization of property, which will take away from a man the temptation to be a highwayman, because he is hungry or cold. But want is not the sole incentive to crime; men desire to gratify some passion which preys upon them, or they are eager to enjoy the pleasures which are unaccompanied with the pain of desire, and therefore they commit crimes.

Now what is the cure of these three disorders? Of the first, moderate possessions and occupation; of the second, habits of temperance; as to the third, if any desire pleasures which depend on themselves, they will find the satisfaction of their desires nowhere but in philosophy; for all other pleasures we are dependent on others. The fact is that the greatest crimes are caused by excess and not by necessity. Men do not become tyrants in order that they may not suffer cold; and hence great is the honour bestowed, not on him who kills a thief, but on him who kills a tyrant. Thus we see that the institutions of Phaleas avail only against petty crimes. . . .

Hippodamus, the son of Euryphon, a native of Miletus, the same who invented the art of planning cities, and who also laid out the Piraeus—a strange man, whose fondness for distinction led him into a general eccentricity of life, which made some think him affected (for he would wear flowing hair and expensive ornaments; and yet he dressed himself in the same cheap warm garment both in winter and summer); he, besides aspiring to be an adept in the knowledge of nature, was the first person not a statesman who made enquiries about the best form of government.

The city of Hippodamus was composed of ten thousand citizens . . . He also divided his laws into three classes, and no more, for he maintained that there are three subjects of lawsuits—insult, injury, and homicide. He likewise instituted a single final court of appeal, to which all causes seeming to have been improperly decided might be referred; this court he formed of elders chosen for the purpose. He was further of opinion that the decisions of the courts ought not to be given by the use of a voting pebble, but that every one should have a tablet on which he might not only write a simple condemnation, or leave the tablet blank for a simple acquittal; but, if he partly acquitted and partly condemned, he was to distinguish accordingly. To the existing law he objected that it obliged the judges to be guilty of perjury, whichever way they voted. He also enacted that those who discovered anything for the good of the state should be rewarded. . . .

Neither is the law to be commended which says that the judges, when a simple issue is laid before them, should distinguish in their judgment; for the judge is thus converted into an arbitrator. Now, in an arbitration, although the arbitrators are many, they confer with one another about the decision, and therefore they can distinguish; but in courts of law this is impossible, and, indeed, most legislators take pains to prevent the judges from holding any communication with one another. Again, will there not be confusion if the judge thinks that damages should be given, but not so much as the suitor demands? He asks, say, for twenty minae, and the judge allows him ten minae, or one judge more and another less; one five, another four minae. In this way they will go on apportioning the damages, and some will grant the whole and others nothing: how is the final reckoning to be taken? Again, no one who votes for a simple acquittal or condemnation is compelled to perjure himself, if the indictment is quite simple and in right form; for the judge who acquits does not decide that the defendant owes nothing, but that he does not owe the twenty minae. He only is guilty of perjury who thinks that the defendant ought not to pay twenty minae, and yet condemns him.

To reward those who discover anything which is useful to the state is a proposal which has a specious sound, but cannot safely be enacted by law, for it may encourage informers, and perhaps even lead to political commotions. This question involves another. It has been doubted whether it is or is not expedient to make any changes in the laws of a country, even if another law be better. Now, if all changes are inexpedient, we can hardly assent to the proposal of Hippodamus; for, under pretence of doing a public service, a man may introduce measures which are really destructive to the laws or to the constitution. But, since we have touched upon this subject, perhaps we had better go a little into detail, for, as I was saying, there is a difference of opinion, and it may sometimes seem desirable to make changes. Such changes in the other arts and sciences have certainly been beneficial; medicine, for example, and gymnastic, and every other art and science have departed from traditional usage. And, if politics be an art, change must be necessary in this as in any other art. The need of improvement is shown by the fact that old customs are exceedingly simple and barbarous. For the ancient Hellenes went about armed and bought their wives of each other. The remains of ancient laws which have come down to us are quite absurd; for example, at Cumae there is a law about murder, to the effect that if the accuser produce a certain number of witnesses from among his own kinsmen, the accused shall be held guilty. Again, men in general desire the good, and not merely what their fathers had. But the primaeval inhabitants, whether they were born of the earth, or were the survivors of some destruction, may be supposed to have been no better than ordinary foolish people among ourselves (such is certainly the tradition concerning the earth-born men); and it would be ridiculous to rest contented with their notions. Even when laws have been written down, they ought not always to remain unaltered. As in other arts, so in making a constitution, it is impossible that all things should be precisely set down in writing; for enactments must be universal, but actions are concerned with particulars. Hence we infer that sometimes and in certain cases laws may be changed; but when we look at the matter from another point of view, great caution would seem to be required. For the habit of lightly changing the laws is an evil, and, when the advantage is small, some errors both of lawgivers and rulers had better be left; the citizen will not gain so much by the change as he will lose by the habit of disobedience. The analogy of the arts is false; a change in a law is a very different thing from a change in an art. For the law has no power to command obedience except that of habit, which can only be given by time, so that a readiness to change from old to new laws enfeebles the power of the law. Even if we admit that the laws are to be changed, are they all to be changed, and in every state? And are they to be changed by anybody who likes, or only by certain persons? These are very important questions; and therefore we had better reserve the discussion of them to a more suitable occasion.

In the governments of Lacedaemon and Crete, and indeed in all governments, two points have to be considered; first, whether any particular law is good or bad, when compared with the perfect state; secondly, whether it is or is not consistent with the idea and character which the lawgiver has set before his citizens. That in a well-ordered state the citizens should have leisure and not have to provide for their daily wants is generally acknowledged, but there is a difficulty in seeing how this leisure is to be attained. [For, if you employ slaves, they are liable to rebel.] The Thessalian Penestae have often risen against their masters . . . Besides, if there were no other difficulty, the treatment or management of slaves is a troublesome affair; for, if not kept in hand, they are insolent, and think that they are as good as their masters, and, if harshly treated, they hate and conspire against them. Now it is clear that when these are the results the citizens of a state have not found out the secret of managing their subject population.

Again, the license of the Lacedaemonian women defeats the intention of the Spartan constitution, and is adverse to the good order

of the state. For a husband and a wife, being each a part of every family, the state may be considered as about equally divided into men and women; and, therefore, in those states in which the condition of the women is bad, half the city may be regarded as having no laws. And this is what has actually happened at Sparta; the legislator wanted to make the whole state hardy and temperate, and he has carried out his intention in the case of the men, but he has neglected the women, who live in every sort of intemperance and luxury. The consequence is that in such a state wealth is too highly valued, especially if the citizens fall under the dominion of their wives, after the manner of all warlike races, except the Celts and a few others who openly approve of male loves. The old mythologer would seem to have been right in uniting Ares and Aphrodite, for all warlike races are prone to the love either of men or of women. This was exemplified among the Spartans in the days of their greatness; many things were managed by their women. But what difference does it make whether women rule, or the rulers are ruled by women? The result is the same. . . .

The mention of avarice naturally suggests a criticism on the inequality of property. While some of the Spartan citizens have quite small properties, others have very large ones; hence the land has passed into the hands of a few. And here is another fault in their laws; for, although the legislator rightly holds up to shame the sale or purchase of an inheritance, he allows anybody who likes to give and bequeath it. Yet both practices lead to the same result. And nearly two-fifths of the whole country are held by women; this is owing to the number of heiresses and to the large dowries which are customary. It would surely have been better to have given no dowries at all, or, if any, but small or moderate ones . . . Again, the law which relates to the procreation of children is adverse to the correction of this inequality. For the legislator, wanting to have as many Spartans as he could, encouraged the citizens to have large families; and there is a law at Sparta that the father of three sons shall be exempt from military service, and he who has four from all the burdens of the state. Yet it is obvious that, if there were many children, the land being distributed as it is, many of them must necessarily fall into poverty.

The Lacedaemonian constitution is defective in another point; I mean the Ephoralty. This magistracy has authority in the highest matters, but the Ephors are all chosen from the people, and so the office is apt to fall into the hands of very poor men, who, being badly off, are open to bribes. There have been many examples at Sparta of this evil in former times; and quite recently, in the matter of the Andrians, certain of the Ephors who were bribed did their best to ruin the state. And so great and tyrannical is their power, that even the kings have been compelled to court them; through their influence the constitution has deteriorated, and from being an aristocracy has turned into a democracy. The Ephoralty certainly does keep the state together; for the people are contented when they have a share in the highest office, and the result, whether due to the legislator or to chance, has been advantageous. For if a constitution is to be permanent, all the parts of the state must wish that it should exist and be maintained. . . .

Again, the council of elders is not free from defects. It may be said that the elders are good men and well trained in manly virtue; and that, therefore, there is an advantage to the state in having them. But that judges of important causes should hold office for life is not a good thing, for the mind grows old as well as the body. And when men have been educated in such a manner that even the legislator himself cannot trust them, there is real danger. Many of the elders are well known to have taken bribes and to have been guilty of partiality in public affairs. And therefore they ought not to be irresponsible; yet at Sparta they are so. But (it may be replied), 'All magistracies are accountable to the Ephors.' Yes, but this prerogative is too great for them, and we maintain that the control should be exercised in some other manner. Further, the mode in which the Spartans elect their elders is childish; and it is improper that the person to be elected should canvass for the office; the worthiest should be appointed, whether he chooses or not. And here the legislator clearly indicates the same intention which appears in other parts of his constitution; he would have his citizens ambitious, and he has reckoned upon this quality in the election of the elders; for no one would ask to be elected if he were not. Yet ambition and avarice, almost more than any other passions, are the motives of crime.

Whether kings are or are not an advantage to states, I will consider at another time; they should at any rate be chosen, not as they are now, but with regard to their personal life and conduct. The legislator himself obviously did not suppose that he could make them really good men; at least he shows a great distrust of their virtue. For this reason the Spartans used to join enemies in the same embassy, and the quarrels between the kings were held to be conservative of the state. . . .

2
Marcus Tullius Cicero
106–43 B.C.

Below an ancient Italian town, Arpinus, in the valley of Lirus lay the villa of a knight called A. T. Cicero. He sired a son, Marcus Tullius, fated to become the greatest orator of all times, and the staunchest Republican and brashest braggart of Rome. Cicero's father was not "noble"; a Roman was a noble only if he or one of his forebears had sat in the senate. But A. T. Cicero was an equestrian—a country gentleman. Plagued by sickness, he spent most of his days in his country home and indulged in literary pretensions.

Plutarch (the famous classical biographer) reports that Cicero's mother was delivered of him without pain or labor. His boyhood was sheltered and studious. After practicing dialectic, rhetoric and reading literature, he studied law under established jurisconsults. He wrote verses, translated Greek authors, and even wrote a book on rhetoric (which he later held in low esteem, but which was taken seriously in the Middle Ages). At sixteen he celebrated rites of donning a *toga virilis*—a ceremony before a magistrate giving him status of a man. His training, however, continued, and even included a military interlude—he saw active service in the social war.

Cicero's career as an advocate started when he was twenty-five, but was soon interrupted by a trip to Athens for more study in philosophy and rhetoric. Some say his Grecian tour was prompted by displeasure of the bloody dictator, Sulla, who was aroused because Cicero took a case against one of Sulla's household. There is evidence to the contrary.

Cicero's prominent part in Roman affairs waited until he returned from Greece almost thirty years old. He came home married to a wealthy woman who may have goaded him into prominence.

Young Roman politicians attracted attention to themselves by undertaking prosecution of some notorious public malefactor. The times were corrupt, and opportunities for such prosecutions were plentiful. Cicero's quarry was Verres, a robber-governor of Sicily, who announced that in his three years of office he would seize enough swag to pay the best lawyers, bribe all the judges, and have enough left over to live in splendor. Cicero pricked this boast and handed him a ruinous conviction. Cicero had more liking, however, for the role of defense counsel, and most of his advocacy was on that side of the bar.

A successful political careerist in Cicero's time mounted a ladder of elective offices. At the top was the plum of provincial or colonial governorship. A young politician sought first to be quaestor (deputy to a more important official), then aedile (in charge of public works and games, police and grain supply), then praetor (magistrate), and finally consul (one of the twin top-administrators of Rome). Each of these offices was held only for one year; candidates had to reach a prescribed age. Cicero realized his ambition to hold each of these offices at minimum age. This was all the more an accomplishment because he was not a noble but was a "novus homo" (new man), an upstart—a fact his political enemies constantly stressed. He was forty three when elected consul. His backers were mostly squires from Italian towns; he did not have enough class for the Roman aristocracy and he was too conservative for the city rabble; as a well brought up country boy he resented first-family exclusiveness and feared popular excesses. His disposition and legal training made him a constitutionalist when military figures were likely to pay only lip service to law while doing as they pleased. Cicero was a canny politician. Like Jim Farley, he knew everybody's name, where he lived, what he did. He bought a home strategically placed so that people who wanted to see him or pay him court could get to him easily without much walking.

Cicero was elected consul when two political giants dominated Rome—Pompey and Caesar. Pompey's leadership had been rewarded with command of forces assigned to put down Mediterranean pirates; the senate gave him dictatorial powers over the sea and fifty miles inland on all coasts. Caesar's star was rising and he was seeking a comparable military command. His rise, however, was interrupted by a desperate revolt led by dissolute Cataline that discredited Caesar's popular party. Cicero's constitutionalism was, for the moment, the popular position, and he was elected consul. Cicero quashed proposals for Caesar's aggrandizement, upset Cataline's plan to assassinate Cicero, and put down the Catalinarian rebellion. Cataline was killed in a skirmish outside the city. Several co-conspirators stayed in Rome and were brought to trial before the senate. Cicero urged death for them—a break from his constitutionalism, since the senate lacked power to decree death for Roman citizens. Cicero's peroration in the senate trial was: "On whatever you decide, decide quickly. Caesar tells you of the Sempronian law— the law, namely, forbidding the death of a Roman citizen—but can he be regarded as a citizen who has been found in arms against the city?" The senate voted with Cicero and the conspirators were executed forthwith. His part and position were to be used tellingly against Cicero in years to come. He, at once, lost support of the popular party;

though his politics at this juncture accorded with the views and interests of nobles, they looked on him as a parvenu and were jealous of his conspicuous riches. Only his opponent, Caesar, offered support; Caesar recognized and hoped to exploit Cicero's talents; Cicero, however, spurned Caesar's offer.

The end of the Republic was near. Pompey made a triumphal return. Caesar went to Spain as colonial governor and returned and placated Pompey. The two joined with rich and influential Crassus in a three-man dictatorship—the first Triumvirate—and controlled Rome to their own liking. It is said that Cicero could have been a fourth in the ruling group if he would, but that his republicanism meant more to him than power. Caesar, before undertaking his command in Gaul, decided that Cicero's power should be neutralized, and inspired Clodius, a colorful enemy of Cicero, to effect Cicero's banishment. Clodius pushed through a law in the people's assembly interdicting giving fire or water to anyone who had wrongfully executed a Roman citizen—aimed, of course, at Cicero's dealing with the Catalinarian conspirators. Later, an interpretive statute was passed applying that law specifically to Cicero and decreeing that he should not come within four hundred miles of Rome. Though Clodius controlled the assembly, the senate was loaded with partisans of Cicero and passed a resolution to wear mourning for him in his trouble—a common Roman expression of sympathy designed to soften threatened discipline. The consuls, however, ordered non-compliance with this resolution. Six short years after Cicero's election to consulship, he was exiled, outlawed, and his property was confiscated.

His banishment lasted only a little over a year, when a tide of feeling favorable to Cicero resulted in repeal legislation. He was received back in Rome with great pomp and honor. Warmth of his welcome fanned his hope that he could reconstruct a solid constitutional party; but he soon saw that this hope was unfounded. In despair he withdrew temporarily, from public life. During this retreat he wrote a work excerpted here-inafter—*De Legibus*—which with his *De Re-publica* is virtually the only extensive Roman writing on legal philosophy.

A shortage of qualified personnel for foreign service led to enactment of a law conscripting all former consuls for colonial governors. Fifty-four-year-old Cicero reluctantly went to govern Cilicia—a group of settlements in Asia Minor and the Island of Cyprus. He stayed not a day over the minimum time required by law. But he was an exemplary governor—the only one of his time to forgo customary exactions and exploitation. He managed affairs of the colony with insight and competence. He also played at the role of military leader and conducted some minor campaigns ably. He had brought with him twelve thousand infantrymen and twenty-six hundred cavalrymen. On this slim base he tried without success to build himself into a military hero.

He returned to a Rome caught in throes preceding civil war between Caesar and Pompey. Though Cicero found it hard to choose sides, and though Caesar had asked him to remain neutral, he thought republicanism might fare better under Pompey and joined Pompey's forces. His military exploits were negligible. Plutarch reports that his wisecracks during the campaign were notable.

Caesar, of course, triumphed and assumed dictatorial powers. Cicero was forgiven and returned to Rome to live again in political silence. He spent his time in literary ways and did some teaching. His family affairs went badly. His thrice married daughter Tullia—the object of his greatest affection—died at the age of twenty-five. His son did not develop to his liking. When his grasping, egotistic wife falsely maneuvered his financial affairs in her own interest, Cicero divorced her and contracted a short, unsatisfactory marriage with a much younger (and very rich) woman.

Three years after Cicero returned to Rome, Caesar was murdered in the Senate by the Brutus-Cassius conspirators. Though Cicero hated the dictatorship he was not a conspirator. (Plutarch says Cicero's cowardice repelled the conspirators and kept his good friend and confidante, Brutus, from asking Cicero to join the conspiracy.) Death of the dictator revived Cicero's hopes for constitutionalism, and he put on a whirlwind campaign for personal support addressed to the senate, the people, and the provincial governors. But the conspirators were not foes of tyranny; they were only enemies of a tyrant. The republic was dead. Cicero's greatest antagonist was Caesar's sycophant, Marc Anthony, against whom Cicero wrote and delivered The Phillippics, a dozen orations. Octavian, Caesar's nephew and heir, was Cicero's hope, but Octavian joined with Anthony and Lepidus to form the Second Triumvirate of dictators. The Triumvirate listed its enemies for death, and Cicero was high on the roster. He made some dispirited moves to escape, but was captured and killed. His dismembered head and hands were carried back to the Senate for unspeakable indignities. Years later when Octavian caught his embarrassed grandson reading Cicero's work, he said, "This was a learned man and a lover of his country."

It is said that Cicero is the channel through which the theory of natural law flowed from Greeks to Early Christians, and then on to great mediaeval Schoolmen. "In this way," says Sabine, "the belief that justice, right, equality and fair dealing should underlie the law became a commonplace in European political philosophy."

LAWS *

Book I

IV. . . . A. . . . But kindly begin without delay the statement of your opinions on the civil law.

M. My opinions? Well then, I believe that there have been most eminent men in our State whose customary function it was to

* Translated by C. W. Keyes, in the Loeb Classical Library. Reprinted by permission of the Harvard University Press.

interpret the law to the people and answer questions in regard to it, but that these men, though they have made great claims, have spent their time on unimportant details. What subject indeed is so vast as the law of the State? But what is so trivial as the task of those who give legal advice? It is, however, necessary for the people. But, while I do not consider that those who have applied themselves to this profession have lacked a conception of universal law, yet they have carried their studies of this civil law, as it is called, only far enough to accomplish their purpose of being useful to the people. Now all this amounts to little so far as learning is concerned, though for practical purposes it is indispensable. What subject is it, then, that you are asking me to expound? To what task are you urging me? Do you want me to write a treatise on the law of eaves and house-walls? Or to compose formulas for contracts and court procedure? These subjects have been carefully treated by many writers, and are of a humbler character, I believe, than what is expected of me.

V. A. Yet if you ask what I expect of you, I consider it a logical thing that, since you have already written a treatise on the constitution of the ideal State, you should also write one on its laws. For I note that this was done by your beloved Plato, whom you admire, revere above all others, and love above all others.

M. Is it your wish, then, that, as he discussed the institutions of States and the ideal laws with Clinias and the Spartan Megillus in Crete on a summer day amid the cypress groves and forest paths of Cnossus, sometimes walking about, sometimes resting—you recall his description—we, in like manner, strolling or taking our ease among these stately poplars on the green and shady river bank, shall discuss the same subjects along somewhat broader lines than the practice of the courts calls for?

A. I should certainly like to hear such a conversation.

M. What does Quintus say?

Q. No other subject would suit me better.

M. And you are wise, for you must understand that in no other kind of discussion can one bring out so clearly what Nature's gifts to man are, what a wealth of most excellent possessions the human mind enjoys, what the purpose is, to strive after and accomplish which we have been born and placed in this world, what it is that unites men, and what natural fellowship there is among them. For it is only after all these things have been made clear that the origin of Law and Justice can be discovered.

A. Then you do not think that the science of law is to be derived from the praetor's edict, as the majority do now, or from the Twelve Tables, as people used to think, but from the deepest mysteries of philosophy?

M. Quite right; for in our present conversation, Pomponius, we are not trying to learn how to protect ourselves legally, or how to answer clients' questions. Such problems may be important, and in fact they are; for in former times many eminent men made a specialty of their solution, and at present one person performs this duty with the greatest authority and skill. But in our present investigation we intend to cover the whole range of universal Justice and Law in such a way that our own civil law, as it is called, will be confined to a small and narrow corner. For we must explain the nature of Justice, and this must be sought for in the nature of man; we must also consider the laws by which States ought to be governed; then we must deal with the enactments and decrees of nations which are already formulated and put in writing; and among these the civil law, as it is called, of the Roman people will not fail to find a place.

VI. Q. You probe deep, and seek, as you should, the very fountain-head, to find what we are after, brother. And those who teach the civil law in any other way are teaching not so much the path of justice as of litigation.

M. There you are mistaken, Quintus, for it is rather ignorance of the law than knowledge of it that leads to litigation. But that will come later; now let us investigate the origins of Justice.

litigate = to carry on a legal contest by judicial process.

Well then, the most learned men have determined to begin with Law, and it would seem that they are right, if, according to their definition, Law is the highest reason, implanted in Nature, which commands what ought to be done and forbids the opposite. This reason, when firmly fixed and fully developed in the human mind, is Law. And so they believe that Law is intelligence, whose natural function it is to command right conduct and forbid wrongdoing. They think that this quality has derived its name in Greek from the idea of granting to every man his own, and in our language I believe it has been named from the idea of choosing. For as they have attributed the idea of fairness to the word law, so we have given it that of selection, though both ideas properly belong to Law. Now if this is correct, as I think it to be in general, then the origin of Justice is to be found in Law, for Law is a natural force; it is the mind and reason of the intelligent man, the standard by which Justice and Injustice are measured. But since our whole discussion has to do with the reasoning of the populace, it will sometimes be necessary to speak in the popular manner, and give the name of law to that which in written form decrees whatever it wishes, either by command or prohibition. For such is the crowd's definition of law. But in determining what Justice is, let us begin with that supreme Law which had its origin ages before any written law existed or any State had been established.

Q. Indeed that will be preferable and more suitable to the character of the conversation we have begun.

M. Well, then, shall we seek the origin of Justice itself at its fountain-head? For when that is discovered we shall undoubtedly have a standard by which the things we are seeking may be tested.

Q. I think that is certainly what we must do.

A. Put me down also as agreeing with your brother's opinion.

M. Since, then, we must retain and preserve that constitution of the state which Scipio proved to be the best in the six books devoted to the subject, and all our laws must be fitted to that type of State, and since we must also inculcate good morals, and not prescribe everything in writing, I shall seek the root of Justice in Nature, under whose guidance our whole discussion must be conducted.

A. Quite right. Surely with her as our guide, it will be impossible for us to go astray.

VII. M. Do you grant us, then, Pomponius (for I am aware of what Quintus thinks), that it is by the might of the immortal gods, or by their nature, reason, power, mind, will, or any other term which may make my meaning clearer, that all Nature is governed? For if you do not admit it, we must begin our argument with this problem before taking up anything else.

A. Surely I will grant it, if you insist upon it, for the singing of the birds about us and the babbling of the streams relieve me from all fear that I may be overheard by any of my comrades in the School.

M. Yet you must be careful; for it is their way to become very angry at times, as virtuous men will; and they will not tolerate your treason, if they hear of it, to the opening passage of that excellent book, in which the author has written, "God troubles himself about nothing, neither his own concerns nor those of others."

A. Continue, if you please, for I am eager to learn what my admission will lead to.

M. I will not make the argument long. Your admission leads us to this: that animal which we call man, endowed with foresight and quick intelligence, complex, keen, possessing memory, full of reason and prudence, has been given a certain distinguished status by the supreme God who created him; for he is the only one among so many different kinds and varieties of living beings who has a share in reason and thought, while all the rest are deprived of it. But what is more divine, I will not say in man only, but in all heaven and earth, than reason? And reason, when it is full grown and perfected, is rightly called wisdom. Therefore, since there is nothing better than reason, and since it exists both in man and God, the first common possession of man and God is reason. But those who have reason in common must also have right reason in common. And since right reason is Law, we must believe that men have Law also in common with the gods. Further, those who share Law must also share Justice; and those who share these are to be regarded as members of the same commonwealth. If indeed they obey the same authorities and powers, this is true in a far greater degree; but as a matter of fact they do obey this celestial system, the divine mind, and the God of transcendent power. Hence we must now conceive of this whole universe as one commonwealth of which both gods and men are members. . . .

X. M . . . Out of all the material of the philosophers' discussions, surely there comes nothing more valuable than the full realization that we are born for Justice, and that right is based, not upon men's opinions, but upon Nature. This fact will immediately be plain if you once get a clear conception of man's fellowship and union with his fellowmen. For no single thing is so like another, so exactly its counterpart, as all of us are to one another. Nay, if bad habits and false beliefs did not twist the weaker minds and turn them in whatever direction they are inclined, no one would be so like his own self as all men would be like all others. And so, however we may define man, a single definition will apply to all. This is a sufficient proof that there is no difference in kind between man and man; for if there were, one definition could not be applicable to all men; and indeed reason, which alone raises us above the level of the beasts and enables us to draw inferences, to prove and disprove, to discuss and solve problems, and to come to conclusions, is certainly common to us all, and, though varying in what it learns, at least in the capacity to learn it is invariable. For the same things are invariably perceived by the senses, and those things which stimulate the senses, stimulate them in the same way in all men; and those rudimentary beginnings of intelligence to which I have referred, which are imprinted on our minds, are imprinted on all minds alike; and speech, the mind's interpreter, though differing in the choice of words, agrees in the sentiments expressed. In fact, there is no human being of any race who, if he finds a guide, cannot attain to virtue.

XI. The similarity of the human race is clearly marked in its evil tendencies as well as in its goodness. For pleasure also attracts all men; and even though it is an enticement to vice, yet it has some likeness to what is naturally good. For it delights us by its lightness and agreeableness; and for this reason, by an error of thought, it is embraced as something wholesome. It is through a similar misconception that we shun death as though it were a dissolution of nature, and cling to life because it keeps us in the sphere in which we were born; and that we look upon pain as one of the greatest of evils, not only because of its cruelty, but also because it seems to lead to the destruction of nature. In the same way, on account of the similarity between moral worth and renown, those who are publicly honoured are considered happy, while those who do not attain fame are thought miserable. Troubles, joys, desires, and fears haunt the minds of all men without distinction, and even if different men have different beliefs, that does not prove, for example, that it is not the same quality of superstition that besets those races which worship dogs and cats as gods, as that which torments other races. But what nation does not love courtesy, kindliness, gratitude, and remembrance of favours bestowed? What people does not hate and despise the haughty, the wicked, the cruel, and the ungrateful? Inasmuch as these considerations prove to us that the whole human race is bound together in unity, it follows, finally, that knowledge of the principles of right living is what makes men better.

If you approve of what has been said, I will go on to what follows. But if there is anything that you care to have explained, we will take that up first.

A. We have no questions, if I may speak for both of us.

XII. M. The next point, then, is that we are so constituted by Nature as to share the sense of Justice with one another and to pass it on to all men. And in this whole discussion I want it understood that what I shall call Nature is [that which is implanted in us by Nature]; that, however, the corruption caused by bad habits is so great that the sparks of fire, so to speak, which Nature has kindled in us are extinguished by this corruption, and the vices which are their opposites spring up and are established. But if the judgments of men were in agreement with Nature, so that, as the poet says, they considered "nothing alien to them which concerns mankind," then Justice would be equally observed by all. For those creatures who have received the gift of reason from Nature have also received right reason, and therefore they have also received the gift of Law, which is right reason applied to command and prohibition. And if they have received Law, they have received Justice also. Now all men have received reason; therefore all men have received Justice. Consequently Socrates was right when he cursed, as he often did, the man who first separated utility from Justice; for this separation, he complained, is the source of all mischief. For what gave rise to Pythagoras' famous words about friendship? . . . From this it is clear that, when a wise man shows toward another endowed with equal virtue the kind of benevolence which is so widely diffused among men, that will then have come to pass which, unbelievable as it seems to some, is after all the inevitable result—namely, that he loves himself no whit more than he loves another. For what difference can there be among things which are all equal? But if the least distinction should be made in friendship, then the very name of friendship would perish forthwith; for its essence is such that, as soon as either friend prefers anything for himself, friendship ceases to exist.

Now all this is really a preface to what remains to be said in our discussion, and its purpose is to make it more easily understood that Justice is inherent in Nature.

After I have said a few words more on this topic, I shall go on to the civil law, the subject which gives rise to all this discourse.

XIII. Q. You certainly need to say very little more on that head, for from what you have already said, Atticus is convinced, and certainly I am, that Nature is the source of Justice.

A. How can I help being convinced, when it has just been proved to us, first, that we have been provided and equipped with what we may call the gifts of the gods; next, that there is only one principle by which men may live with one another, and that this is the same for all, and possessed equally by all; and, finally, that all men are bound together by a certain natural feeling of kindliness and good-will, and also by a partnership in Justice? Now that we have admitted the truth of these conclusions, and rightly, I think, how can we separate Law and Justice from Nature?

M. Quite right; that is exactly the situation. But we are following the method of the philosophers—not those of former times, but those who have built workshops, so to speak, for the production of wisdom. Those problems which were formerly argued loosely and at great length they now discuss systematically, taking them up point by point; and they do not think that a treatment of the topic which we are now considering is complete unless a separate discussion is devoted to the particular point that Justice springs from Nature.

A. And, of course, you have lost your independence in discussion, or else you are the kind of man not to follow your own judgment in a debate, but meekly to accept the authority of others!

M. I do not always do that, Titus. But you see the direction this conversation is to take; our whole discourse is intended to promote the firm foundation of States, the strengthening of cities, and the curing of the ills of peoples. For that reason I want to be especially careful not to lay down first principles that have not been wisely considered and thoroughly investigated. Of course I cannot expect that they will be universally accepted, for that is impossible; but I do look for the approval of all who believe that everything which is right and honourable is to be desired for its own sake, and that nothing whatever is to be accounted a good unless it is praiseworthy in itself, or at least that nothing should be considered a great good unless it can rightly be praised for its own sake. Of all such, I say, I expect the approval, whether they have remained in the Old Academy with Speusippus, Xenocrates, and Polemon; or have followed Aristotle and Theophrastus, who agree with the school just mentioned in doctrine, though differing slightly from it in mode of presentation; or, in agreement with Zeno, have changed the terminology without altering the ideas; or even if they have followed the strict and severe sect of Aristo, now broken up and refuted, and believe everything except virtue and vice to be on an absolute equality. So far, however, as those philosophers are concerned who practise self-indulgence, are slaves to their own bodies, and test the desirability or undesirability of everything on the basis of pleasure and pain, let us, even if they are right (for there is no need to quarrel with them here), bid them carry on their discussions in their own gardens, and even request them to abstain for a while from taking any part in matters affecting the State, which they neither understand nor have ever wished to understand. And let us implore the Academy—the new one, formed by Arcesilaus and Carneades—to be silent, since it contributes nothing but confusion to all these problems; for if it should attack what we think we have constructed and arranged so beautifully, it would play too great havoc with it; at the same time I should like to win over this school, and so do not dare to banish it from the discussion. . . .

XIV. . . There is really no expiation for crimes against men or sacrilege against the gods. And so men pay the penalty, not so much through decisions of the courts (for once there were no courts anywhere, and to-day there are none in many lands; and where they do exist, they often act unjustly

after all); but guilty men are tormented and pursued by the Furies, not with blazing torches, as in the tragedies, but with the anguish of remorse and the torture of a guilty conscience.

But if it were a penalty and not Nature that ought to keep men from injustice, what anxiety would there be to trouble the wicked when the danger of punishment was removed? But in fact there has never been a villain so brazen as not to deny that he had committed a crime, or else invent some story of just anger to excuse its commission, and seek justification for his crime in some natural principle of right. Now if even the wicked dare to appeal to such principles, how jealously should they be guarded by the good! But if it is a penalty, the fear of punishment, and not the wickedness itself, that is to keep men from a life of wrongdoing and crime, then no one can be called unjust, and wicked men ought rather to be regarded as imprudent; furthermore, those of us who are not influenced by virtue itself to be good men, but by some consideration of utility and profit, are merely shrewd, not good. For to what lengths will that man go in the dark who fears nothing but a witness and a judge? What will he do if, in some desolate spot, he meets a helpless man, unattended, whom he can rob of a fortune? Our virtuous man, who is just and good by nature, will talk with such a person, help him, and guide him on his way; but the other, who does nothing for another's sake, and measures every act by the standard of his own advantage—it is clear enough, I think, what he will do! If, however, the latter does deny that he would kill the man and rob him of his money, he will not deny it because he regards it as a naturally wicked thing to do, but because he is afraid that his crime may become known—that is, that he may get into trouble. Oh, what a motive, that might well bring a blush of shame to the cheek, not merely of the philosopher, but even of the simple rustic!

XV. But the most foolish notion of all is the belief that everything is just which is found in the customs or laws of nations.

Would that be true, even if these laws had been enacted by tyrants? If the well-known Thirty had desired to enact a set of laws at Athens, or if the Athenians without exception were delighted by the tyrants' laws, that would not entitle such laws to be regarded as just, would it? No more, in my opinion, should that law be considered just which a Roman interrex proposed, to the effect that a dictator might put to death with impunity any citizen he wished, even without a trial. For Justice is one; it binds all human society, and is based on one Law, which is right reason applied to command and prohibition. Whoever knows not this Law, whether it has been recorded in writing anywhere or not, is without Justice.

But if Justice is conformity to written laws and national customs, and if, as the same persons claim, everything is to be tested by the standard of utility, then anyone who thinks it will be profitable to him will, if he is able, disregard and violate the laws. It follows that Justice does not exist at all, if it does not exist in Nature, and if that form of it which is based on utility can be overthrown by that very utility itself. And if Nature is not to be considered the foundation of Justice, that will mean the destruction [of the virtues on which human society depends]. For where then will there be a place for generosity, or love of country, or loyalty, or the inclination to be of service to others or to show gratitude for favours received? For these virtues originate in our natural inclination to love our fellow-men, and this is the foundation of Justice. Otherwise not merely consideration for men but also rites and pious observances in honour of the gods are done away with; for I think that these ought to be maintained, not through fear, but on account of the close relationship which exists between man and God. XVI. But if the principles of Justice were founded on the decrees of peoples, the edicts of princes, or the decisions of judges, then Justice would sanction robbery and adultery and forgery of wills, in case these acts were approved by the votes or decrees of the populace. But if so great a power belongs to the decisions and decrees of fools that the laws of Nature can be changed by their votes, then why do they not ordain that what is bad and baneful shall be considered good and salutary? Or, if a law can make Justice out of Injustice, can it not also make good out of bad? But in fact we can perceive the difference between good laws and bad by referring them to no other standard than Nature; indeed, it is not merely Justice and Injustice which are distinguished by Nature, but also and without exception things which are honourable and dishonourable. For since an intelligence common to us all makes things known to us and formulates them in our minds, honourable actions are ascribed by us to virtue, and dishonourable actions to vice; and only a madman would conclude that these judgments are matters of opinion, and not fixed by Nature. For even what we, by a misuse of the term, call the virtue of a tree or of a horse, is not a matter of opinion, but is based on Nature. And if that is true, honourable and dishonourable actions must also be distinguished by Nature. For if virtue in general is to be tested by opinion, then its several parts must also be so tested; who, therefore, would judge a man of prudence, and, if I may say so, hard common sense, not by his own character but by some external circumstance? For virtue is reason completely developed; and this certainly is natural; therefore everything honourable is likewise natural. XVII. For just as truth and falsehood, the logical and illogical, are judged by themselves and not by anything else, so the steadfast and continuous use of reason in the conduct of life, which is virtue, and also inconstancy, which is vice, [are judged] by their own nature.

[Or, when a farmer judges the quality of a tree by nature,] shall we not use the same standard in regard to the characters of young men? Then shall we judge character by Nature, and judge virtue and vice, which result from character, by some other standard? But if we adopt the same standard for them, must we not refer the honourable and the base to Nature also? Whatever good thing is praiseworthy must have within itself something which deserves praise, for goodness itself is good by reason not of opinion but of Nature. For, if this were not true, men would also be happy by reason of opinion; and what statement could be more absurd than that? Wherefore since both good and evil are judged by Nature and are natural principles, surely honourable and base actions must also be distinguished in a similar way and referred to the standard of Nature. But we are confused by the variety of men's beliefs and by their disagreements, and because this same variation is not found in the senses, we think that Nature has made these accurate, and say that those things about which different people have different opinions and the same people not always identical opinions are unreal. However, this is far from being the case. For our senses are not perverted by parent, nurse, teacher, poet, or the stage, nor led astray by popular feeling; but against our minds all sorts of plots are constantly being laid, either by those whom I have just mentioned, who, taking possession of them while still tender and unformed, colour and bend them as they wish, or else by that enemy which lurks deep within us, entwined in our every sense—that counterfeit of good, which is, however, the mother of all evils—pleasure. Corrupted by her allurements, we fail to discern clearly what things are by Nature good, because the same seductiveness and itching does not attend them.

XVIII. To close now our discussion of this whole subject, the conclusion, which stands clearly before our eyes from what has already been said is this: Justice and all things honourable are to be sought for their own sake. And indeed all good men love fairness in itself and Justice in itself, and it is unnatural for a good man to make such a mistake as to love what does not deserve love for itself alone. Therefore Justice must be sought and cultivated for her own sake; and if this is true of Justice, it is also true of equity; and if this is the case with equity, then all the other virtues are also to be cherished for their own sake. What of generosity? Is it disinterested or does it look to a recompense? If a man is kind without any reward, then it is disinterested; but if he receives payment, then it is hired. It cannot be doubted that he who is called generous or kind answers the call of duty, not of gain. Therefore equity also demands no reward or price; consequently it is sought for its own sake. And the same motive and purpose characterize all the virtues.

In addition, if it be true that virtue is sought for the sake of other benefits and not for its own sake, there will be only one virtue, which will most properly be called a vice. For in proportion as anyone makes his own advantage absolutely the sole standard of all his actions, to that extent he is absolutely not a good man; therefore those who measure virtue by the reward it brings believe in the existence of no virtue except vice. For where shall we find a kindly man, if no one does a kindness for the sake of anyone else than himself? Who can be considered grateful, if even those who repay favours have no real consideration for those to whom they repay them? What becomes of that sacred thing, friendship, if even the friend himself is not loved for his own sake, "with the whole heart," as people say? Why, according to this theory, a friend should even be deserted and cast aside as soon as there is no longer hope of benefit and profit from his friendship! But what could be more inhuman than that? If, on the other hand, friendship is to be sought for its own sake, then the society of our fellow-men, fairness, and Justice, are also to be sought for their own sake. If this is not the case then there is no such thing as Justice at all, for the very height of injustice is to seek pay for Justice. XIX. But what shall we say of sobriety, moderation, and self-restraint; of modesty, self-respect, and chastity? Is it for fear of disgrace that we should not be wanton, or for fear of the laws and the courts? In that case men are innocent and modest in order to be well spoken of, and they blush in order to gain a good reputation! I am ashamed even to mention chastity! Or rather I am ashamed of those philosophers who believe it honourable to avoid condemnation for a crime without having avoided the crime itself.

And what shall we say of this? Is it possible for us to call those chaste who are kept from lewdness by the fear of disgrace, when the disgrace itself results from the inherent vileness of the deed? For what can properly be either praised or blamed, if you have disregarded the nature of the thing which in your opinion deserves praise or blame? Are bodily defects, if very conspicuous, to offend us, but not a deformity of character? And yet the baseness of this latter can easily be perceived from the very vices which result from it. For what can be thought of that is more loathsome than greed, what more inhuman than lust, what more contemptible than cowardice, what more degraded than stupidity and folly? Well, then, shall we say that those who are sunk deepest in a single vice, or in several, are wretched on account of any penalties or losses or tortures which they incur, or on account of the base nature of the vices themselves? And the same argument can be applied conversely to the praise accorded to virtue. Finally, if virtue is sought on account of other advantages, there must necessarily be something better than virtue. Is it money, then, or public office, or beauty, or health? But these things amount to very little when we possess them, and we can have no certain knowledge as to how long they will remain with us. Or is it—the very mention of such a thing is shameful— is it pleasure? But it is precisely in scorning and repudiating pleasure that virtue is most clearly discerned. . . .

LAWS

Book II

. . . IV. M. Once more, then, before we come to the individual laws, let us look at the character and nature of Law, for fear that, though it must be the standard to which we refer everything, we may now and then be led astray by an incorrect use of terms, and forget the rational principles on which our laws must be based.

Q. Quite so, that is the correct method of exposition.

M. Well, then, I find that it has been the opinion of the wisest men that Law is not a product of human thought, nor is it any enactment of peoples, but something eternal which rules the whole universe by its wisdom in command and prohibition. Thus they have been accustomed to say that Law is the primal and ultimate mind of God, whose reason directs all things either by compulsion or restraint. Wherefore that Law which the gods have given to the human race has been justly praised; for it is the reason and mind of a wise lawgiver applied to command and prohibition.

Q. You have touched upon this subject several times before. But before you come to the laws of peoples, please make the character of this heavenly Law clear to us, so that the waves of habit may not carry us away and sweep us into the common mode of speech on such subjects.

M. Ever since we were children, Quintus, we have learned to call, "If one summon another to court," and other rules of the same kind, laws. But we must come to the true understanding of the matter, which is as follows: this and other commands and prohibitions of nations have the power to summon to righteousness and away from wrong-doing; but this power is not merely older than the existence of nations and States, it is coeval with that God who guards and rules heaven and earth. For the divine mind cannot exist without reason, and divine reason cannot but have this power to establish right and wrong. No written law commanded that a man should take his stand on a bridge alone, against the full force of the enemy, and order the bridge broken down behind him; yet we shall not for that reason suppose that the heroic Cocles was not obeying the law of bravery and following its decrees in doing so noble a deed. Even if there was no written law against rape at Rome in the reign of Lucius Tarquinius, we cannot say on that account that Sextus Tarquinius did not break that eternal Law by violating Lucretia, the daughter of Tricipitinus! For reason did exist, derived from the Nature of the universe, urging men to right conduct and diverting them from wrongdoing, and this reason did not first become Law when it was written down, but when it first came into existence; and it came into existence simultaneously with the divine mind. Wherefore the true and primal Law, applied to command and prohibition, is the right reason of supreme Jupiter.

V. Q. I agree with you, brother, that what is right and true is also eternal, and does not begin or end with written statutes.

M. Therefore, just as that divine mind is the supreme Law, so, when [reason] is perfected in man, [that also is Law; and this perfected reason exists] in the mind of the wise man; but those rules which, in varying forms and for the need of the moment, have been formulated for the guidance of nations, bear the title of laws rather by favour than because they are really such. For every law which really deserves that name is truly praiseworthy, as they prove by approximately the following arguments. It is agreed, of course, that laws were invented for the safety of citizens, the preservation of States, and the tranquillity and happiness of human life, and that those who first put statutes of this kind in force convinced their people that it was their intention to write down and put into effect such rules as, once accepted and adopted, would make possible for them an honourable and happy life; and when such rules were drawn up and put in force, it is clear that men called them "laws." From this point of view it can be readily understood that those who formulated wicked and unjust statutes for nations, thereby breaking their promises and agreements, put into effect anything but "laws." It may thus be clear that in the very definition of the term "law" there inheres the idea and principle of choosing what is just and true. I ask you then, Quintus, according to the custom of the philosophers: if there is a certain thing, the lack of which

in a State compels us to consider it no State at all, must we consider this thing a good?

Q. One of the greatest goods, certainly.

M. And if a State lacks Law, must it for that reason be considered no State at all?

Q. It cannot be denied.

M. Then Law must necessarily be considered one of the greatest goods.

Q. I agree with you entirely.

M. What of the many deadly, the many pestilential statutes which nations put in force? These no more deserve to be called laws than the rules a band of robbers might pass in their assembly. For if ignorant and unskilful men have prescribed deadly poisons instead of healing drugs, these cannot possibly be called physicians' prescriptions; neither in a nation can a statute of any sort be called a law, even though the nation, in spite of its being a ruinous regulation, has accepted it. Therefore Law is the distinction between things just and unjust, made in agreement with that primal and most ancient of all things, Nature; and in conformity to Nature's standard are framed those human laws which inflict punishment upon the wicked but defend and protect the good.

VI. Q. I understand you completely, and believe that from now on we must not consider or even call anything else a law.

M. Then you do not think the Titian or Apuleian Laws were really laws at all?

Q. No; nor the Livian Laws either.

M. And you are right, especially as the Senate repealed them in one sentence and in a single moment. But the Law whose nature I have explained can neither be repealed nor abrogated.

Q. Then the laws you intend to propose will, of course, be the kind that will never be repealed?

M. Certainly, if only they are accepted by both of you. But I think that I should follow the same course as Plato, who was at the same time a very learned man and the greatest of all philosophers, and who wrote a book about the Republic first, and then in a separate treatise described its Laws. Therefore, before I recite the law itself, I will speak in praise of that law. I note that Zaleucus and Charondas did the same thing, though they wrote their laws, not for the interest and pleasure of doing so, but for actual use in their own States. Clearly Plato agreed with their opinion that it was also the function of Law to win some measure of approval, and not always compel by threats of force. . . .

VII. So in the very beginning we must persuade our citizens that the gods are the lords and rulers of all things, and that what is done, is done by their will and authority; that they are likewise great benefactors of man, observing the character of every individual, what he does, of what wrong he is guilty, and with what intentions and with what piety he fulfils his religious duties; and that they take note of the pious and the impious. For surely minds which are imbued with such ideas will not fail to form true and useful opinions. Indeed, what is more true than that no one ought to be so foolishly proud as to think that, though reason and intellect exist in himself, they do not exist in the heavens and the universe, or that those things which can hardly be understood by the highest reasoning powers of the human intellect are guided by no reason at all? In truth, the man that is not driven to gratitude by the orderly courses of the stars, the regular alternation of day and night, the gentle progress of the seasons, and the produce of the earth brought forth for our sustenance—how can such an one be accounted a man at all? And since all things that possess reason stand above those things which are without reason, and since it would be sacrilege to say that anything stands above universal Nature, we must admit that reason is inherent in Nature. Who will deny that such beliefs are useful when he remembers how often oaths are used to confirm agreements, how important to our well-being is the sanctity of treaties, how many persons are deterred from crime by the fear of divine punishment, and how sacred an association of citizens becomes when the immortal gods are made members of it, either as judges or as witnesses? . . .

LAWS

Book III

I. . . . M. You understand, then, that the function of a magistrate is to govern, and to give commands which are just and beneficial and in conformity with the law. For as the laws govern the magistrate, so the magistrate governs the people, and it can truly be said that the magistrate is a speaking law, and the law a silent magistrate. Nothing, moreover, is so completely in accordance with the principles of justice and the demands of Nature (and when I use these expressions, I wish it understood that I mean Law) as is government, without which existence is impossible for a household, a city, a nation, the human race, physical nature, and the universe itself. For the universe obeys God; seas and lands obey the universe, and human life is subject to the decrees of supreme Law.

II. But to return to matters which are closer to us and better known: all ancient nations were at one time ruled by kings. This kind of authority was entrusted at first to those who excelled in justice and wisdom, as was notably the case in our own State while the monarchy lasted. Later the kingship was handed down to the king's descendants, which is still the custom in present-day kingdoms. Now those who objected to monarchy desired, not to have no one to obey, but not always to obey the same man. But we, since we are providing a system of law for free nations, and have presented our conception of the ideal State in our six earlier books, shall now propose laws appropriate to the kind of State there described, which we consider the best. Accordingly we must have magistrates, for without their prudence and watchful care a State cannot exist. In fact the whole character of a republic is determined by its arrangements in regard to magistrates. Not only must we inform them of the limits of their administrative authority; we must also instruct the citizens as to the extent of their obligation to obey them. For the man who rules efficiently must have obeyed others in the past, and the man who obeys dutifully appears fit at some later time to be a ruler. Thus he who obeys ought to expect to be a ruler in the future, and he who rules should remember that in a short time he will have to obey. And we must provide, as Charondas does in his laws, not only that the citizens be obedient and dutiful toward the magistrates, but also that they love and honour them. Indeed my beloved Plato thought that those who rebel against their magistrates, as the Titans did against the gods, are to be classed as of the Titans' brood.

Having established these facts, we shall now proceed to the statement of the laws themselves, if that plan meets with your approval.

A. Indeed I approve not merely of that, but of your whole order of treatment.

III. M. *Commands shall be just, and the citizens shall obey them dutifully and without protest. Upon the disobedient or guilty citizen the magistrate shall use compulsion by means of fines, imprisonment, or stripes, unless an equal or higher authority, or the people, forbid it; the citizen shall have the right of appeal to them. After the Magistrate has pronounced sentence, either of death or fine, there shall be a trial before the people for the final determination of the fine or other penalty. There shall be no appeal from orders given by a commander in the field; while a magistrate is waging war his commands shall be valid and binding.*

There shall be minor magistrates with partial authority who shall be assigned to special functions. In the army they shall command those over whom they are placed, and be their tribunes; in the city they shall be custodians of public money; they shall have charge of the confinement of criminals; they shall inflict capital punishment; they shall coin bronze, silver, and gold money; they shall decide lawsuits; they shall do whatsoever the Senate shall decree.

There shall be aediles, who shall be curators of the city, of the markets, and of the customary games. This magistracy shall be their first step in the advancement to higher office.

Censors shall make a list of the citizens, recording their ages, families, and slaves and other property. They shall have charge of the temples, streets, and aqueducts within the city, and of the public treasury and the revenues. They shall make a division of the citizens into tribes, and other divisions according to wealth, age, and rank. They shall enrol the recruits for the cavalry and infantry; they shall prohibit celibacy; they shall regulate the morals of the people; they shall allow no one guilty of dishonourable conduct to remain in the Senate. They shall be two in number and shall hold office for five years. The other magistrates shall hold office for one year. The office of censor shall never be vacant.

The administrator of justice, who shall decide or direct the decision of civil cases, shall be called praetor; he shall be the guardian of the civil law. There shall be as many praetors, with equal powers, as the Senate shall decree, or the people command.

There shall be two magistrates with royal powers. Since they lead, judge, and confer, from these functions they shall be called praetors, judges, and consuls. In the field they shall hold the supreme military power; they shall be subject to no one; the safety of the people shall be their highest law.

No one shall hold the same office a second time except after an interval of ten years. They shall observe the age limits fixed by a law defining the year.

But when a serious war or civil dissensions arise, one man shall hold, for not longer than six months, the power which ordinarily belongs to the two consuls, if the Senate shall so decree. And after being appointed under favourable auspices, he shall be master of the people. He shall have an assistant to command the cavalry, whose rank shall be equal to that of the administrator of justice.

But when there are neither consuls nor a master of the people, there shall be no other magistrates, and the auspices shall be in the hands of the Senate, which shall appoint one of its number to conduct the election of consuls in the customary manner.

Officials with and without imperium and

ambassadors shall leave the city when the Senate shall so decree or the people so command; they shall wage just wars justly; they shall spare the allies; they shall hold themselves and their subordinates in check; they shall increase the national renown; they shall return home with honour.

No one shall be made an ambassador for the purpose of attending to his own personal affairs.

The ten officials whom the plebeians shall elect to protect them from violence shall be their tribunes. Their prohibitions and resolutions passed by the plebeians under their presidency shall be binding. Their persons shall be inviolable. They shall not leave the plebeians without tribunes.

All magistrates shall possess the right of taking the auspices, and the judicial power. The Senate shall consist of those who have held magistracies. Its decrees shall be binding. But in case an equal or higher authority than the presiding officer shall veto a decree of the Senate, it shall nevertheless be written out and preserved.

The senatorial order shall be free from dishonour, and shall be a model for the rest of the citizens.

When elective, judicial, and legislative acts of the people are performed by vote, the voting shall not be concealed from citizens of high rank, and shall be free to the common people.

IV. But if any acts of administration shall be necessary in addition to those done by the regular magistrates, the people shall elect officials to perform them, and give them the authority to do so.

Consuls, praetors, masters of the people, masters of the horse, and those officials whom the Senate shall appoint to conduct the election of consuls shall have the right to preside over meetings of the people and the Senate. The tribunes chosen by the plebeians shall have the right to preside over the Senate, and shall also refer whatever is necessary to the plebeians.

Moderation shall be preserved in meetings of the people and the Senate.

A senator's absence from a meeting of the Senate shall be either for cause or culpable. A senator shall speak in his turn and at moderate length. He shall be conversant with public affairs.

No violence shall be used at meetings of the people. An equal or higher authority shall have the greater power. But the presiding officer shall be responsible for any disorder which may occur. He who vetoes a bad measure shall be deemed a citizen of distinguished service.

Presiding officers shall observe the auspices and obey the State augur. They shall see that bills, after being read, are filed among the archives in the State treasury. They shall not take the people's vote on more than one question at a time. They shall instruct the people in regard to the matter in hand, and allow them to be instructed by other magistrates and by private citizens.

No law of personal exception shall be proposed. Cases in which the penalty is death or loss of citizenship shall be tried only before the greatest assembly and by those whom the censors have enrolled among the citizens.

No one shall give or receive a present, either during a candidacy or during or after a term of office.

The punishment for violation of any of these laws shall fit the offence.

The censors shall have charge of the official text of the laws. When officials go out of office, they shall refer their official acts to the censors, but shall not receive exemption from prosecution thereby.

The law has been read: "disperse, and I will order the ballots to be distributed."

V. Q. In what brief form, my dear brother, you have placed before us your provisions in regard to the whole body of magistrates! Yet they are practically the same as those of our own State, though you have proposed a few innovations.

M. You are quite right, Quintus. For this is the balanced type of State . . . A government consists of its magistrates and those who direct its affairs, and that different types of States are recognized by their constitution of these magistracies. And since the wisest and most evenly balanced system has been devised by our own ancestors, I had no innovations, or at least only a few, which I thought ought to be introduced into the constitution.

A. And will you now be kind enough to present your reasons for considering these provisions in regard to the magistrates to be the best. . . .

M. I will do as you ask, Atticus, treating the whole subject in accordance with the investigations and discussions of the most learned of the Greek writers. . . .

VII. M. Well, then, these philosophers have considered whether it is best for the State to have one magistrate who shall be obeyed by everyone else. I understand that this was considered the best plan by our ancestors after the expulsion of the kings. But since the monarchy, which had formerly been approved, was later rejected, not so much through the fault of the kingship as that of the king, if one magistrate is to rule over all the others, it will seem that it was merely the name of king that was abolished, the institution remaining. Thus it was not

without good reason that ephors were set up in opposition to the Spartan kings by Theopompus, and tribunes in opposition to the consuls among us. For the consul has the legal right to enforce obedience from all other officials except the tribunes, whose office was instituted later than that of the consul for the purpose of preventing what had taken place from ever happening again. For the existence of an official who was not subject to his orders was the first step in the diminution of the consul's power, the second being the fact that this same official upheld others also, private citizens as well as magistrates, in disobedience to the consul.

Q. What you have just mentioned was a great misfortune. For it was the institution of this office that brought about the decline in the influence of the aristocracy and the growth of the power of the multitude.

M. You are mistaken, Quintus. For was it not inevitable that the consul's authority, when it stood alone, should seem too arrogant and tyrannical to the people? But a moderate and wise limitation of that power has occurred since then. . .

3

Thomas Aquinas
1225–1274

He was a tremendous, silent man with deep, placid eyes. Though his size is not recorded, one authority guesses him taller than six and one-half feet and heavier than three hundred pounds. As a student he was so quiet his fellows thought him dim-witted and called him The Dumb Ox. But he was to flower into the top theologian and philosopher of the Roman Catholic Church.

Thomas was the third son of an Italian count and was related by blood to more than half of the European kings of his day. He was born down-slope from famous Monte Casino Abbey in central Italy. Benedictine monks of the Abbey taught him to read and write and schooled him until he was fourteen. Then he was sent to the University of Naples to study "the seven liberal arts." As soon as he was old enough to have favorite subjects theology attracted him.

Thomas' family were astounded when they heard from Naples that he planned to become a begging Dominican friar. Had he wanted a more stylish and less rigorous religious career his family would have been delighted; but his mother thought the Dominican order beneath his station and forbade the seventeen-year-old from joining. He defiantly entered his noviceship and asked to be sent to Rome. When he got word that his determined mother was following him, he fled north from Rome. Older brothers intercepted him and he was hauled back to the family castle and locked up for a year during which his family tried to change his mind. Their last stratagem was to set his brother's mistress to his seduction. She entered his cell while he slept; he woke and chased her

out of the room with a burning brand seized from the fireplace. The family gave in, and he was allowed to follow his choice.

As a Dominican trainee at Cologne he was not much noticed until he attracted the attention and became the star pupil of Albertus Magnus—a fine scholar and teacher. Albert inducted Thomas into furtive studies of Aristotle, whose works were thought subversive because they were then known only in Moslem versions slanted toward Mohammedanism.

When Thomas was ordained, he left Albertus and went to the University of Paris for a master's and a doctor's degree in theology. There he soon became active in an ongoing quarrel between lay and clerical teachers. The secular side was led by William of St. Amour, who published a pamphlet calling friar-teachers Anti-Christs. As the row became more heated, it went beyond epithets. Street brawls became common, convents were stoned, students and hangers-on fought in taverns. Pope Alexander IV announced he was going to sit in judgment on the dispute. Thomas was chosen to speak on the clerical side. The Pope's judgment was, not surprisingly, for the friars. St. Amour's pamphlet was burned in public, and he was exiled from France.

While Thomas was doing graduate work at Paris he gave public lectures espousing Aristotle's views as a proper rational basis for understanding the Christian faith. This position differed radically from authoritarian orthodox theology of the times. Thomas was soon commanded by the Bishop of Paris to appear before the Inquisition on charges

56

of heresy. He made a brilliant and successful defense.

The mature Thomas was a vigorous teacher, a popular preacher, and a tireless writer. His unfinished *Summa Theologica,* excerpts from which follow this biographical note, was an encyclopedic organization of the knowledge of his times in the guise of theology. He served for several years as personal adviser to Pope Urban IV, who tried unsuccessfully to get Thomas to don a cardinal's hat. After Urban's death Thomas redoubled his writing efforts, but he was no cloistered scholar—he traveled much, occupied teachers' podiums and pulpits, and attended convocations of his order. His last sharp controversy was with Siger of Brabant, leader of the Averroists who lived by an Islamic version of Aristotle. Thomas thought Siger's Aristotle was subverted and anti-Christian. While he sparred with these radicals on his left, he could not neglect attacks on him from the right by Franciscan authoritarians.

In his late forties his health broke, and he went back to Italy. But he could not play the part of a retired, sick man. He still preached and went to general chapters of his order. In the winter of 1274, while he was traveling to a general council of the church at command of the Pope, he died. A century after his birth he was canonized. Five centuries later Pope Leo XIII published an encyclical declaring teachings of St. Thomas the basis of Roman Catholic theology. Of late years there has been an especially active interest in his philosophy by people who call themselves Neo-Thomists.

SUMMA THEOLOGICA *
First Part of the Second Part
Treatise on Law
Question 90
OF THE ESSENCE OF LAW
(In Four Articles)

* Translated by Fathers of the English Dominican Province. Reprinted by permission of Benziger Bros., Inc.

Whether Law Is Something Pertaining to Reason?

We proceed thus to the First Article:—

Objection 1. It would seem that law is not something pertaining to reason. For the Apostle says (*Rom.* vii. 23): *I see another law in my members,* etc. But nothing pertaining to reason is in the members; since the reason does not make use of a bodily organ. Therefore, law is not something pertaining to reason.

Obj. 2. Further, in the reason there is nothing else but power, habit, and act. But law is not the power itself of reason. In like manner, neither is it a habit of reason: because the habits of reason are the intellectual virtues of which we have spoken above (Q. 57). Nor again is it an act of reason: because then law would cease, when the act of reason ceases, for instance, while we are asleep. Therefore law is nothing pertaining to reason.

Obj. 3. Further, the law moves those who are subject to it to act aright. But it belongs properly to the will—to move to act, as is evident from what has been said above (Q. 9, A. 1). Therefore law pertains, not to the reason, but to the will; according to the words of the Jurist (*Lib.* i. ff., *De Const. Prin.* leg. i): *Whatsoever pleaseth the sovereign, has force of law.*

On the contrary, It belongs to the law to command and to forbid. But it belongs to reason to command, as stated above (q. 17, A. 1). Therefore law is something pertaining to reason.

I answer that, Law is a rule and measure of acts, whereby man is induced to act or is restrained from acting: for *lex* (law) is derived from *ligare* (to bind), because it binds one to act. Now the rule and measure of human acts is the reason, which is the first principle of human acts, as is evident from what has been stated above (Q. 1, A. 1 *ad* 3); since it belongs to the reason to direct to the end, which is the first principle in all matters of action, according to the

Philosopher (*Phys.* ii). Now that which is the principle in any genus, is the rule and measure of that genus: for instance, unity in the genus of numbers, and the first movement in the genus of movements. Consequently it follows that law is something pertaining to reason.

Reply Obj. 1. Since law is a kind of rule and measure, it may be something in two ways. First, as in that which measures and rules: and since this is proper to reason, it follows that, in this way, law is in the reason alone.—Secondly, as in that which is measured and ruled. In this way, law is in all those things that are inclined to something by reason of some law: so that any inclination arising from a law, may be called a law, not essentially but by participation as it were. And thus the inclination of the members to concupiscence is called *the law of the members.*

Reply Obj. 2. Just as, in external action, we may consider the work and the work done, for instance the work of building and the house built; so in the acts of reason, we may consider the act itself of reason, i.e., to understand and to reason, and something produced by this act. With regard to the speculative reason, this is first of all the definition; secondly, the proposition; thirdly, the syllogism or argument. And since also the practical reason makes use of a syllogism in respect of the work to be done, as stated above (Q. 13, A. 3; Q. 76, A. 1) and as the Philosopher teaches (*Ethic.* vii. 3); hence we find in the practical reason something that holds the same position in regard to operations, as, in the speculative intellect, the proposition holds in regard to conclusions. Such like universal propositions of the practical intellect that are directed to actions have the nature of law. And these propositions are sometimes under our actual consideration, while sometimes they are retained in the reason by means of a habit.

Reply Obj. 3. Reason has its power of moving from the will, as stated above (Q. 17, A. 1): for it is due to the fact that one wills the end, that the reason issues its commands as regards things ordained to the end.

But in order that the volition of what is commanded may have the nature of law, it needs to be in accord with some rule of reason. And in this sense is to be understood the saying that the will of the sovereign has the force of law; otherwise the the sovereign's will would savor of lawlessness rather than of law.

SECOND ARTICLE

Whether the Law is Always Something Directed to the Common Good?

We proceed thus to the Second Article:—
Objection 1. It would seem that the law is not always directed to the common good as to its end. For it belongs to law to command and to forbid. But commands are directed to certain individual goods. Therefore the end of the law is not always the common good.

Obj. 2. Further, the law directs man in his actions. But human actions are concerned with particular matters. Therefore the law is directed to some particular good.

Obj. 3. Further, Isidore says (*Etym.* v. 3): *If the law is based on reason, whatever is based on reason will be a law.* But reason is the foundation not only of what is ordained to the common good, but also of that which is directed to private good. Therefore the law is not only directed to the good of all, but also to the private good of an individual.

On the Contrary, Isidore says (*Etym.* v. 21) that *laws are enacted for no private profit, but for the common benefit of the citizens.*

I answer that, As stated above (A. 1), the law belongs to that which is a principle of human acts, because it is their rule and measure. Now as reason is a principle of human acts, so in reason itself there is something which is the principle in respect of all the rest: wherefore to this principle chiefly and mainly law must needs be referred.—Now the first principle in practical matters, which are the object of the practical reason, is the last end: and the last end of human life is bliss or happiness, as stated above (Q. 2, A. 7; Q. 3, A. 1). Consequently, the law must needs regard principally the relationship to happiness. Moreover, since every part is ordained to the whole, as imperfect to perfect; and since one man is a part of the perfect community, the law must needs regard properly the relationship to universal happiness. Wherefore the Philosopher, in the above definition of legal matters mentions both happiness and the body politic; for he says (*Ethic.* v. 1) that we call those legal matters *just, which are adapted to produce and preserve happiness and its parts for the body politic:* since the state is a perfect community, as he says in *Polit.* i. 1.

Now in every genus, that which belongs to it chiefly is the principle of the others, and the others belong to that genus in subordination to that thing: thus fire, which is chief among hot things, is the cause of heat in mixed bodies, and these are said to be hot in so far as they have a share of fire. Consequently, since the law is chiefly ordained to the common good, any other precept in regard to some individual work, must needs be devoid of the nature of a law, save in so far as it regards the common good. Therefore every law is ordained to the common good.

Reply Obj. 1. A command denotes an application of a law to matters regulated by the law. Now the order to the common good, at which the law aims, is applicable to particular ends. And in this way commands are given even concerning particular matters.

Reply Obj. 2. Actions are indeed concerned with particular matters: but those particular matters are referable to the common good, not as to a common genus or species, but as to a common final cause, according as the common good is said to be the common end.

Reply Obj. 3. Just as nothing stands firm with regard to the speculative reason except that which is traced back to the first indemonstrable principles, so nothing stands firm with regard to the practical reason, unless it be directed to the last end which is the common good: and whatever stands to

reason in this sense, has the nature of a law.

Whether the Reason of Any Man Is Competent to Make Laws?

We proceed thus to the Third Article:—

Objection 1. It would seem that the reason of any man is competent to make laws. For the Apostle says (Rom. ii. 14) that *when the Gentiles, who have not the law, do by nature those things that are of the law, . . . they are a law to themselves.* Now he says this of all in general. Therefore anyone can make a law for himself.

Obj. 2. Further, as the Philosopher says (*Ethic* ii. 1), *the intention of the lawgiver is to lead men to virtue.* But every man can lead another to virtue. Therefore the reason of any man is competent to make laws.

Obj. 3. Further, just as the sovereign of a state governs the state, so every father of a family governs his household. But the sovereign of a state can make laws for the state. Therefore every father of a family can make laws for his household.

On the contrary, Isidore says (*Etym.* v. 10): *A law is an ordinance of the people, whereby something is sanctioned by the Elders together with the Commonalty.*

I answer that, A law, properly speaking, regards first and foremost the order to the common good. Now to order anything to the common good, belongs either to the whole people, or to someone who is the viceregent of the whole people. And therefore the making of a law belongs either to the whole people or to a public personage who has care of the whole people: since in all other matters the directing of anything to the end concerns him to whom the end belongs.

Reply Obj. 1. As stated above (A. 1 *ad* 1), a law is in a person not only as in one that rules, but also by participation as in one that is ruled. In the latter way each one is a law to himself, in so far as he shares the direction that he receives from one who rules him. Hence, the same text goes on:

Who show the work of the law written in their hearts.

Reply Obj. 2. A private person cannot lead another to virtue efficaciously: for he can only advise, and if his advice be not taken, it has no coercive power, such as the law should have, in order to prove an efficacious inducement to virtue, as the Philosopher says (*Ethic.* x. 9). But this coercive power is vested in the whole people or in some public personage, to whom it belongs to inflict penalties, as we shall state further on (Q. 92, A. 2 *ad* 3; II-II, Q. 64, A. 3). Wherefore the framing of laws belongs to him alone.

Reply Obj. 3. As one man is a part of the household, so a household is a part of the state: and the state is a perfect community, according to *Polit.* i. 1. And therefore, as the good of one man is not the last end, but is ordained to the common good; so too the good of one household is ordained to the good of a single state, which is a perfect community. Consequently he that governs a family, can indeed make certain commands or ordinances, but not such as to have properly the force of law.

FOURTH ARTICLE

Whether Promulgation Is Essential to a Law?

We proceed thus to the Fourth Article:—
Objection 1. It would seem that promulgation is not essential to a law. For the natural law above all has the character of law. But the natural law needs no promulgation. Therefore it is not essential to a law that it be promulgated. . . .

On the contrary. It is laid down in the *Decretals,* dist. 4, that *laws are established when they are promulgated.*

I answer that, As stated above (A. 1), a law is imposed on others by way of a rule and measure. Now a rule or measure is imposed by being applied to those who are to be ruled and measured by it. Wherefore, in order that a law obtain the binding force which is proper to a law, it must needs be applied to the men who have to be ruled by it. Such application is made by its being notified to them by promulgation. Wherefore promulgation is necessary for the law to obtain its force.

Thus from the four preceding articles, the definition of law may be gathered; and it is nothing else than an ordinance of reason for the common good, made by him who has care of the community, and promulgated.

Reply Obj. 1. The natural law is promulgated by the very fact that God instilled it into man's mind so as to be known by him naturally. . . .

Question 91

OF THE VARIOUS KINDS OF LAW
(In Six Articles)

SECOND ARTICLE

Whether There Is in Us a Natural Law?

We proceed thus to the Second Article:—
Objection 1. It would seem that there is no natural law in us. Because man is governed sufficiently by the eternal law: for Augustine says (*De Lib. Arb.* i) that *the eternal law is that by which it is right that all things should be most orderly.* But nature does not abound in superfluities as neither does she fail in necessaries. Therefore no law is natural to man.

Obj. 2. Further, by the law man is directed, in his acts, to the end, as stated above (Q. 90, A. 2). But the directing of human acts to their end is not a function of nature, as is the case in irrational creatures, which act for an end solely by their natural appetite; whereas man acts for an end by his reason and will. Therefore no law is natural to man.

Obj. 3. Further, the more a man is free, the less is he under the law. But man is freer than all the animals, on account of his free-will, with which he is endowed above all other animals. Since therefore other animals are not subject to a natural law, neither is man subject to a natural law.

On the contrary, A gloss on Rom. ii. 14: *When the Gentiles, who have not the law, do by nature those things that are of the law,* comments as follows: *Although they have no written law, yet they have the natural law, whereby each one knows, and is conscious of, what is good and what is evil.*

I answer that, As stated above (Q. 90, A. 1 *ad* 1), law, being a rule and measure, can be in a person in two ways: in one way, as in him that rules and measures; in another way, as in that which is ruled and measured, since a thing is ruled and measured, in so far as it partakes of the rule or measure. Wherefore, since all things subject to Divine providence are ruled and measured by the eternal law, as was stated above (A. 1); it is evident that all things partake somewhat of the eternal law, in so far as, namely, from its being imprinted on them, they derive their respective inclinations to their proper acts and ends. Now among all others, the rational creature is subject to Divine providence in the most excellent way, in so far as it partakes of a share of providence, by being provident both for itself and for others. Wherefore it has a share of the Eternal Reason, whereby it has a natural inclination to its proper act and end: and this participation of the eternal law in the rational creature is called the natural law. Hence the Psalmist after saying (Ps. iv. 6): *Offer up the sacrifice of justice,* as though someone asked what the works of justice are, adds: *Many say, Who showeth us good things?* in answer to which question he says: *The light of Thy Countenance, O Lord, is signed upon us:* thus implying that the light of natural reason, whereby we discern what is good and what is evil, which is the function of the natural law, is nothing else than an imprint on us of the Divine light. It is therefore evident that the natural law is nothing else than the rational creature's participation of the eternal law.

Reply Obj. 1. This argument would hold, if the natural law were something different from the eternal law: whereas it is nothing but a participation thereof, as stated above.

Reply Obj. 2. Every act of reason and will in us is based on that which is according to nature, as stated above (Q. 10, A. 1): for every act of reasoning is based on principles that are known naturally, and every act of appetite in respect of the means is derived from the natural appetite in respect of the last end. Accordingly, the first direction of our acts to their end must needs be in virtue of the natural law.

Reply Obj. 3. Even irrational animals partake in their own way of the Eternal Reason, just as the rational creature does. But because the rational creature partakes thereof in an intellectual and rational manner, therefore the participation of the eternal law in the rational creature is properly called a law, since a law is something pertaining to reason, as stated above (Q. 90, A. 1). Irrational creatures, however, do not partake thereof in a rational manner, wherefore there is no participation of the eternal law in them, except by way of similitude.

THIRD ARTICLE

Whether There Is a Human Law?

We proceed thus to the Third Article:—

Objection 1. It would seem that there is not a human law. For the natural law is a participation of the eternal law, as stated above (A. 2). Now through the eternal law *all things are most orderly,* as Augustine states *(De Lib. Arb.* i. 6). Therefore the natural law suffices for the ordering of all human affairs. Consequently there is no need for a human law. . . .

Obj. 3. Further, a measure should be most certain, as stated in *Metaph.* x, text. 3. But the dictates of human reason in matters of conduct are uncertain, according to Wis. ix. 14: *The thoughts of mortal men are fearful, and our counsels uncertain.* Therefore no law can emanate from human reason.

On the contrary, Augustine *(De Lib. Arb.* i. 6) distinguishes two kinds of law, the one eternal, the other temporal, which he calls human.

I answer that, As stated above (Q. 90, A. 1, *ad* 2), a law is a dictate of the practical reason. Now it is to be observed that the same procedure takes place in the practical and in the speculative reason: for each proceeds from principles to conclusions, as stated above (*ibid.*). Accordingly we conclude that just as, in the speculative reason, from naturally known indemonstrable principles, we draw the conclusions of the various sciences, the knowledge of which is not imparted to us by nature, but acquired by the efforts of reason, so too it is from the precepts of the natural law, as from general and indemonstrable principles, that the human reason needs to proceed to the more particular determination of certain matters. These particular determinations, devised by human reason, are called human laws, provided the other essential conditions of law be observed, as stated above (Q. 90, AA. 2, 3, 4). Wherefore Tully says in his *Rhetoric (De Invent. Rhet. ii)* that *justice has its source in nature; thence certain things came into custom by reason of their utility; afterwards these things which emanated from nature and were approved by custom, were sanctioned by fear and reverence for the law.*

Reply Obj. 1. The human reason cannot have a full participation of the dictate of the Divine Reason, but according to its own mode, and imperfectly. Consequently, as on the part of the speculative reason, by a natural participation of Divine Wisdom, there is in us the knowledge of certain general principles, but not proper knowledge of each single truth, such as that contained in the Divine Wisdom; so too, on the part of the practical reason, man has a natural participation of the eternal law, according to certain general principles, but not as regards the particular determinations of individual cases, which are, however, contained in the eternal law. Hence the need for human reason to proceed further to sanction them by law. . . .

Reply Obj. 3. The practical reason is concerned with practical matters, which are singular and contingent: but not with necessary things, with which the speculative reason is concerned. Wherefore human laws cannot have that inerrancy that belongs to the demonstrated conclusions of sciences. Nor is it necessary for every measure to be altogether unerring and certain, but according as it is possible in its own particular genus.

FOURTH ARTICLE

Whether There Was Any Need for a Divine Law?

We proceed thus to the Fourth Article:—
Objection 1. It would seem that there was no need for a Divine law. Because, as stated above (A. 2), the natural law is a participation in us of the eternal law. But the eternal law is a Divine law, as stated above (A. 1). Therefore there is no need for a Divine law in addition to the natural law, and human laws derived therefrom.

Obj. 2. Further, it is written (*Ecclus.* xv. 14) that *God left man in the hand of his own counsel.* Now counsel is an act of reason, as stated above (Q. 14, A. 1). Therefore man was left to the direction of his reason. But a dictate of human reason is a human law as stated above (A. 3). Therefore there is no need for man to be governed also by a Divine law.

Obj. 3. Further, human nature is more self-sufficing than irrational creatures. But irrational creatures have no Divine law besides the natural inclination impressed on them. Much less, therefore, should the rational creature have a Divine law in addition to the natural law.

On the contrary, David prayed God to set His law before him, saying (*Ps.* cxviii. 33): *Set before me for a law the way of Thy justifications, O Lord.*

I answer that, Besides the natural and the human law it was necessary for the directing of human conduct to have a Divine law. And this for four reasons. First, because it is by law that man is directed how to perform his proper acts in view of his last end. And indeed if man were ordained to no other end than that which is proportionate to his natural faculty, there would be no need for man to have any further direction on the part of his reason, besides the natural law and human law which is derived from it. But since man is ordained to an end of eternal happiness which is inproportionate to man's natural faculty, as stated above (Q. 5, A. 5), therefore it was necessary that, besides the natural and the human law, man should be directed to his end by a law given by God.

Secondly, because, on account of the uncertainty of human judgment, especially on contingent and particular matters, different people form different judgments on human acts; whence also different and contrary laws result. In order, therefore, that man may know without any doubt what he ought to do and what he ought to avoid, it was necessary for man to be directed in his proper acts by a law given by God, for it is certain that such a law cannot err.

Thirdly, because man can make laws in those matters of which he is competent to judge. But man is not competent to judge of interior movements, that are hidden, but only of exterior acts which appear: and yet for the perfection of virtue it is necessary for man to conduct himself aright in both kinds of acts. Consequently human law could not sufficiently curb and direct interior acts; and it was necessary for this purpose that a Divine law should supervene.

Fourthly, because, as Augustine says (*De Lib. Arb.* i. 5, 6), human law cannot punish or forbid all evil deeds: since while aiming at doing away with all evils, it would do away with many good things, and would hinder the advance of the common good, which is necessary for human intercourse. In order, therefore, that no evil might remain unforbidden and unpunished, it was necessary for the Divine law to supervene, whereby all sins are forbidden.

And these four causes are touched upon in Ps. cxviii. 8, where it is said: *The Law of the Lord is unspotted, i.e.,* allowing no foulness of sin; *converting souls,* because it directs not only exterior, but also interior acts; *the testimony of the Lord is faithful,* because of the certainty of what is true and

right; *giving wisdom to little ones,* by directing man to an end supernatural and Divine.

Reply Obj. 1. By the natural law the eternal law is participated proportionately to the capacity of human nature. But to his supernatural end man needs to be directed in a yet higher way. Hence the additional law given by God, whereby man shares more perfectly in the eternal law.

Reply Obj. 2. Counsel is a kind of inquiry: hence it must proceed from some principles. Nor is it enough for it to proceed from principles imparted by nature, which are the precepts of the natural law, for the reasons given above: but there is need for certain additional principles, namely, the precepts of the Divine law.

Reply Obj. 3. Irrational creatures are not ordained to an end higher than that which is proportionate to their natural powers: consequently the comparison fails. . . .

Question 92

OF THE EFFECTS OF LAW

(In Two Articles)

FIRST ARTICLE

Whether an Effect of Law Is to Make Men Good?

We proceed thus to the First Article:—

Objection 1. It seems that it is not an effect of law to make men good. For men are good through virtue, since virtue, as stated in *Ethic.* ii. 6 is *that which makes its subject good.* But virtue is in man from God alone, because He it is Who *works it in us without us,* as we stated above (Q. 55, A. 4) in giving the definition of virtue. Therefore the law does not make men good.

Obj. 2. Further, Law does not profit a man unless he obeys it. But the very fact that a man obeys a law is due to his being good. Therefore in man goodness is presupposed to the law. Therefore the law does not make men good.

Obj. 3. Further, Law is ordained to the

common good, as stated above (Q. 90, A. 2). But some behave well in things regarding the community, who behave ill in things regarding themselves. Therefore it is not the business of the law to make men good.

Obj. 4. Further, some laws are tyrannical, as the Philosopher says (*Polit.* iii. 6). But a tyrant does not intend the good of his subjects, but considers only his own profit. Therefore law does not make men good.

On the contrary, The Philosopher says (*Ethic.* ii. 1) that the *intention of every lawgiver is to make good citizens.*

I answer that, as stated above (Q. 90, A. 1 *ad* 2; AA 3, 4), a law is nothing else than a dictate of reason in the ruler by whom his subjects are governed. Now the virtue of any subordinate thing consists in its being well subordinated to that by which it is regulated: thus we see that the virtue of the irascible and concupiscible faculties consists in their being obedient to reason; and accordingly *the virtue of every subject consists in his being well subjected to his ruler,* as the Philosopher says (*Polit.* i). But every law aims at being obeyed by those who are subject to it. Consequently it is evident that the proper effect of law is to lead its subjects to their proper virtue: and since virtue is *that which makes its subject good,* it follows that the proper effect of law is to make those to whom it is given, good, either simply or in some particular respect. For if the intention of the lawgiver is fixed on true good, which is the common good regulated according to Divine justice, it follows that the effect of the law is to make men good simply. If, however, the intention of the lawgiver is fixed on that which is not simply good, but useful or pleasurable to himself, or in opposition to Divine justice; then the law does not make men good simply, but in respect to that particular government. In this way good is found even in things that are bad of themselves: thus a man is called a good robber, because he works in a way that is adapted to his end.

Reply Obj. 1. Virtue is twofold, as explained above (Q. 63, A. 2), viz., acquired and infused. Now the fact of being accustomed to an action contributes to both, but in different ways; for it causes the acquired virtue; while it disposes to infused virtue, and preserves and fosters it when it already exists. And since law is given for the purpose of directing human acts; as far as human acts conduce to virtue, so far does law make men good. Wherefore the Philosopher says in the second book of the *Politics (Ethic.* ii) that *lawgivers make men good by habituating them to good works.*

Reply Obj. 2. It is not always through perfect goodness of virtue that one obeys the law, but sometimes it is through fear of punishment, and sometimes from the mere dictates of reason, which is a beginning of virtue, as stated above (Q. 63, A. 1).

Reply Obj. 3. The goodness of any part is considered in comparison with the whole; hence Augustine says (*Conf.* iii) that *unseemly is the part that harmonizes not with the whole.* Since then every man is a part of the state, it is impossible that a man be good, unless he be well proportionate to the common good: nor can the whole be well consistent unless its parts be proportionate to it. Consequently the common good of the state cannot flourish, unless the citizens be virtuous, at least those whose business it is to govern. But it is enough for the good of the community, that the other citizens be so far virtuous that they obey the commands of their rulers. Hence the Philosopher says (*Polit.* iii. 2) that *the virtue of a sovereign is the same as that of a good man, but the virtue of any common citizen is not the same as that of a good man.*

Reply Obj. 4. A tyrannical law, through not being according to reason, is not a law, absolutely speaking but rather a perversion of law; and yet in so far as it is something in the nature of a law, it aims at the citizens' being good. For all it has in the nature of a law consists in its being an ordinance made by a superior to his subjects, and aims at being obeyed by them, which is to make them good, not simply, but with respect to that particular government.

Whether the Acts of Law Are Suitably Assigned?

We proceed thus to the Second Article:—
Objection 1. It would seem that the acts of law are not suitably assigned as consisting in *command, prohibition, permission* and *punishment.* For *every law is a general precept,* as the jurist states *(ibid.).* But command and precept are the same. Therefore the other three are superfluous.

Obj. 2. Further, the effect of a law is to induce its subjects to be good, as stated above (A. 1). But counsel aims at a higher good than a command does. Therefore it belongs to law to counsel rather than to command.

Obj. 3. Further, just as punishment stirs a man to good deeds, so does reward. Therefore if to punish is reckoned an effect of law, so also is to reward.

Obj. 4. Further, the intention of a lawgiver is to make men good, as stated above (A. 1). But he that obeys the law, merely through fear of being punished, is not good: because *although a good deed may be done through servile fear, i.e., fear of punishment, it is not done well,* as Augustine says *(Contra duas Epist. Pelag.* ii). Therefore, punishment is not a proper effect of law.

On the contrary, Isidore says *(Etym.* v. 19): *Every law either permits something, as: "A brave man may demand his reward":* or forbids something, as: *"No man may ask a consecrated virgin in marriage":* or punishes, as: *"Let him that commits a murder be put to death."*

I answer that, Just as an assertion is a dictate of reason asserting something, so is a law a dictate of reason, commanding something. Now it is proper to reason to lead from one thing to another. Wherefore just as, in demonstrative sciences, the reason leads us from certain principles to assent to the conclusion, so it induces us by some means to assent to the precept of the law.

Now the precepts of law are concerned with human acts, in which the law directs, as stated above (Q. 90, AA 1, 2; Q. 91, A. 4).

Again, there are three kinds of human acts: for, as stated above (Q. 18, A. 8), some acts are good generically, viz., acts of virtue; and in respect of these the act of the law is a precept or command, for *the law commands all acts of virtue (Ethic.* v. 1). Some acts are evil generically, viz., acts of vice, and in respect of these the law forbids. Some acts are generically indifferent, and in respect of these the law permits; and all acts that are either not distinctly good or not distinctly bad may be called indifferent.—And it is the fear of punishment that law makes use of in order to ensure obedience: in which respect punishment is an effect of law.

Reply Obj. 1. Just as to cease from evil is a kind of good, so a prohibition is a kind of precept: and accordingly, taking precept in a wide sense, every law is a kind of precept.

Reply Obj. 2. To advise is not a proper act of law, but may be within the competency even of a private person, who cannot make a law. Wherefore too the Apostle, after giving a certain counsel (1 Cor. vii. 12) says: *I speak, not the Lord.* Consequently it is not reckoned as an effect of law.

Reply Obj. 3. To reward may also pertain to anyone: but to punish pertains to none but the framer of the law, by whose authority the pain is inflicted. Wherefore to reward is not reckoned an effect of law, but only to punish.

Reply Obj. 4. From becoming accustomed to avoid evil and fulfil what is good, through fear of punishment, one is sometimes led on to do so likewise, with delight and of one's own accord. Accordingly, law, even by punishing, leads men on to being good. . . .

Question 94

OF THE NATURAL LAW

(In Six Articles)

Whether the Natural Law Is a Habit?

We proceed thus to the First Article:—
Objection 1. It would seem that the nat-

ural law is a habit. Because, as the Philosopher says (*Ethic.* ii. 5), *there are three things in the soul, power, habit, and passion.* But the natural law is not one of the soul's powers: nor is it one of the passions; as we may see by going through them one by one. Therefore the natural law is a habit. . . .

On the contrary, Augustine says (*De Bono Conjug.* xxi) that *a habit is that whereby something is done when necessary.* But such is not the natural law: since it is in infants and in the damned who cannot act by it. Therefore the natural law is not a habit.

I answer that, A thing may be called a habit in two ways. First, properly and essentially: and thus the natural law is not a habit. For it has been stated above (Q. 90, A. 1 *ad* 2) that the natural law is something appointed by reason, just as a proposition is a work of reason. Now that which a man does is not the same as that whereby he does it: for he makes a becoming speech by the habit of grammar. Since then a habit is that by which we act, a law cannot be a habit properly and essentially.

Secondly, the term habit may be applied to that which we hold by a habit: thus faith may mean that which we hold by faith. And accordingly, since the precepts of the natural law are sometimes considered by reason actually, while sometimes they are in the reason only habitually, in this way the natural law may be called a habit. Thus, in speculative matters, the indemonstrable principles are not the habit itself whereby we hold those principles, but are the principles the habit of which we possess.

Reply Obj. 1. The Philosopher proposes there to discover the genus of virtue; and since it is evident that virtue is a principle of action, he mentions only those things which are principles of human acts, viz., powers, habits and passions. But there are other things in the soul besides these three: there are acts; thus *to will* is in the one that wills; again, things known are in the knower; moreover its own natural properties are in the soul, such as immortality and the like. . . .

Whether the Natural Law Contains Several Precepts, or One Only?

We proceed thus to the Second Article:—

Objection 1. It would seem that the natural law contains, not several precepts, but one only. For law is a kind of precept, as stated above (Q. 92, A. 2). If therefore there were many precepts of the natural law, it would follow that there are also many natural laws. . . .

On the contrary, The precepts of the natural law in man stand in relation to practical matters, as the first principles to matters of demonstration. But there are several first indemonstrable principles. Therefore there are also several precepts of the natural law.

I answer that, As stated above (Q. 91, A. 3), the precepts of the natural law are to the practical reason, what the first principles of demonstrations are to the speculative reason; because both are self-evident principles. Now a thing is said to be self-evident in two ways: first, in itself; secondly, in relation to us. Any proposition is said to be self-evident in itself, if its predicate is contained in the notion of the subject: although, to one who knows not the definition of the subject, it happens that such a proposition is not self-evident. For instance, this proposition, *Man is a rational being,* is, in its very nature, self-evident, since who says *man,* says *a rational being:* and yet to one who knows not what a man is, this proposition is not self-evident. Hence it is that, as Boethius says (*De Hebdom.*), certain axioms or propositions are universally self-evident to all; and such are those propositions whose terms are known to all, as, *Every whole is greater than its part,* and, *Things equal to one and the same are equal to one another.* But some propositions are self-evident only to the wise, who understand the meaning of the terms of such propositions: thus to one who understands that an angel is not a body, it is self-evident that an angel is not circumscriptively in a place: but this is not evident to the unlearned, for they cannot grasp it.

Now a certain order is to be found in those things that are apprehended universally. For that which, before aught else, falls under apprehension, is *being,* the notion of which is included in all things whatsoever a man apprehends. Wherefore the first indemonstrable principle is that *the same thing cannot be affirmed and denied at the same time,* which is based on the notion of *being* and *not-being:* and on this principle all others are based, as is stated in *Metaph.* iv, text. 9. Now as *being* is the first thing that falls under the apprehension simply, so *good* is the first thing that falls under the apprehension of the practical reason, which is directed to action: since every agent acts for an end under the aspect of good. Consequently the first principle in the practical reason is one founded on the notion of good, viz., that *good is that which all things seek after.* Hence this is the first precept of law, that *good is to be done and pursued, and evil is to be avoided.* All other precepts of the natural law are based upon this: so that whatever the practical reason naturally apprehends as man's good (or evil) belongs to the precepts of the natural law as something to be done or avoided.

Since, however, good has the nature of an end, and evil, the nature of a contrary, hence it is that all those things to which man has a natural inclination, are naturally apprehended by reason as being good, and consequently as objects of pursuit, and their contraries as evil, and objects of avoidance. Wherefore according to the order of natural inclinations, is the order of the precepts of the natural law. Because in man there is first of all an inclination to good in accordance with the nature which he has in common with all substances: inasmuch as every substance seeks the preservation of its own being, according to its nature: and by reason of this inclination, whatever is a means of preserving human life, and of warding off its obstacles, belongs to the natural law. Secondly, there is in man an inclination to

things that pertain to him more specially, according to that nature which he has in common with other animals: and in virtue of this inclination, those things are said to belong to the natural law, *which nature has taught to all animals,* such as sexual intercourse, education of offspring and so forth. Thirdly, there is in man an inclination to good, according to the nature of his reason, which nature is proper to him: thus man has a natural inclination to know the truth about God, and to live in society: and in this respect, whatever pertains to this inclination belongs to the natural law; for instance, to shun ignorance, to avoid offending those among whom one has to live, and other such things regarding the above inclination.

Reply Obj. 1. All these precepts of the law of nature have the character of one natural law, inasmuch as they flow from one first precept. . . .

FOURTH ARTICLE

Whether the Natural Law Is the Same in All Men?

We proceed thus to the Fourth Article:—
Objection 1. It would seem that the natural law is not the same in all. For it is stated in the Decretals (*Dist.* i) that *the natural law is that which is contained in the Law and the Gospel.* But this is not common to all men; because, as it is written (*Rom.* x. 16), *all do not obey the gospel.* Therefore the natural law is not the same in all men.

Obj. 2. Further, *Things which are according to the law are said to be just,* as stated in *Ethic* v. But it is stated in the same book that nothing is so universally just as not to be subject to change in regard to some men. Therefore even the natural law is not the same in all men.

Obj. 3. Further, as stated above (AA. 2, 3), to the natural law belongs everything to which a man is inclined according to his nature. Now different men are naturally inclined to different things; some to the desire of pleasures, others to the desire of honors, and other men to other things. Therefore there is not one natural law for all.

On the contrary, Isidore says *(Etym.* v. 4): *The natural law is common to all nations.*

I answer that, As stated above (AA. 2, 3), to the natural law belongs those things to which a man is inclined naturally: and among these it is proper to man to be inclined to act according to reason. Now the process of reason is from the common to the proper, as stated in *Phys.* i. The speculative reason, however, is differently situated in this matter, from the practical reason. For, since the speculative reason is busied chiefly with necessary things, which cannot be otherwise than they are, its proper conclusions, like the universal principles, contain the truth without fail. The practical reason, on the other hand, is busied with contingent matters, about which human actions are concerned: and consequently, although there is necessity in the general principles, the more we descend to matters of detail, the more frequently we encounter defects. Accordingly then in speculative matters truth is the same in all men, both as to principles and as to conclusions: although the truth is not known to all as regards the conclusions, but only as regards the principles which are called common notions. But in matters of action, truth or practical rectitude is not the same for all, as to matters of detail, but only as to the general principles: and where there is the same rectitude in matters of detail, it is not equally known to all.

It is therefore evident that, as regards the general principles whether of speculative or of practical reason, truth or rectitude is the same for all, and is equally known by all. As to the proper conclusions of the speculative reason, the truth is the same for all, but is not equally known to all: thus it is true for all that the three angles of a triangle are together equal to two right angles, although it is not known to all. But as to the proper conclusions of the practical reason, neither is the truth or rectitude the same

for all, nor, where it is the same, is it equally known by all. Thus it is right and true for all to act according to reason: and from this principle it follows as a proper conclusion, that goods entrusted to another should be restored to their owner. Now this is true for the majority of cases: but it may happen in a particular case that it would be injurious, and therefore unreasonable, to restore goods held in trust; for instance if they are claimed for the purpose of fighting against one's country. And this principle will be found to fail the more, according as we descend further into detail, *e.g.,* if one were to say that goods held in trust should be restored with such and such a guarantee, or in such and such a way; because the greater the number of conditions added, the greater the number of ways in which the principle may fail, so that it be not right to restore or not to restore.

Consequently we must say that the natural law, as to general principles, is the same for all, both as to rectitude and as to knowledge. But as to certain matters of detail, which are conclusions, as it were, of those general principles, it is the same for all in the majority of cases, both as to rectitude and as to knowledge; and yet in some few cases it may fail, both as to rectitude, by reason of certain obstacles (just as natures subject to generation and corruption fail in some few cases on account of some obstacle), and as to knowledge, since in some the reason is perverted by passion, or evil habit, or an evil disposition of nature; thus formerly, theft, although it is expressly contrary to the natural law, was not considered wrong among the Germans, as Julius Caesar relates *(De Bello Gall.* vi).

Reply Obj. 1. The meaning of the sentence quoted is not that whatever is contained in the Law and the Gospel belongs to the natural law, since they contain many things that are above nature; but that whatever belongs to the natural law is fully contained in them. Wherefore Gratian, after saying that *the natural law is what is contained in the Law and the Gospel,* adds at once, by way of example, *by which everyone is commanded to do to others as he would be done by.*

Reply Obj. 2. The saying of the Philosopher is to be understood of things that are naturally just, not as general principles, but as conclusions drawn from them, having rectitude in the majority of cases, but failing in a few.

Reply Obj. 3. As, in man, reason rules and commands the other powers, so all the natural inclinations belonging to the other powers must needs be directed according to reason. Wherefore it is universally right for all men, that all their inclinations should be directed according to reason.

FIFTH ARTICLE

Whether the Natural Law Can Be Changed?

We proceed thus to the Fifth Article:—

Objection 1. It would seem that the natural law can be changed. Because on Ecclus. xvii. 9, *He gave them instructions, and the law of life,* the gloss says: *He wished the law of the letter to be written, in order to correct the law of nature.* But that which is corrected is changed. Therefore the natural law can be changed.

Obj. 2. Further, the slaying of the innocent, adultery, and theft are against the natural law. But we find these things changed by God: as when God commanded Abraham to slay his innocent son (Gen. xxii. 2); and when he ordered the Jews to borrow and purloin the vessels of the Egyptians (Exod. xii. 35); and when He commanded Osee to take to himself *a wife of fornications* (Osee i. 2). Therefore the natural law can be changed.

Obj. 3. Further, Isidore says (*Etym.* v. 4) that *the possession of all things in common, and universal freedom, are matters of natural law.* But these things are seen to be changed by human laws. Therefore it seems that the natural law is subject to change.

On the contrary, It is said in the Decretals (*Dist.* v): *The natural law dates from* the creation of the rational creature. It does not vary according to time, but remains unchangeable.

I answer that, A change in the natural law may be understood in two ways. First, by way of addition. In this sense nothing hinders the natural law from being changed: since many things for the benefit of human life have been added over and above the natural law, both by the Divine law and by human laws.

Secondly, a change in the natural law may be understood by way of subtraction, so that what previously was according to the natural law, ceases to be so. In this sense, the natural law is altogether unchangeable in its first principles: but in its secondary principles, which, as we have said (A. 4), are certain detailed proximate conclusions drawn from the first principles, the natural law is not changed so that what it prescribes be not right in most cases. But it may be changed in some particular cases of rare occurence, through some special causes hindering the observance of such precepts, as stated above (A. 4).

Reply Obj. 1. The written law is said to be given for the correction of the natural law, either because it supplies what was wanting to the natural law; or because the natural law was perverted in the hearts of some men, as to certain matters, so that they esteemed those things good which are naturally evil; which perversion stood in need of correction.

Reply Obj. 2. All men alike, both guilty and innocent, die the death of nature: which death of nature is inflicted by the power of God on account of original sin, according to 1 Kings ii. 6: *The Lord killeth and maketh alive.* Consequently, by the command of God, death can be inflicted on any man, guilty or innocent, without any injustice whatever.—In like manner adultery is intercourse with another's wife; who is allotted to him by the law emanating from God. Consequently intercourse with any woman, by the command of God, is neither adultery nor fornication.—The same applies to theft, which is the taking of another's property. For whatever is taken by the command of God, to Whom all things belong, is not taken against the will of its owner, whereas it is in this that theft consists.—Nor is it only in human things, that whatever is commanded by God is right; but also in natural things, whatever is done by God, is, in some way, natural, as stated in the First Part (Q. 105, A. 6 *ad* 1).

Reply Obj. 3. A thing is said to belong to the natural law in two ways. First, because nature inclines thereto: *e.g.*, that one should not do harm to another. Secondly, because nature did not bring in the contrary: thus we might say that for man to be naked is of the natural law, because nature did not give him clothes, but art invented them. In this sense, *the possession of all things in common and universal freedom* are said to be of the natural law, because to wit, the distinction of possessions and slavery were not brought in by nature, but devised by human reason for the benefit of human life. Accordingly the law of nature was not changed in this respect, except by addition. . . .

Question 95

OF HUMAN LAW

(In Four Articles)

FIRST ARTICLE

Whether It Was Useful for Laws to Be Framed by Men?

We proceed thus to the First Article:— Objection 1. It would seem that it was not useful for laws to be framed by men. Because the purpose of every law is that man be made good thereby, as stated above (Q. 92, A. 1). But men are more to be induced to be good willingly by means of admonitions, than against their will, by means of laws. Therefore there was no need to frame laws.

Obj. 2. Further, As the Philosopher says (*Ethic.* v. 4), *men have recourse to a judge as to animate justice.* But animate justice is better than inanimate justice, which is con-

tained in laws. Therefore it would have been better for the execution of justice to be entrusted to the decision of judges, than to frame laws in addition.

Obj. 3. Further, every law is framed for the direction of human actions, as is evident from what has been stated above (Q. 90, AA. 1, 2). But since human actions are about singulars, which are infinite in number, matters pertaining to the direction of human actions cannot be taken into sufficient consideration except by a wise man, who looks into each one of them. Therefore it would have been better for human acts to be directed by the judgment of wise men, than by the framing of laws. Therefore there was no need of human laws.

On the contrary, Isidore says (*Etym.* v. 20): *Laws were made that in fear thereof human audacity might be held in check, that innocence might be safeguarded in the midst of wickedness, and that the dread of punishment might prevent the wicked from doing harm.* But these things are most necessary to mankind. Therefore it was necessary that human laws should be made.

I answer that, As stated above (Q. 63, A. 1; Q. 94, A. 3), man has a natural aptitude for virtue; but the perfection of virtue must be acquired by man by means of some kind of training. Thus we observe that man is helped by industry in his necessities, for instance, in food and clothing. Certain beginnings of these he has from nature, viz., his reason and his hands; but he has not the full complement, as other animals have, to whom nature has given sufficiency of clothing and food. Now it is difficult to see how man could suffice for himself in the matter of this training: since the perfection of virtue consists chiefly in withdrawing man from undue pleasures, to which above all man is inclined, and especially the young, who are more capable of being trained. Consequently a man needs to receive this training from another, whereby to arrive at the perfection of virtue. And as to those young people who are inclined to acts of virtue, by their good natural disposition, or by custom, or rather by the gift of God, paternal training suffices, which is by admonitions. But since some are found to be depraved, and prone to vice, and not easily amenable to words, it was necessary for such to be restrained from evil by force and fear, in order that, at least, they might desist from evil-doing, and leave others in peace, and that they themselves, by being habituated in this way, might be brought to do willingly what hitherto they did from fear, and thus become virtuous. Now this kind of training, which compels through fear of punishment, is the discipline of laws. Therefore, in order that man might have peace and virtue, it was necessary for laws to be framed: for, as the Philosopher says (*Polit.* i. 2), *as man is the most noble of animals if he be perfect in virtue, so is he the lowest of all, if he be severed from law and righteousness;* because man can use his reason to devise means of satisfying his lusts and evil passions, which other animals are unable to do.

Reply Obj. 1. Men who are well disposed are led willingly to virtue by being admonished better than by coercion: but men who are evilly disposed are not led to virtue unless they are compelled.

Reply Obj. 2. As the Philosopher says (*Rhet.* i. 1), *it is better that all things be regulated by law, than left to be decided by judges:* and this for three reasons. First, because it is easier to find a few wise men competent to frame right laws, than to find the many who would be necessary to judge aright of each single case.—Secondly, because those who make laws consider long beforehand what laws to make; whereas judgment on each single case has to be pronounced as soon as it arises: and it is easier for man to see what is right, by taking many instances into consideration, than by considering one solitary fact.—Thirdly, because lawgivers judge in the abstract and of future events; whereas those who sit in judgment judge of things present, towards which they are affected by love, hatred, or some kind of cupidity; wherefore their judgment is perverted.

Since then the animated justice of the judge is not found in every man, and since it can be deflected, therefore it was necessary,

whenever possible, for the law to determine how to judge, and for very few matters to be left to the decision of men.

Reply Obj. 3. Certain individual facts which cannot be covered by the law *have necessarily to be committed to judges,* as the Philosopher says in the same passage: for instance, *concerning something that has happened or not happened,* and the like.

SECOND ARTICLE

Whether Every Human Law Is Derived from the Natural Law?

We proceed thus to the Second Article:—
Objection 1. It would seem that not every human law is derived from the natural law. For the Philosopher says (*Ethic.* v. 7) that *the legal just is that which originally was a matter of indifference.* But those things which arise from the natural law are not matters of indifference. Therefore, the enactments of human laws are not all derived from the natural law.

Obj. 2. Further, positive law is contrasted with natural law, as stated by Isidore (*Etym.* v. 4) and the Philosopher (*Ethic.* v., *loc. cit.*). But those things which flow as conclusions from the general principles of the natural law belong to the natural law, as stated above (Q. 94, A. 4). Therefore that which is established by human law does not belong to the natural law.

Obj. 3. Further, the law of nature is the same for all; since the Philosopher says (*Ethic.* v. 7) that *the natural just is that which is equally valid everywhere.* If therefore human laws were derived from the natural law, it would follow that they too are the same for all: which is clearly false.

Obj. 4. Further, it is possible to give a reason for things which are derived from the natural law. But *it is not possible to give the reason for all the legal enactments of the lawgivers,* as the jurist says. Therefore not all human laws are derived from the natural law.

On the contrary, Tully says (*Rhetor.* ii): *Things which emanated from nature and were approved by custom, were sanctioned by fear and reverence for the laws.*

I answer that, as Augustine says (*De Lib. Arb.* i. 5), *that which is not just seems to be no law at all:* wherefore the force of a law depends on the extent of its justice. Now in human affairs a thing is said to be just, from being right, according to the rule of reason. But the first rule of reason is the law of nature, as is clear from what has been stated above (Q. 91, A. 2 *ad* 2). Consequently every human law has just so much of the nature of law, as it is derived from the law of nature. But if in any point it deflects from the law of nature, it is no longer a law but a perversion of law.

But it must be noted that something may be derived from the natural law in two ways: first, as a conclusion from premises, secondly, by way of determination of certain generalities. The first way is like to that by which, in sciences, demonstrated conclusions are drawn from the principles: while the second mode is likened to that whereby, in the arts, general forms are particularized as to details: thus the craftsman needs to determine the general form of a house to some particular shape. Some things are therefore derived from the general principles of the natural law, by way of conclusions; *e.g.,* that *one must not kill* may be derived as a conclusion from the principle that *one should do harm to no man:* while some are derived therefrom by way of determination; *e.g.,* the law of nature has it that the evil-doer should be punished; but that he be punished in this or that way, is a determination of the law of nature.

Accordingly both modes of derivation are found in the human law. But those things which are derived in the first way, are contained in human law not as emanating therefrom exclusively, but have some force from the natural law also. But those things which are derived in the second way, have no other force than that of human law.

Reply Obj. 1. The Philosopher is speaking of those enactments which are by way of determination or specification of the precepts of the natural law.

Reply Obj. 2. This argument avails for those things that are derived from the natural law, by way of conclusions.

Reply Obj. 3. The general principles of the natural law cannot be applied to all men in the same way on account of the great variety of human affairs: and hence arises the diversity of positive laws among various people.

Reply Obj. 4. These words of the Jurist are to be understood as referring to decisions of rulers in determining particular points of the natural law: on which determinations the judgment of expert and prudent men is based as on its principles; in so far, to wit, as they see at once what is the best thing to decide.

Hence the Philosopher says (*Ethic.* vi. 11) that in such matters, *we ought to pay as much attention to the undemonstrated sayings and opinions of persons who surpass us in experience, age and prudence, as to their demonstrations . . . .*

Question 96

OF THE POWER OF HUMAN LAW

(In Six Articles)

FIRST ARTICLE

Whether Human Law Should Be Framed for the Community Rather Than for the Individual?

We proceed thus to the First Article:—

Objection 1. It would seem that human law should be framed not for the community, but rather for the individual. For the Philosopher says (*Ethic.* v. 7) that *the legal just . . . includes all particular acts of legislation . . . and all those matters which are the subject of decrees,* which are also individual matters, since decrees are framed about individual actions. Therefore law is framed not only for the community, but also for the individual.

Obj. 2. Further, law is the director of human acts, as stated above (Q. 90, AA. 1, 2). But human acts are about individual matters. Therefore human laws should be framed, not for the community, but rather for the individual.

Obj. 3. Further, law is a rule and measure of human acts, as stated above (Q. 90, AA. 1, 2). But a measure should be most certain, as stated in *Metaph.* x. Since, therefore in human acts no general proposition can be so certain as not to fail in some individual cases, it seems that laws should be framed not in general but for individual cases.

On the contrary, The Jurist says (*Pandect. Justin.* lib, i, tit. iii, art. ii, *De legibus*, etc.) that *laws should be made to suit the majority of instances; and they are not framed according to what may possibly happen in an individual case.*

I answer that, Whatever is for an end should be proportionate to that end. Now the end of law is the common good; because, as Isidore says (*Etym.* v. 21) that *law should be framed, not for any private benefit, but for the common good of all the citizens.* Hence human laws should be proportionate to the common good. Now the common good comprises many things. Wherefore law should take account of many things as to persons, as to matters, and as to times. Because the community of the state is composed of many persons; and its good is procured by many actions; nor is it established to endure for only a short time, but to last for all time by the citizens succeeding one another, as Augustine says (*De Civ. Dei* ii. 21; xxii. 6).

Reply Obj. 1. The Philosopher (*Ethic.* v. 7) divides the legal just, i.e., positive law, into three parts. For some things are laid down simply in a general way: and these are the general laws. Of these he says that *the legal is that which originally was a matter of indifference, but which, when enacted, is so no longer:* as the fixing of the ransom of a captive.—Some things affect the community in one respect, and individuals in another. These are called *privileges*, i.e., *private laws*, as it were, because they regard private persons, although their power extends to many matters; and in regard to these, he adds, *and further, all particular acts of legislation.*—

Other matters are legal, not through being laws, but through being applications of general laws to particular cases: such are decrees which have the force of law; and in regard to these, he adds *all matters subject to decrees.*

Reply Obj. 2. A principle of direction should be applicable to many; wherefore (*Metaph.* x, *text.* 4) the Philosopher says that all things belonging to one genus, are measured by one, which is the principle in that genus. For if there were as many rules or measures as there are things measured or ruled, they would cease to be of use, since their use consists in being applicable to many things. Hence law would be of no use if it did not extend further than to one single act. Because the decrees of prudent men are made for the purpose of directing individual actions; whereas law is a general precept, as stated above (Q. 92, A. 2, Obj. 2).

Reply Obj. 3. We must not seek the same degree of certainty in all things (*Ethic.* i. 3). Consequently in contingent matters, such as natural and human things, it is enough for a thing to be certain, as being true in the greater number of instances, though at times and less frequently it fail.

SECOND ARTICLE

Whether It Belongs to the Human Law to Repress All Vices?

We proceed thus to the Second Article:—

Objection 1. It would seem that it belongs to human law to repress all vices. For Isidore says (*Etym.* v. 20) that *laws were made in order that, in fear thereof, man's audacity might be held in check.* But it would not be held in check sufficiently, unless all evils were repressed by law. Therefore human law should repress all evils . . . .

Obj. 3. Further, human law is derived from the natural law, as stated above (Q. 95, A. 2). But all vices are contrary to the law of nature. Therefore human law should repress all vices.

On the contrary, We read in *De Lib. Arb.* i. 5: *It seems to me that the law which is* written for the governing of the people rightly permits these things, and that Divine providence punishes them. But Divine providence punishes nothing but vices. Therefore human law rightly allows some vices, by not repressing them.

I answer that, As stated above (Q. 90, AA. 1, 2), law is framed as a rule or measure of human acts. Now a measure should be homogeneous with that which it measures, as stated in *Metaph.* x, text. 3, 4, since different things are measured by different measures. Wherefore laws imposed on men should also be in keeping with their condition, for, as Isidore says (*Etym.* v. 21), law should be *possible both according to nature, and according to the customs of the country.* Now possibility or faculty of action is due to an interior habit or disposition: since the same thing is not possible to one who has not a virtuous habit, as is possible to one who has. Thus the same is not possible to a child as to a full-grown man: for which reason the law for children is not the same as for adults, since many things are permitted to children, which in an adult are punished by law or at any rate are open to blame. In like manner many things are permissible to men not perfect in virtue, which would be intolerable in a virtuous man.

Now human law is framed for a number of human beings, the majority of whom are not perfect in virtue. Wherefore human laws do not forbid all vices, from which the virtuous abstain, but only the more grievous vices, from which it is possible for the majority to abstain; and chiefly those that are to the hurt of others, without the prohibition of which human society could not be maintained: thus human law prohibits murder, theft and suchlike.

Reply Obj. 1. Audacity seems to refer to the assailing of others. Consequently it belongs to those sins chiefly whereby one's neighbor is injured: and these sins are forbidden by human law, as stated . . . .

Reply Obj. 3. The natural law is a participation in us of the eternal law: while human law falls short of the eternal law. Now Augustine says (*De Lib. Arb.* i. 5): *The law*

which is framed for the government of states, allows and leaves unpunished many things that are punished by Divine providence. Nor, if this law does not attempt to do everything, is this a reason why it should be blamed for what it does. Wherefore, too, human law does not prohibit everything that is forbidden by the natural law . . . .

Whether Human Law Binds a Man in Conscience?

We proceed thus to the Fourth Article:—
Objection 1. It would seem that human law does not bind a man in conscience. For an inferior power has no jurisdiction in a court of higher power. But the power of man, which frames human law, is beneath the Divine power. Therefore human law cannot impose its precept in a Divine court, such as is the court of conscience.

Obj. 2. Further, the judgment of conscience depends chiefly on the commandments of God. But sometimes God's commandments are made void by human laws, according to Matt. xv. 6: *You have made void the commandment of God for your tradition.* Therefore human law does not bind a man in conscience . . .

On the contrary, It is written (1 Pet. ii. 19): *This is thankworthy, if for conscience . . . a man, endure sorrows, suffering wrongfully.*

I answer that, Laws framed by man are either just or unjust. If they be just, they have the power of binding in conscience, from the eternal law whence they are derived, according to Prov. viii. 15: *By Me kings reign, and lawgivers decree just things.* Now laws are said to be just, both from the end, when, to wit, they are ordained to the common good,—and from their author, that is to say, when the law that is made does not exceed the power of the lawgiver,—and from their form, when, to wit, burdens are laid on the subjects, according to an equality of proportion and with a view to the common good. For, since one man is a part of the community, each man in all that he is and has, belongs to the community; just as a part, in all that it is, belongs to the whole; wherefore nature inflicts a loss on the part, in order to save the whole: so that on this account, such laws as these, which impose proportionate burdens, are just and binding in conscience, and are legal laws.

On the other hand laws may be unjust in two ways: first, by being contrary to human good, through being opposed to the things mentioned above:—either in respect of the end, as when an authority imposes on his subjects burdensome laws, conducive, not to the common good, but rather to his own cupidity or vainglory;—or in respect of the author, as when a man makes a law that goes beyond the power committed to him;—or in respect of the form, as when burdens are imposed unequally on the community, although with a view to the common good. The like are acts of violence rather than laws; because, as Augustine says (*De Lib. Arb.* i. 5), *a law that is not just, seems to be no law at all.* Wherefore such laws do not bind in conscience, except perhaps in order to avoid scandal or disturbance, for which cause a man should even yield his right, according to Matt. v. 40, 41: *If a man . . . take away thy coat, let go thy cloak also unto him; and whosoever will force thee one mile, go with him other two.*

Secondly, laws may be unjust through being opposed to the Divine good: such are the laws of tyrants inducing to idolatry, or to anything else contrary to the Divine law: and laws of this kind must nowise be observed, because, as stated in Acts v. 29, *we ought to obey God rather than men.*

Reply Obj. 1. As the Apostle says (Rom. xiii, 1, 2), all human power is from God . . . *therefore he that resisteth the power,* in matters that are within its scope, *resisteth the ordinance of God;* so that he becomes guilty according to his conscience.

Reply Obj. 2. This argument is true of laws that are contrary to the commandments of God, which is beyond the scope of (human) power. Wherefore in such matters human law should not be obeyed . . . .

SIXTH ARTICLE

Whether He Who Is Under a Law May Act Beside the Letter of the Law?

We proceed thus to the Sixth Article:—

Objection 1. It seems that he who is subject to a law may not act beside the letter of the law. For Augustine says (*De Vera Relig.* xxxi): *Although men judge about temporal laws when they make them, yet when once they are made they must pass judgment not on them, but according to them.* But if anyone disregard the letter of the law, saying that he observes the intention of the lawgiver, he seems to pass judgment on the law. Therefore it is not right for one who is under a law to disregard the letter of the law, in order to observe the intention of the lawgiver.

Obj. 2. Further, he alone is competent to interpret the law who can make the law. But those who are subject to the law cannot make the law. Therefore they have no right to interpret the intention of the lawgiver, but should always act according to the letter of the law.

Obj. 3. Further, every wise man knows how to explain his intention by words. But those who framed the laws should be reckoned wise: for Wisdom says (Prov. viii. 15): *By Me kings reign, and lawgivers decree just things.* Therefore we should not judge of the intention of the lawgiver otherwise than by the words of the law.

On the contrary, Hilary says (*De Trin.* iv): *The meaning of what is said is according to the motive for saying it: because things are not subject to speech, but speech to things.* Therefore we should take account of the motive of the lawgiver, rather than of his very words.

I answer that, As stated above, (A. 4), every law is directed to the common weal of men, and derives the force and nature of law accordingly. Hence the jurist says: *By no reason of law, or favor of equity, is it allowable for us to interpret harshly, and render burdensome, those useful measures which have been enacted for the welfare of man.* Now it happens often that the observance of some point of law conduces to the common weal in the majority of instances, and yet, in some cases, is very hurtful. Since then the lawgiver cannot have in view every single case, he shapes the law according to what happens most frequently, by directing his attention to the common good. Wherefore if a case arise wherein the observance of that law would be hurtful to the general welfare, it should not be observed. For instance, suppose that in a besieged city it be an established law that the gates of the city are to be kept closed, this is good for public welfare as a general rule: but, if it were to happen that the enemy are in pursuit of certain citizens, who are defenders of the city, it would be a great loss to the city, if the gates were not opened to them: and so in that case the gates ought to be opened, contrary to the letter of the law, in order to maintain the common weal, which the lawgiver had in view.

Nevertheless it must be noted, that if the observance of the law according to the letter does not involve any sudden risk needing instant remedy, it is not competent for everyone to expound what is useful and what is not useful to the state: those alone can do this who are in authority, and who, on account of such like cases, have the power to dispense from the laws. If, however, the peril be so sudden as not to allow of the delay involved by referring the matter to authority, the mere necessity brings with it a dispensation, since necessity knows no law.

Reply Obj. 1. He who in a case of necessity acts beside the letter of the law, does not judge of the law; but of a particular case in which he sees that the letter of the law is not to be observed.

Reply Obj. 2. He who follows the intention of the lawgiver, does not interpret the law simply; but in a case in which it is evident, by reason of the manifest harm, that the lawgiver intended otherwise. For if it be a matter of doubt, he must either act according to the letter of the law, or consult those in power.

Reply Obj. 3. No man is so wise as to be able to take account of every single case; wherefore he is not able sufficiently to express in words all those things that are suitable for the end he has in view. And even if a lawgiver were able to take all the cases into consideration, he ought not to mention them all, in order to avoid confusion: but should frame the law according to that which is of most common occurrence.

Question 97

OF CHANGE IN LAWS

(In Four Articles)

FIRST ARTICLE

Whether Human Law Should Be Changed in Any Way?

We proceed thus to the First Article:—
Objection 1. It would seem that human law should not be changed in any way at all. Because human law is derived from the natural law, as stated above (Q. 95, A. 2). But the natural law endures unchangeably. Therefore human law should also remain without any change . . . .

On the contrary, Augustine says (*De Lib. Arb.* i. 6): *A temporal law, however just, may be justly changed in course of time.*

I answer that, As stated above (Q. 91, A. 3), human law is a dictate of reason, whereby human acts are directed. Thus there may be two causes for the just change of human law: one on the part of reason; the other on the part of man whose acts are regulated by law. The cause on the part of reason is that it seems natural to human reason to advance gradually from the imperfect to the perfect. Hence, in speculative sciences, we see that the teaching of the early philosophers was imperfect, and that it was afterwards perfected by those who succeeded them. So also in practical matters: for those who first endeavored to discover something useful for the human community, not being able by themselves to take everything into consideration, set up certain institutions which were deficient in many ways; and these were changed by subsequent lawgivers who made institutions that might prove less frequently deficient in respect of the common weal.

On the part of man, whose acts are regulated by law, the law can be rightly changed on account of the changed condition of man, to whom different things are expedient according to the difference of his condition. An example is proposed by Augustine (*De Lib. Arb.* i. 6): *If the people have a sense of moderation and responsibility, and are most careful guardians of the common weal, it is right to enact a law allowing such a people to choose their own magistrates for the government of the commonwealth. But if, as time goes on, the same people become so corrupt as to sell their votes, and entrust the government to scoundrels and criminals; then the right of appointing their public officials is rightly forfeit to such a people, and the choice devolves to a few good men.*

Reply Obj. 1. The natural law is a participation of the eternal law, as stated above (Q. 91, A. 2), and therefore endures without change, owing to the unchangeableness and perfection of the Divine Reason, the Author of nature. But the reason of man is changeable and imperfect: wherefore his law is subject to change.—Moreover the natural law contains certain universal precepts, which are everlasting: whereas human law contains certain particular precepts, according to various emergencies . . . .

SECOND ARTICLE

Whether Human Law Should Always Be Changed, Whenever Something Better Occurs?

We proceed thus to the Second Article:—Objection 1. It would seem that human law should be changed, whenever something better occurs. Because human laws are devised by human reason, like other arts. But in the other arts, the tenets of former times give place to others, if something better occurs. Therefore the same should apply to human laws.

Obj. 2. Further, by taking note of the past we can provide for the future. Now unless human laws had been changed when it was found possible to improve them, considerable inconvenience would have ensued: because the laws of old were crude in many points. Therefore it seems that laws should be changed, whenever anything better occurs to be enacted.

Obj. 3. Further, human laws are enacted about single acts of man. But we cannot acquire perfect knowledge in singular matters, except by experience, which *requires time,* as stated in *Ethic.* ii. Therefore it seems that as time goes on it is possible for something better to occur for legislation.

On the contrary, It is stated in the Decretals (*Dist.* xii. 5): *It is absurd, and a detestable shame, that we should suffer those traditions to be changed which we have received from the fathers of old.*

I answer that, As stated above (A. 1), human law is rightly changed, in so far as such change is conducive to the common weal. But, to a certain extent, the mere change of law is of itself prejudicial to the common good: because custom avails much for the observance of laws, seeing that what is done contrary to general custom, even in slight matters, is looked upon as grave. Consequently, when a law is changed, the binding power of the law is diminished, in so far as custom is abolished. Wherefore human law should never be changed, unless, in some way or other, the common weal be compensated according to the extent of the harm done in this respect. Such compensation may arise either from some very great and very evident benefit conferred by the new enactment; or from the extreme urgency of the case, due to the fact that either the existing law is clearly unjust, or its observance extremely harmful. Wherefore the jurist says that *in establishing new laws, there should be evidence of the benefit to be derived, before departing from a law which has long been considered just.*

Reply Obj. 1. Rules of art derive their force from reason alone: and therefore whenever something better occurs, the rule followed hitherto should be changed. But *laws derive very great force from custom,* as the Philosopher states (*Polit.* ii. 5): consequently they should not be quickly changed.

Reply Obj. 2. This argument proves that laws ought to be changed: not in view of any improvement, but for the sake of a great benefit or in a case of great urgency, as stated above. This answer applies also to the Third Objection.

THIRD ARTICLE

Whether Custom Can Obtain Force of Law?

We proceed thus to the Third Article:—Objection 1. It would seem that custom cannot obtain force of law, nor abolish a law. Because human law is derived from the natural law and from the Divine law, as stated above (Q. 93, A. 3: Q. 95, A. 2). But human custom cannot change either the law of nature or the Divine law. Therefore neither can it change human law.

Obj. 2. Further, many evils cannot make one good. But he who first acted against the law, did evil. Therefore by multiplying such acts, nothing good is the result. Now a law is something good; since it is a rule of human acts. Therefore law is not abolished by custom, so that the mere custom should obtain force of law.

Obj. 3. Further, the framing of laws belongs to those public men whose business it is to govern the community; wherefore private individuals cannot make laws. But custom grows by the acts of private individuals. Therefore custom cannot obtain force of law, so as to abolish the law.

On the contrary, Augustine says (*Ep. ad Casulan.* xxxvi): *The customs of God's people and the institutions of our ancestors are to be considered as laws. And those who throw contempt on the customs of the Church ought to be punished as those who disobey the law of God.*

I answer that, All law proceeds from the reason and will of the lawgiver; the Divine and natural laws from the reasonable will of God; the human law from the will of man, regulated by reason. Now just as human reason and will, in practical matters, may be made manifest by speech, so may they be made known by deeds: since seemingly a man chooses as good that which he carries into execution. But it is evident that by human speech, law can be both changed and expounded, in so far as it manifests the interior movement and thought of human reason. Wherefore by actions also, especially if they be repeated, so as to make a custom, law can be changed and expounded; and also something can be established which obtains force of law, in so far as by repeated external actions, the inward movement of the will, and concepts of reason are most effectually declared; for when a thing is done again and again, it seems to proceed from a deliberate judgment of reason. Accordingly, custom has the force of a law, abolishes law, and is the interpreter of law.

Reply Obj. 1. The natural and Divine laws proceed from the Divine will, as stated above. Wherefore they cannot be changed by a custom proceeding from the will of man, but only by Divine authority. Hence it is that no custom can prevail over the Divine or natural laws: for Isidore says (*Synon.* ii. 16): *Let custom yield to authority: evil customs should be eradicated by law and reason.*

Reply Obj. 2. As stated above (Q. 96, A. 6), human laws fail in some cases: wherefore it is possible sometimes to act beside the law; namely, in a case where the law fails; yet the act will not be evil. And when such cases are multiplied, by reason of some change in man, then custom shows that the law is no longer useful: just as it might be declared by the verbal promulgation of a law to the contrary. If, however, the same reason remains, for which the law was useful hitherto, then it is not the custom that prevails against the law, but the law that overcomes the custom: unless perhaps the sole reason for the law seeming useless, be that it is not *possible according to the custom of the country,* which has been stated to be one of the conditions of law. For it is not easy to set aside the custom of a whole people.

Reply Obj. 3. The people among whom a custom is introduced may be of two conditions. For if they are free, and able to make their own laws, the consent of the whole people expressed by a custom counts far more in favor of a particular observance, than does the authority of the soverign, who has not the power to frame laws, except as representing the people. Wherefore although each individual cannot make laws, yet the whole people can. If however, the people have not the free power to make their own laws, or to abolish a law made by a higher authority; nevertheless with such a people a prevailing custom obtains force of law, in so far as it is tolerated by those to whom it belongs to make laws for that people: because by the very fact that they tolerate it they seem to approve of that which is introduced by custom. . . .

4

Hugo Grotius

1583–1645

A French ancestor of Hugo Grotius married a well-to-do Dutch woman and founded a Dutch family of importance that prospered for many generations. Grotius was brought up in aristocratic, intellectual surroundings. His grandfather was a student of Hebrew, Greek, and Latin literature. His uncle withdrew from a thriving public career to teach law. His father was a city councillor (pompously called "Senator" in towns of the Low Countries). His father took a law degree, became a leader of the bar, and was appointed curator of Leyden University; he was an early enthusiast in experimental science, and did falling body experiments before Galileo's famous discoveries.

As might be expected, Grotius' literary life began early. At nine he wrote Latin verses said to have been good, but he disdained and destroyed them. He entered college at twelve; in those days, however, many Dutch college freshmen were in their early teens. Influence of Hugo's father and friends told at Leyden University; top professors took personal interest in him; he lived in the home of a distinguished faculty member. He graduated at fourteen—the hope and hero of the Leyden intellectual circle, an articulate and ambitious (but slightly uncertain) youth. Within a year he edited (with paternal and professorial help) and published his first scholarly work—a new edition of a classical school text.

Barneveld, a Dutch statesman, was sent to Paris to seek French support against Spain. He took his son with him and young Grotius went along as the son's companion. Grotius was in Paris for more than a year. He was presented to Henry IV, learned French, and picked up a quick Doctor of Laws degree at the University of Orleans. On his return home he went on with law study for a few months and was admitted to the Dutch bar. In the early days of his law practice he wrote to a friend that a peaceable philosopher like himself was ill-cast in the role of an advocate. His interest in letters drew off much of his energy. He edited classics, wrote top-notch Latin poetry, and published three Latin plays which were translated and republished in both Dutch and English.

At twenty he got his first public appointment—a commission (at a good salary) to write the official history of the United Provinces' struggle for freedom from Spain. Writing executed as a result of this appointment is still highly praised. His law practice, nevertheless, continued to grow. Two years later he wrote a systematic book on law in the scholastic mould, which laid groundwork for later important contributions to jurisprudence. Only one chapter was published—a timely essay championing Freedom of the Seas, inspired by the Dutch East India Company's claim to freedom from Spanish levies of tributes on its ships in Indian waters.

At twenty-five, Grotius was named Advocate-General of the Fisc of Holland, Zeeland, and Friesland, a post entailing important judicial, prosecuting, financial, and administrative functions.

He now had an income big enough for marriage and took the bride his father picked for him—the daughter of an important burgomaster. They were a devoted, well matched couple, and raised a family of six children.

80

His literary output continued; soon after his marriage he wrote a narrative poem about the death of Christ, including a lawyer-like account of the trial. At twenty-seven he published historical material displaying his political theory. He was a states' rights man. With Prince Maurice in mind he set out a theory of autonomy of each of the several provinces allotting to the Prince only limited authority over foreign relations, and no power, without consent of the provinces, to levy taxes, to interfere with ancient laws and customs, or to declare war. He was voicing the stand of the Dutch aristocracy who controlled the provinces and would lose power if national government became potent. But Grotius was still involved in mundane affairs and political activities. He also was party to a conspiratorial religious movement involving James I of England and a French scholar named Casaubon. When Grotius was thirty he was appointed Pensionary of Rotterdam, a civil office second in importance only to Grand Pensionary of the United Provinces.

Soon after this promotion, a Dutch deputation was sent to England to iron out maritime conflicts in eastern waters. Grotius was at the outset only a supernumerary. It is said that he was secretly an agent of the Arminian sect with orders to make common cause with James I and to persuade James to intercede for the sect with the Calvinistic Dutch Government. His three colleagues were content to let all of the mission's business fall into the hands of the smart young supernumerary while they enjoyed English hospitality. Grotius took a position head-on to that which he had taken in his essay on freedom of the seas, written when underdog Dutch were challenging Spain for the East India trade; he argued that the established Dutch had the right to keep the English out of that trade, or, failing that, the Dutch and English should combine against the Iberians. It was the turn of the English to insist—successfully—on Freedom of the Seas. Though he did little to advance the cause of his country, Grotius was personally well-received in England and made a fine impression there. King James liked and entertained him. He hobnobbed with leading English ecclesiastics and scholars.

On his return Grotius became involved in a bitter struggle between Arminians and Calvinists. Theologic differences were not the whole story; Arminians were supporters of aristocratic political power in the several provinces; Calvinists were partisans of Prince Maurice, and stood for nationalism and popular government. Maurice seized control and imposed a powerful national government on the provinces. One of the first acts of this government was trial and conviction of leading Arminians. Grotius, who was second only to Barneveld in Arminian ranks, was sentenced to life imprisonment, and his property was confiscated. While imprisoned in Louvestein Castle Grotius was allowed to study and write. He made several Latin translations of Greek tragedies which were eventually published. He wrote a textbook on Dutch jurisprudence still assigned to Dutch law students. He spent much time in religious meditation, and his most important prison writing was his tolerant *Of the Truth of the Christian Religion,* which has gone through scores of editions and has been translated into many languages, including even Hungarian and Urdu.

In his second year of imprisonment his wife was allowed to live with him. She plotted and effected his escape. They fled to France, where Louis XIII granted (but seldom paid) him an inadequate pension. During a period of bitter poverty he wrote with amazing speed his most famous book, *The Law of War and Peace* (1625)—from which excerpts following this note were taken. This job was facilitated by building on and borrowing from the unpublished jurisprudential work he had written twenty years before. In preparation for this new work, however, Grotius studied prodigously. It is said that he especially conned writings of neo-Scholastic Spanish moralists, and again his work was cast in a scholastic mould. The book especially reflects his abhorrent concern with strife and bloodshed of wars and rebellions of his times. Publication of the book did little to relieve his poverty, but he was at once hailed as a legal scholar the world over. Nearly a hundred editions and translations of the book have been published. W. S. M. Knight (one of Grotius' biographers) explains enthusiasm with which the book was received this way, ". . . Europe, with feudalism in its death-throes and Church and Empire riven asunder, had urgent need of a general theory of the State, of the nation, and its organization. The contractual theory of government was now arising out of the dissolving feudal system, and here was Grotius frankly developing that theory . . . So it was the general course of events, the atmosphere of a rapidly changing Europe, that determined the [great] reputation and influence that *De Jure Belli* was to enjoy and command."

Grotius longed to go back to Holland and hoped his growing fame would make him acceptable in his homeland. Dead Prince Maurice was succeeded by Frederic Henry, who had been Grotius' friend at school. But the Calvinists would have been outraged by pardon for Grotius, and permission to return was denied him. He went back anyway, and scraped together a thriving law practice in short order. The States General decreed his arrest but his great reputation thwarted the decree. A large reward for his arrest was posted and he was frightened into leaving the country. After a dreary sojourn in Hamburg he returned to Paris, renounced his Dutch citizenship and resumed a literary life. His next book was appropriately a Latin tragedy based on the Old Testament Joseph's life.

Honor and importance again came Grotius' way when he was appointed Swedish ambassador to France. Long since, however, he had turned Richelieu against him by refusing to let the Cardinal exploit him. Cardinal Richelieu's unfriendliness was a serious handicap. Grotius did, however, play a signal part in negotiation of an important treaty, and he always exercised diplomatic patience and skill when interests of Sweden called for them. Most of his ten-year diplomatic career was little more than petty

squabbles over precedence and etiquette. His ambassadorial salary came out of funds which France paid Sweden through him, but the French were often in arrears and the embassy was often the site of ornate want.

When Richelieu died, Grotius got along even less well with his successor. He became so ineffective that a coadjutor was sent from Sweden to share his ambassadorial post, and Grotius was virtually shorn of power. He went to Sweden to mend his fences. There he was feted and honored, but given no assignment. Perhaps in his last years as ambassador he had been diverted too much by his writing. He had become obsessed with desire to promote reunification of Christian churches. He wrote biblical criticisms and exegeses which were well received. His theology was tolerant, scholarly and humanistic; he was the proper successor of Erasmus, the great, gentle, Dutch opponent of the vigorous Luther.

The raw Swedish winter and the crude Swedish court were uncongenial to tired, self-important, heavy-humored Grotius. He set sail on a boat bound for Lubeck to a mysteriously unannounced destination. The ship went aground in a storm, and Grotius was carried, sick, to Rostock where he died. His last words to a Lutheran minister who attended his lonely death-bed were, "By undertaking many things I have accomplished nothing." These disspirited words were said by a stalwart, busy public servant who had found time to write outstanding history, literature, theology and jurisprudence, a man who had weathered the change from feudalism to nationalism and saved the best jurisprudential ideas of Scholastics for the modern world.

ON THE
RIGHTS OF WAR AND PEACE *

Preliminary Remarks

1. The Civil Law . . . has been treated of, with a view either to illustrate it or to pre-

* From an abridged translation of William Whewell, published by John W. Parker, London, 1853.

sent it in a compendious form, by many. But International Law . . . has been touched on by few, and has been by no one treated as a whole in an orderly manner. . . .

3. And such a work is the more necessary on this account; that there are not wanting persons in our own time, and there have been also in former times persons, who have despised what has been done in this province of jurisprudence, so far as to hold that no such thing existed, except as a mere name. . . .

5. But since our discussion of Rights is worthless if there are no Rights, it will serve both to recommend our work, and to protect it from objections, if we refute briefly this very grave error. And that we may not have to deal with a mob of opponents, let us appoint them an advocate to speak for them. And whom can we select for this office, fitter than Carneades . . . He undertook to argue against justice; and especially the kind of justice of which we here treat; and in doing so, he found no argument stronger than this:—that men had, as utility prompted, established Rights, different as their manners differed; and even in the same society, often changed with the change of times: but Natural Law there is none: for all creatures, men and animals alike, are impelled by nature to seek their own gratification: and thus, either there is no such thing as justice, or if it exist, it is the height of folly, since it does harm to itself in aiming at the good of others. . . .

6. . . . Man is an animal indeed, but an animal of an excellent kind, differing much more from all other tribes of animals than they differ from one another; which appears by the evidence of many actions peculiar to the human species. And among these properties which are peculiar to man, is a desire for society . . . and not merely spent somehow, but spent tranquilly, and in a manner corresponding to the character of his intellect. This desire the Stoics called *the domestic instinct,* or *feeling of kindred.* And therefore the assertion, that, by nature, every **animal is** impelled only to seek its own ad-

vantage or good, if stated so generally as to include man, cannot be conceded. . . .

8. And this tendency to the conservation of society, which we have now expressed in a rude manner, and which tendency is in agreement with the nature of the human intellect, is the source of *Jus,* or Natural Law, properly so called. To this *Jus* belong the rule of abstaining from that which belongs to other persons; and if we have in our possession anything of another's, the restitution of it, or of any gain which we have made from it; the fulfilling of promises, and the reparation of damage done by fault; and the recognition of certain things as meriting punishment among men.

9. From this signification has flowed another larger sense of *Jus:* for, inasmuch as man is superior to other animals, not only in the social impulse . . . but in his judgment and power of estimating advantages and disadvantages; . . . we may understand that it is congruous to human nature to follow . . . a judgment rightly framed; not to be misled by fear or by the temptation of present pleasure, nor to be carried away by blind and thoughtless impulse; and that what is plainly repugnant to such judgment, is also contrary to *Jus,* that is, to Natural Human Law.

10. And to this exercise of judgment pertains a reasonable and thoughtful assignment, to each individual and each body of men, of the things which peculiarly belong to them; by which exercise of judgment in some cases, the wiser man is preferred to the less wise; in others, our neighbour to a stranger; in others, a poor man to a rich man. . . .

12. . . . We are brought to another origin of *Jus,* besides that natural source; namely, the free will of God, to which, as our reason irresistibly tells us, we are bound to submit ourselves . . . Natural Law of which we have spoken, whether it be that which binds together communities, or that looser kind . . . may yet be rightly ascribed to God; because it was by His will that such principles came to exist in us . . . .

14. Further. The Sacred History, besides

that part which consist in precepts, offers another view which in no small degree excites the social affection of which we have spoken; in that it teaches us that all men are sprung from the same parents. And thus we may rightly say, in this sense also, what Florentinus says in another sense, that there is a kindred established among us by nature: and in virtue of this relation it is wrong for man to intend mischief towards man. . . .

15. In the next place, since it is conformable to Natural Law to observe compacts, (for some mode of obliging themselves was necessary among men, and no other natural mode could be imagined), Civil Rights were derived from this source, mutual compact. For those who had joined any community, or put themselves in subjection to any man or men, those either expressly promised, or from the nature of the case must have been understood to promise tacitly, that they would conform to that which either the majority of the community, or those to whom the power was assigned, should determine.

16. And therefore, what Carneades said (as above), and what others also have said, as Horace,

Utility, Mother of just and right.

if we are to speak accurately, is not true. For the Mother of Right, that is, of Natural Law, is Human Nature; for this would lead us to desire mutual society, even if it were not required for the supply of other wants; and the Mother of Civil Laws, is Obligation by mutual compact; and since mutual compact derives its force from Natural Law, Nature may be said to be the Grandmother of Civil Laws. . . . But Natural Law is *reinforced* by Utility. For the Author of Nature ordained that we should, as individuals, be weak, and in need of many things to make life comfortable, in order that we might be the more impelled to cling to society. But Utility is the *occasion* of Civil Laws; for the association or subjection by mutual compact . . . was at the first instituted for the sake of some utility. And accordingly, they who prescribe laws for others, in doing this,

aim, or ought to aim, at some Utility, to be produced to them for whom they legislate.

17. Further: as the Laws of each Community regard the Utility of that Community, so also between different Communities, all or most, Laws might be established, and it appears that Laws have been established, which enjoined the Utility, not of special communities, but of that great aggregate System of Communities. And this is what is called the Law of Nations, or International Law; when we distinguish it from Natural Law. And this part of Law is omitted by Carneades. . . .

18. And it is without any good reason that Carneades maintains . . . that justice is folly. For since, by his own confession, that Citizen is not foolish who in a Civil Community obeys the Civil Law, although, in consequence of such respect for the Law he may lose something which is useful to himself: so too that People is not foolish which does not so estimate its own utility, as, on account of *that,* to neglect the common Laws between People and People. The reason of the thing is the same in both cases. For as a citizen who violates the Civil Law for the sake of present utility, destroys that institution in which the perpetual utility of himself and his posterity is bound up; so too a people which violates the Laws of Nature and nations, beats down the bulwark of its own tranquillity for future time. . . .

19. And therefore neither is that other saying of Horace universally true:

'Twas fear of wrong that made us make our laws;

an opinion which one of the interlocutors in Plato's *Republic* explains in this way: that Laws were introduced from the fear of receiving wrong, and that men are driven to practise justice by a certain compulsion . . . many, individually feeble, fearing to be oppressed by those who were stronger, combined to establish judicial authorities, and to uphold them by their common strength; that those whom they could not resist singly, they might, united, control. And we may accept in this sense, and in no other, what is also said in Plato, that Right is that which the stronger party likes: namely, that we are to understand that Rights do not attain their external end, except they have force to back them. . . .

20. But still Rights, even unsupported by force, are not destitute of all effect . . . The conscience of honest men approves justice, condemns injustice. . . .

30. . . . Natural Law, as being always the same, can be easily collected into an Art: but that which depends upon institution, since it is often changed, and is different in different places, is out of the domain of Art. . . .

31. If, then, those who have devoted themselves to the study of true justice would separately undertake to treat of separate parts of Natural and Permanent Jurisprudence, omitting all which derives its origin from the will of man alone . . . we might, by collecting all these parts, form a complete body of such Jurisprudence.

32. What course *we* think ought to be followed in the execution of such a task, we shew by act rather than by words, in this present work; in which is contained by far the noblest part of Jurisprudence. . . .

39. . . . The principles of such Natural Law, if you attend to them rightly, are of themselves patent and evident, almost in the same way as things which are perceived by the external senses: which do not deceive us, if the organs are rightly disposed, and if other things necessary are not wanting. . . .

40. In order to give proofs on questions respecting this Natural Law, I have made use of the testimonies of philosophers, historians, poets, and finally orators. Not that I regard these as judges from whose decision there is no appeal: for they are warped by their party, their argument, their cause: but I quote them as witnesses whose conspiring testimony, proceeding from innumerable different times and places, must be referred to some universal cause; which, in the questions with which we are here concerned, can be no other than a right deduction proceeding from the principles of reason, or some common consent. The former cause of agreement points to the Law of Nature; the latter, to the Law of Nations: though the difference of these two is not to be collected from the testimonies themselves, (for writers everywhere confound the Law of Nature and the Law of Nations,) but from the quality of the matter. For what cannot be deduced from certain principles by solid reasoning, and yet is seen and observed everywhere, must have its origin from the will and consent of all.

41. I have, therefore, taken pains to distinguish Natural Law from the Law of Nations, as well as both from the Civil Law. . . .

43. . . . It appears to me that both some of the Platonists and the ancient Christians had good reason to depart from Aristotle's doctrine, in which he placed the very nature of Virtue in a *medium* of the affections and actions. . . .

44. That this foundation of virtue, [that it is the *medium* between two extremes,] is not a right one, appears from the example of Justice itself; for the *too much* and *too little* which are opposed to this, since he cannot find in the affections and the consequent actions, he seeks them in the things with which justice deals; which proceeding is, in the first place, a transition to another genus; a fault which he justly blames in others. And in the next place, to take less than is one's own, may indeed have a vice adventitiously connected with it, growing out of a consideration of what a person, under the circumstances, owes to himself and those who depend on him; but certainly cannot be repugnant to justice, which resides entirely in abstaining from what is another's. And to this mistake that other is similar, that adultery as the fruit of lust, and homicide arising from anger, he will not allow to belong properly to injustice; though injustice is nothing else in its nature than the usurpation of what is another's; nor does it make any difference whether that proceeds from avarice, or from lust, or from anger, or from thoughtless compassion; or on the other hand, from the desire of superiority, in which the greatest examples of unjust aggressions originate. For to resist

all impulses on this account only, that human society may not be violated, is what is really the proper character of justice.

45. . . . it is true that it belongs to the character of certain virtues, that the affections are kept in moderation; but it does not follow that this is the proper and universal character of all virtue; but that Right Reason, which virtue everywhere follows, dictates that in some things a medium course is to be followed, in others, the highest degree of the affection is to be aimed at. Thus for instance, we cannot love God too much. . . .

57. I have refrained from discussing points which belong to another subject; as the Utility of this or that course; for these belong to a special Art, namely, the Art Political; which Aristotle rightly treats as a separate subject, mixing with it nothing of any other kind . . . In some cases, however, I have made mention of the Utility of acts; but collaterally only, and in order to distinguish that question the more plainly from the question of Right.

58. The reader will do me injustice, if he judges me to have written with a regard to any controversies of our own time; either such as already exist, or such as can be foreseen as likely to arise. I profess, in all sincerity, that, as mathematicians consider their figures as abstracted from body, so did I, in treating of Rights, abstract my mind from every particular fact. . . .

Book I

CHAPTER I

What is War.
What are Rights

I. [Questions of Rights among citizens of the same State are settled by the instituted Law of the State; and therefore do not belong to our subject, which is, Rights by nature, not Rights by institution.] . . . .

III. 1. By entitling our Treatise, *Of the Rights of War,* we mean, in the first place, to imply the discussion of the questions just stated, Whether any war is just, and What is just in war. For *Rights, Jus,* in this case, means only what is right, that is, just; and that, rather with a negative than a positive sense; so that *that* comes within the substantive *Right,* which is not unjust, or wrong.

That is unjust which is contrary to the nature of a society of rational creatures. . . .

2. Society is either that of equals, as brothers, friends, allies; or it is unequal, as that of parent and child, master and servant, king and subjects, God and men: and what is just, is different in the two cases. We may call them respectively Equatorial Rights and Rectorial Rights.

IV. *Jus, Right,* has another signification, derived from the former, as when we say *my* Right. In this sense Right is a moral Quality by which a person is competent to have or to do a certain thing justly. . . .

This moral quality, when perfect, is called *facultas,* a jural claim; when less perfect, *aptitudo,* a fitness, or moral claim.

V. A Jural Claim . . . includes, Power; whether over one's self, which is Liberty; or over another, which is Authority, for example, paternal, dominical (that of a master over a servant;)

Ownership; whether full, as of Property; or less full, as of Compact, Pledge,

Credit, to which corresponds Debt on the other side.

VI. But this Right is again twofold: Vulgar, which exists for the purpose of private use; and Eminent, which is superior to vulgar Right, and is the right which the community has over persons and things for the sake of the common good . . .

. . . Every one is more bound to the state in regard to public uses than to his private creditor. . . .

X. 1. Natural Law is the Dictate of Right Reason, indicating that any act, from its agreement or disagreement with the rational nature [of man] has in it a moral turpitude or a moral necessity; and consequently that such act is forbidden or commanded by God, the author of nature.

2. Acts concerning which there is such a Dictate, are obligatory, or are unlawful, in

themselves, and are therefore understood as necessarily commanded or forbidden by God; and in this character, Natural Law differs, not only from Human Law, but from Positive Divine Law, which does not forbid or command acts which, in themselves and by their own nature, are either obligatory or unlawful; but, by forbidding them makes them unlawful, by commanding them makes them obligatory.

3. In order to understand Natural Law, we must remark that some things are said to be according to Natural Law, which are not so properly, but, as the schools love to speak, reductively, Natural Law not opposing them; as we have said [III. 1] that some things are called just, which are not unjust. And again, by an abuse of expression, some things are said to be according to Natural Law which reason shews to be decent, or better than their opposites, though not obligatory. . . .

4. It is to be remarked also that Natural Law deals not only with things made by nature herself, but with things produced by the act of man. Thus property, as it now exists, is the result of human will: but being once introduced, Natural Law itself shews that it is unlawful for me to take what is yours against your will. . . .

5. Natural Law is so immutable that it cannot be changed by God himself . . . Thus God himself cannot make twice two not be four; and in like manner, he cannot make that which is intrinsically bad, not be bad. For as the essence of things, when they exist, and by which they exist, does not depend on anything else, so is it with the properties which follow that essence: and such a property is the baseness of certain actions, when compared with the nature of rational beings. . . .

6. Yet sometimes, in acts directed by Natural Law, there is a seeming of change, which may mislead the unwary; when in fact it is not Natural Law which is changed, but the thing about which that Law is concerned. Thus if a creditor gives me a receipt for my debt, I am no longer bound to pay him; not that Natural Law has ceased to command me to pay what I owe, but because I have ceased to owe it. So if God command any one to be slain or his goods to be taken, this does not make lawful homicide or theft, which words involve crime: but the act will no longer be homicide or theft, being authorized by the supreme Lord of life and of goods.

7. Further; some things are according to Natural Law, not simply, but in a certain state of things. Thus a community in the use of things was natural till property was established; and the right of getting possession of one's own by force existed before instituted law. . . .

XII. 1. That there is such a thing as Natural Law, is commonly proved both *a priori* and *a posteriori;* the former the more subtle, the latter, the more popular proof. It is proved *a priori* by shewing the agreement or disagreement of anything with the rational and social nature of man. It is proved *a posteriori* when by certain or very probable accounts we find anything accepted as Natural Law among all nations, or at least the more civilized. For a universal effect requires a universal cause: now such a universal belief can hardly have any cause except the common sense of mankind. . . .

XIV. 1. Of Human Law, first, as more widely known. This is either the Civil Law, [that is, the National Law,] or Law in a narrower, or in a wider sphere.

The Civil Law is that which governs the State, (*Civitas*).

The State, (*Civitas*) is a perfect [that is, independent] collection of free men, associated for the sake of enjoying the advantages of *jus,* and for common utility.

Law is a narrow sphere, and not derived from the State, though subject to it, is various, as paternal precepts, the commands of a master, and the like.

Law in a wider sphere is *Jus Gentium,* the Law of Nations, that Law which has received an obligatory force from the will of all nations, or of many.

I have added *"or of many,"* because scarce

any Law is found, except Natural Law, (which also is often called *Jus Gentium,*) common to *all* nations. . . .

2. This *Jus Gentium,* Law of Nations, is proved in the same manner as the unwritten Civil Law, by constant usage, and the testimony of those who have made it their study. . . .

CHAPTER II

Whether War Ever be Just

1. 1. . . . Cicero repeatedly speaks of certain First Principles. . . . There is, according to him, a First Principle of Self-preservation. An animal, from its birth, is urged to care for and preserve itself, to choose the means of preserving its good condition, to shun destruction, and every thing which leads to its destruction. Thus there is no one who does not prefer to have the parts of his body sound and whole, rather than maimed and distorted. The first business of each is to preserve himself in the state of nature; the next, to retain what is according to nature, and to reject what is contrary to it.

2. After this Principle, there follows a notion of the Agreement of things with Reason, which is superior to the body; and this Agreement, in which what is reasonable (*honestum*) becomes our object, is seen to be of more importance than those things to which alone the first impulse of appetite tended. The first Principle [of self-preservation] commends us to Right Reason; but Right Reason ought to be dearer to us than those things by which we were first led to use it.

This is allowed by all who are of sound mind, without demonstration. Hence in examining what agrees with Natural Law, we must first see what agrees with that first principle of Self-preservation; and afterwards proceed to that which, though subsequent in origin, is of greater dignity; and must not only accept it, if it be offered, but seek it with all care. . . .

4. In the first principle of nature [Self-preservation] there is nothing which is re-

pugnant to war: indeed all things rather favour it: for the end of war, the preservation of life and limb, and the retention or acquisition of things useful to life, agrees entirely with that principle. . . .

5. Again, Right Reason and the nature of Society . . . do not prohibit all force, but that only which is repugnant to Society; that is, that which is used to attack the Rights of others. For Society has for its object, that every one may have what is his own in safety, by the common help and agreement. Which consideration would still have place, even if property were not introduced: for even then, each one would have a property in his life, limbs, liberty; and these could not be attacked without wrong done to him. And also to use things which lay in common, and to take as much of them as nature should require, would be the right of the person who first took occupation of them; and he who should prevent the exercise of this Right, would do the occupier wrong. And this is much more easily understood now, when property has taken a shape by law or usage. . . .

II. 1. Our doctrine, that all war is not contrary to Natural Law, is further proved from the sacred history. Abraham made war upon the four kings who had plundered Sodom, and was thereupon blessed by Melchisedec. This he did without the special mandate of God, as appears by the history: he must therefore have been justified by the Law of Nature: for he was a most holy and wise man, as even heathen authors declare. . . .

CHAPTER III

Of War Public and Private Of Sovereignty

I. . . . 2. That private war may be lawful, so far as Natural Law goes, I conceive is sufficiently apparent from what has been said above, when it was shewn, that for any one to repel injury, even by force, is not repugnant to Natural Law. But perhaps some may think that after judicial tribunals have been established, this is no longer lawful: for though public tribunals do not proceed from nature, but from the act of man, yet equity and natural reason dictate to us that we must conform to so laudable an institution; since it is much more decent and more conducive to tranquillity among men, that a matter should be decided by a disinterested judge, than that men, under the influence of self-love, should right themselves according to their notions of right. . . .

II. 1. It is not to be doubted, indeed, that the licence which existed before the establishment of public justice is much restricted. Yet still it continues to exist; namely when public justice ends: for the law which forbids us to seek our own by other than judicial proceedings, must be understood to apply only when judicial aid can be had. Now judicial aid ceases either momentarily or continuously. It ceases momentarily when the judge cannot be waited for without certain danger or loss. It ceases continuously either *de jure* or *de facto: de jure,* if any one be in an unsettled place, as at sea, in a desert, in an uninhabited island, or in any other place where there is no political government: *de facto,* if the subjects do not obey the judge, or if the judge openly refuses to take cognizance. . . .

2. . . . By the laws of all nations which we know, he is deemed innocent who defends himself being in peril of life; which manifest consent is a proof that such a course is not at variance with Natural Law. . . .

VIII. 1. And here we must first reject their opinion who say that the Sovereignty everywhere belongs to the People; so that *it* has the power of controlling kings, and of punishing them if they abuse their power. . . .

A man may by his own act make himself the slave of any one: as appears by the Hebrew and the Roman law. Why then may not a people do the same, so as to transfer the whole Right of governing it to one or more persons? . . . Nor is it to the purpose to allege the inconveniences which follow or may follow from such a course: for whatever form of government you take, you will never escape all inconvenience.

2. But as there are many ways of living, one better than another, and each man is free to choose which of them he pleases; so each nation may choose what form of government it will: and its right in this matter is not to be measured by the excellence of this or that form, concerning which opinions may be various, but by its choice.

3. Nor is it difficult to conceive causes why a people may resign the whole power of its own government, and transfer, it to another; as for example, if it be in great peril and cannot find a defender on other conditions: or if it be in want and cannot otherwise obtain sustenance. . . .

4. Add to this that, as Aristotle says that some men are slaves by nature, so some nations are more prone to be governed than to govern. . . .

6. Moreover civil authority, or the right of governing, may also be acquired by legitimate war. . . .

13. The arguments on the other side [that all kings are responsible to the people] are not difficult to answer: for

(1) First, the assertion that he who constitutes any authority is superior to the person so constituted, is only true in that constitution which depends perpetually on the will of the constituent body: not in that which, though voluntary at first, afterwards becomes compulsory: thus a woman constitutes a person her husband, whom afterwards she is obliged forever to obey. . . .

14. (2) The other argument is taken from the maxim of the philosophers, that all government exists for the sake of the governed, not of the governors; whence they conceive it follows that, the end being more noble than the means, the governed are superior to the governors.

But it is not universally true that all government is for the sake of the governed: for some kinds of government are for the sake of the governor, as that of the master in his family; for there the advantage of the servant is extrinsic and adventitious; as the gain of the physician is extrinsic to the art of medicine. Other kinds of government are for the sake of common utility, as the marital. So some kingly governments may be established for the good of the kings, as those which are won by victory: and these are not therefore to be called tyrannies: since *tyranny*, as we now understand it, implies injustice. Some governments too may have respect to the utility both of the governor and the governed; as when a people in distress places a powerful king over it to defend it.

But I do not deny that in most governments, the good of the governed is the object: and that . . . kings are constituted for the sake of justice. But it does not follow, as our opponents infer, that peoples are superior to kings: for guardianship is for the sake of the ward, and yet the guardian has authority over the ward . . . in political government, because we cannot have an infinite gradation of superiors, we must stop at some person or body, whose transgressions, having no superior judge, are the province of God; as he himself declares . . .

IX. 1. Some assert that there is a mutual subjection, so that the whole people ought to obey the king when he rules rightly, but when a king rules ill, he is subject to the people. If these reasoners were to say that those things which are manifestly iniquitous are not to be done, though commanded by the king, they would say what is true, and confessed by all good men. . . .

. . . The most extreme confusion must follow, if the king and the people claim cognisance of the same matter by the allegation of good and evil conduct . . .

XII. 1. Some oppose this, because, they say, men are not things, and cannot be possessed *pleno jure*, as things. But personal liberty is one thing, civil liberty, another. Men may have personal liberty, so as not to be slaves; and yet not have civil liberty, so as to be free citizens. . . .

XVI. 1. . . . Authority does not cease to be sovereign, although the Ruler makes certain promises to his subjects, or to God, even of matters relating to the government. I do not now speak of promises to observe Natural Law and Divine Law, or the *Jus gentium,* to which all kings are bound, even without promise; but of the concession of rules to which they could not be bound without promise. . . .

2. But still it must be confessed, that when this is done, the sovereignty is in some degree, limited . . . an act done against the promise becomes unjust, because, as we shall elsewhere shew, a legitimate promise gives a Right to the promisee. . . .

XVII. 2. . . . Many persons allege many inconveniences against such a two headed Sovereignty; but in political matters nothing is quite free from inconveniences; and Rights arise, not from what seems to one or another convenient, but from the will of him who is the origin of Rights. For example, the kings established by the Heraclidae in Argos, Messena, and Sparta, were bound to govern within the rules of the law; and so long as they did so, the people were bound to preserve the throne to them. . . .

CHAPTER IV

Of Wars of Subjects Against Superiors

I. . . . 2. But we have now to inquire only whether it be lawful either for private or for public persons to carry on war against those who have over them an authority either sovereign or subordinate . . .

3. It is beyond controversy among all good men, that if the persons in authority command any thing contrary to Natural Law or the Divine Precepts, it is not to be done. For the Apostles, in saying that we must obey God rather than man, appealed to an undoubted rule, written in the minds of all. . . .

II. 1. By Natural Law, all have the Right of repelling wrong. But civil society being instituted to secure public tranquillity, the State acquires a Superior Right over us and ours, as far as is necessary for that end. Therefore the State may prohibit that promiscuous Right of resisting, for the sake of public peace and order: and it is to be presumed to have intended this, since it cannot otherwise attain its end. If this prohibition does not exist, there is no State . . . .

IV. . . . 3. If the Rulers at any time are misled by excessive fear or anger, or other passions, so as to deviate from the road that leads to tranquillity, this is to be held as the less usual case, and compensated by the alternation of better times . . . . Exceptional cases must submit to the general rule; for though the reason of the rule does not specially hold in that special case, yet the general reason of the rule remains; and to this special facts must be subjected. This is better than living without a rule, or leaving the rule to everyone's will . . . .

V. 1. The custom of the early Christians, the best interpreters of the law of our Lord, did not deviate from this rule. For though very wicked men held the Roman empire, and there were not wanting persons who opposed them on pretence of relieving the State, the Christians never took part in their attempts. . . .

VI. 1. Some learned men of our time, yielding too much to the influences of time and place, have persuaded first themselves (for so I believe) and then others, that this, though true of private persons, is not true of inferior magistrates; that they have a right of resistance, and ought to use it; which opinion is not to be admitted. For those inferior magistrates, though public persons with regard to their inferiors, are private persons with regard to their superiors. . . .

VII. 1. Whether in a very grave and certain danger the rule of non-resistance holds, is a more difficult question. For the laws of God may admit of exemption in cases of extreme necessity . . . Some laws are of such a nature that it is not credible that they were given with so rigid an intention: still more in human laws.

2. . . . Laws are and ought to be made, with a sense of human weakness. The law of which we speak (that of non-resistance) seems to depend on those who first formed civil society, and from whom the Rights of Rulers are derived. And if these could be asked whether they would impose on all this burthen, that they should prefer to die

rather than in any case resist a superior by force, it is probable they would answer that they would not: unless perhaps with this addition; except resistance would involve extreme disturbance of the State, and the death of many innocent persons. And what benevolence would recommend in such circumstances, we may confidently ascribe to human law.

3. It may be said that the rigid obligation of bearing death rather than resisting a superior, proceeds not from human, but from Divine Law. But it is to be noted that Civil Society is the result, not of Divine precept, but of the experience of the weakness of separate families to protect themselves; and is thus called by Peter an *ordinance of man*, though it is also an ordinance of God, because He approves it. And God, approving a human law, must be conceived approving it as human, and in a human manner.

4. Barclay, the most strenuous asserter of royal authority, yet allows that the people, or a *considerable part* of it, has the Right of protecting itself against extreme cruelty, though he asserts the whole people to be subject to the king. I can understand, that in proportion as what is preserved [by the rule of non-resistance] is more valuable, so much the more serious a matter is the equitable construction, which allows an exception to the words of the law. But still, I do not venture indiscriminately to condemn, either *individuals* or a *minority* of the people who thus have recourse to the ultimate means of necessity, provided they do not desert a respect for the common good. . . .

7. Nor are those who resist to throw false reproaches on any one; but on the king, not even true ones. Still more are they to abstain from laying hands on him. . . .

XI. . . . If the king act, with a really hostile mind, with a view to the destruction of the whole people, Barclay says that the kingdom is forfeited; for the purpose of governing and the purpose of destroying cannot subsist together . . . .

XIII. . . . If the king have a part only of the Sovereignty, another part being in the Senate or the people, and if the king invade the part which is not his, he may justly be opposed by force, because in that part he has not authority. . . .

Book II

CHAPTER I

Of the Causes of War; and First, of Self-Defense and the Defense of Our Property

I. . . . 4. A just cause of War is injury done us, and nothing else. Augustine says, *The Injustice* (that is the injury) *of the adverse party makes a war just.* . . .

II. . . . 2. Most writers state three just causes of war; defense, recovery of property, and punishment of wrong. . . .

3. Such is the natural feeling of Justice among nations . . . .

Therefore the first cause of a just war is an injury not yet done which menaces body or goods.

III. If the body be menaced by present force with danger of life not otherwise evitable, war is lawful, even to the slaying of the aggressor, as we have before said, in proving some private war to be lawful. And this right of defense arises from the natural right of self-protection, not from the injustice or fault of another who makes the danger. And therefore this right of self-protection is not taken away, even if the aggressor be blameless; if, for instance, he be a soldier acting *bona fide;* or if he take me for another than I am, or if he be insane or a sleepwalker, such as we read of; it is sufficient that I am not bound to suffer what he attempts to inflict; just as if a wild beast were to attack me.

IV. . . . 2. Thomas Aquinas well says . . . that a man killed in self-defense is not killed by intention . . . He who is attacked, even then, ought to do anything by which the assailant may be scared away, or deprived of power, rather than by which he may be killed.

V. 1. Present danger is here required, and imminent in a point of time. I confess in-

deed that if the aggressor be taking up weapons, and in such a way that he manifestly does so with the intent to kill, the deed may be anticipated; for in moral things, as in natural, there is no point without a certain latitude: but they are in great error who allow any fear [however slight] as a right of killing for prevention . . . .

2. If any one direct against us violence not present; as if he make a conspiracy, or lay an ambush, or put poison in our way, or assail us with a false accusation, false testimony, or iniquitous judgment; I deny that he may be lawfully slain, if either the danger may be otherwise avoided, or it be not certain that it cannot be otherwise avoided. For delay allows recourse to many remedies and many chances; as we say, between the cup and the lip . . . .

VII. Whether the same be lawful in defense of chastity, can scarcely be doubted, since not only common estimation, but the divine law, makes chastity of the same value as life. . . .

IX. 1. On the other hand, it may happen that because the life of the aggressor is useful to many, he cannot be killed without sin; and that, not only by the divine law, but by Natural Law. For Natural Law not only respects what corrective justice dictates, but also contains in itself acts of other virtues, as temperance, fortitude, prudence, as in certain circumstances not only good but obilgatory. Now benevolence binds to act as we have said.

2. Vasquius says that a prince, when he insults an innocent man, ceases to be a prince: but nothing can be less true or more dangerous. . . .

X. 1. If any one be in danger of receiving a buffet, or the like evil, some hold that he has a right to protect himself by killing his enemy. If merely corrective justice be regarded, I do not dissent. For though a buffet and death are very unequal, yet he who is about to do me an injury, thereby gives me a Right, that is a moral claim against him, *in infinitum,* so far as I cannot otherwise repel the evil. And even benevolence *per se* does not appear to bind us to the advantage of him who does us wrong. But the Gospel law has made every such act unlawful: for Christ commands us to take a buffet, rather than hurt our adversary; how much less may we kill him? We must therefore beware of the doctrine of Covarruvias, that with Natural Law in our minds, we cannot conceive anything permitted by natural reason which is not permitted by God, since God is Nature itself. For God, who is the Author of nature in such a way that he is above Nature, has a right to prescribe laws to us concerning the things which by nature are free and undetermined; much more, that that be duty which by nature is good, though not duty.

2. It is wonderful, since the will of God appears so clearly in the Gospel, that there should be found Theologians, and Christian Theologians, who not only think killing may be permitted to avoid a buffet, but even when a buffet has been received, if the striker flies, for the recovery of honour, as it is called. This seems to me very far removed from reason and piety. For honour is an opinion of one's own excellence; and he who bears such an injury shews himself excellently patient, and so increases his honour rather than diminishes . . . .

3. Hence it appears also that that is wrong which is delivered by most writers, that defense with slaying is lawful, that is by Divine Law, (for I do not dispute that it is by Natural Law,) when flight without danger is possible: namely, because flight is ignominious, especially in a man of noble family. In truth there is, then, no ignominy, but a false opinion of ignominy, to be despised by those who follow virtue and wisdom . . . .

XI. Let us come to injuries by which our property is attacked.

If we regard corrective justice, I do not deny that in order to preserve our goods, the robber, if need be, may be killed; for the difference that there is between things and life, is compensated by the preference to be given to the innocent, and the condemnation incurred by the robber, as we have said. Whence it follows that if we regard Natural Law alone, the thief flying with his plunder may, if the goods cannot otherwise be recovered, be slain with a missile . . . Nor does benevolence oppose this as a command; setting aside human and divine law; except the thing stolen be a trifle which may be contemned. . . .

XII. 1. Let us look at the sense of the Hebrew Law, (Exod. xxii. 2) with which agrees the law of Solon, and of the Twelve Tables, and Plato's *Laws*. These laws all agree in distinguishing the nocturnal from the diurnal thief. Some think that this is because by night we cannot tell whether he is a thief or a murderer, and therefore may kill him as a murderer. Others think it is because by night we have less chance of recovering the property. I think that neither is the true ground; but this; that no one ought to be slain directly for the sake of mere things, which would be done if I were to kill an unarmed flying thief with a missile, and so recover my goods. . . .

2. The difference depends then on this; that by night there is no testimony to be had; and therefore if the thief be found slain, credit is to be given to him who says that he slew him in defending his life. . . .

3. And therefore, as I have said, the presumption is in favour of him who kills the nocturnal thief; but if there be testimony by which it appears that the slayer was not in danger of his life, the presumption ceases, and he is guilty of homicide. . . .

XIV. It is made a question whether the civil law, when it permits us to kill a thief with impunity, does not give us a Right to do so; since the civil law has the Right of life and death. But this is not so. In the first place, the Civil Law has not the Right of life and death in all cases, but only in cases of great crimes . . . And moreover, the law neither does nor ought to give the Right of privately putting to death those who deserve death, except in very atrocious crimes; otherwise tribunals would be useless. Wherefore if the law allows us in any case to kill a thief with impunity, it takes away the punishment, but does not give the Right. . . .

XVII. There is an intolerable doctrine in some writers, that by the Law of Nations we may rightly take arms against a power which is increasing, and may increase, so as to be dangerous. Undoubtedly, in deliberating of war, this may come into consideration, not as a matter of justice, but as a matter of utility; so that if the war be just on other accounts, it may, on this account, be prudent; and this is what the arguments of authors come to. But that the possibility of suffering force gives us the right of using force, is contrary to all notion of equity. Such is human life, that we are never in complete security. We must seek protection against uncertain fears from Divine Providence, and from blameless caution, not from force.

CHAPTER II

Of the Common Rights of Men

II. 1. God gave the human race generally a right to the things of a lower nature, at the Creation, and again, after the Deluge. Every thing was common and undivided, as if all had one patrimony. Hence each man might take for his use what he would, and consume what he could . . . What each one had taken, another could not take from him by force without wrong. . . .

And this state might have continued, if men had remained in great simplicity, or had lived in great mutual good will. . . .

2. But men did not continue in this simple and innocent life, but applied their minds to various arts . . . The oldest arts, agriculture and pasture, appeared in the first brothers (Cain and Abel); not without a division of possessions already shewing itself, and even not without bloodshed. . . .

3. But the concord was especially broken by a more generous vice, ambition: of which the Tower of Babel was the sign; and then different men divided the earth among them and possessed it. Yet still there remained among neighbours a community, not of their flocks and herds, but of their pastures; for there was enough for all for a time: until,

cattle increasing, the land was divided, not according to nations as before, but according to families. And some made and occupied their own wells, things most necessary in a thirsty region, and not sufficing for many. This is the account of the sacred history, sufficiently agreeing with the account given by philosophers and poets.

4. There we learn what was the cause why men departed from the community of things, first of moveables, then of immoveables: namely, because when they were not content to feed on spontaneous produce, to dwell in caves, to go naked, or clothed in bark or in skins, but had sought a more exquisite kind of living, there was need of industry, which particular persons might employ on particular things. And as to the common use of the fruits of the earth, it was prevented by the dispersion of men into different localities, and by the want of justice and kindness which interfered with a fair division of labour and sustenance.

5. And thus we learn how things became Property . . . by a certain pact, either express, as by division, or tacit, as by occupation . . . .

V. Concerning wild beasts, fishes, birds, this also is to be remarked; that he who has the ownership of the land and water, may, on that ground, prevent any one from taking those creatures, and thus acquiring property in them. The reason, is, that it is morally necessary to the government of a people that they who mingle with the people even for a time, which is done by entering the territory, must conform to its institutions. Nor is this disproved by what we often read in the Roman Law, that *jure naturae* or *jure gentium* men are free to pursue animals of chase. For this is true as long as no Civil Law interferes: as the Roman Law left many things in that primeval state which other nations settled otherwise. And when the Civil Law has settled anything otherwise, the Natural Law itself directs that it be obeyed. For though the Civil Law cannot ordain anything which the Natural Law prohibits, nor prohibit what that ordains: yet it may circumscribe natural liberty, and forbid what was lawful by Natural Law; and even interfere to prevent an ownership which might be acquired by Natural Law.

VI. 1. Let us consider whether men have any Common Right to those things which are already made private property . . . .

2. . . . In extreme necessity, the pristine right of using things revives, as if they had remained common: for in all laws, and thus in the law of ownership, extreme necessity is excepted.

3. Hence the rule, that in a voyage, if the provisions run short, what each one has must be thrown into the common stock. So to preserve my house from a conflagration which is raging, my neighbour's house may be pulled down: and ropes or nets may be cut, of which any ship has run foul, if it cannot be extricated otherwise. All which rules are not introduced by the Civil Law, but by the interpretations of it.

4. For among Theologians also, it is a received opinion, that in such a necessity, if any one take what is necessary to his life from any other's property, he does not commit theft: of which rule the reason is, not that which some allege, that the owner of the property is bound to give so much to him that needs it, out of charity: but this, that all things must be understood to be assigned to owners with some such benevolent exception of the Right thus primitively assigned. For if the first dividers had been asked what was their intention, they would have given such a one as we have stated. . . .

XVIII. After the Common Right to things follows the Common Right to acts; and this is given either simply or hypothetically. There is given *simply* a Right to those acts without which life cannot conveniently be sustained, and others which may be compared with these. The same necessity is not required here, as in taking what belongs to another; for here we do not speak of what may be done, the owner being unwilling; but of the mode of acquiring things with the owner's consent; asserting only, that he

may not prevent the acquisition either by law or by conspiracy. For such impediment in such matters is contrary to the nature of human society. . . .

XIX. We say then that these things, all men have a Right to purchase at a fair price; excepting when they from whom they are asked, themselves need them. . . .

XX. We have not the same Right to sell what we have; for every one is free to decide what he will acquire, and what not. Thus formerly the Belgians would not admit wine and other foreign merchandize: and the Arabians admitted some articles and not others.

XXI. 1. In the Right of which we speak is included . . . the Right of seeking and making marriages with neighbouring nations: if for instance, a population entirely male expelled from some other place come thither. For to live without marriage, though not entirely repugnant to human nature, is repugnant to the nature of most men. Celibacy suits only superior minds: therefore men ought not to be deprived of the means of getting wives. . . .

XXII. The Right *hypothetical* to acts, refers to acts which any nation has permitted to strangers generally: in this case, if one people be excluded from such acts, it is wronged. Thus if it be permitted to strangers to catch beasts, fish, birds, in certain places . . . that cannot be denied to one particular people, except on account of a delinquency. . . .

XXIV. I recollect a question raised, Whether it be lawful for one people to make an agreement with another, that they will sell to them alone fruits of a certain kind, which grew nowhere else. I conceive it to be lawful, if the buying people be ready to sell them to others at an equitable price: for it makes no difference to other nations, from whom they buy what gratifies their natural desires. And one party may anticipate another in a gainful trade; especially if the people making this bargain have taken the other people under its protection, and have incurred expense on that account. Such forestalling and monopoly, made with the intention which I have described, is not contrary to Natural Law; although sometimes it is prohibited by Civil Law, on account of public utility. . . .

CHAPTER IV

Of Presumed Dereliction of Property, and the Occupation Which Follows; and How it Differs from Usucaption and Prescription

I. HERE arises a great difficulty concerning the right of usucaption, [by which a thing long used becomes the property of the possessor]. This Right is introduced by the Civil Law, [not by Natural Law], for time, of its own nature, has no effective power . . . .

III. In truth, the effects, as to Rights, which depend on man's will, still do not follow the mere internal act of the mind, except that act be indicated by some external signs. For to assign a jural efficiency to mere acts of the mind, would not be congruous to human nature, which cannot know the acts of the mind, except from outward signs. Yet signs denoting the acts of the mind have never a mathematical, but only a probable certainty; for men may express in words something different from what they feel and will, and may simulate in their acts. But the nature of human society does not suffer that the acts of the mind, sufficiently indicated, should have no efficacy: therefore what is sufficiently indicated in words, is to be held true, as against him who so indicates it.

This doctrine of the force of words is to be applied to derelicts.

IV. 1. A derelict may also be indicated by the fact; thus, that is a derelict which is thrown away; unless the circumstances of the case be such that it may be supposed to be put away for a time and with the intention of taking it again. . . .

2. . . . This rule flows, not only from the Civil Law, but from Natural Law, according to which any one may abdicate what is his; and from the natural presumption by which every one is supposed to intend what he has sufficiently indicated. . . .

V. 1. . . . If any one knows a thing which is his to be held by another, and in the course of a long time says nothing against it, he, except some other reason manifestly appear, must be supposed to have acted with the purpose of no longer having that thing as his. . . .

VI. To establish the assumption of these two conditions, other conjectures are of force: but for the most part, the effect of time, in both points, is great. For in the first place, it can hardly happen that in a long time, a thing pertaining to any one should not come to his knowledge, since time supplies many occasions. And a shorter time is sufficient for this purpose in a case between persons present, than absent, even without referring to the Civil Law. So fear once impressed is understood to last for a certain time, but not for ever, since a long time affords many occasions of taking counsel against the danger, either by one's own means or by means of others; as by going out of the bounds of the authority of him who inspires the fear; or at least, it affords the means of renewing our right by protest, or, what is better, of referring to judges or arbitrators. . . .

IX. And perhaps we may say that this is not merely a matter of presumption, but that this law was introduced by an instituted law of nations, that a possession going beyond memory uninterrupted, and not accompained with any appeal to justice, absolutely transfers ownership. It is credible that nations have agreed upon this, since such a rule tends greatly to peace. . . .

XI. . . . And thus [by the course of usage] the king of any people may lose his authority and become subject to the people; and he who was not king, but only governor, may become king with absolute authority; and the sovereign authority, which at first was in the king or in the people wholly, may be shared between them. . . .

CHAPTER V

Of the Original Acquisition of Rights Over Persons; Wherein of the Rights of Parents; of Marriage; of Corporations; of Rights Over Subjects, and Over Slaves

I. THERE are rights over persons as well as over things; and these may be acquired by generation, consent, or delinquency.

Parents acquire a right over their children by generation; both parents, the father and the mother; but if there be a contention between the authorities, the authority of the father is preferred, as superior in sex.

II. 1. In children, three periods of life are to be distinguished; first the period previous to years of discretion; next, the period when they have come to years of discretion, but remain part of the parents' family; third, the period when they have gone out of the family . . . .

In the first period, all the actions of the children are under the dominion of the parents; for he who cannot govern himself must be governed by another; and the parents are the natural governors. . . .

III. In the second period . . . those actions only are subject to the authority of the parents which have some important bearing upon the state of the paternal or maternal family . . . In other actions, the children have, at that period, the moral right to act; but are bound, even in those, to endeavour to please their parents. But since this obligation is not founded in a jural right . . . but in piety, reverence, and the duty of repaying the benefits they have received, it does not render void what is done in transgression of it; as a donation made contrary to the rules of prudence by the owner is not void. . . .

V. . . . By the Law of Nature, and where the Civil Law does not impede, the father may put his son in pledge, and if necessary, even sell him, when there is no other means of providing for him . . . Nature is conceived to give a right to do every thing without which that cannot be obtained which nature

demands: [as the sustenance of children].

VI. In the third period, the son is independent and *sui juris,* the duty of piety and reverence still remaining, as its cause is perpetual. . . .

VII. Whatever goes beyond this, proceeds from instituted law, which is different in different places. . . .

VIII. 1. The right over persons which arises *ex consensu,* from consent, flows either from partnership or from subjection. The most natural form of partnership appears in marriage; but on account of the difference of sex, the authority is not common to the two; the husband is the head of the wife; namely, in matters relating to the marriage union and to the family: for the wife is part of the husband's family. Thus to determine the place of domicile, is the husband's office. If any further rights are given to the husband, as by the Hebrew law, the right of disallowing the vows of the wife, and in some nations, the right of selling the wife's goods, this is not by Natural Law, but by institution.

The subject requires that we consider the nature of the marriage union.

2. Marriage, by Natural Law, we conceive to be such a cohabitation of the male and female, as places the female under the protection and custody of the male; for such a union we see in some cases in mute animals. But in man, as being a rational creature, to this is added a vow of fidelity by which the woman binds herself to the man.

IX. 1. Nor does nature appear to require any thing more for the existence of marriage. Nor does the divine law seem to have required more, before the propagation of the gospel. For holy men, before the law, had more than one wife; and in the law, precepts are given to those who have more than one . . . .

2. And in like manner a process is appointed for him who wishes to put away his wife; and no one is prohibited from marrying her who is put away, except him who put her away, and a priest. But this liberty of going to another husband is to be so restricted, even by Natural Law, that no con-

fusion of offspring shall arise. Hence the question of pontifical law in Tacitus; *whether after the conception and before the birth of the child a woman might lawfully marry.* By the Hebrew law three months must be interposed between the marriages.

But the law of Christ refers, as other things, so this, to a more perfect rule; and by this, pronounces him who had put away a wife, except an adulteress, and him who married one thus put away, as guilty of adultery; and Paul, his Apostle and Interpreter, not only gives the man a right over the body of the woman, which also was the Natural Law, but also gives the woman right over the body of the man. So Lactantius says that each party may be guilty of adultery. . . .

XVII. Besides marriage, the most natural of partnerships, there are others . . . All partnerships have this in common, that in those matters for which the partnership was instituted, the whole body, and the majority as representing the whole, bind the special members of the partnership. For it must be supposed to have been the intention of those who united to make the society, that there should be some way of promoting business; and it is manifestly unjust that the greater part should follow the less; wherefore by Natural Law, not taking into account pacts and laws which prescribe a form for conducting business, the majority has a right to act for the whole. . . .

XXII. It is to be added however, that when a partnership has its foundation in property which all do not equally share in; as if, in an inheritance or other estate, one person has a half, one a third, one a fourth; then, not only is the order of precedence to follow the order of shares, but also the weight of the votes must be proportional to the shares. And as this is the rule of natural equity, so is it also the rule of the Roman Law. . . .

XXIV. 1. It is often asked, whether citizens may quit the State without leave obtained. We know that there are peoples where this is not permitted, as the Muscovites; nor do we deny that civil society may

be formed on such a pact, and that usage may take the force of a pact. . . .

2. But the question for us is, What ought to be the rule by Natural Law, if no agreement has been made . . . And that the subjects may not depart in large bodies, is evident enough from the necessity of the end, which gives a right in moral matters; for if that were permitted, Civil Society could no longer subsist. With regard to the emigration of individuals, the case is different; as it is one thing to take water out of a river in a vessel, another thing to turn off a part of the river by a side cut. Some hold that each ought to be at liberty to choose his own city . . . But here the rule of natural equity is to be observed, which the Romans followed in winding up the affairs of private societies; that it should not be done, if the interests of the society forbade. . . .

XXVII. 1. The most ignoble species of subjection is that in which a person gives himself into perfect slavery. . . .

XXIX. 1. The question concerning those who are born slaves, is more difficult . . . Let us suppose . . . that both the parents are in slavery; and let us see whether the offspring would be of servile condition by Natural Law. Certainly if there were no other means of bringing up the offspring, the parents might give their future progeny along with themselves into slavery: since on such grounds, parents may even sell their children.

2. But since this Right by Natural Law flows from necessity only, it is not the right of the parents, in any other case, to give their children into slavery. And therefore the right of the owners over the progeny of slaves arises, in this case, from their supplying sustenance and the other necessaries of life. And thus, when the children born of slaves are to be supported for a long time, and the subsequent labour corresponds to the aliment afterwards supplied, it is not lawful for those thus born to escape slavery.

But if the cruelty of the owner be extreme, it is a probable opinion that even those who have given themselves into slavery may seek refuge in flight. . . .

CHAPTER X

Of the Obligation Arising from Ownership

I. . . . 2. From things extant, this obligation arises; that he who has a thing of mine in his power is bound to do so as much as he can that it may come into my power . . . For as in the state of community of things, a certain equality came to be observed, so that one might be able to use those common things not less than another; so when ownership is introduced there is a sort of association established among owners, that he who has in his power a thing belonging to another, is to restore it to the owner. For if ownership were only so far effective, that the thing is to be restored to the owner if he asks for it, ownership would be too feeble, and custody too expensive. . . .

II. 1. Concerning things not extant, this is the rule established by mankind (the *jus gentium*), that if you are made richer by something which is mine, and which I am deprived of, you are bound to make restitution to the extent of your gain. For by what you have gained from my property, you have so much the more, and I the less. But ownership was introduced to preserve equality, that is, each having his own. . . .

CHAPTER XI

Of Promises

I. 1. . . . Here we at once find opposed to us a man of no ordinary erudition, Francis Connanus. For he maintains this opinion, that, *jure naturae ac gentium,* those pacts which have not a consideration do not induce any obligation. . . .

2. He adduces for his opinion . . . these reasons: (1) That there is a fault no less in him who rashly trusts a person who makes a promise for no cause: (2) That there is a great danger thrown upon the fortunes of all, if men be judged to be bound by a promise, which often proceeds more from ostentation than from real purpose; or from

a purpose, but a light and inconsiderate one: (3) That it is right to leave something to each person's honesty, and not to bind men to the necessity of an obligation:—that it is disgraceful not to fulfil promises, not because such a course is unjust, but because thereby the levity of the promise is detected. . . .

3. But this opinion cannot stand, in the general form in which he propounds it. . . .

. . . When the will is sufficiently signified, the ownership of a thing may be transferred, as we have already said: why then may there not also be a transfer of a *jus in personam,* a right to the performance of a person's promise, or a right to transfer ownership, (which is a less thing than ownership itself), or a right to do anything; since we have the same right over our actions as over the things which belong to us? . . .

IV. 1. . . . A strong example of what we say is furnished by the Scriptures, which teach us that God himself, who cannot be compelled by any instituted law, would act contrary to his nature, except he performed his promises. Whence it follows, that the performance of promises proceeds from the nature of immutable justice, which is, in a certain way, common to God and to all rational creatures. . . .

CHAPTER XV

Of Treaties and Sponsions

III. 1. . . . We may take Livy's view, in which he says that *foedera* are treaties made by the sovereign power of the State, in which the people is liable to the Divine wrath if it do not make good its engagements. . . .

VIII. It is often made a question whether it is lawful to make treaties with those who are strangers to the true Religion; which point, in Natural Law, is open to no doubt. For that Law is so far common to all men that it recognizes no distinction of Religion. But the question is put on the ground of the Divine Law, and so treated, not only by Theologians but by Jurists. . . .

IX. 1. First of Divine Law. We have examples of covenants for mutual forbearance, with strangers to true Religion, before the law of Moses, as Jacob with Laban, not to speak of Abimelech. The law of Moses did not change this. . . .

X. 1. The Gospel changed nothing in this matter: it rather favours conventions with all men that we may do them good: as God makes his sun to rise on the just and on the unjust. . . .

3. Familiar intercourse is not forbidden with strangers to Religion, nor even those who have gone back from religion; but only unnecessary familiarity. . . .

XI. . . . 2. But if the strength of the profane is likely thus to be much increased, we must abstain from such alliances, except in case of necessity . . . For it is not mere right which justifies men in doing what may indirectly harm religion. We must seek first the kingdom of God, that is, the propagation of the Gospel. . . .

CHAPTER XVII

Of Damage Done Wrongfully and Consequent Obligation

I. . . . We come to what by Natural Law is due on account of Wrong. We have given the name of *wrong* to every fault, either of doing or of omission, which is at variance with what men ought to do, either on the ground of their common connexion, or of some special quality. From such fault arises by Natural Law an obligation, if the wrong be accompanied with damage: namely, the obligation of repairing the wrong. . . .

XXI. It is to be noted also that the Rule, that if a slave, or any animal, cause any damage or loss, it creates a liability in the master, is a creation of Civil Law. For the master, who is not in fault, is not liable by Natural Law; as also he is not whose ship, without any fault of his, damages another's ship: although by the laws of many nations, and by ours, the damage in such case is commonly divided, on account of the difficulty of proving where the fault lay. . . .

CHAPTER XVIII

Of the Right of Legation

I. HITHERTO we have spoken of things which are due to us by Natural Law, adding only a few points which belong to the instituted Law of Nations . . . It remains to speak of the obligations which that which we call the Instituted Law of Nations has of itself introduced: in which class, the principal head is the Right of Legation. For we everywhere read of the reverence for Embassies; the sacredness of Ambassadors; the Rights of Nations lodged in them by Divine and Human Law . . . To violate this is not only unjust, but impious, by the confession of all. . . .

III. 1. There are two points with regard to ambassadors which we everywhere find referred to the Law of Nations: that they be admitted, and that they be not violated. . . .

. . . The Law of Nations does not prescribe that all ambassadors are to be admitted; but that they are not to be excluded without cause. . . .

IV. 1. The question of the inviolability of ambassadors is more difficult, and variously treated by the able men of our time. . . .

With regard to the persons of ambassadors, some are of opinion that they are protected only from unjust violence: for that their privileges are to be interpreted by common Law. Others think that force may be put upon an ambassador, not for any cause, but only if he violate the Law of Nations; which is a very wide expression; for in the Law of Nations, Natural Law is included: and so, according to this, an ambassador might be punished for any offense, except those which arise from mere Civil Law. Others restrict this to what is done against the state or dignity of the commonwealth to which the ambassador is sent: and others think that even this is dangerous, and that complaints against the ambassador are to be transmitted to him who sent him, and that he is to be left to be judged by him. Some, again, think that kings and nations who are not interested in the question, should be consulted;

which may be a matter of prudence, but cannot be a matter of right.

2. The reasons which each of these parties adduce do not conclude anything definitely; because this Law of Nations is not like Natural Law, which flows in a sure way from certain reasons; but this takes its measure from the will of nations. For nations might either altogether refuse to entertain ambassadors, or with certain exceptions. For on the one side stands the utility of punishment against grave delinquents, [even if they be ambassadors,] and on the other, the utility of ambassadors, the sending of whom is facilitated by their having all possible security. We must consider, therefore, how far nations have agreed; and this cannot be proved by examples alone. For there are many each way. We must recur, therefore to the judgments of good authorities, and to conjectures, that is, probable arguments.

3. There are two judgments of great note, that of Livy, and that of Sallust. Livy's is about Tarquin's ambassadors, who stirred up a treasonable design at Rome: *Though they had behaved so that they might have been treated as enemies, the Law of Nations prevailed:* here we see that the Law of Nations is extended even to those who act as enemies. The dictum of Sallust pertains to the subordinate members of the legation . . . He says thus: *Bomilcar, his companion, who had come to Rome on the public faith, is put under accusation, rather on the ground of equity, than of the Law of Nations.* Equity, that is, mere Natural Law, allows penalties to be demanded when the delinquent can be got hold of; but the Law of Nations makes an exception in favour of ambassadors and those who come under the public faith. Hence to put ambassadors under accusation is contrary to the Law of Nations, which forbids many things which Natural Law permits.

4. Conjecture also is on this side . . . the security of the ambassadors may preponderate over the utility which involves a penalty. For punishment may be had through his means who sent the ambassador; and if he will not afford it, may be demanded

by war of him as the approver of the crime . . . .

. . . The safety of ambassadors is in a very insecure position, if they have to render account of their acts to other persons than him who sent them.

5. Wherefore I quite think thus: that the common rule, that he who is in a foreign territory is subject to that territory, does, by the common consent of nations, suffer an exception in the case of ambassadors . . . Hence, if there be any delict which can be treated lightly, either it is to be overlooked, or the ambassador ordered beyond the borders . . . If the crime be more atrocious, and tending to public mischief, the ambassador must be sent back to him who sent him, with a demand that he be punished or surrendered. . . .

6. But, as we have said above, that all human rights are so conditioned, that they do not bind in cases of extreme necessity, so is this true in this doctrine of the inviolability of ambassadors . . . in order to obviate imminent danger, if there be no other effectual course, ambassadors may both be detained and interrogated. . . .

7. If the ambassador use armed force, he may undoubtedly be killed, not in the way of punishment, but in the way of natural defense. . . .

CHAPTER XX

Of Punishments

I. 1. . . . Punishment . . . is *An Evil of suffering which is inflicted on account of an evil of doing.* For though labour [not pain] may be the sentence of persons as a punishment, yet such labour is considered as it is disagreeable, and therefore is a sort of suffering. . . .

2. Among the things which nature herself dictates as lawful and not unjust, this stands; that he who has done evil should suffer evil . . . .

III. 1. Of such punishment, the subject, that is, the person *to whom* it is due, is not determined by nature itself. Nature dictates that evildoing may be punished, but not who ought to punish: except that nature sufficiently indicates that it is most suitable that it be done by one who is superior: yet not in such way as to shew that this is necessary; except the word *superior* be taken in this sense, that he who has done wrong has, by that very fact, made himself inferior to any other, and has thrust himself out of the class of men into that of the inferior brutes, as some theologians hold . . . .

IV. 1. Another question is of the End of Punishment. For what has been said hitherto only proves that transgressors have no wrong done them if they are punished. But from that, it does not necessarily follow that they must be punished. Nor is it necessary; for many offenders are pardoned for many things both by God and by men, and these are often praised on that account. Plato's saying is celebrated (in his laws), which Seneca translates, *No wise man punishes because wrong has been done, but in order that wrong be not done* . . . .

V. 1. Therefore what has been said by various writers, that the pain of the offender is a remedy of the pain of the injured person, (Publius, Syrus, Plutarch, Cicero,) does indeed agree with the nature which man has in common with brutes; for anger is, in brutes as in man, a heat of the blood arising from the desire of revenge, which appetite is irrational; so that it is often directed against objects which have done them no harm, as against the offspring of the creature which did the harm, or against things which have no sense, as in a dog against the stone which hit him. But such an appetite, considered in itself, does not correspond to our rational part, of which the office is to control the passions; and consequently, not to Natural Law, because that is the dictate of our rational and social nature as such. But reason dictates to man that nothing is to be done by him so as to harm another man, except it have some good purpose. But in the pain of an enemy, so nakedly regarded, there is no good, but a false and imaginary one . . . .

VI. . . . 2. But this must be more minutely examined. We shall say then that in punishment is regarded either the utility of the offender, or of him who suffers by the offense, or of persons in general.

VII. 1. To the first of these ends, pertains punishment which is called reformatory: of which Paulus, Plutarch, and Plato speak; the object of which is to make a better man of the offender. For as repeated acts beget habits, vices are to be cured by taking away the pleasure which they bring, and putting pain for their sweetness . . . .

3. But this kind of punishment cannot extend as far as death, except in what they call a reductive way, in which negations are reduced to the opposite class . . . for incurable dispositions, it is better, that is less evil, to die than to live, since by living they are sure to become worse . . . .

VIII. 1. The utility of him whose interest it was that the fault should not have been committed, consists in this, that he do not in future suffer anything of the same kind from the same person or from others. Gellius, from Taurus, says of this case: *When the dignity or authority of him against whom the offense is committed is to be protected, lest punishment omitted produce contempt thereof, and diminish its honour;* but what is said of injury done to authority, is true of injury done to liberty, or to any other right* . . . .

That he who has been injured may not suffer evil from the same person, may be provided for in three ways: first, by the removal of the delinquent; secondly, by taking away his power of doing harm; thirdly, by teaching him, by suffering, not to offend; which is connected with the amendment of which we have spoken. That the person offended shall not be injured by another, is to be procured, not by any casual punishment, but by a punishment open and conspicuous, of the nature of example.

2. Up to these limits then, if vindicative punishment be directed, and be kept within the bounds of equity, even if inflicted by a private hand, it is not unlawful, if we look at the naked law of nature, that is, abstracting divine and human law, and conditions which are not necessary concomitants of the

thing itself; whether it be inflicted by him who is injured, or by another; since for man to help man is consentaneous to nature . . . .

IX. 1. The utility of persons in general, which was the third end of punishment, offers the same divisions as the utility of the injured man. . . .

2. The right of inflicting such punishment, is also, by Natural Law, in the hands of every man . . . .

4. But since the proof of the fact often requires great care, and the estimate of punishment requires great prudence and great equity, communities of men have chosen, for this office, those whom they thought to be, or hoped to find, the best and most prudent . . . .

X. 1. We must now consider whether the Gospel Law has limited this liberty more narrowly . . . It is not to be wondered at, that some things which are permitted by the Natural and the Civil Laws, are forbidden by the Divine Law; that being both the most perfect of Laws, and one which promises rewards beyond the discovery of mere human nature; and to obtain which, very reasonably, virtues are required which go beyond the mere precepts of nature. But punishments or castigations which neither leave behind them infamy nor permanent damage, and which are necessary, according to the age or other quality of the offender, if they are inflicted by those to whom human laws give such permission, as parents, tutors, masters, teachers, have nothing which is at variance with the evangelical precepts. These are remedies of the soul, as innocent as bitter medicines are. . . .

2. With regard to revenge, the case is different . . . The Hebrew Law permitted men to revenge the graver injuries, not by their own hand, but by recourse to the judge. Christ, however, does not permit the same to us. . . .

8. There remain punishments which provide, not for private but for public good; partly by coercion of the mischievous, partly by the effect of example. And that these are not taken away by Christ, we have elsewhere clearly proved, in that while he gave his pre-

cepts, he declared that he did not destroy the Law. The Law, as long as it continued, rigidly required the magistrates to punish homicide and some other crimes. And if the precepts of Christ could stand along with the law of Moses when it pronounced even capital punishments, they may also stand along with human laws, which in this respect imitate the Divine Law. . . .

XIV. From what has been said, it may be collected, how unsafe it is for a private Christian man to inflict punishment, and especially capital punishment, either for the sake of his own or of the public good, upon a guilty person; although, as we have said, that is sometimes permitted by the Law of Nations. And hence we must approve of the usage of those peoples by whom navigators are provided with commissions from the public power to suppress pirates, if they find any upon the seas; on which commissions they may act, not as of their own motion, but by public command. . . .

XVIII. Let us now consider whether all vicious acts are such that they may be punished by men. It is certain that they are not all such. For, in the first place, mere internal acts, even if they come to be known, for instance by confession, cannot be punished by men; because, as we have said, it is not congruous to human nature that mere internal acts should give rise to right or obligation . . . But that does not prevent that internal acts, so far as they influence external, may not be taken into account in estimating, not themselves properly, but the external acts which receive from them their character of desert. . . .

Book III

CHAPTER I

General Rules as to What is Lawful in War by Natural Law . . .

I . . . . Let us then see what is allowed by Natural Law.

II. 1 . . . if I cannot otherwise preserve my life, I may, by any force which I can use, repel him who assails it, even if he be without fault. . . .

2. Further, I may take possession of a thing belonging to another, from which a certain danger impends over me, without consideration of another's fault: not however so as to become the owner of it, (for that is not a step suitable to the end,) but to keep it till sufficient provision is made for my security . . . .

3. So also when punishment is just, all force is just without which punishment cannot be attained. . . .

III. It is to be noted in the second place, that these rights are not only to be regarded with reference to the origin of the war, but also with reference to causes *subnascent*, that is, growing up during the progress of the war . . . Thus those who join themselves to the party which attacks me, whether as allies or as subjects, give me a right of defending myself against them. . . .

V.1. But the question often arises, what is lawful against those who are not enemies . . . but who provide our enemies with supplies of various kinds. . . .

2. In the first place, we must make a distinction as to the things supplied. For there are some articles of supply which are useful in war only, as arms; others which are of no use in war, but are only luxuries; others which are useful both in war, and out of war, as money, provisions, ships and their furniture. In matters of the first kind . . . they are of the party of the enemy who supply him with what is necessary in war. The second class of objects is not a matter of complaint. . . .

3. In the third class, objects of ambiguous use, the state of war is to be considered. For if I cannot defend myself except by intercepting what is sent, necessity . . . gives us a right to intercept it, but under the obligation of restitution, except there be cause to the contrary. If the supplies sent impede the exaction of my rights, and if he who sends them may know this, as if I were besieging a town, or blockading a port, and if surrender or peace were expected; he will be bound to me for damages . . . But if, besides, the

injustice of my enemy to me be very evident, and he confirm him in a most unjust war, he will then be bound to me not only civilly, for the damage, but also criminally. . . .

4. On this account, belligerents commonly issue manifestos to other nations, to make known both the justice of the cause, and also the probable hope of exacting their rights . . . .

5. We have referred this question to Natural Law because we have not been able to find in history anything on the subject as determined by Instituted Law. . . .

CHAPTER IV

Of the Right of Killing Enemies in Formal War, and of Other Violence Against the Person

II. 1 . . . . Sometimes *that* is said to be lawful which is every way right and pious. . . .

2. In other cases a thing is said to be lawful, not which is agreeable to piety and duty, but which is not liable to punishment. . . .

3. And in this sense, what is lawful is often opposed to what is right. . . .

III. In this latter sense, it is lawful to harm an enemy, both in person and in property; and this, not only for him who is making a just war and who harms the enemy in the way which is allowed by Natural Law . . . but on both sides, and without distinction. . . .

IV. The reason of this rule among nations was this: that for other nations to offer to pronounce on the right of war between two peoples would be dangerous for those who interfered, and who might thus be involved in a war belonging to others. . . . And in the next place, it can scarcely be known by external indications, in a just war, what is the proper limit of self-defense, of recovery of property, or of exaction of punishment; so that it is by all means better to leave this to the conscience of the belligerents, than to appeal to extraneous decision. . . .

VIII. 1. As to those who are truly the subjects of the enemy . . . it is allowable to attack them wherever they are, by this right of nations. . . .

2. Therefore we may slay such persons on our own soil, on the hostile soil, on ground which is no one's, and on the sea. That it is not lawful to slay them, or do them violence, in a peaceful neutral territory, is a consequence, not of their personal rights, but of the rights of the lord of the territory. . . .

IX. 1 . . . the slaughter of infants and women is allowed to have impunity, as comprehended in that right of war . . . .

X. 1. Even captives were not exempted from this liability. No law spares or protects a captive. . . .

XII. Even those who have surrendered unconditionally and been received, you may find, in history, put to death. . . .

XV. 1. As the Laws of Nations permit many things, (in this way of permitting which we have explained), which are forbidden by Natural Law; so they forbid some things which are permitted by Natural Law. For him whom it is lawful to put to death, whether we put to death by the sword or by poison, it makes no difference, if we look to Natural Law . . . But the Laws of Nations, if not of all, at least of the best, have long been, that it is not lawful to kill an enemy by poison. This consent had its rise in common utility, that the dangers of war, which are numerous enough, may not be made too extensive. And it is probable that this rule proceeded from kings, whose life may be defended from other causes, better than the lives of other persons; but is less safe than that of others from poison, except it be defended by the scruples of conscience, and the fear of infamy. . . .

XVI. 1. Somewhat different from poisoning, is the use of poisoned arrows or missiles . . . This, however, is against the Law of Nations, not universal, but of European nations, and those which share in European culture. . . .

XVII. But the same is not true of making waters foul and undrinkable without poisoning them . . . For that is the same thing as turning away a stream, or intercepting a spring of water, which is lawful both by Natural Law and by consent.

XIX. 1. The violation of women in war you may perpetually find both allowed and disallowed. Those who allowed it, looked only at the injury done to the person, and judged that it was not incongruous to the laws of war that what belonged to the enemy should be subject to such injury. But others have judged better, who regarded, not only the injury, but the act of uncontrolled lust; and that the act has no tendency either to security or to punishment; and therefore ought to be no more unpunished in peace than in war: and this latter rule is the Law of Nations, not of all, but of the best. . . .

CHAPTER VII

Of the Right Over Prisoners of War

I. 1. By nature, that is, in the primeval state of nature, and without the act of man, no men are slaves . . . and in this sense we may assent to what the jurists say, that slavery is against nature. But that slavery should have its origin in human act, that is, in convention or delict, is not repugnant to natural justice. . . .

2. But by the laws of nations . . . slavery is more comprehensive, both as to persons, and effects. For, if we regard the persons, it is not those only who surrender themselves, or promise slavery, who are reckoned slaves; but all persons whatever who are taken in a regular war . . . .

II. And not only do they themselves become slaves, but their posterity for ever; that is, those who are born of a slave-mother in slavery. . . .

III. 1. The effects of this right are unlimited, so that the master may do any thing lawfully to the slave, as Seneca says. . . . Even cruelty in the masters, towards persons of servile condition, is unpunished; except so far as the Civil Law imposes limits and punishments for cruelty. . . .

V. 1. All these powers are introduced by the Laws of Nations, for no other cause than this; that the captors, induced by so many advantages, may willingly abstain from the extreme rigour by which they were allowed to put captives to death, either immediately or after any delay. . . .

2. For the same reason, this right is allowed to be transferred to others, like the ownership of things. And this right is extended so as to apply to the offspring, on this account; that otherwise, if the captors had used their extreme right, they would never have been born. From which it follows, that those born before the calamity, if they are not captured, do not become slaves. And therefore it was established that the children should follow the condition of the mother, because the cohabitation of slaves was not guarded, either by law or by sure custody, so that there could be no sufficient presumption to indicate the father. . . .

VIII. This also is to be noted; that this Law of Nations respecting captives, has neither been received always, nor among all nations. . . .

CHAPTER X

Warnings Concerning Things Done in an Unjust War

I. 1. I must now tread back my steps, and take from belligerents nearly all, which I have seemed to grant them; and yet have not really granted; for when I began to explain this part of the Law of Nations, I testified that many things were said to be *law,* or *lawful,* because they are done with impunity . . . while the things themselves either deviate from the rule of right . . . or at least, may more righteously and laudably be omitted. . . .

III. First, then, we say, that if the cause of war be unjust, though the war be regular in manner, all acts thence arising are unjust, according to internal injustice. And all who operate knowingly in such acts, or co-operate, are in the number of those who cannot enter into the kingdom of heaven without repentance for their acts. Now repentance, if time and opportunity be granted, requires restitution. . . .

VI. 1. But also, he who has not caused any damage, or has caused it without any fault, but who has in his possession a thing taken in war from another, is bound to restore it, because there is no cause, naturally just, why the other should be deprived of it; not his consent; not his ill desert; not compensation. . . .

CHAPTER XI

Restraints as to the Right of Killing in War

VII. 1. Even when justice does not require us to spare men's lives in war, it is often agreeable to goodness, to moderation, to magnanimity. . . .

4. An enemy, therefore, who considers, not what human laws permit, but what is his duty, what is righteous and pious, will spare hostile blood: and will never inflict death, except either to avoid death, or evils like death, or to punish crimes which are capital in desert. And even to some who have deserved that, he will remit all, or at least, capital punishment, either out of humanity, or for some other plausible causes. . . .

VIII. . . . If justice do not require, at least mercy does, that we should not, except for weighty causes tending to the safety of many undertake anything which may involve innocent persons in destruction. . . .

5

Thomas Hobbes

1588–1679

His Good Friday birthday was not especially appropriate for Thomas Hobbes; though he was a proper Episcopalian, he was the leading secularist of his times and was often called an atheist. It is said he was born prematurely because his mother panicked at rumors of impending attack of the Spanish Armada. His father, a hot-headed, illiterate vicar, brawled with a visiting clergyman at his church door, and decamped leaving his three small children (Thomas was the second) under the care of his brother—a prosperous glover.

Hobbes' school days were largely spent learning Latin and Greek until he went, at fifteen to a disorderly Oxford where he lived under a boring medieval scholastic regimen. He spent much time in Oxford book stores doing extra-curricular study of maps and charts.

After graduation from Oxford he was hired as a tutor in the powerful Cavendish family at Hardwicke. His pupil was almost as old as Hobbes and was married to a twelve-year-old bride, taken to satisfy a wish of King James. Hobbes—more a companion than a teacher—took his charge on the grand tour; they were abroad long enough for Hobbes to learn French and Italian.

On the continent, to his surprise, wherever he went Hobbes heard attacks on scholastic learning and came to think his Oxford training worthless. He wanted to be a scholar, but had no currently admired competence except skill in the classics. During the next two decades he studied Greek poetry and history (but paid no attention to the great Greek philosophers) and put himself to acquiring a good Latin style. His first publication came out when he was forty, an English translation of history written by Thucydides, preceded by an introduction in which Hobbes showed distaste for democracy and liking for a single ruler.

Young Cavendish became an important figure in England. Hobbes stayed on as his secretary and was thrown with such people as Ben Jonson and Francis Bacon. Though he had close associations with Bacon, he was little influenced by him. Cavendish became Earl of Devonshire when Hobbes was thirty-eight, but the Earl's tenure was short—he died two years later of the plague. Hobbes once said that his twenty years with the Earl were his happiest. The Earl's estate was lean and Hobbes was cast adrift for a while. Soon, however, he became the middle-aged tutor to the thirteen-year-old son of his former master. For seven years he taught the young Earl in rhetoric, logic, astronomy, and law. For the first time Aristotle is mentioned as an influence on Hobbes; he translated *The Rhetoric* for his pupil. With his new charge he made another grand European tour, during which Hobbes (now in his fifties) became engrossed in science and philosophy. He had not studied mathematics at college which was abjured at Oxford as a black art. The story goes that he accidentally opened a copy of Euclid's *Elements* at the forty-seventh proposition of the First Book. After reading it he said, "By God, this is impossible!" But when he considered the proofs, he was convinced and "fell in love with geometry." On this grand tour he sought out philosophers and scientists. He was in time to make a

107

pilgrimage to visit aged Galileo in his last days. A busy scientific circle in Paris led by Pere Mersenne gave him daily contacts with mathematics and physics. During this period his materialism took root; he was taken with the idea that motion in nature is the fundamental datum. He merged rigorous methods of proof in geometry and physics of motion into a basic philosophic system upon which he elaborated for the rest of his life.

Hobbes brought the young Earl back to an England seething with a struggle for power between Parliament and Charles I. The Long Parliament sent important supporters of Charles to the Tower. Hobbes, whose public utterances and writings had favored monarchy, became apprehensive. He exiled himself once again to the Continent.

In Paris he was welcomed back to Mersenne's scientific group. Mersenne submitted work of Descartes to Hobbes for criticism. Hobbes was more eager however to expound his own ideas than to evaluate Descartes'. He wrote superficially about Descartes' theories and at length about his own. Mersenne submitted this criticism anonymously; it infuriated Descartes. These two great thinkers were thus repelled from each other.

Soon the Civil War broke out in England. After the Royalist defeat at Marston Moor many of the King's friends fled to Paris. Hobbes was engaged to tutor the Prince of Wales (later to become Charles II). His slim finances were augmented by this appointment at a time when he was in great need.

Hobbes had published a political philosophy in Latin under the title, *De Cive*. Now he decided the time had come to do a more complete and popular version in English. The result was *Leviathan* (1651), his best known work, excerpts from which follow this biographical note. He wrote much of *Leviathan* in direct reference to the current English scene. Soon after its publication Hobbes was the most praised and most criticized political thinker of his time. He stirred the wrath of Royalists by urging submission to conquerors (Cromwell) in his Review and Conclusion. He vexed Anglican clergy by saying that the only true and lasting way

to peace was by subordinating the church to secular power. He made himself *persona non grata* in Catholic France by attacking the papal system. He was in real physical danger; others had been assassinated for less. He fled back to London with fear in his heart and sent his submission to Cromwell's Council of State; it was accepted.

He lived quietly and studiously in London until the Restoration. Two days after Charles II returned from Paris, he recognized Hobbes on the street. If Charles had ever resented passages of Leviathan that comforted Cromwellians, he did not show it. Of course the book strongly favored monarchy and could now be turned to Charles' support. Charles liked Hobbes' lively wit and made him a figure in his court. Charles enjoyed the discomfort to court clerics that Hobbes' presence caused. The king granted Hobbes a hundred-pound yearly pension—which was not always forthcoming when due.

Hobbes constantly broached and continued public disputes in his old age. He assumed that Oxford education was as bad as it was when he attended and quarrelled with several of the faculty. His longest and bitterest dispute was with a distinguished mathematician, John Wallis—a quarrel punctuated with clever invective for a quarter of a century. Hobbes never knew either that he came off very badly in these disputes or that Wallis was an extremely competent mathematician. At one time Wallis tried to break off, but Hobbes tricked him into continuing by anonymously publishing a mathematical demonstration in French in Paris, only to claim it after Wallis criticized it.

The Great Plague and the London Fire of 1666 widely inspired fear that God was outraged by English unbelief. The House of Commons passed a bill forbidding atheism and profanity. A Parliamentary committee was ordered to look into, among other things, *Leviathan,* and report their opinion back to the House. Seventy-eight-year-old Hobbes was terrified. He studied the law of heresy, and announced his works were not heretical and claimed that no English court had jurisdiction to try heretics. However, he was refused permission to publish further on human conduct, and the Latin edition of his collected works had to be published in Holland. Other late works on political philosophy went unpublished until after his death.

In his declining years Hobbes amused himself by writing a smug autobiography in Latin verse adorned with jokes. He also made interesting translations of the *Odyssey* and the *Iliad*. He spent his last days in the country, where he took walks every morning and wrote every afternoon until a final short illness kept him abed. Important visitors from all over the civilized world called on him often and paid him court.

Hobbes was a tall man, sickly and yellowish in his youth, but healthy and ruddy in his middle age. He was a black-headed youth, a bald old man. He was said to have a cheerful disposition. As he grew older he became both more sardonic and more smug. He enjoyed a nip up to the time he was sixty, after that he gave up wine. He is said to have had an illegitimate daughter, but none of his biographers report any associations with women. During the last third of his long life he contracted an increasing palsy, in spite of which he was still playing tennis at seventy.

Hobbes was a thorough student of all he read. He was fond of saying that if he had read as much as other learned men he would have been as ignorant.

LEVIATHAN *

CHAPTER XIII

Of the NATURALL CONDITION of Mankind, as Concerning Their Felicity, and Misery

Nature hath made men so equall, in the faculties of body, and mind; as that though there bee found one man sometimes mani-

* From A. R. Waller's edition, Cambridge University Press (1904).

festly stronger in body, or of quicker mind then another; yet when all is reckoned together, the difference between man, and man, is not so considerable, as that one man can thereupon claim to himselfe any benefit, to which another may not pretend, as well as he. For as to the strength of body, the weakest has strength enough to kill the strongest, either by secret machination, or by confederacy with others, that are in the same danger with himselfe.

And as to the faculties of the mind . . . I find yet a greater equality amongst men . . . That which may perhaps make such equality incredible, is but a vain conceipt of ones owne wisdome, which almost all men think they have in a greater degree, than the Vulgar; that is, than all men but themselves, and a few others, whom by Fame, or for concurring with themselves, they approve. . . But this proveth rather that men are in that point equall, than unequall. For there is not ordinarily a greater signe of the equall distribution of any thing, than that every man is contented with his share.

From this equality of ability, ariseth equality of hope in the attaining of our Ends. And therefore if any two men desire the same thing, which neverthelesse they cannot both enjoy, they become enemies. . . .

And from this diffidence of one another, there is no way for any man to secure himselfe, so reasonable, as Anticipation; that is, by force, or wiles, to master the persons of all men he can. . . . Also because there be some, that taking pleasure in contemplating their own power in the acts of conquest, which they pursue farther than their security requires; if others, that otherwise would be glad to be at ease within modest bounds, should not by invasion increase their power, they would not be able, long time, by standing only on their defence, to subsist. And by consequence, such augmentation of dominion over men, being necessary to a mans conservation, it ought to be allowed him.

Againe, men have no pleasure, (but on the contrary a great deale of griefe) in keeping company, where there is no power able to over-awe them all. For every man looketh that his companion should value him, at the same rate he sets upon himselfe. . . .

So that in the nature of man, we find three principall causes of quarrell. First Competition; Secondly, Diffidence; Thirdly, Glory.

The first, maketh men invade for Gain; the second, for Safety; and the third, for Reputation. . . .

Hereby it is manifest, that during the time men live without a common Power to keep them all in awe, they are in that condition which is called Warre; and such a warre, as is of every man, against every man. . . .

. . . In such condition, there is no place for Industry; because the fruit thereof is uncertain: and consequently no Culture of the Earth; no Navigation, nor use of the commodities that may be imported by Sea; no commodious Building; no Instruments of moving, and removing such things as require much force; no Knowledge of the face of the Earth; no account of Time; no Arts; no Letters; no Society; and which is worst of all, continuall feare, and danger of violent death; And the life of man, solitary, poore, nasty, brutish, and short. . . .

. . . The Desires, and other Passions of man, are in themselves no Sin. No more are the Actions, that proceed from those Passions, till they know a Law that forbids them: which till Lawes be made they cannot know: nor can any Law be made, till they have agreed upon the Person that shall make it.

It may peradventure be thought, there was never such a time, nor condition of warre as this; and I believe it was never generally so, over all the world: but there are many places, where they live so now. . . .

But though there had never been any time, wherein particular men were in a condition of warre one against another; yet in all times, Kings, and Persons of Soveraigne authority because of their Independency, are in continuall jealousies, and in the state and posture of Gladiators; having their weapons pointing, and their eyes fixed on one another; that is, their Forts, Garrisons, and Guns upon the Frontiers of their King domes; and continuall Spyes upon their neighbours; which is a posture of War. But because they uphold thereby, the Industry of their Subjects; there does not follow from it, that misery, which accompanies the Liberty of particular men.

To this warre of every man against every man, this also is consequent; that nothing can be Unjust. The notions of Right and Wrong, Justice and Injustice have there no place. Where there is no common Power, there is no Law: where no Law, no Injustice. Force, and Fraud, are in warre, the two Cardinall vertues. Justice, and Injustice are none of the Faculties neither of the Body, nor Mind . . . It is consequent also to the same condition, that there be no Propriety, no Dominion, no *Mine* and *Thine* distinct; but onely that to be every mans, that he can get; and for so long, as he can keep it. . . .

CHAPTER XIV

Of the First and Second *NATURALL LAWES, and of CONTRACTS*

The RIGHT OF NATURE, which Writers commonly call *Jus Naturale*, is the Liberty each man hath, to use his own power, as he will himselfe, for the preservation of his own Nature; that is to say, of his own Life; and consequently, of doing any thing, which in his own Judgment, and Reason, hee shall conceive to be the aptest means thereunto.

By LIBERTY, is understood, according to the proper signification of the word, the absence of externall Impediments: which Impediments, may oft take away part of a mans power to do what hee would; but cannot hinder him from using the power left him, according as his judgment, and reason shall dictate to him.

A LAW OF NATURE, *(Lex Naturalis,)* is a Precept, or generall Rule, found out by Reason, by which a man is forbidden to do, that, which is destructive of his life, or taketh away the means of preserving the same; and to omit, that, by which he thinketh it may be best preserved. For though they that speak of this subject, use to confound *Jus,* and *Lex, Right* and *Law;* yet they ought to be distinguished; because RIGHT, consisteth in liberty to do, or to forbeare; Whereas LAW, determineth, and bindeth to one of them: so that Law, and Right, differ as much, as Obligation, and Liberty; which in one and the same matter are inconsistent.

And because the condition of Man, (as hath been declared in the precedent Chapter) is a condition of Warre of every one against every one; in which case every one is governed by his own Reason; and there is nothing he can make use of, that may not be a help unto him, in preserving his life against his enemyes; It followeth, that in such a condition, every man has a Right to every thing; even to one anothers body. And therefore, as long as this naturall Right of every man to every thing endureth, there can be no security to any man, (how strong or wise soever he be,) of living out the time, which Nature ordinarily alloweth men to live. And consequently it is a precept, or generall rule of Reason, *That every man, ought to endeavour Peace, as farre as he has hope of obtaining it; and when he cannot obtain it, that he may seek, and use, all helps, and advantages of Warre.* The first branch of which Rule, containeth the first, and Fundamentall Law of Nature; which is, *to seek Peace, and follow it.* The Second, the summe of the Right of Nature; which is, *By all means we can, to defend our selves.*

From this Fundamentall Law of Nature, by which men are commanded to endeavour Peace, is derived this second Law; *That a man be willing, when others are so too, as farre-forth, as for Peace, and defence of himselfe he shall think it necessary, to lay down this right to all things; and be contented with so much liberty against other men, as he would allow other men against himselfe.* For as long as every man holdeth this Right, of doing any thing he liketh; so long are all men in the condition of Warre. But if other men will not lay down their Right, as well as he; then there is no Reason for any one,

to devest himselfe of his: For that were to expose himselfe to Prey, (which no man is bound to) rather than to dispose himselfe to Peace. This is that Law of the Gospell; *Whatsoever you require that others should do to you, that do ye to them. . . .*

To *lay downe* a mans *Right* to any thing, is to *devest* himselfe of the *Liberty,* of hindring another of the benefit of his own Right to the same. For he that renounceth, or passeth away his Right, giveth not to any other man a Right which he had not before; because there is nothing to which every man had not Right by Nature: but onely standeth out of his way, that he may enjoy his own originall Right, without hindrance from him; not without hindrance from another. So that the effect which redoundeth to one man, by another mans defect of Right, is but so much diminution of impediments to the use of his own Right originall.

Right is layd aside, either by simply Renouncing it; or by Transferring it to another. By *Simply RENOUNCING:* when he cares not to whom the benefit thereof redoundeth. By TRANSFERRING: when he intendeth the benefit thereof to some certain person, or persons. And when a man hath in either manner abandoned, or granted away his Right; then is he said to be OBLIGED, or BOUND, not to hinder those, to whom such Right is granted, or abandoned, from the benefit of it: and that he *Ought,* and it is his DUTY, not to make voyd that voluntary act of his own: and that such hindrance is INJUSTICE, and INJURY, as being *Sine Jure;* the Right being before renounced, or transferred. . . .

Whensoever a man Transferreth his Right, or Renounceth it; it is either in consideration of some Right reciprocally transferred to himselfe; or for some other good he hopeth for thereby. For it is a voluntary act: and of the voluntary acts of every man, the object is some *Good to himselfe.* And therefore there be some Rights, which no man can be understood by any words, or other signes, to have abandoned, or transferred. As first a man cannot lay down the right of resisting them, that assault him by force, to take away his life; because he cannot be understood to ayme thereby, at any Good to himselfe. The same may be sayd of Wounds, and Chayns, and Imprisonment; both because there is no benefit consequent to such patience; as there is to the patience of suffering another to be wounded, or imprisoned: as also because a man cannot tell, when he seeth men proceed against him by violence, whether they intend his death or not. And lastly the motive, and end for which this renouncing, and transferring of Right is introduced, is nothing else but the security of a mans person, in his life, and in the means of so preserving life, as not to be weary of it. And therefore if a man by words, or other signes, seem to despoyle himselfe of the End, for which those signes were intended; he is not to be understood as if he meant it, or that it was his will; but that he was ignorant of how such words and actions were to be interpreted.

The mutuall transferring of Right, is that which men call CONTRACT. . . .

. . . one of the Contractors, may deliver the Thing contracted for on his part, and leave the other to perform his part at some determinate time after, and in the mean time be trusted; and then the Contract on his part, is called PACT, or COVENANT: Or both parts may contract now, to performe heareafter: in which cases, he that is to performe in time to come, being trusted, his performance is called *Keeping of Promise,* or Faith; and the fayling of performance (if it be voluntary) *Violation of Faith.* . . .

If a Covenant be made, wherein neither of the parties performe presently, but trust one another; in the condition of meer Nature, (which is a condition of Warre of every man against every man,) upon any reasonable suspition, it is Voyd: But if there be a common Power set over them both, with right and force sufficient to compell performance; it is not Voyd. For he that performeth first, has no assurance the other will performe after; because the bonds of words are too weak to bridle mens ambition, avarice, anger, and other Passions, without

the feare of some coercive Power; which in the condition of meer Nature, where all men are equall, and judges of the justnesse of their own fears, cannot possibly be supposed. And therefore he which performeth first, does but betray himselfe to his enemy; contrary to the Right (he can never abandon) of defending his life, and means of living.

But in a civill estate, where there is a Power set up to constrain those that would otherwise violate their faith, that feare is no more reasonable; and for that cause, he which by the Covenant is to perform first, is obliged so to do. . . .

Covenants entred into by feare, in the condition of meer Nature, are obligatory. For example, if I Covenant to pay a ransome, or service for my life, to an enemy; I am bound by it. For it is a Contract, wherein one receiveth the benefit of life; the other is to receive mony, or service for it; and consequently, where no other Law (as in the condition, of meer Nature) forbiddeth the performance, the Covenant is valid. Therefore Prisoners of warre, if trusted with the payment of their Ransome, are obliged to pay it: And if a weaker Prince, make a disadvantageous peace with a stronger, for feare; he is bound to keep it; unlesse (as hath been sayd before) there ariseth some new, and just cause of feare, to renew the war. And even in Common-wealths, if I be forced to redeem my selfe from a Theefe by promising him mony, I am bound to pay it, till the Civill Law discharge me. For whatsoever I may lawfully do without Obligation, the same I may lawfully Covenant to do through feare: and what I lawfully Covenant, I cannot lawfully break.

A former Covenant, makes voyd a later. For a man that hath passed away his Right to one man to day, hath it not to passe tomorrow to another: and therefore the later promise passeth no Right, but is null.

A Covenant not to defend my selfe from force, by force, is always voyd. For (as I have shewed before) no man can transferre, or lay down his Right to save himselfe from Death, Wounds, and Imprisonment, (the avoyding whereof is the onely End of laying down any Right, and therefore the promise of not resisting force, in no Covenant transferreth any right; nor is obliging. For though a man may Covenant thus, *Unlesse I do so, or so, kill me;* he cannot Covenant thus, *Unlesse I do so, or so, I will not resist you, when you come to kill me.* For man by nature chooseth the lesser evill, which is danger of death in resisting; rather than the greater, which is certain and present death in not resisting. And this is granted to be true by all men, in that they lead Criminals to Execution, and Prison, with armed men, notwithstanding that such Criminals have consented to the Law, by which they are condemned.

A Covenant to accuse one selfe, without assurance of pardon, is likewise invalide. For in the condition of Nature, where every man is Judge, there is no place for Accusation: and in the Civill State, the Accusation is followed with Punishment; which being Force, a man is not obliged not to resist. The same is also true, of the Accusation of those, by whose Condemnation a man falls into misery; as of a Father, Wife, or Benefactor. For the Testimony of such an Accuser, if it be not willingly given, is praesumed to be corrupted by Nature; and therefore not to be received: and where a mans Testimony is not to be credited, he is not bound to give it. Also Accusations upon Torture, are not to be reputed as Testimonies. For Torture is to be used but as means of conjecture, and light, in the further examination, and search of truth: and what is in that case confessed, tendeth to the ease of him that is Tortured; not to the informing of the Torturers: and therefore ought not to have the credit of a sufficient Testimony: for whether he deliver himselfe by true, or false Accusation, he does it by the Right of preserving his own life.

The force of Words, being (as I have formerly noted) too weak to hold men to the performance of their Covenants; there are in mans nature, but two imaginable helps to strengthen it. And those are either a Feare of the consequence of breaking their word; or a Glory, or Pride in appearing not to need to breake it. This later is a Generosity too rarely found to be presumed on, especially in the pursuers of Wealth, Command, or sensuall Pleasure; which are the greatest part of Mankind. . . . Before the time of Civill Society, or in the interruption thereof by Warre, there is nothing can strengthen a Covenant of Peace agreed on, against the temptations of Avarice, Ambition, Lust, or other strong desire, but the feare of that Invisible Power, which they every one Worship as God; and Feare as a Revenger of their perfidy. All therefore that can be done between two men not subject to Civill Power, is to put one another to swear by the God he feareth: Which *Swearing,* or OATH, is a *Forme of Speech, added to a Promise; by which he that promiseth, signifieth, that unless he performe, he renounceth the mercy of his God, or calleth to him for vengeance on himselfe.* Such was the Heathen Forme, *Let* Jupiter *kill me else, as I kill this Beast.* So is our Forme, *I shall do thus, and thus, so help me God.* And this, with the Rites and Ceremonies, which every one useth in his own Religion, that the feare of breaking faith might be the greater. . . .

It appears also, that the Oath addes nothing to the Obligation. For a Covenant, if lawfull, binds in the sight of God, without the Oath, as much as with it: if unlawfull, bindeth not at all; though it be confirmed with an Oath.

CHAPTER XV

Of Other Lawes of Nature

From that law of Nature, by which we are obliged to transferre to another, such Rights, as being retained, hinder the peace of Mankind, there followeth a Third; which is this, *That men performe their Covenants made:* without which, Covenants are in vain, and but Empty words; and the Right of all men to all things remaining, wee are still in the condition of Warre.

And in this law of Nature, consisteth the Fountain and Originall of JUSTICE. For where no Covenant hath preceded, there hath no Right been transferred, and every man has right to everything; and consequently, no action can be Unjust. But when a Covenant is made, then to break it is *Unjust:* And the definition of INJUSTICE, is no other than *the not Performance of Covenant.* And whatsoever is not Unjust, is *Just.*

But because Covenants of mutuall trust, where there is a feare of not performance on either part, (as hath been said in the former Chapter,) are invalid; though the Originall of Justice be the making of Covenants; yet Injustice actually there can be none, till the cause of such feare be taken away; which while men are in the naturall condition of Warre, cannot be done. Therefore before the names of Just, and Unjust can have place, there must be some coercive Power, to compell men equally to the performance of their Covenants, by the terrour of some punishment, greater than the benefit they expect by the breach of their Covenant; and to make good that Propriety, which by mutuall Contract men acquire, in recompence of the universall Right they abandon: and such power there is none before the erection of a Common-wealth. And this is also to be gathered out of the ordinary definition of Justice in the Schooles: For they say, that *Justice is the constant Will of giving to every man his own.* And therefore where there is no *Own,* that is, no Propriety, there is no Injustice; and where there is no coercive Power erected, that is, where there is no Common-wealth, there is no Propriety; all men having Right to all things: Therefore where there is no Common-wealth, there nothing is Unjust. . . .

The Foole hath sayd in his heart, there is no such thing as Justice; and sometimes also with his tongue; seriously alleaging, that every mans conservation, and contentment, being committed to his own care, there could be no reason, why every man might not do what he thought conduced thereunto: and therefore also to make, or not make; keep, or not keep Covenants, was not against Reason, when it conduced to ones benefit . . . The Kingdome of God is gotten by violence: but

what if it could be gotten by unjust violence? were it against Reason so to get it, when it is impossible to receive hurt by it? and if it be not against Reason, it is not against Justice: or else Justice is not to be approved for good. From such reasoning as this, Successfull wickedness hath obtained the name of Vertue. . . .

. . . Either where one of the parties has performed already; or where there is a Power to make him performe; there is the question whether it be against reason, that is, against the benefit of the other to performe, or not. And I say it is not against reason. For the manifestation whereof, we are to consider; First, that when a man doth a thing, which notwithstanding any thing can be foreseen, and reckoned on, tendeth to his own destruction, howsoever some accident which he could not expect, arriving may turne it to his benefit; yet such events do not make it reasonably or wisely done. Secondly, that in a condition of Warre, wherein every man to every man, for want of a common Power to keep them all in awe, is an Enemy, there is no man can hope by his own strength, or wit, to defend himselfe from destruction, without the help of Confederates; where every one expects the same defence by the Confederation, that any one else does: and therefore he which declares he thinks it reason to deceive those that help him, can in reason expect no other means of safety, than what can be had from his own single Power. He therefore that breaketh his Covenant, and consequently declareth that he thinks he may with reason do so, cannot be received into any Society, that unite themselves for Peace and Defence, but by the errour of them that receive him; nor when he is received, be retayned in it, without seeing the danger of their errour; which errours a man cannot reasonably reckon upon as the means of his security: and therefore if he be left, or cast out of Society, he perisheth; and if he live in Society, it is by the errours of other men, which he could not foresee, nor reckon upon; and consequently against the reason of his preservation; and so, as all men that contribute not to his destruction, forbear him onely out of ignorance of what is good for themselves.

As for the Instance of gaining the secure and perpetuall felicity of Heaven, by any way; it is frivolous: there being but one way imaginable; and that is not breaking, but keeping of Covenant. . . .

There be some that proceed further; and will not have the Law of Nature, to be those Rules which conduce to the preservation of mans life on earth; but to the attaining of an eternall felicity after death; to which they think the breach of Covenant may conduce; and consequently be just and reasonable; (such are they that think it a work of merit to kill, or depose, or rebell against, the Soveraigne Power constituted over them by their own consent.) But because there is no naturall knowledge of mans estate after death; much lesse of the reward that is then to be given to breach of Faith; but onely a beliefe grounded upon other mens saying, that they know it supernaturally, or that they know those, that knew them, that knew others, that knew it supernaturally; Breach of Faith cannot be called a Precept of Reason, or Nature.

Others, that allow for a Law of Nature, the keeping of Faith, do neverthelesse make exception of certain persons; as Heretiques, and such as use not to performe their Covenant to others: And this also is against reason. For if any fault of a man, be sufficient to discharge our Covenant made; the same ought in reason to have been sufficient to have hindred the making of it.

The names of Just, and Injust, when they are attributed to Men, signifie one thing; and when they are attributed to Actions, another. When they are attributed to Men, they signifie Conformity, or Inconformity of Manners, to Reason. But when they are attributed to Actions, they signifie the Conformity, or Inconformity to Reason, not of Manners, or manner of life, but of particular Actions. A Just man therefore, is he that taketh all the care he can, that his Actions may be all Just: and an Unjust man, is he that neglecteth it. And such men are more

often in our Language stiled by the names of Righteous, and Unrighteous; then Just, and Unjust; though the meaning be the same. Therefore a Righteous man, does not lose that Title, by one, or a few unjust Actions, that proceed from sudden Passion, or mistake of Things, or Persons: nor does an Unrighteous man, lose his character, for such Actions, as he does, or forbeares to do, for feare: because his Will is not framed by the Justice, but by the apparent benefit of what he is to do. That which gives to humane Actions the relish of Justice, is a certain Noblenesse or Gallantnesse of courage, (rarely found,) by which a man scorns to be beholding for the contentment of his life, to fraud, or breach of promise. This Justice of the Manners, is that which is meant, where Justice is called a Vertue; and Injustice a Vice.

But the Justice of Actions denominates men, not Just, but Guiltlesse: and the Injustice of the same, (which is also called Injury,) gives them but the name of *Guilty.*

Again, the Injustice of Manners, is the disposition, or aptitude to do Injurie; and is Injustice before it proceed to Act; and without supposing any individuall person injured. But the Injustice of an Action, (that is to say Injury,) supposeth an individual person Injured; namely him, to whom the Covenant was made: And therefore many times the injury is received by one man, when the dammage redoundeth to another. As when the Master commandeth his servant to give mony to a stranger; if it be not done, the Injury is done to the Master, whom he had before Covenanted to obey; but the dammage redoundeth to the stranger, to whom he had no Obligation; and therefore could not Injure him. And so also in Common-wealths, private men may remit to one another their debts; but not robberies or other violences, whereby they are endammaged; because the detaining of Debt, is an Injury to themselves; but Robbery and Violence, are Injuries to the Person of the Common-wealth. . . .

Justice of Actions, is by Writers divided into *Commutative,* and *Distributive:* and the former they say consisteth in proportion Arithmeticall; the later in proportion Geometricall. Commutative therefore, they place in the equality of value of the things contracted for; And Distributive, in the distribution of equall benefit, to men of equall merit. As if it were Injustice to sell dearer than we buy; or to give more to a man than he merits. The value of all things contracted for, is measured by the Appetite of the Contractors: and therefore the just value, is that which they be contented to give. And Merit (besides that which is by Covenant, where the performance on one part, meriteth the performance of the other part, and falls, under Justice Commutative, not Distributive,) is not due by Justice; but is rewarded of Grace onely. And therefore this distinction, in the sense wherein it useth to be expounded, is not right. To speak properly, Commutative Justice, is the Justice of a Contractor; that is, a Performance of Covenant, in Buying, and Selling; Hiring, and Letting to Hire; Lending, and Borrowing; Exchanging, Bartering, and other acts of Contract.

And Distributive Justice, the Justice of an Arbitrator; that is to say, the act of defining what is Just. Wherein, (being trusted by them that make him Arbitrator,) if he performe his Trust, he is said to distribute to every man his own: and this is indeed Just Distribution, and may be called (though improperly) Distributive Justice; but more properly Equity; which also is a Law of Nature, as shall be shewn in due place.

As Justice dependeth on Antecedent Covenant; so does GRATITUDE depend on Antecedent Grace; that is to say Antecedent Free-gift: and is the fourth Law of Nature; which may be conceived in this Forme, *That a man which receiveth Benefit from another of meer Grace, Endeavour that he which giveth it, have no reasonable cause to repent him of his good will.* For no man giveth, but with intention of Good to himselfe; because Gift is Voluntary; and of all Voluntary Acts, the Object is to every man his own Good; of which if men see they shall be frustrated, there will be no beginning of

benevolence, or trust; nor consequently of mutuall help; nor of reconciliation of one man to another; and therefore they are to remain still in the condition of *War;* which is contrary to the first and Fundamentall Law of Nature, which commandeth men to *Seek Peace.* The breach of this Law, is called *Ingratitude. . . .*

A fifth Law of Nature, is COMPLEASANCE; that is to say, *That every man strive to accommodate himselfe to the rest.* For the understanding whereof, we may consider, that there is in mens aptnesse to Society, a diversity of Nature, rising from their diversity of Affections; not unlike to that we see in stones brought together for building of an Ædifice. For as that stone which by the asperity, and irregularity of Figure, takes more room from others, than it selfe fills; and for the hardnesse, cannot be easily made plain, and thereby hindereth the building, is by the builders cast away as unprofitable, and troublesome: so also, a man that by asperity of Nature, will strive to retain those things which to himselfe are superfluous, and to others necessary; and for the stubbornness of his Passions, cannot be corrected, is to be left, or cast out of Society, as combersome thereunto . . . The observers of this Law, may be called SOCIABLE, (the Latines call them *Commodi;*) The contrary, *Stubborn, Insociable, Forward, Intractable.*

A sixth Law of Nature, is this, *That upon caution of the Future time, a man ought to pardon the offences past of them that repenting, desire it.* For PARDON, is nothing but granting of Peace; which though granted to them that persevere in their hostility, be not Peace, but Feare; yet not granted to them that give caution of the Future time, is signe of an aversion to Peace; and therefore contrary to the Law of Nature.

A seventh is, *That in Revenges,* (that is, retribution of Evil for Evil,) *Men look not at the greatnesse of the evill past, but the greatnesse of the good to follow.* Whereby we are forbidden to inflict punishment with any other designe, than for correction of the offender, or direction of others . . . Revenge without respect to the Example, and profit to come, is a triumph, or glorying in the hurt of another, tending to no end; (for the End is alwayes somewhat to Come;) and glorying to no end, is vain-glory, and contrary to reason; and to hurt without reason, tendeth to the introduction of Warre; which is against the Law of Nature; and is commonly stiled by the name of *Cruelty.*

And because all signes of hatred, or contempt, provoke to fight; insomuch as most men choose rather to hazard their life, than not to be revenged; we may in the eighth place, for a Law of Nature, set down this Precept, *That no man by deed, word, countenance, or gesture, declare Hatred, or Contempt of another.* The breach of which Law, is commonly called *Contumely.*

The question who is the better man, has no place in the condition of meer Nature; where, (as has been shewn before,) all men are equall. The inequallity that now is, has bin introduced by the Lawes civill. I know that *Aristotle* in the first booke of his Politiques, for a foundation of his doctrine, maketh men by Nature, some more worthy to Command, meaning the wiser sort (such as he thought himselfe to be for his Philosophy;) others to Serve, (meaning those that had strong bodies, but were not Philosophers as he;) as if Master and Servant were not introduced by consent of men, but by difference of Wit: which is not only against reason; but also against experience. For there are very few so foolish, that had not rather governe themselves, than be governed by others: Nor when the wise in their own conceit, contend by force, with them who distrust their owne wisdome, do they alwaies, or often, or almost at any time, get the Victory. If Nature therefore have made men equall, that equalitie is to be acknowledged: or if Nature have made men unequall, yet because men that think themselves equall, will not enter into conditions of Peace, but upon Equall termes, such equalitie must be admitted. And therefore for the ninth law of Nature, I put this, *That every man acknowledge other for his Equall by Nature.* The breach of this Precept is *Pride.*

On this law, dependeth another, *That at the entrance into conditions of Peace, no man require to reserve to himselfe any Right, which he is not content should be reserved to every one of the rest.* As it is necessary for all men that seek peace, to lay down certaine Rights of Nature; that is to say, not to have libertie to do all they list: so is it necessarie for mans life, to retaine some; as right to governe their owne bodies; enjoy aire, water, motion, waies to go from place to place; and all things else without which a man cannot live, or not live well. If in this case, at the making of Peace, men require for themselves that which they would not have to be granted to others, they do contrary to the precedent law, that commandeth the acknowledgment of naturall equalitie, and therefore also against the law of Nature. The observers of this law, are those we call *Modest,* and the breakers *Arrogant* men . . . .

Also if *a man be trusted to judge between man and man,* it is a precept of the Law of Nature, *that he deale Equally between them.* For without that, the Controversies of men cannot be determined but by Warre. He therefore that is partiall in judgment, doth what in him lies, to deterre men from the use of Judges, and Arbitrators; and consequently, (against the fundamentall Lawe of Nature) is the cause of Warre.

The observance of this law, from the equall distribution to each man, of that which in reason belongeth to him, is called EQUITY, and (as I have sayd before) distributive Justice: the violation, *Acception of persons.* . . .

And from this followeth another law, *That such things as cannot be divided, be enjoyed in Common, if it can be; and if the quantity of the thing permit, without Stint; otherwise Proportionably to the number of them that have Right.* For otherwise the distribution is Unequall, and contrary to Equitie.

But some things there be, that can neither be divided, nor enjoyed in common. Then, The Law of Nature, which prescribeth Equity, requireth, *That the Entire Right;*

or else, (making the use alternate,) the First Possession, be determined by Lot. For equall distribution, is of the Law of Nature; and other means of equall distribution cannot be imagined.

Of *Lots* there be two sorts, *Arbitrary,* and *Naturall.* Arbitrary, is that which is agreed on by the Competitors: Naturall, is either *Primogeniture . . .* or *First Seisure.*

And therefore those things which cannot be enjoyed in common, nor divided, ought to be adjudged to the First Possessor; and in some cases to the First-Borne, as acquired by Lot.

It is also a Law of Nature, *That all men that mediate Peace, be allowed safe Conduct.* For the Law that commandeth Peace, as the *End,* commandeth Intercession, as the *Means;* and to Intercession the Means is safe Conduct.

And because, though men be never so willing to observe these Lawes, there may neverthelesse arise questions concerning a mans action; First, whether it were done, or not done; Secondly (if done) whether against the Law, or not against the Law; the former whereof, is called a question *Of Fact;* the later a question *Of Right;* therefore unlesse the parties to the question, Covenant mutually to stand to the sentence of another, they are as farre from Peace as ever. This other, to whose Sentence they submit, is called an ARBITRATOR. And therefore it is of the Law of Nature, *That they that are at controversie, submit their Right to the judgment of an Arbitrator.*

And seeing every man is presumed to do all things in order to his own benefit, no man is a fit Arbitrator in his own cause: and if he were never so fit; yet Equity allowing to each party equall benefit, if one be admitted to be Judge, the other is to be admitted also; & so the controversie, that is, the cause of War, remains, against the Law of Nature.

For the same reason no man in any Cause ought to be received for Arbitrator, to whom greater profit, or honour, or pleasure apparently ariseth out of the victory of one party, than of the other: for hee hath

taken (though an unavoydable bribe, yet) a bribe; and no man can be obliged to trust him. And thus also the controversie, and the condition of War remaineth, contrary to the Law of Nature.

And in a controversie of *Fact,* the Judge being to give no more credit to one, than to the other, (if there be no other Arguments) must give credit to a third; or to a third and fourth; or more: For else the question is undecided, and left to force, contrary to the Law of Nature.

These are the Lawes of Nature, dictating Peace, for a means of the conservation of men in multitudes; and which onely concern the doctrine of Civill Society. There be other things tending to the destruction of particular men; as Drunkenness, and all other parts of Intemperance; which may, therefore also be reckoned amongst those things which the Law of Nature hath forbidden; but are not necessary to be mentioned, nor are pertinent enough to this place.

And though this may seem too subtile a deduction of the Lawes of Nature, to be taken notice of by all men; whereof the most part are too busie in getting food, and the rest too negligent to understand; yet to leave all men unexcusable, they have been contracted into one easie sum, intelligible, even to the meanest capacity; and that is, *Do not that to another, which thou wouldest not have done to thy selfe. . . .*

The [same] Lawes, because they oblige onely to a desire, and endeavour, I mean an unfeigned and constant endeavour, are easie to be observed. For in that they require nothing but endeavour; he that endeavoureth their performance, fulfilleth them; and he that fulfilleth the Law, is Just.

And the Science of them, is the true and onely Moral Philosophy. For Morall Philosophy is nothing else but the Science of what is *Good,* and *Evill,* in the conversation, and Society of mankind. *Good,* and *Evill,* are names that signifie our Appetites, and Aversions; which in different tempers, customes, and doctrines of men, are different: And divers men, differ not onely in their Judgement, on the senses of what is pleasant, and unpleasant to the tast, smell, hearing, touch, and sight; but also of what is conformable or disagreeable to Reason, in the actions of common life. Nay, the same man, in divers times, differs from himselfe; and one time praiseth, that is, calleth Good, what another time he dispraiseth, and calleth Evil: From whence arise Disputes, Controversies, and at last War. And therefore so long a man is in the condition of meer Nature, (which is a condition of War,) as private Appetite is the measure of Good, and Evill: And consequently all men agree on this, that Peace is Good, and therefore also the way, or means of Peace, which (as I have shewed before) are *Justice, Gratitude, Modesty, Equity, Mercy,* & the rest of the Laws of Nature, are good; that is to say, *Morall Vertues;* and their contrarie *Vices,* Evill. . . .

These dictates of Reason, men use to call by the name of Lawes; but improperly: for they are but Conclusions, or Theoremes concerning what conduceth to the conservation and defence of themselves; whereas Law, properly is the word of him, that by right hath command over others. But yet if we consider the same Theoremes, as delivered in the word of God, that by right commandeth all things; then are they properly called Lawes.

OF

COMMON-WEALTH

CHAPTER XVII

Of the Causes, Generation, and Definition of a COMMON-WEALTH

The finall Cause, End, or Designe of men, (who naturally love Liberty, and Dominion over others,) in the introduction of that restraint upon themselves, (in which wee see them live in Common-wealths,) is the foresight of their own preservation, and of a more contented life thereby; that is to say, of getting themselves out from that miserable condition of Warre . . . and tye them by feare

of punishment to the performance of their Covenants, and observation of those Lawes of Nature set down in the fourteenth and fifteenth Chapters.

For the Lawes of Nature (as *Justice, Equity, Modesty, Mercy,* and (in summe) *doing to others, as wee would be done to,)* of themselves, without the terrour of some Power, to cause them to be observed, are contrary to our naturall Passions, that carry us to Partiality, Pride, Revenge, and the like. And Covenants, without the Sword, are but Words, and of no strength to secure a man at all. Therefore notwithstanding the Lawes of Nature, (which every one hath then kept, when he has the will to keep them, when he can do it safely,) if there be no Power erected, or not great enough for our security; every man will, and may lawfully rely on his own strength and art, for caution against all other men. . . .

And be there never so great a Multitude; yet if their actions be directed according to their particular judgements, and particular appetites, they can expect thereby no defence, nor protection, neither against a Common enemy, nor against the injuries of one another. For being distracted in opinions concerning the best use and application of their strength, they do not help, but hinder one another; and reduce their strength by mutuall opposition to nothing: whereby they are easily, not onely subdued by a very few that agree together; but also when there is no common enemy, they make warre upon each other, for their particular interests. For if we could suppose a great Multitude of men to consent in the observation of Justice, and other Lawes of Nature, without a common Power to keep them all in awe; we might as well suppose all Man-kind to do the same; and then there neither would be, nor need to be any Civill Government, or Common-wealth at all; because there would be Peace without subjection. . . .

The only way to erect such a Common Power, as may be able to defend them from the invasion of Forraigners, and the injuries of one another, and thereby to secure them in such sort, as that by their owne industrie, and by the fruites of the Earth, they may nourish themselves and live contentedly; is, to conferre all their power and strength upon one Man, or upon one Assembly of men, that may reduce all their Wills by plurality of voices, unto one Will. . . . This is more than Consent, or Concord; it is a reall Unitie of them all, in one and the same Person, made by Covenant of every man with every man, in such manner, as if every man should say to every man, *I Authorise and give up my Right of Governing my selfe, to this Man, or to this Assembly of men, on this condition, that thou give up thy Right to him, and Authorise all his Actions in like manner.* This done, the Multitude so united in one Person, is called a COMMON-WEALTH, in latine CIVITAS. This is the Generation of that great LEVIATHAN, or rather (to speake more reverently) of that *Mortall God,* to which wee owe under the *Immortall God,* our peace and defence . . . the Essence of the Common-wealth; which (to define it,) is *One Person, of whose Acts a great Multitude, by mutuall Covenants one with another, have made themselves every one the Author, to the end he may use the strength and means of them all, as he shall think expedient, for their Peace and Common Defence.*

And he that carryeth this Person, is called SOVERAIGNE, and said to have *Soveraigne Power;* and every one besides, his SUBJECT.

The attaining to this Soveraigne Power, is by two wayes. One, by Naturall force; as when a man maketh his children, to submit themselves, and their children to his government, as being able to destroy them if they refuse; or by Warre subdueth his enemies to his will, giving them their lives on that condition. The other, is when men agree amongst themselves, to submit to some Man, or Assembly of men, voluntarily, on confidence to be protected by him against all others. This later, may be called a Politicall Common-wealth, or Common-wealth by *Institution;* and the former, a Common-wealth by *Acquisition.* . . .

CHAPTER XVIII

Of the RIGHTS of Soveraignes by Institution

A *Common-wealth* is said to be *Instituted,* when a *Multitude* of men do Agree, and *Covenant, every one, with every one,* that to whatsoever *Man,* or *Assembly of Men,* shall be given by the major part, the *Right* to *Present* the Person of them all, (that is to say, to be their *Representative;*) every one, as well he that *Voted for it,* as he that *Voted against it,* shall *Authorise* all the Actions and Judgements, of that Man, or Assembly of men, in the same manner, as if they were his own, to the end, to live peaceably amongst themselves, and be protected against other men. . . .

. . . they that have already Instituted a Common-wealth, being thereby bound by Covenant, to own the Actions, and Judgements of one, cannot lawfully make a new Covenant, amongst themselves, to be obedient to any other, in any thing whatsoever, without his permission. And therefore, they that are subjects to a Monarch, cannot without his leave cast off Monarchy . . . they have also every man given the Soveraignty to him that beareth their Person; and therefore if they depose him, they take from him that which is his own, and so again it is injustice. Besides, if he that attempteth to depose his Soveraign, be killed, or punished by him for such attempt, he is author of his own punishment, as being by the Institution, Author of all his Soveraign shall do: And because it is injustice for a man to do any thing, for which he may be punished by his own authority, he is also upon that title, unjust. And whereas some men have pretended for their disobedience to their Soveraign, a new Covenant, made, not with men, but with God; this also is unjust: for there is no Covenant with God, but by mediation of some body that representeth Gods Person; which none doth but Gods Lieutenant, who hath the Soveraignty under God. But this pretence of Covenant with God, is so evident a lye, even in the pretenders own consciences, that it is not onely an act of an unjust, but also of a vile, and unmanly disposition. . . .

. . . there can happen no breach of Covenent on the part of the Soveraigne; and consequently none of his Subjects, by any pretence of forfeiture, can be freed from his Subjection. That he which is made Soveraigne maketh no Covenant with his Subjects before-hand, is manifest; because either he must make it with the whole multitude, as one party to the Covenant; or he must make a severall Covenant with every man. With the whole, as one party, it is impossible; because as yet they are not one Person: and if he make so many severall Covenants as there be men, those Covenants after he hath the Soveraignty are voyd, because what act soever can be pretended by any one of them for breach thereof, is the act both of himselfe, and of all the rest, because done in the Person, and by the Right of every one of them in particular. Besides, if any one, or more of them, pretend a breach of the Covenant made by the Soveraigne at his Institution; and others, or one other of his Subjects, or himselfe alone, pretend there was no such breach, there is in this case, no Judge to decide the controversie: it returns therefore to the Sword again; and every man recovereth the right of Protecting himselfe by his own strength, contrary to the designe they had in the Institution. It is therefore in vain to grant Soveraignty by way of precedent Covenant. . . .

Thirdly, because the major part hath by consenting voices declared a Soveraigne; he that dissented must now consent with the rest; that is, be contented to avow all the actions he shall do, or else justly be destroyed by the rest. For if he voluntarily entered into the Congregation of them that were assembled, he sufficiently declared thereby his will (and therefore tacitely covenanted) to stand to what the major part should ordayne . . . And whether he be of the Congregation, or not; and whether his consent be asked, or not, he must either submit to their decrees, or be left in the condition of warre he was in

before; wherein he might without injustice be destroyed by any man whatsoever.

Fourthly, because every Subject is by this Institution Author of all the Actions, and Judgments of the Soveraigne Instituted; it followes, that whatsoever he doth, it can be no injury to any of his Subjects; nor ought he to be by any of them accused of Injustice. For he that doth any thing by authority from another, doth therein no injury to him by whose authority he acteth . . . It is true that they that have Soveraigne power, may commit Iniquity; but not Injustice, or Injury in the proper signification. . . .

. . . it is annexed to the Soveraignty, to be Judge of what Opinions and Doctrines are averse, and what conducing to Peace; and consequently, on what occasions, how farre, and what, men are to be trusted withall, in speaking to Multitudes of people; and who shall examine the Doctrines of all bookes before they be published . . . Though in matter of Doctrine, nothing ought to be regarded but the Truth; yet this is not repugnant to regulating of the same by Peace. For Doctrine repugnant to Peace, can no more be True, than Peace and Concord can be against the Law of Nature. It is true, that in a Common-wealth, where by the negligence, or unskilfullnesse of Governours, and Teachers, false Doctrines are by time generally received; the contrary Truths may be generally offensive: Yet the most sudden, and rough busling in of a new Truth, that can be, does never breake the Peace, but only somtimes awake the Warre. For those men that are so remissely governed, that they dare take up Armes, to defend, or introduce an Opinion, are still in Warre; and their condition not Peace, but only a Cessation of Armes for feare of one another; and they live as it were, in the procincts of battaile continually. It belongeth therefore to him that hath the Soveraign Power, to be Judge, or constitute all Judges of Opinions and Doctrines, as a thing necessary to Peace; therby to prevent Discord and Civill Warre.

Seventhly, is annexed to the Soveraigntie, the whole power of prescribing the Rules, whereby every man may know, what Goods he may enjoy, and what Actions he may doe, without being molested by any of his fellow Subjects: And this is it men call *Propriety*. For before constitution of Soveraign Power (as hath already been shewn) all men had right to all things; which necessarily causeth Warre: and therefore this Proprietie, being necessary to Peace, and depending on Soveraign Power, is the Act of that Power, in order to the publique peace. These Rules of Propriety (or *Meum* and *Tuum*) and of *Good, Evill, Lawfull,* and *Unlawfull* in the actions of Subjects, are the Civill Lawes. . . .

Eightly, is annexed to the Soveraigntie, the Right of Judicature; that is to say, of hearing and deciding all Controversies, which may arise concerning Law, either Civill, or Naturall, or concerning Fact. For without the decision of Controversies, there is no protection of one Subject, against the injuries of another. . . .

. . . to the Soveraign is committed the Power of Rewarding with riches, or honour; and of Punishing with corporall, or pecuniary punishment, or with ignominy every Subject according to the Law he hath formerly made; or if there be no Law made, according as he shall judge most to conduce to the encouraging of men to serve the Common-wealth, or deterring of them from doing dis-service to the same. . . .

These are the Rights, which make the Essence of Soveraignty; and which are the markes, whereby a man may discern in what Man, or Assembly of men, the Soveraign Power is placed, and resideth . . . if he transferre the *Militia*, he retains the Judicature in vain, for want of execution of the Lawes: Or if he grant away the Power of raising Mony; the *Militia* is in vain . . . And so if we consider any one of the said Rights, we shall presently see, that the holding of all the rest, will produce no effect, in the conservation of Peace and Justice, the end for which all Common-wealths are Instituted. And this division is it, whereof it is said, *a Kingdome divided in it selfe cannot stand:* For unlesse this division precede, division into opposite Armies can never happen. If

there had not first been an opinion received of the greatest part of *England,* that these Powers were divided between the King, and the Lords, and the House of Commons, the people had never been divided, and fallen into this Civill Warre; first between those that disagreed in Politiques; and after between the Dissenters about the liberty of Religion; which have so instructed men in this point of Soveraign Right, that there be few now (in *England,*) that do not see, that these Rights are inseparable, and will be so generally acknowledged, at the next return of Peace. . . .

CHAPTER XXI

Of the LIBERTY of Subjects

. . . A FREE-MAN, *is he that in those things, which by his strength and wit he is able to do, is not hindred to doe what he has a will to* . . .

Feare, and Liberty are consistent; as when a man throweth his goods into the Sea for *feare* the ship should sink, he doth it neverthelesse very willingly, and may refuse to doe it if he will: It is therefore the action, of one that was *free:* so a man sometimes pays his debt, only for *feare* of Imprisonment, which because no body hindred him from detaining, was the action of a man at *liberty*. And generally all actions which men doe in Common-wealths, for *feare* of the law, are actions, which the doers had *liberty* to omit.

Liberty, and *Necessity* are Consistent . . . the Actions which men voluntarily doe; which, because they proceed from their will, proceed from *liberty;* and yet, because every act of mans will, and every desire, and inclination proceedeth from some cause, and that from another cause, in a continuall chaine, (whose first link in the hand of God the first of all causes,) proceed from *necessity.* So that to him that could see the connexion of those causes, the *necessity* of all mens voluntary actions, would appeare manifest. . . .

But as men, for the atteyning of peace, and conservation of themselves thereby, have made an Artificiall Man, which we call a Common-wealth; so also have they made Artificiall Chains, called *Civill Lawes,* which they themselves, by mutuall covenants, have fastned at one end, to the lips of that Man, or Assembly, to whom they have given the Soveraigne Power; and at the other end to their own Ears. These Bonds in their own nature but weak, may nevertheless be made to hold, by the danger, though not by the difficulty of breaking them. . . .

. . . The Liberty of a Subject, lyeth therefore only in those things, which in regulating their actions, the Soveraign hath praetermitted: such as is the Liberty to buy, and sell, and otherwise contract with one another; to choose their own aboad, their own diet, their own trade of life, and institute their children as they themselves think fit; & the like.

Neverthelesse we are not to understand, that by such Liberty, the Soveraign Power of life, and death, is either abolished, or limited. For it has been already shewn, that nothing the Soveraign Representative can doe to a Subject, on what pretence soever, can properly be called Injustice, or Injury; because every Subject is Author of every act the Soveraign doth; so that he never wanteth Right to any thing, otherwise, than as he himself is the Subject of God, and bound thereby to observe the laws of Nature. And therefore it may, and doth often happen in Common-wealths, that a Subject may be put to death, by the command of the Soveraign Power; and yet neither doe the other wrong. . . . For though the action be against the law of Nature, as being contrary to Equitie, (as was the killing of *Uriah,* by *David;)* yet it was not an Injurie to *Uriah;* but to *God.* Not to *Uriah,* because the right to doe what he pleased, was given him by *Uriah* himself: And yet to *God,* because *David* was *Gods* Subject; and prohibited all Iniquitie by the law of Nature. . . .

The Libertie whereof there is so frequent, and honourable mention, in the Histories, and Philosophy of the Antient Greeks, and Romans, and in the writings, and discourse of those that from them have received all their learning in the Politiques, is not the Libertie of Particular men; but the Libertie of the Common-wealth. . . .

. . . It is an easy thing, for men to be deceived, by the specious name of Libertie; and for want of Judgement to distinguish, mistake that for their Private Inheritance, and Birth right, which is the right of the Publique only. And when the same errour is confirmed by the authority of men in reputation for their writings in this subject, it is no wonder if it produce sedition, and change of Government. In these westerne parts of the world, we are made to receive our opinions concerning the Institution, and Rights of Common-wealths, from *Aristotle, Cicero,* and other men, Greeks and Romanes, that living under Popular States, derived those Rights, not from the Principles of Nature, but transcribed them into their books, out of the Practise of their own Common-wealths, which were Popular; as the Grammarians describe the Rules of Language, out of the Practise of the time; or the Rules of Poetry, out of the Poems of *Homer* and *Virgil.* And because the Athenians were taught, (to keep them from desire of changing their Government,) that they were Freemen, and all that lived under Monarchy were slaves; therefore *Aristotle* puts it down in his *Politiques (lib. 6. cap. 2.) In democracy,* Liberty *is to be supposed: for 'tis commonly held, that no man is* Free *in any other Government* . . . And by reading of these Greek and Latine Authors, men from their childhood have gotten a habit (under a false shew of Liberty,) of favouring tumults, and of licentious controlling the actions of their Soveraigns; and again of controlling those controllers, with the effusion of so much blood; as I think I may truly say, there was never any thing so deerly bought, as these Western parts have bought the learning of the Greek and Latine tongues.

To come now to the particulars of the true Liberty of a Subject; that is to say, what are the things, which though commanded by the Soveraign, he may neverthelesse, without Injustice, refuse to do; we are to consider, what Rights we passe away, when we make a Common-wealth. . . .

First therefore, seeing Soveraignty by Institution, is by Covenant of every one to every one; and Soveraignty by Acquisition, by Covenants of the Vanquished to the Victor, or Child to the Parent; It is manifest, that every Subject has Liberty in all those things, the right whereof cannot by Covenant be transferred. I have shewn before in the 14. Chapter, that Covenants, not to defend a mans own body, are voyd. Therefore,

If the Soveraign command a man (though justly condemned,) to kill, wound, or mayme himselfe: or not to resist those that assault him; or to abstain from the use of food, ayre, medicine, or any other thing, without which he cannot live; yet hath that man the Liberty to disobey.

If a man be interrogated by the Soveraign, or his Authority, concerning a crime done by himselfe, he is not bound (without assurance of Pardon) to confesse it; because no man (as I have shewn in the same Chapter) can be obliged by Covenant to accuse himselfe.

Again, the Consent of a Subject to Soveraign Power, is contained in these words, *I Authorise, or take upon me, all his actions:* in which there is no restriction at all, of his own former naturall Liberty: For by allowing him to *kill me,* I am not bound to kill my selfe when he commands me. 'Tis one thing to say, *Kill me, or my fellow, if you please;* another thing to say, *I will kill my selfe, or my fellow. . . .*

To resist the Sword of the Commonwealth, in defence of another man, guilty, or innocent, no man hath Liberty; because such Liberty, takes away from the Soveraign, the means of Protecting us; and is therefore destructive of the very essence of Government. . . .

As for other Lyberties, they depend on the Silence of the Law. In cases where the Soveraign has prescribed no rule, there the Subject hath the Liberty to do, or forbeare, according to his own discretion. And therefore such Liberty is in some places more, and in some lesse; and in some times more, in other times lesse, according as they that have the Soveraignty shall think most convenient.

As for Example, there was a time, when in *England* a man might enter in to his own Land, (and dispossesse such as wrongfully possessed it,) by force. But in after-times, that Liberty of Forcible Entry, was taken away by a Statute made (by the King) in Parliament. And in some places of the world, men have the Liberty of many wives: in other places, such Liberty is not allowed.

If a Subject have a controversie with his Soveraigne, of debt, or of right of possession of lands or goods, or concerning any service required at his hands, or concerning any penalty, corporall, or pecuniary, grounded on a precedent Law; he hath the same Liberty to sue for his right, as if it were against a Subject; and before such Judges, as are appointed by the Soveraign. For seeing the Soveraign demandeth by force of a former Law, and not by vertue of his Power; he declareth thereby, that he requireth no more, then shall appear to be due by that Law. The sute therefore is not contrary to the will of the Soveraign; and consequently the Subject hath the Liberty to demand the hearing of his Cause; and sentence, according to that Law. But if he demand, or take anything by pretence of his Power; there lyeth, in that case, no action of Law: for all that is done by him in Vertue of his Power, is done by the Authority of every Subject, and consequently, he that brings an action against the Soveraign, brings it against himselfe. . . .

CHAPTER XXVI

Of CIVILL LAWES

By CIVILL LAWES, I understand the Lawes, that men are therefore bound to observe, because they are Members, not of this, or that Common-wealth in particular, but of a Common-wealth. For the knowledge of particular Lawes belongeth to them, that professe the study of the Lawes of their severall Countries; but the knowledge of Civill Law in generall, to any man. . . .

And first it is manifest, that Law in generall, is not Counsell, but Command; nor a

Command of any man to any man; but only of him, whose Command is addressed to one formerly obliged to obey him. And as for Civill Law, it addeth only the name of the person Commanding, which is *Persona Civitatis,* the Person of the Common-wealth.

Which considered, I define Civill Law in this manner. CIVILL LAW, *Is to every Subject, those Rules, which the Common-wealth hath Commanded him, by Word, Writing, or other sufficient Sign of the Will, to make use of, for the Distinction of Right, and Wrong; that is to say, of what is contrary, and what is not contrary to the Rule.* . . .

. . . Lawes are the Rules of Just, and Unjust; nothing being reputed Unjust, that is not contrary to some Law. Likewise, that none can make Lawes but the Common-wealth; because our Subjection is to the Common-wealth only: and that Commands, are to be signified by sufficient Signs; because a man knows not otherwise how to obey them. And therefore, whatsoever can from this definition by necessary consequence be deduced, ought to be acknowledged for truth. Now I deduce from it this that followeth.

1. The Legislator in all Common-wealths, is only the Soveraign, be he one Man, as in a Monarchy, or one Assembly of men, as in a Democracy, or Aristocracy. For the Legislator, is he that maketh the Law. And the Common-wealth only, praescribes, and commandeth the observation of those rules, which we call Law: Therefore the Common-wealth is the Legislator. But the Common-wealth is no Person, nor has capacity to doe any thing, but by the Representative, (that is, the Soveraign;) and therefore the Soveraign is the sole Legislator. . . .

2. The Soveraign of a Common-wealth, be it an Assembly, or one Man, is not Subject to the Civill Lawes. For having power to make, and repeale Lawes, he may when he pleaseth, free himselfe from that subjection, by repealing those Lawes that trouble him, and making of new; and consequently he was free before. . . .

3. When long Use obtaineth the authority of a Law, it is not the Length of Time that maketh the Authority, but the Will of the Soveraign signified by his silence . . . our Lawyers account no Customes Law, but such as are reasonable, and that evill Customes are to be abolished: But the Judgement of what is reasonable, and of what is to be abolished, belongeth to him that maketh the Law, which is the Soveraign Assembly, or Monarch.

4. The Law of Nature, and the Civill Law, contain each other, and are of equall extent. For the Lawes of Nature, which consist in Equity, Justice, Gratitude, and other morall Vertues on these depending, in the condition of meer Nature . . . are not properly Lawes, but qualities that dispose men to peace, and to obedience. When a Common-wealth is once settled, then are they actually Lawes, and not before; as being then the commands of the Common-wealth; and therefore also Civill Lawes: For it is the Soveraign Power that obliges men to obey them. For in the differences of private men, to declare, what is Equity, what is Justice, and what is morall Vertue, and to make them binding, there is need of the Ordinances of Soveraign Power, and Punishments to be ordained for such as shall break them; which Ordinances are therefore part of the Civill Law. The Law of Nature therefore is a part of the Civill Law in all Common-wealths of the world. Reciprocally also, the Civill Law is a part of the Dictates of Nature. For Justice, that is to say, Performance of Covenant, and giving to every man his own, is a Dictate of the Law of Nature. But every subject in a Common-wealth, hath covenanted to obey the Civill Law . . . And therefore Obedience to the Civill Law is part also of the Law of Nature. Civill, and Naturall Law are not different kinds, but different parts of Law; whereof one part being written, is called Civill, the other unwritten, Naturall. But the Right of Nature, that is, the naturall Liberty of man, may by the Civill Law be abridged, and restrained: nay the end of making Lawes, is no other, but such Restraint; without the which there cannot possibly be any Peace. And Law was brought into the world for nothing else, but to limit the naturall

liberty of particular men, in such manner, as they might not hurt, but assist one another, and joyn together against a common Enemy.

5. If the Soveraign of one Common-wealth, subdue a People that have lived under other written Lawes, and afterwards govern them by the same Lawes, by which they were governed before; yet those Lawes are the Civill Lawes of the Victor, and not of the Vanquished Common-wealth. For the Legislator is he, not by whose authority the Lawes were first made, but by whose authority they now continue to be Lawes. And therefore where there be divers Provinces, within the Dominion of a Common-wealth, and in those Provinces diversity of Lawes, which commonly are called the Customes of each severall Province, we are not to understand that such Customes have their force, onely from Length of Time; but that they were antiently Lawes written, or otherwise made known, for the Constitutions, and Statutes of their Soveraigns; and are now Lawes, not by vertue of the Praescription of time, but by the Constitutions of their present Soveraigns. But if an unwritten Law, in all the Provinces of a Dominion, shall be generally observed, and no iniquity appear in the use thereof; that Law can be no other but a Law of Nature, equally obliging all man-kind. . . .

7. That Law can never be against Reason, our Lawyers are agreed; and that not the Letter, (that is, every construction of it,) but that which is according to the Intention of the Legislator, is the Law. And it is true: but the doubt is, of whose Reason it is, that shall be received for Law. It is not meant of any private Reason; for then there would be as much contradiction in the Lawes, as there is in the Schooles; nor yet, (as Sr. *Ed Coke* makes it,) an *Artificiall perfection of Reason, gotten by long study, observation, and experience,* (as his was.) For it is possible long study may encrease, and confirm erroneous Sentences: and where men build on false grounds, the more they build, the greater is the ruine: and of those that study, and observe with equall time, and diligence, the reasons and resolutions are, and must remain discordant: and therefore it is not that *Juris prudentia,* or wisedome of subordinate Judges; but the Reason of this our Artificiall Man the Common-wealth, and his Command, that maketh Law: And the Common-wealth being in their Representative but one Person, there cannot easily arise any contradiction in the Lawes; and when there doth, the same Reason is able, by interpretation, or alteration, to take it away. In all Courts of Justice, the Soveraign (which is the Person of the Common-wealth,) is he that Judgeth: The subordinate Judge, ought to have regard to the reason, which moved his Soveraign to make such Law, that his Sentence may be according thereunto; which then is his Soveraigns Sentence; otherwise it is his own, and an unjust one. . . .

8. . . . The Command of the Common-wealth, is Law onely to those, that have means to take notice of it. Over naturall fooles, children, or madmen there is no Law, no more than over brute beasts; nor are they capable of the title of just, or unjust; because they had never power to make any covenant, or to understand the consequences thereof; and consequently never took upon them to authorise the actions of any Soveraign, as they must do that make to themselves a Common-wealth. . . .

And first, if it be a Law that obliges all the Subjects without exception, and is not written, nor otherwise published in such places as they may take notice thereof, it is a Law of Nature. For whatsoever men are to take knowledge of for Law, not upon other mens words, but every one from his own reason, must be such as is agreeable to the reason of all men; which no Law can be, but the Law of Nature. The Lawes of Nature therefore need not any publishing, nor Proclamation; as being contained in this one Sentence, approved by all the world, *Do not that to another, which thou thinkest unreasonable to be done by another to thy selfe.* . . . For whatsoever Law is not written, or some way published by him that makes it Law, can be known no way, but by the reason of him that is to obey it; and is therefore also a Law not only Civill, but Naturall.

For Example, if the Soveraign employ a Publique Minister, without written Instructions what to doe; he is obliged to take for Instructions the Dictates of Reason; As if he make a Judge, The Judge is to take notice, that his Sentence ought to be according to the reason of his Soveraign, which being alwaies understood to be Equity, he is bound to it by the Law of Nature. . . . All which Instructions of Naturall Reason may be comprehended under one name of *Fidelity;* which is a branch of naturall Justice.

The Law of Nature excepted, it belongeth to the essence of all other Lawes, to be made known, to every man that shall be obliged to obey them, either by word, or writing, or some other act, known to proceed from the Soveraign Authority. . . .

The Legislator known; and the Lawes, either by writing, or by the light of Nature, sufficiently published; there wanteth yet another very materiall circumstance to make them obligatory. For it is not the Letter, but the Intendment, or Meaning; that is to say, the authentique Interpretation of the Law (which is the sense of the Legislator,) in which the nature of the Law consisteth; And therefore the Interpretation of all Lawes dependeth on the Authority Soveraign; and the Interpreters can be none but those, which the Soveraign, (to whom only the Subject oweth obedience) shall appoint. For else, by the craft of an Interpreter, the Law may be made to beare a sense, contrary to that of the Soveraign; by which means the Interpreter becomes the Legislator.

All Laws, written, and unwritten, have need of Interpretation. The unwritten Law of Nature, though it be easy to such, as without partiality, and passion, make use of their naturall reason, and therefore leaves the violaters thereof without excuse; yet considering there be very few, perhaps none, that in some cases are not blinded by self love, or some other passion, it is now become of all Laws the most obscure; and has consequently the greatest need of able Interpreters. The written Laws, if they be short, are easily misinterpreted, from the divers significations of a word, or two: if long, they be more obscure by the diverse significations of many words: in so much as no written Law, delivered in few, or many words, can be well understood, without a perfect understanding of the finall causes, for which the Law was made; the knowledge of which finall causes is in the Legislator. To him therefore there can not be any knot in the Law, insoluble; either by finding out the ends, to undoe it by; or else by making what ends he will, (as *Alexander* did with his sword in the Gordian knot,) by the Legislative power; which no other Interpreter can doe.

The Interpretation of the Lawes of Nature, in a Common-wealth, dependeth not on the books of Morall Philosophy. The Authority of writers, without the Authority of the Common-wealth, maketh not their opinions Law, be they never so true. That which I have written in this Treatise, concerning the Morall Vertues, and of their necessity, for the procuring, and maintaining peace, though it bee evident Truth, is not therefore presently Law; but because it is in all Common-wealths in the world, it is part of the Civill Law: For though it be naturally reasonable; yet it is by the Soveraigne Power that it is Law: Otherwise, it were a great errour, to call the Lawes of Nature unwritten Law; whereof wee see so many volumes published, and in them so many contradictions of one another, and of themselves.

The Interpretation of the Law of Nature, is the Sentence of the Judge constituted by the Soveraign Authority, to heare and determine such controversies, as depend thereon; and consisteth in the application of the Law to the present case. For in the act of Judicature, the Judge doth no more but consider, whither the demand of the party, be consonant to naturall reason, and Equity; and the Sentence he giveth, is therefore the Interpretation of the Law of Nature; which Interpretation is Authentique; not because it is his private Sentence; but because he giveth it by Authority of the Soveraign, whereby it becomes the Soveraigns Sentence; which is Law for that time, to the parties pleading.

But because there is no Judge Subordinate, nor Soveraign, but may erre in a Judgement of Equity; if afterward in another like case he find it more consonant to Equity to give a contrary Sentence, he is obliged to doe it. No mans error becomes his own Law; nor obliges him to persist in it. Neither (for the same reason) becomes it a Law to other Judges, though sworn to follow it. For though a wrong Sentence given by authority of the Soveraign, if he know and allow it, in such Lawes as are mutable, be a constitution of a new Law, in cases, in which every little circumstance is the same; yet in Lawes immutable, such as are the Lawes of Nature, they are no Lawes to the same, or other Judges, in the like cases for ever after. Princes succeed one another; and one Judge passeth, another commeth; nay, Heaven and Earth shall passe; but not one title of the Law of Nature shall passe; for it is the Eternall Law of God. Therefore, all the Sentences of precedent Judges that have ever been, cannot all together make a Law contrary to naturall Equity; Nor any Examples of former Judges, can warrant an unreasonable Sentence, or discharge the present Judge of the trouble of studying what is Equity (in the case he is to Judge,) from the principles of his own naturall reason. For example sake, 'Tis against the Law of Nature, *To punish the Innocent;* and Innocent is he that acquitteth himselfe Judicially, and is acknowledged for Innocent by the Judge. Put the case now, that a man is accused of a capitall crime, and seeing the power and malice of some enemy, and the frequent corruption and partiality of Judges, runneth away for feare of the event, and afterwards is taken, and brought to a legall triall, and maketh it sufficiently appear, he was not guilty of the crime, and being thereof acquitted, is nevertheless condemned to lose his goods; this is a manifest condemnation of the Innocent. I say therefore, that there is no place in the world, where this can be an interpretation of a Law of Nature, or be made a Law by the Sentences of Precedent Judges, that had done the same. For he that judged it first, judged unjustly; and no Injustice can be a pattern

of Judgement to succeeding Judges. A written Law may forbid innocent men to fly, and they may be punished for flying: But that flying for feare of injury, should be taken for presumption of guilt, after a man is already absolved of the crime Judicially, is contrary to the nature of a Presumption, which hath no place after Judgement given. Yet this is set down by a great Lawyer for the common Law of *England. If a man* (saith he) *that is Innocent, be accused of Felony, and for feare flyeth for the same; albeit he judicially acquitteth himselfe of the Felony; yet if it be found that he fled for the Felony, he shall notwithstanding his Innocency, Forfeit all his goods, chattells, debts, and duties. For as to the Forfeiture of them, the Law will admit no proofe against the Presumption in Law, grounded upon his flight.* Here you see, *An Innocent man, Judicially acquitted, notwithstanding his Innocency,* (when no written Law forbad him to fly) after his acquitall, *upon a Presumption in Law,* condemned to lose all the goods he hath. If the Law ground upon his flight a Presumption of the fact, (which was Capitall,) the Sentence ought to have been Capitall: if the Presumption were not of the Fact, for what then ought he to lose his goods? This therefore is no Law of *England;* nor is the condemnation grounded upon a Presumption of Law, but upon the Presumption of the Judges. It is also against Law, to say that no Proofe shall be admitted against a Presumption of Law. For all Judges, Soveraign and subordinate, if they refuse to heare Proofe, refuse to do Justice. . . . There be other things of this nature, wherein mens Judgements have been perverted, by trusting to Precedents: but this is enough to shew, that though the Sentence of the Judge, be a Law to the party pleading, yet it is no Law to any Judge, that shall succeed him in that Office.

In like manner, when question is of the Meaning of written Lawes, he is not the Interpreter of them, that writeth a Commentary upon them. For Commentaries are commonly more subject to cavill, than the Text; and therefore need other Commentaries; and so there will be no end of such

Interpretation. And therefore unlesse there be an Interpreter authorised by the Soveraign, from which the subordinate Judges are not to recede, the Interpreter can be no other than the ordinary Judges, in the same manner, as they are in cases of the unwritten Law; and their Sentences are to be taken by them that plead, for Lawes in that particular case; but not to bind other Judges, in like cases to give like judgements. For a Judge may erre in the Interpretation even of written Lawes; but no errour of a subordinate Judge, can change the Law, which is the generall Sentence of the Soveraigne.

In written Lawes, men use to make a difference between the Letter, and the Sentence of the Law: And when by the Letter, is meant whatsoever can be gathered from the bare words, 'tis well distinguished. For the significations of almost all words, are either in themselves, or in the metaphoricall use of them, ambiguous; and may be drawn in argument, to make many senses; but there is onely one sense of the Law. But if by the Letter, be meant the literall sense, then the Letter, and the Sentence or intention of the Law, is all one. For the literall sense is that, which the Legislator intended, should by the letter of the Law be signified. Now the Intention of the Legislator is alwayes supposed to be Equity: For it were a great contumely for a Judge to think otherwise of the Soveraigne. He ought therefore, if the Word of the Law doe not fully authorise a reasonable Sentence, to supply it with the Law of Nature; or if the case be difficult, to respit Judgement till he have received more ample authority. For Example, a written Law ordaineth, that he which is thrust out of his house by force, shall be restored by force: It happens that a man by negligence leaves his house empty, and returning is kept out by force, in which case there is no speciall Law ordained. It is evident, that this case is contained in the same Law: for else there is no remedy for him at all; which is to be supposed against the Intention of the Legislator. Again, the word of the Law, commandeth to Judge according to the Evidence: A man is accused falsely of a fact, which the Judge saw himself done by another; and not by him that is accused. In this case neither shall the Letter of the Law be followed to the condemnation of the Innocent, nor shall the Judge give Sentence against the evidence of the Witnesses; because the Letter of the Law is to the contrary: but procure of the Soveraign that another be made Judge, and himself Witnesse. So that the incommodity that follows the bare words of a written Law, may lead him to the Intention of the Law, whereby to interpret the same the better; though no Incommodity can warrant a Sentence against the Law. For every Judge of Right, and Wrong, is not Judge of what is Commodious, or Incommodious to the Common-wealth.

The abilities required in a good Interpreter of the Law, that is to say, in a good Judge, are not the same with those of an Advocate; namely the study of the Lawes. For a Judge, as he ought to take notice of the Fact, from none but the Witnesses; so also he ought to take notice of the Law, from nothing but the S[t]atutes, and Constitutions of the Soveraign, alledged in the pleading, or declared to him by some that have authority from the Soveraign Power to declare them; and need not take care beforehand, what hee shall Judge; for it shall bee given him what hee shall say concerning the Fact, by Witnesses; and what hee shall say in point of Law, from those that shall in their pleadings shew it, and by authority interpret it upon the place. The Lords of Parliament in *England* were Judges, and most difficult causes have been heard and determined by them; yet few of them were much versed in the study of the Lawes; and fewer had made profession of them; and though they consulted with Lawyers, that were appointed to be present there for that purpose; yet they alone had the authority of giving Sentence. In like manner, in the ordinary trialls of Right, Twelve men of the common People, are the Judges, and give Sentence, not onely of the Fact, but of the Right; and pronounce simply for the Complaynant, or for the Defendant; that is to say, are Judges not onely of the Fact, but also of the Right: and in a question of crime, not onely determine whether done, or not done; but also whether it be *Murder, Homicide, Felony, Assault,* and the like, which are determinations of Law: but because they are not supposed to know the Law of themselves, there is one that hath Authority to enforme them of it, in the Particular case they are to Judge of. But yet if they judge not according to that he tells them, they are not subject thereby to any penalty; unlesse it be made appear, they did it against their consciences, or had been corrupted by reward.

The things that make a good Judge, or good Interpreter of the Lawes, are, first, *A right understanding* of that principall Law of Nature called *Equity;* which depending not on the reading of other mens Writings, but on the goodnesse of a mans own naturall Reason, and Meditation, is presumed to be in those most, that have had most leisure, and had the most inclination to meditate thereon. Secondly, *Contempt of unnecessary Riches,* and Preferments. Thirdly, *To be able in judgement to devest himselfe of all feare, anger, hatred, love,* and *compassion.* Fourthly, and lastly, *Patience to heare; diligent attention in hearings; and memory to retain, digest and apply what he hath heard.* . . .

CHAPTER XXIX

Of Those Things that Weaken, or Tend to the DISSOLUTION of a Common-wealth

. . . A man to obtain a Kingdome, is sometimes content with lesse Power, than to the Peace, and defence of the Common-wealth is necessarily required. From whence it commeth to passe, that when the exercise of the Power layd by, is for the publique safety to be resumed, it hath the resemblance of an unjust act; which disposeth great numbers of men (when occasion is presented) to rebell. . . .

Nor does this happen in Monarchy onely. For whereas the stile of the antient Roman Common-wealth, was, *The Senate, and People of Rome;* neither Senate, nor People pretended to the whole Power; which first caused the seditions, of *Tiberius Gracchus, Caius Gracchus, Lucius Saturninus,* and others; and afterwards the warres between the Senate and the People, under *Marius* and *Sylla;* and again under *Pompey* and *Caesar,* to the Extinction of their Democraty, and the setting up of Monarchy. . . .

. . . I observe the *Diseases* of a Common-wealth, that proceed from the poyson of seditious doctrines; whereof one is, *That every private man is Judge of Good and Evill actions.* This is true in the condition of meer Nature, where there are no Civill Lawes; and also under Civill Government, in such cases as are not determined by the Law. But otherwise, it is manifest, that the measure of Good and Evill actions, is the Civill Law; and the Judge the Legislator, who is alwayes Representative of the Common-wealth. From this false doctrine, men are disposed to debate with themselves, and dispute the commands of the Common-wealth; and afterwards to obey, or disobey them, as in their private judgements they shall think fit. Whereby the Common-wealth is distracted and *Weakened.* . . .

A Fifth doctrine, that tendeth to the Dissolution of a Common-wealth, is, *That every private man has an absolute Propriety in his Goods; such, as excludeth the Right of the Soveraign.* Every man has indeed a Propriety that excludes the Right of every other Subject: And he has it only from the Soveraign Power; without the protection whereof, every other man should have equall Right to the same. But if the Right of the Soveraign also be excluded, he cannot performe the office they have put him into; which is, to defend them both from forraign enemies, and from the injuries of one another; and consequently there is no longer a Common-wealth. . . .

There is a Sixth doctrine, plainly, and directly against the essence of a Common-wealth; and 'tis this, *That the Soveraign Power may be divided.* For what is it to divide the Power of a Common-wealth, but to Dissolve it; for Powers divided mutually destroy each other. And for these doctrines, men are chiefly beholding to some of those, that making profession of the Lawes, endeavour to make them depend upon their own learning, and not upon the Legislative Power.

And as False Doctrine, so also often-times the Example of different Government in a neighbouring Nation, disposeth men to alteration of the forme already setled. . . . And I doubt not, but many men, have been contented to see the late troubles in *England,* out of an imitation of the Low Countries; supposing there needed no more to grow rich, than to change, as they had done, the forme of their Government. . . .

And as to Rebellion in particular against Monarchy; one of the most frequent causes of it, is the Reading of the books of Policy, and Histories of the antient Greeks, and Romans; from which, young men, and all others that are unprovided of the Antidote of solid Reason, receiving a strong, and delightfull impression, of the great exploits of warre, atchieved by the Conductors of their Armies, receive withall a pleasing Idea, of all they have done besides; and imagine their great prosperity, not to have proceeded from the aemulation of particular men, but from the vertue of their popular forme of government: Not considering the frequent Seditions, and Civill warres, produced by the imperfection of their Policy. From the reading, I say, of such books, men have undertaken to kill their Kings, because the Greek and Latine writers, in their books, and discourses of Policy, make it lawfull, and laudable, for any man so to do; provided before he do it, he call him Tyrant. For they say not *Regicide,* that is, killing of a King, but *Tyrannicide,* that is, killing of a Tyrant is lawfull. From the same books, they that live under a Monarch conceive an opinion, that the Subjects in a Popular Common-wealth enjoy Liberty; but that in a Monarchy they are all Slaves. I say, they that live under a Monarchy conceive such an opinion; not they that live under a Popular Government: for they find no such matter. In summe, I cannot imagine, how any thing can be more prejudiciall to a Monarchy, than the allowing of such books to be publikely read, without present applying such correctives of discreet Masters, as are fit to take away their Venime: Which Venime I will not doubt to compare to the biting of a mad Dogge. . . .

As there have been Doctors, that hold there be three Soules in a man; so there be also that think there may be more Soules, (that is, more Soveraigns,) than one, in a Common-wealth; and set up a *Supremacy* against the *Soveraignty; Canons* against *Lawes;* and a *Ghostly Authority* against the *Civill;* working on mens minds, with words and distinctions, that of themselves signifie nothing, but bewray (by their obscurity) that there walketh (as some think invisibly) another Kingdome, as it were a Kingdome of Fayries, in the dark. Now seeing it is manifest, that the Civill Power, and the Power of the Common-wealth is the same thing; and that Supremacy, and the Power of making Canons, and granting Faculties, implyeth a Common-wealth; it followeth, that where one is Soveraign, another Supreme; where one can make Lawes, and another make Cannons; there must needs be two Common-wealths, of one and the same Subjects; which is a Kingdome divided in it selfe, and cannot stand . . . When therefore these two Powers oppose one another, the Common-wealth cannot but be in great danger of Civill warre, and Dissolution. . . .

CHAPTER XXX

Of the OFFICE of the Soveraign Representative

. . . To the care of the Soveraign, belongeth the making of Good Lawes. But what is a good Law? By a Good Law, I mean not a Just Law: for no Law can be Unjust. The Law is made by the Soveraign Power, and all that is done by such Power, is warranted, and owned by every one of the people; and that which every man will have so, no man can say is unjust. It is in the Lawes of a Common-wealth, as in the Lawes of Gaming: whatsoever the Gamesters all agree on, is Injustice to none of them. A Good Law is that, which is *Needfull,* for the *Good of the People,* and withall *Perspicuous.* easily understood

For the use of Lawes, (which are but Rules Authorised) is not to bind the People from all Voluntary actions; but to direct and keep them in such a motion, as not to hurt themselves by their own impetuous desires, rashnesse, or indiscretion; as Hedges are set, not to stop Travellers, but to keep them in the way. And therefore a Law that is not Needfull, having not the true End of a Law, is not Good. . . .

The Perspicuity, consisteth not so much in the words of the Law it selfe, as in a Declaration of the Causes, and Motives, for which it was made. That is it, that shewes us the meaning of the Legislator; and the meaning of the Legislator known, the Law is more easily understood by few, than many words. For all words, are subject to ambiguity; and therefore multiplication of words in the body of the Law, is multiplication of ambiguity: Besides it seems to imply, (by too much diligence,) that whosoever can evade the words, is without the compasse of the Law. And this is a cause of many unnecessary Processes. For when I consider how short were the Lawes of antient times; and how they grew by degrees still longer; me thinks I see a contention between the Penners, and Pleaders of the Law; the former seeking to circumscribe the later; and the later to evade their circumscriptions; and that the Pleaders have got the Victory. It

belongeth therefore to the Office of a Legislator, (such as is in all Common-wealths the Supreme Representative, be it one Man, or an Assembly,) to make the reason Perspicuous, why the Law was made; and the Body of the Law it selfe, as short, but in as proper, and significant termes, as may be.

It belongeth also to the Office of the Soveraign, to make a right application of Punishments, and Rewards. And seeing the end of punishing is not revenge, and discharge of choler; but correction, either of the offender, or of others by his example; the severest Punishments are to be inflicted for those Crimes, that are of most Danger to the Publique. . . . But crimes of Infirmity; such as are those which proceed from great provocation, from great fear, great need, or from ignorance whether the Fact be a great Crime, or not, there is place many times for Lenity, without prejudice to the Common-wealth; and Lenity when there is such place for it, is required by the Law of Nature. . . .

In like manner it belongeth to the Office, and Duty of the Soveraign, to apply his Rewards always so, as there may arise from them benefit to the Common-wealth: wherein consisteth their Use, and End; and is then done, when they that have well served the Common-wealth, are with as little expence of the Common Treasure, as is possible, so well recompenced, as others thereby may be encouraged, both to serve the same as faithfully as they can, and to study the arts by which they may be enabled to do it better. . . .

A Review, and Conclusion

. . . And because I find by divers English Books lately printed, that the Civill warres have not yet sufficiently taught men, in what point of time it is, that a Subject becomes obliged to the Conquerour; nor what is Conquest; nor how it comes about, that it obliges men to obey his Laws: Therefore for farther satisfaction of men therein, I say, the point of time, wherein a man becomes subject to a Conquerour, is that point, wherein having liberty to submit to him, he consenteth, either by expresse words, or by other sufficient sign, to be his Subject. When it is that a man hath the liberty to submit, I have shewed before in the end of the 21. Chapter; namely, that for him that hath no obligation to his former Soveraign but that of an ordinary Subject, it is then, when the means of his life is within the Guards and Garrisons of the Enemy; for it is then, that he hath no longer Protection from him, but is protected by the adverse party for his Contribution. Seeing therefore such contribution is every where, as a thing inevitable, (notwithstanding it be an assistance to the Enemy,) esteemed lawfull; a totall Submission; which is but an assistance to the Enemy, cannot be esteemed unlawfull. . . . But if a man, besides the obligation of a Subject, hath taken upon him a new obligation of a Souldier, then he hath not the liberty to submit to a new Power, as long as the old one keeps the field, and giveth him means of subsistence, either in his Armies, or Garrisons: for in this case, he cannot complain of want of Protection, and means to live as a Souldier: But when that also failes, a Souldier also may seek his Protection wheresoever he has most hope to have it; and may lawfully submit himself to his new master. And so much for the Time when he may do it lawfully, if hee will. . . .

. . . *Conquest* (to define it) is the Acquiring of the Right of Soveraignty by Victory. Which Right, is acquired, in the peoples Submission, by which they contract with the Victor, promising Obedience, for Life and Liberty. . . .

. . . because the name of Tyranny, signifieth nothing more, nor lesse, than the name of Soveraignty, be it in one, or many men, saving that they that use the former word, are understood to bee angry with them they call Tyrants; I think the toleration of a professed hatred of Tyranny, is a Toleration of hatred to Common-wealth in generall, and another evill seed, not differing much from the former. For to the Justification of the Cause of a Conqueror, the Reproach of the Cause of the Conquered, is for the most part necessary: but neither of them necessary for the Obligation of the Conquered. . . .

6

John Locke

1632–1704

The Locke family lived in rural southwest England. John Sr., the philosopher's father, was an estate agent, a good country lawyer, a Puritan, a captain in Parliamentary forces who saw action against the King's army, and a stout believer in political liberty. Little is known about his wife, who was ten years his senior. The pattern of family life was set by her husband. He insisted that his sons live busy, studious lives; he taught them to prize simplicity and to avoid display.

When Locke was fourteen he went to harsh Westminster School. Westminster stressed the classics; Locke had a thorough grounding in Latin and Greek. He excelled and was given a scholarship in his third year. One biographer says Locke might have seen Charles I lose his head in nearby Whitehall Palace Yard.

At twenty he belatedly entered Oxford where he also enjoyed a scholarship. There he spent much of the next thirty years as student and scholar. Oxford had been Royalist, but John Owen, a strong Cromwellian, was a leading force when Locke matriculated. Owen protected tenure of Royalist Anglican teachers, and this example may have quickened Locke's non-sectarianism (which unfortunately never widened to tolerance for non-Protestants). The Oxford curriculum had changed little since Hobbes' student days; the courses were still a scholastic exposition of Aristotelean subjects—grammar, rhetoric, logic, moral philosophy, and Greek. Mathematics had been added, and Locke studied it under Wallis—one of Hobbes' antagonists. Locke complained that Oxford

education was pallid and tiresome, but he plowed through four years of it to get his Bachelor's degree and stayed on for two more for his Master's. Less arid extra-curricular study and skylarking made his Oxford life pleasant, and after graduation he hung on lower faculty rungs with annual appointments to lecture on various subjects. Only clerics were eligible for most Oxford chairs; Locke toyed with the idea of becoming a divine, but his non-sectarianism and his belief in the wisdom of secular supremacy turned him from the ministry. He liked the girls and toyed with the idea of marriage; his reasons for turning back from this course are not known.

Two branches of science attracted him in his post-graduate years—physics and medicine. Sir Robert Boyle, pioneer physicist, lived in the town of Oxford for five years and became Locke's friend. From him Locke learned much about physics and went on to speculate on scientific method. His medical studies were irregular but fitted him to treat patients, which he did on and off for the rest of his life. Most of the medical men at Oxford taught their subject as classic lore learned from authorities like Aristotle and Galen, but the beginnings of modern medicine stirred some to adopt the empirical method. These attracted Locke. He thought traditional Oxford medical instruction futile. When he was thirty-six he tried to use influence to get admitted to candidacy for a Doctor of Medicine degree without attending lectures required for a Bachelor's degree. The Doctor's degree would have made him eligible to become a don without taking religious orders—his heart's desire. But the medical faculty's regularity was stronger than the pressure brought to bear. At forty-two Locke finally got his Bachelor's degree; he was then admitted to candidacy for the M.D., but he never graduated as a doctor.

At thirty-three he enjoyed a short diplomatic interlude as a secretary in a mission to Brandenberg and Cleves. On return he was asked to take more important assignments in foreign service, but the appeal of science and university life drew him back to Oxford.

Two years later, his influential friend, Lord Ashley, persuaded Locke to join his household in London. At first Locke's function seemed medical; it was said he performed life-saving surgery on Ashley. Soon, however, he became Ashley's adviser on politics and affairs of state. Later he chose a wife for Ashley's son. He was thrown with top-drawer politicians, wealthy businessmen, and influential courtiers. In the next half-dozen years Ashley's star rose rapidly; he became Earl of Shaftesbury, President of the Council of Trade and Plantations, and Lord High Chancellor. Locke held a succession of salaried jobs under Shaftesbury.

Locke's latest biographer, Cranston, says in his excellent work, "The world remembers Locke as a great theorist of toleration, but Ashley was a champion of toleration before Locke was, when Locke's views of toleration were indeed quite otherwise. This is not to say that Locke acquired his mature opinions on toleration from Ashley, for by the time he met Ashley, Locke's views had come into line with his, but it was Ashley who made Locke give systematic attention to the subject and furthered his evolution as a liberal."

Locke's health was bad in London; he especially suffered in winter when heavy smoke inflamed his weak lungs and brought on attacks of asthma. He spent short periods in the country and in France. At forty-three he was seriously ill and decided on a long stay in Montpelier, a French health resort. After a quiet year there, he went to Paris to tutor a son of one of Shaftesbury's friends.

He spent a third summer junketing through rural France (and noting particularly the peasants' wretchedness) and a third winter merrily in Paris. During his stay in France he sought the company of scholars, especially if they were gay. His thoughts were often on philosophic subjects; he particularly pondered the then-popular views of Descartes.

In spring Locke reluctantly returned to an England discordant under Charles II. Shaftesbury's fortunes had swung between presidency of Privy Council, imprisonment in London Tower, and back again. Locke rejoined him in a moment of favor, but the pendulum began to swing the other way, and Shaftesbury sent Locke back to Oxford. There he quietly studied science and medicine and said nothing about politics. Because of his Shaftesbury connections, authorship of several seditious pamphlets was erroneously ascribed to him, and he was closely watched by secret agents of the King. Shaftesbury fled to Holland and died there. Locke rightly became concerned for his safety, and in 1683 he sought asylum with the Dutch.

Now in his fifties, Locke continued his quiet scholar's life in Holland. One of his close friends was Limborch of Leyden, a theologian in the Arminian tradition originated by Grotius' group. Locke's political posture was remembered in England. The King's minister demanded he be struck from faculty rolls at Oxford, and after temporizing the head of Christ College reluctantly complied. Charles II died, and James II mounted the throne. A Protestant attempt to unseat Catholic James and enthrone Charles II's bastard, Monmouth, failed. Locke was accused of being party to the plot and his name was on a list of eighty-five men whom the English government tried to extradite from Holland. The Dutch did not take the extradition request seriously. Locke, nevertheless, cautiously assumed a false name and went into seclusion. But this was a period of well-being for him; the Dutch climate agreed with him and he enjoyed life.

In his fifth year of exile, he became an active conspirator against James II and for William of Orange. In the autumn of 1688

William set sail for England. In January 1689 William sent back word that James had fled and Parliament had asked him and Mary jointly to rule England. The Queen was to come at once. Locke was in the party that sailed with her—taking flirtatious care of an attractive Viscountess who was also of the party. Soon after his return Locke was asked to go to the Court of Frederick III, Elector of Brandenburg. He declined because of his ill health and lack of diplomatic experience. Cranston reports: "Besides, he said, a successful diplomatist had to be able to manage the bottle in drawing out men's thoughts; and the 'warm drinking' of the Germans was beyond him. He thought the King should send someone who could 'drink his share' rather than the soberest man in England."

The Whigs who enthroned William and Mary, looked on fifty-six-year-old returning Locke as a national hero and prophet. Soon his published works began to appear. The first two, *Letter on Toleration* and *Two Treatises on Civil Government* (1690) were published anonymously. The *Two Treatises* were a Whig bible for the next century. Excerpts following this note were taken from the second of these treatises. The same year Locke published his most important philosophical work, his *Essay on Human Understanding*. This work was hailed as great and soon became required reading in many universities. Locke saw the *Essay* through five editions, and of course it has been re-published many times since his death. As a man of influence he was tendered several lush appointments, but took only the modest post of Commissioner of Appeals, which paid a small salary and entailed little work.

Soon London smoke began to eat into his health again. Two years after his return from Holland he found the city intolerable. Sir Francis and Lady Masham asked him to take up residence at Oates, their country estate. They were Locke's old friends, particularly Lady Masham who though twenty-six years Locke's junior was greatly attracted to Locke in her youth and had a romantic relation to him before her marriage to Sir Francis. Locke

accepted only on condition that he pay twenty shillings a week board for himself and his servant; the Mashams humored him and agreed. At Oates he spent his time writing and visiting with personal and literary friends. He took a vigorous interest in public affairs and published work on fiscal matters that influenced the course of Parliament. In his sixties his interests and his writings became increasingly theological. Locke had always been deeply religious; his assults on orthodoxy sometimes gave the contrary impression. Cranston says: "His religion was that of the Latitudinarian wing of the Church of England. His creed was short but he held to it with the utmost assurance." Later he approached, but never admitted to, Unitarianism. Locke was not, however, preoccupied with religion; he also wrote on economics, and continued his studies on philosophy and government. His old interest in science flickered as a result of close relations with Newton. At sixty-four he tried to re-enter the great world by accepting an appointment to a new Council of Trade at a salary of one thousand pounds a year. In the Council's first summer, he found London tolerable, met with the Council nearly every day, and virtually established its course. But winter smoke drove him out of town and he tried to quit. The authorities asked him to stay on the Council and do what he could. In the three years following sickness kept him from more than half of the Council's meetings, and he felt uneasy about drawing his large salary. In 1700, sixty-eight-year-old Locke resigned and spent the remainder of his time at Oates.

Locke, during his last years, was able to pay more attention to children, to whom he was much drawn. He edited *Aesop's Fables* to help children learn Latin, putting Latin words above their English equivalents. He took a special interest in his young cousin, Peter King (who later became Lord High Chancellor of England) and in children of his close friends. He often undertook their instruction, was patient and indulgent, and was much loved by them. His last high spot was a celebration for Peter King's bride, a month before Locke died. The party was at Oates. A letter written to King in London instructed him to buy supplies for the feast —the shopping list called for a small mountain of fine meats, game, foul, and fish. After the party was over no new business engaged seventy-two-year-old Locke, and he became listless. The next month his life slowly ebbed away.

Locke was noted for his prudence. He was careful not only of his person and belongings, but also in his thinking. He was prosaic, had little appreciation of art and not much feel for history. He participated actively in many kinds of enterprises, because he believed that truth was likely to hide from those who only sat and thought. Sometimes his actions were over frugal—or even tightfisted. He believed paupers needed stern correction more than care. He usually avoided extremes. But his carefulness was prudence, not caution; he loved many people as individuals and mankind in general. In the preface to *Two Essays*, his proud patriotism and regard for his fellows is indicated by his statement that he wrote the book ". . . to justify to the world the people of England, whose love of their just and natural rights . . . saved the nation when it was on the very brink of slavery and ruin." It has been said that Locke did not merely enlarge men's knowledge, he changed their ways of thinking.

TWO TREATISES OF CIVIL GOVERNMENT *

Book II

AN ESSAY CONCERNING THE TRUE ORIGINAL, EXTENT AND END OF CIVIL GOVERNMENT

CHAPTER II

Of the State of Nature

4. To understand political power aright, and derive it from its original we must

* From number 751, Everyman's Library. Reprinted by permission of E. P. Dutton & Co.

consider what estate all men are naturally in, and that is, a state of perfect freedom to order their actions, and dispose of their possessions and persons as they think fit, within the bounds of the law of Nature, without asking leave or depending upon the will of any other man.

A state also of equality, wherein all the power and jurisdiction is reciprocal, no one having more than another, there being nothing more evident than that creatures of the same species and rank, promiscuously born to all the same advantages of Nature, and the use of the same faculties, should also be equal one amongst another, without subordination or subjection, unless the lord and master of them all should, by any manifest declaration of his will, set one above another, and confer on him, by an evident and clear appointment, an undoubted right to dominion and sovereignty. . . .

6. But though this be a state of liberty, yet it is not a state of license; though man in that state have an uncontrollable liberty to dispose of his person or possessions, yet he has not liberty to destroy himself, or so much as any creature in his possession, but where some nobler use than its bare preservation calls for it. The state of Nature has a law of Nature to govern it, which obliges every one, and reason, which is that law, teaches all mankind who will but consult it, that being all equal and independent, no one ought to harm another in his life, health, liberty or possessions; for men being all the workmanship of one omnipotent and infinitely wise Maker; all the servants of one sovereign Master, sent into the world by His order and about His business; they are His property, whose workmanship they are made to last during His, not one another's pleasure. And, being furnished with like faculties, sharing all in one community of Nature, there cannot be supposed any such subordination among us that may authorise us to destroy one another, as if we were made for one another's uses, as the inferior ranks of creatures are for ours. Every one as he is bound to preserve himself, and not to quit his station wilfully, so by the like reason,

when his own preservation comes not in competition, ought he as much as he can to preserve the rest of mankind, and not unless it be to do justice on an offender, take away or impair the life, or what tends to the preservation of the life, the liberty, health, limb, or goods of another.

7. And that all men may be restrained from invading others' rights, and from doing hurt to one another, and the law of Nature be observed, which willeth the peace and preservation of all mankind, the execution of the law of Nature is in that state put into every man's hands, whereby every one has a right to punish the transgressors of that law to such a degree as may hinder its violation. For the law of Nature would, as all other laws that concern men in this world, be in vain if there were nobody that in the state of Nature had a power to execute that law, and thereby preserve the innocent and restrain offenders; and if any one in the state of Nature may punish another for any evil he has done, every one may do so. . . .

8. And thus, in the state of Nature, one man comes by a power over another, but yet no absolute or arbitrary power to use a criminal, when he has got him in his hands, according to the passionate heats or boundless extravagancy of his own will, but only to retribute to him so far as calm reason and conscience dictate, what is proportionate to his transgression, which is so much as may serve for reparation and restraint. . . . In transgressing the law of Nature, the offender declares himself to live by another rule than that of reason and common equity, which is that measure God has set to the actions of men for their mutual security, and so he becomes dangerous to mankind; the tie which is to secure them from injury and violence being slighted and broken by him, which being a trespass against the whole species, and the peace and safety of it, provided for by the law of Nature, every man upon this score, by the right he hath to preserve mankind in general, may restrain, or where it is necessary, destroy things noxious to them, and so may bring such evil on any

one who hath transgressed that law, as may make him repent the doing of it, and thereby deter him, and, by his example, others from doing the like mischief. . . .

9. I doubt not but this will seem a very strange doctrine to some men; but before they condemn it, I desire them to resolve me by what right any prince or state can put to death or punish an alien for any crime he commits in their country? . . . The legislative authority by which they are in force over the subjects of that commonwealth hath no power over him. . . . And therefore, if by the law of Nature every man hath not a power to punish offences against it, as he soberly judges the case to require, I see not how the magistrates of any community can punish an alien of another country, since, in reference to him, they can have no more power than what every man naturally may have over another.

10. Besides the crime which consists in violating the laws, and varying from the right rule of reason, whereby a man so far becomes degenerate, and declares himself to quit the principles of human nature and to be a noxious creature, there is commonly injury done, and some person or other, some other man, receives damage by his transgression; in which case, he who hath received any damage has (besides the right of punishment common to him, with other men) a particular right to seek reparation from him that hath done it. And any other person who finds it just may also join with him that is injured, and assist him in recovering from the offender so much as may make satisfaction for the harm he hath suffered.

11. . . . The magistrate, who by being magistrate hath the common right of punishing put into his hands, can often, where the public good demands not the execution of the law, remit the punishment of criminal offences by his own authority, but yet cannot remit the satisfaction due to any private man for the damage he has received. . . . The damnified person has this power of appropriating to himself the goods or service of the offender by right of self-preservation. . . .

remit → to refrain from exacting, inflicting punishment.

Cain was so fully convinced that every one had a right to destroy such a criminal, that, after the murder of his brother, he cries out, "Every one that findeth me shall slay me," so plain was it writ in the hearts of all mankind.

12. By the same reason may a man in the state of Nature punish the lesser breaches of that law, it will, perhaps, be demanded, with death? I answer: Each transgression may be punished to that degree, and with so much severity, as will suffice to make it an ill bargain to the offender, give him cause to repent, and terrify others from doing the like. . . . For though it would be beside my present purpose to enter here into the particulars of the law of Nature, or its measures of punishment, yet it is certain there is such a law, and that too as intelligible and plain to a rational creature and a studier of that law as the positive laws of commonwealths, nay, possibly plainer; as much as reason is easier to be understood than the fancies and intricate contrivances of men, following contrary and hidden interests put into words; for truly so are a great part of the municipal laws of countries, which are only so far right as they are founded on the law of Nature, by which they are to be regulated and interpreted.

13. . . . I doubt not but it will be objected that it is unreasonable for men to be judges in their own cases, that self-love will make men partial to themselves and their friends; and, on the other side, ill-nature, passion and revenge will carry them too far in punishing others, and hence nothing but confusion and disorder will follow, and that therefore God hath certainly appointed government to restrain the partiality and violence of men. I easily grant that civil government is the proper remedy for the inconveniences of the state of Nature. . . . But I shall desire those who make this objection to remember that absolute monarchs are but men; and if government is to be the remedy of those evils which necessarily follow from men being judges in their own cases, and the state of Nature is therefore not to be endured, I

desire to know what kind of government that is, and how much better it is than the state of Nature, where one man commanding a multitude has the liberty to be judge in his own case, and may do to all his subjects whatever he pleases without the least question or control of those who execute his pleasure? and in whatsoever he doth, whether led by reason, mistake, or passion, must be submitted to? which men in the state of Nature are not bound to do one to another. And if he that judges, judges amiss in his own or any other case, he is answerable for it to the rest of mankind.

14. It is often asked as a mighty objection, where are, or ever were, there any men in such a state of Nature? To which it may suffice as an answer at present, that since all princes and rulers of "independent" governments all through the world are in a state of Nature, it is plain the world never was, nor never will be, without numbers of men in that state. I have named all governors of "independent" communities, whether they are, or are not, in league with others; for it is not every compact that puts an end to the state of Nature between men, but only this one of agreeing together mutually to enter into one community, and make one body politic; other promises and compacts men may make one with another, and yet still be in the state of Nature. The promises and bargains for truck, etc., between the two men in Soldania, in or between a Swiss and an Indian, in the woods of America, are binding to them, though they are perfectly in a state of Nature in reference to one another for truth, and keeping of faith belongs to men as men, and not as members of society.

15. To those that say there were never any men in the state of Nature, I will not only oppose the authority of the judicious Hooker. . . . But I, moreover, affirm that all men are naturally in that state, and remain so till, by their own consents, they make themselves members of some politic society, and I doubt not, in the sequel of this discourse, to make it very clear.

CHAPTER III

Of the State of War

16. The state of war is a state of enmity and destruction; and therefore declaring by word or action, not a passionate and hasty, but sedate, settled design upon another man's life puts him in a state of war with him against whom he has declared such an intention, and so has exposed his life to the other's power to be taken away by him, or any one that joins with him in his defence, and espouses his quarrel; it being reasonable and just I should have a right to destroy that which threatens me with destruction; for by the fundamental law of Nature, man being to be preserved as much as possible, when all cannot be preserved, the safety of the innocent is to be preferred, and one may destroy a man who makes war upon him, or has discovered an enmity to his being, for the same reason that he may kill a wolf or a lion, because they are not under the ties of the common law of reason, have no other rule but that of force and violence, and so may be treated as a beast of prey, those dangerous and noxious creatures that will be sure to destroy him whenever he falls into their power.

17. And hence it is that he who attempts to get another man into his absolute power does thereby put himself into a state of war with him; it being to be understood as a declaration of a design upon his life. For I have reason to conclude that he would get me into his power without my consent would use me as he pleased when he had got me there, and destroy me too when he had a fancy to it; for nobody can desire to have me in his absolute power unless it be to compel me by force to that which is against the right of my freedom—*i.e.* make me a slave. . . . He that in the state of Nature would take away the freedom that belongs to any one in that state must necessarily be supposed to have a design to take away everything else, that freedom being the foundation of all the rest; as he that in the state of society would take away the freedom belonging to those of that society or commonwealth must be supposed to design to take away from them everything else, and so be looked on as in a state of war.

18. This makes it lawful for a man to kill a thief who has not in the least hurt him, nor declared any design upon his life, any farther than by the use of force, so to get him in his power as to take away his money, or what he pleases, from him; because using force, where he has no right to get me into his power, let his pretence be what it will, I have no reason to suppose that he who would take away my liberty would not, when he had me in his power, take away everything else. And, therefore, it is lawful for me to treat him as one who has put himself into a state of war with me—*i.e.*, kill him if I can. . . .

19. And here we have the plain difference between the state of Nature and the state of war, which however some men have confounded. . . . Thus, a thief whom I cannot harm, but by appeal to the law, for having stolen all that I am worth, I may kill when he sets on me to rob me but of my horse or coat, because the law, which was made for my preservation, where it cannot interpose to secure my life from present force, which if lost is capable of no reparation, permits me my own defence and the right of war, a liberty to kill the aggressor, because the aggressor allows not time to appeal to our common judge, nor the decision of the law, for remedy in a case where the mischief may be irreparable. . . .

20. But when the actual force is over, the state of war ceases between those that are in society and are equally on both sides subject to the judge. . . .

CHAPTER IV

Of Slavery

21. The natural liberty of man is to be free from any superior power on earth, and not to be under the will or legislative authority of man, but to have only the law of Nature for his rule. The liberty of man in society is to be under no other legislative power but that established by consent in the

common-wealth, nor under the dominion of any will, or restraint of any law, but what that legislative shall enact according to the trust put in it. Freedom, then, is not what Sir Robert Filmer tells us: "A liberty for every one to do what he lists, to live as he pleases, and not to be tied by any laws"; but freedom of men under government is to have a standing rule to live by, common to every one of that society, and made by the legislative power erected in it. A liberty to follow my own will in all things where that rule prescribes not, not to be subject to the inconstant, uncertain, unknown, arbitrary will of another man, as freedom of nature is to be under no other restraint but the law of Nature.

22. This freedom from absolute, arbitrary power is so necessary to, and closely joined with, a man's preservation, that he cannot part with it but by what forfeits his preservation and life together. For a man, not having the power of his own life, cannot by compact or his own consent enslave himself to any one, nor put himself under the absolute, arbitrary power of another to take away his life when he pleases. Nobody can give more power than he has himself, and he that cannot take away his own life cannot give another power over it. Indeed, having by his fault forfeited his own life by some act that deserves death, he to whom he has forfeited it may, when he has him in his power, delay to take it, and make use of him to his own service; and he does him no injury by it. For, whenever he finds the hardship of his slavery outweigh the value of his life, it is in his power, by resisting the will of his master, to draw on himself the death he desires.

23. This is the perfect condition of slavery, which is nothing else but the state of war continued between a lawful conqueror and a captive, for if once compact enter between them, and make an agreement for a limited power on the one side, and obedience on the other, the state of war and slavery ceases as long as the compact endures; for, as has been said, no man can by agreement pass over to another that which he hath not in himself—a power over his own life.

I confess, we find among the Jews, as well as other nations, that men did sell themselves; but it is plain this was only to drudgery, not to slavery; for it is evident the person sold was not under an absolute, arbitrary, despotical power, for the master could not have power to kill him at any time, whom at a certain time he was obliged to let go free out of his service; and the master of such a servant was so far from having an arbitrary power over his life that he could not at pleasure so much as maim him, but the loss of an eye or tooth set him free (Exod. xxi.).

CHAPTER V

Of Property

24. Whether we consider natural reason, which tells us that men, being once born, have a right to their preservation, and consequently to meat and drink and such other things as Nature affords for their subsistence, or "revelation," which gives us an account of those grants God made of the world to Adam, and to Noah and his sons, it is very clear that God, as King David says (Psalm cxv. 16), "has given the earth to the children of men," given it to mankind in common. But, this being supposed, it seems to some a very great difficulty how any one should ever come to have a property in anything. . . . I shall endeavour to show how men might come to have a property in several parts of that which God gave to mankind in common, and that without any express compact of all the commoners.

25. God, who hath given the world to men in common, hath also given them reason to make use of it to the best advantage of life and convenience. The earth and all that is therein is given to men for the support and comfort of their being. And though all the fruits it naturally produces, and beasts it feeds, belong to mankind in common . . . yet being given for the use of men,

there must of necessity be a means to appropriate them some way or other before they can be of any use, or at all beneficial, to any particular men. The fruit or venison which nourishes the wild Indian, who knows no enclosure, and is still a tenant in common, must be his . . . before it can do him any good for the support of his life.

26. Though the earth and all inferior creatures be common to all men, yet every man has a "property" in his own "person." This nobody has any right to but himself. The "labour" of his body and the "work" of his hands, we may say, are properly his. Whatsoever, then, he removes out of the state that Nature hath provided and left it in, he hath mixed his labour with it, and joined to it something that is his own, and thereby makes it his property. It being by him removed from the common state Nature placed it in, it hath by this labour something annexed to it that excludes the common right of other men. For this "labour" being the unquestionable property of the labourer, no man but he can have a right to what that is once joined to, at least where there is enough, and as good left in common for others. . . .

30. It will, perhaps, be objected to this, that if gathering the acorns or other fruits of the earth, etc., makes a right to them, then any one may engross as much as he will. To which I answer, Not so. The same law of Nature that does by this means give us property, does also bound that property too. "God has given us all things richly." Is the voice of reason confirmed by inspiration? But how far has He given it us—"to enjoy"? As much as any one can make use of to any advantage of life before it spoils, so much he may by his labour fix a property in. Whatever is beyond this is more than his share, and belongs to others. Nothing was made by God for man to spoil or destroy. . . .

31. But the chief matter of property being now not the fruits of the earth and the beasts that subsist on it but the earth itself, as that which takes in and carries with it all the rest, I think it is plain that property in that

too is acquired as the former. As much land as a man tills, plants, improves, cultivates, and can use the product of, so much is his property. He by his labour does, as it were, enclose it from the common. Nor will it invalidate his right to say everybody else has an equal title to it, and therefore he cannot appropriate, he cannot enclose, without the consent of all his fellow-commoners, all mankind. God, when He gave the world in common to all mankind, commanded man also to labour, and the penury of his condition required it of him. God and his reason commanded him to subdue the earth—*i.e.*, improve it for the benefit of life and therein lay out something upon it that was his own, his labour. He that, in obedience to this command of God, subdued, tilled, and sowed any part of it, thereby annexed to it something that was his property, which another had no title to, nor could without injury take from him.

32. Nor was this appropriation of any parcel of land, by improving it, any prejudice to any other man, since there was still enough and as good left, and more than the yet unprovided could use. So that, in effect, there was never the less left for others because of his enclosure for himself. For he that leaves as much as another can make use of does as good as take nothing at all. . . .

34. It is true, in land that is common in England or any other country, where there are plenty of people under government who have money and commerce, no one can enclose or appropriate any part without the consent of all his fellow-commoners; because this is left common by compact—*i.e.*, by the law of the land, which is not to be violated. . . .

36. . . . This I dare boldly affirm, that the same rule of propriety—viz., that every man should have as much as he could make use of, would hold still in the world, without straitening anybody, since there is land enough in the world to suffice double the inhabitants, had not the invention of money, and the tacit agreement of men to put a value on it, introduced (by consent) larger

possessions and a right to them; which, how it has done, I shall by and by show more at large. . . .

40. Nor is it so strange as, perhaps, before consideration, it may appear, that the property of labour should be able to overbalance the community of land, for it is labour indeed that puts the difference of value on everything; and let any one consider what the difference is between an acre of land planted with tobacco or sugar, sown with wheat or barley, and an acre of the same land lying in common without any husbandry upon it, and he will find that the improvement of labour makes the far greater part of the value. I think it will be but a very modest computation to say, that of the products of the earth useful to the life of man, nine-tenths are the effects of labour. Nay, if we will rightly estimate things as they come to our use, and cast up the several expenses about them—what in them is purely owing to Nature and what to labour—we shall find that in most of them ninety-nine hundredths are wholly to be put on the account of labour. . . .

45. Thus labour, in the beginning, gave a right of property, wherever any one was pleased to employ it, upon what was common, which remained a long while, the far greater part, and is yet more than mankind makes use of. Men at first, for the most part, contented themselves with what unassisted Nature offered to their necessities; and though afterwards, in some parts of the world, where the increase of people and stock, with the use of money, had made land scarce, and so of some value, the several communities settled the bounds of their distinct territories, and, by laws, within themselves, regulated the properties of the private men of their society, and so, by compact and agreement, settled the property which labour and industry began. And the leagues that have been made between several states and kingdoms, either expressly or tacitly disowning all claim and right to the land in the other's possession, have, by common consent, given up their pretences to their natural common right, which origi-

nally they had to those countries; and so have, by positive agreement, settled a property amongst themselves, in distinct parts of the world; yet there are still great tracts of ground to be found, which the inhabitants thereof, not having joined with the rest of mankind in the consent of the use of their common money, lie waste, and are more than the people who dwell on it, do, or can make use of, and so still lie in common; though this can scarce happen amongst that part of mankind that have consented to the use of money.

46. The greatest part of things really useful to the life of man, and such as the necessity of subsisting made the first commoners of the world look after—as it doth the Americans now—are generally things of short duration, such as—if they are not consumed by use—will decay and perish of themselves. Gold, silver, and diamonds are things that fancy or agreement hath put the value on, more than real use and the necessary support of life. Now of those good things which Nature hath provided in common, every one hath a right (as hath been said) to as much as he could use, and had a property in all he could effect with his labour; all that his industry could extend to, to alter from the state Nature had put it in, was his. He that gathered a hundred bushels of acorns or apples had thereby a property in them; they were his goods as soon as gathered. He was only to look that he used them before they spoiled, else he took more than his share, and robbed others. And, indeed, it was a foolish thing, as well as dishonest, to hoard up more than he could make use of. If he gave away a part to anybody else, so that it perished not uselessly in his possession, these he also made use of. And if he also bartered away plums that would have rotted in a week, for nuts that would last good for his eating a whole year, he did no injury; he wasted not the common stock; destroyed no part of the portion of goods that belonged to others, so long as nothing perished uselessly in his hands. Again, if he would give his nuts for a piece of metal, pleased with its colour, or exchange his sheep for shells, or

wool for a sparkling pebble or a diamond, and keep those by him all his life, he invaded not the right of others; he might heap up as much of these durable things as he pleased; the exceeding of the bounds of his just property not lying in the largeness of his possession, but the perishing of anything uselessly in it.

47. And thus came in the use of money; some lasting thing that men might keep without spoiling, and that, by mutual consent, men would take in exchange for the truly useful but perishable supports of life.

48. And as different degrees of industry were apt to give men possessions in different proportions, so this invention of money gave them the opportunity to continue and enlarge them. . . .

50. But since gold and silver, being little useful to the life of man, in proportion to food, raiment, and carriage, has its value only from the consent of men—whereof labour yet makes in great part the measure—it is plain that the consent of men have agreed to a disproportionate and unequal possession of the earth—I mean out of the bounds of society and compact; for in governments the laws regulate it; they having, by consent, found out and agreed in a way how a man may, rightfully and without injury, possess more than he himself can make use of by receiving gold and silver, which may continue long in a man's possession without decaying for the overplus, and agreeing those metals should have a value. . . .

CHAPTER VI

Of Paternal Power

54. Though I have said above (2) "That all men by nature are equal," I cannot be supposed to understand all sorts of "equality." Age or virtue may give men a just precedency. Excellency of parts and merit may place others above the common level. Birth may subject some, and alliance or benefits others, to pay an observance to those to whom Nature, gratitude, or other respects, may have made it due; and yet all this consists with the equality which all men are in in respect of jurisdiction or dominion one over another, which was the equality I there spoke of as proper to the business in hand, being that equal right that every man hath to his natural freedom, without being subjected to the will or authority of any other man.

55. Children, I confess, are not born in this full state of equality, though they are born to it. Their parents have a sort of rule and jurisdiction over them when they come into the world, and for some time after, but it is but a temporary one. The bonds of this subjection are like the swaddling clothes they are wrapt up in and supported by in the weakness of their infancy. Age and reason as they grow up loosen them, till at length they drop quite off, and leave a man at his own free disposal.

56. . . . Adam and Eve, and after them all parents were, by the law of Nature, under an obligation to preserve, nourish and educate the children they had begotten, not as their own workmanship, but the workmanship of their own Maker, the Almighty, to whom they were to be accountable for them.

57. The law that was to govern Adam was the same that was to govern all his posterity, the law of reason. But his offspring having another way of entrance into the world, different from him, by a natural birth, that produced them ignorant, and without the use of reason, they were not presently under that law. For nobody can be under a law that is not promulgated to him; and this law being promulgated or made known by reason only, he that is not come to the use of his reason cannot be said to be under this law; and Adam's children being not presently as soon as born under this law of reason, were not presently free. For law, in its true notion, is not so much the limitation as the direction of a free and intelligent agent to his proper interest, and prescribes no farther than is for the general good of those under that law. Could they be happier without it, the law, as a useless thing, would of itself vanish; and that ill deserves the

name of confinement which hedges us in only from bogs and precipices. So that however it may be mistaken, the end of law is not to abolish or restrain, but to preserve and enlarge freedom. For in all the states of created beings, capable of laws, where there is no law there is no freedom. For liberty is to be free from restraint and violence from others, which cannot be where there is no law; and is not, as we are told, "a liberty for every man to do what he lists." For who could be free, when every other man's humour might domineer over him? But a liberty to dispose and order freely as he lists his person, actions, possessions, and his whole property within the allowance of those laws under which he is, and therein not to be subject to the arbitrary will of another, but freely follow his own.

58. The power, then, that parents have over their children arises from that duty which is incumbent on them, to take care of their offspring during the imperfect state of childhood. To inform the mind, and govern the actions of their yet ignorant nonage, till reason shall take its place and ease them of that trouble, is what the children want, and the parents are bound to. . . .

59. . . . But after that the father and son are equally free, as much as tutor and pupil, after nonage, equally subjects of the same law together, without any dominion left in the father over the life, liberty, or estate of his son, whether they be only in the state and under the law of Nature, or under the positive laws of an established government. . . .

61. Thus we are born free as we are born rational; not that we have actually the exercise of either: age that brings one, brings with it the other too. And thus we see how natural freedom and subjection to parents may consist together, and are both founded on the same principle. A child is free by his father's title, by his father's understanding, which is to govern him till he hath it of his own. The freedom of a man at years of discretion, and the subjection of a child to his parents, whilst yet short of it, are so consistent and so distinguishable that the most blinded contenders for monarchy, "by right of fatherhood," cannot miss of it; the most obstinate cannot but allow of it. . . . If anybody should ask me when my son is of age to be free, I shall answer, just when his monarch is of age to govern. . . .

63. The freedom then of man, and liberty of acting according to his own will, is grounded on his having reason, which is able to instruct him in that law he is to govern himself by, and make him know how far he is left to the freedom of his own will. To turn him loose to an unrestrained liberty, before he has reason to guide him, is not the allowing him the privilege of his nature to be free, but to thrust him out amongst brutes, and abandon him to a state as wretched and as much beneath that of a man as theirs. This is that which puts the authority into the parents' hands to govern the minority of their children. . . .

64. But what reason can hence advance this care of the parents due to their offspring into an absolute, arbitrary dominion of the father, whose power reaches no farther than by such a discipline as he finds most effectual to give such strength and health to their bodies, such vigour and rectitude to their minds, as may best fit his children to be most useful to themselves and others, and, if it be necessary to his condition, to make them work when they are able for their own subsistence; but in this power the mother, too, has her share with the father. . . .

65. . . . And if the father die whilst the children are young, do they not naturally everywhere owe the same obedience to their mother, during their minority, as to their father, were he alive? And will any one say that the mother hath a legislative power over her children that she can make standing rules which shall be of perpetual obligation, by which they ought to regulate all the concerns of their property, and bound their liberty all the course of their lives, and enforce the observation of them with capital punishments? For this is the proper power of the magistrate, of which the father hath not so much as the shadow. His command over his children is but temporary, and

reaches not their life or property. It is but a help to the weakness and imperfection of their nonage, a discipline necessary to their education. . . .

66. But though there be a time when a child comes to be as free from subjection to the will and command of his father as he himself is free from subjection to the will of anybody else, and they are both under no other restraint but that which is common to them both, whether it be the law of Nature or municipal law of their country, yet this freedom exempts not a son from that honour which he ought, by the law of God and Nature, to pay his parents, God having made the parents instruments in His great design of continuing the race of mankind and the occasions of life to their children. . . . From this obligation no state, no freedom, can absolve children. But this is very far from giving parents a power of command over their children, or an authority to make laws and dispose as they please of their lives or liberties. It is one thing to owe honour, respect, gratitude, and assistance; another to require an absolute obedience and submission. The honour due to parents a monarch on his throne owes his mother, and yet this lessens not his authority nor subjects him to her government.

67. . . . The want of distinguishing these two powers which the father hath, in the right of tuition, during minority, and the right of honour all his life, may perhaps have caused a great part of the mistakes about this matter. For, to speak properly of them, the first of these is rather the privilege of children and duty of parents than any prerogative of paternal power. The nourishment and education of their children is a charge so incumbent on parents for their children's good, that nothing can absolve them from taking care of it. And though the power of commanding and chastising them go along with it, yet God hath woven into the principles of human nature such a tenderness for their offspring, that there is little fear that parents should use their power with too much rigour; the excess is

seldom on the severe side, the strong bias of nature drawing the other way. . . .

68. . . . On the other side, honour and support all that which gratitude requires to return; for the benefits received by and from them is the indispensable duty of the child and the proper privilege of the parents. This is intended for the parents' advantage, as the other is for the child's. . . .

71. This shows the reason how it comes to pass that parents in societies, where they themselves are subjects, retain a power over their children and have as much right to their subjection as those who are in the state of Nature, which could not possibly be if all political power were only paternal, and that, in truth, they were one and the same thing; for then, all paternal power being in the prince, the subject could naturally have none of it. But these two powers, political and paternal, are so perfectly distinct and separate, and built upon so different foundations, and given to so different ends, that every subject that is a father has as much a paternal power over his children as the prince has over his. And every prince that has parents owes them as much filial duty and obedience as the meanest of his subjects do to theirs, and can therefore contain not any part or degree of that kind of dominion which a prince or magistrate has over his subject.

72. Though the obligation on the parents to bring up their children, and the obligation on children to honour their parents, contain all the power, on the one hand, and submission on the other, which are proper to this relation, yet there is another power ordinarily in the father, whereby he has a tie on the obedience of his children, which, though it be common to him with other men, yet the occasions of showing it, almost constantly happening to fathers in their private families and in instances of it elsewhere being rare, and less taken notice of, it passes in the world for a part of "paternal jurisdiction." And this is the power men generally have to bestow their estates on those who please them best. . . .

73. This is no small tie to the obedience of children; and there being always annexed to the enjoyment of land a submission to the government of the country of which that land is a part, it has been commonly supposed that a father could oblige his posterity to that government of which he himself was a subject, that his compact held them; whereas, it being only a necessary condition annexed to the land which is under that government, reaches only those who will take it on that condition, and so is no natural tie or engagement, but a voluntary submission; for every man's children being, by Nature, as free as himself or any of his ancestors ever were, may, whilst they are in that freedom, choose what society they will join themselves to, what commonwealth they will put themselves under. But if they will enjoy the inheritance of their ancestors, they must take it on the same terms their ancestors had it, and submit to all the conditions annexed to such a possession. By this power, indeed, fathers oblige their children to obedience to themselves even when they are past minority, and most commonly, too, subject them to this or that political power. But neither of these by any peculiar right of fatherhood, but by the reward they have in their hands to enforce and recompense such a compliance, and is no more power than what a Frenchman has over an Englishman, who, by the hopes of an estate he will leave him, will certainly have a strong tie on his obedience; and if when it is left him, he will enjoy it, he must certainly take it upon the conditions annexed to the possession of land in that country where it lies, whether it be France or England.

74. . . . it is obvious to conceive how easy it was, in the first ages of the world, and in places still where the thinness of people gives families leave to separate into unpossessed quarters, and they have room to remove and plant themselves in yet vacant habitations, for the father of the family to become the prince of it; he had been a ruler from the beginning of the infancy of his children; and when they were grown up, since without some government it would be hard for them to live together, it was likeliest it should, by the express or tacit consent of the children, be in the father, where it seemed, without any change, barely to continue. . . . But that this was not by any paternal right, but only by the consent of his children, was evident. . . .

76. Thus the natural fathers of families, by an insensible change, became the politic monarchs of them too; and as they chanced to live long, and leave able and worthy heirs for several successions or otherwise, so they laid the foundations of hereditary or elective kingdoms under several constitutions and manors, according as chance, contrivance, or occasions happened to mould them. . . .

CHAPTER VII

Of Political or Civil Society

87. Man being born, as has been proved, with a title to perfect freedom and an uncontrolled enjoyment of all the rights and privileges of the law of Nature, equally with any other man, or number of men in the world, hath by nature a power not only to preserve his property—that is, his life, liberty, and estate, against the injuries and attempts of other men, but to judge of and punish the breaches of that law in others, as he is persuaded the offence deserves, even with death itself, in crimes where the heinousness of the fact, in his opinion, requires it. But because no political society can be, nor subsist, without having in itself the power to preserve the property, and in order thereunto punish the offences of all those of that society, there, and there only, is political society where every one of the members hath quitted this natural power, resigned it up into the hands of the community in all cases that exclude him not from appealing for protection to the law established by it. And thus all private judgment of every particular member being excluded, the community comes to be umpire, and by understanding indifferent rules and men authorised by the community for their execution, decides all the differences that

may happen between any members of that society concerning any matter of right, and punishes those offences which any member hath committed against the society with such penalties as the law has established; whereby it is easy to discern who are, and are not, in political society together. Those who are united into one body, and have a common established law and judicature to appeal to, with authority to decide controversies between them and punish offenders, are in civil society one with another; but those who have no such common appeal, I mean on earth, are still in the state of Nature, each being where there is no other, judge for himself and executioner; which is, as I have before showed it, the perfect state of Nature.

88. And thus the commonwealth comes by a power to set down what punishment shall belong to the several transgressions they think worthy of it, committed amongst the members of that society (which is the power of making laws), as well as it has the power to punish any injury done unto any of its members by any one that is not of it (which is the power of war and peace); and all this for the preservation of the property of all the members of that society, as far as is possible. But though every man entered into society has quitted his power to punish offences against the law of Nature in prosecution of his own private judgment, yet with the judgment of offences which he has given up to the legislative, in all cases where he can appeal to the magistrate, he has given up a right to the commonwealth to employ his force for the execution of the judgments of the commonwealth whenever he shall be called to it, which, indeed, are his own judgments, they being made by himself or his representative. And herein we have the original of the legislative and executive power of civil society, which is to judge by standing laws how far offences are to be punished when committed within the commonwealth; and also by occasional judgments founded on the present circumstances of the fact, how far injuries from without are to be vindicated, and in both these to

employ all the force of all the members when there shall be need.

89. Wherever, therefore, any number of men so unite into one society as to quit every one his executive power of the law of Nature, and to resign it to the public, there and there only is a political or civil society. . . .

90. And hence it is evident that absolute monarchy, which by some men is counted for the only government in the world, is indeed inconsistent with civil society, and so can be no form of civil government at all. For the end of civil society being to avoid and remedy those inconveniences of the state of Nature which necessarily follow from every man's being judge in his own case, by setting up a known authority to which every one of that society may appeal upon any injury received, or controversy that may arise, and which every one of the society ought to obey. Wherever any persons are who have not such an authority to appeal to, and decide any difference between them there, those persons are still in the state of Nature. And so is every absolute prince in respect of those who are under his dominion.

91. For he being supposed to have all, both legislative and executive, power in himself alone, there is no judge to be found, no appeal lies open to any one, who may fairly and indifferently, and with authority decide, and from whence relief and redress may be expected of any injury or inconveniency that may be suffered from him, or by his order. So that such a man, however entitled, Czar, or Grand Signior, or how you please, is as much in the state of Nature, with all under his dominion, as he is with the rest of mankind. . . .

92. For he that thinks absolute power purifies men's blood, and corrects the baseness of human nature, need read but the history of this, or any other age, to be convinced to the contrary. . . .

94. . . . No man in civil society can be exempted from the laws of it. For if any man may do what he thinks fit and there be no appeal on earth for redress or security against any harm he shall do, I ask whether

he be not perfectly still in the state of Nature, and so can be no part or member of that civil society, unless any one will say the state of Nature and civil society are one and the same thing, which I have never yet found any one so great a patron of anarchy as to affirm.

CHAPTER VIII

Of the Beginning of Political Societies

95. Men being, as has been said, by nature all free, equal, and independent, no one can be put out of this estate and subjected to the political power of another without his own consent, which is done by agreeing with other men, to join and unite into a community for their comfortable, safe, and peaceable living, one amongst another, in a secure enjoyment of their properties, and a greater security against any that are not of it. This any number of men may do, because it injures not the freedom of the rest; they are left, as they were, in the liberty of the state of Nature. When any number of men have so consented to make one community or government, they are thereby presently incorporated, and make one body politic, wherein the majority have a right to act and conclude the rest. . . .

97. And thus every man, by consenting with others to make one body politic under one government, puts himself under an obligation to every one of that society to submit to the determination of the majority, and to be concluded by it; or else this original compact, whereby he with others incorporates into one society, would signify nothing, and be no compact if he be left free and under no other ties than he was in before in the state of Nature. . . .

98. For if the consent of the majority shall not in reason be received as the act of the whole, and conclude every individual, nothing but the consent of every individual can make anything to be the act of the whole. . . . Such a constitution as this would make the mighty leviathan of a shorter duration than the feeblest creatures, and not let it outlast the day it was born in, which cannot be supposed till we can think that rational creatures should desire and constitute societies only to be dissolved. For where the majority cannot conclude the rest, there they cannot act as one body, and consequently will be immediately dissolved again. . . .

100. To this I find two objections made: 1. That there are no instances to be found in story of a company of men, independent and equal one amongst another, that met together, and in this way began and set up a government. 2. It is impossible of right that men should do so, because all men, being born under government, they are to submit to that, and are not at liberty to begin a new one.

101. To the first there is this to answer: That it is not at all to be wondered that history gives us but a very little account of men that lived together in the state of Nature. The inconveniences of that condition, and the love and want of society, no sooner brought any number of them together, but they presently united and incorporated if they designed to continue together. And if we may not suppose men ever to have been in the state of Nature, because we hear not much of them in such a state, we may as well suppose the armies of Salmanasser or Xerxes were never children, because we hear little of them till they were men and embodied in armies. Government is everywhere antecedent to records, and letters seldom come in amongst a people till a long continuation of civil society has, by other more necessary arts, provided for their safety, ease, and plenty. And then they begin to look after the history of their founders, and search into their original when they have outlived the memory of it. . . .

112. Thus we may see how probable it is that people that were naturally free, and, by their own consent, either submitted to the government of their father, or united together, out of different families, to make a government, should generally put the rule into one man's hands, and choose to be under the conduct of a single person, with-

out so much, as by express conditions, limiting or regulating his power, which they thought safe enough in his honesty and prudence; though they never dreamed of monarchy being *jure Divino,* which we never heard of among mankind till it was revealed to us by the divinity of this last age, nor ever allowed paternal power to have a right to dominion or to be the foundation of all government. And thus much may suffice to show that, as far as we have any light from history, we have reason to conclude that all peaceful beginnings of government have been laid in the consent of the people. I say "peaceful," because I shall have occasion, in another place, to speak of conquest, which some esteem a way of beginning of governments.

The other objection, I find, urged against the beginning of polities, in the way I have mentioned, is this, viz.:

113. "That all men being born under government, some or other, it is impossible any of them should ever be free and at liberty to unite together and begin a new one, or ever be able to erect a lawful government." If this argument be good, I ask, How came so many lawful monarchies into the world? For if anybody, upon this supposition, can show me any one man, in any age of the world, free to begin a lawful monarchy, I will be bound to show him ten other free men at liberty, at the same time, to unite and begin a new government under a regal or any other form. It being demonstration that if any one born under the dominion of another may be so free as to have a right to command others in a new and distinct empire, every one that is born under the dominion of another may be so free too, and may become a ruler or subject of a distinct separate government. And so, by this their own principle, either all men, however born, are free, or else there is but one lawful prince, one lawful government in the world; and then they have nothing to do but barely to show us which that is, which, when they have done, I doubt not but all mankind will easily agree to pay obedience to him. . . .

115. For there are no examples so frequent in history, both sacred and profane, as those of men withdrawing themselves and their obedience from the jurisdiction they were born under, and the family or community they were bred up in, and setting up new governments in other places, from whence sprang all that number of petty commonwealths in the beginning of ages, and which always multiplied as long as there was room enough, till the stronger or more fortunate swallowed the weaker; and those great ones, again breaking to pieces, dissolved into lesser dominions. . . .

116. . . . It is true that whatever engagements or promises any one made for himself, he is under the obligation of them, but cannot by any compact whatsoever bind his children or posterity. For his son, when a man, being altogether as free as the father, any act of the father can no more give away the liberty of the son than it can of anybody else. . . .

117. . . . Commonwealths not permitting any part of their dominions to be dismembered, nor to be enjoyed by any but those of their community, the son cannot ordinarily enjoy the possessions of his father but under the same terms his father did, by becoming a member of the society, whereby he puts himself presently under the government he finds there established, as much as any other subject of that commonweal. And thus the consent of free men, born under government, which only makes them members of it, being given separately in their turns, as each comes to be of age, and not in a multitude together, people take no notice of it, and thinking it not done at all, or not necessary, conclude they are naturally subjects as they are men.

118. . . . A child is born a subject of no country nor government. He is under his father's tuition and authority till he come to age of discretion, and then he is a free man, at liberty what government he will put himself under, what body politic he will unite himself to. . . .

119. . . . Nobody doubts but an express consent of any man, entering into any society, makes him a perfect member of that society,

a subject of that government. The difficulty is, what ought to be looked upon as a tacit consent, and how far it binds—*i.e.,* how far any one shall be looked on to have consented, and thereby submitted to any government, where he has made no expressions of it at all. And to this I say, that every man that hath any possession or enjoyment of any part of the dominions of any government doth hereby give his tacit consent, and is as far forth obliged to obedience to the laws of that government, during such enjoyment, as any one under it, whether this his possession be of land to him and his heirs for ever, or a lodging only for a week; or whether it be barely travelling freely on the highway; and, in effect, it reaches as far as the very being of any one within the territories of that government.

120. To understand this the better, it is fit to consider that every man when he at first incorporates himself into any commonwealth, he, by his uniting himself thereunto, annexes also, and submits to the community those possessions which he has, or shall acquire, that do not already belong to any other government. For it would be a direct contradiction for any one to enter into society with others for the securing and regulating of property, and yet to suppose his land, whose property is to be regulated by the laws of the society, should be exempt from the jurisdiction of that government to which he himself, and the property of the land, is a subject. By the same act, therefore, whereby any one unites his person, which was before free, to any commonwealth, by the same he unites his possessions, which were before free, to it also; and they become, both of them, person and possession, subject to the government and dominion of that commonwealth as long as it hath a being. Whoever therefore, from thence forth, by inheritance, purchases permission, or otherwise enjoys any part of the land so annexed to, and under the government of that commonweal, must take it with the condition it is under—that is, of submitting to the government of the commonwealth, under

whose jurisdiction it is, as far forth as any subject of it.

121. But since the government has a direct jurisdiction only over the land and reaches the possessor of it (before he has actually incorporated himself in the society) only as he dwells upon and enjoys that, the obligation any one is under by virtue of such enjoyment to submit to the government begins and ends with the enjoyment; so that whenever the owner, who has given nothing but such a tacit consent to the government will, by donation, sale or otherwise, quit the said possession, he is at liberty to go and incorporate himself into any other commonwealth, or agree with others to begin a new one *in vacuis locis,* in any part of the world they can find free and unpossessed; whereas he that has once, by actual agreement and any express declaration, given his consent to be of any commonweal, is perpetually and indispensably obliged to be, and remain unalterably a subject to it, and can never be again in the liberty of the state of Nature, unless by any calamity the government he was under comes to be dissolved.

122. But submitting to the laws of any country, living quietly and enjoying privileges and protection under them, makes not a man a member of that society; it is only a local protection and homage due to and from all those who, not being in a state of war, come within the territories belonging to any government, to all parts whereof the force of its law extends. But this no more makes a man a member of that society, a perpetual subject of that commonwealth, than it would make a man a subject to another in whose family he found it convenient to abide for some time, though, whilst he continued in it, he were obliged to comply with the laws and submit to the government he found there. And thus we see that foreigners, by living all their lives under another government, and enjoying the privileges and protection of it, though they are bound, even in conscience, to submit to its administration as far forth as any denizen, yet do not thereby come to be subjects or members of that commonwealth. Nothing

can make any man so but his actually entering into it by positive engagement and express promise and compact. This is that which, I think, concerning the beginning of political societies, and that consent which makes any one a member of any commonwealth.

CHAPTER IX

Of the Ends of Political Society and Government

123. If man in the state of Nature be so free as has been said, if he be absolute lord of his own person and possessions, equal to the greatest and subject to nobody, why will he part with his freedom, this empire, and subject himself to the dominion and control of any other power? To which it is obvious to answer, that though in the state of Nature he hath such a right, yet the enjoyment of it is very uncertain and constantly exposed to the invasion of others. . . . This makes him willing to quit this condition which, however free, is full of fears and continual dangers; and it is not without reason that he seeks out and is willing to join in society with others who are already united, or have a mind to unite for the mutual preservation of their lives, liberties and estates, which I call by the general name—property.

124. The great and chief end, therefore, of men uniting into commonwealths, and putting themselves under government, is the preservation of their property; to which in the state of Nature there are many things wanting.

Firstly, there wants an established, settled, known law. . . .

125. Secondly, in the state of Nature there wants a known and indifferent judge, with authority to determine all differences according to the established law. . . .

126. Thirdly, in the state of Nature there often wants power to back and support the sentence when right, and to give it due execution. . . .

131. But though men when they enter into society give up the equality, liberty, and ex-

ecutive power they had in the state of Nature into the hands of the society, to be so far disposed of by the legislative as the good of the society shall require, yet it being only with an intention in every one the better to preserve himself, his liberty and property (for no rational creature can be supposed to change his condition with an intention to be worse), the power of the society or legislative constituted by them can never be supposed to extend farther than the common good, but is obliged to secure every one's property by providing against those three defects above mentioned that made the state of Nature so unsafe and uneasy. And so, whoever has the legislative or supreme power of any commonwealth, is bound to govern by established standing laws, promulgated and known to the people, and not by extemporary decrees, by indifferent and upright judges, who are to decide controversies by those laws; and to employ the force of the community at home only in the execution of such laws, or abroad to prevent or redress foreign injuries and secure the community from inroads and invasion. And all this to be directed to no other end but the peace, safety, and public good of the people.

CHAPTER XI

Of the Extent of the Legislative Power

135. Though the legislative, whether placed in one or more, whether it be always in being or only by intervals, though it be the supreme power in every commonwealth, yet, first, it is not, nor can possibly be, absolutely arbitrary over the lives and fortunes of the people. For it being but the joint power of every member of the society given up to that person or assembly which is legislator, it can be no more than those persons had in a state of Nature before they entered into society, and gave it up to the community. For nobody can transfer to another more power than he has in himself, and nobody has an absolute arbitrary power over himself, or over any other, to destroy his own life,

or take away the life or property of another. A man, as has been proved, cannot subject himself to the arbitrary power of another; and having, in the state of Nature, no arbitrary power over the life, liberty, or possession of another, but only so much as the law of Nature gave him for the preservation of himself and the rest of mankind, this is all he doth, or can give up to the commonwealth, and by it to the legislative power, so that the legislative can have no more than this. Their power in the utmost bounds of it is limited to the public good of the society.... The obligations of the law of Nature cease not in society, but only in many cases are drawn closer, and have, by human laws, known penalties annexed to them to enforce their observation. Thus the law of Nature stands as an eternal rule to all men, legislators as well as others. The rules that they make for other men's actions must, as well as their own and other men's actions, be conformable to the law of Nature—*i.e.*, to the will of God, of which that is a declaration, and the fundamental law of Nature being the preservation of mankind, no human sanction can be good or valid against it.

136. Secondly, the legislative or supreme authority cannot assume to itself a power to rule by extemporary arbitrary decrees, but is bound to dispense justice and decide the rights of the subject by promulgated standing laws, and known authorised judges .... Men give up all their natural power to the society they enter into, and the community put the legislative power into such hands as they think fit, with this trust, that they shall be governed by declared laws, or else their peace, quiet, and property will still be at the same uncertainty as it was in the state of Nature.

137. ... It cannot be supposed that they should intend, had they a power so to do, to give any one or more an absolute arbitrary power over their persons and estates, and put a force into the magistrate's hand to execute his unlimited will arbitrarily upon them; this were to put themselves into a worse condition than the state of Nature,

wherein they had a liberty to defend their right against the injuries of others, and were upon equal terms of force to maintain it, whether invaded by a single man or many in combination. Whereas by supposing they have given up themselves to the absolute arbitrary power and will of a legislator, they have disarmed themselves, and armed him to make a prey of them when he pleases....

138. Thirdly, the supreme power cannot take from any man any part of his property without his own consent. For the preservation of property being the end of government, and that for which men enter into society, it necessarily supposes and requires that the people should have property, without which they must be supposed to lose that by entering into society which was the end for which they entered into it; too gross an absurdity for any man to own. ...

141. Fourthly. The legislative cannot transfer the power of making laws to any other hands, for it being but a delegated power from the people, they who have it cannot pass it over to others. The people alone can appoint the form of the commonwealth, which is by constituting the legislative, and appointing in whose hands that shall be. And when the people have said, "We will submit, and be governed by laws made by such men, and in such forms," nobody else can say other men shall make laws for them; nor can they be bound by any laws but such as are enacted by those whom they have chosen and authorised to make laws for them.

CHAPTER XIII

Of the Subordination of the Powers of the Commonwealth

149. Though in a constituted commonwealth standing upon its own basis and acting according to its own nature—that is, acting for the preservation of the community, there can be but one supreme power, which is the legislative, to which all the rest are and must be subordinate, yet the legislative being only a fiduciary power to act for certain

ends, there remains still in the people a supreme power to remove or alter the legislative, when they find the legislative act contrary to the trust reposed in them. For all power given with trust for the attaining an end being limited by that end, whenever that end is manifestly neglected or opposed, the trust must necessarily be forfeited, and the power devolve into the hands of those that gave it, who may place it anew where they shall think best for their safety and security. And thus the community perpetually retains a supreme power of saving themselves from the attempts and designs of anybody, even of their legislators, whenever they shall be so foolish or so wicked as to lay and carry on designs against the liberties and properties of the subject. . . .

151. In some commonwealths where the legislative is not always in being, and the executive is vested in a single person who has also a share in the legislative, there that single person, in a very tolerable sense, may also be called supreme; not that he has in himself all the supreme power, which is that of law-making, but because he has in him the supreme execution from whom all inferior magistrates derive all their several subordinate powers, or, at least, the greatest part of them; having also no legislative superior to him, there being no law to be made without his consent, which cannot be expected should ever subject him to the other part of the legislative, he is properly enough in this sense supreme. But yet it is to be observed that though oaths of allegiance and fealty are taken to him, it is not to him as supreme legislator, but as supreme executor of the law made by a joint power of him with others, allegiance being nothing but an obedience according to law, which, when he violates, he has no right to obedience, nor can claim it otherwise than as the public person vested with the power of the law, and so is to be considered as the image, phantom, or representative of the commonwealth, acted by the will of the society declared in its laws, and thus he has no will, no power, but that of the law. But when he quits this representation, this public will,

and acts by his own private will, he degrades himself, and is but a single private person without power and without will; the members owing no obedience but to the public will of the society. . . .

153. It is not necessary—no, nor so much as convenient—that the legislative should be always in being; but absolutely necessary that the executive power should, because there is not always need of new laws to be made, but always need of execution of the laws that are made. When the legislative hath put the execution of the laws they make into other hands, they have a power still to resume it out of those hands when they find cause, and to punish for any maladministration against the laws. . . .

155. . . . In all states and conditions the true remedy of force without authority is to oppose force to it. The use of force without authority always puts him that uses it into a state of war as the aggressor, and renders him liable to be treated accordingly.

CHAPTER XIV

Of Prerogative

159. Where the legislative and executive power are in distinct hands, as they are in all moderated monarchies and well-framed governments, there the good of the society requires that several things should be left to the discretion of him that has the executive power. For the legislators not being able to foresee and provide by laws for all that may be useful to the community, the executor of the laws, having the power in his hands, has by the common law of Nature a right to make use of it for the good of the society, in many cases where the municipal law has given no direction, till the legislative can conveniently be assembled to provide for it; nay, many things there are which the law can by no means provide for, and those must necessarily be left to the discretion of him that has the executive power in his hands, to be ordered by him as the public good and advantage shall require; nay, it is fit that the laws themselves should

in some cases give way to the executive power, or rather to this fundamental law of Nature and government—viz., that as much as may be all the members of the society are to be preserved. For since many accidents may happen wherein a strict and rigid observation of the laws may do harm, as not to pull down an innocent man's house to stop the fire when the next to it is burning; and a man may come sometimes within the reach of the law, which makes no distinction of persons, by an action that may deserve reward and pardon; it is fit the ruler should have a power in many cases to mitigate the severity of the law, and pardon some offenders, since the end of government being the preservation of all as much as may be, even the guilty are to be spared where it can prove no prejudice to the innocent. . . .

163. And therefore they have a very wrong notion of government who say that the people have encroached upon the prerogative when they have got any part of it to be defined by positive laws. For in so doing they have not pulled from the prince anything that of right belonged to him, but only declared that that power which they indefinitely left in his or his ancestors' hands, to be exercised for their good, was not a thing they intended him, when he used it otherwise. For the end of government being the good of the community, whatsoever alterations are made in it tending to that end cannot be an encroachment upon anybody. . . .

168. . . . And where the body of the people, or any single man, are deprived of their right, or are under the exercise of a power without right, having no appeal on earth they have a liberty to appeal to Heaven whenever they judge the cause of sufficient moment. And therefore, though the people cannot be judge, so as to have, by the constitution of that society, any superior power to determine and give effective sentence in the case, yet they have reserved that ultimate determination to themselves which belongs to all mankind, where there lies no appeal on earth, by a law antecedent and paramount to all positive laws of men, whether they have just cause to make their appeal to Heaven. And this judgment they cannot part with, it being out of a man's power so to submit himself to another as to give him a liberty to destroy him; God and Nature never allowing a man so to abandon himself as to neglect his own preservation. And since he cannot take away his own life, neither can he give another power to take it. Nor let any one think this lays a perpetual foundation for disorder; for this operates not till the inconvenience is so great that the majority feel it, and are weary of it, and find a necessity to have it amended. . . .

CHAPTER XVIII

Of Tyranny

199. As usurpation is the exercise of power which another hath a right to, so tyranny is the exercise of power beyond right, which nobody can have a right to; and this is making use of the power any one has in his hands, not for the good of those who are under it, but for his own private, separate advantage. . . .

202. Wherever law ends, tyranny begins, if the law be transgressed to another's harm; and whosoever in authority exceeds the power given him by the law, and makes use of the force he has under his command to compass that upon the subject which the law allows not, ceases in that to be a magistrate, and acting without authority may be opposed, as any other man who by force invades the right of another. . . .

203. May the commands then, of a prince be opposed? May he be resisted, as often as any one shall find himself aggrieved, and but imagine he has not right done him? This will unhinge and over turn all polities, and instead of government and order, leave nothing but anarchy and confusion.

204. To this I answer: That force is to be opposed to nothing but to unjust and unlawful force. Whoever makes any opposition in any other case draws on himself a just condemnation, both from God and man; and so no such danger or confusion will follow, as is often suggested. For—

205. First. As in some countries the person of the prince by the law is sacred, and so whatever he commands or does, his person is still free from all question or violence, not liable to force, or any judicial censure or condemnation. But yet opposition may be made to the illegal acts of any inferior officer or other commissioned by him . . . The harm he can do in his own person not being likely to happen often, nor to extend itself far, nor being able by his single strength to subvert the laws nor oppress the body of the people, should any prince have so much weakness and ill-nature as to be willing to do it. The inconveniency of some particular mischiefs that may happen sometimes when a heady prince comes to the throne are well recompensed by the peace of the public and security of the government in the person of the chief magistrate, thus set out of the reach of danger; it being safer for the body that some few private men should be sometimes in danger to suffer than that the head of the republic should be easily and upon slight occasions exposed.

206. Secondly. But this privilege, belonging only to the king's person, hinders not but they may be questioned, opposed, and resisted, who use unjust force, though they pretend a commission from him which the law authorises not . . . For the king's authority being given him only by the law, he cannot empower any one to act against the law, or justify him by his commission in so doing. The commission or command of any magistrate where he has no authority, being as void and insignificant as that of any private man, the difference between the one and the other being that the magistrate has some authority so far and to such ends, and the private man has none at all; for it is not the commission but the authority that gives the right of acting, and against the laws there can be no authority. But notwithstanding such resistance, the king's person and authority are still both secured, and so no danger to governor or government.

207. Thirdly. Supposing a government wherein the person of the chief magistrate is not thus sacred, yet this doctrine of the lawfulness of resisting all unlawful exercises of his power will not, upon every slight occasion, endanger him or embroil the government; for where the injured party may be relieved and his damages repaired by appeal to the law, there can be no pretence for force, which is only to be used where a man is intercepted from appealing to the law. For nothing is to be accounted hostile force but where it leaves not the remedy of such an appeal, and it is such force alone that puts him that uses it into a state of war, and makes it lawful to resist him. A man with a sword in his hand demands my purse on the highway, when perhaps I have not 12d. in my pocket. This man I may lawfully kill. To another I deliver £100 to hold only whilst I alight, which he refuses to restore me when I am got up again, but draws his sword to defend the possession of it by force. I endeavour to retake it. The mischief this man does me is a hundred, or possibly a thousand times more than the other perhaps intended me (whom I killed before he really did me any); and yet I might lawfully kill the one and cannot so much as hurt the other lawfully. The reason whereof is plain; because the one using force which threatened my life, I could not have time to appeal to the law to secure it, and when it was gone it was too late to appeal. The law could not restore life to my dead carcass. The loss was irreparable; which to prevent the law of Nature gave me a right to destroy him who had put himself into a state of war with me and threatened my destruction. But in the other case, my life not being in danger, I might have the benefit of appealing to the law, and have reparation for my £100 that way.

208. Fourthly. But if the unlawful acts done by the magistrate be maintained (by the power he has got), and the remedy, which is due by law, be by the same power obstructed, yet the right of resisting, even in such manifest acts of tyranny, will not suddenly, or on slight occasions, disturb the government. For if it reach no farther than some private men's cases, though they have a right to defend themselves, and to recover

by force what by unlawful force is taken from them, yet the right to do so will not easily engage them in a contest wherein they are sure to perish; it being as impossible for one or a few oppressed men to disturb the government where the body of the people do not think themselves concerned in it, as for a raving madman or heady malcontent to overturn a well-settled state, the people being as little apt to follow the one as the other.

209. But if either these illegal acts have extended to the majority of the people, or if the mischief and oppression has light only on some few, but in such cases as the precedent and consequences seem to threaten all, and they are persuaded in their consciences that their laws, and with them, their estates, liberties, and lives are in danger, and perhaps their religion too, how they will be hindered from resisting illegal force used against them I cannot tell. This is an inconvenience, I confess, that attends all governments whatsoever, when the governors have brought it to this pass, to be generally suspected of their people, the most dangerous state they can possibly put themselves in; wherein they are the less to be pitied, because it is so easy to be avoided. It being as impossible for a governor, if he really means the good of his people, and the preservation of them and their laws together, not to make them see and feel it, as it is for the father of a family not to let his children see he loves and takes care of them. . . .

CHAPTER XIX

Of the Dissolution of Government

229. The end of government is the good of mankind; and which is best for mankind, that the people should be always exposed to the boundless will of tyranny, or that the rulers should be sometimes liable to be opposed when they grow exorbitant in the use of their power, and employ it for the destruction, and not the preservation, of the properties of their people?

230. Nor let any one say that mischief can arise from hence as often as it shall please a busy head or turbulent spirit to desire the alteration of the government. It is true such men may stir whenever they please, but it will be only to their own just ruin and perdition. For till the mischief be grown general, and the ill designs of the rulers become visible, or their attempts sensible to the greater part, the people, who are more disposed to suffer than right themselves by resistance, are not apt to stir. The examples of particular injustice or oppression of here and there an unfortunate man moves them not. But if they universally have a persuasion grounded upon manifest evidence that designs are carrying on against their liberties, and the general course and tendency of things cannot but give them strong suspicions of the evil intention of their governors, who is to be blamed for it? Who can help it if they, who might avoid it, bring themselves into this suspicion? Are the people to be blamed if they have the sense of rational creatures, and can think of things no otherwise than as they find and feel them? And is it not rather their fault who put things in such a posture that they would not have them thought as they are? I grant that the pride, ambition, and turbulency of private men have sometimes caused great disorders in commonwealths, and factions have been fatal to states and kingdoms. But whether the mischief hath oftener begun in the people's wantonness, and a desire to cast off the lawful authority of their rulers, or in the rulers' insolence and endeavours to get and exercise an arbitrary power over their people, whether oppression or disobedience gave the first rise to the disorder, I leave it to impartial history to determine. This I am sure, whoever, either ruler or subject, by force goes about to invade the rights of either prince or people, and lays the foundation for overturning the constitution and frame of any just government, he is guilty of the greatest crime I think a man is capable of, being to answer for all those mischiefs of blood, rapine, and desolation, which the breaking to pieces of governments

bring on a country; and he who does it is justly to be esteemed the common enemy and pest of mankind, and is to be treated accordingly. . . .

243. To conclude. The power that every individual gave the society when he entered into it can never revert to the individuals again, as long as the society lasts, but will always remain in the community; because without this there can be no community—no commonwealth, which is contrary to the original agreement; so also when the society hath placed the legislative in any assembly of men, to continue in them and their successors, with direction and authority for providing such successors, the legislative can never revert to the people whilst that government lasts; because, having provided a legislative with power to continue for ever, they have given up their political power to the legislative, and cannot resume it. But if they have set limits to the duration of their legislative, and made this supreme power in any person or assembly only temporary; or else when, by the miscarriages of those in authority, it is forfeited; upon the forfeiture of their rulers, or at the determination of the time set, it reverts to the society, and the people have a right to act as supreme, and continue the legislative in themselves or place it in a new form, or new hands, as they think good.

7

Baron de Montesquieu
(Charles Louis de Secondat)
1689–1755

On a cold January day in 1689 a beggar stood up in a Gascony chapel as godfather to the second son of the well-to-do De Secondats; the beggar was chosen as godfather to dispose the babe to look on the poor as his brothers. Judging by results the rite was effective in two ways: Charles Louis de Secondat grew to be a frugal Gascon and as lord over many peasants guarded their welfare.

His early childhood was spent on family estates in south-western France. At seven his mother died. At eleven he was sent north to the college of the Oration Fathers near Meaux, where he was an apt and eager pupil for eleven years. He left college a well-informed man to return to Gascony to study law—and enjoy the brightest associations of Bordeaux society.

When his father died, Baron de Montesquieu, his uncle, became his "guardian." It is unlikely that twenty-four old Charles needed parental guidance; the Baron had lost his own son and was substituting Charles as his heir and protégé. The Baron got Charles a staff appointment to the Parliament of Bordeaux and chose a rich, but plain, bride for him. His marriage was no love match; Charles lived on good terms with his wife, who was a satisfactory housekeeper and mother; they had three children, two girls and a boy.

The guardianship did not last long; the Baron died and Charles inherited the estate and took the name of Montesquieu. Among the assets inherited was the office of *President a mortier* of the Bordeaux Parliament—

a lucrative purchased office which, nevertheless carried great dignity. Six presidents ran Parliament, which had judicial, administrative, and legislative functions. Their duties were rigorous, and business of Parliament consumed much of Montesquieu's time for twelve years. He, nevertheless, was also active in the Bordeaux Academy to which he was elected when twenty-seven. It is believed he wrote many papers for delivery to the Academy, but most of these writings are lost.

First of his three major works, his *Persian Letters,* was written over his ten post-graduate years. The *Letters* were sexy, deft satires on government, manners, morals, and religious practices. Dangerous comment in them was labeled Mohammedan—to keep Montesquieu out of trouble. The book was an immediate success and went through four editions in its first year. It still deserves to be read. *Persian Letters* established Montesquieu as a great wit—an inconvenient reputation when, afterwards, he wanted to be taken seriously. The story is told that years later his daughter picked up a copy of *Letters* and Montesquieu said, "Let it alone my child; it is a work of my youth unsuited to yours."

Montesquieu's new fame could be better exploited in Paris than at home; there he went to be lionized and to make highbrow friends. The Versailles court was riddled with petty intrigue and attracted Montesquieu little. His best times came from membership in the Club de l'Entre-sol, which gathered top Parisian intellectuals. He was elected to the Academy in 1725 but his election was nullified because he was not domiciled in Paris. So he went to Bordeaux, sold his presidency, returned to Paris, and rented a house. He was ruled qualified and seated three years later.

In 1728 when Montesquieu was thirty-nine he embarked on travels to Austria, Italy, Germany, Holland, and England. He kept careful notes. He was well received and met the important people of the western world. The story is told that Pope Benedict XIII granted Montesquieu, as a souvenir of friendship, permission to eat meat on Fridays. Papal messengers next day brought him the enscrolled dispensation with a small bill to cover clerical costs. He frugally refused the scroll saying, "The Pope is an honest man; I will not doubt his word; I hope God has no reason to doubt it either." More than half his time abroad was spent in England, whose ways he especially admired. He later showed his approval of the scheme of English landed proprietorships by reorganizing his own ancestral estate in English style. When he wrote on political philosophy the strength of the English system influenced him much—his description of that system greatly influenced the English who tried to live up to his observations. After his wandering, he reflected: "Germany was made to travel in, Italy to rest in, England to think in, and France to live in."

The next two decades of Montesquieu's life were spent on his estates and in Paris; Gascony claimed more and more of his time as he grew older. He set up an enormous study hall in his country home. Now it was time for him to write his second major work —*Causes of the Rise and Fall of Rome*. This serious historical book contrasted sharply with his witty *Persian Letters*. One of his biographers suggests that when *Causes* was published in 1734, during the ministry of suspicious Cardinal Fleury, ancient history was a safer subject than satire on current politics and society. At first the French shrugged off this studious work. His two books were jokingly referred to as "The Rise and Fall of Montesquieu." But *Causes* had

real merit and was eagerly read abroad; it eventually came into its own in France.

Fourteen years later, Montesquieu published his influential and best known work, *The Spirit of Laws* (1748), excerpts from which follow this note. As was the custom of his day, he submitted the manuscript to a committee of learned friends. The committee unanimously advised him not to publish this important work. Fortunately, he rejected their recommendation. Yet their judgment was not entirely without grounds. The work is loose, often vague, unmethodical, and uncritical; many statements of fact are off-base; many inferences are guesses. Still, this book changed the thought of the western world. Montesquieu was first to approach political and legal sciences as sciences of observation; he took environment into account in judging excellence of laws. He reversed the accepted method and started with data in his search for the truth; most scholars before him began with abstractions and used facts merely as illustrations. For the next hundred years, his *Spirit of Laws,* was a prime source book for constitutional democrats in England, America, and France. Montesquieu planted seeds from which modern relativities grew to replace ancient absolutes.

Montesquieu's writing years were not cloistered. He was a successful and frugal land manager. Though he did not prize money, he made a large income. He often worked among peasants, dressed in their garb, and was sometimes mistaken for one. Scholars came to see him on his estates, and it was not unusual for talk to go 'round the clock. He often took his serene country manners to the most interesting drawing rooms in Paris, where he was a good listener as well as a respected talker. He was witty, yet gentle, profound, yet plain. His eyes were weak, and in his last years he was almost blind. Yet he was always a sprightly and energetic French noble. He died in Paris at the age of sixty-one while on the mission of disposing of his Paris house.

One writer says of Montesquieu: ". . . in his generation he succeeded, with a success beyond his most sanguine hopes; in doing what he tried to do—he made men think."

THE SPIRIT OF LAWS *

Book I

OF LAWS IN GENERAL

CHAPTER I

Of the Relation of Laws to Different Beings

Laws, in their most general signification, are the necessary relations arising from the nature of things. In this sense all beings have their laws: the Deity his laws, the material world its laws, the intelligences superior to man their laws, the beasts their laws, man his laws. . . .

God is related to the universe, as Creator and Preserver; the laws by which he created all things, are those by which he preserves them. He acts according to these rules, because he knows them; he knows them, because he made them; and he made them, because they are relative to his wisdom and power. . . .

Particular intelligent beings may have laws of their own making, but they have some likewise which they never made. Before there were intelligent beings, they were possible; they had therefore possible relations, and consequently possible laws. Before laws were made, there were relations of possible justice. To say that there is nothing just or unjust but what is commanded or forbidden by positive laws, is the same as saying, that before the describing of a circle, all the radii were not equal.

We must therefore acknowledge relations of justice antecedent to the positive law by which they are established: as for instance, that if human societies existed, it would be right to conform to their laws; if there were intelligent beings that had received a benefit of another being, they ought to show their gratitude; if one intelligent being had created another intelligent being, the latter ought to continue in its original state of dependence; if one intelligent being injures another, it deserves a retaliation; and so on.

But the intelligent world is far from being so well governed as the physical. For though the former has also its laws, which of their own nature are invariable, it does not conform to them so exactly as the physical world. This is, because, on the one hand, particular intelligent beings are of a finite nature, and consequently liable to error; and on the other, their nature requires them to be free agents. Hence they do not steadily conform to their primitive laws; and even those of their own instituting they frequently infringe. . . .

Man, as a physical being, is like other bodies, governed by invariable laws. As an intelligent being, he incessantly transgresses the laws established by God, and changes those of his own instituting. He is left to his private direction, though a limited being, and subject, like all finite intelligencies, to ignorance and error: even his imperfect knowledge he loses; and as a sensible creature, he is hurried away by a thousand impetuous passions. Such a being might every instant forget his Creator; God has therefore reminded him of his duty by the laws of religion. Such a being is liable every moment to forget himself; philosophy has provided against this by the laws of morality. Formed to live in society, he might forget his fellow-creatures; legislators have therefore by political and civil laws confined him to his duty.

CHAPTER II

Of the Laws of Nature

Antecedent to the above-mentioned laws are those of nature, so called, because they derive their force entirely from our frame and existence. In order to have a perfect knowledge of these laws, we must consider man before the establishment of society: the laws received in such a state would be those of nature.

. . . Man in a state of nature would have

* Translated by Thomas Nugent, published originally by Thomas Clark & Co. (1873). Reprinted by permission of Appleton-Century-Crofts, Inc.

the faculty of knowing, before he had acquired any knowledge. . . . Such a man would feel nothing in himself at first but impotency and weakness; his fears and apprehensions would be excessive; as appears from instances (were there any necessity of proving it) of savages found in forests, trembling at the motion of a leaf, and flying from every shadow.

In this state every man, instead of being sensible of his equality, would fancy himself inferior. There would therefore be no danger of their attacking one another; peace would be the first law of nature.

The natural impulse or desire which Hobbes attributes to mankind of subduing one another, is far from being well-founded. The idea of empire and dominion is so complex, and depends on so many other notions, that it could never be the first which occurred to the human understanding. . . .

Next to a sense of his weakness man would soon find that of his wants. Hence another law of nature would prompt him to seek for nourishment.

Fear . . . would induce men to shun one another; but the marks of this fear being reciprocal, would soon engage them to associate. Besides, this association would quickly follow from the very pleasure one animal feels at the approach of another of the same species. Again, the attraction arising from the difference of sexes would enhance this pleasure; and the natural inclination they have for each other, would form a third law.

Beside the sense or instinct which man posseses in common with brutes, he has the advantage of acquiring knowledge; and thence arises a second tie, which brutes have not. Mankind have therefore a new motive of uniting; and a fourth law of nature results from the desire of living in society.

CHAPTER III

Of Positive Laws

As soon as mankind enter into a state of society they lose the sense of their weakness; equality ceases, and then commences the state of war.

Each particular society begins to feel its strength, whence arises a state of war betwixt different nations. The individuals likewise of each society become sensible of their force; hence the principal advantages of this society they endeavour to convert to their own emolument, which constitutes a state of war betwixt individuals.

These two different kinds of states give rise to human laws. Considered as inhabitants of so great a planet, which necessarily contains a variety of nations, they have laws relative to their mutual intercourse, which is what we call the *law of nations*. As members of a society that must be properly supported, they have laws relative to the governors and the governed, and this we distinguish by the name of *politic law*. They have also another sort of laws, as they stand in relation to each other; by which is understood the *civil law*. . . .

. . . Some think that nature having established paternal authority, the most natural government was that of a single person. But the example of paternal authority proves nothing. For if the power of a father be relative to a single government, that of brothers after the death of a father, and that of cousin germans after the decease of brothers, refer to a government of many. The political power necessarily comprehends the union of several families.

Better is it to say, that the government most conformable to nature, is that which best agrees with the humour and disposition of the people in whose favour it is established.

The strength of individuals can not be united without a conjunction of all their wills. "The conjunction of those wills," as Gravina again very justly observes, "is what we call the *civil state*."

Law in general is human reason, inasmuch as it governs all the inhabitants of the earth; the political and civil laws of each nation ought to be only the particular cases in which human reason is applied.

They should be adapted in such a manner

to the people for whom they are framed, that it is a great chance if those of one nation suit another.

They should be relative to the nature and principle of each government; whether they form it, as may be said of politic laws; or whether they support it, as in the case of civil institutions.

They should be relative to the climate of each country, to the quality of its soil, to its situation and extent, to the principle occupation of the natives, whether husbandmen, huntsmen, or shepherds: they should have a relation to the degree of liberty which the constitution will bear; to the religion of the inhabitants, to their inclinations, riches, numbers, commerce, manners, and customs. . . .

I have not separated the political from the civil institutions: for as I do not pretend to treat of laws, but of their spirit; and as this spirit consists in the various relations which the laws may have to different objects, it is not so much my business to follow the natural order of laws, as that of these relations and objects. . . .

Book III

OF THE PRINCIPLES OF THE THREE KINDS OF GOVERNMENT

CHAPTER III

Of the Principle of Democracy

There is no great share of probity necessary to support a monarchical or despotic government. The force of laws in one, and the prince's arm in the other, are sufficient to direct and maintain the whole. But in a popular state, one spring more is necessary, namely, *virtue*. . . .

. . . A monarch, who, through bad advice or indolence, ceases to enforce the execution of the laws, may easily repair the evil; he has only to follow other advice; or to shake off this indolence. But when, in a popular government, there is a suspension of the laws, as this can proceed only from the corruption of the republic, the state is certainly undone. . . .

When virtue is banished, ambition invades the minds of those who are disposed to receive it, and avarice possesses the whole community. The objects of their desires are changed; what they were fond of before, is become indifferent; they were free, while under the restraint of laws, but they would fain now be free to act against law; and as each citizen is like a slave who has run away from his master, what was a maxim of equity, he calls rigour; what was a rule of action, he styles constraint; and to precaution, he gives the name of fear. Frugality, and not the thirst of gain, now passes for avarice. Formerly the wealth of individuals constituted the public treasure; but now this is become the patrimony of private persons. The members of the commonwealth riot on the public spoils, and its strength is only the power of a few, and the licentiousness of many.

Athens was possessed of the same number of forces, when she triumphed so gloriously, and when with so much infamy she was enslaved. . . .

CHAPTER V

That Virtue Is not the Principle of a Monarchical Government

In monarchies, policy effects great things with as little virtue as possible. . . .

The state subsists independently of the love of our country, of the thirst of true glory, of self-denial, of the sacrifice of our dearest interests, and of all those heroic virtues which we admire in the ancients, and to us are known only by story.

The laws supply here the place of those virtues. . . .

CHAPTER VI

In what Manner Virtue Is Supplied in a Monarchical Government

But it is high time for me to have done with this subject, lest I should be suspected of writing a satire against monarchical government. Far be it from me; if monarchy wants one spring, it is provided with another. Honour . . . supplies the place of the political virtue of which I have been speaking, and is everywhere her representative: here it is capable of inspiring the most glorious actions, and, joined with the force of laws, may lead us to the end of government as well as virtue itself.

Hence, in well regulated monarchies, they are almost all good subjects, and very few good men; for to be a good man, a good intention is necessary, and we should love our country, not so much on our own account, as out of regard to the community. . . .

CHAPTER IX

Of the Principle of Despotic Government

As virtue is necessary in a republic, and in a monarchy honour, so fear is necessary in a despotic government: with regard to virtue, there is no occasion for it, and honour would be extremely dangerous.

Here the immense power of the prince is devolved entirely upon those whom he is pleased to intrust with the administration. Persons capable of setting a value upon themselves, would be likely to create disturbances. Fear must therefore depress their spirits, and extinguish even the least sense of ambition. . . .

Book VI

CONSEQUENCES OF THE PRINCIPLES OF DIFFERENT GOVERNMENTS WITH RESPECT TO THE SIMPLICITY OF CIVIL AND CRIMINAL LAWS, THE FORM OF JUDGMENTS, AND THE INFLICTING OF PUNISHMENTS

CHAPTER I

Of the Simplicity of Civil Laws in Different Governments

Monarchies do not permit of so great a simplicity of laws as despotic governments.

For in monarchies there must be courts of judicature; these must give their decisions; the decisions must be preserved and learned, that we may judge in the same manner today as yesterday, and that the lives and property of the citizens may be as certain and fixed as the very constitution of the state. . . .

The monarch who knows each of his provinces, may establish different laws, or tolerate different customs. But as the despotic prince knows nothing, and can attend to nothing, he must take general measures, and govern by a rigid and inflexible will, which throughout his whole dominions produces the same effect; in short, every thing bends under his feet.

In proportion as the decisions of the courts of judicature are multiplied in monarchies, the law is loaded with decrees that sometimes contradict one another; either because succeeding judges are of a different way of thinking, or because the same causes are sometimes well, and at other times ill defended; or, in fine, by reason of an infinite number of abuses, to which all human regulations are liable. This is a necessary evil, which the legislator redresses from time to time, as contrary even to the spirit of moderate governments. For when people are obliged to have recourse to courts of judicature, this should come from the nature of the constitution, and not from the contradiction or uncertainty of the law.

In governments where there are necessary distinctions of persons, there must likewise be privileges. This also diminishes the simplicity, and creates a thousand exceptions. . . .

CHAPTER II

Of the Simplicity of Criminal Laws in Different Governments

We hear it generally said, that justice ought to be administered with us as in Turkey. Is it possible, then, that the most ignorant of all nations should be the most clear sighted in a point which it most behoves mankind to know?

If we examine the set forms of justice with

respect to the trouble the subject undergoes in recovering his property, or in obtaining satisfaction for an injury or affront, we shall find them doubtless too numerous; but if we consider them in the relation they bear to the liberty and security of every individual, we shall often find them too few; and be convinced that the trouble, expense, delays, and even the very dangers of our judiciary proceedings, are the price that each subject pays for his liberty.

In Turkey, where little regard is shown to the honour, life, or estate of the subject, all causes are speedily decided. The method of determining them is a matter of indifference, provided they be determined. The bashaw, after a quick hearing, orders which party he pleases to be bastinadoed, and then sends them about their business. . . .

But in moderate governments, where the life of the meanest subject is deemed precious, no man is stript of his honour or property but after a long inquiry. . . .

. . . When a person renders himself absolute, he immediately thinks of reducing the number of laws. In a government thus constituted, they are more affected with particular inconveniences, than with the liberty of the subject, which is very little minded.

In republics, it is plain, that as many formalities at least are necessary as in monarchies. In both governments they increase in proportion to the value which is set on the honour, fortune, liberty and life of the subject.

In republican governments, men are all equal; equal they are also in despotic governments; in the former, because they are every thing; in the latter, because they are nothing.

CHAPTER III

In what Governments and in what Cases the Judges Ought to Determine According to the Express

Letter of the Law

The nearer a government approaches towards a republic, the more the manner of judging becomes settled and fixed . . .

. . . In republics, the very nature of the constitution requires the judges to follow the letter of the law; otherwise the law might be explained to the prejudice of every citizen, in cases where their honour, property, or life are concerned. . . .

CHAPTER IV

Of the Manner of Passing Judgment

Hence arises the different manner of passing judgment. In monarchies the judges choose the method of arbitration; they deliberate together, they communicate their sentiments for the sake of unanimity; they moderate their opinions, in order to render them conformable to those of others; and the lesser number are obliged to give way to the majority. But this is not agreeable to the nature of a republic. At Rome, and in the cities of Greece, the judges never entered into a consultation; each gave his opinion one of these three ways, "I absolve, I condemn, it does not appear clear to me"; this was because the people judged, or were supposed to judge. But the people are far from being civilians; all these restrictions and methods of arbitration are above their reach; they must have only one object, and one single fact set before them; and then they have only to see whether they ought to condemn, to acquit, or to suspend their judgment.

The Romans introduced set forms of actions . . . and established a rule, that each cause should be directed by its proper action. This was necessary in their manner of judging; it was necessary to fix the state of the question, that the people might have it always before their eyes. Otherwise, in a long process, this state of the question would continually change, and be no longer distinguished.

Hence it followed, that the Roman judges granted only the simple demand, without making any addition, deduction, or limitation. . . .

CHAPTER IX

Of the Severity of Punishments in Different Governments

The severity of punishments is fitter for despotic governments, whose principle is terror, than for a monarchy or a republic, whose spring is honour and virtue.

In moderate governments, the love of one's country, shame, and the fear of blame, are restraining motives, capable of preventing a multitude of crimes. Here the greatest punishment of a bad action is conviction. The civil laws have therefore a softer way of correcting, and do not require so much force and severity.

In those states a good legislator is less bent upon punishment, than preventing crimes; he is more attentive to inspire good morals, than to inflict penalties. . . .

It would be an easy matter to prove, that in all, or almost all, the governments of Europe, penalties have increased or diminished in proportion as those governments favoured or discouraged liberty. . . .

In moderate governments, a good legislator may make use of every thing by way of punishment. Is it not very extraordinary, that one of the chief penalties at Sparta was, to deprive a person of the power of lending out his wife, or of receiving the wife of another man, and to oblige him to have no company at home but virgins? In short, whatever the law calls a punishment, is such effectively. . . .

CHAPTER XII

Of the Power of Punishments

Experience shews that in countries remarkable for the lenity of their laws, the spirit of the inhabitants is as much affected by slight penalties, as in other countries by severer punishments.

If an inconveniency or abuse arises in the state, a violent government endeavours suddenly to redress it; and instead of putting the old laws in execution, it establishes some cruel punishment, which instantly puts a stop to the evil. But the spring of government hereby loses its elasticity; the imagination grows accustomed to the severe as well as the milder punishment; and as the fear of the latter diminishes, they are soon obliged in every case to have recourse to the former. Robberies on the highway were grown common in some countries; in order to remedy this evil, they invented the punishment of breaking upon the wheel, the terror of which put a stop for a while to this mischievous practice. But soon after robberies on the highways became as common as ever. . . .

. . . If we inquire into the cause of all human corruptions, we shall find that they proceed from the impunity of criminals, and not from the moderation of punishments.

Let us follow nature, who has given shame to man for his scourge; and let the heaviest part of the punishment be the infamy attending it.

But if there be some countries where shame is not a consequence of punishment, this must be owing to tyranny, which has inflicted the same penalties on villains and honest men.

And if there are others where men are deterred only by cruel punishments, we may be sure that this must, in a great measure, arise from the violence of the government, which has used such penalties for slight transgressions. . . .

CHAPTER XIII

Insufficiency of the Laws of Japan

Excessive punishments may even corrupt a despotic government; of this we have an instance in Japan. . . .

. . . The excessive severity of the laws hinders . . . their execution: when the punishment surpasses all measure, they are frequently obliged to prefer impunity to it. . . .

CHAPTER XVI

Of the Just Proportion Betwixt Punishments and Crimes

It is an essential point, that there should be a certain proportion in punishments, because it is essential that a great crime should be avoided rather than a smaller, and that which is more pernicious to society rather than that which is less. . . .

It is a great abuse amongst us to condemn to the same punishment a person that only robs on the highway, and another who robs and murders. Surely, for the public security, some difference should be made in the punishment. . . .

CHAPTER XVIII

Of Pecuniary and Corporal Punishments

Our ancestors, the Germans, admitted of none but pecuniary punishments. Those free and warlike people were of opinion, that their blood ought not to be spilt but with sword in hand. On the contrary, these punishments are rejected by the Japanese, under pretence that the rich might elude them. But are not the rich afraid of being stripped of their property? And might not pecuniary penalties be proportioned to people's fortunes? and in fine, might not infamy be added to those punishments?

A good legislator takes a just medium; he ordains neither always pecuniary, nor always corporal punishments. . . .

Book X

OF LAWS IN THE RELATION THEY BEAR TO OFFENSIVE FORCE

CHAPTER II

Of War

The life of governments is like that of man. The latter has a right to kill in case of natural defence; the former have a right to wage war for their own preservation.

In the case of natural defence I have a right to kill, because my life is in respect to me, what the life of my antagonist is to him: in the same manner a state wages war, because its preservation is like that of any other being.

With individuals the right of natural defence does not imply a necessity of attacking. Instead of attacking they need only have recourse to proper tribunals. They cannot therefore exercise this right of defence, but in sudden cases, when immediate death would be the consequence of waiting for the assistance of the law. But with states the right of natural defence carries along with it sometimes the necessity of attacking; as for instance, when one nation sees that a continuance of peace will enable another to destroy her, and that to attack that nation instantly is the only way to prevent her own destruction. . . .

The right therefore of war is derived from necessity and strict justice. If those who direct the conscience or councils of princes do not abide by this maxim the consequence is dreadful: when they proceed on arbitrary principles of glory, conveniency, and utility, torrents of blood must overspread the earth. . . .

CHAPTER III

Of the Right of Conquest

. . . The right the conqueror has over a conquered people is directed by four sorts of laws: the law of nature which makes everything tend to the preservation of the species; the law of natural reason, which teaches us to do to others what we would have done to ourselves; the law that forms political societies, whose duration nature has not limited; and, in fine, the law derived from the nature of the thing itself. Conquest is an acquisition, and carries with it the spirit of preservation and use, not of destruction.

The inhabitants of a conquered country are treated by the conqueror one of the four following ways. Either he continues to rule them according to their own laws, and assumes to himself only the exercise of the political and civil government; or he gives them new political and civil government; or he destroys and disperses the society; or, in fine, he exterminates the people. . . .

The authors of our public law, guided by

ancient histories, without confining themselves to cases of strict necessity, have fallen into very great errors. They have adopted tyrannical and arbitrary principles, by supposing the conquerors to be invested with I know not what right to kill. . . . It is a plain case, that when the conquest is completed, the conqueror has no longer a right to kill, because he has no longer the plea of natural defence and self-preservation.

What has lead them into this mistake is, that they imagined a conqueror had a right to destroy the state; from whence they inferred that he had a right to destroy the men that compose it; a wrong consequence from a false principle. For from the destruction of the state it does not at all follow, that the people who compose it ought to be also destroyed. The state is the association of men, and not the men themselves; the citizen may perish, and the man remain.

From the right of killing in the case of conquest, politicians have drawn that of reducing to slavery; a consequence as ill grounded as the principle.

There is no such thing as a right of reducing people to slavery, but when it becomes necessary for the preservation of the conquest. Preservation, and not servitude, is the end of conquest; though servitude may happen sometimes to be a necessary means of preservation.

Even in that case it is contrary to the nature of things that the slavery should be perpetual. The people enslaved ought to be rendered capable of becoming subjects. Slavery in conquests is an accidental thing. When after the expiration of a certain space of time all the parts of the conquering state are connected with the conquered nation, by custom, marriages, laws, associations, and by a certain conformity of disposition, there ought to be an end of the slavery. . . .

A conqueror, therefore, who reduces the conquered people to slavery, ought always to reserve to himself the means (for means there are without number) of restoring them to their liberty. . . .

CHAPTER IV

Some Advantages of a Conquered People

. . . Conquered countries are, generally speaking, degenerated from their original institution. . . . Who can question but such a state would be a gainer, and derive some advantages from the very conquest itself, if it did not prove destructive? . . .

It is a conqueror's business to repair a part of the mischief he has occasioned. The right, therefore, of conquest I define thus: a necessary, lawful, but unhappy power, which leaves the conqueror under a heavy obligation of repairing the injuries done to humanity. . . .

CHAPTER XI

Of the Manners of a Conquered People

It is not sufficient in those conquests to let the conquered nation enjoy their own laws; it is, perhaps, more necessary to leave them also their manners, because people in general have a stronger attachment to these than to their laws.

The French have been driven nine times out of Italy, because, as historians say, of their insolent familiarities with the fair sex. It is too much for a nation to be obliged to bear not only with the pride of conquerors, but with their incontinence and indiscretion; these are, without doubt, most grievous and intolerable, as they are the source of infinite outrages. . . .

Book XI

OF THE LAWS WHICH ESTABLISH POLITICAL LIBERTY, WITH REGARD TO THE CONSTITUTION

CHAPTER II

Different Significations of the Word "Liberty"

There is no word that admits of more various significations, and has made more different impressions on the human mind, than that of *Liberty*. Some have taken it for a facility of deposing a person on whom they had conferred a tyrannical authority; others for the power of choosing a superior whom they are obliged to obey; others for the right of bearing arms, and of being thereby enabled to use violence; others, in fine, for the privilege of being governed by a native of their own country, or by their own laws. A certain nation, for a long time thought liberty consisted in the privilege of wearing a long beard. Some have annexed this name to one form of government exclusive of others . . . they have all applied the name of *liberty* to the government most suitable to their own customs and inclinations. . . . In fine, as in democracies the people seem to act almost as they please; this sort of government has been deemed the most free; and the power of the people has been confounded with their liberty.

CHAPTER III

In What Liberty Consists

It is true, that in democracies the people seem to act as they please; but political liberty does not consist in an unlimited freedom. In governments, that is, in societies directed by laws, liberty can consist only in the power of doing what we ought to will, and in not being constrained to do what we ought not to will.

We must have continually present to our minds the difference between independence and liberty. Liberty is a right of doing whatever the laws permit; and if a citizen could do what they forbid, he would be no longer possessed of liberty, because all his fellow-citizens would have the same power.

CHAPTER IV

The Same Subject Continued

Democratic and aristocratic states are not in their own nature free. Political liberty is to be found only in moderate governments;

and even in these, it is not always found. It is there only when there is no abuse of power; but constant experience shews us, that every man invested with power is apt to abuse it, and to carry his authority as far as it will go. Is it not strange, though true, to say, that virtue itself has need of limits?

To prevent this abuse, it is necessary from the very nature of things, power should be a check to power. A government may be so constituted, as no man shall be compelled to do things to which the law does not oblige him, nor forced to abstain from things which the law permits. . . .

CHAPTER VI

Of the Constitution of England

. . . The political liberty of the subject is a tranquility of mind arising from the opinion each person has of his safety. In order to have this liberty, it is requisite the government be so constituted as one man needs not be afraid of another.

When the legislative and executive powers are united in the same person, or in the same body of magistrates, there can be no liberty; because apprehensions may arise, lest the same monarch or senate should enact tyrannical laws, to execute them in a tyrannical manner.

Again, there is no liberty, if the judiciary power be not separated from the legislative and executive. Were it joined with the legislative, the life and liberty of the subject would be exposed to arbitrary control; for the judge would be then the legislator. Were it joined to the executive power, the judge might behave with violence and oppression.

There would be an end of every thing, were the same man, or the same body, whether of the nobles or of the people, to exercise those three powers, that of enacting laws, that of executing the public resolutions, and of trying the causes of individuals.

In what a situation must the poor subject be, under those republics! The same body of magistrates are possessed, as executors of the laws, of the whole power they have given themselves in quality of legislators. They may plunder the state by their general determinations; and as they have likewise the judiciary power in their hands, every private citizen may be ruined by their particular decisions. . . .

In accusations of a deep and criminal nature, it is proper the person accused should have the privilege of choosing, in some measure, his judges, in concurrence with the law; or at least he should have a right to except against so great a number, that the remaining part may be deemed his own choice.

The other two powers may be given rather to magistrates or permanent bodies, because they are not exercised on any private subject; one being no more than the general will of the state, and the other the execution of that general will.

But though the tribunals ought not to be fixed, the judgments ought; and to such a degree as to be ever conformable to the letter of the law. Were they to be the private opinion of the judge, people would then live in society, without exactly knowing the nature of their obligations.

The judges ought likewise to be of the same rank as the accused, or in other words, his peers; to the end that he may not imagine he is fallen into the hands of persons inclined to treat him with rigour. . . .

The executive power ought to be in the hands of a monarch, because this branch of government, having need of dispatch, is better administered by one than by many: on the other hand, whatever depends on the legislative power, is oftentimes better regulated by many than by a single person. . . .

Though, in general, the judiciary power ought not to be united with any part of the legislative, yet this is liable to three exceptions, founded on the particular interest of the party accused.

The great are always obnoxious to popular envy; and were they to be judged by the people, they might be in danger from their judges, and would, moreover, be deprived of the privilege which the meanest subject is possessed of in a free state, of being tried by his peers. The nobility, for this reason, ought not to be cited before the ordinary courts of judicature, but before that part of the legislature which is composed of their own body.

It is possible that the law, which is clear sighted in one sense, and blind in another, might, in some cases, be too severe. But as we have already observed, the national judges are no more than the mouth that pronounces the words of the law, mere passive beings, incapable of moderating either its force or rigour. That part, therefore, of the legislative body, which we have just now observed to be a necessary tribunal on another occasion is also a necessary tribunal in this; it belongs to its supreme authority to moderate the law in favour of the law itself, by mitigating the sentence.

It might also happen that a subject intrusted with the administration of public affairs, may infringe the rights of the people, and be guilty of crimes which the ordinary magistrates either could not, or would not punish. But, in general, the legislative power cannot try causes: and much less can it try this particular case, where it represents the party aggrieved, which is the people. It can only, therefore, impeach. But before what court shall it bring its impeachment; must it go and demean itself before the ordinary tribunals which are its inferiors, and being composed, moreover, of men who are chosen from the people as well as itself, will naturally be swayed by the authority of so powerful an accuser! No: in order to preserve the dignity of the people, and the security of the subject, the legislative part which represents the people, must bring in its charge before the legislative part which represents the nobility, who have neither the same interests, nor the same passions. . . .

Book XII

OF THE LAWS THAT FORM POLITICAL
LIBERTY, AS RELATIVE TO THE
SUBJECT

CHAPTER II

Of the Liberty of the Subject

Philosophical liberty consists in the free exercise of the will; or at least, if we must speak agreeably to all systems, in an opinion that we have the free exercise of our will. Political liberty consists in security, at least, in the opinion that we enjoy security.

This security is never more dangerously attacked than in public or private accusations. It is, therefore, on the goodness of criminal laws, that the liberty of the subject principally depends.

Criminal laws did not receive their full perfection all at once. Even in places where liberty has been most sought after, it has not been always found. Aristotle informs us, that at Cumae, the parents of the accuser might be witnesses. So imperfect was the law under the kings of Rome, that Servius Tullius pronounced sentence against the children of Ancus Martius, who were charged with having assassinated the king, his father-in-law. Under the first kings of France, Clotarius made a law, that nobody should be condemned without being heard; which shows that a contrary custom had prevailed in some particular case or among some barbarous people. . . .

CHAPTER III

The Same Subject continued

Those laws which condemn a man to death on the deposition of a single witness, are fatal to liberty. In right reason there should be two, because a witness who affirms, and the accused who denies, make an equal balance, and a third must incline the scale. . . .

CHAPTER IV

That Liberty is Favoured by the Nature and Proportion of Punishments

Liberty is in its highest perfection, when criminal laws derive each punishment from the particular nature of the crime. There are then no arbitrary decisions; the punishment does not flow from the capriciousness of the legislator, but from the very nature of the thing; and man uses no violence to man.

There are four sorts of crimes. Those of the first species are prejudicial to religion, the second to morals, the third to the public tranquillity, and the fourth to the security of the subject. The punishment inflicted for these crimes ought to proceed from the nature of each of these species. . . .

In order to derive the punishment of simple sacrileges from the nature of the thing, it should consist in depriving people of the advantages conferred by religion in expelling them out of the temples, in a temporary or perpetual exclusion from the society of the faithful, in shunning their presence, in execrations, comminations, and conjurations.

In things that prejudice the tranquillity or security of the state, secret actions are subject to human jurisdiction. But in those which offend the Deity, where there is no public act, there can be no criminal matter, the whole passes betwixt man and God, who knows the measure and time of his vengeance. Now if magistrates confounding things, should inquire also into hidden sacrileges, this inquisition would be directed to a kind of action that does not at all require it; the liberty of the subject would be subverted by arming the zeal of timorous, as well as of presumptuous consciences against him.

The mischief arises from a notion which some people have entertained of revenging the cause of the Deity. But we must honour the Deity and leave him to avenge his own cause. . . .

The second class consists of those crimes which are prejudicial to morals. Such is the violation of public or private continence, that is of the police directing the manner in which the pleasure annexed to the conjunction of the sexes is to be enjoyed. The punishment of those crimes ought to be also derived from the nature of the thing; the privation of such advantages as society has attached to the purity of morals, fines, shame, necessity of concealment, public infamy, expulsion from home and society, and in fine all such punishments as belong to a corrective jurisdiction, are sufficient to repress the temerity of the two sexes. In effect these things are less founded on malice, than on carelessness and self-neglect. . . .

The crimes of the third class are those which disturb the public tranquillity. The punishments ought therefore to be derived from the nature of the thing, and to be relative to this tranquillity; such as imprisonment, exile, and other like chastisements, proper for reclaiming turbulent spirits, and obliging them to conform to the established order.

I confine those crimes that injure the public tranquillity to things which imply a bare offence against the police; for as to those which by disturbing the public peace, attack at the same time the security of the subject, they ought to be ranked in the fourth class.

The punishments inflicted upon the latter crimes are such as are properly distinguished by that name. They are a kind of retaliation, by which the society refuses security to a member, who has actually or intentionally deprived another of his security. These punishments are derived from the nature of the thing, founded on reason, and drawn from the very source of good and evil. A man deserves death when he has violated the security of the subject so far as to deprive, or attempt to deprive another man of his life. The punishment of death is the remedy, as it were, of a sick society. When there is a breach of security with regard to property, there may be some reasons for inflicting a capital punishment: but it would be much better, and perhaps more natural, that crimes committed against the security of property should be punished with the loss of property; and this ought, indeed, to be the case if men's fortunes were common or equal. But as those who have no property of their own are generally the readiest to attack that of others, it has been found necessary, instead of a pecuniary, to substitute a corporal punishment.

All that I have here advanced, is founded in nature, and extremely favourable to the liberty of the subject.

CHAPTER V

Of Certain Accusations that Require Particular Moderation and Prudence

It is an important *maxim,* that we ought to be very circumspect in the prosecution of witchcraft and heresy. The accusation of these two crimes may be vastly injurious to liberty, and productive of infinite oppression, if the legislator knows not how to set bounds to it. For as it does not directly point at a person's actions, but at his character, it grows dangerous in proportion to the ignorance of the people; and then a man is sure to be always in danger, because the most exceptionable conduct, the purest morals, and the constant practice of every duty in life, are not a sufficient security against the suspicion of his being guilty of the like crimes. . . .

CHAPTER XIX

In what Manner the Use of Liberty Is Suspended in a Republic

In countries where liberty is most esteemed, there are laws by which a single person is deprived of it, in order to preserve it for the whole community. Such are in England what they call *Bills of Attainder.* These are relative to those Athenian laws by which a private person was condemned, provided they were made by the unanimous suffrage of six thousand citizens. They are relative also to those laws which were made at Rome against private citizens, and were called *privileges.* These were never passed but in the great meetings of the people.

But in what manner soever they were enacted, Cicero was for having them abolished, because the force of a law consists in its being made for the whole community. I must own, notwithstanding, that the practice of the freest nation that ever existed, induces me to think, that there are cases in which a veil should be drawn for a while over liberty, as it was customary to cover the statues of the gods. . . .

Book XV

IN WHAT MANNER THE LAWS OF CIVIL SLAVERY ARE RELATIVE TO THE NATURE OF THE CLIMATE

CHAPTER I

Of Civil Slavery

. . . The state of slavery is in its own nature bad. It is neither useful to the master nor to the slave; not to the slave, because he can do nothing through a motive of virtue; nor to the master, because by having an unlimited authority over his slaves, he insensibly accustoms himself to the want of all moral virtues, and from thence becomes fierce, hasty, severe, choleric, voluptuous, and cruel. . . .

CHAPTER II

Origin of the Right of Slavery Among the Roman Civilians

One would never have imagined that slavery should owe its birth to pity, and that this should have been excited three different ways.

The law of nations, to prevent prisoners from being put to death, has allowed them to be made slaves. The civil law of the Romans empowered debtors, who were subject to be ill-used by their creditors, to sell themselves. . . .

. . . It is false, that killing in war is lawful, unless in a case of absolute necessity: but when a man has made another his slave, he cannot be said to have been under a necessity of taking away his life, since he actually did not take it away. War gives no other right over prisoners than to disable them from doing any farther harm, by securing their persons. All nations concur in detesting the murdering of prisoners in cold blood.

Neither is it true, that a freeman can sell himself. . . . If it is not lawful for a man to kill himself, because he robs his country of his person, for the same reason he is not allowed to barter his freedom. The freedom of every citizen constitutes a part of the public liberty; and in a democratical state is even a part of the sovereignty. To sell one's freedom is so repugnant to all reason, as can scarce be supposed in any man. If liberty may be rated with respect to the buyer, it is beyond all price to the seller. . . .

If it be pretended, that it has been beneficial to him, as his master has provided for his subsistence, slavery, at this rate, should be limited to those who are incapable of earning their livelihood. But who will take up with such slaves? . . .

Nor is slavery less opposite to the civil law than to that of nature. What civil law can restrain a slave from running away, since he is not a member of society, and consequently has no interest in any civil institutions? He can be retained only by a family law, that is, by the master's authority. . . .

Book XVI

HOW THE LAWS OF DOMESTIC SLAVERY HAVE A RELATION TO THE NATURE OF THE CLIMATE

CHAPTER II

That in the Countries of the South There is a Natural Inequality Between the Two Sexes

Women, in hot climates, are marriageable at eight, nine, or ten years of age; thus, in those countries, infancy and marriage generally go together. They are old at twenty: their reason therefore never accompanies their beauty. When beauty demands the empire, the want of reason forbids the claim; when reason is obtained, beauty is no more. These women ought then to be in a state of dependence; for reason cannot procure in old age, that empire which even youth and beauty could not give. It is therefore extremely natural that in these places, a man, when no law opposes it, should leave one wife to take another, and that polygamy should be introduced.

In temperate climates, where the charms of women are best preserved, where they arrive later at maturity, and have children at a more advanced season of life, the old age of their husbands in some degree follows theirs; and as they have more reason and knowledge at the time of marriage, if it be only on account of their having continued longer in life, it must naturally introduce a kind of equality between the two sexes; and, in consequence of this, the law of having only one wife.

In cold countries the almost necessary custom of drinking strong liquors, establishes intemperance amongst men. Women, who in this respect have a natural restraint, because they are always on the defensive, have therefore the advantage of reason over them.

Nature, which has distinguished men by their reason and bodily strength, has set no other bounds to their power than those of this strength and reason. It has given charms to women, and ordained that their ascendant over man shall end with these charms: but in hot countries, these are found only at the beginning, and never in the progress of life.

Thus the law which permits only one wife, is physically conformable to the climate of Europe, and not to that of Asia. . . .

Book XIX

OF LAWS IN RELATION TO THE PRINCI-
PLES WHICH FORM THE GENERAL
SPIRIT, THE MORALS AND CUS-
TOMS OF A NATION

CHAPTER II

That it is Necessary People's Minds Should be Prepared for the Reception of the Best Laws

. . . Liberty itself has appeared intolerable to those nations, who have not been accustomed to enjoy it. Thus a pure air is sometimes disagreeable to such as have lived in a fenny country. . . .

CHAPTER III

Of Tyranny

There are two sorts of tyranny: one real, which arises from oppression; the other is seated in opinion, and is sure to be felt, whenever those who govern, establish things shocking to the present ideas of a nation.

Dio tells us, that Augustus was desirous of being called Romulus; but having been informed that the people feared that he would cause himself to be crowned king, he changed his design. The old Romans were averse to a king; because they could not suffer any man to enjoy such power; these would not have a king, because they could not bear his manners. For though Caesar, the Trimuvirs, and Augustus were really invested with regal power, they had preserved all the outward appearance of equality, while their private lives were a kind of contrast to the pomp and luxury of foreign monarchs; so that when the Romans were resolved to have no king, this only signified that they would preserve their customs, and not imitate those of the African and eastern nations. . . .

CHAPTER IV

Of the General Spirit of Mankind

Mankind are influenced by various causes, by the climate, by the religion, by the laws, by the maxims of government, by precedents, morals, and customs; from whence is formed a general spirit of nations.

In proportion as, in every country, any one of these causes acts with more force, the others in the same degree are weakened. Nature and the climate rule almost alone over the savages; customs govern the Chinese; the laws tyrannize in Japan; morals had formerly all their influence at Sparta; maxims of government, and the ancient simplicity of manners, once prevailed at Rome.

CHAPTER V

How Far We Should be Attentive Lest the General Spirit of a Nation be Changed

Should there happen to be a country, whose inhabitants were of a sociable temper, open-hearted, cheerful, endowed with taste and a facility in communicating their thoughts; who were sprightly and agreeable; sometimes imprudent, often indiscreet; and besides had courage, generosity, frankness, and a certain notion of honour; no one ought to endeavour to restrain their manners by laws, unless he would lay a constraint on their virtues. . . .

It is the business of the legislature to follow the spirit of the nation, when it is not contrary to the principles of government; for we do nothing so well as when we act with freedom, and follow the bent of our natural genius. . . .

CHAPTER XIV

What Are the Natural Means of Changing the Manners and Customs of a Nation

We have said, that the laws were the particular and precise institutions of a legislator, and manners and customs the institutions of a nation in general. From hence it follows, that when these manners and customs are to be changed, it ought not to be done by laws; this would have too much the air of tyranny; it would be better to change them by introducing other manners and other customs.

Thus when a prince would make great alterations in his kingdom, he should reform by law what is established by law, and change by custom what is settled by custom; for it is very bad policy to change by law, what ought to be changed by custom. . . .

Nations are in general very tenacious of their customs; to take them away by violence is to render them unhappy: we should not therefore change them, but engage the people to make the change themselves.

All punishment which is not derived from necessity, is tyrannical. The law is not a mere act of power; things in their own nature indifferent are not within its province. . . .

Book XXIV

OF LAWS AS RELATIVE TO RELIGION CONSIDERED IN ITSELF, AND IN ITS DOCTRINES

CHAPTER VII

Of the Laws of Perfection in Religion

Human laws, made to direct the will, ought to give precepts, and not counsels; religion, made to influence the heart, should give many counsels, and few precepts.

When, for instance, it gives rules, not for what is good, but for what is better; not to direct to what is right, but to what is perfect; it is expedient that these should be counsels, and not laws: for perfection can have no relation to the universality of men or things. Besides, if these were laws, there would be a necessity for an infinite number of others, to make people observe the first. Celibacy was advised by Christianty; when they made it a law in respect to a certain order of men, it became necessary to make new ones every day, in order to oblige those men to observe it. The legislator wearied himself, and he wearied society, to make men execute by precept, what those, who love perfection, would have executed as counsel. . . .

CHAPTER XIV

In what Manner Religion Has an Influence on Civil Laws

As both religion and the civil laws ought to have a peculiar tendency to render men good citizens, it is evident, that when one of these deviates from this end, the tendency of the other ought to be strengthened. The less severity there is in religion, the more there ought to be in the civil laws.

Thus the reigning religion of Japan having few doctrines, and proposing neither future rewards nor punishments, the laws to supply these defects have been made with the spirit of severity, and are executed with an extraordinary punctuality.

When the doctrine of necessity is established by religion, the penalties of the laws ought to be more severe, and the magistrate more vigilant; to the end that men, who would otherwise become abandoned, might be determined by these motives; but it is quite otherwise, where religion has established the doctrine of liberty.

From the inactivity of the soul springs the Mahometan doctrine of predestination, and from this doctrine of predestination springs the inactivity of the soul. This, they say, is in the decrees of God; they must therefore indulge their repose. In a case like this the magistrate ought to waken by the laws, those who are lulled asleep by religion. . . .

Book XXVI

OF LAWS AS RELATIVE TO THE ORDER OF THINGS ON WHICH THEY DETERMINE

CHAPTER I

Idea of this Book

Men are governed by several kinds of laws: by the law of nature; by the divine law, which is that of religion; by ecclesiastical, otherwise called canon law, which is that of religious polity; by the law of nations, which may be considered as the civil law of the whole globe, in which sense every nation is a citizen; by the general political law, which relates to that human wisdom from whence all societies derive their origin; by the particular political law, the object of which is each society; by the law of conquest founded on this, that one nation has been willing and able, or has had a right to offer violence to another; by the civil law of every society, by which a citizen may defend his possessions and his life, against the attacks of any other citizen; in fine, by domestic law which

proceeds from a society's being divided into several families, all which have need of a particular government.

There are therefore different orders of laws, and the sublimity of human reason consists in perfectly knowing to which of these orders the things that are to be determined ought to have a principal relation, and not to throw into confusion those principles which should govern mankind.

CHAPTER II

Of Laws Divine and Human

. . . 1. It is in the nature of human laws to be subject to all the accidents which can happen, and to vary in proportion as the will of man changes; on the contrary, by the nature of the laws of religion, they are never to vary. Human laws appoint for some good; those of religion for the best: good may have another object, because there are many kinds of good; but the best is but one, it cannot therefore change. We may alter laws, because they are reputed no more than good; but the institutions of religion are always supposed to be the best.

2. There are kingdoms, in which the laws are of no value, as they depend only on the capricious and fickle humour of the sovereign. If in these kingdoms the laws of religion were of the same nature as the human institutions, the laws of religion too would be of no value. It is, however, necessary to the society that it should have something fixed; and it is religion that has this stability.

3. The influence of religion proceeds from its being believed; that of human laws, from their being feared. Antiquity suits with religion, because we have frequently a firmer belief of things, in proportion to their distance; for we have no ideas annexed to them drawn from those times, which can contradict them. Human laws, on the contrary, receive advantage from their novelty, which implies the actual and particular attention of the legislator to put them in execution.

CHAPTER III

Of Civil Laws Contrary to the Law of Nature

If a slave, says Plato, defends himself, and kills a freeman, he ought to be treated as a parricide. This is a civil law which punishes self-defence, though dictated by nature.

The law of Henry VIII, which condemned a man without being confronted by witnesses, was contrary to self-defence. In order to pass sentence of condemnation, it is necessary that the witnesses should know whether the man against whom they make their deposition, is he whom they accuse, and that this man be at liberty to say, I am not the person you mean. . . .

There has been much talk of a law in England, which permitted girls seven years old to choose a husband. This law was shocking two ways: it had no regard to the time when nature gives maturity to the understanding, nor to that in which she gives maturity to the body.

Amongst the Romans, a father might oblige his daughter to repudiate her husband, though he himself had consented to the marriage. But it is contrary to nature, for a divorce to be in the power of a third person.

A divorce can be agreeable to nature, only when it is by consent of the two parties, or at least of one of them: but when neither consents, it is a monstrous separation. . . .

CHAPTER V

Cases, in Which We May Judge by the Principles of the Civil Law, in Limiting the Principles of the Law of Nature

An Athenian law obliged children to provide for their fathers, when fallen into poverty, it excepted those who were born of a courtezan, those whose chastity had been infamously prostituted by their father, and those to whom he had not given any means of gaining a livelihood.

The law considered, that, in the first case,
the father being uncertain, he had rendered the natural obligation precarious; that in the second, he had sullied the life he had given, and done the greatest injury he could do to his children, in depriving them of their reputation; that in the third, he had rendered insupportable a life which had no means of subsistence. The law suspended the natural obligation of children, because the father had violated his; it looked upon the father and the son as no more than two citizens, and determined in respect to them, only from civil and political views; ever considering, that a good republic ought to have a particular regard to manners. I am apt to think, that Solon's law was a wise regulation in the first two cases, whether that in which nature has left the son in ignorance with regard to his father, or that in which she even seems to ordain he should not own him; but it cannot be approved with respect to the third, where the father had only violated a civil institution.

CHAPTER VI

That the Order of Succession or Inheritance Depends on the Principles of Political or Civil Law, and not on those of the Law of Nature

. . . The law of nature ordains, that fathers shall provide for their children; but it does not oblige them to make them their heirs. The division of property, the laws of this division, and the succession after the death of the person who has had this division, can be regulated only by the community, and consequently by political or civil laws.

True it is, that a political or civil order frequently demands that children should succeed to their father's estate; but it does not always make this necessary. . . .

CHAPTER VII

That We Ought not to Decide by the Precepts of Religion, what Belongs Only to the Law of Nature

The Abassines have a most severe Lent of fifty days, which weakens them to such a degree, that for a long time they are incapable of business: the Turks do not fail to attack them after their Lent. Religion ought, in favour of the natural right of self-defence, to set bounds to these customs. . . .

. . . Who does not see that self-defence is a duty superior to every precept. . . .

CHAPTER IX

That Things which Ought to be Regulated by the Principles of Civil Law, can Seldom be Regulated by Those of Religion

The laws of religion have a greater sublimity; the civil laws a greater extent.

The laws of perfection drawn from religion, have more in view the goodness of the person that observes them, than of the society in which they are observed; the civil laws, on the contrary, have more in view the moral goodness of men in general, than that of individuals.

Thus, venerable as those ideas are which immediately spring from religion, they ought not always to serve as a first principle to the civil laws; because these have another, the general welfare of society.

The Romans made regulations amongst themselves, to preserve the morals of their women; these were political institutions. . . . When the Christian religion became predominant, the new laws that were then made, had less relation to the general rectitude of morals, than to the holiness of marriage; they had less regard to the union of the two sexes in a civil than in a spiritual state. . . .

Formerly, when a woman, whose husband was gone to war, heard no longer any tidings of him, she might easily marry again, because she had in her hands the power of making a divorce. . . . But Justinian decreed, that let the time be never so long after the departure of her husband, she should not marry, unless, by the deposition and oath of the general, she could prove the death of her husband. . . . He injured the commonwealth,

by obliging women to live out of marriage; he injured individuals, by exposing them to a thousand dangers.

The law of Justinian . . . was entirely opposite to the principles of the civil laws. . . .

CHAPTER XIII

In what Cases, with Regard to Marriage, We Ought to Follow the Laws of Religion; and in what Cases we Should Follow the Civil Laws

It has happened in all ages and countries, that religion has been blended with marriages. . . .

On the other hand, as marriage is of all human actions that in which society is most interested, it became proper that this should be regulated by the civil laws. . . .

The consequences of this union, with regard to property, the reciprocal advantages, every thing which has a relation to the new family, to that from which it sprung, and to that which is expected to arise; all this relates to the civil laws.

As one of the great objects of marriage is to take away that uncertainty which attends unlawful conjunctions, religion here stamps its seal, and the civil laws join theirs to it: to the end that it may be as authentic as possible. Thus besides the conditions required by religion to make a marriage valid, the civil laws may still exact others.

The civil laws receive this power from their being additional obligations, and not contradictory ones. The law of religion insists upon certain ceremonies, the civil laws on the consent of fathers; in this case, they demand something more than that of religion, but they demand nothing contrary to it.

It follows from hence, that the religious law must decide whether the bond be indissoluble, or not; for if the laws of religion had made the bound indissoluble, and the civil laws had declared it might be broken, they would be contradictory to each other. . . .

CHAPTER XIV

In what Instances Marriages Between Relations Should be Regulated by the Laws of Nature; and in what Instances by the Civil Laws

With regard to the prohibition of marriage between relations, it is a thing extremely delicate, to fix exactly the point at which the laws of nature stop, and where the civil laws begin. For this purpose, we must establish some principles.

The marriage of the son with the mother confounds the state of things: the son ought to have an unlimited respect to his mother, the wife an unlimited respect for her husband; therefore the marriage of the mother to her son, would subvert the natural state of both.

Besides, nature has forwarded in women the time in which they are able to have children, but has retarded it in men; and, for the same reason, women sooner lose this ability and men later. If the marriage between the mother, and the son were permitted, it would almost always be the case, that when the husband was capable of entering into the views of nature, the wife would be incapable. . . .

It has ever been the natural duty of fathers to watch over the chastity of their children. Intrusted with the care of their education, they are obliged to preserve the body in the greatest perfection, and the mind from the least corruption; to encourage whatever has a tendency to inspire them with virtuous desires, and to nourish a becoming tenderness. Fathers, always employed in preserving the morals of their children, must have a natural aversion to every thing that can render them corrupt. Marriage, you will say, is not a corruption: but before marriage they must speak, they must make their persons beloved, they must seduce; it is this seduction which ought to inspire us with horror. . . .

The horror that arises against the incest of the brother with the sister, should proceed from the same source. The desire of fathers and mothers to preserve the morals of their children and families untainted, is sufficient to inspire their offspring with a detestation of every thing that can lead to the union of the two sexes.

The prohibition of marriage between cousin-germans, has the same original. In the early ages . . . it was customary for children, upon their marriage, not to remove from their parents, but to settle in the same house . . . The children of two brothers, or cousin-germans, were considered both by others and themselves, as brothers. The estrangement then between the brothers and sisters, as to marriage, subsisted also between the cousin-germans.

These principles are so strong and so natural, that they have had their influence almost over all the earth, independently of any communication. . . .

But if some nations have not rejected marriages between fathers and children, sisters and brothers, we have seen in the first book, that intelligent beings do not always follow the law of nature. . . . Religious ideas have frequently made men fall into these mistakes. . . .

As children dwell, or are supposed to dwell in their father's house, and consequently the son-in-law with the mother-in-law, the father-in-law with the daughter-in-law, or wife's daughter; the marriage between them is forbidden by the law of nature. In this case the resemblance has the same effect as the reality, because it springs from the same cause; the civil law neither can, nor ought to permit these marriages.

There are nations, as we have already observed, amongst whom cousin-germans are considered as brothers, because they commonly dwell in the same house: there are others, where this custom is not known. Among the first, the marriage of cousin-germans ought to be regarded as contrary to nature; not so among the others.

But the laws of nature cannot be local. Therefore, when these marriages are forbidden or permitted, they are, according to the circumstances, permitted or forbidden by a civil law.

It is not a necessary custom for the brother-in-law and the sister-in-law to dwell in the same house. The marriage between them is not then prohibited to preserve chastity in the family; and the law which forbids or permits it, is not a law of nature, but a civil law, regulated by circumstances, and dependent on the customs of each country: these are cases in which the laws depend on the morals or customs of the inhabitants.

The civil laws forbid marriages, when by the customs received in a certain country, they are found to be in the same circumstances as those forbidden by the law of nature; and they permit them when this is not the case. The prohibitions of the laws of nature are invariable, because the thing on which they depend is invariable; the father, the mother, and the children, necessarily dwell in the same house. But the prohibitions of the civil laws are accidental, because they depend on an accidental circumstance; cousin-germans and others dwelling in the house by accident. . . .

CHAPTER XV

That we Should not Regulate by the Principles of Political Law those Things which Depend on the Principles of Civil Law

As men have given up their natural independence to live under political laws, they have given up the natural community of goods to live under civil laws.

By the first, they acquired liberty; by the second, property. We should not decide by the laws of liberty, which, as we have already said, is only the government of the community, what ought to be decided by the laws concerning property. It is a paralogism to say, that the good of the individual should give way to that of the public: this can never take place, but when the government of the community, or, in other words, the liberty of the subject is concerned; this does not affect such cases as relate to private property, because the public good consists in every one's having their property, which was given

him by the civil laws, invariably preserved.

Cicero maintains, that the Agrarian laws were unjust; because the community was established with no view, but that every one might be able to preserve his property.

Let us, therefore, lay down a certain maxim, that whenever the public good happens to be the matter in question, it is not for the advantage of the public to deprive an individual of his property, or even to retrench the least part of it by law, or a political regulation. In this case we should follow the rigour of the civil law, which is the *Palladium* of property.

Thus when the public has occasion for the estate of an individual, it ought never to act by the rigour of political law; it is here that the civil law ought to triumph, who, with the eyes of a mother, regards every individual as the whole community.

If the political magistrate would erect a public edifice, or make a new road, he must indemnify those who are injured by it: the public is in this respect like an individual, who treats with an individual. It is full enough that it can oblige a citizen to sell his inheritance, and that it can strip him of this great privilege which he holds from the civil law, the not being forced to alienate his possessions. . . .

CHAPTER XVI

That we Ought not to Decide by the Rules of the Civil Law, when it is Proper to Decide by those of the Political Law

Most difficulties on this subject may be easily solved, by not confounding the rules derived from property with those which spring from liberty.

Is the demesne of a state or government alienable, or is it not? This question ought to be decided by the political law, and not by the civil. It ought not to be decided by the civil law, because it is as necessary that there should be demesnes for the subsistence of a state, as that the state should have civil laws to regulate the disposal of property.

If then they alienate the demesne, the state will be forced to make a new fund for another. But this expedient overturns the political government, because, by the nature of the thing, for every demesne that shall be established, the subject will always be obliged to pay more, and the sovereign to receive less; in a word, the demesne is necessary, and the alienation is not.

The order of succession is, in monarchies, founded on the welfare of the state: this makes it necessary that such an order should be fixed, to avoid the misfortunes, which I have said, must arise in a despotic kingdom, where all is uncertain, because all is arbitrary.

The order of succession is not fixed for the sake of the reigning family; but because it is the interest of the state that it should have a reigning family. The law which regulates the succession of individuals, is a civil law, whose view is the interest of individuals; that which regulates the succession to monarchy, is a political law, which has in view the welfare and preservation of the kingdom. . . .

It is ridiculous to pretend to decide the rights of kingdoms, of nations, and of the whole globe, by the same maxims on which . . . we should determine the right of a gutter between individuals. . . .

CHAPTER XVIII

That it is Necessary to Inquire, Whether the Laws which Seem Contradictory, Are of the Same Class

At Rome the husband was permitted to lend his wife to another. . . .

On the other hand, a husband who suffered his wife to be debauched, who did not bring her to justice, or who took her again after her condemnation, was punished. These laws seem to contradict each other, and yet are not contradictory. The law which permitted a Roman to lend his wife, was visibly a Lacedaemonian institution, established with a view of giving the republic children

of a good species, if I may be allowed the term; the other had in view the preservation of morals. The first was a law of politics, the second a civil law.

CHAPTER XIX

That we Should not Decide those Things by the Civil Law, which Ought to be Decided by Domestic Laws

The law of the Visigoths enjoins that the slaves of the house shall be obliged to bind the man and woman they surprise in adultery, and to present them to the husband and to the judge. . . .

. . . In countries where women are not guarded, it is ridiculous to subject those who govern the family to the inquisition of their slaves.

This inquisition may, in certain cases, be at the most a particular domestic regulation, but never a civil law.

CHAPTER XX

That We Ought not to Decide by the Principles of the Civil Laws those Things which Belong to the Law of Nations

Liberty consists principally in not being forced to do a thing where the laws do not oblige: people are in this state only as they are governed by civil laws; and because they live under those civil laws, they are free.

It follows from hence, that princes who live not among themselves under civil laws, are not free; they are governed by force; they may continually force, or be forced. From hence it follows, that treaties made by force, are as obligatory as those made by free consent. When we who live under civil laws, are, contrary to law, constrained to enter into a contract, we may, by the assistance of the law, recover from the effects of violence: but a prince, who is always in that state in which he forces, or is forced, cannot complain of a treaty which he has been compelled to sign. This would be to complain of his natural state; it would seem as if he would be a prince with respect to other princes, and as if other princes should be subjects with respect to him; that is, it would be contrary to the nature of things.

CHAPTER XXI

That We Should not Decide by Political Laws, Things which Belong to the Law of Nations

Political laws demand that every man be subject to the natural and civil courts of the country where he resides, and to the censure of the sovereign.

The law of nations requires that princes shall send ambassadors; and a reason drawn from the nature of things does not permit these ambassadors to depend either on the sovereign to whom they are sent, or on his tribunals. They are the voice of the prince who sends them, and this voice ought to be free; no obstacle should hinder the execution of their office: they may frequently offend, because they speak for a man entirely independent; they might be wrongfully accused, if they were liable to be punished for crimes: if they could be arrested for debts, these might be forged. Thus a prince, who has naturally a bold and enterprizing spirit, would speak by the mouth of a man who had everything to fear. We must then be guided, with respect to ambassadors, by reasons drawn from the law of nations, and not by those derived from political law. But if they make an ill use of their representative character, a stop may be put to it by sending them back. They may even be accused before their master, who becomes either their judge or their accomplice. . . .

CHAPTER XXIV

That the Regulations of the Police Are of a Different Class from Other Civil Laws

There are criminals, whom the magistrate punishes, there are others whom he reproves.

The former are subject to the power of the law, the latter to his authority: those are cut off from society; these they oblige to live according to the rules of society.

In the exercise of the police, it is rather the magistrate who punishes, than the law; in the sentence passed on crimes, it is rather the law which punishes than the magistrate. The business of the police consists in the affairs which arise every instant, and are commonly of a trifling nature: there is then but little need of formalities. The actions of the police are quick; they are exercised over things which return every day; it would be therefore improper for it to inflict severe punishments. It is continually employed about minute particulars; great examples are therefore not designed for its purpose. It is governed rather by regulations than laws; those who are subject to its jurisdiction, are incessantly under the eye of the magistrate: it is therefore his fault if they fall into excess. Thus we ought not to confound a flagrant violation of the laws, with a simple breach of the police; these things are of a different order. . . .

Book XXIX

OF THE MANNER OF COMPOSING LAWS

CHAPTER I

Of the Spirit of a Legislator

I say it, and methinks I have undertaken this work with no other view than to prove it, the spirit of a legislator ought to be that of moderation; political, like moral good, lying always between two extremes. Let us produce an example.

The set forms of justice are necessary to liberty; but the number of them might be so great as to be contrary to the end of the very laws that established them; processes would have no end; property would be uncertain; the goods of one of the parties would be adjudged to the other without examining, or they would both be ruined by examining too much.

The citizens would lose their liberty and

security, the accusers would no longer have any means to convict, nor the accused to justify themselves. . . .

CHAPTER IV

Of the Laws Contrary to the Views of the Legislator

There are laws so little understood by the legislator, as to be contrary to the very end he proposed. Those who made this regulation among the French, that when one of the two competitors died, the benefice should devolve to the survivor, had in view without doubt, the extinction of quarrels: but the very reverse falls out; we see the clergy at variance every day, and like English mastiffs worrying one another to death. . . .

CHAPTER XI

How We Are to Judge of the Difference of Laws

In France, the punishment against false witnesses is capital; in England it is not. Now, to be able to judge which of these two laws is the best, we must add, that in France the rack is used against criminals, but not in England; that in France the accused is not allowed to produce his witnesses; and that they very seldom admit of circumstantial evidence in favour of the prisoner; in England they allow of witnesses on both sides. These three French laws form a close and well-connected system; and so do the three English laws. The law of England, which does not allow of the racking of criminals, has but very little hopes to draw from the accused a confession of his crime; for this reason it invites witnesses from all parts, and does not venture to discourage them by the fear of a capital punishment. The French law, which has one resource more, is not afraid of intimidating the witnesses: on the contrary, reason requires they should be intimidated; it listens only to the witnesses on one side, which are those produced by the attorney-general, and the fate of the accused depends entirely on their testimony. But in England they admit of witnesses on both sides, and the affair is discussed in some measure between them; consequently false witness is there less dangerous, the accused having a remedy against the false witness which he has not in France. —Wherefore, to determine which of those laws are most agreeable to reason, we must not consider them singly, but compare the whole together. . . .

CHAPTER XVI

Things to be Observed in the Composing of Laws

They who have a genius sufficient to enable them to give laws to their own, or to another nation, ought to be particularly attentive to the manner of forming them.

The style ought to be concise. The laws of the Twelve Tables are a model of conciseness; the very children used to learn them by heart. . . .

The style should also be plain and simple; a direct expression being better understood than an indirect one. There is no majesty at all in the laws of the lower empire: princes are made to speak like rhetoricians. When the style of laws is tumid, they are looked upon only as a work of parade and ostentation.

It is an essential article that the words of the laws should excite in everybody the same ideas. Cardinal Richelieu agreed that a minister might be accused before the king; but he would have the accuser punished, if the facts he proved were not matters of moment. This was enough to hinder people from telling any truth whatsoever against the minister; because a matter of moment is entirely relative, and what may be of moment to one is not so to another. . . .

The laws ought not to be subtle; they are designed for people of common understanding, not as an art of logic, but as the plain reason of the father of a family.

When there is no necessity for exceptions and limitations in a law, it is much better to omit them: details of that kind throw people into new details.

No alteration should be made in a law without sufficient reason. Justinian ordained, that a husband might be repudiated, and yet the wife not lose her portion, if for the space of two years he had been incapable of consummating the marriage. He altered his law afterwards, and allowed the poor wretch three years. But in a case of that nature, two years are as good as three, and three are not worth more than two.

When a legislator condescends to give the reason of his law, it ought to be worthy of its majesty. . . .

As useless laws debilitate such as are necessary, so those that may be easily eluded, weaken the legislation. Every law ought to have its effect, and no one should be suffered to deviate from it by a particular exception. . . .

There very seldom happens to be a necessity of prohibiting a thing which is not bad under pretence of some imaginary perfection.

There ought to be a certain simplicity and candour in the laws; made to punish the iniquity of men, they themselves should be clad with the robes of innocence. . . .

CHAPTER XVII

A Bad Method of Giving Laws

The Roman emperors manifested their will like our princes, by decrees and edicts; but they permitted, which our princes do not, both the judges and private people to interrogate them by letters in their several differences; and their answers were called rescripts. The decretals of the popes are rescripts, strictly speaking. It is plain, that this is a bad method of legislation. Those who thus apply for laws are improper guides to the legislator; the facts are always wrong stated. Julius Capitolinus says, that Trajan often refused to give this kind of rescripts, lest a single decision, and frequently a particular favour, should be extended to all cases. . . .

I would advise those who read the Roman laws, to distinguish carefully between this sort of hypotheses, and the Senatus Consulta, the Plebiscita, the general constitutions of the emperors, and all the laws founded on the nature of things, on the frailty of women, the weakness of minors, and the public utility.

CHAPTER XVIII

Of the Ideas of Uniformity

There are certain ideas of uniformity, which sometimes strike great geniuses (for they even affected Charlemain), but infallibly make an impression on little souls. They discover therein a kind of perfection, because it is impossible for them not to see it; the same weights, the same measures in trade, the same laws in the state, the same religion in all its parts. But is this always right and without exception? Is the evil of changing constantly less than that of suffering? And does not a greatness of genius consist rather in distinguishing between those cases in which uniformity is requisite, and those in which there is a necessity for differences? . . .

CHAPTER XIX

Of Legislators

. . . The laws always meet the passions and prejudices of the legislator; sometimes they pass through, and imbibe only a tincture; sometimes they stop, and are incorporated with them. . . .

8

David Hume

1711–1776

The Humes were an old Scotch country family—educated, cultured, comfortable, but far from rich. Sweetly named *Ninewells,* their home in southern Scotland was not a castle. There were three children, two boys and a girl; David was the second son. Their father died when the children were quite young. They were gently raised by their beautiful, placid mother.

The Hume library was furnished with a collection of good books, and David was early a bookish lad. He was taught at home until he was eleven, probably by young tutors. David got little formal education. He spent about three years at Edinburgh University, returning home when he was about fourteen. The family, impressed by his love of books, urged him to study law; at seventeen he tried it, but law did not interest him, and he soon quit. He clerked for an English merchant at Bristol for a few months, but had no taste for business. His income as the second son was enough for a meager living. He decided to get along as best he could and spend his time in scholarship.

At twenty Hume was tall, scrawny, and raw boned. A sudden disorder (probably scurvy) made him ravenously hungry. He stuffed himself to ruddy robustness and was obese for the rest of his days. He was usually the typical cheery fat man—except that he developed the habit of staring annoyingly at those who talked to him.

When Hume was twenty-three he began an inexpensive three-year stay in rural France, mostly in the company of Jesuits at their college in La Fleche. During this period he wrote his first work, *Treatise of Human Nature,* subtitled, *an Attempt to Introduce the Experimental Method of Reasoning into Moral Subjects.* The work was divided into three books. The first two were published in 1739 and the third, a year later. Excerpts which follow this biographical note are from the third book. The first book dealt with logic and metaphysics to supply a psychological underpinning for the ethics and jurisprudence which followed. The publisher paid well for the *Treatise,* but it attracted little notice and sold poorly; reviews were few and not very favorable. Hume was dispirited. His morale rose when his second work, *Essays, Moral and Political* (1741-2), was a well-received sell-out; in his early thirties he enjoyed a substantial reputation. Hume aspired to a vacant philosophy chair at Edinburgh University. The town council could not be won over because Hume's books and talk had fairly well established that he was an atheist. The appointment went to another.

The Marquis of Annandale was attracted to Hume, and in 1745 he invited Hume to live on his estate and help with the Marquis' literary efforts. The Marquis had talent, but was on the verge of insanity. His dementia deepened. Hume's discomfort was aggravated by shabby treatment from members of the Marquis' family. They were even slow in paying salary due when he quit at the end of an unhappy year to become secretary to General St. Clair.

St. Clair was in command of forces scheduled for Canada, but was sent instead on an abortive mission against the French at

Lorient. The expedition came quietly back to England, and St. Clair was sent to the courts at Vienna and Turin. Hume went along as secretarial aide-de-camp, his fat body unbecomingly dressed in a military uniform. Nevertheless, he had a grand time and found many good companions.

When the mission ended, Hume went home to *Ninewells* and a country literary life with his brother and sister. It was a little too quiet for him. He had saved money and his published works brought in more. He moved to Edinburgh and bought a house. Shortly after he wrote to a friend, "I can reach, I find, cleanliness, warmth, light, and contentment. What would you have more? Independence? I have it in a supreme degree. Honour? That is not altogether wanting. Grace? That will come in time. A wife? That is none of the indispensable requisites of life. . . ." At times, however, he waivered about staying in Edinburgh. The Church of Scotland was divided. The Highflier party was orthodox and outraged by atheism; they proposed measures against Hume and his writings in church councils. The Moderates —many of whom were Hume's friends— blocked his condemnation. But the attacks must have been harassing. One of Hume's 1759 letters says, "Scotland suits my fortune best, and is the seat of my principal friendships; but it is too narrow a place for me, and it mortifies me that I sometimes hurt my friends." Sometimes Hume hankered for London and Paris. Sometimes, too, he was not so sure about the joys of bachelorhood. His last serious temptation to propose marriage came when he was sixty, but failing health and other forces held him back.

In Edinburgh Hume changed the direction of his literary interest and launched into a multi-volume English history. The Faculty of Advocates named him Librarian, giving him access to a fine collection of books and making little demand on his time. As his history came out, the volumes sold well and were praised. His literary earnings, it is said, were the largest that any English author had made up to that time.

In 1759 he went to London to see part of his history through the presses. The early part of his visit was frolicsome and sociable. His reputation as a good companion grew and his social life expanded. A letter to Adam Smith on the publication of his *Theory of Moral Sentiments,* illustrates Hume's wit at this time. ". . . your book has been very unfortunate. For the public seem to be disposed to applaud it extremely. . . . Three bishops called yesterday at Millar's shop in order to buy copies and ask questions about the author. You may conclude what an opinion true philosophers will entertain of it when these retainers to superstition praise it so highly. The Duke of Argyle is more decisive . . . in its favor. I suppose he either considers it an exotic or thinks the author will be serviceable to him in the Glasgow elections. . . ."

Hume's delight in London began to wane. The temper of intellectual circles was changing; England under George III was forging ahead as a nation and a world power; notables' interest turned toward politics and foreign relations and away from philosophy and history. By 1761 Hume decided against permanent residence in England and reestablished himself in Edinburgh. After his return he wrote a friend, "I do not believe there is one Englishman in fifty, who if he heard I broke my neck tonight, would not be rejoiced with it. Some hate me because I am not a Tory, some because I am not a Whig, some because I am not a Christian, and all because I am a Scotsman."

But Hume was not too fixed in Edinburgh to say, "No," when pious Lord Hertford, ambassador to France, surprisingly asked Hume to join his staff. Hume accepted more for amusement than advancement. For twenty-six months Hume was the rage of Paris; his literary reputation opened all doors. Leaders of Paris society sought to be seen with "Fat David" in their theatre and opera boxes. The first time he came to the French court, three future kings of France (aged six to nine) recited little set speeches about him and his work. He spent many evenings in discussions in fashionable sâlons. One of these was the sâlon of Comtesse de

Boufflers, with whom his relationship was not entirely intellectual.

When Jean Jaques Rousseau was exiled from France and found his position in Switzerland untenable, Hume befriended him and took him to England. Rousseau transplanted poorly and crazily suspected everyone of plotting against him—especially Hume. Their relationship became a topic of public gossip and was discussed in the press. Hume was very unhappy to find his attempt to help a great man had misfired and that he was faced with unjust charges of persecution. The affair ended when Rousseau, with unnecessary furtiveness, slunk out of England.

Hertford returned to England from foreign service and became Lord Chamberlain. His nomination got Hume the post of Under Secretary of State. He held that post for almost a year, enjoying the easy pace with which he could still be a model civil servant. He had plenty of time for cards, club life, and London high society. When he left office he replied to a publisher's prod, that he would write no more because he was too old, too fat, too lazy, and too rich.

He went back to Edinburgh and built a fine house in a new part of town. In his letters of this period he boasted of his cooking talents and recipes for tasty soups and meats. His house became a center of liberal intellectual life and often attracted travellers. Benjamin Franklin spent almost a month with Hume in 1771—his visit being the occasion of a constant round of dinners and discussions.

Six years after Hume's return to Edinburgh he began to feel a debility which increased gradually, but surely, until Hume knew that he was mortally ill. He stoically made a medical pilgrimage to London and Bath, but soon set back for home to die. He wrote letters ahead, asking friends to a farewell dinner. They gathered at his house on July 4, 1776—the last of his beloved parties. Six weeks later, he was dead at sixty-four.

In his later years, Hume found criticism hard to take. To forestall some of his detractors he wrote an "advertisement" to be printed in future editions of his *Essays,* in which he characterized his *Treatise of Human Nature* as a work published prematurely and said that his ideas were recast and corrected in his later work. "Henceforth," he wrote, "the author desires that the following pieces may alone be regarded as containing his philosophical sentiments and principles." Mossner, in his great biography of Hume, comments, "Happily, few philosophers have taken the 'advertisement' seriously; and the *Treatise of Human Nature ...* is generally and properly regarded as his masterpiece."

A TREATISE OF HUMAN NATURE *

Volume II, Book III

OF MORALS

Part I

OF VIRTUE AND VICE IN GENERAL

SECTION I

Moral Distinctions not Derived from Reason

... Those who affirm that virtue is nothing but a conformity to reason; that there are eternal fitnesses and unfitnesses of things, which are the same to every rational being that considers them; that the immutable measure of right and wrong impose an obligation, not only on human creatures, but also on the Deity himself: all these systems concur in the opinion, that morality, like truth, is discerned merely by deas, and by their juxtaposition and comparison. In order, therefore, to judge of these systems, we need only consider whether it be possible from reason alone, to distinguish betwixt moral good and evil, or whether there must concur some other principles to enable us to make that distinction.

If morality had naturally no influence on

* From number 549, Everyman's Library. Reprinted by permission of E. P. Dutton & Co., Inc.

human passions and actions, it were in vain to take such pains to inculcate it; and nothing would be more fruitless than that multitude of rules and precepts with which all moralists abound. Philosophy is commonly divided into *speculative* and *practical;* and as morality is always comprehended under the latter division, it is supposed to influence our passions and actions, and to go beyond the calm and indolent judgments of the understanding. And this is confirmed by common experience, which informs us that men are often governed by their duties, and are deterred from some actions by the opinion of injustice, and impelled to others by that of obligation.

Since morals, therefore, have an influence on the actions and affections, it follows that they cannot be derived from reason; and that because reason alone . . . can never have any such influence. Morals excite passions, and produce or prevent actions. Reason of itself is utterly impotent in this particular. The rules of morality, therefore, are not conclusions of our reason. . . .

Reason is the discovery of truth or falsehood. Truth or falsehood consists in an agreement or disagreement either to the *real* relations of ideas, or to *real* existence and matter of fact. Whatever therefore is not susceptible of this agreement or disagreement, is incapable of being true or false, and can never be an object of our reason. Now, it is evident our passions, volitions, and actions, are not susceptible of any such agreement or disagreement; being original facts and realities, complete in themselves, and implying no reference to other passions, volitions, and actions. It is impossible, therefore, they can be pronounced either true or false, and be either contrary or conformable to reason.

This argument is of double advantage to our present purpose. For it proves *directly,* that actions do not derive their merit from a conformity to reason, nor their blame from a contrariety to it; and it proves the same truth more *indirectly,* by showing us, that as reason can never immediately prevent or produce any action by contradicting or approving of it, it cannot be the source of moral good and evil, which are found to have that influence. Actions may be laudable or blamable; but they cannot be reasonable or unreasonable: laudable or blamable, therefore, are not the same with reasonable or unreasonable. . . .

It has been observed that reason, in a strict and philosophical sense, can have an influence on our conduct only after two ways: either when it excites a passion, by informing us of the existence of something which is a proper object of it; or when it discovers the connection of causes and effects, so as to afford us means of exerting any passion. These are the only kinds of judgment which can accompany our actions, or can be said to produce them in any manner; and it must be allowed, that these judgments may often be false and erroneous. A person may be affected with passion, by supposing a pain or pleasure to lie in an object which has no tendency to produce either of these sensations, or which produces the contrary to what is imagined. A person may also take false measures for the attaining of his end, and may retard, by his foolish conduct, instead of forwarding the execution of any object. These false judgments may be thought to affect the passions and actions, which are connected with them, and may be said to render them unreasonable, in a figurative and improper way of speaking. But though this be acknowledged, it is easy to observe, that these errors are so far from being the source of all immorality, that they are commonly very innocent, and draw no manner of guilt upon the person who is so unfortunate as to fall into them. They extend not beyond a mistake of *fact*, which moralists have not generally supposed criminal, as being perfectly involuntary. . . .

If the thought and understanding were alone capable of fixing the boundaries of right and wrong, the character of virtuous and vicious either must lie in some relations of objects, or must be a matter of fact which is discovered by our reasoning. This consequence is evident. As the operations of human understanding divide themselves into two kinds, the comparing of ideas, and the inferring of matter of fact, were virtue discovered by the understanding, it must be an object of one of these operations; nor is there any third operation of the understanding which can discover it. There has been an opinion very industriously propagated by certain philosophers, that morality is susceptible of demonstration; and though no one has ever been able to advance a single step in those demonstrations, yet it is taken for granted that this science may be brought to an equal certainty with geometry or algebra. . . .

If you assert that vice and virtue consist in relations susceptible of certainty and demonstration, you must confine yourself to those *four* relations which alone admit of that degree of evidence; and in that case you run into absurdities from which you will never be able to extricate yourself. For as you make the very essence of morality to lie in the relations, and as there is no one of these relations but what is applicable, not only to an irrational but also to an inanimate object, it follows that even such objects must be susceptible of merit or demerit. *Resemblance, contrariety, degrees in quality,* and *proportions in quantity and number;* all these relations belong as properly to matter as to our actions, passions, and volitions. It is unquestionable, therefore, that morality lies not in any of these relations, nor the sense of it in their discovery. . . .

I must therefore, on this occasion, rest contented with requiring the two following conditions of any one that would undertake to clear up this system. *First,* as moral good and evil belong only to the actions of the mind, and are derived from our situation with regard to external objects, the relations from which these moral distinctions arise must lie only betwixt internal actions and external objects, and must not be applicable either to internal actions, compared among themselves, or to external objects, when placed in opposition to other external objects. For as morality is supposed to attend certain relations, if these relations could belong to internal actions considered singly, it would

follow, that we might be guilty of crimes in ourselves, and independent of our situation with respect to the universe; and in like manner, if these moral relations could be applied to external objects, it would follow that even inanimate beings would be susceptible of moral beauty and deformity. Now, it seems difficult to imagine that any relation can be discovered betwixt our passions, volitions, and actions, compared to external objects, which relation might not belong either to these passions and volitions, or to these external objects, compared among *themselves.*

But it will be still more difficult to fulfil the *second* condition, requisite to justify this system. According to the principles of those who maintain an abstract rational difference betwixt moral good and evil, and a natural fitness and unfitness of things, it is not only supposed, that these relations, being eternal and immutable, are the same, when considered by every rational creature, but their *effects* are also supposed to be necessarily the same; and it is concluded they have no less, or rather a greater, influence in directing the will of the Deity, than in governing the rational and virtuous of our own species. These two particulars are evidently distinct. It is one thing to know virtue, and another to conform the will to it. In order, therefore, to prove that the measures of right and wrong are eternal laws, *obligatory* on every rational mind, it is not sufficient to show the relations upon which they are founded: we must also point out the connection betwixt the relation and the will; and must prove that this connection is so necessary, that in every well-disposed mind, it must take place and have its influence; though the difference betwixt these minds be in other respects immense and infinite. . . .

Thus it will be impossible to fulfil the *first* condition required to the system of eternal rational measures of right and wrong; because it is impossible to show those relations, upon which such a distinction may be founded: and it is as impossible to fulfil the *second* condition; because we cannot prove *a priori,* that these relations, if they really existed and were perceived, would be universally forcible and obligatory.

But to make these general reflections more clear and convincing, we may illustrate them by some particular instances, wherein this character of moral good or evil is the most universally acknowledged. Of all crimes that human creatures are capable of committing, the most horrid and unnatural is ingratitude, especially when it is committed against parents, and appears in the more flagrant instances of wounds and death. This is acknowledged by all mankind, philosophers as well as the people: the question only arises among philosophers, whether the guilt or moral deformity of this action be discovered by demonstrative reasoning, or be felt by an internal sense, and by means of some sentiment, which the reflecting on such an action naturally occasions. This question will soon be decided against the former opinion, if we can show the same relations in other objects, without the notion of any guilt or iniquity attending them. Reason or science is nothing but the comparing of ideas, and the discovery of their relations; and if the same relations have different characters, it must evidently follow, that those characters are not discovered merely by reason. To put the affair, therefore, to this trial, let us choose any inanimate object, such as an oak or elm; and let us suppose, that, by the dropping of its seed, it produces a sapling below it, which, springing up by degrees, at last overtops and destroys the parent tree: I ask, if, in this instance, there be wanting any relation which is discoverable in parricide or ingratitude? Is not the one tree the cause of the other's existence; and the latter the cause of the destruction of the former, in the same manner as when a child murders his parent? It is not sufficient to reply, that a choice or will is wanting. For in the case of parricide, a will does not give rise to any *different* relations, but is only the cause from which the action is derived; and consequently produces the *same* relations, that in the oak or elm arise from some other principles. It is a will or choice that determines

a man to kill his parent: and they are the laws of matter and motion that determine a sapling to destroy the oak from which it sprung. Here then the same relations have different causes; but still the relations are the same: and as their discovery is not in both cases attended with a notion of immorality, it follows, that that notion does not arise from such a discovery.

But to choose an instance still more resembling; I would fain ask any one, why incest in the human species is criminal, and why the very same action, and the same relations in animals, have not the smallest moral turpitude and deformity? If it be answered, that this action is innocent in animals, because they have not reason sufficient to discover its turpitude; but that man, being endowed with that faculty, which *ought* to restrain him to his duty, the same action instantly becomes criminal to him. Should this be said, I would reply, that this is evidently arguing in a circle. For, before reason can perceive this turpitude, the turpitude must exist; and consequently is independent of the decisions of our reason, and is their object more properly than their effect. . . .

Nor does this reasoning only prove, that morality consists not in any relations that are the objects of science; but if examined, will prove with equal certainty, that it consists not in any *matter of fact*, which can be discovered by the understanding. This is the *second* part of our argument; and if it can be made evident, we may conclude that morality is not an object of reason. But can there be any difficulty in proving that vice and virtue are not matters of fact, whose existence we can infer by reason? Take any action allowed to be vicious; wilful murder, for instance. Examine it in all lights, and see if you can find that matter of fact, or real existence, which you call *vice*. In whichever way you take it, you find only certain passions, motives, volitions, and thoughts. There is no other matter of fact in the case. The vice entirely escapes you, as long as you consider the object. You never can find it, till you turn your reflection into your own breast, and find a sentiment of disprobation, which arises in you, towards this action. Here is a matter of fact; but it is the object of feeling, not of reason. It lies in yourself, not in the object. So that when you pronounce any action or character to be vicious, you mean nothing, but that from the constitution of your nature you have a feeling or sentiment of blame from the contemplation of it. . . .

. . . In every system of morality which I have hitherto met with, I have always remarked, that the author proceeds for some time in the ordinary way of reasoning, and establishes the being of a God, or makes observations concerning human affairs; when of a sudden I am surprised to find, that instead of the usual copulations of propositions, *is,* and *is not,* I meet with no proposition that is not connected with an *ought,* or an *ought not.* This change is imperceptible; but is, however, of the last consequence. For as this *ought,* or *ought not,* expresses some new relation or affirmation, it is necessary that it should be observed and explained; and at the same time that a reason should be given, for what seems altogether inconceivable, how this new relation can be a deduction from others, which are entirely different from it. But as authors do not commonly use this precaution, I shall presume to recommend it to the readers; and am persuaded, that this small attention would subvert all the vulgar systems of morality, and let us see that the distinction of vice and virtue is not founded merely on the relations of objects, nor is perceived by reason.

SECTION II

Moral Distinctions Derived from a Moral Sense

Thus the course of the argument leads us to conclude, that since vice and virtue are not discoverable merely by reason, or the comparison of ideas, it must be by means of some impression or sentiment they occasion, that we are able to mark the difference betwixt them. Our decisions concerning moral rectitude and depravity are evidently perceptions; and as all perceptions are either impressions or ideas, the exclusion of the one is a convincing argument for the other. Morality, therefore, is more properly felt than judged of. . . .

. . . To have the sense of virtue, is nothing but to *feel* a satisfaction of a particular kind from the contemplation of a character. The very *feeling* constitutes our praise or admiration. We go no further; nor do we inquire into the cause of the satisfaction. We do not infer a character to be virtuous, because it pleases; but in feeling that it pleases after such a particular manner, we in effect feel that it is virtuous. The case is the same as in our judgments concerning all kinds of beauty, and tastes, and sensations. Our approbation is implied in the immediate pleasure they convey to us. . . .

It may now be asked, *in general,* concerning this pain or pleasure that distinguishes moral good and evil, *From what principle is it derived, and whence does it arise in the human mind?* To this I reply, *first,* that it is absurd to imagine that, in every particular instance, these sentiments are produced by an *original* quality and *primary* constitution. For as the number of our duties is in a manner infinite, it is impossible that our original instinct should extend to each of them, and from our very first infancy impress on the human mind all that multitude of precepts which are contained in the completest system of ethics. Such a method of proceeding is not conformable to the usual maxims by which nature is conducted, where a few principles produce all that variety we observe in the universe, and everything is carried on in the easiest and most simple manner. It is necessary, therefore, to abridge these primary impulses, and find some more general principles upon which all our notions of morals are founded. . . .

Meanwhile, it may not be amiss to observe, from these definitions of *natural* and *unnatural,* that nothing can be more unphilosophical than those systems which assert that virtue is the same with what is natural, and vice with what is unnatural. For, in the first sense of the word, nature, as opposed to miracles, both vice and virtue are equally natural; and, in the second sense, as opposed to what is unusual, perhaps virtue will be found to be the most unnatural. At least it must be owned, that heroic virtue, being as unusual, is as little natural as the most brutal barbarity. As to the third sense of the word, it is certain that both vice and virtue are equally artificial and out of nature. For, however it may be disputed, whether the notion of a merit or demerit in certain actions, be natural or artificial, it is evident that the actions themselves are artificial, and performed with a certain design and intention; otherwise they could never be ranked under any of these denominations. It is impossible, therefore, that the character of natural and unnatural can ever, in any sense, mark the boundaries of vice and virtue. . . .

Part II

OF JUSTICE AND INJUSTICE

SECTION I

Justice, Whether a Natural or Artificial Virtue?

I have already hinted, that our sense of every kind of virtue is not natural; but that there are some virtues that produce pleasure and approbation by means of an artifice or contrivance, which arises from the circumstances and necessity of mankind. Of this kind I assert *justice* to be; and shall endeavour to defend this opinion by a short, and, I hope, convincing argument, before I examine the nature of the artifice, from which the sense of that virtue is derived.

It is evident that, when we praise any actions, we regard only the motives that produced them, and consider the actions as signs or indications of certain principles in the mind and temper. The external performance has no merit. We must look within to find the moral quality. This we cannot do directly; and therefore fix our attention on actions, as on external signs. But these actions are still considered as signs; and the ultimate object of our praise and approbation is the motive that produced them. . . .

. . . The first virtuous motive which bestows a merit on any action, can never be a regard to the virtue of that action, but must be some other natural motive or principle. To suppose that the mere regard to the virtue of the action, may be the first motive which produced the action, and rendered it virtuous, is to reason in a circle. Before we can have such a regard, the action must be really virtuous; and this virtue must be derived from some virtuous motive: and, consequently, the virtuous motive must be different from the regard to the virtue of the action. . . .

. . . We blame a father for neglecting his child. Why? because it shows a want of natural affection, which is the duty of every parent. Were not natural affection a duty, the care of children could not be a duty; and it were impossible we could have the duty in our eye in the attention we give to our offspring. In this case, therefore, all men suppose a motive to the action distinct from a sense of duty.

Here is a man that does many benevolent actions; relieves the distressed, comforts the afflicted, and extends his bounty even to the greatest strangers. No character can be more amiable and virtuous. We regard these actions as proofs of the greatest humanity. This humanity bestows a merit on the actions. A regard to this merit is, therefore, a secondary consideration, and derived from the antecedent principles of humanity, which is meritorious and laudable.

In short, it may be established as an undoubted maxim, *that no action can be virtuous, or morally good, unless there be in human nature some motive to produce it distinct from the sense of its morality.*

But may not the sense of morality or duty produce an action, without any other motive? I answer, it may: but this is no objection to the present doctrine. When any virtuous motive or principle is common in human nature, a person who feels his heart devoid of that motive, may hate himself upon that account, and may perform the ac-

justice – artifice or contrivance, which arises from the circumstances & necessity of mankind.

tion without the motive, from a certain sense of duty, in order to acquire, by practice, that virtuous principle, or at least to disguise to himself, as much as possible, his want of it. A man that really feels no gratitude in his temper, is still pleased to perform grateful actions, and thinks he has, by that means, fulfilled his duty. Actions are at first only considered as signs of motives: but it is usual, in this case, as in all others, to fix our attention on the signs, and neglect, in some measure, the thing signified. But though, on some occasions, a person may perform an action merely out of regard to its moral obligation, yet still this supposes in human nature some distinct principles, which are capable of producing the action, and whose moral beauty renders the action meritorious.

Now, to apply all this to the present case; I suppose a person to have lent me a sum of money, on condition that it be restored in a few days; and also suppose, that after the expiration of the term agreed on, he demands the sum: I ask, *What reason or motive have I to restore the money?* It will perhaps be said, that my regard to justice, and abhorrence of villainy and knavery, are sufficient reasons for me, if I have the least grain of honesty, or sense of duty and obligation. And this answer, no doubt, is just and satisfactory to man in his civilised state, and when trained up according to a certain discipline and education. But in his rude and more *natural* condition, if you are pleased to call such a condition natural, this answer would be rejected as perfectly unintelligible and sophistical. For one in that situation would immediately ask you, *Wherein consists this honesty and justice, which you find in restoring a loan, and abstaining from the property of others?* It does not surely lie in the external action. It must, therefore, be placed in the motive from which the external action is derived. This motive can never be a regard to the honesty of the action. For it is a plain fallacy to say, that a virtuous motive is requisite to render an action honest, and, at the same time, that a regard to the honesty is the motive

of the action. We can never have a regard to the virtue of an action, unless the action be antecedently virtuous. No action can be virtuous, but so far as it proceeds from a virtuous motive. A virtuous motive, therefore, must precede the regard to the virtue; and it is impossible that the virtuous motive and the regard to the virtue can be the same.

It is requisite, then, to find some motive to acts of justice and honesty, distinct from our regard to the honesty; and in this lies the great difficulty. For should we say, that a concern for our private interest or reputation, is the legitimate motive to all honest actions: it would follow that wherever that concern ceases, honesty can no longer have place. But it is certain that self-love, when it acts at its liberty, instead of engaging us to honest actions, is the source of all injustice and violence; nor can a man ever correct those vices, without correcting and restraining the *natural* movements of that appetite.

But should it be affirmed that the reason or motive of such actions is the *regard to public interest*, to which nothing is more contrary than examples of injustice and dishonesty; should this be said, I would propose the three following considerations as worthy of our attention. *First,* Public interest is not naturally attached to the observation of the rules of justice; but is only connected with it, after an artificial convention for the establishment of these rules, as shall be shown more at large hereafter. *Secondly,* If we suppose that the loan was secret, and that it is necessary for the interest of the person, that the money be restored in the same manner (as when the lender would conceal his riches), in that case the example ceases, and the public is no longer interested in the actions of the borrower; though I suppose there is no moralist who will affirm that the duty and obligation ceases. *Thirdly,* Experience sufficiently proves that men, in the ordinary conduct of life, look not so far as the public interest, when they pay their creditors, perform their promises, and abstain from theft, and robbery, and injustice of every kind. That is a motive too remote and too sublime to affect the generality of mankind, and operate with any force in actions so contrary to private interest as are frequently those of justice and common honesty.

In general, it may be affirmed, that there is no such passion in human minds as the love of mankind, merely as such, independent of personal qualities, of services, or of relation to ourself. It is true, there is no human, and indeed no sensible creature, whose happiness or misery does not, in some measure, affect us, when brought near us, and represented in lively colours: but this proceeds merely from sympathy, and is no proof of such an universal affection to mankind, since this concern extends itself beyond our own species. . . .

If public benevolence, therefore, or a regard to the interests of mankind, cannot be the original motive to justice, much less can *private benevolence,* or a *regard to the interests of the party concerned,* be this motive. For what if he be my enemy, and has given me just cause to hate him? What if he be a vicious man, and deserves the hatred of all mankind? What if he be a miser, and can make no use of what I would deprive him of? What if he be a profligate debauchee, and would rather receive harm than benefit from large possessions? What if I be in necessity, and have urgent motives to acquire something to my family? In all these cases, the original motive to justice would fail; and consequently the justice itself, and along with it all property, right, and obligation. . . .

A man's property is supposed to be fenced against every mortal, in every possible case. But private benevolence is, and ought to be, weaker in some persons than in others: and in many, or indeed in most persons, must absolutely fail. Private benevolence, therefore, is not the original motive of justice.

From all this it follows, that we have no real or universal motive for observing the laws of equity, but the very equity and merit of that observance; and as no action can be equitable or meritorious, where it cannot arise from some separate motive, there is here an evident sophistry and reasoning in a circle. Unless, therefore, we will allow that nature has established a sophistry, and rendered it necessary and unavoidable, we must allow, that the sense of justice and injustice is not derived from nature, but arises artificially, though necessarily, from education and human conventions. . . .

To avoid giving offence, I must here observe, that when I deny justice to be a natural virtue, I make use of the word *natural,* only as opposed to *artificial.* In another sense of the word, as no principle of the human mind is more natural than a sense of virtue, so no virtue is more natural than justice. Mankind is an inventive species; and where an invention is obvious and absolutely necessary, it may as properly be said to be natural as anything that proceeds immediately from original principles, without the intervention of thought or reflection. Though the rules of justice be *artificial,* they are not *arbitrary.* Nor is the expression improper to call them *Laws of Nature;* if by natural we understand what is common to any species, or even if we confine it to mean what is inseparable from the species.

SECTION II

Of the Origin of Justice and Property

We now proceed to examine two questions, viz. *concerning the manner in which the rules of justice are established by the artifice of men;* and *concerning the reasons which determine us to attribute to the observance or neglect of these rules a moral beauty and deformity.* These questions will appear afterwards to be distinct. We shall begin with the former.

Of all the animals with which this globe is peopled, there is none toward whom nature seems, at first sight, to have exercised more cruelty than towards man, in the numberless wants and necessities with which she has loaded him, and in the slender means which she affords to the relieving these necessities. In other creatures, these two particulars generally compensate each other. If we consider the lion as a voracious and carnivorous animal, we shall easily discover him to be very necessitous; but if we turn our eye to his make and temper, his agility, his courage, his arms, and his force, we shall find that his advantages hold proportion with his wants. The sheep and ox are deprived of all these advantages; but their appetites are moderate, and their food is of easy purchase. In man alone this unnatural conjunction of infirmity and of necessity may be observed in its greatest perfection. Not only the food which is required for his sustenance flies his search and approach, or at least requires his labour to be produced, but he must be possessed of clothes and lodging to defend him against the injuries of the weather; though, to consider him only in himself, he is provided neither with arms, nor force, nor other natural abilities which are in any degree answerable to so many necessities.

It is by society alone he is able to supply his defects, and raise himself up to an equality with his fellow-creatures, and even acquire a superiority above them. By society all his infirmities are compensated; and though in that situation his wants multiply every moment upon him, yet his abilities are still more augmented, and leave him in every respect more satisfied and happy than it is possible for him, in his savage and solitary condition, ever to become. When every individual person labours apart, and only for himself, his force is too small to execute any considerable work; his labour being employed in supplying all his different necessities, he never attains a perfection in any particular art; and as his force and success are not at all times equal, the least failure in either of these particulars must be attended with inevitable ruin and misery. Society provides a remedy for these *three* inconveniences. By the conjunction of forces, our power is augmented; by the partition of employments, our ability increases; and by mutual succour, we are less exposed to fortune and accidents. It is by this additional *force, ability,* and *security,* that society becomes advantageous.

But, in order to form society, it is requisite not only that it be advantageous, but also that men be sensible of these advantages; and it is impossible, in their wild uncultivated state, that by study and reflection alone they should ever be able to attain this knowledge. Most fortunately, therefore, there is conjoined to those necessities, whose remedies are remote and obscure, another necessity, which, having a present and more obvious remedy, may justly be regarded as the first and original principle of human society. This necessity is no other than that natural appetite betwixt the sexes, which unites them together, and preserves their union, till a new tie takes place in their concern for their common offspring. This new concern becomes also a principle of union betwixt the parents and offspring, and forms a more numerous society, where the parents govern by the advantage of their superior strength and wisdom, and at the same time are restrained in the exercise of their authority by that natural affection which they bear their children. In a little time, custom and habit, operating on the tender minds of the children, makes them sensible of the advantages which they may reap from society, as well as fashions them by degrees for it, by rubbing off those rough corners and untoward affections which prevent their coalition.

For it must be confessed, that however the circumstances of human nature may render a union necessary, and however those passions of lust and natural affection may seem to render it unavoidable, yet there are other particulars in our *natural temper,* and in our *outward circumstances,* which are very incommodious, and are even contrary to the requisite conjunction. Among the former we may justly esteem our *selfishness* to be the most considerable. I am sensible that, generally speaking, the representations of this quality have been carried much too far; and that the descriptions which certain philosophers delight so much to form of mankind in this particular, are as wide of nature as any accounts of monsters which we meet with in fables and romances. So far from thinking that men have no affection for anything beyond themselves, I am of opinion that, though it be rare to meet with one who loves any single person better than himself, yet it is as rare to meet with one in whom all the kind affections, taken together, do not overbalance all the selfish. Consult common experience; do you not see, that though the whole expense of the family be generally under the direction of the master of it, yet there are few that do not bestow the largest part of their fortunes on the pleasures of their wives and the education of their children, reserving the smallest portion for their own proper use and entertainment? This is what we may observe concerning such as have those endearing ties; and may presume, that the case would be the same with others, were they placed in a like situation. . . .

. . . There are three different species of goods which we are possessed of; the internal satisfaction of our minds; the external advantages of our body; and the enjoyment of such possessions as we have acquired by our industry and good fortune. We are perfectly secure in the enjoyment of the first. The second may be ravished from us, but can be of no advantage to him who deprives us of them. The last only are both exposed to the violence of others, and may be transferred without suffering any loss or alteration; while at the same time there is not a sufficient quantity of them to supply every one's desire and necessities. As the improvement, therefore, of these goods is the chief advantage of society, so the *instability* of their possession, along with their *scarcity*, is the chief impediment.

In vain should we expect to find, in *uncultivated nature*, a remedy to this inconvenience; or hope for any inartificial principle of the human mind which might control those partial affections, and make us overcome the temptations arising from our circumstances. The idea of justice can never serve to this purpose, or be taken for a natural principle, capable of inspiring men with an equitable conduct towards each other . . . Our natural uncultivated ideas of morality, instead of providing a remedy for the partiality of our affections, do rather conform themselves to that partiality, and give it an additional force and influence.

The remedy, then, is not derived from nature, but from *artifice;* or, more properly speaking, nature provides a remedy, in the judgment and understanding, for what is irregular and incommodious in the affections. For when men, from their early education in society, have become sensible of the infinite advantages that result from it, and have besides acquired a new affection to company and conversation, and when they have observed that the principal disturbance in society arises from those goods, which we call external, and from their looseness and easy transition from one person to another, they must seek for a remedy, by putting these goods, as far as possible, on the same footing with the fixed and constant advantages of the mind and body. This can be done after no other manner, than by a convention entered into by all the members of the society to bestow stability on the possession of those external goods, and leave every one in the peaceable enjoyment of what he may acquire by his fortune and industry. By this means every one knows what he may safely possess; and the passions are restrained in their partial and contradictory motions. Nor is such a restraint contrary to these passions; for, if so, it could never be entered into nor maintained; but it is only contrary to their heedless and impetuous movement. Instead of departing from our own interest, or from that of our nearest friends, by abstaining from the possessions of others, we cannot better consult both these interests than by such a convention; because it is by that means we maintain society, which is so necessary to their well-being and subsistence, as well as to our own.

This convention is not of the nature of a *promise;* for even promises themselves, as we shall see afterwards, arise from human conventions. It is only a general sense of common interest; which sense all the members of the society express to one another, and which induces them to regulate their conduct by certain rules. I observe, that it will be for my interest to leave another in the possession of his goods, *provided* he will act in the same manner with regard to me. He is sensible of a like interest in the regulation of his conduct. When this common sense of interest is mutually expressed, and is known to both, it produces a suitable resolution and behaviour. And this may properly enough be called a convention or agreement betwixt us, though without the interposition of a promise; since the actions of each of us have a reference to those of the other, and are performed upon the supposition that something is to be performed on the other part. Two men who pull the oars of a boat, do it by an agreement or convention, though they have never given promises to each other. . . .

After this convention, concerning abstinence from the possessions of others, is entered into, and every one has acquired a stability in his possessions, there immediately arise the ideas of justice and injustice; as also those of *property, right,* and *obligation.* The latter are altogether unintelligible, without first understanding the former. Our property is nothing but those goods, whose constant possession is established by the laws of society; that is, by the laws of justice. Those, therefore, who make use of the words *property,* or *right,* or *obligation,* before they have explained the origin of justice, or even make use of them in that explication, are guilty of a very gross fallacy, and can never reason upon any solid foundation. A man's property is some object related to him. This relation is not natural, but moral, and founded on justice. It is very preposterous, therefore, to imagine that we can have any idea of property, without fully comprehending the nature of justice, and showing its origin in the artifice and contrivance of men. The origin of justice explains that of property. The same artifice gives rise to both. As our first and most natural sentiment of morals is founded on the nature of our passions, and gives the preference to ourselves and friends above strangers, it is impossible there can be naturally any such thing as a fixed right or property,

while the opposite passions of men impel them in contrary directions, and are not restrained by any convention or agreement. . . .

. . . No affection of the human mind has both a sufficient force and a proper direction to counterbalance the love of gain, and render men fit members of society, by making them abstain from the possessions of others. Benevolence to strangers is too weak for this purpose; and as to the other passions, they rather inflame this avidity, when we observe, that the larger our possessions are, the more ability we have of gratifying all our appetites. There is no passion, therefore, capable of controlling the interested affection, but the very affection itself, by an alteration of its direction. Now, this alteration must necessarily take place upon the least reflection; since it is evident that the passion is much better satisfied by its restraint than by its liberty, and that, in preserving society, we make much greater advances in the acquiring possessions, than in the solitary and forlorn condition which must follow upon violence and an universal licence. The question, therefore, concerning the wickedness or goodness of human nature, enters not in the least into that other question concerning the origin of society; nor is there anything to be considered but the degrees of men's sagacity or folly. For whether the passion of self-interest be esteemed vicious or virtuous, it is all a case, since itself alone restrains it; so that if it be virtuous, men become social by their virtue; if vicious, their vice has the same effect.

Now, as it is by establishing the rule for the stability of possession that this passion restrains itself, if that rule be very abstruse and of difficult invention, society must be esteemed in a manner accidental, and the effect of many ages. But if it be found that nothing can be more simple and obvious than that rule; that every parent, in order to preserve peace among his children, must establish it; and that these first rudiments of justice must every day be improved, as the society enlarges: if all this appear evident, as it certainly must, we may conclude that it is utterly impossible for men to remain any considerable time in that savage condition which precedes society, but that his very first state and situation may justly be esteemed social. This, however, hinders not but that philosophers may, if they please, extend their reasoning to the supposed *state of nature;* provided they allow it to be a mere philosophical fiction, which never had, and never could have, any reality. Human nature being composed of two principal parts, which are requisite in all its actions, the affections and understanding, it is certain that the blind motions of the former, without the direction of the latter, incapacitate men for society; and it may be allowed us to consider separately the effects that result from the separate operations of these two component parts of the mind. The same liberty may be permitted to moral, which is allowed to natural philosophers; and it is very usual with the latter to consider any motion as compounded and consisting of two parts separate from each other, though at the same time they acknowledge it to be in itself uncompounded and inseparable.

This *state of nature,* therefore, is to be regarded as a mere fiction, not unlike that of the *golden age* which poets have invented; only with this difference, that the former is described as full of war, violence, and injustice; whereas the latter is painted out to us as the most charming and most peaceable condition that can possibly be imagined. . . .

. . . I have already observed, that justice takes its rise from human conventions; and that these are intended as a remedy to some inconveniences, which proceed from the concurrence of certain *qualities* of the human mind with the *situation* of external objects. The qualities of the mind are *selfishness* and *limited generosity:* and the situation of external objects is their *easy change,* joined to their *scarcity* in comparison of the wants and desires of men. But however philosophers may have been bewildered in those speculations, poets have been guided more infallibly, by a certain taste or common instinct, which, in most kinds of reasoning, goes further than any of that art and philosophy with which we have been yet acquainted.

They easily perceived, if every man had a tender regard for another, or if nature supplied abundantly all our wants and desires, that the jealousy of interest, which justice supposes, could no longer have place; nor would there be any occasion for those distinctions and limits of property and possession, which at present are in use among mankind. . . .

Nor need we have recourse to the fictions of poets to learn this; but, beside the reason of the thing, may discover the same truth by common experience and observation. It is easy to remark, that a cordial affection renders all things common among friends; and that married people, in particular, mutually lose their property, and are unacquainted with the *mine* and *thine,* which are so necessary, and yet cause such disturbance in human society. The same effect arises from any alteration in the circumstances of mankind; as when there is such a plenty of anything as satisfies all the desires of men: in which case the distinction of property is entirely lost, and everything remains in common. This we may observe with regard to air and water, though the most valuable of all external objects; and may easily conclude, that if men were supplied with everything in the same abundance, or if *every one* had the same affection and tender regard for *every one* as for himself, justice and injustice would be equally unknown among mankind.

Here then is a proposition, which, I think, may be regarded as certain, *that it is only from the selfishness and confined generosity of man, along with the scanty provision nature has made for his wants, that justice derives its origin.* If we look backward we shall find, that this proposition bestows an additional force on some of those observations which we have already made on this subject.

First, We may conclude from it, that a regard to public interest, or a strong extensive benevolence, is not our first and original motive for the observation of the rules of justice; since it is allowed, that if men were endowed with such a benevolence, these rules would never have been dreamed of.

Secondly, We may conclude from the same

principle, that the sense of justice is not founded on reason, or on the discovery of certain connections and relations of ideas, which are eternal, immutable, and universally obligatory. For since it is confessed, that such an alteration as that above mentioned, in the temper and circumstances of mankind, would entirely alter our duties and obligations, it is necessary upon the common system, *that the sense of virtue is derived from reason,* to show the change which this must produce in the relations and ideas. But it is evident, that the only cause why the extensive generosity of man, and the perfect abundance of everything, would destroy the very idea of justice, is, because they render it useless; and that, on the other hand, his confined benevolence, and his necessitous condition, give rise to that virtue, only by making it requisite to the public interest, and to that of every individual. It was therefore a concern for our own and the public interest which made us establish the laws of justice; and nothing can be more certain, than that it is not any relation of ideas which gives us this concern, but our impressions and sentiments, without which everything in nature is perfectly indifferent to us, and can never in the least affect us. The sense of justice, therefore, is not founded on our ideas, but on our impressions.

Thirdly, We may further confirm the foregoing proposition, *that those impressions, which give rise to this sense of justice, are not natural to the mind of man, but arise from artifice and human conventions.* For, since any considerable alteration of temper and circumstances destroys equally justice and injustice; and since such an alteration has an effect only by changing our own and the public interest, it follows that the first establishment of the rules of justice depends on these different interests. But if men pursued the public interest naturally, and with a hearty affection, they would have never dreamed of restraining each other by these rules; and if they pursued their own interest, without any precaution, they would run headlong into every kind of injustice and violence. These rules, therefore, are artificial,

and seek their end in an oblique and indirect manner; nor is the interest which gives rise to them of a kind that could be pursued by the natural and inartificial passions of men.

To make this more evident, consider, that, though the rules of justice are established merely by interest, their connection with interest is somewhat singular, and is different from what may be observed on other occasions. A single act of justice is frequently contrary to *public interest;* and were it to stand alone, without being followed by other acts, may, in itself, be very prejudicial to society. When a man of merit, of a beneficent disposition, restores a great fortune to a miser, or a seditious bigot, he has acted justly and laudably; but the public is a real sufferer. Nor is every single act of justice, considered apart, more conducive to private interest than to public; and it is easily conceived how a man may impoverish himself by a single instance of integrity, and have reason to wish, that, with regard to that single act, the laws of justice were for a moment suspended in the universe. But, however single acts of justice may be contrary, either to public or private interest, it is certain that the whole plan or scheme is highly conducive, or indeed absolutely requisite, both to the support of society, and the well-being of every individual. It is impossible to separate the good from the ill. Property must be stable, and must be fixed by general rules. Though in one instance the public be a sufferer, this momentary ill is amply compensated by the steady prosecution of the rule, and by the peace and order which it establishes in society. And even every individual person must find himself a gainer on balancing the account; since, without justice, society must immediately dissolve, and every one must fall into that savage and solitary condition, which is infinitely worse than the worst situation that can possibly be supposed in society. When, therefore, men have had experience enough to observe, that, whatever may be the consequence of any single act of justice, performed by a single person, yet the whole system of actions concurred in by the whole society, is infinitely advantageous to the whole, and to every part, it is not long before justice and property take place. Every member of society is sensible of this interest: every one expresses this sense to his fellows, along with the resolution he has taken of squaring his actions by it, on condition that others will do the same. No more is requisite to induce any one of them to perform an act of justice, who has the first opportunity. This becomes an example to others; and thus justice establishes itself by a kind of convention or agreement, that is, by a sense of interest, supposed to be common to all, and where every single act is performed in expectation that others are to perform the like. Without such a convention, no one would ever have dreamed that there was such a virtue as justice, or have been induced to conform his actions to it. Taking any single act, my justice may be pernicious in every respect; and it is only upon the supposition that others are to imitate my example, that I can be induced to embrace that virtue; since nothing but this combination can render justice advantageous, or afford me any motives to conform myself to its rules.

We come now to the *second* question we proposed, viz. *Why we annex the idea of virtue to justice, and of vice to injustice.* . . .

After men have found by experience, that their selfishness and confined generosity, acting at their liberty, totally incapacitate them for society; and at the same time have observed that society is necessary to the satisfaction of those very passions, they are naturally induced to lay themselves under the restraint of such rules, as may render their commerce more safe and commodious. To the imposition, then, and observance of these rules, both in general, and in every particular instance, they are at first induced only by a regard to interest; and this motive, on the first formation of society, is sufficiently strong and forcible. But when society has become numerous, and has increased to a tribe or nation, this interest is more remote; nor do men so readily perceive that disorder and confusion follow upon every breach of these

rules, as in a more narrow and contracted society. But though, in our own actions, we may frequently lose sight of that interest which we have in maintaining order, and may follow a lesser and more present interest, we never fail to observe the prejudice we receive, either mediately or immediately, from the injustice of others; as not being in that case either blinded by passion, or biased by any contrary temptation. Nay, when the injustice is so distant from us as no way to affect our interest, it still displeases us; because we consider it as prejudicial to human society, and pernicious to every one that approaches the person guilty of it. We partake of their uneasiness by *sympathy;* and as everything which gives uneasiness in human actions, upon the general survey, is called Vice, and whatever produces satisfaction, in the same manner, is denominated Virtue, this is the reason why the sense of moral good and evil follows upon justice and injustice. And though this sense, in the present case, be derived only from contemplating the actions of others, yet we fail not to extend it even to our own actions. The *general rule* reaches beyond those instances from which it arose; while, at the same time, we naturally *sympathise* with others in the sentiments they entertain of us.

Though this progress of the sentiments be *natural,* and even necessary, it is certain that it is here forwarded by the artifice of politicians, who, in order to govern men more easily, and preserve peace in human society, have endeavoured to produce an esteem for justice, and an abhorrence of injustice. This, no doubt, must have its effect; but nothing can be more evident than that the matter has been carried too far by certain writers on morals, who seem to have employed their utmost efforts to extirpate all sense of virtue from among mankind. Any artifice of politicians may assist nature in the producing of those sentiments, which she suggests to us, and may even, on some occasions, produce alone an approbation or esteem for any particular action; but it is impossible it should be the sole cause of the distinction we make betwixt vice and virtue. For if nature did not aid us in this particular, it would be in vain for politicians to talk of *honourable* or *dishonourable, praiseworthy* or *blamable.* These words would be perfectly unintelligible, and would no more have any idea annexed to them, than if they were of a tongue perfectly unknown to us. The utmost politicians can perform, is to extend the natural sentiments beyond their original bounds; but still nature must furnish the materials, and give us some notion of moral distinctions.

As public praise and blame increase our esteem for justice, so private education and instruction contribute to the same effect. For as parents easily observe, that a man is the more useful, both to himself and others, the greater degree of probity and honour he is endowed with, and that those principles have greater force when custom and education assist interest and reflection: for these reasons they are induced to inculcate on their children, from their earliest infancy, the principles of probity, and teach them to regard the observance of those rules by which society is maintained, as worthy and honourable, and their violation as base and infamous. By this means the sentiments of honour may take root in their tender minds, and acquire such firmness and solidity, that they may fall little short of those principles which are the most essential to our natures, and the most deeply radicated in our internal constitution.

What further contributes to increase their solidity, is the interest of our reputation, after the opinion, *that a merit or demerit attends justice or injustice,* is once firmly established among mankind. There is nothing which touches us more nearly than our reputation, and nothing on which our reputation more depends than our conduct with relation to the property of others. For this reason, every one who has any regard to his character, or who intends to live on good terms with mankind, must fix an inviolable law to himself, never, by any temptation, to be induced to violate those principles which are essential to a man of probity and honour.

I shall make only one observation before I leave this subject, viz. that, though I assert that, in the *state of nature,* or that imaginary state which preceded society, there be neither justice nor injustice, yet I assert not that it was allowable, in such a state, to violate the property of others. I only maintain, that there was no such thing as property; and consequently could be no such thing as justice or injustice. I shall have occasion to make a similar reflection with regard to *promises,* when I come to treat of them; and I hope this reflection, when duly weighed, will suffice to remove all odium from the foregoing opinions, with regard to justice and injustice.

SECTION III

Of the Rules which Determine Property

Though the establishment of the rule, concerning the stability of possession, be not only useful, but even absolutely necessary to human society, it can never serve to any purpose, while it remains in such general terms. Some method must be shown, by which we may distinguish what particular goods are to be assigned to each particular person, while the rest of mankind are excluded from their possession and enjoyment. Our next business, then, must be to discover the reasons which modify this general rule, and fit it to the common use and practice of the world.

It is obvious that those reasons are not derived from any utility or advantage, which either the *particular* person or the public may reap from his enjoyment of any *particular* goods, beyond what would result from the possession of them by any other person. It were better, no doubt, that every one were possessed of what is most suitable to him, and proper for his use: But besides, that this relation of fitness may be common to several at once, it is liable to so many controversies, and men are so partial and passionate in judging of these controversies, that such a loose and uncertain rule would be absolutely incompatible with the peace of human society. The convention concerning the stability of possession is entered into, in order to cut off all occasions of discord and contention; and this end would never be attained were we allowed to apply this rule differently in every particular case, according to every particular utility which might be discovered in such an application. Justice, in her decisions, never regards the fitness or unfitness of objects to particular persons, but conducts herself by more extensive views. Whether a man be generous, or a miser, he is equally well received by her, and obtains, with the same facility, a decision in his favour, even for what is entirely useless to him.

It follows, therefore, that the general rule, *that possession must be stable,* is not applied by particular judgments, but by other general rules, which must extend to the whole society, and be inflexible either by spite or favour. To illustrate this, I propose the following instance. I first consider men in their savage and solitary condition; and suppose that, being sensible of the misery of that state, and foreseeing the advantages that would result from society, they seek each other's company, and make an offer of mutual protection and assistance. I also suppose that they are endowed with such sagacity as immediately to perceive that the chief impediment to this project of society and partnership lies in the avidity and selfishness of their natural temper; to remedy which, they enter into a convention for the stability of possession, and for mutual restraint and forbearance. I· am sensible that this method of proceeding is not altogether natural; but, besides that, I here only suppose those reflections to be formed at once, which, in fact, arise insensibly and by degrees; besides this, I say, it is very possible that several persons, being by different accidents separated from the societies to which they formerly belonged, may be obliged to form a new society among themselves; in which case they are entirely in the situation above mentioned.

It is evident, then, that their first difficulty in this situation, after the general convention for the establishment of society, and for the constancy of possession, is, how to separate their possessions, and assign to each his particular portion, which he must for the future unalterably enjoy. This difficulty will not detain them long; but it must immediately occur to them, as the most natural expedient, that every one continue to enjoy what he is at present master of, and that property or constant possession be conjoined to the immediate possession. Such is the effect of custom, that it not only reconciles us to anything we have long enjoyed, but even gives us an affection for it, and makes us prefer it to other objects, which may be more valuable, but are less known to us. What has long lain under our eye, and has often been employed to our advantage, *that* we are always the most unwilling to part with; but can easily live without possessions which we never have enjoyed, and are not accustomed to. It is evident, therefore, that men would easily acquiesce in this expedient, *that every one continue to enjoy what he is at present possessed of:* and this is the reason why they would so naturally agree in preferring it.

But we may observe, that, though the rule of the assignment of property to the present possessor be natural, and by that means useful, yet its utility extends not beyond the first formation of society; nor would anything be more pernicious than the constant observance of it; by which restitution would be excluded, and every injustice would be authorised and rewarded. We must, therefore, seek for some other circumstance, that may give rise to property after society is once established; and of this kind I find four most considerable, viz. Occupation, Prescription, Accession, and Succession. We shall briefly examine each of these, beginning with *occupation.*

The possession of all external goods is changeable and uncertain; which is one of the most considerable impediments to the establishment of society, and is the reason why, by universal agreement, express or tacit, men restrain themselves by what we now call the rules of justice and equity. The misery of the condition which precedes this restraint is the cause why we submit to that remedy as quickly as possible; and this affords us an easy reason why we annex the idea of property to the first possession, or to *occupation*. Men are unwilling to leave property in suspense, even for the shortest time, or open the least door to violence and disorder. To which we may add, that the first possession always engages the attention most; and did we neglect it, there would be no colour of reason for assigning property to any succeeding possession. . . .

But if it often happens that the title of first possession becomes obscure through time, and that it is impossible to determine many controversies which may arise concerning it; in that case, long possession or *prescription* naturally takes place, and gives a person a sufficient property in anything he enjoys. . . . A man's title that is clear and certain at present, will seem obscure and doubtful fifty years hence, even though the facts on which it is founded should be proved with the greatest evidence and certainty. The same facts have not the same influence after so long an interval of time. And this may be received as a convincing argument for our preceding doctrine with regard to property and justice. Possession during a long tract of time conveys a title to any object. . . .

We acquire the property of objects by *accession*, when they are connected in an intimate manner with objects that are already our property, and at the same time are inferior to them. Thus, the fruits of our garden, the offspring of our cattle, and the work of our slaves, are all of them esteemed our property, even before possession. . . .

The right of *succession* is a very natural one, from the presumed consent of the parent or near relation, and from the general interest of mankind, which requires that men's possessions should pass to those who are dearest to them, in order to render them more industrious and frugal. Perhaps these causes are seconded by the influence of *relation*, or the association of ideas, by which we are naturally directed to consider the son after the parent's decease, and ascribe to him a title to his father's possessions. Those

goods must become the property of somebody; but *of whom* is the question. Here it is evident the person's children naturally present themselves to the mind; and being already connected to those possessions by means of their deceased parent, we are apt to connect them still further by the relation of property. . . .

Of the Transference of Property by Consent

However useful, or even necessary, the stability of possession may be to human society, it is attended with very considerable inconveniences. The relation of fitness or suitableness ought never to enter into consideration, in distributing the properties of mankind; but we must govern ourselves by rules which are more general in their application, and more free from doubt and uncertainty. Of this kind is *present* possession upon the first establishment of society; and afterwards *occupation, prescription, accession,* and *succession*. As these depend very much on chance, they must frequently prove contradictory both to men's wants and desires; and persons and possessions must often be very ill adjusted. This is a grand inconvenience, which calls for a remedy. To apply one directly, and allow every man to seize by violence what he judges to be fit for him, would destroy society; and therefore the rules of justice seek some medium betwixt a rigid stability and this changeable and uncertain adjustment. But there is no medium better than that obvious one, that possession and property should always be stable, except when the proprietor consents to bestow them on some other person. This rule can have no ill consequence in occasioning wars and dissensions, since the proprietor's consent, who alone is concerned, is taken along in the alienation; and it may serve to many good purposes in adjusting property to persons. Different parts of the earth produce different commodities; and not only so, but different men both are by nature fitted for different employments, and attain to greater perfection in any one, when they confine themselves to it alone. All this requires a mutual exchange and commerce; for which reason the translation of property by consent is founded on a law of nature, as well as its stability without such a consent.

So far is determined by a plain utility and interest. But perhaps it is from more trivial reasons, that *delivery,* or a sensible transference of the object is commonly required by civil laws, and also by the laws of nature, according to most authors, as a requisite circumstance in the translation of property. The property of an object, when taken for something real, without any reference to morality, or the sentiments of the mind, is a quality perfectly insensible, and even inconceivable; nor can we form any distinct notion, either of its stability or translation. This imperfection of our ideas is less sensibly felt with regard to its stability, as it engages less our attention, and is easily passed over by the mind, without any scrupulous examination. But as the translation of property from one person to another is a more remarkable event, the defect of our ideas becomes more sensible on that occasion and obliges us to turn ourselves on every side in search of some remedy. Now, as nothing more enlivens any idea than a present impression, and a relation betwixt that impression and the idea; it is natural for us to seek some false light from this quarter. In order to aid the imagination in conceiving the transference of property, we take the sensible object, and actually transfer its possession to the person on whom we would bestow the property. The supposed resemblance of the actions, and the presence of this sensible delivery, deceive the mind, and make it fancy that it conceives the mysterious transition of the property. And that this explication of the matter is just, appears hence, that men have invented a *symbolical* delivery, to satisfy the fancy where the real one is impracticable. Thus the giving the keys of a granary is understood to be the delivery of the corn contained in it; the giving of stone and earth represents the delivery of a manor. . . .

SECTION V

Of the Obligation of Promises

That the rule of morality, which enjoins the performance of promises, is not *natural,* will sufficiently appear from these two propositions, which I proceed to prove, viz. *that a promise would not be intelligible before human conventions had established it;* and *that even if it were intelligible, it would not be attended with any moral obligation.*

I say, *first,* that a promise is not intelligible naturally, nor antecedent to human conventions; and that a man, unacquainted with society, could never enter into any engagements with another, even though they could perceive each other's thoughts by intuition. If promises be natural and intelligible, there must be some act of the mind attending these words, *I promise;* and on this act of the mind must the obligation depend. Let us therefore run over all the faculties of the soul, and see which of them is exerted in our promises.

The act of the mind, expressed by a promise, is not a *resolution* to perform anything; for that alone never imposes any obligation. Nor is it a *desire* of such a performance; for we may bind ourselves without such a desire, or even with an aversion, declared and avowed. Neither is it the *willing* of that action which we promise to perform; for a promise always regards some future time, and the will has an influence only on present actions. It follows, therefore, that since the act of the mind, which enters into a promise, and produces its obligation, is neither the resolving, desiring, nor willing any particular performance, it must necessarily be the *willing* of that *obligation* which arises from the promise. Nor is this only a conclusion of philosophy, but is entirely conformable to our common ways of thinking and of expressing ourselves, when we say that we are bound by our own consent, and that the obligation arises from our mere will and pleasure. The only question then is, whether there be not a manifest absurdity in supposing this act of the mind, and such an absurdity as no man could fall into, whose ideas are not confounded with prejudice and the fallacious use of language.

All morality depends upon our sentiments; and when any action or quality of the mind pleases us *after a certain manner,* we say it is virtuous; and when the neglect or non-performance of it displeases us *after a like manner,* we say that we lie under an obligation to perform it. A change of the obligation supposes a change of the sentiment; and a creation of a new obligation supposes some new sentiment to arise. But it is certain we can naturally no more change our own sentiments than the motions of the heavens; nor by a single act of our will, that is, by a promise, render any action agreeable or disagreeable, moral or immoral, which, without that act, would have produced contrary impressions, or have been endowed with different qualities. It would be absurd, therefore, to will any new obligation, that is, any new sentiment of pain or pleasure; nor is it possible that men could naturally fall into so gross an absurdity. A promise, therefore, is *naturally* something altogether unintelligible, nor is there any act of the mind belonging to it.[1]

But, *secondly,* if there was any act of the mind belonging to it, it could not *naturally* produce any obligation. This appears evidently from the foregoing reasoning. A promise creates a new obligation. A new obligation supposes new sentiments to arise. The will never creates new sentiments. There could not naturally, therefore, arise any obligation from a promise, even supposing the

mind could fall into the absurdity of willing that obligation.

The same truth may be proved still more evidently by that reasoning which proved justice in general to be an artificial virtue. No action can be required of us as our duty, unless there be implanted in human nature some actuating passion or motive capable of producing the action. This motive cannot be the sense of duty. A sense of duty supposes an antecedent obligation; and where an action is not required by any natural passion, it cannot be required by any natural obligation; since it may be omitted without proving any defect or imperfection in the mind and temper, and consequently without any vice. Now, it is evident we have no motive leading us to the performance of promises, distinct from a sense of duty. If we thought that promises had no moral obligation, we never should feel any inclination to observe them. This is not the case with the natural virtues. Though there was no obligation to relieve the miserable, our humanity would lead us to it; and when we omit that duty, the immorality of the omission arises from its being a proof that we want the natural sentiments of humanity. A father knows it to be his duty to take care of his children, but he has also a natural inclination to it. And if no human creature had that inclination, no one could lie under any such obligation. But as there is naturally no inclination to observe promises distinct from a sense of their obligation, it follows that fidelity is no natural virtue, and that promises

---

[1] Were morality discoverable by reason, and not by sentiment, it would be still more evident that promises could make no alteration upon it. Morality is supposed to consist in relation. Every new imposition of morality, therefore, must arise from some new relation of objects; and consequently the will could not produce *immediately* any change in the morals, but could have that effect only by producing a change upon the objects. But as the moral obligation of a promise is the pure effect of the will, without the least change in any part of the universe, it follows that promises have no *natural* obligation.

Should it be said, that this act of the will, being in effect a new object, produces new relations and new duties; I would answer, that this is a pure sophism, which may be detected by a very moderate share of accuracy and exactness. To will a new obligation is to will a new relation of objects; and therefore, if this new relation of objects were formed by the volition itself, we should, in effect, will the volition, which is plainly absurd and impossible. The will has here no object to which it could tend, but must return upon itself *in infinitum.* The new obligation depends upon new relations. The new relations depend upon a new volition. The new volition has for object a new obligation, and consequently new relations, and consequently a new volition; which volition, again, has in view a new obligation, relation, and volition, without any termination. It is impossible, therefore, we could ever will a new obligation; and consequently it is impossible the will could ever accompany a promise, or produce a new obligation of morality.

have no force antecedent to human conventions.

If any one dissent from this, he must give a regular proof of these two propositions, viz. *that there is a peculiar act of the mind annexed to promises;* and *that consequent to this act of the mind, there arises an inclination to perform, distinct from a sense of duty.* I presume that it is impossible to prove either of these two points; and therefore I venture to conclude, that promises are human inventions, founded on the necessities and interests of society.

In order to discover these necessities and interests, we must consider the same qualities of human nature which we have already found to give rise to the preceding laws of society. Men being naturally selfish, or endowed only with a confined generosity, they are not easily induced to perform any action for the interest of strangers, except with a view to some reciprocal advantage, which they had no hope of obtaining but by such a performance. Now, as it frequently happens that these mutual performances cannot be finished at the same instant, it is necessary that one party be contented to remain in uncertainty, and depend upon the gratitude of the other for a return of kindness. But so much corruption is there among men, that, generally speaking, this becomes but a slender security; and as the benefactor is here supposed to bestow his favours with a view to self-interest, this both takes off from the obligation, and sets an example of selfishness, which is the true mother of ingratitude. Were we, therefore, to follow the natural course of our passions and inclinations, we should perform but few actions for the advantage of others from disinterested views, because we are naturally very limited in our kindness and affection; and we should perform as few of that kind out of regard to interest, because we cannot depend upon their gratitude. Here, then, is the mutual commerce of good offices in a manner lost among mankind, and every one reduced to his own skill and industry for his well-being and subsistence. The invention of the law of nature, concerning the *stability* of possession,

has already rendered men tolerable to each other; that of the *transference* of property and possession by consent has begun to render them mutually advantageous; but still these laws of nature, however strictly observed, are not sufficient to render them so serviceable to each other as by nature they are fitted to become. Though possession be *stable,* men may often reap but small advantage from it, while they are possessed of a greater quantity of any species of goods than they have occasion for, and at the same time suffer by the want of others. The *transference* of property, which is the proper remedy for this inconvenience, cannot remedy it entirely; because it can only take place with regard to such objects as are *present* and *individual,* but not to such as are *absent* or *general.* One cannot transfer the property of a particular house, twenty leagues distant, because the consent cannot be attended with delivery, which is a requisite circumstance. Neither can one transfer the property of ten bushels of corn, or five hogsheads of wine, by the mere expression and consent, because these are only general terms, and have no distinct relation to any particular heap of corn or barrels of wine. Besides, the commerce of mankind is not confined to the barter of commodities, but may extend to services and actions, which we may exchange to our mutual interest and advantage. Your corn is ripe to-day; mine will be so to-morrow. It is profitable for us both that I should labour with you to-day, and that you should aid me tomorrow. I have no kindness for you, and know you have as little for me. I will not, therefore, take any pains upon your account; and should I labour with you upon my own account, in expectation of a return, I know I should be disappointed, and that I should in vain depend upon your gratitude. Here, then, I leave you to labour alone: you treat me in the same manner. The seasons change; and both of us lose our harvests for want of mutual confidence and security.

All this is the effect of the natural and inherent principles and passions of human nature; and as these passions and principles are unalterable, it may be thought that our conduct, which depends on them, must be so too, and that it would be in vain, either for moralists or politicians, to tamper with us, or attempt to change the usual course of our actions, with a view to public interest. And, indeed, did the success of their designs depend upon their success in correcting the selfishness and ingratitude of men, they would never make any progress, unless aided by Omnipotence, which is alone able to new-mould the human mind, and change its character in such fundamental articles. All they can pretend to is, to give a new direction to those natural passions, and teach us that we can better satisfy our appetites in an oblique and artificial manner, than by their headlong and impetuous motion. Hence I learn to do a service to another, without bearing him any real kindness; because I foresee that he will return my service, in expectation of another of the same kind, and in order to maintain the same correspondence of good offices with me or with others. And accordingly, after I have served him, and he is in possession of the advantage arising from my action, he is induced to perform his part, as foreseeing the consequences of his refusal. . . .

Afterwards a sentiment of morals concurs with interest, and becomes a new obligation upon mankind. This sentiment of morality, in the performance of promises, arises from the same principles as that in the abstinence from the property of others. *Public interest, education,* and *the artifices of politicians,* have the same effect in both cases. . . .

. . . It is evident that the will alone is never supposed to cause the obligation, but must be expressed by words or signs, in order to impose a tie upon any man. The expression being once brought in as subservient to the will, soon becomes the principal part of the promise; nor will a man be less bound by his word, though he secretly give a different direction to his intention, and withhold himself both from a resolution, and from willing an obligation. But though the expression makes on most occasions the whole of the promise, yet it does not always so; and one who should make use of any expression of which he knows not the meaning, and which he uses without any intention of binding himself, would not certainly be bound by it. Nay, though he knows its meaning, yet if he uses it in jest only, and with such signs as show evidently he has no serious intention of binding himself, he would not lie under any obligation of performance; but it is necessary that the words be a perfect expression of the will, without any contrary signs. Nay, even this we must not carry so far as to imagine, that one, whom, by our quickness of understanding, we conjecture, from certain signs, to have an intention of deceiving us, is not bound by his expression or verbal promise, if we accept of it; but must limit this conclusion to those cases where the signs are of a different kind from those of deceit. All these contradictions are easily accounted for, if the obligation of promises be merely a human invention for the convenience of society; but will never be explained, if it be something *real* and *natural,* arising from any action of the mind or body.

I shall further observe, that, since every new promise imposes a new obligation of morality on the person who promises, and since this new obligation arises from his will; it is one of the most mysterious and incomprehensible operations that can possibly be imagined, and may even be compared to *transubstantiation* or *holy orders* [1] where a certain form of words, along with a certain intention, changes entirely the nature of an external object, and even of a human creature. But though these mysteries be so far alike, it is very remarkable that they differ widely in other particulars, and that this difference may be regarded as a strong proof of the difference of their origins. As the obligation of promises is an invention for the interest of society, it is warped into as many different forms as that interest requires, and even runs into direct contradictions, rather than lose sight of its object. But as those

[1] I mean so far as holy orders are supposed to produce the *indelible character.* In other respects they are only a legal qualification.

other monstrous doctrines are mere priestly
inventions, and have no public interest in
view, they are less disturbed in their progress
by new obstacles; and it must be owned,
that, after the first absurdity, they follow
more directly the current of reason and good
sense. Theologians clearly perceived that
the external form of words, being mere
sound, require an intention to make them
have any efficacy; and that this intention being once considered as a requisite circumstance, its absence must equally prevent the
effect, whether avowed or concealed, whether
sincere or deceitful. Accordingly, they have
commonly determined, that the intention of
the priest makes the sacrament, and that
when he secretly withdraws his intention, he
is highly criminal in himself; but still destroys the baptism, or communion, or holy
orders. The terrible consequences of this
doctrine were not able to hinder its taking
place; as the inconvenience of a similar doctrine, with regard to promises, have prevented that doctrine from establishing itself.
Men are always more concerned about the
present life than the future; and are apt to
think the smallest evil which regards the
former more important than the greatest
which regards the latter.

We may draw the same conclusion concerning the origin of promises, from the
force which is supposed to invalidate all contracts, and to free us from their obligation.
Such a principle is a proof that promises
have no natural obligation, and are mere
artificial contrivances for the convenience
and advantage of society. If we consider
aright of the matter, force is not essentially
different from any other motive of hope or
fear, which may induce us to engage our
word, and lay ourselves under any obligation. A man, dangerously wounded, who
promises a competent sum to a surgeon to
cure him, would certainly be bound to performance; though the case be not so much
different from that of one who promises a
sum to a robber, as to produce so great a
difference in our sentiments of morality, if
these sentiments were not built entirely on
public interest and convenience.

SECTION VI

Some Further Reflections Concerning Justice and Injustice

We have now run over the three fundamental laws of nature, *that of the stability of
possession, of its transference by consent,* and
of the performance of promises. It is on the
strict observance of those three laws that the
peace and security of human society entirely
depend; nor is there any possibility of establishing a good correspondence among men,
where these are neglected. Society is absolutely necessary for the wellbeing of men;
and these are as necessary to the support of
society. Whatever restraint they may impose
on the passions of men, they are the real offspring of those passions, and are only a more
artful and more refined way of satisfying
them. Nothing is more vigilant and inventive than our passions; and nothing is more
obvious than the convention for the observance of these rules. Nature has, therefore,
trusted this affair entirely to the conduct of
men, and has not placed in the mind any
peculiar original principles, to determine us
to a set of actions, into which the other principles of our frame and constitution were
sufficient to lead us. And to convince us the
more fully of this truth, we may here stop a
moment, and, from a review of the preceding
reasonings, may draw some new arguments,
to prove that those laws, however necessary,
are entirely artificial, and of human invention; and consequently, that justice is an artificial, and not a natural virtue.

I. The first argument I shall make use of
is derived from the vulgar definition of justice. Justice is commonly defined to be *a
constant and perpetual will of giving every
one his due.* In this definition it is supposed
that there are such things as right and property, independent of justice, and antecedent
to it; and that they would have subsisted,
though men had never dreamt of practising
such a virtue. I have already observed, in a
cursory manner, the fallacy of this opinion,
and shall here continue to open up, a little
more distinctly, my sentiments on that subject.

I shall begin with observing that this quality, which we call *property,* is like many of the imaginary qualities of the *Peripatetic* philosophy, and vanishes upon a more accurate inspection into the subject, when considered apart from our moral sentiments. It is evident property does not consist in any of the sensible qualities of the object. For these may continue invariably the same, while the property changes. Property, therefore, must consist in some relation of the object. But it is not in its relation with regard to other external and inanimate objects. For these may also continue invariably the same, while the property changes. This quality, therefore, consists in the relations of objects to intelligent and rational beings. But it is not the external and corporeal relation which forms the essence of property. For that relation may be the same betwixt inanimate objects, or with regard to brute creatures; though in those cases it forms no property. It is therefore in some internal relation that the property consists; that is, in some influence which the external relations of the object have on the mind and actions. Thus the external relation which we call *occupation* or first possession, is not of itself imagined to be the property of the object, but only to cause its property. Now, it is evident this external relation causes nothing in external objects, and has only an influence on the mind, by giving us a sense of duty in abstaining from that object, and in restoring it to the first possessor. These actions are properly what we call *justice;* and consequently it is on that virtue that the nature of property depends, and not the virtue on the property.

If any one, therefore, would assert that justice is a natural virtue, and injustice a natural vice, he must assert that abstracting from the notions of *property* and *right* and *obligation* a certain conduct and train of actions, in certain external relations of objects, has naturally a moral beauty or deformity, and causes an original pleasure or uneasiness. Thus the restoring a man's goods to him is considered as virtuous, not because nature has annexed a certain sentiment of pleasure to such a conduct with regard to the property of others, but because she has annexed that sentiment to such a conduct, with regard to those external objects of which others have had the first or long possession, or which they have received by the consent of those who have had first or long possession. If nature has given us no such sentiment, there is not naturally, nor antecedent to human conventions, any such thing as property. Now, though it seems sufficiently evident, in this dry and accurate consideration of the present subject, that nature has annexed no pleasure or sentiment of approbation to such a conduct, yet, that I may leave as little room for doubt as possible, I shall subjoin a few more arguments to confirm my opinion.

First, If nature had given us a pleasure of this kind, it would have been as evident and discernible as on every other occasion; nor should we have found any difficulty to perceive that the consideration of such actions, in such a situation, gives a certain pleasure and sentiment of approbation. We should not have been obliged to have recourse to notions of property in the definition of justice, and at the same time make use of the notions of justice in the definition of property. This deceitful method of reasoning is a plain proof that there are contained in the subject some obscurities and difficulties which we are not able to surmount, and which we desire to evade by this artifice.

Secondly, Those rules by which properties, rights, and obligations are determined, have in them no marks of a natural origin, but many of artifice and contrivance. They are too numerous to have proceeded from nature; they are changeable by human laws; and have all of them a direct and evident tendency to public good, and the support of civil society. This last circumstance is remarkable upon two accounts. *First,* Because, though the cause of the establishment of these laws had been a *regard* for the public good, as much as the public good is their natural tendency, they would still have been artificial, as being purposely contrived and directed to a certain end. *Secondly,* Because, if men had been endowed with such a strong regard for public good, they would never have restrained themselves by these rules; so that the laws of justice arise from natural principles, in a manner still more oblique and artificial. It is self-love which is their real origin; and as the self-love of one person is naturally contrary to that of another, these several interested passions are obliged to adjust themselves after such a manner as to concur in some system of conduct and behaviour. This system, therefore, comprehending the interest of each individual, is of course advantages to the public, though it be not intended for that purpose by the inventors.

II. In the *second* place, we may observe that all kinds of vice and virtue run insensibly into each other, and may approach by such imperceptible degrees as will make it very difficult, if not absolutely impossible, to determine when the one ends, and the other begins; and from this observation we may derive a new argument for the foregoing principle. For, whatever may be the case with regard to all kinds of vice and virtue, it is certain that rights, and obligations, and property, admit of no such insensible gradation, but that a man either has a full and perfect property, or none at all; and is either entirely obliged to perform any action, or lies under no manner of obligation. However civil laws may talk of a perfect *dominion,* and of an imperfect, it is easy to observe, that this arises from a fiction, which has no foundation in reason, and can never enter into our notions of natural justice and equity. A man that hires a horse, though but for a day, has as full a right to make use of it for that time, as he whom we call its proprietor has to make use of it any other day; and it is evident that, however the use may be bounded in time or degree, the right itself is not susceptible of any such gradation, but is absolute and entire, so far as it extends. Accordingly, we may observe that this right both arises and perishes in an instant; and that a man entirely acquires the property of any object by occupation, or the consent of the proprietor; and loses it by his own consent, without any of that insensible grada-

tion which is remarkable in other qualities and relations. Since, therefore, this is the case with regard to property, and rights, and obligations, I ask, how it stands with regard to justice and injustice? After whatever manner you answer this question, you run into inextricable difficulties. If you reply, that justice and injustice admit of degree, and run insensibly into each other, you expressly contradict the foregoing position, that obligation and property are not susceptible of such a gradation. These depend entirely upon justice and injustice, and follow them in all their variations. Where the justice is entire, the property is also entire: where the justice is imperfect, the property must also be imperfect. And *vice versa,* if the property admit of no such variations, they must also be incompatible with justice. If you assent, therefore, to this last proposition, and assert that justice and injustice are not susceptible of degrees, you in effect assert that they are not *naturally* either vicious or virtuous; since vice and virtue, moral good and evil, and indeed all *natural* qualities, run insensibly into each other, and are on many occasions undistinguishable.

And here it may be worth while to observe, that though abstract reasoning and the general maxims of philosophy and law establish this position, *that property, and right, and obligation, admit not of degrees,* yet, in our common and negligent way of thinking, we find great difficulty to entertain that opinion, and do even *secretly* embrace the contrary principle. An object must either be in the possession of one person or another. An action must either be performed or not. The necessity there is of choosing one side in these dilemmas, and the impossibility there often is of finding any just medium, oblige us, when we reflect on the matter, to acknowledge that all property and obligations are entire. But, on the other hand, when we consider the origin of property and obligation, and find that they depend on public utility, and sometimes on the propensity of the imagination, which are seldom entire on any side, we are naturally inclined to imagine that these moral relations admit of an insensible gradation. Hence it is that in references, where the consent of the parties leave the referees entire masters of the subject, they commonly discover so much equity and justice on both sides as induces them to strike a medium, and divide the difference betwixt the parties. Civil judges, who have not this liberty, but are obliged to give a decisive sentence on some one side, are often at a loss how to determine, and are necessitated to proceed on the most frivolous reasons in the world. Half rights and obligations, which seem so natural in common life, are perfect absurdities in their tribunal; for which reason they are often obliged to take half arguments for whole ones, in order to terminate the affair one way or the other.

III. The *third* argument of this kind I shall make use of may be explained thus. If we consider the ordinary course of human actions, we shall find that the mind restrains not itself by any general and universal rules, but acts on most occasions as it is determined by its present motives and inclination. As each action is a particular individual event, it must proceed from particular principles, and from our immediate situation within ourselves, and with respect to the rest of the universe. If on some occasions we extend our motives beyond those very circumstances which gave rise to them, and form something like *general rules* for our conduct, it is easy to observe that these rules are not perfectly inflexible, but allow of many exceptions. Since, therefore, this is the ordinary course of human actions, we may conclude that the laws of justice, being universal and perfectly inflexible, can never be derived from nature, nor be the immediate offspring of any natural motive or inclination. No action can be either morally good or evil, unless there be some natural passion or motive to impel us to it, or deter us from it; and it is evident that the morality must be susceptible of all the same variations which are natural to the passion. Here are two persons who dispute for an estate; of whom one is rich, a fool, and a bachelor; the other poor, a man of sense, and has a numerous family: the first is my enemy; the second my friend. Whether I be actuated in this affair by a view to public or private interest, by friendship or enmity, I must be induced to do my utmost to procure the estate to the latter. Nor would any consideration of the right and property of the persons be able to restrain me, were I actuated only by natural motives, without any combination or convention with others. For as all property depends on morality, and as all morality depends on the ordinary course of our passions and actions, and as these again are only directed by particular motives, it is evident such a partial conduct must be suitable to the strictest morality, and could never be a violation of property. Were men, therefore, to take the liberty of acting with regard to the laws of society, as they do in every other affair, they would conduct themselves, on most occasions, by particular judgments, and would take into consideration the characters and circumstances of the persons, as well as the general nature of the question. But it is easy to observe, that this would produce an infinite confusion in human society, and that the avidity and partiality of men would quickly bring disorder into the world, if not restrained by some general and inflexible principles. It was therefore with a view to this inconvenience that men have established those principles, and have agreed to restrain themselves by general rules, which are unchangeable by spite and favour, and by particular views of private or public interest. These rules, then, are artificially invented for a certain purpose, and are contrary to the common principles of human nature, which accommodate themselves to circumstances, and have no stated invariable method of operation.

Nor do I perceive how I can easily be mistaken in this matter. I see, evidently, that when any man imposes on himself general inflexible rules in his conduct with others, he considers certain objects as their property, which he supposes to be sacred and inviolable. But no proposition can be more evident, than that property is perfectly unintelligible without first supposing justice and injustice; and that these virtues and vices are as unintelligible, unless we have motives, independent of the morality, to impel us to just actions, and deter us from unjust ones. Let those motives, therefore, be what they will, they must accommodate themselves to circumstances, and must admit of all the variations which human affairs, in their incessant revolutions, are susceptible of. They are consequently, a very improper foundation for such rigid inflexible rules as the laws of nature; and it is evident these laws can only be derived from human conventions, when men have perceived the disorders that result from following their natural and variable principles.

Upon the whole, then, we are to consider this distinction betwixt justice and injustice, as having two different foundations, viz. that of *interest*, when men observe that it is impossible to live in society without restraining themselves by certain rules; and that of *morality*, when this interest is once observed, and men receive a pleasure from the view of such actions as tend to the peace of society, and an uneasiness from such as are contrary to it. It is the voluntary convention and artifice of men which makes the first interest take place; and therefore those laws of justice are so far to be considered as *artificial*. After that interest is once established and acknowledged, the sense of morality in the observance of these rules follows *naturally*, and of itself; though it is certain that it is also augmented by a new *artifice*, and that the public instructions of politicians, and the private education of parents, contribute to the giving us a sense of honour and duty, in the strict regulation of our actions with regard to the properties of others.

9

Jean Jacques Rousseau

1712–1778

Jean Jacques Rousseau often said his troubles started at birth—his mother died in labor. His father, a watch-maker, was a restless, emotional man. A son, older than Jean Jacques, ran away from the family's Geneva home and Jean Jacques was raised as an only child. He was taught to read early; often he and his father would read romantic trash aloud the whole night through. Solider biographic or historical work was read when romances were not at hand. After ten years of pampering, the lad suffered complete parental rejection; a quarrel and legal involvement led his father to exile himself from Geneva, and Jean Jacques was sent off for schooling in a neighboring town. At twelve Jean Jacques was back in Geneva under guardianship of his uncle who apprenticed him first to a notary and then to an engraver. He learned neither trade. He became a sly, greedy, slovenly adolescent. At sixteen he ran away. _careless, untidy_

He wandered first into Savoy, where an evangelical Catholic group worked at his conversion. After extensive religious instruction in a Turin monastery, he turned Catholic. He loafed and did menial work for a while and then went to the Annecy home of Madame de Warens, one of the group that had sent him to Turin. He stayed with her for eleven years.

Madame de Warens was a woman of twenty-eight with a small pension, a warm heart, and a roving eye. She became mother and mistress to sixteen year-old Rousseau. He had a sticky, chattering affection for her and great love for the beautiful Savoy countryside. She tried to improve his education.

He failed, however, at learning Latin, versification, dancing, fencing, and chess. He did better in music, and in later years he had slight successes in teaching music, writing about it, and composing popular works. Throughout his adult life he occasionally earned subsistence by copying scores. One of his music teachers got into difficulty and left furtively for Lyons; restless Rousseau went with him but abandoned him when he threw an epileptic fit. A few months later Rousseau was back with Madame de Warens. She had enjoyed a whirl in Paris and had hired a grave, but amorous, gardener who also shared her bed. Rousseau later reported in his *Confessions* that this relationship was quite satisfactory to all three until the gardener's death.

Rousseau fell ill. He blamed his poor health on the artificial atmosphere of village life, and persuaded Madame de Warens to set up a retreat just out of the town of Chambery. Here his roaming instincts turned to amateur naturalizing—particularly botanizing and making friends with small animals. Here he turned from conventional Christianity to nature worship, waivering only when he felt passing twinges of fear of damnation to hell. He also studied literature, philosophy and sciences; but his study seemed disorderly and unpromising. In his middle twenties his writing skill began to flower.

He went to Montpelier to see a doctor, and philandered on the way. The doctor could find nothing wrong with him. When money sponged from Madame de Warens ran out, he came back and found her with a new gentleman friend. Rousseau had no stomach for a second triumvirate and so ended his first attachment.

Rousseau wandered to Lyons and took on a tutoring job. He was a poor teacher and became frantic when his charges were inept or wilful. After a year of frustrating tutoring, he moved on to Paris. Soon a patroness got him a post as secretary to the French ambassador at Venice. The ambassador was an avaricious fellow whom Rousseau hated and left after eighteen months. But Rousseau's life in Venice was social and gay, and for the first time in his adult life, he had a circle of friends. When he came back to Paris he met Diderot, the great encyclopedist, and joined the literary group around him. He wrote several items for Diderot on music, and one on political economy.

Since his funds were low, he moved into a dingy, small hotel. There the kitchen maid, Theresa Le Vasseur, became his mistress and lived with him for the rest of his life. She was ignorant, illiterate, and unteachable. Most of Rousseau's friends found her mean, greedy, jealous and brutish. But he wrote of her, "I lived with my Theresa as pleasantly as with the finest genius in the universe." His highbrow pursuits were unpaid, and he got only meagre wages as secretary to a rich woman. Theresa had five unwanted babies in a half dozen years; all were left on the door step of a foundling home. At different times Rousseau gave conflicting rationalizations for these desertations.

Rousseau became the rage in literary circles by writing a prize essay in a Dijon Academy contest. The assigned subject was "Has restoration of the sciences contributed to purify or corrupt manners?" Rousseau took the spectacular position (perhaps on Diderot's urging) that development of civilization resulted in the degradation of man.

In 1754 forty-two-year-old Rousseau made his first trip back to Geneva. He found the simple, industrious, independent community much to his liking and was reconverted to Calvinism so that he could reclaim his citizenship. Nevertheless, events took him soon to live on the outskirts of Paris in a cottage

furnished him by Madame d'Epinay. He loved the country around his "Hermitage" and spent much of his time in botanizing. He became more and more querulous. He picked a quarrel with Diderot. He wrote and published a slighting piece which made Voltaire and D'Alembert his enemies. He fought with the philosopher Grimm, and with his patroness. Nevertheless he found time to have a romantic affair with his patroness' sister-in-law, Madame d'Houdetot, and to write a sugary romantic novel, *The New Heloise. Heloise* was a tremendous hit; copies were rented by the hour at high prices; great ladies missed important soirées to stay home and read it; it is even said that the one day Kant was late on his walk was the day on which he could not lay his copy down. After Rousseau's quarrel with his patroness, he moved from the Hermitage to the nearby estate of the Duke of Luxembourg. There he hobnobbed with nobles, but lived frugally. He complained constantly about feeling unwell and contemplated suicide.

Now came time for publication of his two major works, which appeared almost simultaneously—*The Social Contract* (1762), excerpts from which follow this note, and *Emilius,* a radical book on education. *Heloise* had contained a little dangerous comment, and *Social Contract* was far from pleasing to those in power. But *Emilius* was his telling mistake. His sentimental deism was attacked as sacrilegious and the Parliament of Paris ordered the book burned and its author arrested. He fled to Switzerland and found himself unwelcome in Berne and Geneva. He petitioned Frederick II of Prussia, whom he had formerly criticized, for asylum in Neuchatel, then under Frederick's dominion. Frederick acceded and offered financial support. Rousseau answered, "I have enough to live on, but if I were dying of hunger, I would rather in the present condition of your good Prince and not being of any service to him, go and eat grass and grub out roots, than accept a morsel of bread from him."

In Neuchatel he spent much time botanizing. He adopted outlandish Armenian dress because it was comfortable. Visitors from over the world came out of respect or out of curiosity to plague him. But charges of his heresy were repeated, and the community become more and more hostile. After three years at Neuchatel he was hounded out by real and imaginary fears.

Hume had become interested in Rousseau years earlier. When Hume heard of Rousseau's plight, he invited him to England, and escorted him to London. Theresa followed soon after, escorted by Boswell, who had met and admired Rousseau but, nevertheless, had an affair with Theresa en route. Rousseau was received in London by the king, nobles, and outstanding statesmen. He became unhappy in the city, and Hume arranged for his accommodation in a Derbyshire house. The winter was cold and bleak. Brooding Rousseau soon picked a quarrel with Hume. Rousseau thought Hume was traitorously in league with his French detractors, particularly Voltaire and D'Alembert. Hume thought Rousseau an outrageous ingrate. The quarrel became a subject of comment in the press. Rousseau's mind became more and more warped, and he thought all of England was plotting against him. He fled in demented terror back to France. For a while, under protection of noble friends, he recovered his composure. Soon again, his confusion increased, and he suffered delusions of persecution. Three years of mad vagrancy ensued, followed by eight more bad years in Paris. He wrote his unbalanced *Dialogues,* made a pittance by copying music, and lived in poverty. Theresa failed and could not keep house. An old admirer persuaded them to take up suburban life on his estate. After a few weeks Rousseau died suddenly. Medical attendants said he died from apoplexy but suicide has been suspected.

Rousseau was the prime advocate of the ignobility of civilization. He was a romantic in a world losing its grip on classicism. He was a republican from emotional conviction of the worth of ordinary man. He turned his back on science in a world turning to science.

But his attack on society put its upholders on the defensive and inspired experimentation and reform.

THE SOCIAL CONTRACT *

Book I

I mean to inquire if, in the civil order, there can be any sure and legitimate rule of administration, men being taken as they are and laws as they might be. In this inquiry I shall endeavour always to unite what right sanctions with what is prescribed by interest, in order that justice and utility may in no case be divided. . . .

CHAPTER I

Subject of the First Book

Man is born free; and everywhere he is in chains. . . . How did this change come about? I do not know. What can make it legitimate? That question I think I can answer.

If I took into account only force, and the effects derived from it, I should say: "As long as a people is compelled to obey, and obeys, it does well; as soon as it can shake off the yoke, and shakes it off, it does still better; for, regaining its liberty by the same right as took it away, either it is justified in resuming it, or there was no justification for those who took it away." But the social order is a sacred right which is the basis of all rights. Nevertheless, this right does not come from nature, and must therefore be founded on conventions. Before coming to that, I have to prove what I have just asserted.

CHAPTER II

The First Societies

The most ancient of all societies, and the only one that is natural, is the family: and even so the children remain attached to the

---

* Translated by G. D. H. Cole. Number 660A, Everyman's Library. Reprinted by permission of E. P. Dutton & Co., Inc.

father only so long as they need him for
their preservation. As soon as this need
ceases, the natural bond is dissolved. The
children, released from the obedience they
owed to the father, and the father, released from the care he owed his children,
return equally to independence. If they remain united, they continue so no longer
naturally, but voluntarily; and the family
itself is then maintained only by convention.

This common liberty results from the nature of man. His first law is to provide for
his own preservation, his first cares are those
which he owes to himself; and, as soon as
he reaches years of discretion, he is the sole
judge of the proper means of preserving himself, and consequently becomes his own master.

The family then may be called the first
model of political societies: the ruler corresponds to the father, and the people to the
children; and all, being born free and equal,
alienate their liberty only for their own advantage. The whole difference is that, in the
family, the love of the father for his children
repays him for the care he takes of them,
while, in the State, the pleasure of commanding takes the place of the love which
the chief cannot have for the peoples under
him.

Grotius denies that all human power is
established in favour of the governed, and
quotes slavery as an example. His usual
method of reasoning is constantly to establish right by fact. It would be possible to
employ a more logical method, but none
could be more favourable to tyrants.

It is then, according to Grotius, doubtful
whether the human race belongs to a hundred men, or that hundred men to the human race: and, throughout his book, he
seems to incline to the former alternative,
which is also the view of Hobbes. On this
showing, the human species is divided into
so many herds of cattle, each with its ruler,
who keeps guard over them for the purpose
of devouring them. . . .

. . . Aristotle, before any of them, had said
that men are by no means equal naturally,
but that some are born for slavery, and
others for dominion.

Aristotle was right; but he took the effect
for the cause. . . . Slaves lose everything in
their chains, even the desire of escaping from
them. . . . If then there are slaves by nature,
it is because there have been slaves against
nature. . . .

CHAPTER III

The Right of the Strongest

The strongest is never strong enough to
be always the master, unless he transforms
strength into right, and obedience into
duty. . . . Force is a physical power, and I
fail to see what moral effect it can have.
To yield to force is an act of necessity, not
of will—at the most, an act of prudence. In
what sense can it be a duty? . . . Clearly, the
word "right" adds nothing to force: in this
connection, it means absolutely nothing.

. . . All power comes from God, I admit;
but so does all sickness; does that mean that
we are forbidden to call in the doctor? . . .

CHAPTER IV

Slavery

. . . If an individual, says Grotius, can
alienate his liberty and make himself the
slave of a master, why could not a whole
people do the same and make itself subject
to a king? . . . Now, a man who becomes the
slave of another . . . sells himself, at the least
for his subsistence: but for what does a people sell itself? A king is so far from furnishing his subjects with their subsistence that he
gets his own only from them. . . .

It will be said that the despot assures his
subjects civil tranquillity. Granted; but what
do they gain, if the wars his ambition brings
down upon them, his insatiable avidity, and
the vexatious conduct of his ministers press
harder on them than their own dissensions
would have done? . . .

To say that a man gives himself gratui-
tously, is to say what is absurd and inconceivable; such an act is null and illegitimate,

from the mere fact that he who does it is out of his mind. To say the same of a whole people is to suppose a people of madmen; and madness creates no right.

Even if each man could alienate himself, he could not alienate his children. . . . It would therefore be necessary, in order to legitimize an arbitrary government, that in every generation the people should be in a position to accept or reject it; but, were this so, the government would be no longer arbitrary.

To renounce liberty is to renounce being a man, to surrender the rights of humanity and even its duties. . . . Such a renunciation is incompatible with man's nature; to remove all liberty from his will is to remove all morality from his acts. Finally, it is an empty and contradictory convention that sets up, on the one side, absolute authority, and, on the other, unlimited obedience. . . .

Grotius and the rest find in war another origin for the so-called right of slavery. The victor having, as they hold, the right of killing the vanquished, the latter can buy back his life at the price of his liberty; and this convention is the more legitimate because it is to the advantage of both parties.

But it is clear that this supposed right to kill the conquered is by no means deducible from the state of war. Men, from the mere fact that, while they are living in their primitive independence, they have no mutual relations stable enough to constitute either the state of peace or the state of war, cannot be naturally enemies . . . War of man with man, can exist neither in the state of nature, where there is no constant property, nor in the social state, where everything is under the authority of the laws. . . .

War then is a relation . . . between State and State, and individuals are enemies only accidentally, not as men, nor even as citizens, but as soldiers; not as members of their country, but as its defenders. Finally, each State can have for enemies only other States, and not men; for between things disparate in nature there can be no real relation.

. . . Even in real war, a just prince, while

laying hands, in the enemy's country, on all that belongs to the public, respects the lives and goods of individuals. . . . The object of the war being the destruction of the hostile State, the other side has a right to kill its defenders, while they are bearing arms; but as soon as they lay them down and surrender, they cease to be enemies or instruments of the enemy, and become once more merely men, whose life no one has any right to take. . . .

The right of conquest has no foundation other than the right of the strongest. If war does not give the conqueror the right to massacre the conquered peoples, the right to enslave them cannot be based upon a right which does not exist. . . .

. . . a slave made in war, or a conquered people, is under no obligation to a master, except to obey him as far as he is compelled to do so. . . .

CHAPTER V

That We Must Always go Back to a First Convention

. . . There will always be a great difference between subduing a multitude and ruling a society. Even if scattered individuals were successively enslaved by one man, however numerous they might be, I still see no more than a master and his slaves, and certainly not a people and its ruler. . . .

A people, says Grotius, can give itself to a king. Then according to Grotius, a people is a people before it gives itself. . . . It would be better, before examining the act by which a people gives itself to a king, to examine that by which it has become a people; for this act, being necessarily prior to the other, is the true foundation of society.

Indeed, if there were no prior convention, where, unless the election were unanimous, would be the obligation on the minority to submit to the choice of the majority? . . . The law of majority voting is itself something established by convention, and presupposes unanimity, on one occasion at least.

CHAPTER VI

The Social Compact

I suppose men to have reached the point at which the obstacles in the way of their preservation in the state of nature show their power of resistance to be greater than the resources at the disposal of each individual for his maintenance in that state. That primitive condition can then subsist no longer; and the human race would perish unless it changed its manner of existence.

But, as men cannot engender new forces, but only unite and direct existing ones, they have no other means of preserving themselves than the formation, by aggregation, of a sum of forces great enough to overcome the resistance. . . .

. . . as the force and liberty of each man are the chief instruments of his self-preservation, how can he pledge them without harming his own interests, and neglecting the care he owes to himself? This difficulty, in its bearing on my present subject, may be stated in the following terms:

"The problem is to find a form of association which will defend and protect with the whole common force the person and goods of each associate, and in which each, while uniting himself with all, may still obey himself alone, and remain as free as before." This is the fundamental problem of which the *Social Contract* provides the solution.

The clauses of this contract are so determined by the nature of the act that the slightest modification would make them vain and ineffective; so that, although they have perhaps never been formally set forth, they are everywhere the same and everywhere tacitly admitted and recognized, until, on the violation of the social compact, each regains his original rights and resumes his natural liberty. . . .

These clauses, properly understood, may be reduced to one—the total alienation of each associate, together with all his rights, to the whole community; for, in the first place, as each gives himself absolutely, the conditions are the same for all; and, this

being so, no one has any interest in making them burdensome to others.

Moreover, the alienation being without reserve, the union is as perfect as it can be, and no associate has anything more to demand: for, if the individuals retained certain rights, as there would be no common superior to decide between them and the public, each, being on one point his own judge, would ask to be so on all; the state of nature would thus continue, and the association would necessarily become inoperative or tyrannical.

Finally, each man, in giving himself to all, gives himself to nobody; and as there is no associate over which he does not acquire the same right as he yields others over himself, he gains an equivalent for everything he loses and an increase of force for the preservation of what he has.

. . . It reduces itself to the following terms: *"Each of us puts his person and all his power in common under the supreme direction of the general will, and, in our corporate capacity, we receive each member as an indivisible part of the whole."*

At once, in place of the individual personality of each contracting party, this act of association creates a moral and collective body, composed of as many members as the assembly contains voters, and receiving from this act its unity, its common identity, its life, and its will. . . .

CHAPTER VII

The Sovereign

This formula shows us that the act of association comprises a mutual undertaking between the public and the individuals, and that each individual, in making a contract, as we may say, with himself, is bound in a double capacity; as a member of the Sovereign he is bound to the individuals, and as a member of the State to the Sovereign. . . .

. . . Public deliberation . . . cannot . . . bind the Sovereign to itself, and . . . it is consequently against the nature of the body politic for the Sovereign to impose on itself a law which it cannot infringe. Being able to regard itself in only one capacity, it is in the position of an individual who makes a contract with himself; and this makes it clear that there neither is nor can be any kind of fundamental law binding on the body of the people—not even the social contract itself. . . .

But the body politic or the Sovereign, drawing its being wholly from the sanctity of the contract, can never bind itself, even to an outsider, to do anything derogatory to the original act, for instance, to alienate any part of itself, or to submit to another Sovereign. . . .

As soon as this multitude is so united in one body, it is impossible to offend against one of the members without attacking the body, and still more to offend against the body without the members resenting it. Duty and interest therefore equally oblige the two contracting parties to give each other help; and the same men should seek to combine, in their double capacity, all the advantages dependent upon that capacity.

Again, the Sovereign, being formed wholly of the individuals who compose it, neither has nor can have any interest contrary to theirs; and consequently the sovereign power need give no guarantee to its subjects, because it is impossible for the body to wish to hurt all its members. We shall also see later on that it cannot hurt any in particular. The Sovereign, merely by virtue of what it is, is always what it should be.

This, however, is not the case with the relation of the subjects to the Sovereign, which, despite the common interest, would have no security that they would fulfil their undertakings, unless it found means to assure itself of their fidelity.

In fact, each individual, as a man, may have a particular will contrary or dissimilar to the general will which he has as a citizen. His particular interest may speak to him quite differently from the common interest: his absolute and naturally independent existence may make him look upon what he owes to the common cause as a gratuitous contribution, the loss of which will do less harm to others than the payment of it is burdensome to himself; and, regarding the moral person which constitutes the State as a *persona ficta,* because not a man, he may wish to enjoy the rights of citizenship without being ready to fulfil the duties of a subject. The continuance of such an injustice could not but prove the undoing of the body politic.

In order then that the social compact may not be an empty formula, it tacitly includes the undertaking, which alone can give force to the rest, that whoever refuses to obey the general will shall be compelled to do so by the whole body. This means nothing less than that he will be forced to be free; for this is the condition which, by giving each citizen to his country, secures him against all personal dependence. In this lies the key to the working of the political machine; this alone legitimizes civil undertakings, which, without it, would be absurd, tyrannical, and liable to the most frightful abuses.

CHAPTER VIII

The Civil State

The passage from the state of nature to the civil state produces a very remarkable change in man, by substituting justice for instinct in his conduct, and giving his actions the morality they had formerly lacked. Then only, when the voice of duty takes the place of physical impulses and right of appetite, does man, who so far had considered only himself, find that he is forced to act on different principles, and to consult his reason before listening to his inclinations. . . .

. . . What man loses by the social contract is his natural liberty and an unlimited right to everything he tries to get and succeeds in getting; what he gains is civil liberty and the proprietorship of all he possesses. If we are to avoid mistake in weighing one against the other, we must clearly distinguish natural liberty, which is bounded only by the strength of the individual, from civil liberty, which is limited by the general will; and possession, which is merely the effect of force or the right of the first occupier, from property, which can be founded only on a positive title. . . .

CHAPTER IX

Real Property

Each member of the community gives himself to it, at the moment of its foundation, just as he is, with all the resources at his command, including the goods he possesses. This act does not make possession, in changing hands, change its nature, and becomes property in the hands of the Sovereign; but, as the forces of the city are incomparably greater than those of an individual, public possession is also, in fact, stronger and more irrevocable, without being any more legitimate. . . .

The right of the first occupier, though more real than the right of the strongest, becomes a real right only when the right of property has already been established. . . . In this right we are respecting not so much what belongs to another as what does not belong to ourselves.

In general, to establish the right of the first occupier over a plot of ground, the following conditions are necessary: first, the land must not yet be inhabited; secondly, a man must occupy only the amount he needs for his subsistence; and, in the third place, possession must be taken, not by an empty ceremony, but by labour and cultivation, the only sign of proprietorship that should be respected by others, in default of a legal title. . . .

. . . in taking over the goods of individuals, the community, so far from despoiling them, only assures them legitimate possession, and changes usurpation into a true right and enjoyment into proprietorship. . . .

. . . However the acquisition be made, the right which each individual has to his own estate is always subordinate to the right which the community has over all: without this, there would be neither stability in the social tie, nor real force in the exercise of Sovereignty.

I shall end this chapter and this book by remarking on a fact on which the whole social system should rest: i.e. that, instead of destroying natural inequality, the fundamental compact substitutes, for such physical inequality as nature may have set up between men, an equality that is moral and legitimate, and that men, who may be unequal in strength or intelligence, become every one equal by convention and legal right.

Book II

CHAPTER I

That Sovereignty is Inalienable

The first and most important deduction from the principles we have so far laid down is that the general will alone can direct the state according to the object for which it was instituted, i.e. the common good. . . .

. . . Sovereignty, being nothing less than the exercise of the general will, can never be alienated, and . . . the Sovereign, who is no less than a collective being, cannot be represented except by himself. . . .

In reality, if it is not impossible for a particular will to agree on some point with the general will, it is at least impossible for the agreement to be lasting and constant; for the particular will tends, by its very nature, to partiality, while the general will tends to equality. It is even more impossible to have any guarantee of this agreement; for even if it should always exist, it would be the effect not of art, but of chance. . . . If then the people promises simply to obey, by that very act it dissolves itself and loses what makes it a people; the moment a master exists, there is no longer a Sovereign, and from that moment the body politic has ceased to exist.

This does not mean that the commands of the rulers cannot pass for general wills, so long as the Sovereign, being free to oppose them, offers no opposition. In such a case, universal silence is taken to imply the consent of the people. . . .

CHAPTER II

That Sovereignty is Indivisible

Sovereignty, for the same reason as makes it inalienable, is indivisible; for will either is, or is not, general; it is the will either of the body of the people, or only of a part of it. In the first case, the will, when declared, is an act of Sovereignty and constitutes law: in the second, it is merely a particular will, or act of magistracy—at the most a decree.

But our political theorists, unable to divide Sovereignty in principle, divide it according to its object: into force and will; into legislative power and executive power; into rights of taxation, justice, and war; into internal administration and power of foreign treaty. . . .

This error is due to a lack of exact notions concerning the Sovereign authority, and to taking for parts of it what are only emanations from it. Thus, for example, the acts of declaring war and making peace have been regarded as acts of Sovereignty; but this is not the case, as these acts do not constitute law, but merely the application of a law. . . .

when factions arise, and partial associations are formed at the expense of the great association, the will of each of these associations becomes general in relation to its members, while it remains particular in relation to the State. . . . The differences become less numerous and give a less general result. Lastly, when one of these associations is so great as to prevail over all the rest, the result is no longer a sum of small differences, but a single difference; in this case there is no longer a general will, and the opinion which prevails is purely particular.

It is therefore essential, if the general will is to be able to express itself, that there should be no partial society within the State, and that each citizen should think only his own thoughts: which was indeed the sublime and unique system established by the great Lycurgus. But if there are partial societies, it is best to have as many as possible and to prevent them from being unequal. . . .

CHAPTER III

Whether the General Will is Fallible

It follows from what has gone before that the general will is always right and tends to the public advantage; but it does not follow that the deliberations of the people are always equally correct. Our will is always for our own good, but we do not always see what that is; the people is never corrupted, but it is often deceived, and on such occasions only does it seem to will what is bad.

There is often a great deal of difference between the will of all and the general will; the latter considers only the common interest, while the former takes private interest into account, and is no more than a sum of particular wills: but take away from these same wills the pluses and minuses that cancel one another, and the general will remains as the sum of the differences.

If, when the people, being furnished with adequate information, held its deliberations, the citizens had no communication one with another, the grand total of the small differences would always give the general will, and the decision would always be good. But

CHAPTER IV

The Limits of the Sovereign Power

If the State is a moral person whose life is in the union of its members, and if the most important of its cares is the care for its own preservation, it must have a universal and compelling force, in order to move and dispose each part as may be most advantageous to the whole. As nature gives each man absolute power over all his members, the social compact gives the body politic absolute power over all its members also; and it is this power which, under the direction of the general will, bears, as I have said, the name of Sovereignty. . . .

Each man alienates, I admit, by the social compact, only such part of his powers, goods, and liberty as it is important for the community to control; but it must also be granted that the Sovereign is sole judge of what is important.

Every service a citizen can render the State he ought to render as soon as the Sovereign demands it; but the Sovereign, for its part, cannot impose upon its subjects any fetters that are useless to the community, nor can it even wish to do so; for no more by the law of reason than by the law of nature can anything occur without a cause.

The undertakings which bind us to the social body are obligatory only because they are mutual; and their nature is such that in fulfilling them we cannot work for others without working for ourselves. Why is it that the general will is always in the right, and that all continually will the happiness of each one, unless it is because there is not a man who does not think of "each" as meaning him, and consider himself in voting for all? This proves that equality of rights and the idea of justice which such equality creates originate in the preference each man gives to himself, and accordingly in the very nature of man. It proves that the general will, to be really such, must be general in its object as well as its essence; that it must both come from all and apply to all; and that it loses its natural rectitude when it is directed to some particular and determinate object, because in such a case we are judging of something foreign to us and have no true principle of equity to guide us.

Indeed, as soon as a question of particular fact or right arises on a point not previously regulated by a general convention, the matter becomes contentious. It is a case in which the individuals concerned are one party, and the public the other, but in which I can see neither the law that ought to be followed nor the judge who ought to give the decision. In such a case, it would be absurd to propose to refer the question to an express decision of the general will, which can be only the conclusion reached by one of the parties and in consequence will be, for the other party, merely an external and particular will, inclined on this occasion to injustice and subject to error. Thus, just as a particular will cannot stand for the general will, the general will, in turn, changes its nature, when its object is particular, and, as general, cannot pronounce on a man or a fact. When, for instance, the people of Athens nominated or displaced its rulers, decreed honours to one, and imposed penalties on another, and,

by a multitude of particular decrees, exercised all the functions of government indiscriminately, it had in such cases no longer a general will in the strict sense; it was acting no longer as Sovereign, but as magistrate. . . .

. . . What makes the will general is less the number of voters than the common interest uniting them; for, under this system, each necessarily submits to the conditions he imposes on others: and this admirable agreement between interest and justice gives to the common deliberations an equitable character which at once vanishes when any particular question is discussed, in the absence of a common interest to unite and identify the ruling of the judge with that of the party.

From whatever side we approach our principle, we reach the same conclusion, that the social compact sets up among the citizens an equality of such a kind, that they all bind themselves to observe the same conditions and should therefore all enjoy the same rights. Thus, from the very nature of the compact, every act of Sovereignty, i.e. every authentic act of the general will, binds or favours all the citizens equally; so that the Sovereign recognizes only the body of the nation, and draws no distinctions between those of whom it is made up. What, then, strictly speaking, is an act of Sovereignty? It is not a convention between a superior and an inferior, but a convention between the body and each of its members. It is legitimate, because based on the social contract, and equitable, because common to all; useful, because it can have no other object than the general good, and stable, because guaranteed by the public force and the supreme power. . . .

When these distinctions have once been admitted, it is seen to be so untrue that there is, in the social contract, any real renunciation on the part of the individuals, that the position in which they find themselves as a result of the contract is really preferable to that in which they were before. Instead of a renunciation, they have made an advantageous exchange: instead of an uncertain and precarious way of living they have got one that is better and more secure; instead of natural independence they have got liberty; instead of the power to harm others security for themselves, and instead of their strength, which others might overcome, a right which social union makes invincible. . . . All have indeed to fight when their country needs them; but then no one has ever to fight for himself. Do we not gain something by running, on behalf of what gives us our security, only some of the risks we should have to run for ourselves, as soon as we lost it?

CHAPTER V

The Right of Life and Death

The question is often asked how individuals, having no right to dispose of their own lives, can transfer to the Sovereign a right which they do not possess. . . . Every man has a right to risk his own life in order to preserve it. . . .

The social treaty has for its end the preservation of the contracting parties. He who wills the end wills the means also, and the means must involve some risks, and even some losses. He who wishes to preserve his life at others' expense should also, when it is necessary, be ready to give it up for their sake. Furthermore, the citizen is no longer the judge of the dangers to which the law desires him to expose himself; and when the prince says to him: "It is expedient for the State that you should die," he ought to die, because it is only on that condition that he has been living in security up to the present, and because his life is no longer a mere bounty of nature, but a gift made conditionally by the State.

The death-penalty inflicted upon criminals may be looked on in much the same light: it is in order that we may not fall victims to an assassin that we consent to die if we ourselves turn assassins. . . .

But, it will be said, the condemnation of a criminal is a particular act. I admit it: but such condemnation is not a function of the Sovereign; it is a right the Sovereign can con-

fer without being able itself to exert it. . . .

. . . Frequent punishments are always a sign of weakness or remissness on the part of the government. There is not a single illdoer who could not be turned to some good. The State has no right to put to death, even for the sake of making an example, any one whom it can leave alive without danger. . . .

CHAPTER VI

Law

By the social compact we have given the body politic existence and life; we have now by legislation to give it movement and will. . . .

What is well and in conformity with order is so by the nature of things and independently of human conventions. All justice comes from God, who is its sole source; but if we knew how to receive so high an inspiration, we should need neither government nor laws. Doubtless, there is a universal justice emanating from reason alone; but this justice, to be admitted among us, must be mutual. Humanly speaking, in default of natural sanctions, the laws of justice are ineffective among men: they merely make for the good of the wicked and the undoing of the just, when the just man observes them towards everybody and nobody observes them towards him. Conventions and laws are therefore needed to join rights to duties and refer justice to its object. In the state of nature, where everything is common, I owe nothing to him whom I have promised nothing; I recognize as belonging to others only what is of no use to me. In the state of society all rights are fixed by law, and the case becomes different.

But what, after all, is a law? . . . when we have defined a law of nature, we shall be no nearer the definition of a law of the State. . . .

. . . When the whole people decrees for the whole people, it is considering only itself; and if a relation is then formed, it is between two aspects of the entire object, without there being any division of the whole. In that case the matter about which the decree is made is, like the decreeing will, general. This act is what I call a law.

When I say that the object of laws is always general, I mean that law considers subjects *en masse* and actions in the abstract, and never a particular person or action. Thus the law may indeed decree that there shall be privileges, but cannot confer them on anybody by name. It may set up several classes of citizens, and even lay down the qualifications for membership of these classes, but it cannot nominate such and such persons as belonging to them; it may establish a monarchical government and hereditary succession, but it cannot choose a king, or nominate a royal family. In a word, no function which has a particular object belongs to the legislative power.

On this view, we at once see that it can no longer be asked whose business it is to make laws, since they are acts of the general will; nor whether the prince is above the law, since he is a member of the State; nor whether the law can be unjust, since no one is unjust to himself; nor how we can be both free and subject to the laws, since they are but registers of our wills. . . .

I therefore give the name "Republic" to every State that is governed by laws, no matter what the form of its administration may be: for only in such a case does the public interest govern, and the *res publica* rank as a *reality.* . . .

Laws are, properly speaking, only the conditions of civil association. The people, being subject to the laws, ought to be their author: the conditions of the Society ought to be regulated solely by those who come together to form it. But how are they to regulate them? . . . Who can give it the foresight to formulate and announce its acts in advance? . . . How can a blind multitude, which often does not know what it wills, because it rarely knows what is good for it, carry out for itself so great and difficult an enterprise as a system of legislation? . . . public enlightenment leads to the union of understanding and will in the social body: the parts are made to work exactly together, and

the whole is raised to its highest power. This makes a legislator necessary.

CHAPTER VII

The Legislator

In order to discover the rules of society best suited to nations, a superior intelligence beholding all the passions of men without experiencing any of them would be needed. This intelligence would have to be wholly unrelated to our nature, while knowing it through and through; its happiness would have to be independent of us, and yet ready to occupy itself with ours; and lastly, it would have, in the march of time, to look forward to a distant glory, and, working in one century, to be able to enjoy in the next. It would take gods to give men laws. . . .

The legislator occupies in every respect an extraordinary position in the State. If he should do so by reason of his genius, he does so no less by reason of his office, which is neither magistracy, nor Sovereignty. This office, which sets up the Republic, nowhere enters into its constitution; it is an individual and superior function, which has nothing in common with human empire; for if he who holds command over men ought not to have command over the laws, he who has command over the laws ought not any more to have it over men; or else his laws would be the ministers of his passions and would often merely serve to perpetuate his injustices: his private aims would inevitably mar the sanctity of his work.

When Lycurgus gave laws to his country, he began by resigning the throne. It was the custom of most Greek towns to entrust the establishment of their laws to foreigners . . . Rome, when it was most prosperous, suffered a revival of all the crimes of tyranny, and was brought to the verge of destruction, because it put the legislative authority and the sovereign power into the same hands. . . .

He, therefore, who draws up the laws has, or should have, no right of legislation, and the people cannot, even if its wishes, deprive itself of this incommunicable right, because, according to the fundamental compact, only the general will can bind the individuals, and there can be no assurance that a particular will is in conformity with the general will, until it has been put to the free vote of the people. . . .

. . . Wise men, if they try to speak their language to the common herd instead of its own, cannot possibly make themselves understood. There are a thousand kinds of ideas which it is impossible to translate into popular language. . . . For a young people to be able to relish sound principles of political theory and follow the fundamental rules of statecraft, the effect would have to become the cause; the social spirit, which should be created by these institutions, would have to preside over their very foundation; and men would have to be before law what they should become by means of law. The legislator therefore, being unable to appeal to either force or reason, must have recourse to an authority of a different order, capable of constraining without violence and persuading without convincing.

This is what has, in all ages, compelled the fathers of nations to have recourse to divine intervention and credit the gods with their own wisdom, in order that the peoples, submitting to the laws of the State as to those of nature, and recognizing the same power in the formation of the city as in that of man, might obey freely, and bear with docility the yoke of the public happiness.

This sublime reason, far above the range of the common herd, is that whose decisions the legislator puts into the mouth of the immortals, in order to constrain by divine authority those whom human prudence could not move. But it is not anybody who can make the gods speak, or get himself believed when he proclaims himself their interpreter. . . .

CHAPTER VIII

The People

. . . The wise legislator does not begin by laying down laws good in themselves, but by investigating the fitness of the people, for which they are destined, to receive them. . . .

A thousand nations have achieved earthly greatness, that could never have endured good laws; even such as could have endured them could have done so only for a very brief period of their long history. Most peoples, like most men, are docile only in youth; as they grow old they become incorrigible. When once customs have become established and prejudices inveterate, it is dangerous and useless to attempt their reformation. . . .

There are indeed times in the history of States when . . . the State, set on fire by civil wars, is born again, so to speak, from its ashes, and takes on anew, fresh from the jaws of death, the vigour of youth. Such were Sparta at the time of Lycurgus, Rome after the Tarquins, and, in modern times, Holland and Switzerland after the expulsion of the tyrants. . . .

. . . One people is amenable to discipline from the beginning; another, not after ten centuries. Russia will never be really civilized, because it was civilized too soon. Peter had a genius for imitations; but he lacked true genius, which is creative and makes all from nothing. . . .

CHAPTER X

The People (continued)

. . . What people, then, is a fit subject for legislation? One which, already bound by some unity of origin, interest, or convention, has never yet felt the real yoke of law; one that has neither customs nor superstitions deeply ingrained, one which stands in no fear of being overwhelmed by sudden invasion; one which, without entering into its neighbours' quarrels, can resist each of them single-handed, or get the help of one to repel another; one in which every member may be known by every other, and there is no need to lay on any man burdens too heavy for a man to bear; one which can do without other peoples, and without which all others can do; one which is neither rich nor poor, but self-sufficient; and, lastly, one which unites the consistency of an ancient people with the docility of a new one. Legislation is made difficult less by what it is necessary to build up than by what has to be destroyed; and what makes success so rare is the impossibility of finding natural simplicity together with social requirements. All these conditions are indeed rarely found united, and therefore few States have good constitutions. . . .

CHAPTER XI

The Various Systems of Legislation

If we ask in what precisely consists the greatest good of all, which should be the end of every system of legislation, we shall find it reduce itself to two main objects, liberty and equality-liberty, because all particular dependence means so much force taken from the body of the State, and equality, because liberty cannot exist without it.

I have already defined civil liberty by equality, we should understand, not that the degrees of power and riches are to be absolutely identical for everybody; but that power shall never be great enough for violence, and shall always be exercised by virtue of rank and law; and that, in respect of riches, no citizen shall ever be wealthy enough to buy another, and none poor enough to be forced to sell himself: which implies, on the part of the great, moderation in goods and position, and, on the side of the common sort, moderation in avarice and covetousness.

Such equality, we are told, is an unpractical ideal that cannot actually exist. But if its abuse is inevitable, does it follow that we should not at least make regulations concerning it? It is precisely because the force of circumstances tends continually to destroy equality that the force of legislation should always tend to its maintenance.

But these general objects of every good legislative system need modifying in every country in accordance with the local situation and the temper of the inhabitants. . . .

What makes the constitution of a State really solid and lasting is the due observance of what is proper, so that the natural relations are always in agreement with the laws on every point, and law only serves, so to speak, to assure, accompany and rectify them. But if the legislator mistakes his object and adopts a principle other than circumstances naturally direct . . . the laws will insensibly lose their influence, the constitution will alter, and the State will have no rest from trouble till it is either destroyed or changed, and nature has resumed her invincible sway.

CHAPTER XII

The Division of the Laws

. . . First, there is the action of the complete body upon itself, the relation of the whole to the whole, of the Sovereign to the State. . . .

The laws which regulate this relation bear the name of political laws, and are also called fundamental laws. . . .

The second relation is that of the members one to another, or to the body as a whole; and this relation should be in the first respect as unimportant, and in the second as important, as possible. Each citizen would then be perfectly independent of all the rest, and at the same time very dependent on the city; which is brought about always by the same means, as the strength of the State can alone secure the liberty of its members. From this second relation arise civil laws.

We may consider also a third kind of relation between the individual and the law, a relation of disobedience to its penalty. This gives rise to the setting up of criminal laws, which, at bottom, are less a particular class of law than the sanction behind all the rest.

Along with these three kinds of law goes a fourth, most important of all, which is not graven on tablets of marble or brass, but on the hearts of the citizens. This forms the real constitution of the State, takes on every day new powers, when other laws decay or die out, restores them or takes their place, keeps a people in the ways in which it was meant to go, and insensibly replaces authority by the force of habit. I am speaking of morality, of custom, above all of public opinion; a power unknown to political thinkers, on which none the less success in everything else depends. With this the great legislator concerns himself in secret, though he seems to confine himself to particular regulations; for these are only the arc of the arch, while manners and morals, slower to arise, form in the end its immovable keystone.

Among the different classes of laws, the political, which determine the form of the government, are alone relevant to my subject.

Book III

CHAPTER I

Government in General

. . . Every free action is produced by the concurrence of two causes; one moral, i.e. the will which determines the act; the other physical, i.e. the power which executes it. When I walk towards an object, it is necessary first that I should will to go there, and, in the second place, that my feet should carry me. . . . The body politic has the same motive powers; here too force and will are distinguished, will under the name of legislative power and force under that of executive power. Without their concurrence, nothing is, or should be, done.

. . . The legislative power belongs to the people, and can belong to it alone. It may, on the other hand, readily be seen . . . that the executive power cannot belong to the generality as legislature or Sovereign, because it consists wholly of particular acts which fall outside the competency of the law, and consequently of the Sovereign, whose acts must always be laws.

The public force therefore needs an agent of its own to bind it together and set it to work under the direction of the general will. . . . Here we have what is, in the State, the basis of government, often wrongly confused with the Sovereign, whose minister it is.

What then is government? An intermediate body set up between the subjects and the Sovereign, to secure their mutual correspondence, charged with the execution of the laws and the maintenance of liberty, both civil and political.

The members of this body are called magistrates or *kings,* that is to say *governors,* and the whole body bears the name *prince.* Thus those who hold that the act, by which a people puts itself under a prince, is not a contract, are certainly right. It is simply and solely a commission, an employment, in which the rulers, mere officials of the Sovereign, exercise in their own name the power of which it makes them depositaries. This power it can limit, modify, or recover at pleasure; for the alienation of such a right is incompatible with the nature of the social body, and contrary to the end of association.

I call then *government,* or supreme administration, the legitimate exercise of the executive power, and piince or magistrate the man or the body entrusted with that administration. . . .

. . . If the Sovereign desires to govern, or the magistrate to give laws, or if the subjects refuse to obey, disorder takes the place of regularity, force and will no longer act together, and the State is dissolved and falls into despotism or anarchy . . . As countless events may change the relations of a people, not only may different governments be good for different peoples, but also for the same people at different times. . . .

Suppose the State is composed of ten thousand citizens. The Sovereign can only be considered collectively and as a body; but each member, as being a subject, is regarded as an individual: thus the Sovereign is to the subject as ten thousand to one, i.e. each member of the State has as his share only a ten-thousandth part of the sovereign authority, although he is wholly under its control. If the people numbers a hundred thousand, the condition of the subject undergoes no change, and each equally is under the whole authority of the laws, while his vote, being reduced to one hundred thousandth part, has ten times less influence in drawing them up. The subject therefore remaining always a unit, the relation between him and the Sovereign increases with the number of the citizens. From this it follows that, the larger the State, the less the liberty. . . .

. . . the less relation the particular wills have to the general will, that is, morals and manners to laws, the more should the repressive force be increased. The government, then, to be good, should be proportionately stronger as the people is more numerous.

On the other hand, as the growth of the State gives the depositaries of the public authority more temptations and chances of abusing their power, the greater the force with which the government ought to be endowed for keeping the people in hand, the greater too should be the force at the disposal of the Sovereign for keeping the government in hand . . . .

. . . the dominant will of the prince is, or should be, nothing but the general will or the law; his force is only the public force concentrated in his hands, and, as soon as he tries to base any absolute and independent act on his own authority, the tie that binds the whole together begins to be loosened. If finally the prince should come to have a particular will more active than the will of the Sovereign, and should employ the public force in his hands in obedience to this particular will, there would be, so to speak, two Sovereigns, one rightful and the other actual, the social union would evaporate instantly, and the body politic would be dissolved.

However, in order that the government may have a true existence . . . it must have a particular personality, a sensibility common to its members, and a force and will of its own making for its preservation. This particular existence implies assemblies, councils, power of deliberation and decision, rights, titles, and privileges belonging exclusively to the prince and making the office of magistrate more honourable in proportion as it is more troublesome. The difficul-

ties lie in the manner of so ordering this subordinate whole within the whole, that it in no way alters the general constitution by affirmation of its own, and always distinguishes the particular force it possesses, which is destined to aid in its preservation, from the public force, which is destined to the preservation of the State; and, in a word, is always ready to sacrifice the government to the people, and never to sacrifice the people to the government. . . .

CHAPTER II

The Constituent Principle in the Various Forms of Government

. . . We said that the relation of the Sovereign to the subjects was greater in proportion as the people was more numerous, and, by a clear analogy, we may say the same of the relation of the government to the magistrates.

But the total force of the government, being always that of the State, is invariable; so that, the more of this force it expends on its own members, the less it has left to employ on the whole people.

The more numerous the magistrates, therefore, the weaker the government. . . .

In the person of the magistrate we can distinguish three essentially different wills: first, the private will of the individual, tending only to his personal advantage; secondly, the common will of the magistrates, which is relative solely to the advantage of the prince, and may be called corporate will, being general in relation to the government, and particular in relation to the State, of which the government forms part; and, in the third place, the will of the people or the sovereign will, which is general both in relation to the State regarded as the whole, and to the government regarded as a part of the whole.

In a perfect act of legislation, the individual or particular will should be at zero; the corporate will belonging to the government should occupy a very subordinate position; and, consequently, the general or sovereign will should always predominate and should be the sole guide of all the rest.

According to the natural order, on the other hand, these different wills become more active in proportion as they are concentrated. Thus, the general will is always the weakest, the corporate will second, and the individual will strongest of all: so that, in the government, each member is first of all himself, then a magistrate, and then a citizen—in an order exactly the reverse of what the social system requires. . . .

CHAPTER III

The Division of Governments

. . . There has been at all times much dispute concerning the best form of government, without consideration of the fact that each is in some cases the best, and in others the worst.

If, in the different States, the number of supreme magistrates should be in inverse ratio to the number of citizens, it follows that, generally, democratic government suits small states, aristocratic government those of middle size, and monarchy great ones. This rule is immediately deducible from the principle laid down. But it is impossible to count the innumerable circumstances which may furnish exceptions.

CHAPTER IV

Democracy

He who makes the law knows better than any one else how it should be executed and interpreted. It seems then impossible to have a better constitution than that in which the executive and legislative powers are united; but this very fact renders the government in certain respects inadequate, because things which should be distinguished are confounded, and the prince and the Sovereign, being the same person, form, so to speak, no more than a government without government.

It is not good for him who makes the laws

to execute them, or for the body of the people to turn its attention away from a general standpoint and devote it to particular objects. Nothing is more dangerous than the influence of private interests in public affairs, and the abuse of the laws by the government is a less evil than the corruption of the legislator, which is the inevitable sequel to a particular standpoint. . . .

If we take the term in the strict sense, there never has been a real democracy, and there never will be. It is against the natural order for the many to govern and the few to be governed. It is unimaginable that the people should remain continually assembled to devote their time to public affairs, and it is clear that they cannot set up commissions for that purpose without the form of administration being changed. . . .

. . . There is no government so subject to civil wars and intestine agitations as democratic or popular government, because there is none which has so strong and continual a tendency to change to another form, or which demands more vigilance and courage for its maintenance as it is. . . .

Were there a people of gods, their government would be democratic. So perfect a government is not for men.

CHAPTER V

Aristocracy

. . . The first societies governed themselves aristocratically. The heads of families took council together on public affairs. The young bowed without question to the authority of experience . . . .

But, in proportion as artificial inequality produced by institutions became predominant over natural inequality, riches or power were put before age, and aristocracy became elective. Finally, the transmission of the father's power along with his goods to his children, by creating patrician families, made government hereditary, and there came to be senators of twenty.

There are then three sorts of aristocracy—natural, elective, and hereditary. The first is only for simple peoples; the third is the worst of all governments; the second is the best, and is aristocracy properly so called.

. . . here magistracy is confined to a few, who become such only by election. By this means uprightness, understanding, experience, and all other claims to pre-eminence and public esteem become so many further guarantees of wise government.

Moreover, assemblies are more easily held, affairs better discussed and carried out with more order and diligence, and the credit of the State is better sustained abroad by venerable senators than by a multitude that is unknown or despised.

In a word, it is the best and most natural arrangement that the wisest should govern the many, when it is assured that they will govern for its profit, and not for their own . . . .

But if aristocracy does not demand all the virtues needed by popular government, it demands others which are peculiar to itself; for instance, moderation on the side of the rich and contentment on that of the poor; for its seems that thorough-going equality would be out of place. . . .

CHAPTER VI

Monarchy

. . . if no government is more vigorous than this, there is also none in which the particular will holds more sway and rules the rest more easily. Everything moves towards the same end indeed, but this end is by no means that of the public happiness, and even the force of the administration constantly shows itself prejudicial to the State.

Kings desire to be absolute, and men are always crying out to them from afar that the best means of being so is to get themselves loved by their people. This precept is all very well, and even in some respects very true. Unfortunately, it will always be derided at court. The power which comes of a people's love is no doubt the greatest; but it is precarious and conditional, and

princes will never rest content with it. The best kings desire to be in a position to be wicked, if they please, without forfeiting their mastery: political sermonizers may tell them to their hearts' content that, the people's strength being their own, their first interest is that the people should be prosperous, numerous, and formidable; they are well aware that this is untrue. Their first personal interest is that the people should be weak, wretched, and unable to resist them. I admit that, provided the subjects remained always in submission, the prince's interest would indeed be that it should be powerful, in order that its power, being his own, might make him formidable to his neighbours; but, this interest being merely secondary and subordinate, and strength being incompatible with submission, princes naturally give the preference always to the principle that is more to their immediate advantage . . . .

An essential and inevitable defect, which will always rank monarchical below republican government, is that in a republic the public voice hardly ever raises to the highest positions men who are not enlightened and capable, and such as to fill them with honour; while in monarchies those who rise to the top are most often merely petty blunderers, petty swindlers, and petty intriguers, whose petty talents cause them to get into the highest positions at court, but, as soon as they have got there, serve only to make their ineptitude clear to the public. The people is far less often mistaken in its choice than the prince; and a man of real worth among the king's ministers is almost as rare as a fool at the head of a republican government. . . .

The disadvantage that is most felt in monarchical government is the want of the continuous succession which, in both the other forms, provides an unbroken bond of union. When one king dies, another is needed; elections leave dangerous intervals and are full of storms. . . .

. . . Crowns have been made hereditary in certain families, and an order of succession has been set up, to prevent disputes . . .

men have chosen rather to risk having children, monstrosities, or imbeciles as rulers to having disputes over the choice of good kings. . . .

Everything conspires to take away from a man who is set in authority over others the sense of justice and reason . . . .

CHAPTER IX

The Marks of a Good Government

. . . What is the end of political association? The preservation and prosperity of its members. And what is the surest mark of their preservation and prosperity? Their numbers and population. Seek then nowhere else this mark that is in dispute. The rest being equal, the government under which, without external aids, without naturalization or colonies, the citizens increase and multiply most is beyond question the best. The government under which a people wanes and diminishes is the worst . . . .

CHAPTER X

The Abuse of Government and Its Tendency to Degenerate

As the particular will acts constantly in opposition to the general will, the government continually exerts itself against the Sovereignty. The greater this exertion becomes, the more the constitution changes; and, as there is in this case no other corporate will to create an equilibrium by resisting the will of the prince, sooner or later the prince must inevitably suppress the Sovereign and break the social treaty . . . .

Government undergoes contraction when it passes from the many to the few. . . .

The dissolution of the State may come about in either of two ways.

First, when the prince ceases to administer the State in accordance with the laws, and usurps the Sovereign power. A remarkable change then occurs: not the government, but the State, undergoes contraction; I mean that the great State is dissolved, and

another is formed within it, composed solely of the members of the government, which becomes for the rest of the people merely master and tyrant. So that the moment the government usurps the Sovereignty, the social compact is broken, and all private citizens recover by right their natural liberty, and are forced, but not bound, to obey.

The same thing happens when the members of the government severally usurp the power they should exercise only as a body . . . There are then, so to speak, as many princes as there are magistrates, and the State, no less divided than the government, either perishes or changes its form . . . .

CHAPTER XI

The Death of the Body Politic

. . . If Sparta and Rome perished, what State can hope to endure for ever? If we would set up a long-lived form of government, let us not even dream of making it eternal. If we are to succeed, we must not attempt the impossible, or flatter ourselves that we are endowing the work of man with a stability of which human conditions do not permit.

The body politic, as well as the human body, begins to die as soon as it is born, and carries in itself the causes of its destruction. But both may have a constitution that is more or less robust and suited to preserve them a longer or a shorter time. . . .

The State subsists by means not of the laws, but of the legislative power. Yesterday's law is not binding to-day; but silence is taken for tacit consent, and the Sovereign is held to confirm incessantly the laws it does not abrogate as it might. All that it has once declared itself to will it wills always, unless it revokes its declaration.

Why then is so much respect paid to old laws? For this very reason. We must believe that nothing but the excellence of old acts of will can have preserved them so long: if the Sovereign had not recognized them as throughout salutary, it would have revoked them a thousand times. This is why, so far from growing weak, the laws continually gain new strength in any well constituted State; the precedent of antiquity makes them daily more venerable: while wherever the laws grow weak as they become old, this proves that there is no longer a legislative power and that the State is dead.

CHAPTER XII

How the Sovereign Authority Maintains Itself

The Sovereign having no force other than the legislative power, acts only by means of the laws; and the laws being solely the authentic acts of the general will, the Sovereign cannot act save when the people is assembled. The people in assembly, I shall be told, is a mere chimera. It is so to-day, but two thousand years ago it was not so. Has man's nature changed? . . .

. . . The last census showed that there were in Rome four hundred thousand citizens capable of bearing arms, and the last computation of the population of the Empire showed over four million citizens, excluding subjects, foreigners, women, children, and slaves.

What difficulties might not be supposed to stand in the way of the frequent assemblage of the vast population of this capital and its neighbourhood. Yet few weeks passed without the Roman people being in assembly, and even being so several times. It exercised not only the rights of Sovereignty, but also a part of those of government. . . .

CHAPTER XIII

The Same (continued)

It is not enough for the assembled people to have once fixed the constitution of the State by giving its sanction to a body of law; it is not enough for it to have set up a perpetual government, or provided once for all for the election of magistrates. Besides the extraordinary assemblies unforeseen circumstances may demand, there must

be fixed periodical assemblies which cannot be abrogated or prorogued so that on the proper day the people is legitimately called together by law, without need of any formal summoning. . . .

The greater or less frequency with which lawful assemblies should occur depends on so many considerations that no exact rules about them can be given. It can only be said generally that the stronger the government the more often should the Sovereign show itself.

This, I shall be told, may do for a single town; but what is to be done when the State includes several? . . .

. . . if the State cannot be reduced to the right limits, there remains still one resource; this is, to allow no capital, to make the seat of government move from town to town, and to assemble by turn in each the Provincial Estates of the country.

People the territory evenly, extend everywhere the same rights, bear to every place in it abundance and life: by these means will the State become at once as strong and as well governed as possible. . . .

CHAPTER XIV

The Same (continued)

The moment the people legitimately assembled as a sovereign body, the jurisdiction of the government wholly lapses, the executive power is suspended, and the person of the meanest citizen is as sacred and inviolable as that of the first magistrate; for in the presence of the person represented, representatives no longer exist. . . .

CHAPTER XV

Deputies or Representatives

As soon as public service ceases to be the chief business of the citizens and they would rather serve with their money than with their persons, the State is not far from its fall. When it is necessary to march out to war, they pay troops and stay at home: when it is necessary to meet in council, they name deputies and stay at home. By reason of idleness and money, they end by having soldiers to enslave their country and representatives to sell it.

It is through the hustle of commerce and the arts, through the greedy self-interest of profit, and through softness and love of amenities that personal services are replaced by money payments. . . .

Sovereignty, for the same reason as makes it inalienable, cannot be represented; it lies essentially in the general will, and will does not admit of representation . . . The deputies of the people, therefore, are not and cannot be its representatives: they are merely its stewards, and can carry through no definitive acts. Every law the people has not ratified in person is null and void . . . The people of England regards itself as free: but it is grossly mistaken: it is free only during the election of members of parliament. As soon as they are elected, slavery overtakes it, and it is nothing. . . .

Book IV

CHAPTER I

That the General Will Is Indestructible

As long as several men in assembly regard themselves as a single body, they have only a single will which is concerned with their common preservation and general well-being. In this case, all the springs of the State are vigorous and simple and its rules clear and luminous; there are no embroilments or conflicts of interests; the common good is everywhere clearly apparent, and only good sense is needed to perceive it. Peace, unity, and equality are the enemies of political subtleties. Men who are upright and simple are difficult to deceive because of their simplicity; lures and ingenious pretexts fail to impose upon them, and they are not even subtle enough to be dupes. When, among the happiest people in the world, bands of peasants are seen regulating affairs of State

under an oak, and always acting wisely, can we help scorning the ingenious methods of other nations, which make themselves illustrious and wretched with so much art and mystery?

A State so governed needs very few laws; and, as it becomes necessary to issue new ones, the necessity is universally seen. The first man to propose them merely says what all have already felt, and there is no question of factions or intrigues or eloquence in order to secure the passage into law of what every one has already decided to do, as soon as he is sure that the rest will act with him.

Theorists are led into error because, seeing only States that have been from the beginning wrongly constituted, they are struck by the impossibility of applying such a policy to them. . . .

But when the social bond begins to be relaxed and the State to grow weak, when particular interests begin to make themselves felt and the smaller societies to exercise an influence over the larger, the common interest changes and finds opponents: opinion is no longer unanimous; the general will ceases to be the will of all. . . .

Finally, when the State, on the eve of ruin, maintains only a vain, illusory, and formal existence, when in every heart the social bond is broken, and the meanest interest brazenly lays hold of the sacred name of "public good," the general will becomes mute . . . and iniquitous decrees directed solely to private interest get passed under the name of laws.

Does it follow from this that the general will is exterminated or corrupted? Not at all: it is always constant, unalterable, and pure; but it is subordinated to other wills which encroach upon its sphere. Each man, in detaching his interest from the common interest, sees clearly that he cannot entirely separate them; but his share in the public mishaps seems to him negligible beside the exclusive good he aims at making his own. Apart from this particular good, he wills the general good in his own interest, as strongly as any one else. . . .

CHAPTER II

Voting

. . . There is but one law which, from its nature, needs unanimous consent. This is the social compact; for civil association is the most voluntary of all acts. Every man being born free and his own master, no one, under any pretext whatsoever, can make any man subject without his consent. To decide that the son of a slave is born a slave is to decide that he is not born a man.

If then there are opponents when the social compact is made, their opposition does not invalidate the contract, but merely prevents them from being included in it. They are foreigners among citizens. When the State is instituted, residence constitutes consent; to dwell within its territory is to submit to the Sovereign.

Apart from this primitive contract, the vote of the majority always binds all the rest. This follows from the contract itself. But it is asked how a man can be both free and forced to conform to wills that are not his own. How are the opponents at once free and subject to laws they have not agreed to?

I retort that the question is wrongly put. The citizen gives his consent to all the laws, including those which are passed in spite of his opposition, and even those which punish him when he dares to break any of them. . . . When in the popular assembly a law is proposed, what the people is asked is not exactly whether it approves or rejects the proposal, but whether it is in conformity with the general will, which is their will. Each man, in giving his vote states his opinion on that point; and the general will is found by counting votes. When therefore the opinion that is contrary to my own prevails, this proves neither more nor less than that I was mistaken, and that what I thought to be the general will was not so. If my particular opinion had carried the day I should have achieved the opposite of what was my will; and it is in that case that I should not have been free.

This presupposes, indeed, that all the qualities of the general will still reside in the majority: when they cease to do so, whatever side a man may take, liberty is no longer possible. . . .

CHAPTER III

Elections

In the elections of the prince and the magistrates . . . there are two possible methods of procedure, choice and lot . . . .

"Election by lot," says Montesquieu, "is democratic in nature." I agree that it is so; but in what sense? "The lot," he goes on, "is a way of making choice that is unfair to nobody; it leaves each citizen a reasonable hope of serving his country." These are not reasons. . . .

In every real democracy, magistracy is not an advantage, but a burdensome charge which cannot justly be imposed on one individual rather than another. . . .

Election by lot would have few disadvantages in a real democracy, in which, as equality would everywhere exist in morals and talents as well as in principles and fortunes, it would become almost a matter of indifference who was chosen. But I have already said that a real democracy is only an ideal.

When choice and lots are combined, positions that require special talents, such as military posts, should be filled by the former; the latter does for cases, such as judicial offices, in which good sense, justice, and integrity are enough, because in a State that is well constituted, these qualities are common to all the citizens. . . .

CHAPTER VI

The Dictatorship

The inflexibility of the laws, which prevents them from adapting themselves to circumstances, may, in certain cases, render them disastrous, and make them bring about, at a time of crisis, the ruin of the State. The order and slowness of the forms they enjoin require a space of time which circumstances sometimes withhold. A thousand cases against which the legislator has made no provision may present themselves, and it is a highly necessary part of foresight to be conscious that everything cannot be foreseen.

It is wrong therefore to wish to make political institutions so strong as to render it impossible to suspend their operation. Even Sparta allowed its laws to lapse.

However, none but the greatest dangers can counterbalance that of changing the public order, and the sacred power of the laws should never be arrested save when the existence of the country is at stake. In these rare and obvious cases, provision is made for the public security by a particular act entrusting it to him who is most worthy. . . .

CHAPTER VIII

Civil Religion

. . . Christianity as a religion is entirely spiritual, occupied solely with heavenly things; the country of the Christian is not of this world. He does his duty, indeed, but does it with profound indifference to the good or ill success of his cares. Provided he has nothing to reproach himself with, it matters little to him whether things go well or ill here on earth. If the State is prosperous, he hardly dares to share in the public happiness, for fear he may grow proud of his country's glory; if the State is languishing, he blesses the hand of God that is hard upon His people.

. . . If by ill hap there should be a single self-seeker or hypocrite . . . he would certainly get the better of his pious compatriots. Christian charity does not readily allow a man to think hardly of his neighbours. As soon as, by some trick, he has discovered the art of imposing on them and getting hold of a share in the public authority, you have a man established in dignity; it is the will of God that he be respected: very soon you have a power; it is God's will that it be obeyed: and if the power is abused by him who wields it, it is the scourge wherewith God punishes His children. There

would be scruples about driving out the usurper: public tranquillity would have to be disturbed, violence would have to be employed, and blood spilt; all this accords ill with Christian meekness; and after all, in this vale of sorrows, what does it matter whether we are free men or serfs? The essential thing is to get to heaven, and resignation is only an additional means of doing so. . . .

. . . The right which the social compact gives the Sovereign over the subjects does not, we have seen, exceed the limits of public expediency. The subjects then owe the Sovereign an account of their opinions only to such an extent as they matter to the community. Now, it matters very much to the community that each citizen should have a religion. That will make him love his duty; but the dogmas of that religion concern the State and its members only so far as they have reference to morality and to the duties which he who professes them is bound to do to others. Each man may have, over and above, what opinions he pleases, without its being the Sovereign's business to take cognizance of them; for, as the Sovereign has no authority in the other world, whatever the lot of its subjects may be in the life to come, that is not its business, provided they are good citizens in this life.

There is therefore a purely civil profession of faith of which the Sovereign should fix the articles, not exactly as religious dogmas, but as social sentiments without which a man cannot be a good citizen or a faithful subject. While it can compel no one to believe them, it can banish from the State whoever does not believe them—it can banish him, not for impiety, but as an anti-social being, incapable of truly loving the laws and justice, and of sacrificing, at need, his life to his duty. If any one, after publicly recognizing these dogmas, behaves as if he does not believe them, let him be punished by death: he has committed the worst of all crimes, that of lying before the law.

The dogmas of civil religion ought to be few, simple, and exactly worded, without explanation or commentary. The existence of a mighty, intelligent, and beneficent Divinity, possessed of foresight and providence, the life to come, the happiness of the just, the punishment of the wicked, the sanctity of the social contract and the laws: these are its positive dogmas. Its negative dogmas I confine to one, intolerance, which is a part of the cults we have rejected.

Those who distinguish civil from theological intolerance are, to my mind, mistaken. The two forms are inseparable. It is impossible to live at peace with those we regard as damned; to love them would be to hate God who punishes them: we positively must either reclaim or torment them. Wherever theological intolerance is admitted, it must inevitably have some civil effect; and as soon as it has such an effect, the Sovereign is no longer Sovereign even in the temporal sphere: thenceforth priests are the real masters, and kings only their ministers.

Now that there is and can be no longer an exclusive national religion, tolerance should be given to all religions that tolerate others, so long as their dogmas contain nothing contrary to the duties of citizenship. But whoever dares to say "Outside the Church is no salvation," ought to be driven from the State, unless the State is the Church, and the prince the pontiff. Such a dogma is good only in a theocratic government; in any other, it is fatal. . . .

10

Immanuel Kant

1724–1804

He was a small man with a large head; he was misshapen and not quite healthy. He rose to fame from a scrimpy craftsman's home, but not till late in life did he come into his own. His only signs of self-doubt were youthful touchiness and too much insistence on his own importance. He followed a spartan regimen in the same provincial locale for all his eighty years. Yet he wrote original philosophy. He recognized the inherent dignity of man while colonial America tolerated slavery and reformulated the Golden Rule into a Categorical Imperative condemning departures from the actor's ideas of proper universal legislation.

Kant was born, lived, and died in Konigsberg, East Prussia. His father, the son of Scotch parents, was an industrious saddler and a stern trainer of his many children. Kant's mother was a low-born Prussian woman with above average intelligence. The family was steeped in the Pietistic movement of the Lutheran Church. Of eleven children, only two boys and three girls survived childhood. The girls lived lower class lives; Kant's brother became a preacher of little distinction; once Kant left home, he had little to do with any of them.

The family's pastor saw promise in Immanuel not readily apparent to others, and helped him get schooling at the Konigsberg gymnasium, where he was rector. Kant studied hard and made good grades, but showed no signs of genius. The gymnasium stressed religion—each school day started with an hour of religious instruction, and all recitation periods began and ended with prayers. This overdose turned Kant against the clerical career planned for him. His Latin teacher made the Latin classics so attractive that he and two companions spent spare time conning them.

At sixteen he entered Konigsberg University—then an isolated provincial school with its faculty strength concentrated largely in theology. Many professors were assigned work in two or more diverse fields. Kant matriculated in theology, probably following parental orders, but spent most of his time studying mathematics, physics and medicine. He tutored to make ends meet. His only recreation was an occasional game of billiards.

After he finished his undergraduate work at twenty he wrote his first book—a work on mathematical physics. His uncle subsidized its publication. In it Kant flouted authorities and said he had done science a considerable service. Little attention was paid to it then, and none now.

Two years after he finished his studies he got a position as a "family tutor." He was not good with children, but nevertheless spent nine years with three families in this uncongenial role. His first place was at Arnsdorf, sixty miles southwest of Konigsberg—his furthest travel from his birthplace in all his eighty years. His last place was in the establishment of Count Kayserling. The Count and Countess were cultivated people who sensed Kant's ability and treated him with respect. In their home he met guests of rank and distinction, learned poise, and made lasting friendships. In the latter part of this tutorial period he published works on astronomy and geology.

When he applied for his magister's degree

and a teaching position at the University of Konigsberg he ably defended well-thought-out philosophical theses. He was qualified as a Privatdozent, which entitled him to lecture to fee-paying students, but did not entitle him to a salary. He was thirty-one when he first lectured on mathematics and physics in the house where he lodged. The next year he added logic and metaphysics, and lectured three or four times a day. As a Privatdozent Kant was not obliged to lecture on any particular topic, but could teach anything appropriate to the philosophical faculty, which included all subjects but medicine, law, and theology. He went as far afield as fortification, a course of lectures which attracted many military officers.

At the beginning of a course of lectures he was likely to state his pedagogic aims in these words: "I do not read for geniuses, their endowments being such that they will make a way for themselves; nor for the stupid, for they are not worth the trouble; but I read for the sake of those who stand between these two classes, and want to be prepared for their future work." He tried to teach his students to think and often said he would not think for them. He was easily annoyed in the lecture hall, and complained when students' sloppy dress, unusual looks, or fidgety deportment distracted him. His meager income from fees necessitated frugality. He abhorred debt; he often sold choice books from his small personal library to buy bed and board.

For fifteen years he stayed a Privatdozent, while lesser and safer men were promoted. When he was forty a chair of poetry and rhetoric was vacated and the Minister of Public Instruction inquired about Kant's fitness for it. Kant sent word that he did not want this chair because its occupant had to teach versification and write official poems for special occasions. Six years later Kant got a professorship of logic and metaphysics. By lecturing on these subjects, he became a specialist in speculative philosophy. In his heyday his lectures were so popular that the hall was filled an hour beforehand. The University was at a low ebb, by contrast, making competent Kant all the more outstanding. Eight years after he got his chair, he was offered one at the well-thought-of University of Halle. This offer would have doubled his salary and boosted his fame. But he would not move from his accustomed niche. He taught at Konigsberg until feebleness forced his overdue resignation at seventy-seven, three years before his death. During his thirty professorial years several times he served terms as dean of his faculty and rector of the university—without distinction.

Though his finances permitted better living in his latter days, he remained frugal and stuck to his iron-clad schedule. He became more and more absorbed in speculations, and more and more absent-minded—one of his biographers thinks Kant did not notice total blindness in his left eye until two or three years after it set in. However, he was anxious about his health, and on the lookout for ways to prolong his life. He got the idea that most medicines were poison and took none until he was quite old. He was a crank on diet, and ate only one meal a day. He was out of bed every morning at the stroke of five, and put in many hard-working, scheduled hours every day of his life. They say Konigsbergers set their clocks by his daily walks.

He had one extravagance once his professor's salary permitted—clothes. He dressed with scrupulous care and preferred bright colors. Until his senility he was be-wigged, silk-stockinged, gold-braided and silver-buckled. When he was nearly sixty he moved, for the first time, into his own house. There he entertained two to five male guests at midday dinner, daily. He gave them simple food and profound talk. Women were not invited; he thought learning unbecoming to ladies and that they lacked talent for serious conversation. On a few occasions his heart was touched by some gentle, attractive woman, but he never got around to any serious courtship.

In his middle years his philosophic interests were entirely self-centered; he paid little attention to systems of his philosopher contemporaries, and did not even bother to look at their reviews of his work. But he did keep track of world developments and was sympathetically interested in the American and French Revolutions, even though the latter was a particularly unpopular cause in Konigsberg. He was so confident of his own powers of deduction that his conclusions became unshakeable. He deduced Napoleon's expedition against Egypt was a feint and that the real blow would fall on Portugal; even after the landing in Egypt was announced, he still maintained his conclusion, saying that the announcement was an attempt to mislead the English.

His stature was shown by his *Critique of Pure Reason* published in 1781 when Kant was fifty-seven. Kant had no idea that the book would be well received. A Konigsberg publisher had turned it down as potentially unprofitable. The Riga publisher who took it could have had it for nothing, but he paid Kant four dollars a page for it and made substantial voluntary payments on each of many editions. Kant regarded this money as gifts. Ten years after its publication the *Critique* was expounded in all German and many foreign universities.

Kant's earlier works were clear and even fluent, but the *Critique* was prolix and obscure. In a letter to a friend he said that though the book was the product of more than twelve years of thought, he had written it out in white heat in four or five months, with no attention to style and no effort to cater to readers. He was too old, he said, to execute an extensive job of writing and at the same time, file in hand, make each part round, smooth, and graceful.

As Kant developed his system he attracted more and more admiration. Students flocked to his lectures. He was adulated, hailed, visited, worshipped, bothered. At sixty-five he began to slip physically and mentally, but he still managed another decade of significant writing and accepted teaching. During these days he wrote *The Science of Right,* 1791, published in translation as *Kant's Philosophy of Law,* from which the excerpts following this note were taken.

His last five years were a period of weakness, fading memory, and mental debility. He died on an unusually bright February day in 1804. One small white cloud was in the sky. The tale is told that a soldier stationed on the Schmiede Bridge said, "See, that is Kant's soul flying heavenward"—which goes to show that common Konigsbergers not only knew their famous townsman, but also knew about the fluffy whiteness of his soul. Perhaps the story-teller was not devoted to the stern truth called for by the Categorical Imperative.

KANT'S PHILOSOPHY OF LAW *

(AN EXPOSITION
OF THE
FUNDAMENTAL PRINCIPLES
OF JURISPRUDENCE
AS
THE SCIENCE OF RIGHT)

GENERAL INTRODUCTION TO THE META-
PHYSICS OF MORALS

I

*The Relation of the Faculties of the
Human Mind to the Moral Laws*

* * *

The Will as the Faculty of Practical Principles.—Under the Will, taken generally, may be included the volitional act of *Choice* . . . The act of Choice that can be determined by *pure Reason,* constitutes the act of Free-Will. That act which is determinable only by Inclination as a sensuous impulse or stimulus would be irrational brute Choice. The human act of Choice, however, as human, is in fact *affected* by such impulses or stimuli, but is not *determined* by them; and it is, therefore, not pure in itself when taken apart from the acquired habit of determination by Reason. But it may be determined to action by the pure Will. The *Freedom*

* Translated by W. Hastie, reprinted by permission of T. & T. Clark, Edinburgh.

of the act of volitional Choice, is its independence of being *determined* by sensuous
impulses or stimuli. This forms the *negative*
conception of the Freewill. The *positive*
Conception of Freedom is given by the fact
that the Will is the capability of Pure Reason to be practical of itself. But this is not
possible otherwise than by the Maxim
of every action being subjected to the
condition of being practicable as a universal Law. Applied as Pure Reason to the
act of Choice, and considered apart from its
objects, it may be regarded as the Faculty of
Principles; and, in this connection, it is the
source of Practical Principles. Hence it is to
be viewed as a lawgiving Faculty. But as the
material upon which to construct a Law is
not furnished to it, it can only make the
form of the Maxim of the act of Will, in so
far as it is available as a universal Law, the
supreme Law and determining Principle of
the Will. And as the Maxims, or Rules of
human action derived from subjective causes,
do not of themselves necessarily agree with
those that are objective and universal, Reason can only prescribe this supreme Law as
an absolute Imperative of prohibition or
command.

The Laws of Freedom as Moral, Juridical,
and Ethical.—The Laws of Freedom, as distinguished from the Laws of Nature, are
moral Laws. So far as they refer only to external actions and their lawfulness, they are
called *Juridical;* but if they also require
that, as Laws, they shall themselves be the
determining Principles of our actions, they
are *Ethical.* The agreement of an action with
Juridical Laws, is its *Legality;* the agreement
of an action with Ethical Laws, is its *Morality* . . . .

II

The Idea and Necessity of a Metaphysic of Morals

Moral Laws a priori and Necessary— . . .
conceptions and judgments regarding ourselves and our conduct have no *moral* significance, if they contain only what may be
learned from experience; and when any one

is, so to speak misled into making a Moral
Principle out of anything derived from this
latter source, he is already in danger of falling into the coarsest and most fatal errors.

If the Philosophy of Morals were nothing
more than a Theory of Happiness it would
be absurd to search after Principles *a priori*
as a foundation for it . . . It is only Experience that can show what will bring us enjoyment. The natural impulses directed
towards nourishment, the sexual instinct, or
the tendency to rest and motion, as well as
the higher desires of honour, the acquisition
of knowledge, and such like, as developed
with our natural capacities, are alone capable of showing in what those enjoyments are
to be *found*. And, further, the knowledge
thus acquired, is available for each individual merely in his own way; and it is only
thus he can learn the means by which he has
to *seek* those enjoyments. . . .

But it is quite otherwise with the Principles of Morality. They lay down Commands
for every one without regard to his particular inclinations, and merely because and so
far as he is free, and has a practical Reason.
Instruction in the Laws of Morality is not
drawn from observation of oneself or of our
animal nature, nor from perception of the
course of the world in regard to what happens, or how men act. But Reason commands how we *ought* to act, even although
no example of such action were to be found;
nor does Reason give any regard to the Advantage which may accrue to us by so acting, and which Experience could alone
actually show . . . .

IV

General Preliminary Conceptions Defined and Explained

* * *

Natural and Positive Laws.—Obligatory
Laws for which an external Legislation is
possible, are called generally *External Laws*.
Those External Laws, the obligatoriness of
which can be recognised by Reason *a priori*
even without an external Legislation, are
called NATURAL LAWS. Those Laws,

there are things that are obligatory

again, which are not obligatory without actual External Legislation, are called POSITIVE LAWS. An External Legislation, containing pure Natural Laws, is therefore conceivable; but in that case a previous Natural Law must be presupposed to establish the authority of the Lawgiver by the Right to subject others to Obligation through his own act of Will.

Maxims—The Principle which makes a certain action a Duty, is a Practical Law. The Rule of the Agent or Actor, which he forms as a Principle for himself on subjective grounds, is called his MAXIM. Hence, even when the Law is one and invariable, the Maxims of the Agent may yet be very different.

The Categorical Imperative.—The Categorical Imperative only expresses generally what constitutes Obligation. It may be rendered by the following Formula: 'Act according to a Maxim which can be adopted at the same time as a Universal Law' . . . Reason brings the principle or maxim of any action to the test, by calling upon the Agent to think of himself in connection with it as at the same time laying down a Universal Law, and to consider whether his action is so qualified as to be fit for entering into such a Universal Legislation. . . .

. . . The Principle of Duty is what Reason absolutely, and therefore objectively and universally, lays down in the form of a Command to the individual, as to how he *ought* to act.

The SUPREME PRINCIPLE of the Science of Morals accordingly is this: 'Act according to a Maxim which can likewise be valid as a Universal Law.'—Every Maxim which is not qualified according to this condition, is contrary to Morality. . . .

INTRODUCTION TO THE SCIENCE OF RIGHT: GENERAL DEFINITIONS AND DIVISIONS

A

What the Science of Right is

THE SCIENCE OF RIGHT has for its object the Principles of all the Laws which it is possible to promulgate by external legislation. Where there is such a legislation, it becomes in actual application to it, a system of *positive* Right and Law . . . A professional Lawyer, is one who is skilled in the knowledge of positive external Laws, and who can apply them to cases that may occur in experience. Such practical knowledge of positive Right, and Law, may be regarded as belonging to *Jurisprudence* in the original sense of the term. But the theoretical knowledge of Right and law in Principle, as distinguished from positive Laws and empirical cases, belongs to the pure SCIENCE OF RIGHT. The Science of Right thus designates the philosophical and systematic knowledge of the Principles of Natural Right. And it is from this Science that the immutable Principles of all positive Legislation must be derived by practical Jurists and Lawgivers.

B

What is Right?

. . . A reference to what holds true merely of the laws of some one country at a particular time, is not a solution of the general problem thus proposed. It is quite easy to state what may be right in particular cases as being what the laws of a certain place and of a certain time say or may have said; but it is much more difficult to determine whether what they have enacted is right in itself, and to lay down a universal Criterion by which Right and Wrong in general, and what is just and unjust, may be recognised. . . .

1. The conception of RIGHT,—as referring to a corresponding Obligation which is the moral aspect of it,—in the *first* place, has regard only to the external and practical relation of one Person to another, in so far as they can have influence upon each other, immediately or mediately, by their *Actions* as facts. 2. In the *second* place, the conception of Right does not indicate the relation of the action of an individual to the *wish* or the mere desire of another, as in acts of benevolence or of unkindness, but only the

relation of his free action to the freedom of *action* of the other. 3. And, in the *third* place, in this reciprocal relation of voluntary actions, the conception of Right does not take into consideration the *matter* of the act of Will in so far as the end which any one may have in view in willing it, is concerned. In other words, it is not asked in a question of Right whether any one on buying goods for his own business realizes a profit by the transaction or not; but only the *form* of the transaction is taken into account, in considering the relation of the mutual acts of Will. Acts of Will or voluntary Choice are thus regarded only in so far as they are *free,* and as to whether the action of one can harmonize with the Freedom of another, according to a universal Law.

RIGHT, therefore, comprehends the whole of the conditions under which the voluntary actions of any one Person can be harmonized in reality with the voluntary actions of every other Person, according to a universal Law of Freedom.

C

Universal Principle of Right

'Every Action is *right* which in itself, or in the maxim on which it proceeds, is such that it can co-exist along with the Freedom of the Will of each and all in action, according to a universal Law.'

If, then, my action or my condition generally can co-exist with the freedom of every other, according to a universal Law, any one does me a wrong who hinders me in the performance of this action, or in the maintenance of this condition. For such a hindrance or obstruction cannot co-exist with Freedom according to universal Laws.

It follows also that it cannot be demanded as a matter of Right, that this universal Principle of all maxims shall itself be adopted as my maxim, that is, that I shall make it the *maxim* of my actions. For any one may be free, although his Freedom is entirely indifferent to me, or even if I wished in my heart to infringe it, so long as

I do not actually violate that freedom by *my external action.* Ethics, however, as distinguished from Jurisprudence, imposes upon me the obligation to make the fulfilment of Right a *maxim* of my conduct.

The universal Law of Right may then be expressed, thus: 'Act externally in such a manner that the free exercise of thy Will may be able to co-exist with the Freedom of all others, according to a universal Law.' This is undoubtedly a Law which imposes obligation upon me; but it does not at all imply and still less command that I *ought,* merely on account of this obligation, to limit my freedom to these very conditions. Reason in this connection says only that it *is* restricted thus far by its Idea, and may be likewise thus limited in fact by others; and it lays this down as a Postulate which is not capable of further proof . . . .

D

Right is Conjoined with the Title or Authority to Compel

. . . Everything that is wrong is a hindrance of freedom, according to universal Laws. . . . If a certain exercise of Freedom is itself a hindrance of the Freedom that is according to universal Laws, it is wrong; and the compulsion or constraint which is opposed to it is right . . . All Right is accompanied with an implied Title or warrant to bring compulsion to bear on any one who may violate it in fact.

E

Strict Right May be Also Represented as the Possibility of a Universal Reciprocal Compulsion in Harmony with the Freedom of All According to Universal Laws

. . . As Right in general has for its object only what is external in actions, Strict Right, as that with which nothing ethical is intermingled, requires no other motives of action than those that are merely external; for it is then pure Right, and is unmixed with any prescriptions of Virtue . . . It founds upon the principle of the possibility of an external Compulsion, such as may co-exist with the freedom of every one according to universal Laws. Accordingly, then, where it is said that a Creditor has a right to demand from a Debtor the payment of his debt, this does not mean merely that he can bring him to feel in his mind that Reason obliges him to do this; but it means that he can apply an external compulsion to force any such one so to pay, and that this compulsion is quite consistent with the Freedom of all, including the parties in question, according to a universal Law. Right and the Title to compel, thus indicate the same thing . . . .

F

Supplementary Remarks on Equivocal Right

With every Right, in the strict acceptation there is conjoined a Right to compel. But it is possible to think of other Rights of a *wider* kind in which the Title to compel cannot be determined by any Law. Now there are two real or supposed Rights of this kind—EQUITY and THE RIGHT OF NECESSITY. The first alleges a Right that is without compulsion; the second adopts a compulsion that is without Right. . . .

I. Equity

EQUITY regarded objectively, does not properly constitute a claim upon the moral Duty of benevolence or beneficience on the part of others; but whoever insists upon anything on the ground of Equity, founds upon his *Right* to the same. In this case, however, the conditions are awanting that are requisite for the function of a Judge in order that he might determine what or what kind of satisfaction can be done to this claim. When one of the partners of a Mercantile Company, formed under the condition of Equal profits, has, however, *done more* than

the other members, and in consequence has also *lost more,* it is *in accordance with Equity* that he should demand from the Company more than merely an equal share of advantage with the rest. But, in relation to *strict Right,*—if we think of a Judge considering his case,—he can furnish no definite data to establish how much more belongs to him by the contract; and in case of an action at law, such a demand would be rejected. A domestic servant, again, who might be paid his wages due to the end of his year of service in a coinage that became depreciated within that period, so that it would not be of the same value to him as it was when he entered on his engagement, cannot claim by Right to be kept from loss on account of the unequal value of the money if he receives the due amount of it. He can only make an appeal on the ground of Equity,—a dumb goddess who cannot claim a hearing of Right,—because there was nothing bearing on this point in the Contract of Service, and a Judge cannot give a decree on the basis of vague or indefinite conditions.

Hence it follows, that a COURT OF EQUITY for the decision of disputed questions of Right, would involve a contradiction . . . .

The *Dictum* of Equity may be put thus: 'The strictest Right is the greatest Wrong.' But this evil cannot be obviated by the forms of Right although it relates to a matter of Right; for the grievance that it gives rise to can only be put before a 'Court of Conscience' whereas every question of Right must be taken before a CIVIL COURT.

II. The Right of Necessity

The so-called Right of Necessity is the supposed Right or Title, in case of the danger of losing my own life, to take away the life of another who has, in fact, done me no harm. It is evident that, viewed as a doctrine of Right, this must involve a contradiction . . . It is a question of the allowableness of using violence against one who has used none against me.

It is clear that the assertion of such a

Right is not to be understood objectively as being in accordance with what a Law would prescribe, but merely subjectively, as proceeding on the assumption of how a sentence would be pronounced by a Court in the case. There can, in fact, be no *Criminal Law* assigning the penalty of death to a man who, when shipwrecked and struggling in extreme danger for his life, and in order to save it, may thrust another from a plank on which he had saved himself. For the punishment threatened by the Law could not possibly have greater power than the fear of the loss of life in the case in question. Such a Penal Law would thus fail altogether to exercise its intended effect; for the threat of an Evil which is still *uncertain*—such as Death by a judicial sentence—could not overcome the fear of an Evil which is *certain,* as Drowning is in such circumstances. An act of violent self-preservation, then, ought not to be considered as altogether beyond condemnation; it is only to be adjudged as exempt from punishment. Yet this *subjective* condition of impunity, by a strange confusion of ideas, has been regarded by Jurists as equivalent to *objective* lawfulness. . . .

DIVISION OF THE SCIENCE OF RIGHT

A

General Division of the Duties of Right (Juridical Duties)

In this Division we may very conveniently follow Ulpian . . . if his three Formulae are taken in a general sense, which may not have been quite clearly in his mind, but which they are capable of being developed into or of receiving. . . .

1. "Live rightly." Juridical Rectitude, or Honour, consists in maintaining one's own worth as a man in relation to others. This Duty may be rendered by the proposition, "Do not make thyself a mere Means for the use of others, but be to them likewise an End." This Duty will be explained in the next Formula as an Obligation arising out of the *Right* of Humanity in our own Person.

2. "Do Wrong to no one." This Formula may be rendered so as to mean, "Do no Wrong to any one, even if thou shouldst be under the necessity, in observing this Duty, to cease from all connection with others and to avoid all Society."

3. "Assign to every one what is his own." This may be rendered, "Enter, if Wrong cannot be avoided, into a Society with others in which every one may have *secured* to him what is his own."—If this Formula were to be simply translated, "Give every one *his own,*" it would express an absurdity, for we cannot *give* any one what he already has. If it is to have a definite meaning, it must therefore run thus, "Enter into a state in which every one can have what is his own secured against the action of every other" . . . .

B

Universal Division of Rights

I. Natural Right and Positive Right

The System of Rights, viewed as a scientific System of Doctrines, is divided into NATURAL RIGHT and POSITIVE RIGHT. Natural Right rests upon pure rational Principles *a priori;* Positive or Statutory Right is what proceeds from the Will of a Legislator.

II. Innate Right and Acquired Right

. . . Innate Right is that Right which belongs to every one by Nature, independent of all juridical acts of experience. ACQUIRED RIGHT is that Right which is founded upon such juridical acts.

Innate Right may also be called the "Internal Mine and Thine"; for External Right must always be acquired.

There is only one Innate Right, the Birthright of Freedom.

FREEDOM is Independence of the compulsory Will of another; and in so far as it can co-exist with the Freedom of all according to a universal Law, it is the one sole original, inborn Right belonging to every man in virtue of his Humanity. There is, indeed, an innate EQUALITY belonging to every man which consists in his Right to be independent of being bound by others to anything more than that to which he may also reciprocally bind them. It is, consequently, the inborn quality of every man in virtue of which he ought to be *his own master by Right....*

PRIVATE RIGHT: THE PRINCIPLES OF THE EXTERNAL MINE AND THINE GENERALLY

CHAPTER FIRST

Of the Mode of Having Anything External as One's Own

1. The Meaning of "Mine" in Right

ANYTHING is *"Mine" by Right,* or is rightfully Mine, when I am so connected with it, that if any other Person should make use of it without my consent, he would do me a lesion or injury. The subjective condition of the use of anything, is *Possession* of it.

An *external* thing, however, as such could only be mine, if I may assume it to be possible that I can be wronged by the use which another might make of it *when it is not actually in my possession.* Hence it would be a contradiction to have anything External as one's own, were not the conception of Possession capable of two different meanings, as *sensible* Possession that is perceivable by the senses, and *rational* Possession that is perceivable only by the Intellect. By the former is to be understood a *physical* Possession, and by the latter, a purely *juridical* Possession of the same object....

2. Juridical Postulate of the Practical Reason

It is possible to have any external object of my Will as Mine. In other words, a Maxim to this effect—were it to become law —that any object on which the Will can be

exerted must remain objectively in itself *without an owner,* as 'res nullius,' is contrary to the Principle of Right

. . . suppose there were things that *by right* should absolutely not be in our power, or, in other words, that it would be wrong or inconsistent with the freedom of all, according to universal Law, to make use of them. On this supposition, Freedom would so far be depriving itself of the use of its voluntary activity, in thus putting *useable* objects out of all possibility of *use.* In practical relations, this would be to annihilate them, by making them *res nullius,* notwithstanding the fact that acts of Will in relation to such things would formally harmonize, in the actual use of them, with the external freedom of all according to universal Laws . . . The practical Reason cannot contain, in reference to such an object, an absolute prohibition of its use, because this would involve a contradiction of external freedom with itself . . . It is therefore an assumption *a priori* of the practical Reason, to regard and treat every object within the range of my free exercise of Will as objectively a possible Mine or Thine . . . .

5. Definition of the Conception of the External Mine and Thine

Definitions are *nominal* or *real.* A nominal Definition is sufficient merely to *distinguish* the object defined from all other objects, and it springs out of a complete and definite *exposition* of its conception. A real Definition further suffices for a *Deduction* of the conception defined, so as to furnish a knowledge of the reality of the object.—The *nominal Definition* of the external 'Mine' would thus be: 'The external Mine is anything outside of myself, such that any hindrance of my use of it at will, would be doing me an injury or wrong as an infringement of that Freedom of mine which may coexist with the freedom of all others according to a universal Law.' The *real Definition* of this conception may be put thus: 'The external Mine is anything outside of myself, such that any prevention of my use of it would be a wrong, *although I may not be in possession of it* so as to be actually holding it as an object.'—I must be in some kind of possession of an external object, if the object is to be regarded as *mine;* for, otherwise, any one interfering with this object would not, in doing so, affect me; nor consequently, would he thereby do me any wrong . . . .

6. Deduction of the Conception of a Purely Juridical Possession of an External Object

. . . a first appropriator acquires originally by primary possession a particular portion of the ground; and by Right he resists every other person who would hinder him in the private use of it, although while the 'state of Nature' continues, this cannot be done by juridical means because a public Law does not yet exist.

And although a piece of ground should be regarded as free, or declared to be such, so as to be for the public use of all without distinction, yet it cannot be said that it is thus free by nature and *originally* so, prior to any juridical act. For there would be a real relation already incorporated in such a piece of ground by the very fact that the possession of it was denied to any particular individual; and as this public freedom of the ground would be a prohibition of it to every particular individual, this presupposes a common possession of it which cannot take effect without a Contract. A piece of ground, however, which can only become publicly free by contract, must actually be in the possession of all those associated together, who mutually interdict or suspend each other, from any particular of private use of it.

This *original* Community of the soil and of the things upon it, is an idea which has objective and practical Juridical reality, and is entirely different from the idea of a *primitive* community of things which is a fiction. For the latter would have had to be *founded* as a form of Society, and must have taken its rise from a Contract by which all renounced the Right of Private Possession, so that by

uniting the property owned by each into a whole, it was thus transformed into a common possession. But had such an event taken place, History must have presented some evidence of it. To regard such a procedure as the original mode of taking possession, and to hold that the particular possessions of every individual may and ought to be grounded upon it, is evidently a contradiction. . . .

7. Application of the Principle of the Possibility of an External Mine and Thine to Objects of Experience

. . . The mode, of having something External to myself as Mine, consists in a specially juridical connection of the Will of the Subject with that object, independently of the empirical relations to it in Space and in Time, and in accordance with the conception of a rational possession.—A particular spot on the earth is not externally Mine because I occupy it with my body . . . But if I continue to be in possession of the spot, although I have taken myself away from it and gone to another place, only under that condition is my external Right concerned in connection with it. And to make the continuous possession of this spot by my person a condition of having it as mine, must either be to assert that it is not possible at all to have anything External as one's own . . . or to require, in order that this external Possession may be possible, that I shall be in two places at the same time. . . .

8. To Have Anything External as One's Own is Only Possible in a Juridical or Civil State of Society Under the Regulation of a Public Legislative Power

If, by word or deed, I declare my Will that some external thing shall be mine, I make a declaration that every other person is obliged to abstain from the use of this object of my exercise of Will; and this imposes an Obligation which no one would be under, without such a juridical act on my part. But the assumption of this Act, at the same time involves the admission that I am obliged reciprocally to observe a similar abstention towards every other in respect to what is externally theirs; for the Obligation in question arises from a universal Rule regulating the external juridical relations . . . This guarantee of reciprocal and mutual abstention from what belongs to others, does not require a special juridical act for its establishment, but is already involved in the Conception of an external Obligation of Right, on account of the universality and consequently the reciprocity of the obligatoriness arising from a universal Rule.—Now a single Will, in relation to an external and consequently contingent Possession, cannot serve as a compulsory Law for all, because that would be to do violence to the Freedom which is in accordance with universal Laws. Therefore it is only a Will that binds every one, and as such a common, collective, and authoritative Will, that can furnish a guarantee of security to all. But the state of men under a universal, external and public Legislation, conjoined with authority and power, is called the Civil state. There can therefore be an external Mine and Thine only in the Civil state of Society . . . .

9. There May, However, be an External Mine and Thine Found as a Fact in the State of Nature, but it is Only Provisory

. . . a Civil constitution is only the juridical condition under which every one has what is his own merely secured to him, as distinguished from its being specially assigned and determined to him.—All Guarantee, therefore, assumes that every one to whom a thing is secured, is already in possession of it as his own. Hence, prior to the Civil Constitution—or *apart* from it—an external Mine and Thine must be assumed as possible, and along with it a Right to compel every one with whom we could come into any kind of intercourse, to enter with us into a constitution in which what is Mine or

Thine can be secured.—There may thus be a Possession in expectation or in preparation for such a state of security, as can only be established on the Law of the Common Will; and as it is therefore in accordance with the *possibility* of such a state, it constitutes a *provisory* or temporary juridical Possession; whereas that Possession which is found in reality in the Civil state of Society will be a *peremptory* or guaranteed Possession . . . The mode in which anything external may be held as one's own in the *state of Nature,* is just *physical* possession with a *presumption* of Right thus far in its favour, that by union of the Wills of all in a public Legislation, it will be made *juridical;* and in this expectation it holds *comparatively,* as a kind of potential juridical Possession . . . .

CHAPTER SECOND

The Mode of Acquiring Anything External

FIRST SECTION

Principles of Real Right

11. What is a Real Right?

The usual Definition of Real Right, or "Right in a Thing" is that "it is a Right as *against every possessor of it.*" This is a correct Nominal Definition. But what is it that entitles me to claim an external object from any one who may appear as its possessor, and to compel him, *per vindicationem,* to put me again, in place of himself, into possession of it? Is this external juridical relation of my Will a kind of *immediate* relation to an external thing? . . . It is . . . absurd to think of an obligation of Persons towards Things, and conversely. . . .

The Real Definition would run thus: "RIGHT IN A THING is a Right to the Private Use of a Thing, of which I am in possession—original or derivative—in common with all others." For this is the one condition under which it is alone possible that I can exclude every other possessor from the private use of the Thing ... For, except by presupposing such a common collective possession, it cannot be conceived how, when I am not in actual possession of a thing, I could be injured or wronged by others who are in possession of it and use it.—By an individual act of my own Will I cannot oblige any other person to abstain from the use of a thing in respect of which he would otherwise be under no obligation; and, accordingly, such an Obligation can only arise from the collective Will of all united in a relation of common possession. Otherwise, I would have to think of a Right in a Thing, as if the *Thing* had an Obligation towards me, and as if the Right as against every Possessor of it had to be derived from this Obligation in the Thing, which is an absurd way of representing the subject.

Further, by the term "Real Right" is meant not only the "Right in a Thing" but also the *constitutive principle* of all the Laws which relate to the real Mine and Thine.—It is, however, evident that a man entirely alone upon the earth could properly neither have nor acquire any external thing as his own; because between him as a Person and all external Things as material objects, there could be no relations of Obligation. There is therefore, literally, no *direct* Right in a Thing, but only that Right is to be properly called "real" which belongs to any one as constituted against a Person, who is in common possession of things with all others in the Civil state of Society.

13. *Every Part of the Soil May be Originally Acquired; and the Principal of the Possibility of such Acquisition is the Original Community of the Soil Generally ...*

All Men are originally and before any juridical act of Will in rightful possession of the Soil; that is, they have a Right to be wherever Nature or Chance has placed them without their will. Possession which is to be distinguished from residential settlement as a voluntary, acquired, and *permanent* possession, becomes *common* possession, on account of the connection with each other of all the places on the surface of the Earth as a globe. For, had the surface of the earth been an infinite plain, men could have been so dispersed upon it that they might not have come into any necessary communion with each other, and a state of social Community would not have been a necessary consequence of their existence upon the Earth.—Now that Possession proper to all men upon the earth which is prior to all their particular juridical acts, constitutes *an original possession in common.* The Conception of such an original, common Possession of things is not derived from experience, nor is it dependent on conditions of time, as is the case with the imaginary and indemonstrable fiction of *a primaeval Community of possession* in actual history. Hence it is a practical conception of Reason, involving in itself the only Principle according to which Men may use the place they happen to occupy on the surface of the Earth, in accordance with Laws of Right.

15. *It is Only Within a Civil Constitution that Anything can be Acquired Peremptorily, Whereas in the State of Nature Acquisition Can Only be Provisory*

... Every one is justified or entitled to exercise that compulsion by which it alone becomes possible to pass out of the state of Nature, and to enter into that state of Civil Society which alone can make all Acquisition peremptory.

It is a question as to how far the right of taking possession of the Soil extends? The answer is, so far as the capability of having it under one's power extends, that is, just as far as he who wills to appropriate it can defend it, as if the Soil were to say, "If you cannot protect me, neither can you command me." In this way the controversy about what constitutes a *free* or *closed* Sea must be decided. Thus, within the range of a cannonshot no one has a right to intrude on the coast of a country that already belongs to a certain State, in order to fish or gather amber on the shore, or such like.— Further, the question is put, "Is Cultivation of the Soil, by building, agriculture, drainage, etc. necessary in order to its Acquisition?" *No.* For, as these processes as forms of specification are only Accidents, they do not constitute objects of immediate possession. . . .

As a further question, it may be asked: Whether, when neither Nature nor Chance, but merely our own Will, brings us into the neighbourhood of a people that gives no promise of a prospect of entering into Civil Union with us, we are to be considered entitled in any case to proceed with force in the intention of founding such a Union, and bringing into a juridical state such men as the savage American Indians, the Hottentots, and the New Hollanders; Or—and the case is not much better—whether we may establish Colonies by deceptive purchase, and so become owners of their soil, and, in general, without regard to their first possession, make use at will of our superiority in relation to them? Further, may it not be held that Nature herself, as abhorring a vacuum, seems to demand such a procedure, and that large regions in other Continents, that are now magnificently peopled, would otherwise have remained unpossessed by civilised inhabitants, and might have for ever remained thus, so that the end of Creation would have so far been frustrated? It is almost unnecessary to answer; for it is easy to see through all this flimsy veil of injustice, which just amounts to the Jesuitism of making a good End justify any Means. This mode of acquiring the Soil is, therefore, to be repudiated. . . .

Property

An external Object, which, in respect of its Substance, can be claimed by some one as his own, is called the PROPERTY of that Person to whom all the Rights in it as a thing belong . . . and which, therefore, he

as the Proprietor can dispose of at will. But from this it follows at once, that such an object can only be a Corporeal Thing towards which there is no direct personal Obligation. Hence a man may be HIS OWN MASTER but not the Proprietor *of himself* so as to be able to dispose of himself at will, to say nothing of the possibility of such a relation to other men; because he is responsible to Humanity in his own person . . . .

SECOND SECTION

Principles of Personal Right

18. Nature and Acquisition of Personal Right

. . . The Acquisition of a Personal Right can never be primary or arbitrary; for such a mode of acquiring it would not be in accordance with the Principle of the harmony of the freedom of my will with the freedom of every other, and it would therefore be wrong. Nor can such a Right be acquired by means of any *unjust* act of another as being itself contrary to Right; for if such a wrong as it implies were perpetrated on me, and I could demand satisfaction from the other, in accordance with Right, yet in such a case I would only be entitled to maintain undiminished what was mine, and not to acquire anything more than what I formerly had. . . .

. . . It is only by positive TRANSFERENCE, or CONVEYANCE, that a Personal Right can be acquired; and this is only possible by means of a common Will, through which objects come into the power of one or other . . . The act of the united Wills of two Persons, by which what belonged to one passes to the other, constitutes CONTRACT.

19. Acquisition by Contract

. . . The two Acts of Promise and Acceptance are not regarded as *following* one another in time, but, in the manner of a *pactum re initum,* as proceeding from a *common* Will, which is expressed by the term "at the same time," or "simultaneous," and the object promised *(promissum)* is represented, under elimination of empirical conditions, as acquired according to the Law of the pure Practical Reason.

That this is the true and only possible Deduction of the idea of Acquisition by Contract, is sufficiently attested by the laborious yet always futile striving of writers on Jurisprudence—such as Moses Mendelssohn in his *Jerusalem*—to adduce a proof of its rational possibility.—The question is put thus: 'Why *ought* I to keep my Promise?' for it is assumed as understood by all that I *ought* to do so. It is, however, absolutely impossible to give any further proof of the Categorical Imperative implied; just as it is impossible for the Geometrician to prove by rational Syllogisms that in order to construct a Triangle, I must take three Lines—so far an Analytical Proposition—of which three Lines any two together must be greater than the third—a Synthetical Proposition, and like the former *a priori*. It is a Postulate of the Pure Reason that we ought to abstract from all the sensible conditions of Space and Time in reference to the conception of Right; and the theory of the possibility of such Abstraction from these conditions without taking away the reality of the Possession, just constitutes the Transcendental Deduction of the Conception of Acquisition by Contract. . . .

THIRD SECTION

Principles of Personal Right that is Real in Kind: . . . The Rights of the Family as a Domestic Society

TITLE FIRST

Conjugal Right (Husband and Wife)

24. *The Natural Basis of Marriage*

The domestic Relations are founded on Marriage, and Marriage is founded upon the natural Reciprocity or intercommunity of the Sexes. This natural union of the sexes proceeds either according to the mere animal Nature or according to Law. The latter is MARRIAGE, which is the Union of two Persons of different sex for life-long reciprocal possession of their sexual faculties.—The End of producing and educating children may be regarded as always the End of Nature in implanting mutual desire and inclination in the sexes; but it is not necessary for the rightfulness of marriage that those who marry should set this before themselves as the End of their Union, otherwise the Marriage would be dissolved of itself when the production of children ceased.

And even assuming that enjoyment in the reciprocal use of the sexual endowments is an end of marriage yet the Contract of Marriage is not on that account a matter of arbitrary will, but is a Contract necessary in its nature by the Law of Humanity. In other words, if a man and a woman have the will to enter on reciprocal enjoyment in accordance with their sexual nature, they *must* necessarily marry each other; and this necessity is in accordance with the juridical Laws of Pure Reason.

25. *The Rational Right of Marriage*

. . . In this relation the human individual makes himself a *"res,"* which is contrary to the Right of Humanity in his own Person. This, however, is only possible under the one condition, that as the one Person is acquired by the other as a *res,* that same Person also equally acquires the other reciprocally, and thus regains and re-establishes the rational Personality . . . The Personal Right thus acquired is at the same time, *real in kind;* and this characteristic of it is established by the fact that if one of the married Persons run away or enter into the possession of another, the other is entitled, at any time, and incontestably, to bring such a one back to the former relation, as if that Person were a Thing.

26. *Monogamy and Equality in Marriage*

For the same reasons, the relation of the Married Persons to each other is a relation of EQUALITY as regards the mutual possession of their Persons, as well as of their

Goods. Consequently Marriage is only truly realized in MONOGAMY: for in the relation of Polygamy the Person who is given away on the one side, gains only a part of the one to whom that Person is given up, and therefore becomes a mere *res* . . . .

. . . The question may be raised as to whether it is not contrary to the Equality of married Persons when the Law says in any way of the Husband in relation to the Wife, 'he shall be thy master,' so that he is represented as the one who commands, and she as the one who obeys. This, however, cannot be regarded as contrary to the natural Equality of a human pair, if such legal Supremacy is based only upon the natural superiority of the faculties of the Husband compared with the Wife, in the effectuation of the common interest of the household; and if the Right to command, is based merely upon this fact. For this Right may thus be deduced from the very duty of Unity and Equality in relation to the *End* involved. . . .

TITLE SECOND

Parental Right (Parent and Child)

28. The Relation of Parent and Child

. . . From the fact of *Procreation* . . . there follows the Duty of preserving and rearing *Children* . . . Accordingly, Children as Persons, have, at the same time, an original congenital Right—distinguished from mere hereditary Right—to be reared by the care of their Parents till they are capable of maintaining themselves; and this provision becomes immediately theirs by Law, without any particular juridical Act being required to determine it.

For what is thus produced is a *Person,* and it is impossible to think of a Being endowed with personal Freedom as produced merely by a physical process. And hence, *in the practical relation,* it is quite a correct and even a necessary Idea to regard the act of generation as a process by which a Person is brought without his consent into the world, and placed in it by the responsible free will of others. This Act, therefore, attaches an obligation to the Parents to make their Children—as far as their power goes—contented with the condition thus acquired. Hence Parents cannot regard their Child as, in a manner, a Thing *of their own making,* for a Being endowed with Freedom cannot be so regarded. Nor, consequently, have they a Right to destroy it as if it were their own property, or even to leave it to chance; because they have brought a Being into the world who becomes in fact a Citizen of the world, and they have placed that Being in a state which they cannot be left to treat with indifference, even according to the natural conceptions of Right. . . .

29. The Rights of the Parent

From the Duty thus indicated, there further necessarily arises the Right of the Parents to THE MANAGEMENT AND TRAINING OF THE CHILD, so long as it is itself incapable of making proper use of its body as an Organism, and of its mind as an Understanding . . . All this training is to be continued till the Child reaches the period of Emancipation . . . The Parents then virtually renounce the parental Right to command, as well as all claim to repayment for their previous care and trouble . . . They can only appeal to the Children by way of any claim, on the ground of the Obligation of Gratitude as a Duty of Virtue.

From the fact of Personality in the Children, it further follows that they can never be regarded as the Property of the Parents. . . .

CHAPTER THIRD

Acquisition Conditioned by the Sentence of a Public Judicatory

36. How and What Acquisition is Subjectively Conditioned by the Principle of a Public Court

NATURAL RIGHT, understood simply as that Right which is not statutory, and which is knowable purely *a priori,* by every man's Reason, will include Distributive Justice as well as Commutative Justice. It is manifest that the latter as constituting the

Justice that is valid between Persons in their reciprocal relations of intercourse with one another, must belong to Natural Right. But this holds also of Distributive Justice, in so far as it can be known *a priori;* and Decisions or Sentences regarding it, must be regulated by the Law of Natural Right.

The Moral Person who presides in the sphere of Justice and administers it, is called the COURT of Justice, and as engaged in the process of official duty, the Judicatory; the Sentence delivered in a case, is the Judgment. All this is to be here viewed *a priori,* according to the rational Conditions of Right, without taking into consideration how such a Constitution is to be actually established or organized, for which particular Statutes, and consequently empirical Principles, are requisite.

The question, then, in this connection, is not merely "What is *right in itself?*" in the sense in which every man must determine it by the Judgment of Reason; but "What is Right as applied to this case?" that is, what is right and just as viewed by a Court? The rational and the judicial points of view, are therefore to be distinguished. . . .

Transition: From the Mine and Thine in the State of Nature to the Mine and Thine in the Juridical State Generally

41. Public Justice as Related to the Natural and the Civil State

The Juridical state is that relation of men to one another which contains the conditions, under which it is alone possible for every one to obtain the Right that is his due. The formal Principle of the possibility of actually *participating* in such Right, viewed in accordance with the idea of a universally legislative Will, is PUBLIC JUSTICE. Public Justice may be considered in relation either to the Possibility, or Actuality, or Necessity of the Possession of objects—regarded as the matter of the activity of the Will—according to laws. It may thus be divided into *Protective Justice, Commutative Justice,* and *Distributive Justice.* In the *first* mode of Justice, the Law declares merely what Relation is internally *right* in respect of Form; in the *second,* it declares what is likewise externally in accord with a Law in respect of the Object, and what Possession is rightful; and in the *third,* it declares what is right, and what is *just,* and to what extent, by the Judgment of a Court in any particular case coming under the given Law. In this latter relation, the Public Court is called the *Justice* of the Country; and the question whether there actually is or is not such an administration of Public Justice, may be regarded as the most important of all juridical interests.

The non-juridical state is that condition of Society in which there is no Distributive Justice. It is commonly called the *Natural* state, or the state of Nature. It is not the *"Social State,"* as Achenwall puts it, for this may be in itself an *artificial* state, that is to be contradistinguished from the "Natural" state. The opposite of the state of Nature is the *Civil* state as the condition of a Society standing under a Distributive Justice . . . .

The Natural or non-juridical Social state may be viewed as the sphere of PRIVATE RIGHT, and the Civil state may be specially regarded as the sphere of PUBLIC RIGHT. The latter state contains no more and no other Duties of men towards each other than what may be conceived in connection with the former state; the Matter of Private Right is, in short, the very same in both. The Laws of the Civil state, therefore, only turn upon the juridical Form of the co-existence of men under a common Constitution; and in this respect these Laws must necessarily be regarded and conceived as Public Laws.

The Civil Union cannot, in the strict sense, be properly called a *Society;* for there is no sociality in common between the Ruler and the Subject under a Civil Constitution. They are not co-ordinated as Associates in a Society with each other, but the one is *subordinated* to the other. Those who may be co-ordinated with one another must consider themselves as mutually equal, in so far as they stand under common Laws. The

Civil Union may therefore be regarded not so much as *being,* but rather as *making* a Society.

42. The Postulate of Public Right

From the conditions of Private Right in the Natural state, there arises, the Postulate of Public Right. It may be thus expressed: "In the relation of unavoidable co-existence with others, thou shalt pass from the state of Nature into a juridical Union constituted under the condition of a Distributive Justice." . . .

No one is under obligation to abstain from interfering with the Possession of others, unless they give him a reciprocal guarantee for the observance of a similar abstention from interference with his Possession. Nor does he require to wait for proof by experience of the need of this guarantee, in view of the antagonistic disposition of others. He is therefore under no obligation to wait till he acquires practical prudence at his own cost; for he can perceive in himself evidence of the natural Inclination of men to play the master over others, and to disregard the claims of the Right of others, when they feel themselves their superiors by Might or Fraud. . . .

So long as the intention to live and continue in this state of externally lawless Freedom prevails, men may be said to do no wrong or injustice at all *to one another,* even when they wage war against each other. . . .

Part Second

PUBLIC RIGHT: THE SYSTEM OF THOSE
LAWS WHICH REQUIRE PUBLIC
PROMULGATION

I

Right of the State and Constitutional Law

44. Origin of the Civil Union and Public Right

It is not from any Experience prior to the appearance of an external authoritative Legislation, that we learn of the maxim of natural violence among men, and their evil tendency to engage in war with each other. Nor is it assumed here that it is merely some particular historical condition or fact, that makes public legislative constraint necessary; for however well-disposed or favourable to Right men may be considered to be of themselves, the rational Idea of a state of Society not yet regulated by Right, must be taken as our starting-point. This Idea implies that before a legal state of Society can be publicly established, individual Men, Nations and States can never be safe against violence from each other; and this is evident from the consideration that every one of his own Will naturally does *what seems good and right in his own eyes,* entirely independent of the opinion of others. Hence . . . the first thing incumbent on men is to accept the Principle that it is necessary to leave the state of Nature . . . and to form a union of all those who cannot avoid coming into reciprocal communication, and thus subject themselves in common to the external restraint of public compulsory Laws. Men thus enter into a Civil Union, in which every one has it determined by Law what shall be recognised as his; and this is secured to him by a competent external Power distinct from his own individuality. Such is the primary Obligation, on the part of all men, to enter into the relations of a Civil State of Society.

The natural condition of mankind need not, on this ground, be represented as a state of absolute *Injustice,* as if there could have been no other relation originally among men but what was merely determined by force. . . .

If men were not disposed to recognise any Acquisition at all as rightful—even in a provisional way—prior to entering into the Civil state, this state of Society would itself be impossible. For the Laws regarding the Mine and Thine in the state of Nature, contain formally the very same thing as they prescribe in the Civil state, when it is viewed merely according to rational conceptions: only that in the forms of the Civil state the conditions are laid down under which the formal prescriptions of the state of Nature attain realization conformable to Distributive Justice.—Were there, then, not even *provisionally,* an external Meum and Tuum in the state of Nature, neither would there be any juridical Duties in relation to them; and, consequently, there would be no obligation to pass out of that state into another.

45. The Form of the State and its Three Powers

Every State contains in itself THREE POWERS, the universal united Will of the People being thus personified in a political triad. These are *the Legislative Power, the Executive Power,* and *the Judiciary Power* . . .

46. The Legislative Power and the Members of the State

The Legislative Power, viewed in its rational Principle, can only belong to the united Will of the People. For, as all Right ought to proceed from this Power, it is necessary that its Laws should be unable to do wrong to any one whatever. Now, if any *one* individual determines anything in the State in contradistinction to *another,* it is always possible that he may perpetrate a wrong on that other; but this is never possible when *all* determine and decree what is to be Law to themselves. *"Volenti non fit injuria."* Hence it is only the united and consenting Will of all the People—in so far as Each of them determines the same thing about all, and All determine the same thing about each—that ought to have the power of enacting Law in the State.

The Members of a Civil Society thus united . . . are called its CITIZENS: and there are three juridical attributes that inseparably belong to them by Right. These are—1. Constitutional FREEDOM, as the Right of every Citizen to have to obey no other Law than that to which he has given his consent or approval; 2. Civil EQALITY, as the Right of the Citizen to recognise no

one as a Superior among the people in relation to himself, except in so far as such a one is as subject to *his* moral power to impose obligations, as that other has power to impose obligations upon him; and 3. Political INDEPENDENCE, as The Right to owe his existence and continuance in Society not to the arbitrary Will of another, but to his own Rights and Powers as a Member of the Commonwealth; and, consequently, the possession of a Civil Personality, which cannot be represented by any other than himself. . . .

. . . The last of the three qualities involved necessarily constitutes the distinction between *active* and *passive* Citizenship; although the latter conception appears to stand in contradiction to the definition of a Citizen as such . . . The resident Tutor as distinguished from the Schoolmaster; the Ploughman as distinguished from the Farmer and such like, illustrate the distinction in question. In all these cases, the former members of the contrast are distinguished from the latter by being mere subsidiaries of the Commonwealth and not active independent Members of it, because they are of necessity commanded and protected by others, and consequently possess no political Self-sufficiency in themselves. Such Dependence on the Will of others and the consequent Inequality are, however, not inconsistent with the Freedom and Equality of the individuals *as Men* helping to constitute the people. Much rather is it the case that it is only under such conditions, that a People can become a State and enter into a Civil Constitution. But all are not equally qualified to exercise the Right of the Suffrage under the Constitution, and to be full Citizens of the State, and not mere passive Subjects under its protection. For, although they are entitled to demand to be treated by all the other Citizens according to laws of natural Freedom and Equality, as *passive* parts of the State, it does not follow that they ought themselves to have the Right to deal with the State as active Members of it, to reorganize it, or to take action by way of introducing certain laws. All they have a right in their circumstances to claim, may be no more than that whatever be the mode in which the positive laws are enacted, these laws must not be contrary to the natural Laws that demand the Freedom of all the people and the Equality that is conformable thereto; and it must therefore be made possible for them to raise themselves from this passive condition in the State, to the condition of active Citizenship.

47. Dignities in the State and the Original Contract

All these three Powers in the State are DIGNITIES. . . . They imply the relation between a universal SOVEREIGN as Head of the State—which according to the laws of freedom can be none other than the People itself united into a Nation—and the mass of the individuals of the Nation as SUBJECTS. . . .

The act by which a People is represented as constituting itself into a State, is termed THE ORIGINAL CONTRACT. This is properly only an outward mode of representing the idea by which the rightfulness of the process of organizing the Constitution, may be made conceivable. According to this representation, all and each of the people give up their external Freedom in order to receive it immediately again as Members of a Commonwealth. The Commonwealth is the people viewed as united altogether into a State. And thus it is not to be said that the individual in the State has sacrificed *a part* of his inborn external Freedom for a particular purpose; but he has abandoned his wild lawless Freedom wholly, in order to find all his proper Freedom again entire and undiminished, but in the form of a regulated order of dependence, that is, in a Civil state regulated by laws of Right. This relation of Dependence thus arises out of his own regulative law-giving Will. . . .

49. Distinct Functions of the Three Powers. Autonomy of the State

. . . Regarded as a Moral Person, this Executive Authority constitutes the Government. The Orders issued by the Government to the People and the Magistrates as well as to the higher Ministerial *Administrators* of the State are Rescripts or *Decrees,* and not Laws; for they terminate in the decision of particular cases, and are given forth as unchangeable. . . .

The Legislative Authority ought not at the same time to be the Executive or Governor; for the Governor, as Administrator, should stand under the authority of the Law, and is bound by it under the supreme control of the Legislator. . . .

. . . Neither the Legislative Power nor the Executive Power ought to exercise the *judicial* Function, but only appoint Judges as Magistrates. It is the People who ought to judge themselves, through those of the Citizens who are elected by free Choice as their Representatives for this purpose, and even specially for every process or cause. For the judicial Sentence is a special act of public Distributive Justice performed by a Judge or Court as a constitutional Administrator of the Law, to a Subject as one of the People. Such an act is not invested inherently with the power to determine and assign to any one what is his. Every individual among the people being merely passive in this relation to the Supreme Power, either the Executive or the Legislative Authority might do him wrong in their determinations in cases of dispute regarding the property of individuals. It would not be the people themselves who thus determined, or who pronounced the judgments of "guilty" or "not guilty" regarding their fellow-citizens. For it is to the determination of this issue in a cause, that the Court has to apply the Law; and it is by means of the Executive Authority, that the Judge holds power to assign to every one his own. Hence it is only the *People* that properly can judge in a cause—although indirectly—by Representatives elected and deputed by themselves, as in a Jury.—It would even be beneath the dignity of the sovereign Head of the State to play the Judge; for this would be to put himself into a position in which it would be possible to do Wrong, and thus to subject himself to the demand for an appeal to a still higher Power. . . .

It is by the co-operation of these three Powers—the Legislative, the Executive, and the Judicial—that the State realizes its *Autonomy*. This Autonomy consists in its organizing, forming, and maintaining itself in accordance with the Laws of Freedom. In their union the *Welfare* of the State is realized. . . . By this is not to be understood merely the individual *well-being* and *happiness* of the Citizens of the State; for—as Rousseau asserts—this End may perhaps be more agreeably and more desirably attained in the state of Nature, or even under a despotic Government. But the Welfare of the State as its own Highest Good, signifies that condition in which the greatest harmony is attained between its Constitution and the Principles of Right,—a condition of the State which Reason by a Categorical Imperative makes it obligatory upon us to strive after. . . .

Constitutional and Juridical Consequences Arising from the Nature of the Civil Union

A. Right of the Supreme Power . . .

The Origin of the Supreme Power is *practically inscrutable* by the People who are placed under its authority. In other words, the Subject need not *reason too curiously* in regard to its origin in the practical relation, as if the Right of the obedience due to it were to be doubted. . . . The question has been raised as to whether an actual Contract of Subjection originally preceded the Civil Government as a fact; or whether the Power arose first, and the Law only followed afterwards, or may have followed in this order. But such questions, as regards the People already actually living under the Civil Law, are either entirely aimless, or even fraught with subtle danger to the State. For, should the Subject, after having dug down to the ultimate origin of the State, rise in opposition to the present ruling Authority, he would expose himself as a Citizen, according

to the Law and with full Right, to be punished, destroyed, or outlawed. A Law which is so holy and inviolable that it is *practically* a crime even to cast doubt upon it, or to suspend its operation for a moment, is represented of itself as necessarily derived from some Supreme, unblameable Lawgiver. And this is the meaning of the maxim, "All Authority is from God"; which proposition does not express the *historical foundation* of the Civil Constitution, but an ideal Principle of the Practical Reason. It may be otherwise rendered thus, "It is a Duty to obey the Law of the existing Legislative Power, be its origin what it may."

. . . If the Ruler or Regent, as the organ of the Supreme Power, proceeds in violation of the Laws, as in imposing taxes, recruiting soldiers, and so on, contrary to the Law of Equality in the distribution of the political burdens, the Subject may oppose *complaints* and *objections* to this injustice, but not active resistance.

There cannot even be an Article contained in the political Constitution that would make it possible for a Power in the State, in case of the transgression of the Constitutional Laws by the Supreme Authority, to resist or even to restrict it in so doing. For, whoever would restrict the Supreme Power of the State must have more, or at least equal power as compared with the Power that is so restricted . . . Such a one, and not the actual Authority, would then be the Supreme Power; which is contradictory . . . The so-called limited political Constitution, as a Constitution of the internal Rights of the State, is an unreality; and instead of being consistent with Right, it is only a Principle of Expediency. And its aim is not so much to throw all possible obstacles in the way of a powerful violator of popular Rights by his arbitrary influence upon the Government, as rather to cloak it over under the illusion of a Right of opposition conceded to the People.

. . . It is only by submission to the universal Legislative Will, that a condition of law and order is possible. Hence there is no Right of Sedition, and still less of Rebellion, belonging to the People. . . . It is the duty of the People to bear any abuse of the Supreme Power, even then though it should be considered to be unbearable. . . .

C. Relief of the Poor. Foundling Hospitals. The Church

. . . The People have in fact united themselves by their common Will into a Society, which has to be perpetually maintained; and for this purpose they have subjected themselves to the internal Power of the State, in order to preserve the members of this Society even when they are not able to support themselves. By the fundamental principle of the State, the Government is justified and entitled to compel those who are able, to furnish the means necessary to preserve those who are not themselves capable of providing for the most necessary wants of Nature. For the existence of persons with property in the State, implies their submission under it for protection and the provision by the State of what is necessary for their existence; and accordingly the State founds a Right upon an obligation on their part to contribute of their means for the preservation of their fellow-citizens. . . .

The State has also a Right to impose upon the People the duty of preserving Children exposed from want or shame, and who would otherwise perish; for it cannot knowingly allow this increase of its power to be destroyed, however unwelcome in some respects it may be. . . .

The *Church* is here regarded as an Ecclesiastical Establishment merely, and as such it must be carefully distinguished from Religion, which as an internal mode of feeling lies wholly beyond the sphere of the action of the Civil Power. Viewed as an Institution for public *Worship* founded for the people,— to whose opinion or conviction it owes its origin,—the Church Establishment responds to a real want in the State. This is the need felt by the people to regard themselves as also Subjects of a Supreme *Invisible* Power to which they must pay homage, and which may often be brought into a very undesir-

able collision with the Civil Power. The State has therefore a Right in this relation; but it is not to be regarded as the Right of Constitutional Legislation in the Church, so as to organize it as may seem most advantageous for itself, or to prescribe and command its faith and ritual forms of worship; for all this must be left entirely to the teachers and rulers which the Church has chosen for itself. The function of the State in this connection, only includes the *negative* Right of regulating the influence of these public teachers upon the *visible* political Commonwealth, that it may not be prejudicial to the public peace and tranquillity. Consequently the State has to take measures, on occasion of any internal conflict in the Church, or on occasion of any collision of the several Churches with each other, that Civil-concord is not endangered; and this Right falls within the province of the Police. It is *beneath the dignity* of the Supreme Power to interpose in determining what particular faith the Church shall profess. . . . For in doing so, the Supreme Power would be mixing itself up in a scholastic wrangle, on a footing of equality with its subjects. . . .

E. The Right of Punishing

. . . Juridical Punishment can never be administered merely as a means for promoting another Good either with regard to the Criminal himself or to Civil Society, but must in all cases be imposed only because the individual on whom it is inflicted *has committed a Crime.* For one man ought never to be dealt with merely as a means subservient to the purpose of another, nor be mixed up with the subjects of Real Right. Against such treatment his Inborn Personality has a Right to protect him, even although he may be condemned to lose his Civil Personality. . . . The Penal Law is a Categorical Imperative; and woe to him who creeps through the serpent-windings of Utilitarianism to discover some advantage that may discharge him from the Justice of Punishment, or even from the due measure of it, according to the Pharisaic maxim: "It is better that *one* man should die than that the whole people should perish." For if Justice and Righteousness perish, human life would no longer have any value in the world.—What, then, is to be said of such a proposal as to keep a Criminal alive who has been condemned to death, on his being given to understand that if he agreed to certain dangerous experiments being performed upon him, he would be allowed to survive if he came happily through them? It is argued that Physicians might thus obtain new information that would be of value to the Commonweal. But a Court of Justice would repudiate with scorn any proposal of this kind if made to it by the Medical Faculty; for Justice would cease to be Justice, if it were bartered away for any consideration whatever.

But what is the mode and measure of Punishment which Public Justice takes as its Principle and Standard? It is just the Principle of Equality, by which the pointer of the Scale of Justice is made to incline no more to the one side than the other. It may be rendered by saying that the undeserved evil which any one commits on another, is to be regarded as perpetrated on himself. Hence it may be said: 'If you slander another, you slander yourself; if you steal from another, you steal from yourself; if you strike another, you strike yourself; if you kill another, you kill yourself.' This is the Right of RETALIATION: and properly understood, it is the only Principle which in regulating a Public Court, as distinguished from mere private judgment, can definitely assign both the quality and the quantity of a just penalty. All other standards are wavering and uncertain; and on account of other considerations involved in them, they contain no principle conformable to the sentence of pure and strict Justice ... Whoever has committed Murder, must *die*. There is, in this case, no juridical substitute or surrogate, that can be given or taken for the satisfaction of Justice. There is no *Likeness* or proportion between Life, however painful, and Death; and therefore there is no Equality between the crime of Murder and the retalia-

tion of it but what is judicially accomplished by the execution of the Criminal. His death, however, must be kept free from all maltreatment that would make the humanity suffering in his Person loathsome or abominable. Even if a Civil Society resolved to dissolve itself with the consent of all its members—as might be supposed in the case of a People inhabiting an island resolving to separate and scatter themselves throughout the whole world—the last Murderer lying in the prison ought to be executed before the resolution was carried out. This ought to be done in order that every one may realize the desert of his deeds, and that bloodguiltiness may not remain upon the people; for otherwise they might all be regarded as participators in the murder as a public violation of Justice. . . .

However many they may be who have committed a murder, or have even commanded it, or acted as art and part in it, they ought all to suffer death; for so Justice wills it, in accordance with the Idea of the juridical Power as founded on the universal Laws of Reason. But the number of the Accomplices in such a deed might happen to be so great that the State, in resolving to be without such criminals, would be in danger of soon also being deprived of subjects. But it will not thus dissolve itself, neither must it return to tɦ⁣e much worse condition of Nature, in which there would be no external Justice. Nor, above all, should it deaden the sensibilities of the People by the spectacle of Justice being exhibited in the mere carnage of a slaughtering bench. In such circumstances the Sovereign must always be allowed to have it in his power to take the part of the Judge upon himself as a case of Necessity,—and to deliver a Judgment which, instead of the penalty of death, shall assign some other punishment to the Criminals, and thereby preserve a multitude of the People. . . .

Against these doctrines, the Marquis BECCARIA has given forth a different view. Moved by the compassionate sentimentality of a humane feeling, he has asserted that all Capital Punishment is wrong in itself and unjust. He has put forward this view on the ground that the penalty of death could not be contained in the original Civil Contract; for, in that case, every one of the People would have had to consent to lose his life if he murdered any of his fellow-citizens. But, it is argued, such a consent is impossible, because no one can thus dispose of his own life.—All this is mere sophistry and perversion of Right. No one undergoes Punishment because he has willed to be punished, but because he has willed *a punishable Action*. . . . If any one, then, enact a Penal Law against himself as a Criminal, it must be the pure juridically law-giving Reason which subjects him as one capable of crime, and consequently as another Person along with all the others in the Civil Union, to this Penal Law. In other words, it is not the People taken distributively, but the Tribunal of public Justice, as distinct from the Criminal, that prescribes Capital Punishment; and it is not to be viewed as if the Social Contract contained the Promise of all the individuals to allow themselves to be punished, thus disposing of themselves and their lives. . . .

II

The Right of Nations and International Law (Jus Gentium)

* * *

54. Elements of the Right of Nations

The elements of the Right of Nations are as follow:

1. STATES, viewed as NATIONS, in their external relations to one another—like lawless savages—are naturally in a non-juridical condition;

2. This natural condition is a STATE OF WAR in which the Right of the stronger prevails; and although it may not in fact be always found as a state of actual war and incessant hostility, and although no real wrong is done to any one therein, yet the condition is wrong in itself in the highest degree, and the Nations which form States contiguous to each other are bound mutually to pass out of it;

3. An ALLIANCE OF NATIONS, in accordance with the idea of an original Social Contract, is necessary to protect each other against external aggression and attack, but not involving interference with their several internal difficulties and disputes;

4. This mutual connection by Alliance must dispense with a distinct Sovereign Power, such as is set up in the Civil Constitution; it can only take the form of a FEDERATION, which as such may be revoked on any occasion, and must consequently be renewed from time to time. . . .

55. Right of Going to War as Related to the Subjects of the State

. . . The question arises as to what Right the State has in *relation to its own Subjects,* to use them in order to make war against other States. . . .

. . . The following, then, is such a deduction as a mere Jurist would put forward.

. . . The inhabitants of any country would be but sparsely sown here and there were it not for the protection of Government; because without it they could not spread themselves with their households upon a territory which was always in danger of being devastated by enemies or by wild beasts of prey; and further, so great a multitude of men as now live in any one country could not otherwise obtain sufficient means of support. Hence, as it can be said of vegetable growths, such as potatoes, as well as of domesticated animals, that because the abundance in which they are found is a *product* of human labour, they may be used, destroyed, and consumed by man; so it seems that it may be said of the Sovereign as the Supreme Power in the State, that he has the Right to lead his Subjects, as being for the most part productions of his own to war, as if it were to the chase, and even to march them to the field of battle, as if it were on a pleasure excursion.

. . . But such a principle will not at all apply to men, especially when viewed as citizens who must be regarded as members of the State, with a share in the legislation, and not merely as means for others but as Ends in themselves. As such they must give their free consent, through their representatives, not only to the carrying on of war generally, but to every separate declaration of war; and it is only under this limiting condition that the State has a Right to demand their services in undertakings so full of danger. . . .

60. Right as Against an Unjust Enemy

. . . But what then is an *unjust* enemy according to the conceptions of the Right of Nations, when, as holds generally of the state of Nature, every State is judge in its own cause? It is one whose publicly expressed Will, whether in word or deed, betrays a maxim which, if it were taken as a universal rule, would make a state of Peace among the nations impossible, and would necessarily perpetuate the state of Nature. Such is the violation of public Treaties, with regard to which it may be assumed that any such violation concerns all nations by threatening their freedom, and that they are thus summoned to unite against such a wrong, and to take away the power of committing it. . . .

61. Perpetual Peace and a Permanent Congress of Nations

The natural state of Nations as well as of individual men is a state which it is a duty to pass out of, in order to enter into a legal state. Hence, before this transition occurs, all the Right of Nations and all the external property of States acquirable or maintainable by war, are merely *provisory;* and they can only become *peremptory* in a universal Union of States analogous to that by which a Nation becomes a State. It is thus only that a real *state of Peace* could be established. But with the too great extension of such a Union of States over vast regions any government of it, and consequently the protection of its individual members, must at last become impossible; and thus a multitude of such corporations would again bring round a state of war. Hence the *Perpetual Peace,* which is the ultimate end of all the Right of Nations, becomes in fact an impracticable idea. The political principles, however, which aim at such an end, and which enjoin the formation of such unions among the States as may promote a continuous *approximation* to a Perpetual Peace, are not impracticable. . . .

CONCLUSION

. . . The state of Peace is the only condition of the Mine and Thine that is secured and guaranteed by *Laws* in the relationship of men living in numbers contiguous to each other, and who are thus combined in a Constitution whose rule is derived not from the mere experience of those who have found it the best as a normal guide for others, but which must be taken by the Reason *a priori* from the ideal of a juridical Union of men under public laws generally. For all particular examples or instances, being able only to furnish illustration but not proof, are deceptive, and at all events require a Metaphysic to establish them by its necessary principles. And this is conceded indirectly even by those who turn Metaphysics into ridicule, when they say, as they often do, "The best Constitution is that in which not Men but Laws exercise the power." For what can be more metaphysically sublime in its own way than this very Idea of theirs, which according to their own assertion has, notwithstanding, the most objective reality? . . . If the idea is carried forward by gradual Reform, and in accordance with fixed Principles, it may lead by a continuous approximation to the highest political Good, and to Perpetual Peace.

11

Jeremy Bentham

1748–1832

The small-boned skeleton of Jeremy Bentham is kept in University College's London anatomical museum—The Great Ultilitarian, true to his philosophy, willed his corpse to the college for dissection for advancement of science.

He was a son of an ambitious scrivener, grandson of a dignified lawyer, and great-grandson of a prosperous pawnbroker. He was raised in an intellectual hot-house, where (it is said) he read and enjoyed adult history books before he was four. Among his father's papers were Latin lines certified by the father to have been written by Jeremy at five. At seven he had a French tutor who made him study hard and kept him away from fiction. He liked music and played both harpsichord and violin well.

He was sent to Oxford before he was thirteen and was given little money. He was small for his age, lonely and unhappy. He worked hard and took his degree at fifteen.

Next Bentham turned to law study at Lincoln's Inn. He visited courts and reported being delighted by Mansfield's opinions delivered from Queen's Bench. (Later he was to rail at Mansfield for judicial legislation). He attended Blackstone's lectures reluctantly and disdainfully. He dawdled at fitting himself for law practice; instead of memorizing Coke on Littleton he experimented with chemicals and speculated on law reform. When he was called to the bar he could not warm to advocacy. He decided to live economically on a small legacy left by his mother and dedicate himself to improving law.

His first book, *A Fragment on Govern-ment,* was cavalierly critical of Blackstone's smug belief that the common law was the embodiment of reason and had flowered to perfection. He published anonymously and the book had great vogue; its authorship was attributed to several tall political personages. When its obscure writer was identified the book's popularity plummeted. The *Fragment* did attract prominent Lord Shelburne to Bentham. Shelburne hated Blackstone's work and sought out Bentham. Often in the next decade was Bentham to visit Bowood, Shelburne's country estate. These country days were happy ones. Women of the household liked his company and enjoyed his music; he played chess and billiards with the men. His scrivener father basked in his son's acceptance and almost forgave Jeremy's reluctance to push himself forward.

At Bowood Bentham tried out ideas on law reform with men of political force. He was writing what later became his *Introduction to the Principles of Morals and Legislation.* Shelburne was rhapsodic about this analytical work, and insisted that it be read aloud to the ladies. Qualified critics, however, thought it too abstruse and dry, which discouraged Bentham from publishing the work. He eventually did publish part of it in 1789, but not until 1945 was the last half published under the title, *The Limits of Jurisprudence Defined.* Excerpts that follow this biographical note are from these two books.

Bentham's brother, Samuel, an engineer, worked for Russian Prince Potemkin who was trying to introduce civilization into a barbarous region. Jeremy, in his late thirties, set out to visit Samuel in Russia, hoping he could further law reform there more effectively than he had in England. The trip was hard; it took three months via Italy and Istanbul. Bentham's dream of reforming Russian law under Catherine the Great proved empty. During his stay in Russia he got interested in economics. He adopted Adam Smith's newly stated *laissez faire* theory—which he carried further than Smith himself in a *Defense of Usury* which he sent back to England for publication.

The visit to Russia lasted three years. Soon after Bentham came home, the first edition of his *Introduction to the Principles of Morals and Legislation* was brought out. His reputation as "The Great Utilitarian" stems from this work; its publication brought him fame which built up gradually over the years; France gave him honorary citizenship in 1792; English kudos came his way; statesmen from the world over sought his opinions.

In his early forties Bentham made a protracted and disappointing try at practical reform by espousing a "Panopticon"—a prison in which convicts were always under surveillance without their knowledge. He spent much of his own money in building and housing a complicated series of mirrors to demonstrate the structure. Bentham thought that parliamentary support for this scheme was killed by George III, who looked askance at Bentham's political views. Years later Parliament appropriated money to reimburse Bentham for his "Panopticon" expense. Other of Bentham's proposals fared better: his poor-law reform proposals were adopted near the time of his death; he advocated digging canals at Suez and Panama —for which he was called an impractical visionary.

When he was forty-four he inherited from his father a home and money enough for a comfortable living. He called his house the Hermitage—a charming hideaway in a London blind alley that widened into a gardened courtyard. As an amiable bachelor, he was the center of a group of congenial friends and important disciples—including John Stuart Mill, John Austin, and a host of other intellectuals. Company was unwelcome, however, before nightfall—his days were spent in a regimen of prodigious writing. As he grew older he got crotchety. Routine could not be interrupted; he refused to receive important personages and sometimes would not see old friends. But his mind remained vigorous and words flowed from his pen until his last illness.

Young Bentham's interest in reform was legal and not political. Only as he grew older did he come to admire democracy. In 1822 (Bentham was seventy-four) he wrote that the English government was least bad of all bad governments, and that the United States was the first of all governments which could properly be called good.

AN INTRODUCTION TO THE PRINCIPLES OF MORALS AND LEGISLATION *

CHAPTER I

Of the Principle of Utility

1. NATURE has placed mankind under the governance of two sovereign masters, *pain* and *pleasure*. It is for them alone to point out what we ought to do, as well as to determine what we shall do. On the one hand the standard of right and wrong, on the other the chain of causes and effects, are fastened to their throne. They govern us in all we do, in all we say, in all we think: every effort we can make to throw off our subjection, will serve but to demonstrate and confirm it. In words a man may pretend to abjure their empire: but in reality he will remain subject to it all the while. The *principle of utility* recognizes this subjection, and assumes it for the foundation of that system, the object of which is to rear the fabric of felicity by the hands of reason and of law. Systems which attempt to question it, deal in sounds instead of senses, in caprice instead of reason, in darkness instead of light. . . .

* Reprinted by permission of Basil Blackwell, Oxford.

2. . . . By the principle of utility is meant that principle which approves or disapproves of every action whatsoever, according to the tendency which it appears to have to augment or diminish the happiness of the party whose interest is in question: or, what is the same thing in other words, to promote or to oppose that happiness. I say of every action whatsoever; and therefore not only of every action of a private individual, but of every measure of government.

3. By utility is meant that property in any object, whereby it tends to produce benefit, advantage, pleasure, good, or happiness, (all this in the present case comes to the same thing) or (what comes again to the same thing) to prevent the happening of mischief, pain, evil, or unhappiness to the party whose interest is considered: if that party be the community in general, then the happiness of the community: if a particular individual, then the happiness of that individual.

4. The interest of the community is one of the most general expressions that can occur in the phraseology of morals: no wonder that the meaning of it is often lost. When it has a meaning, it is this. The community is a fictitious *body*, composed of the individual persons who are considered as constituting as it were its *members*. The interest of the community then is, what?—the sum of the interests of the several members who compose it. . . .

10. Of an action that is conformable to the principle of utility one may always say either that it is one that ought to be done, or at least that it is not one that ought not to be done. One may say also, that it is right it should be done; at least that it is not wrong it should be done: that it is a right action; at least that it is not a wrong action. When thus interpreted, the words *ought*, and *right* and *wrong*, and others of that stamp, have a meaning: when otherwise, they have none.

11. Has the rectitude of this principle been ever formally contested? It should seem that it had, by those who have not known what they have been meaning. Is it susceptible of any direct proof? it should seem not:

for that which is used to prove every thing else, cannot itself be proved: a chain of proofs must have their commencement somewhere. To give such proof is as impossible as it is needless. . . .

CHAPTER II

Of Principles Adverse to that of Utility

1. If the principle of utility be a right principle to be governed by, and that in all cases, it follows . . . that whatever principle differs from it in any case must necessarily be a wrong one. To prove any other principle, therefore, to be a wrong one, there needs no more than just to show it to be what it is, a principle of which the dictates are in some point or other different from those of the principle of utility: to state it is to confute it.

2. A principle may be different from that of utility in two ways: 1. By being constantly opposed to it: this is the case with a principle which may be termed the principle of *asceticism*. 2. By being sometimes opposed to it, and sometimes not, as it may happen: this is the case with another, which may be termed the principle of *sympathy* and *antipathy*.

3. By the principle of asceticism I mean that principle, which . . . approves or disapproves of any action, according to the tendency which it appears to have to augment or diminish the happiness of the party whose interest is in question; but in an inverse manner: approving of actions in as far as they tend to diminish his happiness; disapproving of them in as far as they tend to augment it.

4. It is evident that any one who reprobates any the least particle of pleasure, as such, from whatever source derived, is *pro tanto* a partizan of the principle of asceticism. It is only upon that principle, and not from the principle of utility, that the most abominable pleasure which the vilest of malefactors ever reaped from his crime would be reprobated, if it stood alone. The case is, that it never does stand alone; but is

necessarily followed by such a quantity of pain (or, what comes to the same thing, such a chance for a certain quantity of pain) that the pleasure in comparison of it, is as nothing: and this is the true and sole, but perfectly sufficient, reason for making it a ground for punishment.

5. There are two classes of men of very different complexions, by whom the principle of asceticism appears to have been embraced; the one a set of moralists, the other a set of religionists. Different accordingly have been the motives which appear to have recommended it to the notice of these different parties. Hope, that is the prospect of pleasure, seems to have animated the former: hope, the aliment of philosophic pride: the hope of honour and reputation at the hands of men. Fear, that is the prospect of pain, the latter: fear the offspring of superstitious fancy: the fear of future punishment at the hands of a splenetic and revengeful Deity. . . .

6. The religious party, however, appear to have carried it farther than the philosophical: they have acted more consistently and less wisely. The philosophical party have scarcely gone farther than to reprobate pleasure: the religious party have frequently gone so far as to make it a matter of merit and of duty to court pain. The philosophical party have hardly gone farther than the making pain a matter of indifference. It is no evil, they have said: they have not said, it is a good. They have not so much as reprobated all pleasure in the lump. They have discarded only what they have called the gross; . . . they have even cherished and magnified the refined. Yet this, however, not under the name of pleasure: to cleanse itself from the sordes of its impure original, it was necessary it should change its name: the honourable, the glorious, the reputable, the becoming, the *honestum,* the *decorum,* it was to be called: in short, any thing but pleasure. . . .

8. The principle of asceticism, however, with whatever warmth it may have been embraced by its partizans as a rule of private conduct, seems not to have been carried to any considerable length, when applied to the business of government. In a few instances it has been carried a little way by the philosophical party: witness the Spartan regimen. Though then, perhaps, it may be considered as having been a measure of security: and an application, though a precipitate and perverse application, of the principle of utility. Scarcely in any instances, to any considerable length, by the religious. . . . We read of saints, who for the good of their souls, and the mortification of their bodies, have voluntarily yielded themselves a prey to vermin: but though many persons of this class have wielded the reins of empire, we read of none who have set themselves to work, and made laws on purpose, with a view of stocking the body politic with the breed of highwaymen, housebreakers, or incendiaries. If at any time they have suffered the nation to be preyed upon by swarms of idle pensioners, or useless placemen, it has rather been from negligence and imbecility, than from any settled plan for oppressing and plundering of the people. . . .

9. The principle of asceticism seems originally to have been the reverie of certain hasty speculators, who having perceived, or fancied, that certain pleasures, when reaped in certain circumstances, have, at the long run, been attended with pains more than equivalent to them, took occasion to quarrel with every thing that offered itself under the name of pleasure. Having then got thus far, and having forgot the point which they set out from, they pushed on, and went so much further as to think it meritorious to fall in love with pain. Even this, we see, is at bottom but the principle of utility misapplied.

10. The principle of utility is capable of being consistently pursued; and it is but tautology to say, that the more consistently it is pursued, the better it must ever be for humankind. The principle of asceticism never was, nor ever can be, consistently pursued by any living creature. . . .

11. Among principles adverse to that of utility, that which at this day seems to have most influence in matters of government, is what may be called the principle of sym-

pathy and antipathy. By the principle of sympathy and antipathy, I mean that principle which approves or disapproves of certain actions, not on account of their tending to augment the happiness, nor yet on account of their tending to diminish the happiness of the party whose interest is in question, but merely because a man finds himself disposed to approve or disapprove of them: holding up that approbation or disapprobation as a sufficient reason for itself, and disclaiming the necessity of looking out for any extrinsic ground. Thus far in the general department of morals: and in the particular department of politics, measuring out the quantum (as well as determining the ground) of punishment, by the degree of the disapprobation.

12. It is manifest, that this is rather a principle in name than in reality: it is not a positive principle of itself, so much as a term employed to signify the negation of all principle. What one expects to find in a principle is something that points out some external consideration, as a means of warranting and guiding the internal sentiments of approbation and disapprobation: this expectation is but ill fulfilled by a proposition, which does neither more nor less than hold up each of those sentiments as a ground and standard for itself. . . .

14. The various systems that have been formed concerning the standard of right and wrong, may all be reduced to the principle of sympathy and antipathy. One account may serve for all of them. They consist all of them in so many contrivances for avoiding the obligation of appealing to any external standard, and for prevailing upon the reader to accept of the author's sentiment or opinion as a reason for itself. The phrases different, but the principle the same.[1]

1 It is curious enough to observe the variety of inventions men have hit upon, and the variety of phrases they have brought forward, in order to conceal from the world, and, if possible, from themselves, this very general and therefore very pardonable self-sufficiency.

1. One man says, he has a thing made on purpose to tell him what is right and what is wrong; and that it is called a *moral sense*: and then he goes to work at his ease, and says, such a thing is right, and such a thing is wrong—why? "because my moral sense tells me it is."

2. Another man comes and alters the phrase: leaving out *moral*, and putting in *common*, in the room of it. He then tells you, that his common sense teaches him what is right and wrong, as surely as the other's moral sense did: meaning by common sense, a sense of some kind or other, which, he says, is possessed by all mankind: the sense of those, whose sense is not the same as the author's, being struck out of the account as not worth taking. This contrivance does better than the other; for a moral sense, being a new thing, a man may feel about him a good while without being able to find it out: but common sense is as old as the creation; and there is no man but would be ashamed to be thought not to have as much of it as his neighbours. It has another great advantage: by appearing to share power, it lessens envy . . .

3. Another man comes, and says, that as to a moral sense indeed, he cannot find that he has any such thing: that however he has an *understanding*, which will do quite as well. This understanding, he says, is the standard of right and wrong: it tells him so and so. All good and wise men understand as he does: if other men's understandings differ in any point from

his, so much the worse for them: it is a sure sign they are either defective or corrupt.

4. Another man says, that there is an eternal and immutable Rule of Right: that the rule of right dictates so and so: and then he begins giving you his sentiments upon any thing that comes uppermost: and these sentiments (you are to take for granted) are so many branches of the eternal rule of right.

5. Another man, or perhaps the same man (it's no matter) says, that there are certain practices conformable, and others repugnant, to the Fitness of Things; and then he tells you, at his leisure, what practices are conformable and what repugnant: just as he happens to like a practice or dislike it.

6. A great multitude of people are continually talking of the Law of Nature; and then they go on giving you their sentiments about what is right and what is wrong: and these sentiments, you are to understand, are so many chapters and sections of the Law of Nature.

7. Instead of the phrase, Law of Nature, you have sometimes, Law of Reason, Right Reason, Natural Justice, Natural Equity, Good Order. Any of them will do equally well. This latter is most used in politics. The three last are much more tolerable than the others, because they do not very explicitly claim to be any thing more than phrases: they insist but feebly upon the being looked upon as so many positive standards of themselves, and seem content to be taken, upon occasion, for phrases expressive of the conformity of the thing in question to the proper standard, whatever that may be. On most occasions, however, it will be better to say *utility: utility* is clearer, as referring more explicitly to pain and pleasure. . . .

15. It is manifest that the dictates of this principle will frequently coincide with those of utility, though perhaps without intending any such thing. Probably more frequently than not: and hence it is that the business of penal justice is carried on upon that tolerable sort of footing upon which we see it carried on in common at this day. For what more natural or more general ground of hatred to a practice can there be, than the mischievousness of such practice? What all men are exposed to suffer by, all men will be disposed to hate. It is far yet, however, from being a constant ground: for when a man suffers, it is not always that he knows what it is he suffers by. A man may suffer grievously, for instance, by a new tax, without being able to trace up the cause of his sufferings to the injustice of some neighbour, who has eluded the payment of an old one. . . .

18. It may be wondered, perhaps, that in all this while no mention has been made of the *theological* principle; meaning that principle which professes to recur for the standard of right and wrong to the will of God. But the case is, this is not in fact a distinct principle. It is never any thing more or less than one or other of the three beforementioned principles presenting itself under another shape. . . .

CHAPTER IV

Value of a Lot of Pleasure or Pain, How to be Measured

5. To take an exact account then of the general tendency of any act, by which the interests of a community are affected proceed as follows. Begin with any one person of those whose interests seem most immediately to be affected by it: and take an account,

1. Of the value of each distinguishable *pleasure* which appears to be produced by it in the *first* instance.

2. Of the value of each *pain* which appears to be produced by it in the *first* instance.

3. Of the value of each pleasure which appears to be produced by it *after* the first. This constitutes the *fecundity* of the first *pleasure* and the *impurity* of the first *pain*.

4. Of the value of each *pain* which appears to be produced by it after the first. This constitutes the *fecundity* of the first *pain,* and the *impurity* of the first pleasure.

5. Sum up all the values of all the *pleasures* on the one side, and those of all the pains on the other. The balance, if it be on the side of pleasure, will give the *good* tendency of the act upon the whole, with respect to the interests of that *individual* person; if on the side of pain, the *bad* tendency of it upon the whole.

6. Take an account of the *number* of persons whose interests appear to be concerned; and repeat the above process with respect to each. *Sum up* the numbers expressive of the degrees of *good* tendency, which the act has, with respect to each individual, in regard to whom the tendency of it is *good* upon the whole: do this again with respect to each individual, in regard to whom the tendency of it is *good* upon the whole: do this again with respect to each individual, in regard to whom the tendency of it is *bad* upon the whole. Take the *balance;* which, if on the side of *pleasure,* will give the general *good tendency* of the act, with respect to the total number or community of individuals concerned; if on the side of pain, the general *evil tendency,* with respect to the same comn.unity.

6. It is not to be expected that this process should be strictly pursued previously to every moral judgment, or to every legislative or judicial operation. It may, however, be always kept in view: and as near as the process actually pursued on these occasions approaches to it, so near will such process approach to the character of an exact one. . . .

CHAPTER V

Pleasures and Pains, Their Kinds

2. The several simple pleasures of which human nature is susceptible, seem to be as

follows: 1. The pleasures of sense. 2. The pleasures of wealth. 3. The pleasures of skill. 4. The pleasures of amity. 5. The pleasures of a good name. 6. The pleasures of power. 7. The pleasures of piety. 8. The pleasures of benevolence. 9. The pleasures of malevolence. 10. The pleasures of memory. 11. The pleasures of imagination. 12. The pleasures of expectation. 13. The pleasures dependent on association. 14. The pleasures of relief.

3. The several simple pains seem to be as follows: 1. The pains of privation. 2. The pains of the senses. 3. The pains of awkwardness. 4. The pains of enmity. 5. The pains of an ill name. 6. The pains of piety. 7. The pains of benevolence. 8. The pains of malevolence. 9. The pains of the memory. 10. The pains of the imagination. 11. The pains of expectation. 12. The pains dependent on association. . . .

33. Of all these several sorts of pleasures and pains, there is scarce any one which is not liable, on more accounts than one, to come under the consideration of the Law. Is an offence committed? It is the tendency which it has to destroy, in such or such persons, some of these pleasures, or to produce some of these pains, that constitutes the mischief of it, and the ground for punishing it. It is the prospect of some of these pleasures, or of security from some of these pains, that constitutes the motive or temptation, it is the attainment of them that constitutes the profit of the offence. Is the offender to be punished? It can be only by the production of one or more of these pains, that the punishment can be inflicted.

CHAPTER VII

Of Human Actions in General

1. The business of government is to promote the happiness of the society, by punishing and rewarding. That part of its business which consists in punishing, is more particularly the subject of penal law. In proportion as an act tends to disturb that happiness, in proportion as the tendency of it is pernicious, will be the demand it creates for punishment. What happiness consists of we have already seen: enjoyment of pleasures, security from pains. . . .

21. So much with regard to acts considered in themselves: we come now to speak of the *circumstances* with which they may have been accompanied. These must necessarily be taken into the account before any thing can be determined relative to the consequences. What the consequences of an act may be upon the whole can never otherwise be ascertained: it can never be known whether it is beneficial, or indifferent, or mischievous. In some circumstances even to kill a man may be a beneficial act: in others, to set food before him may be a pernicious one. . . .

23. We have already had occasion to make mention for a moment of the *consequences* of an act: these were distinguished into material and immaterial. In like manner may the circumstances of it be distinguished. Now *materiality* is a relative term: applied to the consequences of an act, it bore relation to pain and pleasure: applied to the circumstances, it bears relation to the consequences. A circumstance may be said to be material, when it bears a visible relation in point of causality to the consequences: immaterial, when it bears no such visible relation.

24. The consequences of an act are events. A circumstance may be related to an event in point of causality in any one of four ways: 1. In the way of causation or production. 2. In the way of derivation. 3. In the way of collateral connexion. 4. In the way of conjunct influence. It may be said to be related to the event in the way of causation, when it is of the number of those that contribute to the production of such event: in the way of derivation, when it is of the number of the events to the production of which that in question has been contributory: in the way of collateral connexion, where the circumstance in question, and the event in question, without being either of them instrumental in the production of the other,

are related, each of them, to some common object, which has been concerned in the production of them both: in the way of conjunct influence, when, whether related in any other way or not, they have both of them concurred in the production of some common consequence. . . .

26. These several relations do not all of them attach upon an event with equal certainty. In the first place, it is plain, indeed, that every event must have some circumstance or other, and in truth, an indefinite multitude of circumstances, related to it in the way of production: it must of course have a still greater multitude of circumstances related to it in the way of collateral connexion. But it does not appear necessary that every event should have circumstances related to it in the way of derivation: nor therefore that it should have any related to it in the way of conjunct influence. But of the circumstances of all kinds which actually do attach upon an event, it is only a very small number that can be discovered by the utmost exertion of the human faculties: it is a still smaller number that ever actually do attract our notice: when occasion happens, more or fewer of them will be discovered by a man in proportion to the strength, partly of his intellectual powers, partly of his inclination.[2] It appears therefore that the multitude and description of such of the circumstances belonging to an act, as may appear to be material, will be determined by two considerations: 1. By the nature of things themselves. 2. By the strength or weakness of the faculties of those who happen to consider them . . . .

CHAPTER XII

Of the Consequences of a Mischievous Act

1. Shapes in Which the Mischief of an Act May Show Itself

1. . . . We now come to speak of *consequences* or tendency: an article which forms the concluding link in all this chain of causes and effects, involving in it the materiality of the whole. Now, such part of this tendency as is of a mischievous nature, is all that we have any direct concern with; to that, therefore, we shall here confine ourselves.

2. The tendency of an act is mischievous when the consequences of it are mischievous; that is to say, either the certain consequences or the probable. The consequences, how many and whatsoever they may be, of an act, of which the tendency is mischievous, may, such of them as are mischievous, be conceived to constitute one aggregate body, which may be termed the mischief of the act.

3. This mischief may frequently be distinguished, as it were, into two shares or parcels: the one containing what may be called the primary mischief; the other, what may be called the secondary. That share may be termed the *primary*, which is sustained by an assignable individual, or a multitude of assignable individuals. That share may be termed the *secondary*, which, taking its origin from the former, extends itself either over the whole community, or over some

---

[2] The more remote a connexion of this sort is, of course the more obscure. It will often happen that a connexion, the idea of which would at first sight appear extravagant and absurd, shall be rendered highly probable, and indeed indisputable, merely by the suggestion of a few intermediate circumstances.

At Rome, 390 years before the Christian aera, a goose sets up a cackling: two thousand years afterwards a king of France is murdered. To consider these two events, and nothing more, what can appear more extravagant than the notion that the former of them should have had any influence on the production of the latter? Fill up the gap, bring to mind a few intermediate circumstances, and nothing can

appear more probable. It was the cackling of a parcel of geese, at the time the Gauls had surprised the Capitol, that saved the Roman commonwealth: had it not been for the ascendancy that commonwealth acquired afterwards over most of the nations of Europe, amongst others over France, the Christian religion, humanly speaking, could not have established itself in the manner it did in that country. Grant then, that such a man as Henry IV. would have existed, no man, however, would have had those motives, by which Ravaillac, misled by a mischievous notion concerning the dictates of that religion, was prompted to assassinate him.

other multitude of unassignable individuals. . . .

5. The secondary mischief, again, may frequently be seen to consist of two other shares or parcels: the first consisting of *pain:* the other of *danger.* The pain which it produces is a pain of apprehension: a pain grounded on the apprehension of suffering such mischiefs or inconveniences, whatever they may be, as it is the nature of the primary mischief to produce. It may be styled, in one word, the *alarm.* The danger is the *chance,* whatever it may be, which the multitude it concerns may in consequence of the primary mischief stand exposed to, of suffering such mischiefs or inconveniences. For danger is nothing but the chance of pain, or, what comes to the same thing, of loss of pleasure.

6. An example may serve to make this clear. A man attacks you on the road, and robs you. You suffer a pain on the occasion of losing so much money: you also suffered a pain at the thoughts of the personal ill-treatment you apprehended he might give you, in case of your not happening to satisfy his demands. These together constitute the original branch of the primary mischief, resulting from the act of robbery. A creditor of yours, who expected you to pay him with part of that money, and a son of yours, who expected you to have given him another part, are in consequence disappointed. You are obliged to have recourse to the bounty of your father, to make good part of the deficiency. These mischiefs together make up the derivative branch. The report of this robbery circulates from hand to hand, and spreads itself in the neighbourhood. It finds its way into the newspapers, and is propagated over the whole country. Various people, on this occasion, call to mind the danger which they and their friends, as it appears from this example, stand exposed to in traveling; especially such as may have occasion to travel the same road. On this occasion they naturally feel a certain degree of pain: slighter or heavier, according to the degree of ill-treatment they may understand you to have received; the frequency of the occasion each person may have to travel in that same road, or its neighbourhood; the vicinity of each person to the spot; his personal courage; the quantity of money he may have occasion to carry about with him; and a variety of other circumstances. This constitutes the first part of the secondary mischief, resulting from the act of robbery; viz., the alarm. But people of one description or other, not only are disposed to conceive themselves to incur a chance of being robbed, in consequence of the robbery committed upon you, but (as will be shown presently) they do really incur such a chance. And it is this chance which constitutes the remaining part of the secondary mischief of the act of robbery; viz., the danger.

7. Let us see what this chance amounts to; and whence it comes. How is it, for instance, that one robbery can contribute to produce another? In the first place, it is certain that it cannot create any direct motive. A motive must be the prospect of some pleasure, or other advantage, to be enjoyed in future: but the robbery in question is past. . . .

8. The means, then, by which one robbery tends, as it should seem, to produce another robbery, are two. 1. By suggesting to a person exposed to the temptation, the idea of committing such another robbery (accompanied, perhaps, with the belief of its facility). In this case the influence it exerts applies itself, in the first place, to the understanding. 2. By weakening the force of the tutelary motives which tend to restrain him from such an action, and thereby adding to the strength of the temptation. In this case the influence applies itself to the will. . . .

9. The way in which a past robbery may weaken the force with which the *political* sanction tends to prevent a future robbery, may be thus conceived. The way in which this sanction tends to prevent a robbery, is by denouncing some particular kind of punishment against any who shall be guilty of it: the *real* value of which punishment will of course be diminished by the *real* uncertainty: as also, if there be any difference, the *apparent* value by the *apparent* uncertainty. Now this uncertainty is proportionably in-

creased by every instance in which a man is known to commit the offence, without undergoing the punishment. This, of course, will be the case with every offence for a certain time; in short, until the punishment allotted to it takes place. If punishment takes place at last, this branch of the mischief of the offence is then at last, but not till then, put a stop to.

10. The way in which a past robbery may weaken the force with which the *moral* sanction tends to prevent a future robbery, may be thus conceived. The way in which the moral sanction tends to prevent a robbery, is by holding forth the indignation of mankind as ready to fall upon him who shall be guilty of it. Now this indignation will be the more formidable, according to the number of those who join in it: it will be the less so, the fewer they are who join in it. But there cannot be a stronger way of showing that a man does not join in whatever indignation may be entertained against a practice, than the engaging in it himself. It shows not only that he himself feels no indignation against it, but that it seems to him there is no sufficient reason for apprehending what indignation may be felt against it by others. Accordingly, where robberies are frequent, and unpunished, robberies are committed without shame. It was thus amongst the Grecians formerly. It is thus among the Arabs still. . . .

CHAPTER XIII

Cases Unmeet for Punishment

1. General View of Cases Unmeet for Punishment

1. The general object which all laws have, or ought to have, in common, is to augment the total happiness of the community; and therefore, in the first place, to exclude, as far as may be, every thing that tends to subtract from that happiness: in other words, to exclude mischief.

2. But all punishment is mischief: all punishment in itself is evil. Upon the principle of utility, if it ought at all to be admitted, it

ought only to be admitted in as far as it promises to exclude some greater evil.[1]

3. It is plain, therefore, that in the following cases punishment ought not to be inflicted.

I. Where it is *groundless:* where there is no mischief for it to prevent: the act not being mischievous upon the whole.

II. Where it must be *inefficacious:* where it cannot act so as to prevent the mischief.

III. Where it is *unprofitable,* or too *expensive:* where the mischief it would produce would be greater than what it prevented.

IV. Where it is *needless:* where the mischief may be prevented, or cease of itself, without it: that is, at a cheaper rate. . . .

CHAPTER XVI

Division of Offences

1. Classes of Offences

1. It is necessary, at the outset, to make a distinction between such acts as *are* or *may*

[1] The immediate principal end of punishment is to control action. This action is either that of the offender, or of others· that of the offender it controls by its influence, either on his will, in which case it is said to operate in the way of *reformation*; or on his physical power, in which case it is said to operate by *disablement*: that of others it can influence no otherwise than by its influence over their wills; in which case it is said to operate in the way of *example*. A kind of collateral end, which it has a natural tendency to answer, is that of affording a pleasure or satisfaction to the party injured, where there is one, and, in general, to parties whose ill-will, whether on a self-regarding account, or on the account of sympathy or antipathy, has been excited by the offence. This purpose, as far as it can be answered *gratis*, is a beneficial one. But no punishment ought to be allotted merely to this purpose, because (setting aside its effects in the way of control) no such pleasure is ever produced by punishment as can be equivalent to the pain. The punishment, however, which is allotted to the other purpose, ought, as far as it can be done without expense, to be accommodated to this. Satisfaction thus administered to a party injured, in the shape of a dissocial pleasure, may be styled a vindictive satisfaction or compensation: as a compensation, administered in the shape of a self-regarding profit, or stock of pleasure, may be styled a lucrative one. . . . Example is the most important end of all, in proportion as the *number* of the persons under temptation to offend is to one.

be, and such as *ought* to be offences. Any act *may* be an offence, which they whom the community are in the habit of obeying shall be pleased to make one: that is, any act which they shall be pleased to prohibit or to punish. But, upon the principle of utility, such acts alone *ought* to be made offences, as the good of the community requires should be made so.

2. The good of the community cannot require, that any act should be made an offence, which is not liable, in some way or other, to be detrimental to the community. For in the case of such an act, all punishment is *groundless*.

3. But if the whole assemblage of any number of individuals be considered as constituting an imaginary compound *body*, a community or political state; any act that is detrimental to any one or more of those *members* is, as to so much of its effects, detrimental to the *state*. . . .

CHAPTER XVII

Of the Limits of the Penal Branch of Jurisprudence

1. Limits Between Private Ethics and the Art of Legislation

8. Now private ethics has happiness for its end: and legislation can have no other. Private ethics concerns every member, that is, the happiness and the actions of every member, of any community that can be proposed; and legislation can concern no more. Thus far, then, private ethics and the art of legislation go hand in hand. The end they have, or ought to have, in view, is of the same nature . . . There is no case in which a private man ought not to direct his own conduct to the production of his own happiness, and of that of his fellow-creatures: but there are cases in which the legislator ought not (in a direct way at least, and by means of punishment applied immediately to particular *individual* acts) to attempt to direct the conduct of the several other members of the community. . . .

9 . . . . If legislation interferes in a direct

manner, it must be by punishment. Now the cases in which punishment, meaning the punishment of the political sanction, ought not to be inflicted, have been already stated. If then there be any of these cases in which, although legislation ought not, private ethics does or ought to interfere, these cases will serve to point out the limits between the two arts or branches of science. . . .

12. As to the cases where punishment would be *unprofitable*. These are the cases which constitute the great field for the exclusive interference of private ethics. When a punishment is unprofitable, or in other words too expensive, it is because the evil of the punishment exceeds that of the offence . . . It remains to show how it may happen, that there should be acts really pernicious, which, although they may very properly come under the censure of private ethics, may yet be no fit objects of the legislator to control.

13. Punishment then, as applied to delinquency, may be unprofitable in both or either of two ways: 1. By the expense it would amount to, even supposing the application of it to be confined altogether to delinquency: 2. By the danger there may be of its involving the innocent in the fate designed only for the guilty. First then, with regard to the cases in which the expense of the punishment as applied to the guilty, would outweigh the profit to be made by it. These cases, it is evident, depend upon a certain proportion between the evil of the punishment and the evil of the offence. Now were the offence of such a nature, that a punishment which, in point of *magnitude*, should but just exceed the profit of it, would be sufficient to prevent it, it might be rather difficult perhaps to find an instance in which such punishment would clearly appear to be unprofitable. But the fact is, there are many cases in which a punishment, in order to have any chance of being efficacious, must, in point of magnitude, be raised a great deal above that level. Thus it is, wherever the danger of detection is, or, what comes to the same thing, is likely to appear to be, so small, as to make the pun-

ishment appear in a high degree uncertain. In this case it is necessary . . . if punishment be at all applied, to raise it in point of magnitude as much as it falls short in point of certainty. It is evident, however, that all this can be but guess-work: and that the effect of such a proportion will be rendered precarious, by a variety of circumstances: by the want of sufficient promulgation on the part of the law: by the particular circumstances of the temptation: and by the circumstances influencing the sensibility of the several individuals who are exposed to it. Let the *seducing* motives be strong, the offence then will at any rate be frequently committed. Now and then indeed, owing to a coincidence of circumstances more or less extraordinary, it will be detected, and by that means punished. But for the purpose of example, which is the principal one, an act of punishment, considered in itself, is of no use: what use it can be of, depends altogether upon the expectation it raises of similar punishment, in future cases of similar delinquency. But this future punishment, it is evident, must always depend upon detection. If then the want of detection is such as must in general (especially to eyes fascinated by the force of the seducing motives) appear too improbable to be reckoned upon, the punishment, though it should be inflicted, may come to be of no use. Here then will be two opposite evils running on at the same time, yet neither of them reducing the quantum of the other: the evil of the disease and the evil of the painful and inefficacious remedy. It seems to be partly owing to some such considerations, that fornication, for example, or the illicit commerce between the sexes, has commonly either gone altogether unpunished, or been punished in a degree inferior to that in which, on other accounts, legislators might have been disposed to punish it.

14. Secondly, with regard to the cases in which political punishment, as applied to delinquency, may be unprofitable, in virtue of the danger there may be of its involving the innocent in the fate designed only for the guilty. Whence should this danger then arise? From the difficulty there may be of

fixing the idea of the guilty action: that is, of subjecting it to such a definition as shall be clear and precise enough to guard effectually against misapplication. This difficulty may arise from either of two sources: the one permanent, to wit, the nature of the *actions* themselves: the other occasional, I mean the qualities of the *men* who may have to deal with those actions in the way of government. In as far as it arises from the latter of these sources, it may depend partly upon the use which the *legislator* may be *able* to make of language; partly upon the use which, according to the apprehension of the legislator, the *judge* may be *disposed* to make of it. As far as legislation is concerned, it will depend upon the degree of perfection to which the arts of language may have been carried, in the first place, in the nation in general; in the next place, by the *legislator* in particular. It is to a sense of this difficulty . . . that we may attribute the caution with which most legislators have abstained from subjecting to censure, on the part of the law, such actions as come under the notion of rudeness, for example, or treachery, or ingratitude. The attempt to bring acts of so vague and questionable a nature under the control of law, will argue either a very immature age, in which the difficulties which give birth to that danger are not descried; or a very enlightened age, in which they are overcome.

15. . . . Of the rules of moral duty, those which seem to stand least in need of the assistance of legislation are the rules of *prudence*. It can only be through some defect on the part of the understanding, if a man be ever deficient in point of duty to himself . . . With what chance of success, for example, would a legislator go about to extirpate drunkenness and fornication by dint of legal punishment? Not all the tortures which ingenuity could invent would compass it: and, before he had made any progress worth regarding, such a mass of evil would be produced by the punishment, as would exceed, a thousand-fold, the utmost possible mischief of the offence. The great difficulty would be in the procuring evidence; an ob-

ject which could not be attempted, with any probability of success, without spreading dismay through every family, tearing the bonds of sympathy asunder, and rooting out the influence of all the social motives. All that he can do then, against offences of this nature, with any prospect of advantage, in the way of direct legislation, is to subject them, in cases of notoriety, to a slight censure, so as thereby to cover them with a slight shade of artificial disrepute . . . .

17. The mischief of this sort of interference is more particularly conspicuous in the article of religion. The reasoning, in this case, is of the following stamp. There are certain errors, in matters of belief, to which all mankind are prone: and for these errors in judgment, it is the determination of a Being of infinite benevolence, to punish them with an infinity of torments. But from these errors the legislator himself is necessarily free: for the men, who happen to be at hand for him to consult with, being men perfectly enlightened, unfettered, and unbiassed, have such advantages over all the rest of the world, that when they sit down to enquire out the truth relative to points so plain and so familiar as those in question, they cannot fail to find it. This being the case, when the sovereign sees his people ready to plunge headlong into an abyss of fire, shall he not stretch out a hand to save them? . . .

18 . . . . There are few cases in which it *would* be expedient to punish a man for hurting *himself:* but there are few cases, if any, in which it would *not* be expedient to punish a man for injuring his neighbour. With regard to that branch of probity which is opposed to offences against property, private ethics depends in a manner for its very existence upon legislation. Legislation must first determine what things are to be regarded as each man's property, before the general rules of ethics, on this head, can have any particular application. The case is the same with regard to offences against the state. Without legislation there would be no such thing as a *state:* no particular persons invested with powers to be exercised for the benefit of the rest. . . .

19. As to the rules of beneficence, these, as far as concerns matters of detail, must necessarily be abandoned in great measure to the jurisdiction of private ethics. In many cases the beneficial quality of the act depends essentially upon the disposition of the agent; that is, upon the motives by which he appears to have been prompted to perform it: upon their belonging to the head of sympathy, love of amity, or love of reputation; and not to any head of self-regarding motives, brought into play by the force of political constraint: in a word, upon their being such as denominate his conduct *free* and *voluntary,* according to one of the many senses given to those ambiguous expressions.[2] The limits of the law on this head seem, however, to be capable of being extended a good deal farther than they seem ever to have been extended hitherto. In particular, in cases where the person is in danger, why should it not be made the duty of every man to save another from mischief, when it can be done without prejudicing himself, as well as to abstain from bringing it on him? This accordingly is the idea pursued in the body of the work.[1] . . .

2. *Jurisprudence, its Branches*

21. Jurisprudence is a fictitious entity: nor can any meaning be found for the word, but by placing it in company with some

[2] If we may believe M. Voltaire, there was a time when the French ladies who thought themselves neglected by their husbands, used to petition *pour être embesoignées*: the technical word which, he says, was appropriated to this purpose. This sort of law-proceedings seems not very well calculated to answer the design: accordingly we hear nothing of them now-a-days. The French ladies of the present age seem to be under no such difficulties.

[1] A woman's head-dress catches fire: water is at hand: a man, instead of assisting to quench the fire, looks on, and laughs at it. A drunken man, falling with his face downwards into a puddle, is in danger of suffocation: lifting his head a little on one side would save him: another man sees this and lets him lie. A quantity of gunpowder lies scattered about a room: a man is going into it with a lighted candle: another, knowing this, lets him go in without warning. Who is there that in any of these cases would think punishment misapplied?

word that shall be significative of a real entity. To know what is meant by jurisprudence, we must know, for example, what is meant by a book of jurisprudence. A book of jurisprudence can have but one or the other of two objects: 1. To ascertain what the *law* is: 2. to ascertain what it ought to be. In the former case it may be styled a book of *expository* jurisprudence; in the latter, a book of *censorial* jurisprudence: or, in other words, a book on the *art of legislation.* . . .

23. Now *law,* or *the law,* taken indefinitely, is an abstract and collective term; which, when it means any thing, can mean neither more nor less than the sum total of a number of individual laws taken together.[2] . . .

24. . . . Now of the infinite variety of nations there are upon the earth, there are no two which agree exactly in their laws: certainly not in the whole: perhaps not even in any single article: and let them agree to-day, they would disagree tomorrow . . . However among the words that are appropriated to the subject of law, there are some that in all languages are pretty exactly correspondent to one another: which comes to the same thing nearly as if they were the same. Of this stamp, for example, are those which correspond to the words *power, right, obligation, liberty,* and many others.

It follows, that if there are any books which can, properly speaking, be styled books of universal jurisprudence, they must be looked for within very narrow limits.

---

[2] In most of the European languages there are two different words for distinguishing the abstract and the concrete senses of the word *law*: which words are so wide asunder as not even to have any etymological affinity. In Latin, for example, there is *lex* for the concrete sense, *jus* for the abstract: in Italian, *legge* and *diritto*: in French, *loi* and *droit*: in Spanish, *ley* and *derecho*: in German, *gesetz* and *recht*. The English is at present destitute of this advantage.

In the Anglo-Saxon, besides *lage,* and several other words, for the concrete sense, there was the word *right,* answering to the German *recht,* for the abstract as may be seen in the compound *folc-right,* and in other instances. But the word *right* having long ago lost this sense, the modern English no longer possesses this advantage.

Among such as are expository, there can be none that are authoritative . . . To be susceptible of an universal application, all that a book of the expository kind can have to treat of, is the import of words: to be, strictly speaking, universal, it must confine itself to terminology. . . .

It is in the censorial line that there is the greatest room for disquisitions that apply to the circumstances of all nations alike: and in this line what regards the substance of the laws in question is as susceptible of an universal application, as what regards the words. That the laws of all nations, or even of any two nations, should coincide in all points, would be as ineligible as it is impossible: some leading points, however, there seem to be, in respect of which the laws of all civilized nations might, without inconvenience, be the same. . . .

THE LIMITS OF JURISPRUDENCE DEFINED *

CHAPTER 1

Distinction Between Penal Law and Civil

. . . We come now to speak of what is called civil law or jurisprudence on the one hand and penal law or jurisprudence on the other . . . They are inextricably interwoven. . . . In every law must be comprised two things: 1. a specification of the cases in which the punishment is to attach; 2. a specification of the punishment itself . . . .

. . . That book belongs to the subject of penal jurisprudence which has most in it about punishment: that book belongs to the civil branch which has least in it about punishment itself, and most about the cases in which punishment is or is not to be applied.

The book indeed may be a large book; it may indeed be of any size, and yet be a book of law, and yet not say a syllable in any part

---

* Edited by Charles Warren Everett. Reprinted by permission of the Columbia University Press.

of it about punishment: still however it has a tacit reference to punishment: else the law which it delivers or professes to deliver would be nugatory, and the book useless.

A great book for example is written about Wills . . . It says a great deal about the nature of a Will: about the sort of persons who are empowered to make them: about the cases in which these persons may and those in which they may not exercise that power: about the different sorts of Wills when made: about the number of witnesses which must attest them: about the places where they must be registered: about the construction that is to be given them, and so on for evermore: all this while without intimating a syllable about punishment. Has punishment however no concern in this? If that were the case the whole affair would amount to nothing. In fact all this is of no further use than as it serves to fix the application of punishment: distinguishing the one person who would *not* be punished in case of his meddling with and using that thing in question, from the multitude of other persons (amounting in fact to no fewer than all the rest of mankind) who would. You claim to be the sole proprietor of yonder house . . . You maintain that you are the person named . . . by the will of your deceased friend: who possessed the house: who was of the number of those persons who are allowed to make a will: who was so circumstanced as to have a right to dispose of this house by his will: who made such and such a will accordingly in your favor; took care to have it attested by so many witnesses, etc. All this is only to give other persons to understand that were they to offer to meddle with the house they would be punished, and that you alone are left free to deal with it as you please. . . .

CHAPTER 2

Analysis and Exposition

Analysis

Power, right, prohibition, duty, obligation, burthen, immunity, exemption, privilege, property, security, liberty—all these with a multitude of others that might be named are so many fictitious entities which the law upon one occasion or another is spoken of in common speech as creating or disposing of . . . Would a man know what it is that the law really does in any case, and in what condition it leaves the parties that are concerned? He must know in such case the acts which it takes into contemplation, and the aspect which it bears to them. He must know who the persons, and what the things, if any, which are in question: what the acts are of those persons, whether for their termination they look to other persons or to things: and in what circumstances if in any the act is prohibited or permitted, commanded or left uncommanded. Knowing this much, we shall have ideas to our words: not knowing it, we shall have none. . . .

Exposition

. . . Now there can be no such thing as an act which is not the act of some person or of some sentient thing: nor can there be any act of law which is not either a command or a prohibition, or the reverse of the one or the other of those operations: nor lastly, can there be any command or prohibition which has not for its object some sort of act . . . By this means alone can the import of such words as duty, obligation, power, right and other names of fictitious moral entities be laid open: by these means alone can a regular analysis of the contents of a body of laws be exhibited . . . .

. . . It follows that whatever number of these fictitious entities may be created or brought into play, it must all be done in the course of some or other of those operations by which the several sorts of offences are created. They are a sort of vapours which during the course of the legislative process are as it were generated and sublimed . . . .

As yet there is no law in the land. . . . This is the first day of the political creation: the state is without form and void. As yet then you and I and everyone are at liberty. Understand always, as against the law: for as against one another this may be far from being the case. . . . You and your neighbour, suppose, are at variance: he has bound you hand and foot, or has fastened you to a tree: in this case you are certainly not at liberty as against him . . . Since the legislator then takes an active part, how is it that he must demean himself? He must either command or prohibit: for there is nothing else that he can do . . . Liberty then is of two or even more sorts, according to the number of quarters from whence coercion, which it is the absence of, may come: liberty as against the law, and liberty as against those who first in consideration of the effect of their conduct upon the happiness of society, and afterwards in consideration of the course taken against them by the law, may be styled *wrong-doers.* These two sorts of liberty are directly opposed to one another: and in as far as it is in favour of an individual, that the law exercises its authority over another, the generation of the one sort is, as far as it extends, the destruction of the other. . . .

The law, after certain exceptions made, prohibits in one and in others all such acts as it thinks advisable to prevent . . . What then is the result? To me and the rest of the community, restraint: to you, personal security and protection. . . .

. . . Now property before it can be offended against must be created: and the creation of it is the work of law . . . Conceive any material thing at pleasure: a piece of land for instance. The law issues no mandate at all to me or anyone with respect to that piece of land . . . What is the result? on all sides liberty as before. Moreover, considering that it might have commanded us all, you and me and others, not to exercise any act upon that land, and that such are the commands which to you to me and to everybody but one or a few it actually does give with respect to by far the greatest part of the land under its dominion, it is on that account frequently spoken of as if it had done something in favour of those whom it has left thus at liberty: it is spoken of as having given them or rather left them a *power over* the land: it may also be said to have left them a *property in* the land. As this same

sort of property is given not to you only, but to me and everybody else, no restraint with respect to the use of the land being laid on anybody, that which is given to you may on that account be styled *inexclusive:* an inexclusive power over the land: an inexclusive property in the land. The land in this case is said to be the common property of us all: and each of us is said to have a property in it in common with the rest: and each man may even be said to have *the* property of it, so as this phrase be added *"in common with the rest.".* . . .

The law forbids everybody but you from exercising any act upon the land. In this case it gives you alone a power over the land: it makes the land your property, your estate: it makes you sole owner, the proprietor of the land: it gives you not only *an* estate, an interest, in the land in severalty, but *the* property *of* the land, *the* estate *of* the land, both also in severalty.

As to this case it may be proper to observe that in reality it is never completely verified. Under any system of law some occasions there are in which for the carrying on of government it is necessary that any man's ownership over any object of property would be liable to be suspended: as if for instance there were need to make use of the land in question for the encampment of an army. But when these periods are not long, and the commencement of them is casual only and contingent, as in the case just stated, such slight exceptions are not in common speech considered as derogating from the general rule. . . .

The error against which these observations are leveled is at least a general one among jurists, not to say a universal one. It is by no means an innocent one: from speculation it creeps into practice, producing obstinacy, ill humour, blindness, turbulence, and in the end disobedience to law. The right I have to my property, to my possessions is derived from physical, from natural acts: being derived from natural acts it is a natural right: being derived from nature it is not derived from law: its origin, its existence was antecedent to law: for nature existed before law. Being antecedent to law, it was not created by law: not being created by law it cannot be taken away by law. Law was instituted to protect a man in the enjoyment of such his rights, not to deprive him of them, or of any part of them: these rights like all other natural rights are sacred and indefeasible. So far as it protects him accordingly, it is comfortable to natural justice: so far as it deprives him of such his rights or any part of them it is repugnant to natural justice. Laws conformable to natural justice are valid, and ought to be observed: laws repugnant to natural justice are *ipso facto* void, and instead of being observed ought to be resisted. Those who make them are tyrants, those who attempt to enforce them are the tools of tyrants: both the one and the other ought to be resisted, made war upon, and destroyed. . . .

Of rights thus self-evident the existence requires not to be proved but only to be declared: to prove it is impossible because the demonstration of that which is self-evident is impossible: to doubt of it argues of want of sense: to express a doubt of it argues not only a want of sense but a want of honesty.

All this talk about nature, natural rights, natural justice and injustice proves two things and two things only, the heat of the passions, and the darkness of the understanding. . . .

Property the creature of law?—Oh, no—Why not?—because if it were the law that gave everything, the law might take away every thing. . . .

The case is that in a society in any degree civilized, all the rights a man can have, all the expectation he can entertain of enjoying any thing that is said to be his is derived solely from the law. Even the expectation which a thief may entertain of enjoying the thing which he has stolen forms no exception: for till it is known to have been stolen the law will as fully protect him in the enjoyment of it, as much as if he had bought or made it.

But what it may be said was the ground the law went upon at first in choosing whom it should take for the object of its protec-

tion, and for what things? a time there must always have been in which men were entertaining a *natural* expectation of enjoying certain things, an expectation derived from sources anterior to law.—Certainly occasions there must have originally been, and will have been still in which one man must have found a greater facility in securing to himself the enjoyment of certain things than any other man: but how narrow and how fleeting the security! Without the aid of law a savage, it is true, who has hid in a cave some fruits he has gathered or some animals which he has killed may keep them to himself so long as the cave remains undiscovered, without the aid of law . . . An expectation in any degree strong and permanent can only be derived from law. Till law existed, property could scarcely be said to exist.

CHAPTER 3.

Of a Law and its Parts

A Law may be defined as an assemblage of signs declarative of a volition conceived or adopted by the *sovereign* in a state, concerning the conduct to be observed in a certain *case* by a certain person or class of persons, who in the case in question are or are supposed to be subject to his power: such volition trusting for its accomplishment to the expectation of certain events which it is intended such declaration should upon occasion be a means of bringing to pass, and the prospect of which it is intended should act as a motive upon those whose conduct is in question . . . .

The latitude here given to the import of the word *law* is it must be confessed rather greater than what seems to be given to it in common: the definition being such as is applicable to various objects which are not commonly characterized by that name. Taking this definition for the standard it matters not whether the expression of will in question, so as it have but the authority of the sovereign to back it, were his by immediate conception or only by adoption: whether it be of the most public or of the most private or even domestic nature: whether the sovereign from whom it derives its force be an individual or a body: whether it be issued . . . on account of some positive act or event which is understood to warrant it (as is the case with an order of the judicial kind made in the course of a cause); or without the assignment of any such special ground: or whether it be susceptible of an indefinite duration or whether it be *sua natura* temporary and undurable: as is most commonly the case with such expressions of will the uttering of which is looked upon as a *measure of administration:* whether it be a command or a countermand: whether it be expressed in the way of statute, or of customary law. Under the term *law* then if this definition be admitted of, we must include a judicial order, a military or any other kind of executive order, or even the most trivial and momentary order of the domestic kind, so it be not illegal: that is, so as the issuing of it be not forbidden by some other law. . . .

CHAPTER 4

Source of a Law

. . . The will of which it is the expression must, as the definition intimates, be the will of the sovereign in *a* state. Now by a sovereign I mean any person or assemblage of persons to whose will a whole political community are (no matter on what account) supposed to be in a disposition to pay obedience: and that in preference to the will of any other person. Suppose the will in question not to be the will of *a* sovereign, that is of some sovereign or other; in such case, if it come backed with motives of a coercive nature, it is not a law, but an illegal mandate: and the act of issuing it is an offence. . . .

Now a given will or mandate may be the will or mandate of a given person in either of two ways: in the way of *conception* . . . (that is of original conception) or 2. in the way of *adoption*. A will or mandate may be said to belong to a sovereign in the way of conception when it was he himself . . . who

first issued it, in the words or other signs in which it stands expressed: it may be said to belong to him by adoption when the person from whom it immediately comes is not the sovereign himself . . . but some other person: insomuch that all the concern which he to whom it belongs by adoption has in the matter is the being known to entertain a will that in case such or such another person should have expressed . . . a will concerning the act or sort of act in question, such will should be observed and looked upon as his. . . .

. . . The mandates of the master, the father, the husband, the guardian, are all of them the mandates of the sovereign: if not, then neither are those of the general nor of the judge. Not a cook is bid to dress a dinner, a nurse to feed a child, an usher to whip a school boy, an executioner to hang a thief, an officer to drive the enemy from a post, but it is by his orders. If anyone should find a difficulty in conceiving this, he has only to suppose the several mandates in question to meet with resistance: in one case as well as in another the business of enforcing them must rest ultimately with the sovereign. To deny it is as much as to say that it is God Almighty indeed that keeps up the race of elephants, but it is somebody else that keeps up the race of mites. Nor is there anything of fiction in all this: if there were, this is the last place in which it should be found.

Fiction, the bane of science, which is frequently wickedness and which is at best but nonsense, can never be requisite for explanation. . . .

It is in this very way that conveyances and covenants acquire all the validity they can possess, all the connection they have with the System of the laws: adopted by the sovereign, they are converted into mandates. If you give your coat to a man, and the gift is valid, and nobody else has a right to meddle with your coat, it is because a mandate subsists on the part of the sovereign, commanding all persons whatever to refrain from meddling with it, he to whom you gave it alone excepted, upon the event of your declaring such to be your pleasure. If a man engages or covenants to mend your coat for you, and such an engagement is valid, it is because on the part of the sovereign a mandate hath been issued, commanding any person upon the event of his entering into any engagement, (exceptions excepted) and thereby that particular person in consequence of his having entered into that particular engagement, (it not being within the exceptions) to perform it: in other words to render you that particular service which is rendered to you by performance of the act which he has engaged for. . . .

CHAPTER 5

Ends which a Law May Have in View

. . . As to the general and ultimate end, this upon the principle of utility can be no other than the greatest good of the whole community. But the good of the community is the sum of the several particular *goods* (if the term may be employed) of the several individuals of which it is composed: so that to augment the good of any one such individual is *pro tanto* to augment the good of the whole community. A law therefore of which the immediate end is no other than the good or benefit of the person whose law it is does not on that account cease to be such a law as is capable of being warranted by the principle of utility: much less does it cease to be entitled to the appellation of a law. Now by *end* is here meant not the eventual end, which is a matter of chance, but the intended end, which is a matter of design. . . .

It is to be remembered that law may belong to the sovereign either in the way of conception or in the way of adoption: in the latter case there are necessarily two persons whose law in these two different senses it may be said to be. These two persons it may happen may in regard to the parts they have necessarily taken in the establishment of the law, have been actuated by two different motives: they may have had in view two different ends.

As to the sovereign, the end or external motive he can have had in view in adopting the law, can upon the principle of utility, have been no other than the greatest good of the community: which end we suppose his measures to be directed to of course: since it is only in as far as that is the case that these enquiries are calculated or designed to be of any use to him. But with regard to the party to whom the law appertains in the way of conception and from whom it immediately ensues, the case is different. In many instances it may happen, and that properly enough, that the end which he has in view is no other than his own particular benefit or satisfaction: . . . in this case are all the mandates for instance of the master acting as such, as also those of the parent and of the husband in as far as the parent and the husband are allowed to act in the capacity of a master. . . .

But the more conspicuous case and the more common with such mandates as in consideration of their generality and their permancy are usually distinguished by the name of *laws* is that in which the proper end of the sovereign who adopts, and that of the subordinate magistrate who issues the mandate, coincide: being each of them not the particular good of the author of the mandate but the general good of the community at large. . . .

Wherein then consists the good of the community? A question this which is to be answered not by vague declamation, not by point and metaphor, but by minute analysis and sober estimation . . . .

Those who cry out against pleasure, as such, know not what it is they say. They swerve manifestly from the principle of utility. . . .

. . . For matter of censure or approbation I appeal solely to this principle. The principle such as it is, is not of my own invention. The merit of discovering it is none of mine. The legitimate consequences of it, should any of them prove obnoxious are not chargeable upon me. I had it from Epicurus, from Carneades, from Horace, from Helvetius, from Beccaria. All that remains for me is only to apply it to particular cases as they come under review. . . .

The learned Grotius . . . bethinks himself of the line of Horace, in which the heathen poet, adopting . . . the doctrine of the Greek philosopher Carneades, expressly places the whole fabric of moral science on the foundation of this principle. "Utility" says that philosopher in the figurative language given him by his poetical commentator, "is the mother of Justice and Equity." This genealogy Grotius positively objects to: whereupon he enters into an investigation which is not altogether of the clearest, but the result of which is that utility, though not the parent of natural Law, is however a distant relation to it, being first cousin to its Great-Grandmother.

After this he assures us that although no utility were to be looked for from the observance of the Law, it would be the part of a wise man, not of a fool to be led by it, as being prompted thereto by nature. . . .

Our own Lord Coke in his *Commentary on Littleton* in the course of the Chapter on Fee Simple bethinks himself of giving a catalogue of the several principles or "fountains" from whence his Author (in whose works are the very sum and substance of the Law) may be observed to draw his arguments. There are twenty of them in all. In the tenth place after a variety of arguments of very different complexion, comes in the *argumentum ab inconvenienti;* and in the fifteenth place with a variety of arguments of a nature still more disparate, between them enters in the guise of a different sort of argument, the argument *ab utili et inutili.* . . .

CHAPTER 11

The Generality of a Law

. . . To begin with the deficiencies to which the power of general legislation or legislation *de classibus* is exposed.

The commands of a sovereign will like any other communications be liable to receive a tinge from the channel through which they are conveyed . . . A legislator in uttering a law which shall be general must in as far as it is intended to be general make use of general terms or names. . . .

Conceive him then on any occasion to have taken up any such generic name. By this name a class suppose of subjects (no matter what) is brought to view. This class taken at a given period is composed of a certain number of individuals. As to these individuals then, by what means is it that they have come to be aggregated to this class? to be looked upon as belonging to it? to be the individuals who are deemed to have been had in view upon the mention of this name? By whatever means the event of their belonging to this class has come to pass, such event either depended or did not depend upon the will of a human being: if it did, such person has thereby a power: in the former case, whatever limitation the power of the legislator is subject to on this account, the power which remains to him, whatever it be, is still so far his own, that no other person is a sharer in it. In the other case, the power of imperation does not belong to him alone; he has a sharer or partner in it: and this partner is the person on whose will the event above mentioned has a dependence. The share which this person has in the entire power of imperation may be termed the *accensitive power* or power of right of *aggregation* with regard to the class in question. . . .

. . . To every class of persons who in any manner stand affected by a law a certain condition or station in life is attributed by the fashion of language: a person being said to be of such or such a condition in virtue of his belonging to such or such a class. To aggregate a man then to a class is the same thing as to invest him with a condition. . . .

To juries, in most cases belongs in conjunction with the regular Judges as also with prosecutors, witnesses and individual officers of justice, and other persons whose share in this power however inconspicuous is not the less real, the power of aggregating persons in most cases to the disadvantageous class of delinquents, a class which is branched out into the various classes we have seen. They thence become the persons from whom the legislator has taken such and such rights, whom he has subjected to such and such obligations, and rendered obnoxious in the way of punishment or for other purposes to such and such applications of the *impressive* power, this branch of the *accensitive power*. . . .

It is by this time, I suppose, sufficiently manifest that the legislative power ordinarily so called, I mean the power of legislating *de classibus* even though it be supreme, can never of itself be absolute and unlimited. It can never so much as amount to the entire power of imperation: it will fall short of being equal to that power by so much as is contained in whatever powers of aggregation or disaggregation are established in the state. . . .

CHAPTER 15

Signs of a Law

. . . A law is an *expression* of will: that is an assemblage of signs expressive of an act of the will. These signs then may by possibility be any signs whatever which are capable of expressing such a will: the behaviour of him who instead of saying, put to death the chief leaders of the people, smote off the tallest heads among a parcel of poppies, might instead of being an advice, have been a command. But the only signs which can answer this purpose in a manner tolerably commodious are those conventional signs the assemblage of which forms what is called *discourse*. Now the signs of which discourse is composed may either be of the *transient* kind, of which those most in use are articulate sounds: or they may be a sort of secondary symbols, permanent signs of the before mentioned transient ones, composing what is commonly called *written,* and what by a more comprehensive mode of appellation might be styled *graphical* discourse. Of the last description of all are what are commonly called statute or written laws. Of the first kind, are what in the English language are usually styled *common* or *unwritten,* but which might more aptly be styled *customary* laws. For the second, it being for so many

ages out of date among civilized nations, no distinct denomination seems to ever have been in common use: they might be styled *traditional* statute laws: or more shortly traditionary laws.

When the nature of those laws which are here called customary comes to be precisely understood, which it seems hardly to have been hitherto, the doubt above expressed will not be wondered at. These laws are nothing but so many autocratic acts or orders, which in virtue of the more extensive interpretation which the people are disposed to put upon them, have somewhat of the effect of general laws. Here it is to be observed that all verbal discourse is out of the question. Perhaps there shall have been no verbal discourse made use of on the occasion: but if there be, it is not this verbal discourse that makes the law. For the verbal discourse containing the mandate of the judge is in point of extent particular, being confined to the assignable individuals to whom it is addressed: whereas what there is of law in the case must be general, applicable to an indefinite multitude of individuals not then assignable. A magistrate exercises some act of power over a particular individual: the assemblage of acts by which this is done serves as a sign to the people at large expressing that the like act of power will probably be exercised in future in a like case. A Cadi comes by a Baker shop, and finds the bread short of weight: the baker is hanged in consequence. This, if it be part of the design that other bakers should take notice of it, is a sort of law forbidding the selling of bread short of weight under the pain of hanging. Whether the Cadi makes a record in writing attesting that the baker has sold bread short of weight, and issues an order to a public executioner to strangle him, or whether the Cadi himself without saying a word strangles him on the spot, is what to this purpose makes no difference. The silent act of hanging when thus made a consequence of the offence has as good a title in point of extent to the appellation of a law as anything that could be made out of a whole shelf full of pleadings put together. Written law then is the law of those who can both speak and write: traditionary law, of those who can speak but can not write: customary law, of those who neither know how to write, nor how to speak. Written law is the law for civilized nations: traditionary law, for barbarians: customary law, for brutes.

Not but that there are plenty of books purporting to be books of customary or as it is more frequently called *unwritten* law: for if the written law is written, so is the unwritten too. But what are they? Books written not by the legislator but by private individuals: Books not of authoritative but of unauthoritative jurisprudence. In none of all these books is there so much as a single article which can with propriety receive the appellation of *a* law. It is owing rather to an imperfection which as we have seen is peculiar to the English tongue, if in that language they can with any degree of propriety be termed books of law: They contain *jus* indeed but not *leges: Le droit,* but not *des loix.*

If in all that has been ever written of this nature there be a single paragraph which (not being a passage copied from some statute) is seriously meant to pass for a paragraph of *a* law, I mean in the sense in which the word *law* is used in contradistinction to the word *order,* it is a forgery. Whether there be anything in it or not that has been marked with the stamp of authority, makes no difference: if authoritative, it is particular; and therefore no law: if general, it is unauthoritative: and therefore again no law. But of this a little farther on. . . .

CHAPTER 16

Completeness of a Law

. . . Now completeness is a word of reference: It supposes a standard of reference: This standard then may be either what actually was the will entertained by the legislator relative to the matters in question, or what on a certain contingency it is supposed, *would* have been his will: his *actual* will as it may be styled, or his *hypothetical* will. . . .

. . . Were a legislator to take a book of any size whatever, containing any quantity of imperative matter whatsoever, and exhibit it as comprehending a complete collection of all the laws he thinks proper should be looked upon as being in force, as many imperative provisions as it contained would, with the help of such qualifications as were to be found, be all and every of them complete laws: I mean always in point of expression: in this point the laws in a complete code, such as they are, cannot be otherwise than complete. For from what other sources can his will be collected, than from the signs and those the only ones which he has made choice of to express it? In searching after his will there may be occasion indeed to travel from one passage of this instrument to another: but out of this instrument so long as the words of it are intelligible, there can be no pretense for travelling. If indeed there should be any words in it which notwithstanding everything that can be done in the view of collecting the import of them from the instrument itself still continue ambiguous or unintelligible, in such case, as a means of finding out the sense of them it may indeed be necessary to have recourse to some other instrument. But such explanatory instrument can not be said to detract from the completeness of the principal one considered as a book of law. If it could, then a common dictionary might be considered as a book of law. The evidence derived from any such foreign source being only presumptive evidence can never be considered as outweighing any direct intrinsic evidence that may be to be had from the body of the code itself. To recur to the old instance of a law against the exportation of corn. A doubt arises what sort of articles are to be understood under the name of corn: whether *maize,* for example is to be looked upon as included in the number. The opinions of persons conversant in the trade being doubtful or divided, a dictionary of commerce or a dictionary of botany is recurred to; and it there appears that maize is looked upon as a species of the commodity in question. The law being totally silent, the interpretation thus obtained may be considered as conclusive, without any disparagement to the completeness of the law. This however can never be the case if the contrary sense could justly be collected from any passage contained in the law itself. In such case to decide according to the dictionary would be to deny the completeness of the code, and recognizing the author of the dictionary as being *pro tanto* the superior legislator.

Secondly in regard to the completeness of a law in point of *connection*. A single law, even of the narrowest pattern, may consist . . . of a great multitude of provisions: a greater multitude by far than from anything that has hitherto been observed would easily be suspected. These provisions in order to have the effect they are designed to have, it is necessary that the influence they are meant to have on one another should by some means or other be made appear. This there are two ways of doing: the one is by making them follow one another in the same instrument without interruption: this may be styled connection by juxtaposition: the other is by sending the reader from the place at which the chain of provisions is broken off, to the place where it is resumed again: this may be styled connection by reference. . . .

Thirdly with regard to the completeness of the law in point of *design:* that is with reference to what would, it is supposed, have been the will of the legislator had such or such a case been present to his view. Every law that is made may be said to have been made upon the consideration of some mischief: of a sort of mischief regarded as being apt to ensue from the sort of act which the legislator is thereby inclined to prohibit: which general idea of mischief must originally have been suggested by the idea of some particular mischief which appeared to result from some particular act of the sort in question. In as far then as the general idea which (to judge from the act as described in the prohibition) he appears to have formed to himself of the mischief of the case deviates from that which from the view of that case it is thought he should and might have formed to himself, in so far the law

may be looked upon as incomplete in point of design. If then the law be considered as deviating from the standard thus assigned, it must be considered as deviating from it in one or other of two ways: as falling short of it, or as stretching beyond it: in the former case it may be said to be deficient or incomplete in point of *amplitude:* in the latter, in point of *discrimination.* . . .

"Whoso draweth blood in the streets shall be severely punished." This is a law that may serve at the same time as an example of every fault in point of extent of which a law is susceptible . . . 1. Want of original amplitude: For drawing blood is but one out of a great variety of ways in which a mischief the same in substance may be produced: a bruise, a scald, a burn, and so forth may be as hurtful as a wound. 2. Want of proper discrimination. For how many disorders are there with which a man is as liable to be seized in the streets as anywhere else for which instant bleeding is the only remedy? And what if a man has no other way of defending or otherwise saving his life or limbs, or a woman her chastity. 3. Want of residuary amplitude through improper discrimination. For why must the act be confined to the streets in order to come within the censure of the law? Is it less mischievous if committed in the market-place, or in a church? . . . .

If the will which a legislator manifests with relation to a given act fails of being what it ought to be, such failure . . . must arise from one or other of two causes: the state of his understanding, or the state of his affections. In the former case it must be owing either to inadvertency, or to wrong judgment: the facts which may go to constitute or those which may serve to control the mischief may not have been, all of them, present to his *apprehension:* or being present, the judgment formed by him concerning their existence or their tendency may have been a wrong one.

Interpretation may be distinguished into *strict* and *liberal.* It may be styled strict where you attribute to the legislator the will which at the time of making the law, as you suppose, he really entertained. It may be styled liberal where the will you attribute to him is not that which you suppose he really entertained, but a will which as you suppose he failed of entertaining only through inadvertency: insomuch that had the individual case which calls for interpretation been present to his view, he would have entertained that will, which by the interpretation put upon his law you act up to, as if it had been his in reality.

I say through inadvertency: for to attribute to the legislator a will which you suppose him to have failed of entertaining through any other cause than inadvertency, that is from wrong judgment or perverse affections, and to act accordingly is not to interpret the law, but to act against it: which in a judge or other officer invested with powers of a public nature is as much as to over-rule it.

It appears then to interpret the law according to the liberal mode of interpretation is *pro tanto* to apply to the imperative provision either an extensive or a qualificative clause. . . . The only circumstance that can serve to distinguish the alteration itself, when made in this way, from alteration at large is, that the alteration goes no farther than from what it appears was the legislator's will to what, it is supposed, would have been his will had the case in question been present to his view: from his actual to his hypothetical will. . . .

CHAPTER 17

No Customary Law Complete

. . . A customary law is not expressed in words, now in what words should it present itself? it has no parts: how should it exhibit any? It is one single indivisible act, capable of all manner of constructions. Under the customary law there can scarcely be said to be a right or a wrong in any case. How should there? right is the conformity to a rule, wrong the deviation from it: but here there is no rule established, no measure to discern by, no standard to appeal to: all is uncertainty, darkness, and confusion.

It is evident enough that the sign, the act of punishment, which is all there is properly speaking of a customary law, can express nothing of itself to any who have not some other means of informing themselves of the occasion on which it was given. . . . If then it can serve as a rule to any distance or for any length of time, some account of the case must be taken and handed down by somebody: which somebody stands then in the place of a legislator. But of the boundless group of circumstances with which the act punished must necessarily have been attended, how many and which of them were considered as material? what were received as exculpative? what were not suffered to operate in the way of exculpation? to what circumstances was it owing that the punishment was so great? to what others that it was no greater? These and a multitude of other circumstances which it would be needless to repeat must all be taken into the account in the description of the case. But let the case be delineated ever so exactly, it is still but that individual case that is delineated: to make a rule that can serve for cases yet to come, a new process must be carried on: the historian must give place to the metaphysician: and a general rule must be created by abstraction out of this particular proceeding. And by whom then shall the abstraction be performed? by every man for himself, or by some one for all the rest? In the latter case that one man, be he whoever he will, if his rule comes to be adopted and adhered to, that one man becomes in effect the legislator. . . .

But the rule extracted no matter how, from these particular *data,* and which if there were a law in the case, would be the law, is after all absurd and mischievous: perhaps it was so from the very first, that is the decisions on which it is grounded were so at the first moment of their being made. But at any rate it would be so if applied now to the matter at present in dispute. To decide then according to *this* rule would be mischievous in one way: but to depart from *any* rule which is to be deemed to have been establi̇̀hed would be mischievous in another way: It is only in as far as subsequent decisions are rendered conformable to the rules that are fairly to be drawn from prior decisions that such prior decisions can answer, in any even the most imperfect degree, the purpose of a law. Whenever the chain of conformity, such as it is, is broken, the anomalous decision whatever it is, does all the mischief that can be done by an *ex post facto* law. . . .This it does by its own single efficacy: add to which that in the way of example it gives a shock which from hand to hand is felt by the whole future of customary law. Nor is the mischief cured till a strong body of connected decisions either in confirmation of the first anomalous one or in opposition to it have repaired the broken thread of analogy and brought back the current of reputation to its old channel. I speak in metaphors: since in metaphors only on a subject like the present can one speak. This being the case, whenever any past decision, in itself apparently absurd, is brought in the character of a law to govern the proposed decision in the case in litigation, there are two maxims that point different ways and press for opposite determinations. As this dilemma is occurring at every turn, lawyers are of course continually called upon to embrace the one side of it or the other. Accordingly then as the inconveniences on the one side or those on the other have been accustomed to press upon their imaginations with the greatest force they insensibly contract a general propensity to lean on the one side or on the other. They form themselves like the Proculians and the Sabinians of old, though on a ground of much greater extent and importance into different parties: *Stare decisis* is the maxim of the one; *salus respublicae* or something like it, the motto of the other: both perhaps partisans of utility, though of utility viewed through a different medium: the one of the general utility which results from the adherence to established precedents: the other, of the particular utility which results from the bringing back the current of decision at any rate into the channel of original utility

from which the force of precedent they suppose had drawn it aside: the one, enamoured of uniformity, the mother of security and peace: the other, of natural Justice or Equity or Right Reason or by whatever other name the phantom has but his own.

From a set of *data* like these a law is to be extracted by every man who can fancy that he is able: by each man, perhaps a different law: and these *monades* which meeting together, constitute that inimitable and unimprovable production of enlightened reason, that fruit of concord and pledge of liberty in every country in which it is found, the common or customary law. . . .

It appears then, that the customary law is a fiction from beginning to end: and it is in the way of fiction if at all that we must speak of it. . . .

CHAPTER 21

Analysis, and Uses of the Preceding Chapters

. . . At present we may boldly affirm that among all the systems of law which prevail among the several nations of the world, there is not one which does not exist more or less of it in the form of customary law: so that as yet no instance of a complete code of statute law is anywhere to be found. It follows not, however, by any means that if a complete code of that kind were given to any nation it must thereby be deprived of so much as a single article of those ancient and respected institutions to which the people in many instances with great reason are so strenuously attached. . . .

. . . No system of laws will ever . . . be altogether perfect: none so good but that a greater share either of information or judgment or of probity might make it better. Even if at any given instant it were really perfect, at the next instant, owing to some change in national affairs it might be otherwise. . . . But such a system if constructed upon a regular and measured plan such as that appears to be which we have been attempting to sketch out, would not only have the advantage of every other which remained untouched, but alterations, whenever any were made, would give less disturbance to it: provided that such alterations, as often as any were made in point of form, were accommodated as they easily might be to that of the original government. The effects and influence of every such provision whether it were an entire law, a provision expositive, limitative, or exceptive, might then with certainty and precision be traced on and out by reference throughout the whole body of the laws. At present such is the entanglement, that when a new statute is applied it is next to impossible to follow it through and discover the limits of its influence. . . .

. . . The fundamental principle which is the basis of the system of laws here sketched out is the principle of utility: and the method here proposed is particularly calculated to shew how far that principle has been deferred to, and where if anywhere it has been deviated from. . . .

. . . it tends to check the license of interpretation. I mean of course, what has been distinguished by the name of *liberal* interpretation: that delicate and important branch of judiciary power, the concession of which is dangerous, the denial ruinous.

Now this necessity supposing it to exist from whence does it arise? From the want of circumspection or advertency, from the want of amplitude or discrimination in the views of the legislator. In the beginning, one might almost say till now, legislators have felt their way rather than seen it, taking up the ground by bits and parcels and without so much as attempting any general survey of the whole. In consequence no order, no connexity: no steps taken for guarding against oversights and omissions. The best-imagined provision might perhaps have done more mischief than good unless molded into form by the prudence of the Judge. On the one hand, the obligative part was not wide enough to embrace the mischief: on the other hand the qualificative parts were not wide enough to yield shelter to innocence or to afford the necessary range to power. But the incidents which foresight could not

present to the legislator, experience would from time to time be presenting to the Judge. What was to be done? Was the continual recurrency of partial evil to be suffered to reduce, to fritter away into nothing the hopes of general good? This was not to be endured. Here then in the very cradle of legislative empire grew up another power, in words the instrument of the former, in reality continually its censor and not infrequently its successful rival. How difficult to distinguish what the legislator would have adopted had he adverted to it, from what he did actually advert to and reject. How easy to establish the one under pretense of looking for the other? especially when if truth refused her aid, fiction was ready at their call. The legislator, perhaps an unlettered soldier, perhaps a narrow-minded priest, perhaps an interrupted, unwieldy, heterogeneous, unconnected multitude: the judicature, a permanent, compact experienced body, composed of connected individuals, participating in the same affections and pursuing the same views. And thus sprung up by degrees another branch of customary law, which striking its roots into the substance of the statute law, infected it with its own characteristic obscurity, uncertainty and confusion.

For disorders proceeding from the want of plan, a regular plan may at length, it is hoped, provide a powerful palliative at least, and in time it is hoped, a complete and effectual remedy. To supersede as far as may be the necessity of discretionary interpretation, the business is to give amplitude enough in the first place to the imperative matter in the code. . . .

. . . Human reason does not seem to be yet far enough advanced to warrant our laying the discretionary mode of interpretation under an absolute prohibition in all cases whatsoever. It remains therefore to contrive some expedient for guarding that power from abuses during the exercise of it, from the inconveniences it is attended with, and confining it within its proper limits. For these purposes a plan is contrived, which will be developed at length in a subsequent part of the work. Let the judge be required wheresoever he determines in the way of liberal interpretation, to declare openly his having done so: at the same time drawing up *in terminis* a general provision expressive of the attention he thinks the case requires, which let him certify to the legislator: and let the alteration so made if not negatived by the legislator within such a time have the force of law. By this means the legislator would see what the Judge was doing: the Judge would be a counsel to him, not a control, the sceptre would remain unshaken in his hands. The experiments of the one would be corrected by the experience of the other: the simplicity of the legislative plan would be preserved from violation: the corrective applied would be applied, not in the obscure, voluminous and unsteady form of customary jurisprudence, but in the concise and perspicuous form of statute law. . . .

Legislation is a state of warfare: political mischief is the enemy: the legislator is the commander: the moral and religious sanctions his allies: punishments and rewards (raised some of them out of his own resources, others borrowed from those allies) the forces he has under his command: punishments his regular standing force; rewards an occasional subsidiary force too weak to act alone: the mechanical branch of legislation, the branch we have been treating of in the present chapter, the art of tactics: direct legislation a formal attack made with the main body of his forces in the open field: indirect legislation a secret plan of connected and long-concerted operations to be executed in the way of stratagem or *petite guerre*. All these heads except this last have been discussed already. It remains that we should say something of this irregular system of warfare. . . .

. . . But to love power is one thing: and to love the labour which alone can qualify a man to exercise it as he should do, is another.

Laws that are hasty have often been cited in proof of the necessity of interpretation: but methinks it might also have been well at the same time to have observed that they are indications equally strong of imbecility and short sightedness on the part of the legislator: that they bespeak the infancy of the science: and that when once it shall have been brought to a state of tolerable maturity the demand for interpretation will have been in great measure if not altogether taken away.

Now the mischief in cases of this sort being manifest, it was necessary to apply a remedy. Such a remedy if applied by the legislature itself would at any rate be attended with some of the inconveniences of an *ex post facto* law if extensive of the obligation, none if limitative of it. But perhaps the legislative power is vested in a body: and that body is not or cannot be assembled: or it is so constituted that it is next to impossible to consult it: or cases which call for an interpretation of this sort are so frequent and many of them so trifling that there would be no end of consultations: for these reasons or for others not so good, properly or improperly this power has always been assumed and exercised by the Judge. As fast as it has been exercised the cases in which it has been exercised have been noted down: general rules have been formed from the observation of those cases: and thus the customary law breaking through its original barriers has spread itself like a plague over the surface of the statute law, infecting it with its own characteristic obscurity, uncertainty and confusion.

To a mischief thus flagrant it is impossible to turn our thoughts without looking eagerly after a remedy. Let us not despair. . . . Let the legislator have carried his views over the whole field of human action, let him have given a certain degree of perfection to his method, of regularity and consistency to his laws, he may bring them to such a degree of perfection, that they shall need no more interpretation than he himself is equal to supply.

In a system thus constructed upon this plan, a man need but open the book in order to inform himself what the aspect borne by the law bears to every imaginable act that can come within the possible sphere of human agency. . . .

In a map of the law executed upon such a plan there are no *terrae incognitae*, no blank spaces: nothing is at least omitted, no thing unprovided for: the vast and hitherto shapeless expanse of Jurisprudence is collected and condensed into a compact sphere which the eye at a moment's warning can traverse in all imaginable directions.

Such are the fruits of a method planned under the auspices of the principle of utility, in which the laws are ranged according to the ends they have in view.

12

Friedrich Carl von Savigny

1779–1861

Savigny's ancestors were upper-class citizens of Lorraine who moved into Germany when Lorraine first became a division of France. The Savignys were important people who held high public office, wrote notable books, and associated with nobles of the upper Rhine.

Though Friedrich Carl was an orphan, he was well cared for and well educated. At sixteen he was ready for university and entered Marburg. He followed the current fad of educational wandering and spent terms at several different German universities. He returned to Marburg for a doctor's degree when he was twenty-one.

For several years he stayed on at Marburg lecturing on legal subjects. At twenty-four he published his first work of importance—a treatise on the law of possession. It was hailed by leading jurists as a landmark in legal thought. John Austin said of it, "Of all books on law, the most consummate and masterly."

At twenty-five he married a sister of the poet, Brentano, and journeyed to Paris for research in the French National Library. Four years later he was called to Bavaria University to teach Roman Law. Soon after he was called to Berlin University as Professor of Roman Law. At Berlin he organized a faculty court of appeals to review cases submitted by trial courts—a common pattern of German judicial organization at the time. He also served both as third rector of the university and as private law tutor to the Crown Prince of Prussia.

In 1814 he wrote *Of the Vocation of Our Age for Legislation and Jurisprudence,* excerpts from which follow this note. *Vocation* was a reply to a pamphlet written by the then-prominent German jurist Thibaut. Napoleon's yoke had just been thrown off Germany, and Thibaut proposed cleansing German honor by a new code of laws for the German States to replace the imposed Code Napoleon. Savigny opposed this codification. In the next two decades Savigny's published works were mountainous. He did a multi-volumed history of Roman Law in the Middle Ages and a tremendous systematic work on Modern Roman Law. He was a founder of a journal for the "historical school" of jurisprudence. For a while he left teaching to be Great Counsellor of Prussia, and accomplished important reforms in commercial and family law.

His declining years were marked by appreciation and honor. He produced legal writing down to the day of his death at eighty-two. In the preceding generation, Jeremy Bentham had made the outstanding case for codification. Savigny, the foe of codes, does not mention Bentham in *Vocation.*

OF
THE VOCATION
OF
OUR AGE
FOR
LEGISLATION AND
JURISPRUDENCE *

II

Origin of Positive Law

. . . In the earliest times to which authentic history extends, the law will be found to have already attained a fixed character, peculiar to the people, like their language, manners and constitution. Nay, these phenomena have no separate existence, they are but the particular faculties and tendencies of an individual people, inseparably united in nature, and only wearing the semblance of distinct attributes to our view. That which binds them into one whole is the common conviction of the people, the kindred consciousness of an inward necessity, excluding all notion of an accidental and arbitrary origin. . . .

This youth of nations is poor in ideas, but enjoys a clear perception of its relations and circumstances, and feels and brings the whole of them into play; whilst we, in our artificial complicated existence, are overwhelmed by our own riches, instead of enjoying and controlling them. This plain natural state is particularly observable in the law; and as, in the case of an individual, his family relations and patrimonial property may possess an additional value in his eyes from the effect of association,—so on the same principle, it is possible for the rules of the law itself to be amongst the objects of popular faith. But these moral faculties require some bodily existence to fix them. Such, for language, is its constant uninterrupted use; such, for the constitution, are palpable and public powers,—but what supplies its place with regard to the law? In our times it is

* Translated by Abram Hayward, published by Littlewood & Co., London (1831).

supplied by rules, communicated by writing and word of mouth. This mode of fixation, however, presupposes a high degree of abstraction, and is, therefore, not practicable in the early time alluded to. On the contrary, we then find symbolical acts universally employed where rights and duties were to be created or extinguished: it is their palpableness which externally retains law in a fixed form; and their solemnity and weight correspond with the importance of the legal relations themselves, which have been already mentioned as peculiar to this period. . . . These formal acts may be considered as the true grammar of law in this period; and it is important to observe that the principal business of the early Roman jurists consisted in the preservation and accurate application of them. We in latter times, have often made light of them as the creation of barbarism and superstition, and have prided ourselves on not having them, without considering that we, too, are at every step beset with legal forms, to which, in fact, only the principal advantages of the old forms are wanting,—namely, their palpableness, and the popular prejudice in their favour, whilst ours are felt by all as something arbitrary, and therefore burthensome. In such partial views of early times we resemble the travellers, who remark, with great astonishment, that in France the little children, nay, even the common people, speak French with perfect fluency.

But this organic connection of law with the being and character of the people, is also manifested in the progress of the times; and here, again, it may be compared with language. For law, as for language, there is no moment of absolute cessation; it is subject to the same movement and development as every other popular tendency; and this very development remains under the same law of inward necessity, as in its earliest stages. Law grows with the growth, and strengthens with the strength of the people, and finally dies away as the nation loses its nationality. . . .

. . . With the progress of civilization, national tendencies become more and more distinct, and what otherwise would have remained common, becomes appropriated to particular classes; the jurists now become more and more a distinct class of the kind; law perfects its language, takes a scientific direction, and, as formerly it existed in the consciousness of the community, it now devolves upon the jurists, who thus, in this department, represent the community. Law is henceforth more artificial and complex, since it has a twofold life; first, as part of the aggregate existence of the community, which it does not cease to be; and, secondly, as a distinct branch of knowledge in the hands of the jurists. All the latter phenomena are explicable by the co-operation of those two principles of existence; and it may now be understood, how even the whole of that immense detail might arise from organic causes, without any exertion of arbitrary will or intention. For the sake of brevity, we call technically speaking, the connection of law with the general existence of the people—the political element; and the distinct scientific existence of law—the technical element.

At different times, therefore, amongst the same people, law will be natural law (in a different sense from our law of nature), or learned law, as the one or the other principle prevails, between which a precise line of demarcation is obviously impossible . . . The sum, therefore, of this theory is that all law is originally formed in the manner, in which, in ordinary but not quite correct language, customary law is said to have been formed: i.e. that it is first developed by custom and popular faith, next by jurisprudence,—everywhere, therefore, by internal silently-operating powers, not by the arbitrary will of a law-giver.

This state of things has hitherto been only historically set forth; whether it be praiseworthy and desirable, the following enquiry will show. . . .

III

Legislative Provisions and Law Books

Legislation, properly so called, not unfrequently exercises an influence upon particular portions of the law; but the causes of this influence vary greatly. In the first place, the legislator, in altering the existing law, may be influenced by high reasons of state . . . That enactments of this kind easily become a baneful corruption of the law, and that they should be most sparingly employed, must strike any one who consults history. In these, the technical part of law is only looked at for the sake of the form and the connection with the whole remaining law, which connection makes this branch of legislation more difficult than it is commonly supposed to be. Of a much less doubtful character is a second influence of legislation upon the law. Particular rules, indeed, may be doubtful, or from their very nature may have varying and ill-defined limits, as, for example, all prescription; whilst the administration of the law requires limits defined with the greatest possible precision. Here a kind of legislation may be introduced, which comes to the aid of custom, removes these doubts and uncertainties, and thus brings to the light, and keeps pure, the real law, the proper will of the people. . . .

But these kinds of partial influence are not intended when, as in our times, the necessity of a code is spoken of. Rather, in this case, the following is meant:—The nation is to examine its whole stock of law, and put it into writing, so that the book, thus formed, shall henceforth be not one amongst other legal authorities, but that all others which have been hitherto in force, shall be in force no longer. The first question, therefore, is, where are the materials for this code to come from? According to a theory already mentioned, it has been maintained by many, that these are to be supplied by the universal law of nature, without reference to any thing existing. But those who had to do with the execution of such plans, or were otherwise acquainted with practical law, have laid no stress upon this extravagant and wholly groundless theory; and it is unanimously agreed that the existing law is to be laid down with merely such alterations and improvements as might be thought necessary on grounds of expediency . . . The substance of a code would, accordingly, be two-fold; it would be composed partly of the existing law, and partly of new provisions. So far as the last are concerned, their occurrence on the occasion of a code, is obviously a matter of accident; they might have been proposed singly at any other time . . . Not, therefore, to confuse our inquiry, we will lay new laws entirely aside, and look only to the essentials of the code. In this case we must consider the code as the exposition of the aggregate existing law, with exclusive validity conferred by the state itself. . . .

. . . This in every case is wholly technical, and as such belongs to the jurists; since, as regards the substance of the code we are supposing, the political element of the law has long worked itself out, and there is nothing to do but to discriminate and expound the result, which is the peculiar function of technical jurisprudence.

The requisites of such a code, and the expectations from it, are of two kinds. With regard to the condition of the law itself, the highest degree of precision is to be looked for, and, at the same time, the highest degree of uniformity in the application. The limits of its jurisdiction are to be more clearly defined and regulated, since a general national law is to replace a varying customary law. . . .

That this first benefit depends upon the excellence of the execution, must be obvious to all, and, therefore, in this respect, it is just as possible to lose as to gain. Well deserving of consideration is what Bacon, from the magnitude of his intellect and his experience, said of a work of the kind. He is of opinion, that it should never be engaged in without a pressing necessity, and even then with particular care of the legal authorities in force; by, in the first place, the scrupulous adoption of every thing that is applicable in them, and, secondly, by their being preserved and constantly consulted. Above all, he says, the work should only be undertaken in times which in civilization and knowledge surpass the preceding, for it would be truly lamentable were the produc-

tions of former times to be mutilated by the ignorance of the present . . . The existing law, which is not to be changed, but retained, must be thoroughly understood and properly expressed. *That* (the understanding of it) concerns the substance, *this* (the expression) the form.

As regards the substance, the most important and difficult part is the completeness of the code. . . .

The code, then, as it is intended to be the only law-authority, is actually to contain, by anticipation, a decision for every case that may arise. This has been often conceived, as if it were possible and advantageous to obtain, by experience, a perfect knowledge of the particular cases, and then to decide each by a corresponding provision of the code. But whoever has considered law-cases attentively, will see at a glance that this undertaking must fail, because there are positively no limits to the varieties of actual combinations of circumstances. In all the new codes, indeed, all appearance of an attempt to obtain this material perfection has been given up, without, however, establishing any thing in its stead. But there is certainly a perfection of a different kind, which may be illustrated by a technical expression of geometry. In every triangle, namely, there are certain data, from the relations of which all the rest are necessarily deducible: thus, given two sides and the included angle, the whole triangle is given. In like manner, every part of our law has points by which the rest may be given: these may be termed the leading axioms. To distinguish these, and deduce from them the internal connection, and the precise degree of affinity which subsist between all juridical notions and rules, is amongst the most difficult of the problems of jurisprudence. Indeed, it is peculiarly this which gives our labours the scientific character. If then the code be formed in a time which is unequal to this art, the following evils are inevitable: The administration of justice is ostensibly regulated by the code, but really by something else, external to the code, acting as the true dominant authority. This false appearance, however, is productive of the most disastrous effects. For the code, by its novelty, its connection with the prevailing notions of the age, and its external influence, will infallibly attract all attention to itself, away from the real law-authority; so that the latter, left in darkness and obscurity, will derive no assistance from the moral energies of the nation, by which alone it can attain to a satisfactory state . . . If to this imperfect knowledge of the leading principles, be added the above mentioned aim at material completeness, particular decisions unnoticed by the framers, will be constantly crossing and contradicting each other, which will gradually come to light by practice only, and, in the case of a bad administration of justice, not even by that. . . .

But, besides the substance, the form of the code must be taken into consideration, for the framer may have fully studied the law on which he is at work, and his production may, notwithstanding, fail of its end, if he have not withal the art of exposition. What this exposition ought to be, is better shown by instances of successful or unsuccessful application, than by general rules. It is commonly required that the language of the law should be particularly distinguished by brevity. Certainly brevity may be extremely effective, as is clear from the examples of the Roman Decrees and Edicts. But there is also a dry, inexpressive brevity, adopted by him who does not understand the use of language as an instrument, and which remains wholly ineffective; numerous examples of it are to be found in the laws and records of the middle ages. On the other hand, diffuseness in law authorities may be very exceptionable, nay, wholly intolerable, as in many of the constitutions of Justinian, and in most of the novels of the Theodosian Code; but there is also an intelligent and very effective diffuseness, and this is discernible in many parts of the Pandects.

Putting together what has been said above concerning the requisites of a really good code, it is clear that very few ages will be found qualified for it. Young nations, it is true, have the clearest perception of their law, but their codes are defective in language and logical skill . . . In declining ages, on the other hand, almost every thing is wanting—knowledge of the matter, as well as language. There thus remains only a middle period; that which, (as regards the law, although not necessarily in any other respect,) may be accounted the summit of civilization. But such an age has no need of a code for itself: it would merely compose one for a succeeding and less fortunate age, as we lay up provisions for winter. But an age is seldom disposed to be so provident for posterity.

IV

Roman Law

. . . If, in the first place, we consider the juridical works of Justinian, consequently, that form in which the Roman law has come down to modern Europe, we cannot but remark a season of decline in them. The nucleus of these codes is a compilation from the works of a classical age, which must now be regarded as lost and irrecoverable, and Justinian himself does not conceal this. . . .

. . . Every thing depends upon the possession of the leading principles, and it is this very possession which constitutes the greatness of the Roman jurists. The notions and axioms of their science do not appear to have been arbitrarily produced; these are actual beings, whose existence and genealogy have become known to them by long and intimate acquaintance. For this reason, their whole mode of proceeding has a certainty which is found no where else, except in mathematics; and it may be said, without exaggeration, that they calculate with their notions. But this method is by no means the exclusive peculiarity of one or a few great writers; on the contrary, it is common to all, and although a very different measure of felicitous application falls to the lot of each, still the method is universally the same. Indeed, had we their works complete before us, we should discover in them much less individuality than in any other literature; they all co-operate, as it were, in one and the same great work; and the idea upon which the compilation of the Pandects is based, is, therefore, not to be altogether rejected . . . Their theory and practice are the same; their theory is framed for immediate application, and their practice is uniformly ennobled by scientific treatment. They see in every principle a case of application, in every case the rule by which it is to be decided; and in the ease with which they pass from generals to particulars, and back again from particulars to generals, their mastery is undeniable . . . Their art is, at the same time, adapted to the perception and communication of science, without however losing the palpableness and vigour which are ordinarily peculiar to early times.

This highly cultivated state of jurisprudence amongst the Romans at the beginning of the third century of the Christian aera, is so well worthy of note, that we must also pay some attention to its history. It would be very wrong to regard it as the pure creation of a highly favoured age, unconnected with the preceding. On the contrary, the materials of their science were handed down to the jurists of this time, a great part of them even from the time of the free republic. But not only these materials, but that admirable method itself, had root in the time of freedom. What, indeed, made Rome great, was the quick, lively, political spirit, which made her ever ready so to renovate the forms of her constitution, that the new merely ministered to the development of the old,—a judicious mixture of the adhesive and progressive principles. This spirit was equally operative in the constitution and the law; but, in the former, it was extinguished before the end of the republic, whilst, in the latter, it might still operate for centuries to come, because the same causes of corruption did not exist in it as in the constitution. In the law, consequently, the general Roman character was strongly marked,—the holding fast by the long-established, without allowing themselves to be fettered by it, when it no longer harmonised with a new popular prevailing theory. For

this reason, the history of the Roman law, down to the classical age, exhibits everywhere a gradual, wholly-organic development. If a new form is framed, it is immediately bound up with an old established one, and thus participates in the maturity and fixedness of the latter . . . Just as it has been observed above, that jurisprudence in its classical days was common to the jurists in general,—in like manner do we now perceive a similar community between the most different ages, and we are compelled to ascribe that juridical genius to which the excellence of the Roman law is attributable, not to one particular age, but to the nation in general. . . .

. . . the Roman law, like customary law, has formed itself almost entirely from within; and the more detailed history of it shows how little, on the whole, express legislation affected it, so long as it continued in a living state. Even with regard to what has been said above of the necessity for a code, the history of the Roman law is exceedingly instructive. So long as the law was in active progression, no code was discovered to be necessary, not even at the time when circumstances were most favourable for it. For in the times of the classical jurists, there would have been no difficulty in framing an excellent code. The three most celebrated jurists, too—Papinian, Ulpian and Paulus,— were *praefecti praetorio.* These assuredly were wanting neither in interest for the law nor in power to procure the formation of a code, had they deemed it advantageous or necessary; yet we find no trace of such an experiment. But when, at an earlier period, Caesar, in the consciousness of his power and of the corruption of the age, resolved on being absolute in Rome, he is said to have formed the conception of a code in our meaning of the term. And when, in the sixth century, all intellectual life was dead, the wrecks of better times were collected to supply the demand of the moment . . . The idea of these codes, however, was evidently suggested only by the extreme decay of the law. . . .

v
Civil Law in Germany

Up to a very recent period a uniform system of law was in practical operation throughout the whole of Germany under the name of the common law, more or less modified by the provincial laws, but nowhere altogether without force. The principal sources of this common law were the lawbooks of Justinian . . . The Roman law, it is said, has deprived us of our nationality, and nothing but the exclusive attention paid to it by our jurists, has hindered our indigenous law from attaining to an equally independent and scientific condition. Complaints of this kind have a degree of hollowness and groundlessness about them, insomuch as they assume that to be accidental and arbitrary, which would never have come to pass, or, at any rate, would never have endured, without some internal necessity. Besides, an exclusive national development, like that of the ancients, is not generally to be met with in the course, which nature has indicated to the moderns. As the religion of nations is not peculiarly their own, and their literature as little free from the most powerful external influence,—upon the same principle, their having also a foreign and general system of law, does not appear unnatural . . . But there is another radical mistake in this theory. Even without the intermixture of the Roman law, an undisturbed progressive formation of German law would have been impossible . . . Rome itself, the original state, having remained its focus till the downfall of the Western Empire; whilst the German races emigrated—conquered and were conquered by turns . . . The very changes in the constitution under Augustus and Constantine had no immediate effect upon the law . . . In Germany, on the contrary, as soon as the feudal system was completely established, nothing peculiar to the old race of people was left; every thing, even to forms and names, had undergone a radical change, and this entire revolution was already decided, when the Roman law was introduced.

. . . Not only is there in the provincial laws themselves, much law purely Roman, and only intelligible in its original Roman context; but even in those parts where its decisions have been designedly passed by, it has often decided the interpretation and execution of the newly introduced law, so that the question which ought to be solved by this new law, cannot be understood without the Roman law. . . .

Of this extremely complicated state of the sources of law in Germany, arising from the connection of the common law (very complicated in itself) with the provincial laws, the loudest complaints have been raised . . . .

In the first place, the excessive duration of lawsuits in many countries of Germany, is said to have been occasioned by it . . . It is really paying too high a compliment to the judges in such countries, to believe that so much time is devoted to the anxious consideration of difficult points. They are aided, in such matters, by the first compendium or manual that comes to hand . . . This evil is attributable to faulty forms of proceeding, and the reform of these is one of the most pressing necessities; the sources of the law are guiltless of it. . . .

In the second place, the great diversity of the provincial laws is complained of; and this complaint is not confined to the differences between different German states; for often, even in the same country, provinces and towns have systems peculiar to themselves. . . .

The most important argument urged in favour of the uniformity of the law, is, that our love for our common country is enhanced by it, but weakened by a multiplicity of particular laws . . . .

The well-being of every organic being, (consequently of states,) depends on the maintenance of an equipoise between the whole and its parts—on each having its due . . . A lively affection for the whole can only proceed from the thorough participation in all particular relations; and he only who takes good care of his own family, will be a truly good citizen. It is, therefore, an error to suppose that the common weal would gain new life by the annihilation of all individual relations. Were it possible to generate a peculiar corporate spirit in every class, every town, nay, every village, the common weal would gain new strength from this heightened and multiplied individuality. When, therefore, the influence of law on the love of country, is the question, the particular laws of particular provinces and states are not to be regarded as obstacles. In this point of view, the law merits praise, in so far as it falls in, or is adapted to fall in, with the feelings and consciousness of the people; blame, if, like an uncongenial and arbitrary thing, it leaves the people without participation. That, however, will be oftener and more easily the case with the distinct systems of particular districts, although it certainly is not every municipal law that will be truly popular.

Indeed, for this political end, no state of law appears more favourable than that which was formerly general in Germany: great variety and individuality in particulars, but with the common law for the general foundation, constantly reminding all the Germanic nations of their indissoluble unity. The most pernicious, however, in this point of view, is the light and capricious alteration of law; and even were uniformity and fitness attainable by change, the advantage would not be worth naming in comparison with the political disadvantage just alluded to. That which is thus constructed by men's hands before our eyes, will always hold a very different place in popular estimation from that which has not so plain and palpable an origin; and when we, in our praiseworthy zeal, inveigh against this decision as a blind prejudice, we ought not to forget that all faith in, and feeling for, that which is not on a level with us, but more exalted than we, depends upon the same kind of spirit. This consideration might well lead us to doubt of the impropriety of the decision.

VI

Our Vocation for Legislation

. . . Bacon required that the age in which a code should be formed, should excel preceding ages in intelligence . . . Very recently, the opponents of the Roman law have not unfrequently laid particular stress upon such arguments as the following:—Reason is common to all nations and ages alike, and as we have, moreover, the experience of former times to resort to, all that we do must infallibly be better than all that has been done before.—But even this opinion, that every age has a vocation for every thing, is a prejudice of the most dangerous kind. In the fine arts we are obliged to acknowledge the contrary; why are we unwilling to make the same admission, with respect to the government and the law? . . .

. . . If, at any time, a decided and commendable tendency be distinguishable in the public mind, this may be preserved and confirmed, but it cannot be produced, by legislation; and where it is altogether wanting, every attempt that may be made to establish an exhaustive system of legislation, will but increase the existing uncertainty, and add to the difficulties of the cure. . . .

Unluckily, during the whole of the eighteenth century Germany was very poor in great jurists. There were numbers of laborious men, it is true, by whom very valuable preparatory labours were executed, but more than this was seldom done. A twofold spirit is indispensable to the jurist; the historical, to seize with readiness the peculiarities of every age and every form of law; and the systematic, to view every notion and every rule in lively connection and co-operation with the whole, that is, in the only true and natural relation. This twofold scientific spirit is very rarely found amongst the jurists of the eighteenth century; and, in particular, some superficial speculations in philosophy had an extremely unfavourable effect. A just appreciation of the time in which one lives is very difficult: still, unless all signs deceive, a spirit has come upon our science, capable of elevating it for the future to the rank of a national system. Little, indeed, of this improvement is yet produced, and upon this ground I deny our capacity for the production of a good code. . . .

If then, we have really nothing which is necessary to the formation of a good code, we are not to believe that the actual undertaking would be nothing more than a disappointment, which, at the worst, would merely not have advanced us. The great danger inevitably impending when a very defective and shallow state of knowledge is fixed by positive authority, has been already spoken of; and this danger would be great in proportion to the vastness of the undertaking and its connection with the wakening spirit of nationality . . . Vigorous exertions are undeniably making, and it is impossible to say how much good we subtract from the future by confirming present deficiencies. . . .

An important point still remains to be considered,—the language. I ask of any one who knows what good appropriate expression is, and who does not regard language as a common tool, but as a scientific instrument, whether we possess a language in which a code could be composed? I am far from questioning the strength of the old German language; but that even this is not now fit for the purpose, is to me a proof the more, that we are behindhand in this circle of thought. The moment our science improves, it will be seen of how much avail our language, by its freshness and primitive vigour, will prove. What is more, I believe that, of late, we have even retrograded in this respect. . . .

I know what answer might be given to these reasons; even admitting all of them, it may be said, the powers of the human mind are boundless, and by reasonable exertion a work, even in these times, might be soon produced, in which none of these defects would be traceable. Well, any one may

make the attempt, our age is not an inattentive one, and there is no danger that actual success will be overlooked. . . .

VIII

What Are We to do Where There Are no Codes

. . . In the countries where the common law prevails, as in all others, a good state of the law will depend on three things; first, sufficient authorities; secondly, a sufficient ministry of justice; lastly, good forms of procedure. . . .

With regard, in the first place, to the authorities, to which even the proposed code was to conform, the same mixed system of common-law and provincial-law, which formerly prevailed throughout the whole of Germany, ought, in my opinion, to be substituted for the code, or retained where the code was not in force: I hold these authorities to be sufficient, nay, excellent, provided jurisprudence does what it ought to do, and what can only be done by means of it. For if we consider our actual condition, we find ourselves in the midst of an immense mass of juridical notions and theories which have descended, and been multiplied, from generation to generation. At present, we do not possess and master this matter, but are controlled and mastered by it, whether we will or not. This is the ground of all the complaints of the present state of our law, which I admit to be well-founded: this, also, is the sole cause of the demand for codes. This matter encompasses and hems us in on all sides, often without our knowing it. People might think to annihilate it, by severing all historical associations, and beginning an entirely new life. But such an undertaking would be built on a delusion. For it is impossible to annihilate the impressions and modes of thought of the jurists now living,— impossible to change completely the nature of existing legal relations; and on this twofold impossibility rests the indissoluble organic connection of generations and ages; between which, development only, not absolute end and absolute beginning, is conceivable. In particular, the altering of single, nay of many, legal doctrines, is doing absolutely nothing towards this object; for, as before observed, the modes of thought, with the speculations and questions that may arise, will still be influenced by the pre-existing system, and the subserviency of the past to the present will manifest itself even where the present is purposely opposed to the past. There is consequently no mode of avoiding this overruling influence of the existing matter; it will be injurious to us so long as we ignorantly submit to it; but beneficial, if we oppose to it a vivid creative energy,—obtain the mastery over it by a thorough grounding in history, and thus appropriate to ourselves the whole intellectual wealth of preceding generations. . . .

Only when by zealous study we shall have perfected our knowledge, and, more particularly, sharpened our historical and political sense, will a sound judgment on the matter that has come down to us be possible. Until then it might be more prudent to pause before considering the existing law as loose practice, impolitic exclusiveness, and mere juridical apathy: but, most especially, to hesitate upon the application of the dissecting knife to our present system. In applying it we might strike unawares upon sound flesh, and thus charge ourselves with the heaviest of all responsibilities to posterity. The historical spirit, too, is the only protection against a species of self-delusion, which is ever and anon reviving in particular men, as well as in whole nations and ages; namely, the holding that which is peculiar to ourselves to be common to human nature in general . . . We meet with people daily, who hold their juridical notions and opinions to be the offspring of pure reason, for no earthly reason but because they are ignorant of their origin. When we lose sight of our individual connection with the great entirety of the world and its history, we necessarily see our thoughts in a false light

of universality and originality. There is only the historical sense to protect us against this, to turn which upon ourselves is indeed the most difficult of applications.

One might be tempted to admit this historical grounding of the matter in which we are necessarily involved, to be necessary in our present position, but, at the same time, to consider it an evil, from its engrossing energies which might be directed to more useful ends. This would be a melancholy view, because the feeling of an inevitable evil would be excited by it; but we may console ourselves with the conviction that it is false. On the contrary, this necessity is to be deemed a great good in itself. In the history of all considerable nations we find a transition from circumscribed, but fresh and vigorous, individuality, to undefined universality. The law undergoes the same, and in it, likewise, the consciousness of nationality may, in the end, be lost. Thus it happens, that, when old nations reflect how many peculiarities of their law have already dropped off, they easily fall into the error just mentioned, holding all the residue of their law to be a *jus quod naturalis ratio apud omnes homines constituit.* That, at the same time, the peculiar advantage, by which the old law was characterised, is lost, is obvious. To talk of going back to this past time, were a vain and idle proposition; but it is a wholly different affair to keep its distinguishing excellencies fully in view, and thus guard our minds against the narrowing influence of the present,—which is certainly both practicable and salutary. History, even in the infancy of a people, is ever a noble instructress, but in ages such as ours she has yet another and holier duty to perform. For only through her can a lively connection with the primitive state of the people be kept up; and the loss of this connection must take away from every people the best part of its spiritual life. That, consequently, by which according to this theory, the common law and the provincial laws are to become truly useful and unobjectionable as authorities, is the strict historical method of jurisprudence . . . Its object is to trace every established system to its root, and thus discover an organic principle, whereby that which still has life, may be separated from that which is lifeless and only belongs to history. . . .

. . . It is not difficult to say how the old jurists are to be studied, though difficult to make it obvious without actual trial; they are not merely to remain a dead letter in the schools, but to be regenerated; we are to read and think in their spirit, as in that of any other authors whom we thoroughly appreciate; we are to familiarize ourselves with their modes of thought, and be so thoroughly imbued with them, as to compose in their style, and on their principles, and thus continue, in its true spirit, the work they were prevented from consummating. That this is possible, is one of my liveliest convictions. The first requisite is certainly a sound knowledge of legal history, and (which necessarily results from it) the confirmed habit of viewing every notion and every doctrine in its proper historical light. . . .

. . . A free communication between the Law-Faculties and the Courts, which has been recently proposed, would be an excellent mode of bringing about this approximation of Theory and Practice . . . This connection of practice with a vigorous constantly progressing theory, is the only means of gaining a constant supply of men of talent for the Bench. The situation of judge, it is true, may be honourable and respectable without this; he may, moreover, be constantly improving himself by occupations, unconnected with his vocation, such as the disposition of the individual may incline him to; but it will be a very different matter, should the vocation itself, from its connexion with the whole, assume a scientific character and become itself a means of improvement. Such a state of things alone will satisfy all demands. The individual judge will no longer serve as a mere instrument, but be of a liberal and honourable calling, and the administration of justice will be really and scientifically complete . . . The most unfavourable state of things, in this respect, is undeniably that, in which the judge is to be tied down to the mechanical application of a given text, which he is not allowed to interpret; if this be considered as the extreme point upon the one side, the extreme point on the other would be, that the judge should have to find the law for every case; all arbitrary discretion, however, being excluded by the certainty resulting from a strict scientific method. But to this second point, it is not impossible to approximate, at least; and, on attaining it, the most ancient judicial organization of Germany would be revived in a renovated form.

I have above assumed three things to be necessary:—law-authorities, ministry of justice, and forms of procedure, all in good condition. How the authorities are to be based on a profound and comprehensive science, has been shown; as also how, by the same means, the ministry of justice may be rendered truly fit for this vocation. But both will be insufficient, if the form of procedure be bad. In this respect many countries of Germany require a speedy and effectual reform. . . .

According to this view, therefore, no code, it is true, would be formed in countries where the common law prevails; but it by no means follows that civil legislation would be altogether dispensed with. Independently of legislative provisions on political grounds (which do not belong to this place), it might be employed for two purposes: the decision of controversies (disputed points), and the recording of old customs . . . These controversies are not so very bad in reality. In the first place, we must not set down as a controversy every instance in which ignorance or stupidity has ever prosecuted an unsuccessful inquiry. In the second place, legislation need not trouble itself with such controversies as do indeed exist in the books, but are seldom forthcoming in practice. Deduct these two descriptions of cases, and much still remains to be done . . . These controversies, however, had perhaps better be decided in the form of provisional ordinances or directions to the courts, than by regular enactments, since the former would be less likely to prejudice the chance of a better foundation in theory.

The second object of legislation would be the recording of customary law, which might in this manner be subjected to a superintendance, such as that effected by means of the edict in Rome. It is not to be imagined that the code, hitherto opposed, would, after all, be let in in this manner, only under a different name; on the contrary, the difference concerns the very essence of the thing. For in this customary law, that only will be comprised which has been decided in actual practice, and this, now that the legislator has the decisions before him, will, beyond a doubt, be thoroughly comprehended; the code, on the contrary, is obliged to speak on every subject,—even when there is no immediate motive thereto, and no special observation supplies the requisite capacity,—merely in anticipation of future possible cases. . . .

. . . Let jurisprudence be once generally diffused amongst the jurists in the manner above-mentioned, and we again possess, in the legal profession, a subject for living customary law,—consequently, for real improvement . . . The historical matter of law, which now hems us in on all sides, will then be brought under subjection, and constitute our wealth. We shall then possess a truly national law, and a powerful expressive language will not be wanting to it. We may then give up the Roman law to history, and we shall have, not merely a feeble imitation of the Roman system, but a truly national and new system of our own. We shall have reached somewhat higher than to a merely sure and speedy administration of justice; that state of clear perceptiveness which is ordinarily peculiar to the law of young nations, will be combined with the height of scientific development. Then too, may future degenerate times be provided for, and then will be the time for considering whether this be done best by codes or in another form. . . .

13

Georg Wilhelm Friedrich Hegel

1770–1831

Many of the Hegels were petty officials. Georg's father was an orderly and conservative revenue officer. His mother came from a rung higher up the social ladder; she was an educated woman and taught Georg Latin in his early youth. She died when Georg was thirteen.

Georg was a conscientious school boy who took prizes for academic excellence and good conduct in every grade. He kept a compendium of writings on mathematics and morals. He wrote a diary in Latin—thin in substance but good practice for him.

At eighteen Hegel enrolled in the theological seminary at Tübigen. Extracurricular reading and writing often diverted him from religious subjects—he read Rousseau and wrote two translations of *Antigone* (one in prose and one in verse). Fellow students marked his wizened looks by calling him "Old Man." Some of his companions liked to engage him in serious discussion of Greek and Latin classics, but he and his friends found time for carousing German student life. Hegel got his doctor's degree on schedule and was awarded a theological certificate when he was twenty-three. He was certified to have high ability, average knowledge and work habits, but deficient in philosophy.

After he left the seminary, he took a job as a private tutor in an aristocratic family in Bern, Switzerland. Life was lonely in Bern, and Hegel became silent and self-absorbed. His leisure was spent in reading and essay writing. He studied politics (Bern's fiscal system, Hume, Montesquieu) and religion (the original records of Christianity). One of his writings was a Life of Jesus (ig-noring the doctrine of virgin birth) espousing the thesis that Jesus revealed man's destiny in his unity with God. Hegel's interest in polity and religion edged him toward philosophy, which became his central interest after he moved to a new tutoring job in Frankfort where he renewed his friendship with college companions given to philosophic speculations. In this period Hegel concluded that specialization is an enemy of wisdom, and he set about synthesizing religion, morality, government, art, and commerce. After the fashion of Savigny he invested national groups with personality and unity, with changing and developing national consciences.

Just before Hegel turned thirty his father died and left him a tiny legacy. He boldly quit family tutoring, moved to Jena, and set about qualifying for university teaching. His funds held out until his thesis was accepted and· he was certified as a Privatdozent and licensed to lecture to students for fees. He was not a popular lecturer and made only a bare living.

Napoleon's invasion of Jena in 1806 engulfed him in exciting and disrupting experiences. The fall of the Prussian government bothered him little; he thought it corrupt and stuffy. Plundering French soldiers broke into Hegel's lodging house; one had on a Legion of Honor ribbon; Hegel said to him that from one wearing that badge a simple man of letters had the right to expect honorable treatment; the appeal, for the moment, saved his meagre possessions. But when fire spread through the neighborhood, Hegel swept up the last pages of his *Pha-

nomenologie des Geistes and fled. After the battle of Jena, Hegel caught a glimpse of Napoleon riding through town on a white horse. He wrote a friend, "It is in truth a strange feeling to see an individual before one, who here, from one point, as he rides on his horse, is reaching over the world and remoulding it." One of his pupils wrote Hegel in despair about the Prussian defeat. He replied,

"Science . . . alone can keep us from taking events with the stupid astonishment of an animal, or with short-sighted cleverness, ascribing them to the accidents of the moment or the talents of an individual. . . . The French nation by the bath of its revolution, has been freed of many institutions . . . which . . . weighed upon it . . . as lifeless fetters. What, however, is more, the individuals of that nation have, in the shock of revolution, cast off the fear of death and the life of custom. . . . Hence especially comes their preponderance over the cloudy and undeveloped spirit of the Germans, who, however, if they are once forced to cast off their inertia, will rouse themselves into action, and preserving in their contact with outward things the intensity of their inner life, will perchance surpass their teachers."

Later his estimate of the effect of the French revolution was modified as he viewed history as a progressive manifestation of reason and concluded that true reform must be development, rather than departure, that true progress is the spirit of the years-to-come yearning to mix with current life.

In 1807 thirty-seven-year-old Hegel published his first important book, the *Phanomenologie*. But the war had left him destitute, and his living in post-war Jena was precarious. His editor's post on a Bamberg newspaper lasted a year. The work was deadly, since Napoleon let papers publish only the bare record of events without editorial comment. He was glad to leave to become Gymnasium Rector (high school principal) at Nuremberg—a post he held with grace and distinction for eight years. The students liked him and worked hard for him. In his classes he encouraged questions and interruptions and often spent a whole period discussing extemporaneously a difficulty raised by some student. He ran an orderly school, but allowed students almost complete freedom in sports and clubs. He contemptuously spurned the Pestalozzian version of progressive education (built on Rousseau's *Emilius*) which was permissive and individualized.

At forty-one Hegel married a girl of nineteen from an old Nuremberg family. They raised two sons; one (Karl) became a German historian of note. About this time Hegel wrote to a friend, "When a man has got work that suits him and a wife whom he loves, he may be said to have made up his accounts with life." But Hegel was far from resting on his accomplishments. The first two of his three volume *Wissenshaft der Logik* were published in 1812 and the third in 1816. Administrative work was becoming irksome. The older Hegel got, the more immature his gymnasium students seemed. His *Logik* was so well-received that he had calls to three universities.

He answered the call to Heidelberg. In his opening lecture he said to the Heidelbergers, "History shows us that even when all but the name of philosophy was lost in other lands, it has maintained itself as the peculiar possession of the German nation. We have received from nature the high calling to be guardians of this sacred fire . . ." During his two years at Heidelberg Hegel was withdrawn and studious. Students tagged him as idle because he spent so much time looking out of his study window. He seemed absent-minded; he was reported to have unknowingly stepped out of a shoe stuck in the mud and tramped on in one stockinged foot.

Two years later he moved to a professorship at Berlin University. Here he flowered as a lecturer; he was sometimes awkwardly halting on the podium, but he was capable of great eloquence and attracted hundreds to his classes. No longer did he welcome interruptions and questions; scholars out of sympathy with his system found him unbending. He drove his system home to Berlin students. His fame and influence transcended technical philosophy. He was often consulted by the government on academic appointments and policies. During this period Hegel wrote his *Philosophy of Right,* classroom lectures which were published in 1831; excerpts from that work follow this note. In 1830 he was Rector of Berlin University and in 1831 he was decorated by Frederick William III.

As Hegel matured his love of art grew; he spent time in galleries and most of his vacation trips took him to see important paintings and sculptures.

Hegel fell victim to the first great cholera epidemic. The plague hit Berlin in the summer of 1831. The Hegels moved to the suburbs to evade it. When the new school year started Hegel came back to town to resume his lectures. His first class was on a Thursday; that day and the following day he taught with special fire. Saturday he was around the university attending to trivial business. Sunday he was desperately ill and he died in his sleep that night.

Morris R. Cohen, writing in the *Encyclopaedia of Social Sciences* says, "If government and religion are no longer viewed exclusively as inventions but rather as natural growths in which continuity and inertia of the past are always to be reckoned with, the credit is largely due to Hegel." He also says, "Hegel's philosophy of law is in the main of a metaphysical type which clings to concepts that are high above, but do not advance, the analysis of actual problems."

PHILOSOPHY OF RIGHT *

PREFACE

. . . The truth about Right, Ethics, and the state is as old as its public recognition and formulation in the law of the land, in the morality of everyday life, and in religion. What more does this truth require—since the thinking mind is not content to possess it in this ready fashion? It requires to be grasped in thought as well; the content which is already rational in principle must win the *form* of rationality and so appear

* Translated by T. M. Knox, published by Clarendon Press, Oxford.

well-founded to untrammelled thinking. . . .

The unsophisticated heart takes the simple line of adhering with trustful conviction to what is publicly accepted as true . . . There may at once be raised the alleged difficulty of how it is possible, in an infinite variety of opinions, to distinguish and discover what is universally recognized and valid. . . . If they had been serious with what is universally accepted instead of busying themselves with the vanity and particularity of opinions and things, they would have clung to what is substantively right, namely to the commands of the ethical order and the state, and would have regulated their lives in accordance with these.

A more serious difficulty arises, however, from the fact that man thinks and tries to find in thinking both his freedom and the basis of ethical life. . . .

At the present time, the idea that freedom of thought, and of mind generally, evinces itself only in divergence from, indeed in hostility to, what is publicly recognized, might seem to be most firmly rooted in connexion with the state, and it is chiefly for this reason that a philosophy of the state might seem essentially to have the task of discovering and promulgating still another theory, and a special and original one at that. In examining this idea . . . we might suppose that no state or constitution had ever existed in the world at all or was even in being at the present time, but that . . . we had to start all over again from the beginning, and that the ethical world had just been waiting for such present-day projects, proofs, and investigations. So far as nature is concerned, people grant that . . . nature is inherently rational, and that what knowledge has to investigate and grasp in concepts is this actual reason present in it . . . The ethical world, on the other hand, the state, . . . is not allowed to enjoy the good fortune which springs from the fact that it is reason which has achieved power and mastery within that element and which maintains itself and has its home there. The universe of mind is supposed rather to be left to the mercy of chance and caprice, to be God-forsaken, and the result is that if the ethical world is Godless, truth lies outside it, and at the same time, since even so reason is supposed to be in it as well, truth becomes nothing but a problem. But it is this also that is to authorize . . . every thinker to take his own road . . . those who live their lives in the state as it actually exists here and now and find satisfaction there for their knowledge and volition, . . . laugh at these operations and affirmations, and regard them as an empty game. . . .

. . . What we have seen recent philosophical publications proclaiming with the maximum of pretension about the state has really justified anybody who cared to busy himself with the subject in this conviction that he could manufacture a philosophy of this kind himself without ado . . . besides this self-styled "philosophy" has expressly stated that 'truth itself cannot be known,' that that only is true which each individual allows to rise out of his heart, emotion, and inspiration about ethical institutions, especially about the state, the government, and the constitution. . . .

A ringleader of these hosts of superficiality, of these self-styled "philosophers," Herr Fries, did not blush . . . to express the following ideas . . . "In the people ruled by a genuine communal spirit, life for the discharge of all public business would come from below, from the people itself; living associations, indissolubly united by the holy chain of friendship, would be dedicated to every single project of popular education and popular service," and so on. This is the quintessence of shallow thinking, to base philosophic science not on the development of thought and the concept but on immediate sense-perception and the play of fancy. . . . According to a view of this kind, the world of ethics . . . should be given over—as in fact of course it is not—to the subjective accident of opinion and caprice. . . . Such sentiments assume even the guise of piety. . . . With godliness and the Bible, however, it has arrogated to itself the highest of justifications for despising the ethical order and the objectivity of law . . . But if it is piety of the right sort, it sheds the form of this emotional region so soon as it leaves the inner life, enters upon the daylight of the Idea's development and revealed riches, and brings with it, out of its inner worship of God, reverence for law and for an absolute truth exalted above the subjective form of feeling.

. . . Right and ethics, and the actual world of justice and ethical life, are understood through thoughts; through thoughts they are invested with a rational form, i.e. with universality and determinacy. This form is law . . . Law is the reason of the thing, and reason refuses to allow feeling to warm itself at its own private hearth. . . .

What is rational is actual and what is actual is rational. On this conviction the plain man like the philosopher takes his stand, and from it philosophy starts in its study of the universe of mind as well as the universe of nature . . . The great thing is to apprehend in the show of the temporal and transient the substance which is immanent and the eternal which is present. . . . The infinite variety of circumstance which is developed in this externality by the light of the essence glinting in it—this endless material and its organization—this is not the subject matter of philosophy.

This book, then, containing as it does the science of the state, is to be nothing other than the endeavour to apprehend and portray the state as something inherently rational. As a work of philosophy, it must be poles apart from an attempt to construct a state as it ought to be. . . . It is just as absurd to fancy that a philosophy can transcend its contemporary world as it is to fancy that an individual can overleap his own age, jump over Rhodes. If his theory really goes beyond the world as it is and builds an ideal one as it ought to be, that world exists indeed, but only in his opinions. . . .

BERLIN, *June 25,* 1820

INTRODUCTION

1. **The subject-matter of the philosophical science of right is the Idea of right, i.e. the**

concept of right together with the actualization of that concept. . . .

2. The science of right is a section of philosophy. Consequently, its task is to develop the Idea—the Idea being the rational factor in any object of study—out of the concept, or, what is the same thing, to look on at the proper immanent development of the thing itself. . . .

According to the abstract, non-philosphical, method of the sciences, the first thing sought and demanded is a definition . . . But the deduction of the definition is derived . . . so that it is based on human feelings and ideas. The correctness of the definition is then made to lie in its correspondence with current ideas. This method neglects what is all-essential for science—i.e. in respect of content, the absolute necessity of the thing (right, in this instance), and, in respect of form, the nature of the concept.

The truth is that in philosophical knowledge the necessity of a concept is the principal thing; and the process of its production as a result is its proof and deduction. Then, once its content has been shown in this way to be necessary on its own account, the second step is to look round for what corresponds to it in our ideas and language. But this concept as it actually is in its truth not only may be different from our common idea of it, but in fact must be different from it in form and outline. . . .

But while the above-mentioned abstract way of knowing with its formal definitions, syllogisms, proofs, and the like, is more or less a thing of the past, still it is a poor substitute which a different artifice has provided, namely to adopt and uphold Ideas . . . as immediate 'facts of consciousness' and to make into the source of right our natural or our worked up feelings and the inspirations of our own hearts. . . .

3. Right is positive in general (a) when it has the *form* of being valid in a particular state, and this legal authority is the guiding principle for the knowledge of right in this positive form, i.e. for the science of positive law. (b) Right in this positive form acquires a positive element in its *content*

(1) through the particular national character of a people, its stage of historical development, and the whole complex of relations connected with the necessities of nature;

(2) because a system of positive law must necessarily involve the application of the universal concept to particular, externally given, characteristics of objects and cases. . . .

(3) through the finally detailed provisions requisite for actually pronouncing judgment in court.

. . . That force and tyranny may be an element in law is accidental to law and has nothing to do with its nature. . . .

Natural law, or law from the philosophical point of view, is distinct from positive law; but to pervert their difference into an opposition and a contradiction would be a gross misunderstanding. . . .

As for the historical element in positive law . . . Montesquieu proclaimed the genuinely philosophical position, namely that legislation . . . is to be treated not as something isolated and abstract but rather as a subordinate moment in a whole, interconnected with all the other features which make up the character of a nation and an epoch . . . To consider particular laws as they appear and develop in time is a purely historical task. . . . This task is appreciated and rewarded in its own sphere and has no relation whatever to the philosophical study of the subject . . . Even if particular laws *are* both right and reasonable, still it is one thing to *prove* that they have that character . . . and quite another to describe their appearance in history or the circumstances, contingencies, needs, and events which brought about their enactment. . . .

. . . Once the origination of an institution has been shown to be wholly to the purpose and necessary in the circumstances of the time, the demands of history have been fulfilled. But if this is supposed to pass for a general justification of the thing itself, it turns out to be the opposite, because, since those circumstances are no longer present, the institution so far from being justified has by their disappearance lost its meaning and its right. . . .

4. The basis of right is, in general, mind; its precise place and point of origin is the will. The will is free, so that freedom is both the substance of right and its goal, while the system of right is the realm of freedom made actual, the world of mind brought forth out of itself like a second nature. . . .

19. In the demand for the *purification* of impulses there lies the general notion that they should be freed both from their form as immediate and natural determinations, and also from the subjectivity and contingency of their content, and so brought back to their substantial essence. The truth behind this vague demand is that the impulses should become the rational system of the will's volitions. . . .

20. When reflection is brought to bear on impulses, they are imaged, estimated, compared with one another, with their means of satisfaction and their consequences, etc., and with a sum of satisfaction, (i.e. with happiness). In this way reflection invests this material with abstract universality and in this external manner purifies it from its crudity and barbarity. . . .

21. . . . It is only as thinking intelligence that the will is genuinely a will and free. The slave does not know his essence, his infinity, his freedom; . . . and he lacks this knowledge of himself because he does not think himself. This self-consciousness which apprehends itself through thinking as essentially human, and thereby frees itself from the contingent and the false, is the principle of right, morality, and all ethical life. . . .

29. An existent of any sort embodying the free will, this is what right is. Right therefore is by definition freedom as Idea.

The crucial point in both the Kantian and the generally accepted definition of right . . . is the *"restriction* which makes it possible for my freedom or self-will to co-exist with the self-will of each and all according to a universal law." . . . This definition contains only a negative category, restriction . . . The definition of right which I have

quoted involves that way of looking at the matter, especially popular since Rousseau, according to which what is fundamental, substantive, and primary is supposed to be the will of a single person in his own private self-will. . . . Once this principle is adopted, of course the rational can come on the scene only as a restriction on the type of freedom which this principle involves, and so also not as something immanently rational but only as an external abstract universal. This view is devoid of any speculative thinking and is repudiated by the philosophic concept. . . .

30. It is only because right is the embodiment of the absolute concept or of self-conscious freedom that it is something sacrosanct. . . .

31. The method whereby, in philosophic science, the concept develops itself out of itself is expounded in logic and is here likewise presupposed. Its development is a purely immanent progress. . . . Its advance is not effected by the assertion that various things exist and then by the application of the universal to extraneous material. . . .

The concept's moving principle, which alike engenders and dissolves the particularizations of the universal, I call "dialectic" . . . This dialectic is not an activity of subjective thinking applied to some matter externally, but is rather the matter's very soul putting forth its branches and fruit organically. This development of the Idea is the proper activity of its rationality, and thinking, as something subjective, merely looks on at it without for its part adding to it any ingredient of its own. To consider a thing rationally means not to bring reason to bear on the object from the outside and so to tamper with it, but to find that the object is rational on its own account. . . .

First Part

ABSTRACT RIGHT

34. The absolutely free will, at the stage when its concept is abstract, has the determinate character of immediacy. Accordingly

Appt. w/ CCEC → 825-5850

X 11-1
T 11-1
W ½ F 11-1

212
188
24

Things to do this week

1) Write to Rio Hondo formission?

2) Go to CCFE, Friday at 11:00 A.m. - "St. reall" &
   for Insurance

3) Go to Education Dept. to inquire
   about Teaching Credential Program

4) Go to Bullocks (Friday)

5) Go to Brant

this stage is its negative actuality, an actuality contrasted with the real world, only an abstractly self-related actuality—the inherently single will of a subject. Pursuant to the moment of the particularity of the will, it has in addition a content consisting of determinate aims and, as exclusive individuality, it has this content at the same time as an external world directly confronting it.

35. . . . Personality implies that as *this* person: (i) I am completely determined on every side . . . and so finite, yet (ii) none the less I am simply and solely self-relation, and therefore in finitude I know myself as something infinite, universal, and free. . . .

36. (1) Personality essentially involves the capacity for rights and constitutes the concept and the basis (itself abstract) of the system of abstract and therefore formal right. Hence the imperative of right is: "Be a person and respect others as persons."

37. (2) The particularity of the will is a moment in the consciousness of the will as a whole, but it is not yet contained in abstract personality as such. Therefore, it is present at this point, but as still sundered from personality, . . . present as desire, need, impulse, casual whim, and so forth. In formal right, therefore, there is no question of particular interests, of my advantage or my welfare. . . .

38. In relation to action in the concrete and to moral and ethical ties, abstract right is . . . only a possibility, and to have a right is therefore to have only a permission or a warrant. The unconditional commands of abstract right are restricted, once again because of its abstractness, to the negative: "Do not infringe personality and what personality entails." . . .

39. (3) As *immediate* individuality, a person in making decisions is related to a world of nature directly confronting him, and thus the personality of the will stands over against this world as something subjective. . . . Personality is that which struggles to lift itself above this restriction and to give itself reality, or in other words to claim that external world as its own. . . .

SUB-SECTION 1

Property

* * *

42. What is immediately different from free mind is that which, both for mind and in itself, is the external pure and simple, a thing. . . .

44. A person has as his substantive end the right of putting his will into any and every thing and thereby making it his, because it has no such end in itself and derives its destiny and soul from his will. . . .

45. To have power over a thing *ab extra* constitutes possession. The particular aspect of the matter, the fact that I make something my own as a result of my natural need, impulse, and caprice, is the particular interest satisfied by possession. But I as free will am an object to myself in what I possess and thereby also for the first time am an actual will, and this is the aspect which constitutes the category of *property*, the true and right factor in possession.

If emphasis is placed on my needs, then the possession of property appears as a means to their satisfaction, but the true position is that, from the standpoint of freedom, property is the first embodiment of freedom and so is in itself a substantive end.

46. . . . In the Roman agrarian laws there was a clash between public and private ownership of land. The latter is the more rational and therefore had to be given preference even at the expense of other rights.

. . . The specific characteristics pertaining to private property may have to be subordinated to a higher sphere of right (e.g. to a society or the state). . . .

The general principle that underlies Plato's ideal state violates the right of personality by forbidding the holding of private property. The idea of a pious or friendly and even a compulsory brotherhood of men holding their goods in common and rejecting the principle of private property may readily present itself to the disposition which mistakes the true nature of the freedom of mind and right. . . .

49. . . . The demand sometimes made for an equal division of land, and other available resources, is an intellectualism all the more empty . . . in that at the heart of particular differences there lies not only the external contingency of nature but also the whole compass of mind, endlessly particularized and differentiated, and the rationality of mind developed into an organism.

We may not speak of the injustice of nature in the unequal distribution of possessions and resources, since nature is not free and therefore is neither just nor unjust. That everyone ought to have subsistence enough for his needs is a moral wish and thus vaguely expressed is well enough meant, but like anything that is only well meant it lacks objectivity. On the other hand, subsistence is not the same as possession and belongs to another sphere, i.e. to civil society.

50. The principle that a thing belongs to the person who happens to be the first in time to take it into his possession is immediately self-explanatory and superfluous, because a second person cannot take into his possession what is already the property of another.

51. Since property is the *embodiment* of personality, my inward idea and will that something is to be mine is not enough to make it my property; to secure this end occupancy is requisite. . . .

62. . . . It is about a millennium and a half since the freedom of personality began through the spread of Christianity to blossom and gain recognition as a universal principle from a part, though still a small part, of the human race. But it was only yesterday, we might say, that the principle of the freedom of property became recognized in some places. This example from history may serve to rebuke the impatience of opinion and to show the length of time that mind requires for progress in its self-consciousness.

63. A thing in use is a single thing. . . . But its specific utility . . . is . . . comparable with . . . other things of like utility. Similarly, the specific need which it satisfies is . . . need in general and thus is comparable . . . with other needs . . . This, the thing's

universality . . . is the thing's *value,* wherein its genuine substantiality becomes determinate and an object of consciousness. . . .

64. . . . Use, employment, or some other mode in which the will expresses itself, is an event in time, and what is objective in time is the continuance of this expression of the will. Without this the thing becomes a *res nullius,* because it has been deprived of the actuality of the will and possession. Therefore I gain or lose possession of property through prescription.

Prescription, therefore, has not been introduced into law solely . . . with a view to truncating the disputes and confusions which old claims would introduce into the security of property. On the contrary, prescription rests at bottom on the specific character of property as "real," on the fact that the will to possess something must express itself.

65. The reason I can alienate my property is that it is mine only in so far as I put my will into it. Hence I may abandon . . . anything that I have or yield it to the will of another. . . .

66. Therefore those goods . . . which constitute my own private personality and the universal essence of my self-consciousness are inalienable and my right to them is imprescriptible. Such characteristics are my personality as such, my universal freedom of will, my ethical life, my religion. . . .

71. . . . The sphere of contract is made up of . . . mediation whereby I hold property not merely by means of a thing and my subjective will, but by means of another person's will as well and so hold it in virtue of my participation in a common will.

Reason makes it just as necessary for men to enter into contractual relationships—gift, exchange, trade, &c.—as to possess property. . . . While all they are conscious of is that they are led to make contracts by need in general, by benevolence, advantage, &c., the fact remains that they are led to do this by reason implicit within them, i.e. by the Idea of the real existence of free personality, "real" here meaning "present in the will alone."

Contract

* * *

75. . . . The object about which a contract is made is a single external thing, since it is only things of that kind which the parties' purely arbitrary will has it in its power to alienate. . . .

To subsume marriage under the concept of contract is thus quite impossible; this subsumption—though shameful is the only word for it—is propounded in Kant's *Philosophy of Law*. It is equally far from the truth to ground the nature of the state on the contractual relation, whether the state is supposed to be a contract of all with all, or of all with the monarch and the government.

. . . However different these two points of view may be, they have this in common, that they have transferred the characteristics of private property into a sphere of a quite different and higher nature. . . .

79. In contract it is the will, and therefore the substance of what is right in contract, that the stipulation enshrines . . . If then I agree to stipulated terms, I am by rights at once bound to carry them out. . . .

Fichte at one time maintained that my obligation to keep a contract begins only when the other party starts fulfilling his side of it; his reason was that up to that point I am uncertain whether the other party's declarations are seriously meant. . . . But the expression of the stipulation . . . embodies a common will which has been brought into existence and which has superseded the arbitrary and alterable dispositions of the parties. The question therefore is not whether the other party *could* have had different private intentions when the contract was made or afterwards, but whether he had any *right* to have them. . . .

81. . . . If the particular will is explicitly at variance with the universal, it assumes a way of looking at things and a volition which are capricious and fortuitous and comes on the scene in opposition to the principle of rightness. This is *wrong*. . . .

Wrong

* * *

C. Coercion and Crime

90. In owning property I place my will in an external thing, and this implies that my will . . . may be seized in it and brought under compulsion. . . .

91. . . . The free will cannot be coerced at all. . . . Only the will which allows itself to be coerced can in any way be coerced.

92. Since it is only in so far as the will has an existence in something determinate that it is Idea or actually free, and since the existent in which it has laid itself is freedom in being, it follows that force or coercion is in its very conception directly self-destructive because it is an expression of a will which annuls the expression or determinate existence of a will. Hence force or coercion, taken abstractly, is wrong.

93. That coercion is in its conception self-destructive is exhibited in the world of reality by the fact that coercion is annulled by coercion; coercion is thus shown to be not only right under certain conditions but necessary, i.e. as a second act of coercion which is the annulment of one that has preceded.

Breaking a contract by failing to carry out its stipulated terms, or neglect of duty rightly owed to family or state, or action in defiance of that duty, is the first act of coercion or at least force, in that it involves depriving another of his property or evading a service due to him.

Coercion by a schoolmaster, or coercion of savages and brutes, seems at first sight to be an initial act of coercion, not a second, following on one that has preceded. But the merely natural will is implicitly a force against the implicit Idea of freedom which must be protected against such an uncivilized will and be made to prevail in it. Either an ethical institution has already been established in family or government, and the natural will is a mere display of force against it; or else there is only a state of nature, a state of affairs where mere force prevails and against which the Idea establishes a right of Heroes.

94. Abstract right is a right to coerce, because the wrong which transgresses it is an exercise of force against the existence of my freedom in an external thing. . . .

95. The initial act of coercion as an exercise of force by the free agent, an exercise of force which infringes the existence of freedom in its concrete sense, infringes the right as right, is crime—a negatively infinite judgement in its full sense, whereby not only the particular . . . is negated, but also the universality and infinity in the predicate "mine." . . .

98. In so far as the infringement of the right is only an injury to a possession or to something which exists externally, it is a *malum* or damage to some kind of property or asset. The annulling of the infringement, so far as the infringement is productive of damage, is the satisfaction given in a civil suit, i.e. compensation for the wrong done, so far as any such compensation can be found. . . .

99. But the injury which has befallen the *implicit* will (and this means the implicit will of the *injuring* party as well as that of the injured and everyone else) has as little positive existence in this implicit will as such as it has in the mere state of affairs which it produces. In itself this implicit will (i.e. the right or law implicit) is rather that which has no external existence and which for that reason cannot be injured. Consequently, the injury from the point of view of the particular will of the injured party and of onlookers is only something negative. The sole positive existence which the injury possesses is that it is the particular will of the criminal. Hence to injure [or penalize] this particular will as a will determinately existent is to annul the crime, which otherwise would have been held valid, and to restore the right.

The theory of punishment is one of the topics which have come off worst in the recent study of the positive science of law, because in this theory the Understanding is in-sufficient; the essence of the matter depends on the concept.

If crime and its annulment . . . are treated as if they were unqualified evils, it must, of course, seem quite unreasonable to will an evil merely because "another evil is there already." To give punishment this superficial character of an evil is . . . the fundamental presupposition of those which regard it as a preventive, a deterrent, a threat, as reformative, &c., and what on these theories is supposed to result from punishment is characterized equally superficially as a good. . . . The precise point at issue is wrong, and the righting of it. If you adopt that superficial attitude to punishment, you brush aside the objective treatment of the righting of wrong . . . and the natural consequence is that you take as essential the moral attitude, i.e. the subjective aspect of crime, intermingled with trivial psychological ideas of stimuli, impulses too strong for reason, and psychological factors coercing and working on our ideas (as if freedom were not equally capable of thrusting an idea aside and reducing it to something fortuitous!). . . . The only important things are, first, that crime is to be annulled, not because it is the producing of an evil, but because it is an infringement of the right as right, and secondly, the question of what that positive existence is which crime possesses and which must be annulled. . . .

100. The injury [the penalty] which falls on the criminal is not merely *implicitly* just. . . .

As is well known, Beccaria denied to the state the right of inflicting capital punishment. His reason was that it could not be presumed that the readiness of individuals to allow themselves to be executed was included in the social contract. . . . On the contrary, it is that higher entity which even lays claim to this very life and property and demands its sacrifice. Further, what is involved in the action of the criminal is not only the concept of crime . . . but also the abstract rationality of the individual's *volition*. Since that is so, punishment is regarded as containing the criminal's right and hence by being punished he is honoured as a rational being. He does not receive this due of honour unless the concept and measure of his punishment are derived from his own act. Still less does he receive it if he is treated either as a harmful animal who has to be made harmless, or with a view to deterring and reforming him. . . .

101. . . . Empirical science requires that the definition of a class concept (punishment in this case) shall be drawn from ideas universally present to conscious psychological experience. This method would prove that the universal feeling of nations and individuals about crime is and has been that it deserves punishment, that as the criminal has done, so should it be done to him. . . .

But a point of great difficulty has been introduced into the idea of retribution by the category of equality, though it is still true that the justice of specific types or amounts of punishment is a further matter, subsequent to the substance of the thing itself . . . Crime, as the will which is implicitly null, *eo ipso* contains its negation in itself and this negation is manifested as punishment. It is this inner identity whose reflection in the external world appears to the Understanding as "equality." . . . No absolute determinacy is possible in this sphere; . . . in the field of the finite, absolute determinacy remains only a demand, a demand which the Understanding has to meet by continually increasing delimitation . . . which allows only of perennially approximate satisfaction.

. . . It is easy enough . . . to exhibit the retributive character of punishment as an absurdity (theft for theft, robbery for robbery, an eye for an eye, a tooth for a tooth —and then you can go on to suppose that the criminal has only one eye or no teeth). But the concept has nothing to do with this absurdity, for which indeed the introduction of this specific equality is solely to blame. Value, as the inner equality of things which in their outward existence are specifically different from one another in every way, is a category which has appeared already . . . and by means of it our idea of a thing is

raised above its immediate character to its universality. In crime . . . the purely external specific character vanishes all the more obviously, and equality remains the fundamental regulator of the essential thing, to wit the deserts of the criminal. . . .

102. . . . Revenge, because it is a positive action of a particular will, becomes a new transgression. . . .

103. The demand that this contradiction, which is present here in the manner in which wrong is annulled, be resolved like contradictions in the case of other types of wrong, . . . is the demand for a justice freed from subjective interest and a subjective form and no longer contingent on might, i.e. it is the demand for justice not as revenge but as punishment. Fundamentally, this implies the demand for a will which, though particular and subjective, yet wills the universal as such. . . .

Second Part

MORALITY

SUB-SECTION 2

Intention and Welfare

* * *

120. The right of intention is that the universal quality of the action shall not merely be implicit but shall be known by the agent, and so shall have lain from the start in his subjective will. Vice versa, what may be called the right of the objectivity of action is the right of the action to evince itself as known and willed by the subject as a *thinker*.

This right to insight of this kind entails the complete, or almost complete, irresponsibility of children, imbeciles, lunatics, &c., for their actions.—But just as actions on their external side as events include accidental consequences, so there is involved in the subjective agent an indeterminacy whose degree depends on the strength and force of his self-consciousness and circumspection. This indeterminacy, however, may not be taken into account except in connexion with childhood or imbecility, lunacy, &c., since it is only such well marked states of mind that nullify the trait of thought and freedom of will, and permit us to treat the agent as devoid of the dignity of being a thinker and a will. . . .

124. Since the subjective satisfaction of the individual himself (including the recognition which he receives by way of honour and fame) is also part and parcel of the achievement of ends of absolute worth, it follows that the demand that such an end alone shall appear as willed and attained . . . is an empty dogmatism. . . .

The right of the subject's particularity, his right to be satisfied, . . . is the pivot and centre of the difference between antiquity and modern times. . . . Amongst the primary shapes which this right assumes are love, romanticism, the quest for the eternal salvation of the individual, &c.; next come moral convictions and conscience; and, finally, the other forms, some of which come into prominence in what follows as the principle of civil society and as moments in the constitution of the state, while others appear in the course of history, particularly the history of art, science, and philosophy.

Now this principle of particularity is, to be sure, one moment of the antithesis, and in the first place at least it is just as much identical with the universal as distinct from it. Abstract reflection, however, fixes this moment in its distinction from and opposition to the universal and so produces a view of morality as nothing but a bitter, unending, struggle against self-satisfaction, as the command: "Do with abhorrence what duty enjoins."

It is just this type of ratiocination which adduces that familiar psychological view of history which understands how to belittle and disparage all great deeds and great men by transforming into the main intention and operative motive of actions the inclinations and passions which likewise found their satisfaction from the achievement of something substantive, the fame and honour, &c., consequential on such actions; in a word, their particular aspect, the aspect which it has

decreed in advance to be something in itself pernicious . . . This is the view of those valet psychologists "for whom there are no heroes, not because there are no heroes, but because these psychologists are only valets."

125. The subjective element of the will, with its particular content—welfare, is reflected into itself and infinite and so stands related to the universal element, to the principle of the will. This moment of universality, posited first of all within this particular content itself, is the welfare of others also, or, specified completely, though quite emptily, the welfare of all. The welfare of many other unspecified particulars is thus also an essential end and right of subjectivity. . . .

126. . . . An intention to secure my welfare or that of others . . . cannot justify an action which is wrong.

It is one of the most prominent of the corrupt maxims of our time to enter a plea for the so-called "moral" intention behind wrong actions and to imagine bad men with well-meaning hearts, i.e. hearts willing their own welfare and perhaps that of others also. . . .

Incidentally, however, attention must be paid to the point of view from which right and welfare are being treated here. We are considering right as abstract right and welfare as the particular welfare of the single agent. The so-called "general good," the welfare of the state . . . is quite a different sphere, a sphere in which abstract right is a subordinate moment like particular welfare and the happiness of the individual. . . . It is one of the commonest blunders of abstract thinking to make private rights and private welfare count as *absolute* in opposition to the universality of the state.

127. The particularity of the interests of the natural will, taken in their entirety as a single whole, is personal existence or life. In extreme danger and in conflict with the rightful property of someone else, this life may claim (as a right, not a mercy) a right of distress, because in such a situation there is on the one hand an infinite injury to a man's existence and the consequent loss of rights altogether, and on the other hand only

in injury to a single restricted embodiment of freedom, and this implies a recognition both of right as such and also of the injured man's capacity for rights, because the injury affects only *this* property of his. . . .

Good and Conscience

129. The good is the Idea as the unity of the concept of the will with the particular will. In this unity, abstract right, welfare, the subjectivity of knowing and the contingency of external fact, have their independent self-subsistence superseded, though at the same time they are still contained and retained within it in their essence. The good is thus freedom realized, the absolute end and aim of the world.

130. . . . Welfare without right is not a good. Similarly, right without welfare is not the good . . . Consequently, since the good must of necessity be actualized through the particular will and is at the same time its substance, it has absolute right in contrast with the abstract right of property and the particular aims of welfare. If either of these moments becomes distinguished from the good, it has validity only in so far as it accords with the good and is subordinated to it.

131. For the subjective will, the good and the good alone is the essential, and the subjective will has value and dignity only in so far as its insight and intention accord with the good. . . .

132. The right of the subjective will is that whatever it is to recognize as valid shall be seen by it as good, and that an action, as its aim entering upon external objectivity, shall be imputed to it as right or wrong, good or evil, legal or illegal, in accordance with its *knowledge* of the worth which the action has in this objectivity.

The good is in principle the essence of the will in its substantiality and universality, i.e. of the will in its truth, and therefore it exists simply and solely in thinking and by means of thinking. Hence assertions such as "man cannot know the truth but has to do only with phenomena," or "thinking injures the good will" are dogmas depriving mind not only of intellectual but also of all ethical worth and dignity. . . .

. . . I may demand from myself, and regard it as one of my subjective rights, that my insight into an obligation shall be based on good reasons . . . This in no way detracts from the right of objectivity.

This right of insight into the good is distinct from the right of insight in respect of action as such . . . ; the form of the right of objectivity which corresponds to the latter is this, that since action is an alteration which is to take place in an actual world and so will have recognition in it, it must in general accord with what has validity there. Whoever wills to act in this world of actuality has *eo ipso* submitted himself to its laws and recognized the right of objectivity.

Similarly, in the state as the objectivity of the concept of reason, legal responsibility cannot be tied down to what an individual may hold to be or not to be in accordance with his reason. . . . By means of the publicity of the laws and the universality of manners, the state removes from the right of insight its formal aspect and the contingency which it still retains for the subject at the level of morality . . . To turn momentary blindness, the goad of passion, intoxication, or, in a word, what is called the strength of sensual impulse . . . into *reasons* when the imputation, specific character, and culpability of a crime are in question, and to look upon such circumstances as if they took away the criminal's guilt again means . . . failing to treat the criminal in accordance with the right and honour due to him as a man. . . .

The claim is made that the criminal in the moment of his action must have had a "clear idea" of the wrong and its culpability before it can be imputed to him as a crime. At first sight, this claim seems to preserve the right of his subjectivity, but the truth is that it deprives him of his indwelling nature as intelligent. . . .

The sphere in which these extenuating

circumstances come into consideration as grounds for the mitigation of punishment is a sphere other than that of rights, the sphere of pardon. . . .

134. Because every action explicitly calls for a particular content and a specific end, while duty as an abstraction entails nothing of the kind, the question arises: what is my duty? As an answer nothing is so far available except: (a) to do the right, and (b) to strive after welfare, one's own welfare, and welfare in universal terms, the welfare of others. . . .

135. . . . Specific duties, however, are not contained in the definition of duty itself. . . .

Kant's further formulation, the possibility of visualizing an action as a *universal* maxim, does lead to the more concrete visualization of a situation, but in itself it contains no principle beyond abstract identity and the "absence of contradiction" already mentioned.

The absence of property contains in itself just as little contradiction as the non-existence of this or that nation, family, &c., or the death of the whole human race. But if it is already established on other grounds and presupposed that property and human life are to exist and be respected, then indeed it is a contradiction to commit theft or murder; a contradiction must be a contradiction of something, i.e. of some content presupposed from the start as a fixed principle. . . .

138. . . . As one of the commoner features of history (e.g. in Socrates, the Stoics, and others), the tendency to look deeper into oneself and to know and determine from within oneself what is right and good appears in ages when what is recognized as right and good in contemporary manners cannot satisfy the will of better men. When the existing world of freedom has become faithless to the will of better men, that will fails to find itself in the duties there recognized and must try to find in the ideal world of the inner life alone the harmony which actuality has lost. . . .

140. . . . Theft, cowardice, murder, and so forth, as actions, i.e. as achievements of a subjective will, have the immediate charac-

ter of being satisfactions of such a will and therefore of being something positive. In order to make the action a good one, it is only a question of recognizing this positive aspect of the action as my intention, and this then becomes the essential aspect in virtue of which the action is made good, simply because I recognize it as the good in my intention. Theft in order to do good to the poor, theft or flight from battle for the sake of fulfilling one's duty to care for one's life or one's family (a poor family perhaps into the bargain), murder out of hate or revenge (i.e. in order to satisfy one's sense of one's own rights . . . by extirpating this wicked individual . . . and thereby contributing at least one's quota to the project of uprooting the bad)—all these actions are made well-intentioned and therefore good by this method of taking account of the positive aspect of their content . . . Everyone always wills something positive, and therefore, on the view we are considering, something good. In this abstract good the distinction between good and evil has vanished together with all concrete duties; for this reason, simply to will the good and to have a good intention in acting is more like evil than good, because the good willed is only this abstract form of good and therefore to make it concrete devolves on the arbitrary will of the subject.

To this context there also belongs the notorious maxim: "The end justifies the means." . . .

But when someone says that the end justifies the means, . . . he understands by the words . . . that to use as means to a good end something which in itself is simply not a means at all, . . . to commit a crime as a means to a good end, is permissible and even one's bounden duty . . . Now what is set up against such a determinate crime . . . is the justifying end, and this is simply subjective opinion about what is good and better. What happens here is . . . the absolute and valid determinate character assigned to good and evil, right and wrong, is entirely swept away and the determination of them as ascribed instead to the individual's feeling, imagination, and caprice. . . .

. . . The law is no agent; it is only the actual human being who acts . . . The only question, in estimating the worth of human actions, is how far he has taken up the law into his conviction. But if . . . it is not actions which are to be judged, i.e. measured generally, by that law, it is impossible to see what the law is for and what end it is to serve. Such a law is degraded to a mere external letter, in fact to an empty word, if it is only my conviction which makes it a law and invests it with obligatory force.

Such a law may claim its authority from God or the state. It may even have behind it the authority of tens of centuries during which it was the bond which gave men, with all their deeds and destiny, coherence and subsistence. And these are authorities which enshrine the convictions of countless individuals. Now if I set against these the authority of my single conviction . . . that at first seems a piece of monstrous self-conceit, but in virtue of the principle that subjective conviction is to be the measuring-rod, it is pronounced not to be self-conceit at all.

Even if reason and conscience—which shallow science and bad sophistry can never altogether expel—admit with a noble illogicality that error is possible, still by describing crime, and evil generally, as only an error, we minimize the fault . . . The difference between importance and triviality vanishes if everything turns on the subjectivity of conviction and on persistence in it. . . .

. . . It follows further, on this principle of justification by conviction, that logic requires me, in dealing with the way others act against my action, to admit that they are quite in the right—so far at any rate as they maintain with faith and conviction that my action is criminal. . . .

Third Part

ETHICAL LIFE

142. . . . Ethical life is the concept of freedom developed into the existing world and the nature of self-consciousness. . . .

146. . . . The sun, the moon, mountains, rivers, and the natural objects of all kinds by which we are surrounded, *are*. For consciousness they have the authority not only of mere being but also of possessing a particular nature which it accepts and to which it adjusts itself in dealing with them, using them, or in being otherwise concerned with them. The authority of ethical laws is infinitely higher, because natural objects conceal rationality under the cloak of contingency and exhibit it only in their utterly external and disconnected way.

147. On the other hand, they are not something alien to the subject. On the contrary, his spirit bears witness to them as to its own essence, the essence in which he has a feeling of his selfhood, and in which he lives as in his own element which is not distinguished from himself. . . .

148. As substantive in character, these laws and institutions are duties binding on the will of the individual, because as subjective, as inherently undetermined, or determined as particular, he distinguishes himself from them and hence stands related to them as to the substance of his own being. . . .

A "doctrine of duties" which is other than a philosophical science takes its material from existing relationships and shows its connexion with the moralist's personal notions or with principles and thoughts, purposes, impulses, feelings, &c., that are forthcoming everywhere; and as reasons for accepting each duty in turn, it may tack on its further consequences in their bearing on the other ethical relationships or on welfare and opinion. But an immanent and logical "doctrine of duties" can be nothing except the serial exposition of the relationships which are necessitated by the Idea of freedom and are therefore actual in their entirety, to wit in the state.

149. . . . In duty the individual finds his liberation; first, liberation from dependence on mere natural impulse and from the depression which as a particular subject he cannot escape in his moral reflections on what ought to be and what might be; secondly, liberation from the indeterminate subjec-

tivity which, never reaching reality or the objective determinacy of action, remains self-enclosed and devoid of actuality. In duty the individual acquires his substantive freedom.

150. Virtue is the ethical order reflected in the individual character so far as that character is determined by its natural endowment. When virtue displays itself solely as the individual's simple conformity with the duties of the station to which he belongs, it is rectitude.

In an *ethical* community, it is easy to say what man must do, what are the duties he has to fulfil in order to be virtuous: he has simply to follow the well-known and explicit rules of his own situation. Rectitude is the general character which may be demanded of him by law or custom. But from the standpoint of *morality*, rectitude often seems to be something comparatively inferior, something beyond which still higher demands must be made on oneself and others, because the craving to be something special is not satisfied with what is absolute and universal; it finds consciousness of peculiarity only in what is exceptional. . . .

In an existing ethical order in which a complete system of ethical relations has been developed and actualized, virtue in the strict sense of the word is in place and actually appears only in exceptional circumstances or when one obligation clashes with another. The clash, however, must be a genuine one, because moral reflection can manufacture clashes of all sorts to suit its purpose and give itself a consciousness of being something special and having made sacrifices. It is for this reason that the phenomenon of virtue proper is commoner when societies and communities are uncivilized, since in those circumstances ethical conditions and their actualization are more a matter of private choice or the natural genius of an exceptional individual. . . . In the states of antiquity, ethical life had not grown into this free system of an objective order self-subsistently developed, and consequently it was by the personal genius of individuals that this defect had to be made good. . . .

151. But when individuals are simply identified with the actual order, ethical life . . . appears as their general mode of conduct, i.e. as custom, . . . while the habitual practice of ethical living appears as a second nature which, put in the place of the initial, purely natural will, is the soul of custom permeating it through and through, the significance and the actuality of its existence. . . .

153. The right of individuals to be subjectively destined to freedom is fulfilled when they belong to an actual ethical order. . . .

When a father inquired about the best method of educating his son in ethical conduct, a Pythagorean replied: "Make him a citizen of a state with good laws." . . .

156. The ethical substance, as containing independent self-consciousness united with its concept, is the actual mind of a family and a nation. . . .

SUB-SECTION 1

The Family

158. The family, as the immediate substantiality of mind, is specifically characterized by love, which is mind's feeling of its own unity Hence in a family, one's frame of mind is to have self-consciousness of one's individuality within this unity as the absolute essence of oneself, with the result that one is in it not as an independent person but as a member.

159. The right which the individual enjoys on the strength of the family unity and which is in the first place simply the individual's life within this unity, takes on the *form* of right . . . only when the family begins to dissolve. At that point those who should be family-members both in their inclination and in actuality begin to be self-subsistent persons, and whereas they formerly constituted one specific moment within the whole, they now receive their share separately and so only in an external fashion by way of money, food, educational expenses, and the like. . . .

A. Marriage

162. On the subjective side, marriage may have a more obvious source in the particular inclination of the two persons who are entering upon the marriage tie, or in the foresight and contrivance of the parents, and so forth. But its objective source lies in the free consent of the persons, especially in their consent to make themselves one person, to renounce their natural and individual personality to this unity of one with the other. . . .

164. . . . The solemn declaration by the parties of their consent to enter the ethical bond of marriage, and its corresponding recognition and confirmation by their family and community, constitutes the formal completion and actuality of marriage. The knot is tied and made ethical only after this ceremony, whereby . . . the substantial thing in the marriage is brought completely into being. As a result, the sensuous moment . . . is put into its ethical place as something only consequential and accidental, belonging to the external embodiment of the ethical bond, which indeed can subsist exclusively in reciprocal love and support.

If with a view to framing or criticizing legal enactments, the question is asked: what should be regarded as the chief end of marriage?, the question may be taken to mean: which single facet of marriage in its actuality is to be regarded as the most essential one? No one facet by itself, however, makes up the whole range of its implicit and explicit content, i.e. of its ethical character, and one or other of its facets may be lacking in an existing marriage without detriment to the essence of marriage itself. . . .

168. Further, marriage results from the free surrender by both sexes of their personality . . . Consequently, it ought not to be entered by two people identical in stock who are already acquainted and perfectly known to one another; for individuals in the same circle of relationship have no special personality of their own in contrast with that of others in the same circle. On the contrary, the parties should be drawn from separate families and their personalities should be different in origin. Since the very conception of marriage is that it is a freely undertaken ethical transaction, not a tie directly grounded in the physical organism and its desires, it follows that the marriage of blood-relations runs counter to this conception and so also to genuine natural feeling.

. . . External arguments in support of monogamy have been drawn from physical considerations such as the number of men and women. Dark feelings of repulsion are advanced as the sole ground for prohibiting consanguineous marriage. The basis of all these views is the fashionable idea of a state of nature and a natural origin for rights, and the lack of the concept of rationality and freedom. . . .

174. Children have the right to maintenance and education at the expense of the family's common capital. The right of the parents to the service as service of their children is based upon and is restricted by the common task of looking after the family generally. Similarly, the right of the parents over the wishes of their children is determined by the object in view—discipline and education. The punishment of children does not aim at justice as such; the aim is more subjective and moral in character, i.e. to deter them from exercising a freedom still in the toils of nature and to lift the universal into their consciousness and will.

175. Children are potentially free and their life directly embodies nothing save potential freedom. . . . The child's education has the positive aim of instilling ethical principles into him in the form of an immediate feeling for which differences are not yet explicit, so that thus equipped with the foundation of an ethical life, his heart may live its early years in love, trust, and obedience. In respect of the same relation, this education has the negative aim of raising children out of the instinctive, physical, level on which they are originally, to self-subsistence and freedom of personality and so to the level on which they have power to leave the natural unity of the family. . . .

The necessity for education is present in children as their own feeling of dissatisfaction with themselves as they are, as the desire to belong to the adult world whose superiority they divine, as the longing to grow up. The play theory of education assumes that what is childish is itself already something of inherent worth and presents it as such to the children; in their eyes it lowers serious pursuits, and education itself, to a form of childishness for which the children themselves have scant respect. . . .

SUB-SECTION 2

Civil Society

182. The concrete person . . . is, as a totality of wants and a mixture of caprice and physical necessity, one principle of civil society. But the particular person is essentially so related to other particular persons that each establishes himself and finds satisfaction by means of the others, and at the same time purely and simply by means of the form of universality, the second principle here.

183. In the course of the actual attainment of selfish ends . . . there is formed a system of complete interdependence . . . On this system, individual happiness, &c., depend, and only in this connected system are they actualized and secured. . . .

184. The Idea in this its stage of division imparts to each of its moments a characteristic embodiment; to particularity it gives the right to develop and launch forth in all directions: and to universality the right to prove itself not only the ground and necessary form of particularity, but also the authority standing over it and its final end. . . .

185. Particularity by itself, given free rein in every direction to satisfy its needs, accidental caprices, and subjective desires, destroys itself and its substantive concept in this process of gratification. At the same time, the satisfaction of need, necessary and accidental alike, is accidental because it breeds new desires without end, is in thoroughgoing dependence on caprice and external accident, and is held in check by the power of universality. In these contrasts and their complexity, civil society affords a spectacle of extravagance and want as well as of the physical and ethical degeneration common to them both. . . .

186. But in developing itself independently to totality, the principle of particularity passes over into universality, and only there does it attain its truth and the right to which its positive actuality is entitled. . . .

187. Individuals in their capacity as burghers in this state are private persons whose end is their own interest. This end is *mediated* through the universal which thus *appears* as a *means* to its realization. Consequently, individuals can attain their ends only in so far as they themselves determine their knowing, willing, and acting in a universal way and make themselves links in this chain of social connexions. . . .

The idea that the state of nature is one of innocence and that there is a simplicity of manners in uncivilized . . . peoples, implies treating education . . . as something purely external, the ally of corruption. Similarly, the feeling that needs, their satisfaction, the pleasures and comforts of private life, and so forth, are absolute ends, implies treating education as a mere means to these ends . . . The end of reason . . . is to banish natural simplicity . . . It aims in the first instance at securing for this, its external condition, the rationality of which it is capable, i.e. the form of universality or the Understanding. . . . By this means alone does mind become at home with itself within this pure externality. . . . The final purpose of education, therefore, is liberation and the struggle for a higher liberation still; education is the absolute transition from an ethical substantiality which is immediate and natural to the one which is intellectual and so both infinitely subjective and lofty enough to have attained universality of form. In the individual subject, this liberation is the hard struggle against . . . the empty subjectivity of feeling and the caprice of inclination . . . It is through this educational struggle that the subjective will itself attains objectivity within. . . .

Moreover, this form of universality . . . brings it about at the same time that particularity becomes individuality genuinely existent in its own eyes . . . Particularity itself is present in ethical life as infinitely independent free subjectivity. This is the position which reveals education as a moment immanent in the Absolute and which makes plain its infinite value. . . .

A. The System of Needs

189. Particularity is in the first instance characterized . . . by . . . subjective need . . . The aim here is the satisfaction of subjective particularity, but the universal asserts itself in the bearing which this satisfaction has on the needs of others and their free arbitrary wills. . . .

190. An animal's needs and its ways and means of satisfying them are both alike restricted in scope. Though man is subject to this restriction too, yet at the same time he evinces his transcendence of it and his universality, first by the multiplication of needs and means of satisfying them, and secondly by the differentiation and division of concrete need into single parts and aspects which in turn become different needs, particularized and so more abstract. . . .

192. Needs and means, as things existent *realiter*, become something which has being for others by whose needs and work satisfaction for all alike is conditioned. When needs and means become abstract in quality . . . abstraction is also a character of the reciprocal relation of individuals to one another. . . .

194. . . . In social needs . . . the strict natural necessity of need is obscured and man is concerned with his own opinion, indeed with an opinion which is universal, and with a necessity of his own making alone, instead of with an external necessity, an inner contingency, and mere caprice. . . .

195. . . . When social conditions tend to multiply and subdivide needs, means, and enjoyments indefinitely—a process which . . . has no qualitative limits—this is luxury. In this same process, however, dependence and

want increase *ad infinitum,* and the material to meet these is permanently barred to the needy man because it consists of external objects with the special character of being property, the embodiment of the free will of others, and hence from his point of view its recalcitrance is absolute.

196. . . . Through work the raw material directly supplied by nature is specifically adapted to . . . numerous ends by all sorts of different processes. Now this formative change confers value on means and gives them their utility, and hence man in what he consumes is mainly concerned with the products of men. . . .

197. . . . Practical education, acquired through working, consists first in the automatically recurrent need for something to do and the habit of simply being busy; next, in the strict adaptation of one's activity according not only to the nature of the material worked on, but also, and especially, to the pleasure of other workers; and finally, in a habit, produced by this discipline, of objective activity and universally recognized aptitudes.

198. The universal and objective element in work, on the other hand, lies in the abstracting process which effects the subdivision of needs and means and thereby *eo ipso* subdivides production and brings about the division of labour. By this division, the work of the individual becomes less complex, and consequently his skill at his section of the job increases, like his output. At the same time, this abstraction of one man's skill and means of production from another's completes and makes necessary everywhere the dependence of men on one another and their reciprocal relation in the satisfaction of their other needs. Further, the abstraction of one man's production from another's makes work more and more mechanical, until finally man is able to step aside and install machines in his place.

199. When men are thus dependent on one another . . . subjective self-seeking turns into a contribution to the satisfaction of the needs of everyone else. That is to say, by a dialectical advance, subjective self-seeking

turns into the mediation of the particular through the universal, with the result that each man in earning, producing, and enjoying on his own account is *eo ipso* producing and earning for the enjoyment of everyone else. . . .

200. A particular man's . . . opportunity of sharing in the general resources, [is] conditioned, however, partly by his own unearned principal (his capital), and partly by his skill; this in turn is itself dependent . . . on accidental circumstances whose multiplicity introduces differences in the development of natural, bodily, and mental characteristics, which were already in themselves dissimilar. . . .

. . . Men are made unequal by nature, where inequality is in its element, and in civil society the right of particularity is so far from annulling this natural inequality that it produces it out of mind and raises it to an inequality of skill and resources, and even to one of moral and intellectual attainment. To oppose to this right a demand for equality is a folly of the Understanding which takes as real and rational its abstract equality and its "ought-to-be." . . .

201. The infinitely complex, criss-cross movements of reciprocal production and exchange, and the equally infinite multiplicity of means therein employed, become crystallized . . . As a result, the entire complex is built up into . . . class-divisions. . . .

203. The substantial [or agricultural] class has its capital in the natural products of the soil which it cultivates . . . In face of the connexion of [agricultural] work and its fruits with separate and fixed times of the year, and the dependence of harvests on the variability of natural processes, the aim of need in this class turns into provision for the future; but . . . the agricultural mode of subsistence remains one which owes comparatively little to reflection and independence of will, and this mode of life is in general such that this class has the substantial disposition of an ethical life which is immediate, resting on family relationship and trust . . . .

204. The business class has for its task the adaptation of raw materials . . . For what this class produces and enjoys, it has mainly itself, its own industry, to thank. . . .

205. The universal class [the class of civil servants] has for its task the universal interests of the community. It must therefore be relieved from direct labour to supply its needs, either by having private means or by receiving an allowance from the state which claims its industry, with the result that private interest finds its satisfaction in its work for the universal . . . .

207. A man actualizes himself only in becoming something definite, i.e. something specifically particularized; this means restricting himself exclusively to one of the particular spheres of need. In this class-system, the ethical frame of mind therefore is rectitude and *esprit de corps,* i.e. the disposition to make oneself a member of one of the moments of civil society by one's own act, through one's energy, industry, and skill, to maintain oneself in this position, and to fend for oneself only through this process of mediating oneself with the universal, while in this way gaining recognition both in one's own eyes and in the eyes of others. . . .

At first (i.e. especially in youth) a man chafes at the idea of resolving on a particular social position, and looks upon this as a restriction on his universal character and as a necessity imposed on him purely *ab extra.* This is because his thinking is still of that abstract kind which refuses to move beyond the universal and so never reaches the actual. It does not realize that if the concept is to be determinate, it must first of all advance into the distinction between the concept and its real existence and thereby into determinacy and particularity . . . It is only thus that the concept can win actuality and ethical objectivity. . . .

211. The principle of rightness becomes the law . . . when, in its objective existence, it is posited . . . i.e. when thinking makes it determinate for consciousness and makes it known as what is right and valid; and in acquiring this determinate character, the right becomes positive law in general. . . .

Since it is only animals which have their law as instinct, while it is man alone who has law as custom, even systems of customary law contain the moment of being thoughts and being known. Their difference from positive law consists solely in this, that they are known only in a subjective and accidental way, with the result that in themselves they are less determinate and the universality of thought is less clear in them. (And apart from this, knowledge of a system of law either in general or in its details, is the accidental possession of a few.) The supposition that it is customary law, on the strength of its character as custom, which possesses the privilege of having become part of life is a delusion, since the valid laws of a nation do not cease to be its customs by being written and codified. . . . When a nation begins to acquire even a little culture, its customary law must soon come to be collected and put together. Such a collection is a legal code, but one which, as a mere collection, is markedly formless, indeterminate, and fragmentary. The main difference between it and a code properly so-called is that in the latter the principles of jurisprudence in their universality, and so in their determinacy, have been apprehended in terms of thought and expressed. English national law or municipal law is contained . . . in statutes (written laws) and in so-called "unwritten" laws . . . The monstrous confusion, however, which prevails both in English law and its administration is graphically portrayed by those acquainted with the matter. In particular, they comment on the fact that since this unwritten law is contained in court verdicts and judgements, the judges are continually legislators. The authority of precedent is binding on them, since their predecessors have done nothing but give expression to the unwritten law; and yet they are just as much exempt from its authority, because they are themselves repositories of the unwritten law and so have the right to criticize previous judgements and pronounce whether they accorded with the unwritten law or not. . . .

No greater insult could be offered to a civilized people or to its lawyers than to deny them ability to codify their law; for such ability cannot be that of constructing a legal system with a novel content, but only that of apprehending, i.e. grasping in thought, the content of existing laws in its determinate universality and then applying them to particular cases.

212. . . . In being posited in positive law, the right acquires determinant existence. Into such existence there may enter the contingency of self-will and other particular circumstances and hence there may be a discrepancy between the content of the law and the principle of rightness.

In positive law, therefore, it is the legal which is the source of our knowledge of what is right . . . Thus, the science of positive law is to that extent an historical science with authority as its guiding principle. Anything over and above this historical study is matter for the Understanding and concerns the collection of laws, their classification on external principles, deductions from them, their application to fresh details, &c. When the Understanding meddles with the nature of the thing itself, its theories, e.g. of criminal law, show what its deductive argumentation can concoct.

The science of positive law has not only the right, but even the inescapable duty, to study given laws, to deduce from its positive data their progress in history, their applications and subdivisions, down to the last detail, and to exhibit their implications. On the other hand, if, after all these deductions have been proved, the further question about the rationality of a specific law is still raised, the question may seem perverse to those who are busied with these pursuits, but their astonishment at it should at least stop short of dismay. . . .

214. . . . Right by being embodied in positive law becomes applicable to the single case. . . . In this sphere, the concept merely lays down a general limit, within which vacillation is still allowed. This vacillation must be terminated, however, in the interest of getting something done, and for this reason

there is a place within that limit for contingent and arbitrary decisions.

... Reason cannot determine, nor can the concept provide any principle whose application could decide whether justice requires for an offence (i) a corporal punishment of forty lashes or thirty-nine, or (ii) a fine of five dollars or four dollars ninety-three, four, &c., cents. . . .

215. If laws are to have a binding force, it follows that, in view of the right of self-consciousness . . . they must be made universally known.

To hang the laws so high that no citizen could read them (as Dionysius the Tyrant did) is injustice of one and the same kind as to bury them in row upon row of learned tomes, collections of dissenting judgements and opinions, records of customs, &c., and in a dead language too, so that knowledge of the law of the land is accessible only to those who have made it their professional study. . . .

216. For a public legal code, simple general laws are required, and yet the nature of the *finite* material to which law is applied leads to the further determining of general laws *ad infinitum*. . . .

A fruitful source of complexity in legislation is the gradual intrusion of reason, of what is inherently and actually right, into primitive institutions which have something wrong at their roots and so are purely historical survivals. . . .

217. The principle of rightness passes over in civil society into law. My individual right, whose embodiment has hitherto been immediate and abstract, now similarly becomes embodied in the existent will and knowledge of everyone, in the sense that it becomes recognized. Hence property acquisitions and transfers must now be undertaken and concluded only in the form which that embodiment gives to them. . . .

... It is either feeling, refusing to move beyond the subjective, or reflection, clinging to its abstract essences, which casts formalities aside, while the dry-as-dust Understanding may for its part cling to formalities in-

stead of the real thing and multiply them indefinitely.

Apart from this, however, the march of mental development is the long and hard struggle to free a content from its sensuous and immediate form, endow it with its appropriate form of thought, and thereby give it simple and adequate expression. It is because this is the case that when the development of law is just beginning, ceremonies and formalities are more circumstantial and count rather as the thing itself than as its symbol. . . .

218. Since property and personality have legal recognition and validity in civil society, wrongdoing now becomes an infringement, not merely of what is subjectively infinite, but of the universal thing which is existent with inherent stability and strength. Hence a new attitude arises: the action is seen as a danger to society and thereby the magnitude of the wrongdoing is increased. On the other hand, however, the fact that society has become strong and sure of itself diminishes the external importance of the injury and so leads to a mitigation of its punishment. . . .

219. By taking the form of law, right . . . is then something on its own account, and in contrast with particular willing and opining of the right, it is self-subsistent and has to vindicate itself as something universal. This is achieved by recognizing it and making it actual in a particular case without the subjective feeling of private interest; and this is the business of a public authority—the court of justice. . . .

... To regard the introduction of a legal system as no more than an optional act of grace or favour on the part of monarchs and governments . . . is a piece of . . . mere thoughtlessness . . . Legal and political institutions are rational in principle and therefore absolutely necessary, and the question of the form in which they arose or were introduced is entirely irrelevant. . . .

... The administration of justice must be regarded as the fulfilment of a duty by the public authority, no less than as the exercise of a right; and so far as it is a right, it does not depend upon an optional delegation to one authority by the individual members of society.

220. When the right against crime has the form of revenge . . . it is only right implicit, not right in the form of right, i.e. no *act* of revenge is justified. Instead of the injured party, the injured *universal* now comes on the scene, and this has its proper actuality in the court of law. . . .

223. . . . A legal process, in itself in any case a means . . . begins to be something external to its end and contrasted with it. This long course of formalities . . . may be turned into an evil, and even an instrument of wrong, and for this reason it is by law made the duty of the parties to submit themselves to the simple process of arbitration (before a tribunal of arbitrators) and to the attempt to reconcile their differences out of court, in order that they . . . may be protected against legal processes and their misuse.

Equity involves a departure from formal rights owing to moral or other considerations . . . A court of equity, however, comes to mean a court which decides in a single case without insisting on the formalities of a legal process . . . Further, it decides on the merits of the single case as a unique one, not with a view to disposing of it in such a way as to create a binding legal precedent for the future.

224. Amongst the rights of the subjective consciousness are . . . the publicity of judicial proceedings. The reason for this is that a trial is implicitly an event of universal validity,· and although the particular content of the action affects the interests of the parties alone, its universal content . . . affects the interests of everybody. . . .

234. . . . There is . . . no inherent line of distinction between what is and what is not injurious, even where crime is concerned . . . These details are determined by custom, the spirit of the rest of the constitution, contemporary conditions, the crisis of the hour, and so forth. . . .

236. The differing interests of producers and consumers may come into collision with each other; and although a fair balance be-

tween them on the whole may be brought about automatically, still their adjustment also requires a control which stands above both and is consciously undertaken. The right to the exercise of such control in a single case (e.g. in the fixing of the prices of the commonest necessaries of life) depends on the fact that, by being publicly exposed for sale, goods in absolutely universal daily demand are offered not so much to an individual as such but rather to a universal purchaser, the public; and thus both the defence of the public's right not to be defrauded, and also the management of goods inspection, may lie, as a common concern, with a public authority. But public care and direction are most of all necessary in the case of the larger branches of industry, because these are dependent on conditions abroad and on combinations of distant circumstances which cannot be grasped as a whole by the individuals tied to these industries for their living.

At the other extreme to freedom of trade and commerce in civil society is public organization to provide for everything and determine everyone's labour—take for example in ancient times the labour on the pyramids and the other huge monuments in Egypt and Asia which were constructed for public ends, and the worker's task was not mediated through his private choice and particular interest. This interest invokes freedom of trade and commerce against control from above; but the more blindly it sinks into self-seeking aims, the more it requires such control to bring it back to the universal. Control is also necessary to diminish the danger of upheavals arising from clashing interests and to abbreviate the period in which their tension should be eased through the working of a necessity of which they themselves know nothing. . . .

238. Originally the family is the substantive whole whose function it is to provide for the individual on his particular side by giving him either the means and the skill necessary to enable him to earn his living out of the resources of society, or else subsistence and maintenance in the event of his suffer-

ing a disability. But civil society tears the individual from his family ties, estranges the members of the family from one another, and recognizes them as self-subsistent persons . . . Thus the individual becomes a son of civil society which has as many claims upon him as he has rights against it.

239. In its character as a universal family, civil society has the right and duty of superintending and influencing education, inasmuch as education bears upon the child's capacity to become a member of society. . . .

241. . . . Contingencies, physical conditions, and factors grounded in external circumstances . . . may reduce men to poverty. The poor still have the needs common to civil society, and yet since society has withdrawn from them the natural means of acquisition . . . and broken the bond of the family . . . their poverty leaves them more or less deprived of all the advantages of society . . . The public authority takes the place of the family where the poor are concerned in respect not only of their immediate want but also of laziness of disposition, malignity, and the other vices which arise out of their plight and their sense of wrong.

242. . . . Casual almsgiving and casual endowments, e.g. for the burning of lamps before holy images, &c., are supplemented by public almshouses, hospitals, street-lighting, and so forth. There is still quite enough left over and above these things for charity to do on its own account. . . .

SUB-SECTION 3

The State

257. The state is the actuality of the ethical Idea. It is ethical mind *qua* the substantial will manifest and revealed to itself, knowing and thinking itself, accomplishing what it knows and in so far as it knows it. The state exists immediately in custom, mediately in individual self-consciousness, knowledge, and activity, while self-consciousness in virtue of its sentiment towards the state finds in the state, as its essence and the end and product of its activity, its substantive freedom. . . .

258. The state is absolutely rational inasmuch as it is the actuality of the substantial will which it possesses in the particular self-consciousness once that consciousness has been raised to consciousness of its universality. This substantial unity is an absolute unmoved end in itself, in which freedom comes into its supreme right. On the other hand this final end has supreme right against the individual, whose supreme duty is to be a member of the state.

If the state is confused with civil society, and if its specific end is laid down as the security and protection of property and personal freedom, then the interest of the individuals as such becomes the ultimate end of their association, and it follows that membership of the state is something optional. But the state's relation to the individual is quite different from this. Since the state is mind objectified, it is only as one of its members that the individual himself has objectivity, genuine individuality, and an ethical life. Unification pure and simple is the true content and aim of the individual, and the individual's destiny is the living of a universal life. . . .

. . . If we ask what is or has been the historical origin of the state in general, still more if we ask about the origin of any particular state; . . . or finally if we ask in what light the basis of the state's rights has been conceived and consciously established, whether this basis has been supposed to be positive divine right, or contract, custom, &c.—all these questions are no concern of the Idea of the state. We are here dealing exclusively with the philosophic science of the state, and from that point of view all these things are mere appearance and therefore matters for history. . . .

The philosophical treatment of these topics is concerned only with their inward side, with the thought of their concept. The merit of Rousseau's contribution to the search for this concept is that, by adducing the will as the principle of the state, he is adducing a principle which has thought both for its form and its content . . . Unfortunately, however, . . . he takes the will only in a determinate form as the individual will, and he regards the universal will . . . only as a "general" will which proceeds out of this individual will. . . . The result is that he reduces the union of individuals in the state to a contract and therefore to something based on . . . their capriciously given express consent; and abstract reasoning proceeds to draw the logical inferences which destroy the absolutely divine principle of the state, together with its majesty and absolute authority. For this reason, when these abstract conclusions came into power, they afforded for the first time in human history the prodigious spectacle of the overthrow of the constitution of a great actual state and its complete reconstruction *ab initio* on the basis of pure thought alone, after the destruction of all existing and given material. The will of its re-founders was to give it what they alleged was a purely rational basis, but it was only abstractions that were being used; the Idea was lacking; and the experiment ended in the maximum of frightfulness and terror. . . .

260. The state is the actuality of concrete freedom. But concrete freedom consists in this, that personal individuality and its particular interests not only achieve their complete development and gain explicit recognition for their right (as they do in the sphere of the family and civil society) but, for one thing, they also pass over of their own accord into the interest of the universal, and, for another thing, they know and will the universal; they even recognize it as their own substantive mind; they take it as their end and aim and are active in its pursuit. The result is that the universal does not prevail or achieve completion except along with particular interests and through the co-operation of particular knowing and willing; and individuals likewise do not live as private persons for their own ends alone, but in the very act of willing these they will the universal. . . .

264. Mind is the nature of human beings *en masse* and their nature is therefore two-

fold; (i) at one extreme, explicit individuality of consciousness and will, and (ii) at the other extreme, universality which knows and wills what is substantive. Hence they attain their right in both these respects only in so far as both their private personality and its substantive basis are actualized. Now in the family and civil society they acquire their right in the first of these respects directly and in the second indirectly, in that they find their substantive self-consciousness in social institutions which are the universal implicit in their particular interests. . . .

265. These institutions are the components of the constitution (i.e. of rationality developed and actualized) in the sphere of particularity. They are, therefore, the firm foundation not only of the state but also of the citizen's trust in it and sentiment towards it. They are the pillars of public freedom since in them particular freedom is realized and rational, and therefore there is *implicitly* present even in them the union of freedom and necessity. . . .

267. This necessity in ideality is the inner self-development of the Idea. As the substance of the individual subject, it is his political sentiment [patriotism]; . . . it is the organism of the state. . . .

268. The political sentiment, patriotism pure and simple, is assured conviction with truth as its basis . . . and a volition which has become habitual. In this sense it is simply a product of the institutions subsisting in the state, since rationality is *actually* present in the state, while action in conformity with these institutions gives rationality its practical proof. This sentiment is, in general, trust (which may pass over into a greater or lesser degree of educated insight), or the consciousness that my interest, both substantive and particular, is contained and preserved in another's (i.e. in the state's) interest and end, i.e. in the other's relation to me as an individual. In this way, this very other is immediately not an other in my eyes, and in being conscious of this fact, I am free.

Patriotism is often understood to mean only a readiness for exceptional sacrifices and actions. Essentially, however, it is the sentiment which, in the relationships of our daily life and under ordinary conditions, habitually recognizes that the community is one's substantive groundwork and end. . . .

269. The patriotic sentiment acquires its specifically determined content from the various members of the organism of the state . . . This organism is the constitution of the state.

270. . . . The state . . . knows what it wills and knows it in its universality, i.e. as something thought. Hence it works and acts by reference to consciously adopted ends, known principles, and laws which are not merely implicit but are actually present to consciousness; and further, it acts with precise knowledge of existing conditions and circumstances, inasmuch as its actions have a bearing on these.

. . . Religion is a relation to the Absolute, a relation which takes the form of feeling, representative thinking, faith; and, brought within its all-embracing circumference, everything becomes only accidental and transient. Now if, in relation to the state, we cling to this form of experience and make it the authority for the state and its essential determinant, the state must become a prey to weakness, insecurity, and disorder, because it is an organism in which firmly fixed distinct powers, laws, and institutions have been developed. In contrast with the form of religion, a form which draws a veil over everything determinate, and so comes to be purely subjective, the objective and universal element in the state, i.e. the laws, acquires a negative instead of a stable and authoritative character, and the result is the production of maxims of conduct like the following: "To the righteous man no law is given; only be pious, and for the rest, practise what thou wilt; yield to thine own caprice and passion, and if thereby others suffer wrong, commend them to the consolations and hopes of religion, or better still, call them irreligious and condemn them to perdition." This negative attitude, however, may not confine itself to an inner disposition and attitude of mind; it may turn instead to the outside world and assert its authority there, and then there is

an outbreak of the religious fanaticism which . . . discards all government and legal order as barriers cramping the inner life . . . and at the same time proscribes private property, marriage, the ties and work involved in civil society, &c., &c., as degrading to love and the freedom of feeling. But since even then decisions must somehow be made for everyday life and practice, the same doctrine which we had before . . . turns up again here, namely that subjective ideas, i.e. opinion and capricious inclination, are to do the deciding.

In contrast with the truth thus veiled behind subjective ideas and feelings, the genuine truth is the prodigious transfer of the inner into the outer, the building of reason into the real world, and this has been the task of the world during the whole course of its history. It is by working at this task that civilized man has actually given reason an embodiment in law and government and achieved consciousness of the fact. Those who 'seek guidance from the Lord' and are assured that the whole truth is directly present in their unschooled opinions, fail to apply themselves to the task of exalting their subjectivity to consciousness of the truth and to knowledge of duty and objective right. . . .

. . . The difference of their two domains may be pushed by the church into sheer antagonism . . . It may think that it is an end in itself, while the state is a mere means. These claims produce the demand . . . that the state should not only allow the church to do as it likes with complete freedom, but that it should pay unconditional respect to the church's doctrines as doctrines, whatever their character, because their determination is supposed to be the task of the church alone. The church bases this claim on the wide ground that the whole domain of mind . . . is its property. But science and all types of knowledge also have a footing in that domain . . . and, with even better justification, may regard themselves as occupying the position which the church claims. Hence science also may in the same way demand to be independent of the state, which is then supposed to be a mere means with the task of providing for science as though science were an end in itself.

. . . It is philosophic insight which sees that while church and state differ in form, they do not stand opposed in content, for truth and rationality are the content of both. . . .

. . . Since ethical principles and the organization of the state in general are drawn into the domain of religion and not only may, but also should, be established by reference thereto, this reference gives religious credentials to the state itself. On the other hand, however, the state retains the right and the form of self-conscious, objective, rationality, the right to make this form count and to maintain it against pretensions springing from truth in a subjective dress, no matter how such truth may girdle itself with certitude and authority.

The state is universal in form, a form whose essential principle is thought. This explains why it was in the state that freedom of thought and science had their origin. It was a church, on the other hand, which burnt Giordano Bruno, forced Galileo to recant on his knees his exposition of the Copernican view of the solar system, and so forth. Science too, therefore, has its place on the side of the state since it has one element, its form, in common with the state, and its aim is knowledge, knowledge of objective truth and rationality in terms of thought. Such knowledge may, of course, fall from the heights of science into opinion and deductive argumentation, and, turning its attention to ethical matters and the organization of the state, set itself against their basic principles. And it may perhaps do this while making for this opining—as if it were reason and the right of subjective self-consciousness —the same pretentious claim as the church makes for its own sphere, the claim, namely, to be free from restraint in its opinions and convictions.

. . . On the one hand, in so far as opining is mere opining, a purely subjective matter, it is without any genuine inherent force of power, plume itself as it may; and from this point of view the state may be . . . totally

indifferent to it . . . On the other hand, however, when this opining of bad principles embodies itself in a general organization corrosive of the actual order, the state has to set its face against it and protect objective truth and the principles of ethical life (and it must do the same in face of the formulae of unconditioned subjectivity if these have proposed to take the starting point of science as their basis, and turn state educational institutions against the state by encouraging them to make against it claims as pretentious as those of a church); while, vice versa, in face of a church claiming unrestricted and unconditional authority, the state has in general to make good the formal right of self-consciousness to its own insight, its own conviction, and, in short, its own thought of what is to hold good as objective truth.

. . . If the state is to come into existence as the self-*knowing* ethical actuality of mind, it is essential that its form should be distinct from that of authority and faith. But this distinction emerges only in so far as the church is subjected to inward divisions. It is only thereafter that the state, in contrast with the particular sects, has attained to universality of thought—its formal principle —and is bringing this universality into existence. . . . Hence so far from its being or its having been a misfortune for the state that the church is disunited, it is only as a result of that disunion that the state has been able to reach its appointed end as a self-consciously rational and ethical organization. Moreover, this disunion is the best piece of good fortune which could have befallen either the church or thought so far as the freedom and rationality of either is concerned. . . .

272. The constitution is rational in so far as the state inwardly differentiates and determines its activity in accordance with the nature of the concept. . . .

273. The state as a political entity is . . . cleft into three substantive divisions:

(a) the power to determine and establish the universal—the Legislature;

(b) the power to subsume single cases and the

spheres of particularity under the universal
—the Executive;

(c) the power of subjectivity, as the will with
the power of ultimate decision—the Crown.
In the crown, the different powers are
bound into an individual unity which is
thus at once the apex and basis of the
whole, i.e. of constitutional monarchy.

The development of the state to constitutional monarchy is the achievement of the
modern world, a world in which the substantial Idea has won the infinite form. . . .

Another question readily presents itself
here: "Who is to frame the constitution?"
This question seems clear, but closer inspection shows at once that it is meaningless, for
it presupposes that there is no constitution
there, but only an agglomeration of atomic
individuals. How an agglomeration of individuals could acquire a constitution . . .
it would have to be allowed to settle for
itself, since with an agglomeration the concept has nothing to do. But if the question
presupposes an already existent constitution,
then it is not about framing, but only about
altering the constitution, and the very presupposition of a constitution directly implies
that its alteration may come about only
by constitutional means. In any case, however, it is absolutely essential that the
constitution should not be regarded as something made, even though it has come into
being in time. It must be treated rather as
something simply existent in and by itself,
as divine therefore, and constant, and so as
exalted above the sphere of things that are
made.

274. . . . The state, as the mind of a nation, is both the law permeating all relationships within the state and also at the same
time the manners and consciousness of its
citizens. It follows, therefore, that the constitution of any given nation depends in general on the character and development of its
self-consciousness. . . .

278. . . . Sovereignty depends on the fact
that the particular functions and powers of
the state are not self-subsistent or firmly
grounded either on their own account or in
the particular will of the individual func-

tionaries, but have there roots ultimately in
the unity of the state as their single self. . . .

In feudal times, . . . not only was the monarch not sovereign at all, but the state itself
was not sovereign either. For one thing, the
particular functions and powers of the state
and civil society were arranged . . . into independent Corporations and societies, so that
the state as a whole was rather an aggregate
than an organism; and, for another thing,
office was the private property of individuals,
and hence what they were to do in their
public capacity was left to their own opinion and caprice. . . .

The fact that the sovereignty of the state
is the ideality of all particular authorities
within it gives rise to the easy and also very
common misunderstanding that this ideality
is only might and pure arbitrariness while
"sovereignty" is a synonym for "despotism."
But despotism means any state of affairs
where law has disappeared and where the
particular will as such, whether of a monarch or a mob . . . counts as law or rather
takes the place of law; while it is precisely
in legal, constitutional, government that sovereignty is to be found as . . . the ideality
of the particular spheres and functions. That
is to say, sovereignty brings it about that
each of these spheres is not something independent . . . but that instead, even in these
aims and modes of working, each is determined by and dependent on the aim of the
whole. . . .

This ideality manifests itself in a twofold
way:

(i) In times of peace, the particular
spheres and functions pursue the path of
satisfying their particular aims and minding
their own business, and it is in part only by
way of the unconscious necessity of the thing
that their self-seeking is turned into a contribution to reciprocal support and to the
support of the whole . . . In part, however,
it is by the direct influence of higher authority that they are not only continually
brought back to the aims of the whole and
restricted accordingly . . . but are also constrained to perform direct services for the
support of the whole.

(ii) In a situation of exigency, however . . . the organism of which these particular spheres are members fuses into the single concept of sovereignty. The sovereign is entrusted with the salvation of the state at the sacrifice of these particular authorities whose powers are valid at other times, and it is then that the ideality comes into its proper actuality. . . .

279. . . . The usual sense, however, in which men have recently begun to speak of the "sovereignty of the people" is that it is something opposed to the sovereignty existent in the monarch. . . . Taken without its monarch and the articulation of the whole which is the indispensable and direct concomitant of monarchy, the people is a formless mass and no longer a state. It lacks every one of those determinate characteristics—sovereignty, government, judges, magistrates, class-divisions, &c.,—which are to be found only in a whole which is inwardly organized. . . .

If the "people" is represented . . . as an inwardly developed, genuinely organic, totality, then sovereignty is there as the personality of the whole, and this personality is there, in the real existence adequate to its concept, as the person of the monarch.

. . . Leaders must either be available already . . . or . . . they may rise to the top . . . This must happen, since everything done and everything actual is inaugurated and brought to completion by the single decisive act of a leader. . . .

281. Both moments in their undivided unity—(a) the will's ultimate ungrounded self, and (b) therefore its similarly ungrounded objective existence (existence being the category which is at home in nature)—constitute the Idea of something against which caprice is powerless, the "majesty" of the monarch. In this unity lies the actual unity of the state, and it is only through this, its inward and outward immediacy, that the unity of the state is saved from the risk of being drawn down into the sphere of particularity and its caprices, ends, and opinions, and saved too from the war of factions round the throne and from the enfeeblement and overthrow of the power of the state. . . .

If succession to the throne is rigidly determined, i.e. if it is hereditary, then faction is obviated at a demise of the crown. . . . This aspect, however, is only consequential, and to make it the reason for hereditary succession is to drag down the majesty of the throne into the sphere of argumentation, to ignore its true character as ungrounded immediacy and ultimate inwardness, and to base it not on the Idea of the state immanent within it, but on something external to itself, on some extraneous notion such as the "welfare of the state" or the "welfare of the people." . . . Hence, the majesty of the monarch is a topic for thoughtful treatment by philosophy alone, since every method of inquiry, other than the speculative method of the infinite Idea which is purely self-grounded, annuls the nature of majesty altogether. . . .

. . . In an elective monarchy . . . the nature of the relation between king and people implies that the ultimate decision is left with the particular will, and hence the constitution becomes a Compact of Election, i.e. a surrender of the power of the state at the discretion of the particular will. The result of this is that the particular offices of state turn into private property, the sovereignty of the state is enfeebled and lost, and finally the state disintegrates within and is overthrown from without. . . .

287. There is a distinction between the monarch's decisions and their execution and application, or in general between his decisions and the continued execution or maintenance of past decisions, existing laws, regulations, organizations for the securing of common ends, and so forth. This task of merely subsuming the particular under the universal is comprised in the executive power, which also includes the powers of the judiciary and the police. . . .

288. Particular interests which are common to everyone fall within civil society and lie outside the absolutely universal interest of the state proper . . . The administration of these is in the hands of Corporations . . . commercial and professional as well as mu-

nicipal, and their officials, directors, managers, and the like. . . . Their authority rests on the confidence of their commonalties and professional equals. On the other hand, however, these circles of particular interests must be subordinated to the higher interests of the state, and hence the filling of positions of responsibility in Corporations, &c., will generally be effected by a mixture of popular election by those interested with appointment and ratification by higher authority. . . .

297. Civil servants and the members of the executive constitute the greater part of the middle class, the class in which the consciousness of right and the developed intelligence of the mass of the people is found. The sovereign working on the middle class at the top, and Corporation-rights working on it at the bottom, are the institutions which effectually prevent it from acquiring the isolated position of an aristocracy and using its education and skill as means to an arbitrary tyranny. . . .

298. The legislature is concerned (a) with the laws as such in so far as they require fresh and extended determination; and (b) with the content of home affairs affecting the entire state. . . .

299. . . . The proper object of universal legislation may be distinguished in a general way from the proper function of administrative officials or of some kind of state regulation, in that the content of the former is wholly universal, i.e. determinate laws, while it is what is particular in content which falls to the latter. . . . This distinction, however, is not a hard and fast one, because a law, by being a law, is *ab initio* something more than a mere command in general terms. . . . A law must in itself be something determinate, but the more determinate it is, the more readily are its terms capable of being carried out as they stand. At the same time, however, to give to laws such a fully detailed determinacy would give them empirical features subject inevitably to alteration in the course of their being actually carried out, and this would contravene their character as laws. The organic unity of the powers of

the state itself implies that it is one single mind which both firmly establishes the universal and also brings it into its determinate actuality and carries it out. . . .

300. In the legislature as a whole the other powers are . . . (i) the monarchy as that to which ultimate decisions belong; (ii) the executive as the advisory body since it is the moment possessed of (a) a concrete knowledge and oversight of the whole state in its numerous facets and the actual principles firmly established within it, and (b) a knowledge in particular of what the state's power needs. The last moment in the legislature is the Estates.

301. The Estates have the function of bringing public affairs into existence not only implicitly, but also actually, i.e. of bringing into existence the moment of subjective formal freedom, the public consciousness as an empirical universal, of which the thoughts and opinions of the Many are particulars. . . .

. . . The idea uppermost in men's minds when they speak about the necessity or the expediency of "summoning the Estates" is generally something of this sort: (i) The deputies of the people, or even the people themselves, must know best what is in their best interest, and (ii) their will for its promotion is undoubtedly the most disinterested . . . However, the truth is that if "people" means a particular section of the citizens, then it means precisely that section which does *not* know what it wills. To know what one wills, and still more to know what the absolute will, Reason, wills, is the fruit of profound apprehension and insight, precisely the things which are *not* popular.

The Estates are a guarantee of the general welfare and public freedom. A little reflection will show that this guarantee does not lie in their particular power of insight, because the highest civil servants necessarily have a deeper and more comprehensive insight into the nature of the state's organization and requirements. . . . No, the guarantee lies on the contrary (a) in the *additional* insight of the deputies, insight in the first place into the activity of such officials as are not immediately under the eye of the higher functionaries of state, and in particular into the more pressing and more specialized needs and deficiencies which are directly in their view; (b) in the fact that the anticipation of criticism from the Many, particularly of public criticism, has the effect of inducing officials to devote their best attention beforehand to their duties and the schemes under consideration, and to deal with these only in accordance with the purest motives. This same compulsion is effective also on the members of the Estates themselves.

. . . As for the general guarantee which is supposed to lie peculiarly in the Estates, each of the other political institutions shares with the Estates in being a guarantee of public welfare and rational freedom . . . .

Hence the specific function which the concept assigns to the Estates is to be sought in the fact that in them the subjective moment in universal freedom—the private judgement and private will of the sphere called "civil society" in this book—comes into existence integrally related to the state. . . .

302. Regarded as a mediating organ, the Estates stand between the government in general on the one hand and the nation broken up into particulars (people and associations) on the other . . . They are a middle term preventing both the extreme isolation of the power of the crown, which otherwise might seem a mere arbitrary tyranny, and also the isolation of the particular interests of persons, societies, and Corporations. Further, and more important, they prevent individuals from having the appearance of a mass or an aggregate and so from acquiring an unorganized opinion and volition and from crystallizing into a powerful *bloc* in opposition to the organized state. . . .

303. . . . The Many, as units—a congenial interpretation of "people," are of course something connected, but they are connected only as an aggregate, a formless mass whose commotion and activity could therefore only be elementary, irrational, barbarous, and frightful. When we hear speakers on the con-

stitution expatiating about the "people"—this unorganized collection—we know from the start that we have nothing to expect but generalities and perverse declamations.

The circles of association in civil society are already communities. To picture these communities as once more breaking up into a mere conglomeration of individuals as soon as they enter the field of politics, i.e. the field of the highest concrete universality, is *eo ipso* to hold civil and political life apart from one another. . . .

305. The principle of one of the classes of civil society is in itself capable of adaptation to this political position. The class in question is the one whose ethical life is natural, whose basis is family life, and, so far as its livelihood is concerned, the possession of land. Its particular members attain their position by birth, just as the monarch does, and, in common with him, they possess a will which rests on itself alone.

306. This class is more particularly fitted for political position and significance in that its capital is independent alike of the state's capital, the uncertainty of business, the quest for profit, and any sort of fluctuation in possessions. It is likewise independent of favour, whether from the executive or the mob. It is even fortified against its own wilfulness, because those members of this class who are called to political life are not entitled, as other citizens are, either to dispose of their entire property at will, or to the assurance that it will pass to their children, whom they love equally, in similarly equal divisions. Hence their wealth becomes inalienable, entailed, and burdened by primogeniture.

307. . . . This class is summoned and entitled to its political vocation by birth without the hazards of election. . . . While it mirrors in itself . . . the moment of the monarchial power, it also shares in other respects the needs and rights of the other extreme [i.e. civil society] and hence it becomes a support at once of the throne and society.

308. The second section of the Estates comprises the fluctuating element in civil society. This element can enter politics only

through its deputies; the multiplicity of its members is an external reason for this, but the essential reason is the specific character of this element and its activity. Since these deputies are the deputies of civil society, it follows as a direct consequence that their appointment is made by the society as a society . . . It makes the appointment as a society, articulated into associations, communities, and Corporations, which although constituted already for other purposes, acquire in this way a connexion with politics. . . .

311. A further point about the election of deputies is that, since civil society is the electorate, the deputies should themselves be conversant with and participate in its special needs, difficulties, and particular interests. . . .

As for popular suffrage, it may be further remarked that especially in large states it leads inevitably to electoral indifference, since the casting of a single vote is of no significance where there is a multitude of electors . . . The result of an institution of this kind is more likely to be the opposite of what was intended; election actually falls into the power of a few, of a caucus, and so of the particular and contingent interest which is precisely what was to have been neutralized . . . .

314. . . . Knowledge of public business . . . is extended by the publicity of Estates debates.

315. The opening of this opportunity to know has a more universal aspect because by this means public opinion first reaches thoughts that are true and attains insight into the situation and concept of the state and its affairs, and so first acquires ability to estimate these more rationally. By this means also, it becomes acquainted with and learns to respect the work, abilities, virtues, and dexterity of ministers and officials. . . .

316. The formal subjective freedom of individuals consists in their having and expressing their own private judgments, opinions, and recommendations on affairs of state. This freedom is collectively manifested as what is called "public opinion," in which

what is absolutely universal, the substantive and the true, is linked with its opposite, the purely particular and private opinions of the Many. Public opinion as it exists is thus a standing self-contradiction. . . .

317. Public opinion, therefore, is a repository not only of the genuine needs and correct tendencies of common life, but also . . . of the eternal, substantive principles of justice, the true content and result of legislation, the whole constitution, and the general position of the state. At the same time . . . it becomes infected by all the accidents of opinion, by its ignorance and perversity, by its mistakes and falsity of judgement. . . .

. . . The substantial, however, is the heart of public opinion, and therefore it is with that alone that it is truly serious. What the substantial is, though, is not discoverable from public opinion, because its very substantiality implies that it is known in and from itself alone. . . .

318. Public opinion therefore deserves to be as much respected as despised. . . . Thus to be independent of public opinion is the first formal condition of achieving anything great or rational whether in life or in science. . . .

319. Freedom of public communication . . . is directly assured by the laws . . . which control or punish its excesses. But it is assured indirectly by the innocuous character which it acquires as a result, principally, of the rationality of the constitution, the stability of government, and secondly, of the publicity of Estates Assemblies. The reason why the latter makes free speech harmless is that what is voiced in these Assemblies is a sound and mature insight into the concerns of the state, with the result that members of the general public are left with nothing of much importance to say, and above all are deprived of the opinion that what they say is of peculiar importance and efficacy. A further safeguard of free speech is the indifference and contempt speedily and necessarily visited on shallow and cantankerous talking.

To define freedom of the press as freedom to say and write whatever we please is parallel to the assertion that freedom as such means freedom to do as we please. . . .

But the substance of the matter is and remains that traducing the honour of anyone, slander, abuse, the contemptuous caricature of government, its ministers, officials, and in particular the person of the monarch, defiance of the laws, incitement to rebellion, &c., &c., are all crimes or misdemeanours in one or other of their numerous gradations. . . .

320. Subjectivity is manifested in its most external form as the undermining of the established life of the state by opinion and ratiocination when they endeavour to assert the authority of their own fortuitous character and so bring about their own destruction. But its true actuality is attained in the opposite of this, i.e. in the subjectivity identical with the substantial will of the state, the subjectivity which constitutes the concept of the power of the crown and which, as the ideality of the whole state, has not up to this point attained its right or its existence. . . .

337. The substantial welfare of the state is its welfare as a particular state in its specific interest and situation and its no less special foreign affairs, including its particular treaty relations. Its government therefore is a matter of particular wisdom, not of universal Providence. . . .

At one time the opposition between morals and politics, and the demand that the latter should conform to the former, were much canvassed. . . . The welfare of a state has claims to recognition totally different from those of the welfare of the individual. The ethical substance, the state, has its determinate being, i.e. its right, directly embodied in something existent, something not abstract but concrete, and the principle of its conduct and behaviour can only be this concrete existent and not one of the many universal thoughts supposed to be moral commands. When politics is alleged to clash with morals and so to be always wrong, the doctrine propounded rests on superficial ideas about morality, the nature of the state,

and the state's relation to the moral point of view. . . .

340. . . . The principles of the national minds are wholly restricted on account of their particularity, for it is in this particularity that, as existent individuals, they have their objective actuality and their self-consciousness. Their deeds and destinies in their reciprocal relations to one another are the dialectic of the finitude of these minds, and out of it arises the universal mind, the mind of the world, free from all restriction, producing itself as that which exercises its right —and its right is the highest right of all— over these finite minds in the "history of the world which is the world's court of judgement." . . .

343. The history of mind is its own act. Mind is only what it does, and its act is to make itself the object of its own consciousness. In history its act is to gain consciousness of itself as mind, to apprehend itself in its interpretation of itself to itself. . . .

344. In the course of this work of the world mind, states, nations, and individuals arise animated by their particular determinate principle which has its interpretation and actuality in their constitutions and in the whole range of their life and condition. While their consciousness is limited to these and they are absorbed in their mundane interests, they are all the time the unconscious tools and organs of the world mind at work within them. The shapes which they take pass away, while the absolute mind prepares and works out its transition to its next higher stage. . . .

347. . . . The history of a single world-historical nation contains (a) the development of its principle from its latent embryonic stage until it blossoms into the self-conscious freedom of ethical life and presses in upon world history; and (b) the period of its decline and fall, since it is its decline and fall that signalizes the emergence in it of a higher principle as the pure negative of its own. When this happens, mind passes over into the new principle and so marks out another nation for world-historical significance. . . .

349. A nation does not begin by being a state. The transition from a family, a horde, a clan, a multitude, &c., to political conditions is the realization of the Idea in the form of that nation. Without this form, a nation, as an ethical substance—which is what it is implicitly, lacks the objectivity of possessing in its own eyes and in the eyes of others, a universal and universally valid embodiment in laws, i.e. in determinate thoughts, and as a result it fails to secure recognition from others. So long as it lacks objective law and an explicitly established rational constitution, its autonomy is formal only and is not sovereignty.

. . . Before history actually begins, we have on the one hand dull innocence, devoid of interest, and, on the other, the courage of revenge and of the struggle for formal recognition. . . .

350. It is the absolute right of the Idea to step into existence in clear-cut laws and objective institutions . . . This right is the right of heroes to found states.

351. The same consideration justifies civilized nations in regarding and treating as barbarians those who lag behind them in institutions which are the essential moments of the state . . . The civilized nation is conscious that the rights of barbarians are unequal to its own and treats their autonomy as only a formality.

14

John Austin

1790–1859

John Austin's career of frustrations began in the British army. He had had a comfortable childhood in the English countryside as son of a prosperous Ipswich flour miller. He enlisted at sixteen, served overseas, and advanced to a commission. But his bookish ways and tastes unsuited him for military life. He resigned at twenty-one and spent seven years in study.

Austin was called to the bar in 1818. Though his teachers said he would be a brilliant lawyer, he had misgivings. He specialized in drafting equity pleadings, then at the height of prolixity and formality. His health was not good in the early days of his practice; he had a recurrent, debilitating fever which pounced on him whenever practice made rigorous demands and which seemed to be aggravated by the atmosphere of courts and law offices. He was tediously exacting, and even took endless care of insignificant details.

His attraction for handsome Sarah Taylor was puzzling to her friends, who were much surprised when she married the grave young man in 1820. The couple set up an establishment almost next door to James Mill, and windows of their house overlooked Jeremy Bentham's garden, where Austin's daughter, Lucie, played with John Stuart Mill.

At thirty-five poor health and dwindling clientele led Austin to quit his practice. Next year, however, newly founded London University offered him a Jurisprudence chair. His lectures were not to start for two years, so he went to Germany to prepare. He soon settled at Bonn University and quickly became adept in using German with precision. His studies in systematic German jurisprudence re-enforced his natural admiration for careful and laborious analysis and laid groundwork for his leadership in Anglo-American analytical jurisprudence. This German interlude was a high spot in the lives of the Austin family, who were warmly and respectfully received into Bonn's intellectual and social upper crust.

Austin began his teaching in high spirits and improved health. Notes he made for closing remarks after his first lecture showed that he preferred to speak informally but did not dare to; he invited discussion at the end of each lecture from which he hoped to learn to teach without reading a script. His exact and overly qualified style made his lectures dry. His classes were never large. At first he had a respectful roomful of apt young men—including John Stuart Mill. But Austin's course had little to do with everyday law, and vocationally oriented students elected to study under his undistinguished colleague, one Amos. Austin's chair was not endowed, and he attracted little tuition; he soon found himself without income as well as without students. In 1832 he resigned. His wife said that collapse of his university teaching was the tragic blow from which he never recovered.

After his resignation he published his introductory lectures under the title, *The Province of Jurisprudence Determined*, (1832) excerpts from which follow this note. He worried about the loss he thought the publisher was sure to sustain, and was surprised and relieved when the printing sold out. His fears were not groundless; the book was ignored by serious journals and sold only after it had slowly attracted appreciation.

Some of his friends got him a place on a Parliamentary commission on criminal law. His year spent with the commission was agonizing; he felt he was virtually taking public money under false pretenses because the commission worked only at a superficial level and rejected his plans to go to roots of the subject.

He then got a second chance at teaching; Inner Temple engaged him to lecture on jurisprudence. The lectures were an experiment, and their trial status robbed Austin of confidence. These students, too, proved apathetic to instruction unrelated to practice. Austin's health went down hill. Again he resigned.

Then came a trip to Boulogne in search of inexpensive tranquility and better health. It was at this time he said to his wife, "I was born out of place. I ought to have been a schoolman of the twelfth century or a German professor."

After a year and a half of recuperation, he accepted a proposal of the British Colonial Office that he go to Malta as a Royal Commissioner to look into dissatisfactions of the populace. He enjoyed this assignment and did it well; he had enough sympathy to understand real grievances and enough judgment to reject fantastic proposals and fake complaints. The Colonial Office adopted all of his recommendations. But this work, too, was to end in frustration. Recommendations on administrative and social reforms were all in, and Austin was eagerly starting to work on the Maltese legal and judicial system, when a change of administration resulted in Austin's abrupt recall without explanation.

Perhaps his labors in Malta were already too much for him; his health broke badly shortly after. Fifty-year-old Austin went back to the continent where he spent most of the next decade; first at Carlsbad, where the waters seemed to help him, and where he returned for several summers; then to Dresden and Berlin; and finally to Paris.

Again he evoked respect and found intellectual company on the continent. German scholars (including Savigny) sought him out, and in France he was almost immediately elected to the Institute. His book on jurisprudence had become a classic. There were many demands for a new edition and he toyed with the idea of extensive revisions and expansion.

The revolution of 1848 drove the Austins out of France and increased John's fear of popular rule. They settled into quiet English life at Weybridge—close enough to London for an occasional visit from their daughter, Lucie, now Lady Duff Gordon and a glamorous minor literary figure in her own right. Here Austin gave up all thought of career and accomplishment. He forgot about re-editing his book and spent a gentle decade interested in his garden, his books, and English politics. His death was little noted; it was not reported in legal journals. His widow, Sarah, had published several works on her own in various literary fields; it was she who edited his London University lectures, adding a heavy volume and a half to the slight first edition published by her careful, slow working, thwarted husband.

Sir Henry Maine, the famous Cambridge legal historian, revived interest in Austin's jurisprudence, and made him, perhaps, the most influential force in the last quarter of nineteenth century Anglo-American legal thought.

LECTURES ON JURISPRUDENCE *

THE PROVINCE OF JURISPRUDENCE DETERMINED

ANALYSIS LECTURES I-VI

LAWS PROPER, or properly so-called, are commands; laws which are not commands, are laws improper or improperly so called. Laws properly so called, with laws improp-

* Reprinted by permission of John Murray, Ltd., London.

erly so called, may be aptly divided into the four following kinds.

1. The divine laws, or the laws of God: that is to say, the laws which are set by God to his human creatures.

2. Positive laws: that is to say, laws which are simply and strictly so called, and which form the appropriate matter of general and particular jurisprudence.

3. Positive morality, rules of positive morality, or positive moral rules.

4. Laws metaphorical or figurative, or merely metaphorical or figurative.

The divine laws and positive laws are laws properly so called.—Of positive moral rules, some are laws properly so called, but others are laws improper. The positive moral rules which are laws improperly so called, may be styled laws or rules set or imposed by opinion: for they are merely opinions or sentiments held or felt by men in regard to human conduct. A law set by opinion and a law imperative and proper are allied by analogy merely; although the analogy by which they are allied is strong or close.— Laws metaphorical or figurative, or merely metaphorical or figurative, are laws improperly so called. A law metaphorical or figurative and a law imperative and proper are allied by analogy merely; and the analogy by which they are allied is slender or remote.

Consequently, positive laws (the appropriate matter of jurisprudence) are related in the way of resemblance, or by close or remote analogies, to the following objects. 1. In the way of resemblance, they are related to the laws of God. 2. In the way of resemblance, they are related to those rules of positive morality which are laws properly so called: And by a close or strong analogy, they are related to those rules of positive morality which are laws set by opinion. 3. By a remote or slender analogy, they are related to laws metaphorical, or laws merely metaphorical . . . .

LECTURE I

The matter of jurisprudence is positive law: law, simply and strictly so called: or law set by political superiors to political inferiors . . . I begin my projected Course with determining the province of jurisprudence, or with distinguishing the matter of jurisprudence from those various related objects: trying to define the subject of which I intend to treat, before I endeavour to analyze its numerous and complicated parts.

A law . . . may be said to be a rule laid down for the guidance of an intelligent being by an intelligent being having power over him . . . The term *law* embraces the following objects:—Laws set by God to his human creatures, and laws set by men to men.

The whole or a portion of the laws set by God to men is frequently styled the law of nature or natural law: being, in truth, the only natural law, of which it is possible to speak without a metaphor, or without a blending of objects which ought to be distinguished broadly. But rejecting the appellation Law of Nature as ambiguous and misleading, I name those laws or rules, as considered collectively or in a mass, the *Divine law,* or the *law of God.*

Laws set by men to men are of two leading or principal classes. . . .

Of the laws or rules set by men to men, some are established by *political* superiors, sovereign and subject: by persons exercising supreme and subordinate *government,* in independent nations, or independent political societies. The aggregate of the rules thus established . . . is the appropriate matter of jurisprudence . . . But as contradistinguished to *natural* law, or to the law *of nature* (meaning, by those expressions, the law of God), the aggregate of the rules, established by political superiors, is frequently styled *positive* law, or law existing *by position.* . . .

Though *some* of the laws or rules, which are set by men to men, are established by political superiors, *others* are *not* established by political superiors, or are *not* established by political superiors, in that capacity or character.

Closely analogous to human laws of this second class, are a set of objects frequently but *improperly* termed *laws,* being rules set and enforced by *mere opinion,* that is, by the opinions or sentiments held or felt by an indeterminate body of men in regard to human conduct. Instances of such a use of the term *law* are the expressions—"The law of honour"; "The law set by fashion"; and rules of this species constitute much of what is usually termed "International law."

The aggregate of human laws properly so called belonging to the second of the classes above mentioned, with the aggregate of objects *improperly* but by *close analogy* termed laws, I place together in a common class, and denote them by the term *positive morality*. The name *morality* severs them from *positive law*, while the epithet *positive* disjoins them from the *law of God*. . . .

. . . There are numerous applications of the term law, which rest upon a slender analogy and are merely metaphorical or figurative. Such is the case when we talk of *laws* observed by the lower animals; of *laws* regulating the growth or decay of vegetables; of *laws* determining the movements of inanimate bodies or masses. For where *intelligence* is not, or where it is too bounded to take the name of *reason*, and, therefore, is too bounded to conceive the purpose of a law, there is not the *will* which law can work on, or which duty can incite or restrain. . . .

. . . Laws or rules, properly so called, are a *species* of commands. . . .

. . . I shall endeavour, in the first instance, to analyze the meaning of *"command"*: . . . .

If you express or intimate a wish that I shall do or forbear from some act, and if you will visit me with an evil in case I comply not with your wish, the *expression* or *intimation* of your wish is a *command*. A command is distinguished from other significations of desire, not by the style in which the desire is signified, but by the power and the purpose of the party commanding to inflict an evil or pain in case the desire be disregarded. If you cannot or will not harm me in case I comply not with your wish, the expression of your wish is not a command, although you utter your wish in imperative phrase. If you are able and willing to harm me in case I comply not with your wish, the

expression of your wish amounts to a command, although you are prompted by a spirit of courtesy to utter it in the shape of a request. . . .

Being liable to evil from you if I comply not with a wish which you signify, I am *bound* or *obliged* by your command, or I lie under a *duty* to obey it. If, in spite of that evil in prospect, I comply not with the wish which you signify I am said to disobey your command, or to violate the duty which it imposes . . . .

The evil which will probably be incurred in case a command be disobeyed . . . is frequently called a *sanction*, or an *enforcement of obedience* . . . .

. . . The evil to be incurred by disobedience is frequently styled a *punishment*. But as punishments, strictly so called, are only a *class* of sanctions, the term is too narrow to express the meaning adequately. . . .

. . . The greater the eventual evil, and the greater the chance of incurring it, the greater is the efficacy of the command, and the greater is the strength of the obligation: Or (substituting expressions exactly equivalent) the greater is the *chance* that the command will be obeyed, and that the duty will not be broken. But where there is the smallest chance of incurring the smallest evil, the expression of a wish amounts to a command, and, therefore, imposes a duty. The sanction, if you will, is feeble or insufficient; but still there *is* a sanction, and, therefore, a duty and a command.

By some celebrated writers (by Locke, Bentham, and, I think, Paley), the term *sanction*, or *enforcement of obedience* is applied to conditional good as well as to conditional evil: to reward as well as to punishment. But, with all my habitual veneration for the names of Locke, and Bentham, I think that this extension of the term is pregnant with confusion and perplexity. . . .

If *you* expressed a desire that *I* should render a service and if you proffered a reward as the motive or inducement to render it, *you* would scarcely be said to *command* the service, nor should *I*, in ordinary language, be *obliged* to render it. In ordinary language, *you* would *promise* me a reward, on condition of my rendering the service, whilst *I* might be *incited* or *persuaded* to render it by the hope of obtaining the reward.

Again: If a law hold out a *reward* as an inducement to do some act, an eventual *right* is conferred, and not an *obligation* imposed, upon those who shall act accordingly: The *imperative* part of the law being addressed or directed to the party whom it requires to *render* the reward . . . .

Commands are of two species. Some are *laws* or *rules*. The others have not acquired an appropriate name, nor does language afford an expression which will mark them briefly and precisely. I must, therefore, note them as well as I can, by the ambiguous and inexpressive name of "*occasional* or *particular* commands.". . . .

Now where it obliges *generally* to acts or forbearances of a *class*, a command is a law or rule. But where it obliges to a *specific* act or forbearance, or to acts or forbearances which it determines *specifically* or *individually*, a command is occasional or particular. . . .

The statement which I have given in abstract expressions, I will now endeavour to illustrate by apt examples.

If you command your servant to go on a given errand, or *not* to leave your house on a given evening, or to rise at such an hour on such a morning, or to rise at that hour during the next week or month, the command is occasional or particular. For the act or acts enjoined or forbidden are specially determined or assigned.

But if you command him *simply* to rise at that hour, or to rise at that hour *always*, or to rise at that hour *till further orders*, it may be said, with propriety, that you lay down a *rule* for the guidance of your servant's conduct. . . .

If Parliament prohibited simply the exportation of corn, either for a given period or indefinitely, it would establish a law or rule: a *kind* or *sort* of acts being determined by the command, and acts of that kind or sort being *generally* forbidden. But an order

issued by Parliament to meet an impending scarcity, and stopping the exportation of corn *then shipped and in port*, would not be a law or rule, though issued by the sovereign legislature. The order regarding exclusively a specified quantity of corn, the negative acts or forbearances, enjoined by the command, would be determined specifically or individually by the determinate nature of their subject.

As issued by a sovereign legislature, and as wearing the form of a law, the order which I have now imagined would probably be *called* a law. And hence the difficulty of drawing a distinct boundary between laws and occasional commands. . . .

. . . *Judicial commands* are commonly occasional or particular, although the commands, which they are calculated to enforce, are commonly laws or rules.

For instance, the lawgiver commands that thieves shall be hanged. A specific theft and a specified thief being given, the judge commands that the thief shall be hanged, agreeably to the command of the lawgiver.

Now the lawgiver determines a class or description of acts; prohibits acts of the class generally and indefinitely; and commands, with the like generality, that punishment shall follow transgression. The command of the lawgiver is, therefore, a law or rule. But the command of the judge is occasional or particular. For he orders a specific punishment, as the consequence of a specific offence. . . .

A different line of separation has been drawn by Blackstone and others. According to Blackstone and others, a law and a particular command are distinguished in the following manner.—A law obliges *generally* the members of the given community, or a law obliges *generally* persons of a given class. A particular command obliges a *single* person, or persons whom it determines *individually*.

That laws and particular commands are not to be distinguished thus, will appear on a moment's reflection.

For, *first*, commands which oblige generally the members of the given community, or commands which oblige generally persons of given classes, are not always laws or rules.

... Suppose the sovereign to issue an order enforced by penalties, for a general mourning, on occasion of a public calamity. Now, though it is addressed to the community at large, the order is scarcely a rule, in the usual acceptation of the term. For, though it obliges generally the members of the entire community, it obliges to acts which it assigns specifically, instead of obliging generally to acts or forbearances of a class. If the sovereign commanded that *black* should be the dress of his subjects, his command would amount to a law. But if he commanded them to wear it on a specified occasion, his command would be merely particular.

And, *secondly*, a command which obliges exclusively persons individually determined, may amount, notwithstanding, to a law or rule.

For example, A father may set a *rule* to his child or children: a guardian, to his ward: a master, to his slave or servant. And certain of God's *laws* were as binding on the first man, as they are binding at this hour on the millions who have sprung from his loins.

... To frame a system of duties for every individual of the community, were simply impossible: and if it were possible, it were utterly useless. Most of the laws established by political superiors are, therefore, *general* in a twofold manner: as enjoining or forbidding generally acts of kinds or sorts; and as binding the whole community, or, at least, whole classes of its members.

But if we suppose that Parliament creates and grants an office, and that Parliament binds the grantee to services of a given description, we suppose a law established by political superiors, and yet exclusively binding a specified or determinate person. . . .

Laws and other commands are said to proceed from *superiors,* and to bind or oblige *inferiors.* . . .

Superiority is often synonymous with *precedence* or *excellence.* We talk of superiors in rank; of superiors in wealth; of superiors in virtue: comparing certain persons with certain other persons; and meaning that the former precede or excel the latter, in rank, in wealth, or in virtue.

But, taken with the meaning wherein I here understand it, the term *superiority* signifies *might:* the power of affecting others with evil or pain and of forcing them, through fear of that evil, to fashion their conduct to one's wishes.

For example, God is emphatically the *superior* of Man. For his power of affecting us with pain, and of forcing us to comply with his will, is unbounded and resistless.

To a limited extent, the sovereign One or Number is the superior of the subject or citizen: the master, of the slave or servant: the father, of the child.

In short, whoever can *oblige* another to comply with his wishes, is the *superior* of that other, so far as the ability reaches: The party who is obnoxious to the impending evil, being, to that same extent, the *inferior.*

The might or superiority of God, is simple or absolute. But in all or most cases of human superiority, the relation of superior and inferior, and the relation of inferior and superior, are reciprocal. Or (changing the expression) the party who is the superior as viewed from one aspect, is the inferior as viewed from another.

For example, To an indefinite, though limited extent, the monarch is the superior of the governed: his power being commonly sufficient to enforce compliance with his will. But the governed, collectively or in mass, are also the superior of the monarch: who is checked in the abuse of his might by his fear of exciting their anger; and of rousing to active resistance the might which slumbers in the multitude.

A member of a sovereign assembly is the superior of the judge: the judge being bound by the law which proceeds from that sovereign body. But, in his character of citizen or subject, he is the inferior of the judge: the judge being the minister of the law, and armed with the power of enforcing it.

It appears, then, that the term *superiority* (like the terms *duty* and *sanction*) is implied by the term *command*. For superiority is the power of enforcing compliance with a wish. . . .

I have already indicated, and shall hereafter more fully describe, the objects improperly termed laws, which are *not* within the province of jurisprudence (being either rules enforced by opinion and closely analogous to laws properly so called, or being laws so called by a metaphorical application of the term merely). There are other objects improperly termed laws (not being commands) which yet may properly be included within the province of jurisprudence. These I shall endeavour to particularize:

1. Acts on the part of legislatures to *explain* positive law, can scarcely be called laws, in the proper signification of the term. Working no change in the actual duties of the governed, but simply declaring what those duties *are,* they properly are acts of *interpretation* by legislative authority. . . .

It often, indeed, happens (as I shall show in the proper place), that laws declaratory in name are imperative in effect: Legislative, like judicial interpretation, being frequently deceptive; and establishing new law, under guise of expounding the old.

2. Laws to repeal laws, and to release from existing duties, must also be excepted from the proposition "that laws are a species of commands." In so far as they release from duties imposed by existing laws, they are not commands, but revocations of commands. . . .

Remotely and indirectly, indeed, permissive laws are often or always imperative. For the parties released from duties are restored to liberties or rights: and duties answering those rights are, therefore, created or revived. . . .

3. Imperfect laws, or laws of imperfect obligation, must also be excepted from the proposition "that laws are a species of commands."

An imperfect law (with the sense wherein the term is used by the Roman jurists) is a law which wants a sanction, and which, therefore, is not binding. A law declaring that certain acts **are** crimes, but annexing no punishment to the commission of acts of the class, is the simplest and most obvious example. . . .

Examples of imperfect laws are cited by the Roman jurists. But with us in England, laws professedly imperative are always (I believe) perfect or obligatory. Where the English legislature affects to command, the English tribunals not unreasonably presume that the legislature exacts obedience. And, if no specific sanction be annexed to a given law, a sanction is supplied by the courts of justice, agreeably to a general maxim which obtains in cases of the kind.

. . . Many of the writers on *morals,* and on the so called *law of nature,* have annexed a different meaning to the term *imperfect.* Speaking of imperfect obligations, they commonly mean duties which are *not legal:* duties imposed by commands of God, or duties imposed by positive morality, as contradistinguished to duties imposed by positive law. An imperfect obligation, in the sense of the Roman jurists, is exactly equivalent to no obligation at all. For the term *imperfect* denotes simply, that the law wants the sanction appropriate to laws of the kind. An imperfect obligation, in the other meaning of the expression, is a religious or a moral obligation. The term *imperfect* does not denote that the law imposing the duty wants the appropriate sanction. It denotes that the law imposing the duty is *not* a law established by a political superior: that it wants that *perfect,* or that surer or more cogent sanction, which is imparted by the sovereign or state.

. . . There are certain laws (properly so called) which may *seem* not imperative. Accordingly, I will subjoin a few remarks upon laws of this dubious character.

1. There are laws, it may be said, which *merely* create *rights:* And, seeing that every command imposes a *duty,* laws of this nature are not imperative.

But, as I have intimated already, and shall show completely hereafter, there are no laws *merely* creating *rights.* There are laws, it is true, which *merely* create *duties:* duties not correlating with correlating rights, and which, therefore, may be styled *absolute.* But every law, really conferring a right, imposes expressly or tacitly a *relative* duty, or a duty correlating with the right. If it specify the remedy to be given, in case the right shall be infringed, it imposes the relative duty expressly. If the remedy to be given be not specified, it refers tacitly to pre-existing law, and clothes the right which it purports to create with a remedy provided by that law. . . .

2. According to an opinion . . . *customary laws* must be excepted from the proposition "that laws are a species of commands."

By many of the admirers of customary laws (and, especially, of their German admirers), they are thought to oblige legally (independently of the sovereign or state), *because* the citizens or subjects have observed or kept them. Agreeably to this opinion, they are not the *creatures* of the sovereign or state, although the sovereign or state may abolish them at pleasure. Agreeably to this opinion, they are positive law (or law, strictly so called), inasmuch as they are enforced by the courts of justice: But, that notwithstanding, they exist *as positive law* by the spontaneous adoption of the governed, and not by position or establishment on the part of political superiors. Consequently, customary laws, considered as positive law, are not commands. And, consequently, customary laws, considered as positive law, are not laws or rules properly so called.

An opinion less mysterious, but somewhat allied to this, is not uncommonly held by the adverse party: by the party which is strongly opposed to customary law; and to all law made judicially, or in the way of judicial legislation. According to the latter opinion, all judge-made law, or all judge-made law established by *subject* judges, is purely the creature of the judges by whom it is established immediately. To impute it to the sovereign legislature, or to suppose that it speaks the will of the sovereign legislature, is one of the foolish or knavish *fictions* with which lawyers, in every age and nation, have perplexed and darkened the simplest and clearest truths.

I think it will appear, on a moment's re-

flexion, that each of these opinions is groundless: that customary law is *imperative,* in the proper signification of the term; and that all judge-made law is the creature of the sovereign or state.

At its origin, a custom is a rule of conduct which the governed observe spontaneously, or not in pursuance of a law set by a political superior. The custom is transmuted into positive law, when it is adopted as such by the courts of justice, and when the judicial decisions fashioned upon it are enforced by the power of the state. But before it is adopted by the courts, and clothed with the legal sanction, it is merely a rule of positive morality: a rule generally observed by the citizens or subjects; but deriving the only force, which it can be said to possess, from the general disapprobation falling on those who transgress it.

Now when judges transmute a custom into a legal rule . . . the legal rule which they establish is established by the sovereign legislature. A subordinate or subject judge is merely a minister. The portion of the sovereign power which lies at his disposition is merely delegated. The rules which he makes derive their legal force from authority given by the state: an authority which the state may confer expressly, but which it commonly imparts in the way of acquiescence. For, since the state may reverse the rules which he makes, and yet permits him to enforce them by the power of the political community, its sovereign will 'that his rules shall obtain as law' is clearly evinced by its conduct, though not by its express declaration.

. . . Considered as moral rules turned into positive laws, customary laws are established by the state: established by the state directly, when the customs are promulged in its statutes; established by the state circuitously, when the customs are adopted by its tribunals. . . .

LECTURE II

. . . The Divine laws, or the laws of God, are laws set by God to his human creatures. . . . They are laws or rules, *properly* so called.

Of the Divine laws, or the laws of God, some are *revealed* or promulged, and others are *unrevealed*. Such of the laws of God as are unrevealed are not unfrequently denoted by the following names or phrases: "the law of nature"; "natural law"; "the law manifested to man by the light of nature or reason"; "the laws, precepts, or dictates of natural religion."

The *revealed* law of God, and the portion of the law of God which is *unrevealed*, are manifested to men in different ways, or by different sets of signs.

With regard to the laws which God is pleased to *reveal*, the way wherein they are manifested is easily conceived. They are *express* commands: portions of the *word* of God: commands signified to men through the medium of human language; and uttered by God directly, or by servants whom he sends to announce them.

Such of the Divine laws as are *unrevealed* are laws set by God to his human creatures, but not through the medium of human language, or not expressly. . . .

. . . We must look for many of the duties, which God has imposed upon us, to the marks or signs of his pleasure which are styled the *light of nature.* . . .

But if God has given us laws which he has not revealed or promulged, how shall we know them? . . .

The hypotheses or theories which attempt to resolve this question, may be reduced, I think, to two.

According to one of them, there are human actions which all mankind approve, human actions which all men disapprove; and these universal sentiments arise at the thought of those actions, spontaneously, instantly, and inevitably. Being common to all mankind, and inseparable from the thoughts of those actions, these sentiments are marks or signs of the Divine pleasure. They are proofs that the actions which excite them are enjoined or forbidden by the Deity.

The rectitude or pravity of human conduct, or its agreement or disagreement with the laws of God, is instantly inferred from these sentiments, without the possibility of mistake. He has resolved that our happiness shall depend on our keeping his commandments: and it manifestly consists with his manifest wisdom and goodness, that we should know them promptly and certainly. Accordingly, he has not committed us to the guidance of our slow and fallible *reason.* He has wisely endowed us with *feelings,* which warn us at every step; and pursue us, with their importunate reproaches, when we wander from the path of our duties.

These simple or inscrutable feelings have been compared to those which we derive from the outward senses, and have been referred to a peculiar faculty called the *moral sense.* . . .

The hypothesis, however, of a *moral sense,* is expressed in other ways.

The laws of God, to which these feelings are the index, are not unfrequently named *innate practical principles,* or *postulates of practical reason:* or they are said to be written on our hearts, by the finger of their great Author, in broad and indelible characters.

Common sense (the most yielding and accommodating of phrases) has been moulded and fitted to the purpose of expressing the hypothesis in question. In all their decisions on the rectitude or pravity of conduct (its agreement or disagreement with the unrevealed law), mankind are said to be determined by *common sense:* this same *common sense* meaning, in this instance, the simple or inscrutable sentiments which I have endeavoured to describe.

Considered as affecting the soul, when the man thinks especially of *his own* conduct, these sentiments, feelings, or emotions, are frequently styled his *conscience.*

According to the other of the adverse theories or hypotheses, the laws of God, which are not revealed or promulged, must be gathered by man from the goodness of God, and from the tendencies of human actions. In other words, the benevolence of God, with the principle of general utility, is our only index or guide to his unrevealed law.

God designs the happiness of all his sentient creatures. Some human actions forward that benevolent purpose, or their tendencies are beneficient or useful. Other human actions are adverse to that purpose, or their tendencies are mischievous or pernicious, The former, as promoting his purpose, God has enjoined. The latter, as opposed to his purpose, God has forbidden. He has given us the faculty of observing; of remembering; of reasoning: and, by duly applying those faculties, we may collect the tendencies of our actions. Knowing the tendencies of our actions, and knowing his benevolent purpose, we know his tacit commands. . . .

The theory is this: . . . From the probable effects of our actions on the greatest happiness of all, or from the tendencies of human actions to increase or diminish that aggregate, we may infer the laws which he has given, but has not expressed or revealed.

Now the *tendency* of a human action (as its tendency is thus understood) is the whole of its tendency: the sum of its probable consequences, in so far as they are important or material: the sum of its remote and collateral, as well as of its direct consequences, in so far as any of its consequences may influence the general happiness.

Trying to collect its tendency . . . we must not consider the action as if it were *single* and *insulated,* but must look at the *class* of actions to which it belongs. The probable *specific* consequences of doing that single act, of forbearing from that single act, or of omitting that single act, are not the objects of the inquiry. The question to be solved is this: If acts of the *class* were *generally* done, or *generally* forborne or omitted, what would be the probable effect on the general happiness or good?

Considered by itself, a mischievous act may seem to be useful or harmless. Considered by itself, a useful act may seem to be pernicious.

For example, If a poor man steal a handful from the heap of his rich neighbour, the act, considered by itself, is harmless or positively good. One man's poverty is assuaged with the superfluous wealth of another.

But suppose that thefts were general (or

that the useful right of property were open to frequent invasions), and mark the result.

Without security for property, there were no inducement to save. Without habitual saving on the part of proprietors, there were no accumulation of capital. Without accumulation of capital, there were no fund for the payment of wages, no division of labour, no elaborate and costly machines: there were none of those helps to labour which augment its productive power, and, therefore, multiply the enjoyments of every individual in the community. Frequent invasions of property would bring the rich to poverty; and, what were a greater evil, would aggravate the poverty of the poor. . . .

. . . In other cases, an act or omission is evil, considered as single or insulated; but, considered with the rest of its class, is good.

For example, A punishment, as a solitary fact, is an evil: the pain inflicted on the criminal being added to the mischief of the crime. But, considered as part of a system, a punishment is useful or beneficent. By a dozen or score of punishments, thousands of crimes are prevented. . . .

It, therefore, is true generally (for the proposition admits of exceptions), that, to determine the true tendency of an act, forbearance or omission, we must resolve the following question.—What would be the probable effect on the general happiness or good, if *similar* acts, forbearances, or omissions were general or frequent? . . .

. . . If the tendencies of actions be the index to the will of God, it follows that most of his commands are general or universal. The useful acts which he enjoins, and the pernicious acts which he prohibits, he enjoins or prohibits, for the most part, not singly, but by classes: not by commands which are particular, or directed to insulated cases; but by laws or rules which are general, and commonly inflexible. . . .

. . . If utility be our only index to the tacit commands of the Deity, it is idle to object its imperfections. We must even make the most of it.

If we were endowed with a *moral sense,* or with a *common sense,* or with a *practical reason,* we scarcely should construe his commands by the principle of general utility. If our souls were furnished out with *innate practical principles,* we scarcely should read his commands in the tendencies of human actions. For, by the supposition, man would be gifted with a peculiar organ for acquiring a knowledge of his duties. The duties imposed by the Deity would be subjects of immediate consciousness, and completely exempted from the jurisdiction of observation and induction. An attempt to displace that invincible consciousness, and to thrust the principle of utility into the vacant seat, would be simply impossible and manifestly absurd. An attempt to taste or smell by force of syllogism, were not less hopeful or judicious.

But, if we are not gifted with that peculiar organ, we must take to the principle of utility, let it be never so defective. . . .

Whether there be any ground for the hypothesis of a *moral sense,* is a question which I shall duly examine in a future lecture. . . .

. . . Objection is founded on the following assumption.—That, if we adjusted our conduct to the principle of general utility, every election which we made between doing and forbearing from an act would be preceded by a *calculation:* by an attempt to conjecture and compare the respective probable consequences of action and forbearance. . . .

. . . Granting their assumption, I grant their inference. I grant that the principle of utility were a halting and purblind guide.

'But their assumption is groundless. . . .

For, according to that theory, our conduct would conform to *rules* inferred from the tendencies of actions, but would not be determined by a direct resort to the principle of general utility. Utility would be the test of our conduct, ultimately, but not immediately: the immediate test of the rules to which our conduct would conform, but not the immediate test of specific or individual actions. Our rules would be fashioned on utility; our conduct, on our rules. . . .

. . . To preface each act or forbearance by a conjecture and comparison of consequences, were clearly superfluous and mischievous. It were clearly superfluous, inasmuch as the result of that process would be embodied in a known *rule.* It were clearly mischievous, inasmuch as the *true* result would be expressed by that rule, whilst the process would probably be faulty, if it were done on the spur of the occasion.

Speaking generally, human conduct, including the human conduct which is subject to the Divine commands, is inevitably guided by *rules,* or by *principles* or *maxims.*

If our experience and observation of particulars were not *generalized,* our experience and observation of particulars would seldom avail us in *practice* . . . The inferences suggested to our minds by repeated experience and observation are, therefore, drawn into *principles,* or compressed into *maxims.* These we carry about us ready for use, and apply to individual cases promptly or without hesitation: without reverting to the process by which they were obtained; or without recalling, and arraying before our minds, the numerous and intricate considerations of which they are handy abridgments. . . .

The human conduct which is subject to the Divine commands, is not only guided by *rules,* but also by *moral sentiments* associated with those rules.

If I believe (no matter why) that acts of a class or description are enjoined or forbidden by the Deity, a moral sentiment or feeling . . . is inseparably connected in my mind with the thought or conception of such acts. And by this I am urged to do, or restrained from doing such acts, although I advert not to the reason in which my belief originated, nor recall the Divine rule which I have inferred from that reason.

Now, if the reason in which my belief originated be the useful or pernicious tendency of acts of the class, my conduct is truly adjusted to the principle of general utility, but my conduct is not determined by a direct resort to it. It is directly determined by a *sentiment* associated with acts of the class, and with the rule which I have inferred from their tendency. . . .

For example, Reasons which are quite satisfactory, but somewhat numerous and intricate, convince me that the institution of property is necessary to the general good. Convinced of this, I am convinced that thefts are pernicious. Convinced that thefts are pernicious, I infer that the Deity forbids them by a general and inflexible rule.

Now the train of induction and reasoning by which I arrive at this rule, is somewhat long and elaborate. But I am not compelled to repeat the process, before I can know with certainty that I should forbear from taking your purse. . . .

. . . Calculation is the guide, and not the antagonist of sentiment. Sentiment without calculation were blind and capricious; but calculation without sentiment were inert.

To crush the moral sentiments, is not the scope or purpose of the true theory of utility. . . .

But these conclusions (like most conclusions), must be taken with limitations.

There certainly are cases (of comparatively rare occurrence) wherein the specific considerations balance or outweigh the general . . . It were mischievous to depart from a rule which regarded any of these cases; since every departure from a rule tends to weaken its authority. But so important were the *specific* consequences which would follow our resolves, that the evil of observing the rule might surpass the evil of breaking it. Looking at the reasons from which we had inferred the rule, it were absurd to think it inflexible. We should, therefore, dismiss the *rule;* resort directly to the *principle* upon which our rules were fashioned; and calculate *specific* consequences to the best of our knowledge and ability. . . .

. . . Though the principle of utility would afford no certain solution, the community would be fortunate, if their opinions and sentiments were formed upon it. The pretensions of the opposite parties being tried by an intelligible test, a peaceable compromise of their difference would, at least, be possible . . . In short, if the object of each party were measured by the standard of utility, each might compare the worth of its object with the cost of a violent pursuit.

But, if the parties were led by their ears, and not by the principle of utility; if they appealed to unmeaning abstractions, or to senseless fictions; if they mouthed of "the rights of man," or "the sacred rights of sovereigns"; of "unalienable liberties," or "eternal and immutable justice;" of an "original contract or covenant," or "the principles of an inviolable constitution"; neither could compare its object with the cost of a violent pursuit, nor would the difference between them admit of a peaceable compromise. A sacred or unalienable right is truly and indeed *invaluable:* For, seeing that it means nothing, there is nothing with which it can be measured. Parties who rest their pretensions on the jargon to which I have adverted, must inevitably push to their objects through thick and thin, though their objects be straws or feathers as weighed in the balance of utility. Having bandied their fustian phrases, and 'bawled till their lungs be spent," they must even take to their weapons, and fight their difference out. . . .

For example, If the bulk of the people of England had thought and reasoned with Mr. Burke, had been imbued with the spirit and had seized the scope of his arguments, her needless and disastrous war with her American colonies would have been stifled at the birth. The stupid and infuriate majority who rushed into that odious war, could perceive and discourse of nothing but the *sovereignty* of the mother country, and her so called *right* to tax her colonial subjects. . . .

. . . If a serious difference shall arise between ourselves and Ireland, an attempt will probably be made to cram us with the same stuff. But, such are the mighty strides which reason has taken in the interval, that I hope we shall not swallow it with the relish of our good ancestors. It will probably occur to us to ask, whether she be worth keeping, and whether she be worth keeping at the cost of a war? . . .

LECTURE III

. . . If the Divine laws must be gathered from the tendencies of actions, how can they, who are bound to keep them, know them fully and correctly?

So numerous are the classes of actions to which those laws relate, that no single mind can mark the whole of those classes, and examine completely their respective tendencies. If every single man must learn their respective tendencies . . . on many or most of the occasions which require him to act or forbear, he will be forced on the dangerous process of calculating specific consequences.

Besides, ethical, like other wisdom, "cometh by opportunity of leisure": And, since they are busied with earning the means of living, the many are unable to explore the field of ethics, and to learn their numerous duties by learning the tendencies of actions. . . .

In so far as law and morality are what they *ought* to be . . . legal and moral rules have been fashioned on the principle of utility . . . But . . . it is not necessary that all whom they bind should know or advert to the process through which they have been gotten. If all whom they bind keep or observe them, the ends to which they exist are sufficiently accomplished. . . .

. . . If a system of law and morality were exactly fashioned to utility, all its constituent *rules* might be known by all or most. But all the numerous *reasons,* upon which the system would rest, could scarcely be compassed by any: while most must limit their inquiries to a few of those numerous reasons; or, without an attempt to examine the reasons, must receive the whole of the rules from the teaching and example of others.

But this inconvenience is not peculiar to law and morality. It extends to all the sciences, and to all the arts. . . .

In the mathematical and physical sciences, and in the arts which are founded upon them, we may commonly trust the conclusions which we take upon authority. For the adepts in these sciences and arts mostly agree in their results, and lie under no temptation to cheat the ignorant with error. . . .

But the case is unhappily different with the important science of ethics, and also with the various sciences—such as legislation, politics, and political economy—which are nearly related to ethics. Those who have inquired, or affected to inquire into ethics, have rarely been impartial, and, therefore, have differed in their results . . . Most of them have been advocates rather than inquirers. . . .

Many of the legal and moral rules which obtain in the most civilized communities, rest upon brute custom, and not upon manly reason. They have been taken from preceding generations without examination, and are deeply tinctured with barbarity. . . .

. . . These obstacles, I am firmly convinced, will gradually disappear . . . In every civilized community of the Old and New World, the *leading principles* of the science of ethics, and also of the various sciences which are nearly related to ethics, are gradually finding their way, in company with other knowledge, amongst the great mass of the people: whilst those who accurately study, and who labour to advance these sciences, are proportionally increasing in number, and waxing in zeal and activity. . . .

. . . The multitude are fully competent to conceive the *leading principles,* and to apply those leading principles to particular cases. And, if they were imbued with those principles, and were practised in the art of applying them, they would be docile to the voice of reason, and armed against sophistry and error. . . .

If utility be the proximate test of positive law and morality, it is simply impossible that positive law and morality should be free from defects and errors. . . .

For, *first,* positive law and morality, fashioned on the principle of utility, are gotten by observation and induction from the tendencies of human actions . . . Consequently, till these actions shall be marked and classed with perfect completeness, and their effects observed and ascertained with similar completeness, positive law and morality, fashioned on the principle of utility, must be more or less defective, and more or less erroneous. And, these actions being infinitely various, and their effects being infinitely diversified, the work of classing them completely, and of collecting their effects completely, transcends the limited faculties of created and finite beings. . . .

And, *secondly,* if utility be the proximate test of positive law and morality, the defects and errors of *popular* or *vulgar* ethics will scarcely admit of a remedy . . . Most of the ethical maxims, which govern the sentiments of the multitude, must be taken, without examination, from human authority. And where is the *human* authority upon which they can safely rely? . . . We find conflicting maxims taught with equal confidence, and received with equal docility. We find the guides of the multitude moved by sinister interests, or by prejudices which are the offspring of such interests. We find them stifling inquiry, according to the measure of their means: upholding with fire and sword, or with sophistry, declamation and calumny, the theological and ethical dogmas which they impose upon their prostrate disciples. . . .

In the *first* place, the *diffusion* of ethical science amongst the great bulk of mankind will gradually remove the obstacles which prevent or retard its *advancement.* . . .

Secondly: Though the many must trust to authority for a number of subordinate truths, they are competent to examine the elements which are the groundwork of the science of ethics, and to infer the more momentous of the derivative practical consequences.

And, *thirdly,* as the science of ethics advances, and is cleared of obscurity and uncertainties, they who are debarred from opportunities of examining the science extensively, will find an authority, whereon they may rationally rely, in the unanimous or general agreement of searching and impartial inquirers.

LECTURE IV

In my last lecture, I endeavoured to answer an objection which may be urged against the theory of utility . . . .

But this answer . . . grants that law and morality fashioned on the principle of utility is inevitably defective and erroneous: that, if the laws established by the Deity must be construed by the principle of utility, the most perfect system of ethics which the wit of man could conceive, were a partial and inaccurate copy of the Divine original or pattern.

And this (it may be urged) disproves the theory which makes the principle of utility the index to the Divine pleasure. For it consists not with the known wisdom and the known benevolence of the Deity, that he should signify his commands defectively and obscurely to those upon whom they are binding. . . .

Owing to causes which are hidden from human understanding, all the works of the Deity which are open to human observation are alloyed with imperfection or evil. That the Deity should signify his commands defectively and obscurely, is strictly in keeping or unison with the rest of his inscrutable ways. . . .

The objection is founded on the alleged inconsistency of evil with his perfect wisdom and goodness. But the notion or idea of evil or imperfection is involved in the connected notions of law, duty, and sanction. For, seeing that every law imposes a restraint, every law is an evil of itself: and, unless it be the work of malignity, or proceed from consummate folly, it also supposes an evil which it is designed to prevent or remedy. Law, like medicine, is a preventive or remedy of *evil:* and, if the world were free from evil, the notion and the name would be unknown. . . .

. . . To reconcile the existence of evil with the wisdom and goodness of God is a task which surpasses the powers of our narrow and feeble understandings. This is a deep which our reason is too short to fathom. . . .

Now, if we reject *utility* as the index to God's commands, we must assent to the theory or hypothesis which supposes *a moral sense.* . . .

The first of the two assumptions involved by the hypothesis in question, may be stated, in general expressions, thus:

Certain sentiments or feelings of approbation or disapprobation accompany our conceptions of certain human actions. They are neither effects of reflection upon the tendencies of the actions which excite them, nor are they effects of education. A conception of any of these actions would be accompanied by certain of these sentiments, although we had not adverted to its good or evil tendency, nor knew the opinions of others with regard to actions of the class. . . .

That these inscrutable sentiments are signs of the Divine will, or are proofs that the actions which excite them are enjoined or forbidden by God, is the second of the two assumptions involved by the hypothesis in question. . . .

. . . We cannot mistake the laws which God has prescribed to mankind, although we may often be seduced by the blandishments of present advantage from the plain path of our duties. The understanding is never at a fault, although the will may be frail.

But here arises a small question.—Is there any *evidence* that we are gifted with feelings of the sort?

That this question is possible, or is seriously asked and agitated, would seem of itself a sufficient proof that we are *not* endowed with such feelings.—According to the hypothesis of a moral sense, we are conscious of the feelings which indicate God's commands, as we are conscious of hunger or thirst . . . If I were really gifted with feelings or sentiments of the sort, I could no more seriously question whether I had them or not, and could no more blend and confound them with my other feelings or sentiments, than I can seriously question the existence of hunger or thirst, or can mistake the feeling which affects me when I am hungry for the different feeling which affects me when I am thirsty. . . .

The two current arguments in favour of the hypothesis in question are raised on the following assertions. 1. The judgments which we pass internally upon the rectitude or pravity of actions are immediate and involuntary. In other words, our moral sentiments or feelings arise directly and inevitably with our conceptions of the actions which excite them. 2. The moral sentiments of all men are precisely alike.

Now the first of these venturous assertions is not universally true. In numberless cases, the judgments which we pass internally upon the rectitude or pravity of actions are hesitating and slow. And it not unfrequently happens that we cannot arrive at a conclusion, or are utterly at a loss to determine whether we shall praise or blame.

And, granting that our moral sentiments are always instantaneous and inevitable, this will not demonstrate that our moral sentiments are instinctive. Sentiments which are factitious, or begotten in the way of association, are not less prompt and involuntary than feelings which are instinctive or inscrutable . . . .

. . . It is boldly asserted . . . that the moral sentiments of all men are precisely alike.

The argument . . . may be stated briefly in the following manner.—No opinion or sentiment which is a result of observation and induction is held or felt by all mankind. Observation and induction, as applied to the same subject, lead different men to different conclusions. But the judgments which are passed internally upon the rectitude or pravity of actions, or the moral sentiments or feelings which actions excite, are precisely alike with all men. Consequently, our moral sentiments or feelings were not gotten by our inductions from the tendencies of the actions which excite them: nor were these sentiments or feelings gotten by inductions of others, and then impressed upon our minds by human authority and example. Consequently, our moral sentiments are instinctive, or are ultimate or inscrutable facts.

. . . Though the moral sentiments of all men were precisely alike, it would hardly follow that moral sentiments are instinctive.

But . . . respective moral sentiments of different ages and nations, and of different men in the same age and nation, have differed to infinity. This proposition is so notoriously true, and to every instructed mind the facts upon which it rests are so familiar, that I should hardly treat my hearers with due respect if I attempted to establish it by proof. . . .

. . . To affirm "that they are alike with all men," is merely to hazard a bold assertion contradicted by notorious facts. If they are different with different men, it follows that God has not set to men a *common* rule. If they are different with different men, there is no *common* test of human conduct: there is no test by which one man may try the conduct of another. It were folly and presumption in *me* to sit in judgment upon *you*. That which were pravity in *me* may, for aught I can know, be rectitude in *you*. . . .

. . . With regard to actions of a few classes, the moral sentiments of most, though not of all men, have been alike. But, with regard to actions of other classes, their moral sentiments have differed, through every shade or degree, from slight diversity to direct opposition.

And this is what might be expected, supposing that the principle of general utility is our only guide or index to the tacit commands of the Deity. The fact accords exactly with that hypothesis or theory. For, first, the positions wherein men are, in different ages and nations, are, in many respects, widely different: whence it inevitably follows, that much which was useful there and then were useless or pernicious here and now. And, secondly, since human tastes are various, and since human reason is fallible, men's moral sentiments must often widely differ even in respect of the circumstances wherein their positions are alike. But, with regard to actions of a few classes, the dictates of utility are the same at all times and places, and are also so obvious that they hardly admit of mistake or doubt. And hence would naturally ensue what observation shows us is the fact: namely, a general resemblance, with infinite variety, in the systems of law and morality which have actually obtained in the world. . . .

Now (speaking generally) every individual person is the best possible judge of his own interests: of what will affect himself with the greatest pleasures and pains. Compared with his intimate consciousness of his own peculiar interests, his knowledge of the interests of others is vague conjecture.

Consequently, the principle of general utility imperiously demands that he commonly shall attend to his own rather than to the interests of others: that he shall not habitually neglect that which he knows accurately in order that he may habitually pursue that which he knows imperfectly. . . .

The principle of general utility does not demand of us, that we shall always or habitually intend the general good: though the principle of general utility does demand of us, that we shall never pursue our own peculiar good by means which are inconsistent with that paramount object.

For example: The man who delves or spins, delves or spins to put money in his purse, and not with the purpose or thought of promoting the general well-being. But by delving or spinning, he adds to the sum of commodities: and he therefore promotes that general well-being, which is not, and ought not to be, his practical end. General utility is not his motive to action. But his action conforms to utility considered as the standard of conduct: and, when tried by utility considered as the test of conduct, his action deserves approbation. . . .

Even where utility requires that benevolence shall be our motive, it commonly requires that we shall be determined by partial, rather than by general benevolence: by the love of the narrower circle which is formed of family or relations, rather than by sympathy with the wider circle which is formed of friends or acquaintance: by sympathy with friends or acquaintance, rather than by patriotism: by patriotism, or love of country, rather than by the larger humanity which embraces mankind. . . .

LECTURE V

. . . *The science of jurisprudence* . . . is concerned with positive laws . . . as considered without regard to their goodness or badness.

Positive morality, as considered without regard to its goodness or badness, *might* be the subject of a science closely analogous to jurisprudence . . . Only in one of its branches (. . . international law) . . . positive morality . . . has been treated by writers in a scientific or systematic manner. . . .

The science of ethics . . . may be defined in the following manner—It affects to determine the test of positive law and morality, or it affects to determine the principles whereon they must be fashioned in order that they may merit approbation. . . .

The science of ethics . . . consists of two departments: one relating specifically to positive law, the other relating specifically to positive morality. The department which relates specifically to positive law, is commonly styled . . . *legislation*. The department which relates specifically to positive morality is commonly styled . . . *morals* . . . .

. . . Every positive law . . . is set by a sovereign person, or a sovereign body of persons, to a member or members of the independent political society wherein that person or body is sovereign or supreme. Or (changing the expression) it is set by a monarch, or sovereign number, to a person or persons in a state of subjection to its author. . . .

. . . Of positive moral rules which are laws properly so called, and are not established by men in a state of subjection, some are established by men living in the negative state which is styled a state of nature or a state of anarchy: that is to say, by men who are *not* in the state which is styled a state of government, or are *not* members, sovereign or subject, of any political society. . . .

. . . A man living in a state of nature may impose an imperative law: though, since the man *is* in a state of nature, he cannot impose the law in the character of sovereign, and cannot impose the law in pursuance of a legal right. And the law being *imperative* (and therefore proceeding from a *determinate* source) is a law properly so called: though, for want of a sovereign author proximate or remote, it is not a positive law but a rule of positive morality.

. . . Since no supreme government is in a state of subjection to another, an imperative law set by a sovereign to a sovereign is not set by its author in the character of political superior. Nor is it set by its author in pursuance of a legal right: for every legal right is conferred by a supreme government, and is conferred on a person or persons in a state of subjection to the granter. Consequently, an imperative law set by a sovereign to a sovereign is not a positive law or a law strictly so called. But being *imperative* (and therefore proceeding from a *determinate* source), it amounts to a law in the proper signification of the term, although it is purely or simply a rule of positive morality.

If they be set by subjects as private persons, and be not set by their authors in pursuance of legal rights, the laws following are examples of rules of the third kind: namely, imperative laws set by parents to children; imperative laws set by masters to servants; imperative laws set by lenders to borrowers; imperative laws set by patrons to parasites. Being *imperative* (and therefore proceeding from *determinate* sources), the laws foregoing are laws properly so called: though, if they be set by subjects as private persons, and be not set by their authors in pursuance of legal rights, they are not positive laws but rules of positive morality.

Again: A club or society of men, signifying its collective pleasure by a vote of its assembled members, passes or makes a law to be kept by its members severally under pain of exclusion from its meetings. Now if it be made by subjects as private persons, and be not made by its authors in pursuance of a legal right, the law voted and passed by the assembled members of the club is a further example of rules of the third kind. If it be made by subjects as private persons, and be not made by its authors in pursuance of a legal right, it is not a positive law or a law strictly so called. But being an *imperative* law (and the body by which it is set being therefore *determinate),* it may be styled a *law* or *rule* with absolute precision and propriety, although it is purely or simply a rule of positive morality.

The positive moral rules which are laws improperly so called, are *laws set* or *imposed by general opinion:* that is to say, by the general opinion of any class or any society of persons. For example, Some are set or imposed by the general opinion of persons who are members of a profession or calling: others, by that of persons who inhabit a town or province: others, by that of a nation or independent political society: others, by that of a larger society formed of various nations.

A few species of the laws which are set by general opinion have gotten appropriate names.—For example, there are laws or rules imposed upon gentlemen by opinions current amongst gentlemen. And these are usually styled *the rules of honour,* or *the laws* or *law of honour.*—There are laws or rules imposed upon people of fashion by opinions current in the fashionable world. And these are usually styled *the law set by fashion.*— There are laws which regard the conduct of independent political societies in their various relations to one another: Or, rather, there are laws which regard the conduct of sovereigns or supreme governments in their various relations to one another. And laws or rules of this species, which are imposed upon nations or sovereigns by opinions current amongst nations, are usually styled *the laws of nations* or *international law.*

Now a law set or imposed by general opinion is a law improperly so called. It is styled a *law* or *rule* by an analogical extension of the term . . . Some *indeterminate* body or *uncertain* aggregate of persons regards a kind of conduct with a sentiment of aversion or liking . . . In *consequence* of that opinion, it is likely that they or some of them will be displeased with a party who shall pursue or not pursue conduct of that kind. And, in *consequence* of that displeasure, it is likely that *some* party *(what* party being undetermined) will visit the party provoking it with some evil or another.

The body by whose opinion the law is said to be set, does not *command,* expressly or tacitly, that conduct of the given kind shall be forborne or pursued. . . .

It follows from the foregoing reasons, that a so called law set by general opinion is not a law in the proper signification of the term. It also follows from the same reasons, that it is not armed with a sanction, and does not impose a duty, in the proper acceptation of the expressions. For a sanction properly so called is an evil annexed to a command. And duty properly so called is an obnoxiousness to evils of the kind.

But a so called law set by general opinion is closely analogous to a law in the proper signification of the term. And, by consequence, the so called sanction with which the former is armed, and the so called duty which the former imposes, are closely analogous to a sanction and a duty in the proper acceptation of the expressions . . . .

. . . The character or essential difference of a law imposed by opinion, is this: that the law is not a *command,* issued expressly or tacitly, but is merely an *opinion* or *sentiment,* relating to conduct of a kind, which is held or felt by an uncertain body, or by a determinate party . . . The opinion or sentiment is merely an opinion or sentiment, although it subjects a transgressor to the chance of a consequent evil, and may even lead to a command regarding conduct of the kind.

Between the opinion or sentiment of the indeterminate body, and the opinion or sentiment of the precisely determined party, there is merely the following difference.— The precisely determined party is *capable* of issuing a command in pursuance of the opinion or sentiment. But the uncertain body is not. For, being essentially incapable of joint or corporate conduct, it cannot, as a body, signify a wish or desire, and cannot, as a body, hold an intention or purpose. . . .

The body or aggregate of laws which may be styled the law of God, the body or aggregate of laws which may be styled positive law, and the body or aggregate of laws which may be styled positive morality, sometimes *coincide,* sometimes do *not* coincide, and sometimes *conflict.*

. . . The killing which is styled *murder* is forbidden by the positive law of every political society: it is also forbidden by a so called law which the general opinion of the society has set or imposed: it is also forbidden by the law of God as known through the principle of utility. The murderer commits a crime, or he violates a positive law: he commits a conventional immorality, or he violates a so called law which general opinion has established: he commits a sin, or he violates the law of God. He is obnoxious to punishment, or other evil, to be inflicted by sovereign authority: he is obnoxious to the hate and the spontaneous ill-offices of the generality or bulk of the society: he is obnoxious to evil or pain to be suffered here or hereafter by the immediate appointment of the Deity.

One of these bodies of laws does *not* coincide with another, when acts, which are enjoined or forbidden by the former, are not enjoined, or are not forbidden by the latter. —For example, Though smuggling is forbidden by positive law, and (speaking generally) is not less pernicious than theft, it is not forbidden by the opinions or sentiments of the ignorant or unreflecting. Where the impost or tax is itself of pernicious tendency, smuggling is hardly forbidden by the opinions or sentiments of any: And it is therefore practised by any without the slightest shame, or without the slightest fear of incurring general censure. . . .

. . . The practice of duelling is forbidden by positive law. It is also at variance with the law which is received in most of those nations as having been set by the Deity in the way of express revelation. But in spite of positive law, and in spite of his religious convictions, a man of the class of gentlemen may be forced by the law of honour to give or to take a challenge. If he forbore from giving, or if he declined a challenge, he might incur the general contempt of gentlemen or men of honour, and might meet with slights and insults sufficient to embitter his existence. . . .

The simple and obvious considerations to which I have now adverted, are often overlooked by legislators . . . They forget that positive law may be superfluous or impotent, and therefore may lead to nothing but purely gratuitous vexation. They forget that the moral or the religious sentiments of the community may already suppress the practice as completely as it can be suppressed: or that, if the practice is favoured by those moral or religious sentiments, the strongest possible fear which legal pains can inspire may be mastered by a stronger fear of other and conflicting sanctions.

In consequence of the frequent coincidence of positive law and morality, and of positive law and the law of God, the true nature and fountain of positive law is often absurdly mistaken by writers upon jurisprudence. Where positive law has been fashioned on positive morality, or where positive law has been fashioned on the law of God, they forget that the copy is the creature of the sovereign, and impute it to the author of the model.

For example: Customary laws are positive laws fashioned by judicial legislation upon preexisting customs. Now, till they become the grounds of judicial decisions upon cases, and are clothed with legal sanctions by the sovereign one or number, the customs are merely rules set by opinions of the governed, and sanctioned or enforced morally: Though, when they become the reasons of judicial decisions upon cases, and are clothed with legal sanctions by the sovereign one or number, the customs are rules of positive law as well as of positive morality. But, because the customs were observed by the governed before they were clothed with sanctions by the sovereign one or number, it is fancied that customary laws exist *as positive laws* by the institution of the private persons with whom the customs originated.— Admitting the conceit, and reasoning by analogy, we ought to consider the sovereign the author of the positive morality which is often a consequence of positive law. Where a positive law, not fashioned on a custom, is favourably received by the governed, and enforced by their opinions or sentiments, we must deem the so called law, set by those opinions or sentiments, a law imperative and proper of the supreme political superior.

Again: The portion of positive law which

is parcel of the *law of nature* (or, in the language of the classical jurists, which is parcel of the *jus gentium*) is often supposed to emanate, even as positive law, from a Divine or Natural source. But (admitting the distinction of positive law into law natural and law positive) it is manifest that law natural, considered as a portion of positive, is the creature of human sovereigns, and not of the Divine monarch. To say that it emanates, as positive law, from a Divine or Natural source, is to confound positive law with law whereon it is fashioned, or with law whereunto it conforms. . . .

The analogy borne to a law proper by a law which opinion imposes, lies mainly in the following point of resemblance. In the case of a law set by opinion, as well as in the case of a law properly so called, a rational being or beings are obnoxious to contingent evil, in the event of their not complying with a known or presumed desire of another being or beings of a like nature . . . The analogy, therefore, by which the laws are related, mainly lies in the resemblance of the improper sanction and duty to the sanction and duty properly so called. The contingent evil in prospect which enforces the law improper, and the present obnoxiousness to that contingent evil, may be likened to the genuine sanction which enforces the law proper, and the genuine duty or obligation which the law proper imposes. —The analogy . . . is therefore, strong or close. The defect which excludes the latter from the rank of a law proper, merely consists in this: that the wish or desire of its authors has not been duly *signified,* and that they have no formed *intention* of inflicting evil or pain upon those who may break or transgress it.

But, beside the laws improper which are set or imposed by opinion, there are laws improperly so called which are related to laws proper by slender or remote analogies. And, since they have gotten the name of *laws* from their slender or remote analogies to laws properly so called, I style them laws metaphorical. . . .

. . . Laws metaphorical, though numerous and different, have the following common and negative nature.—No property or character of any metaphorical law can be likened to a sanction or a duty. . . .

The most frequent and remarkable of those metaphorical applications is suggested by that uniformity, or that stability of conduct, which is one of the ordinary consequences of a law proper.—By reason of the sanction working on their wills or desires, the parties obliged by a law proper commonly adjust their conduct to the pattern which the law prescribes. Consequently, wherever we observe a uniform order of events, or a uniform order of co-existing phenomena, we are prone to impute that order to a *law* set by its author, though the case presents us with nothing that can be likened to a sanction or a duty.

For example: We say that the movements of lifeless bodies are determined by certain *laws* . . . We mean that they move in certain uniform modes, and that they move in those uniform modes through the pleasure and appointment of God: just as parties obliged behave in a uniform manner through the pleasure and appointment of the party who imposes the law and the duty.—Again: We say that certain actions of the lower and irrational animals are determined by certain *laws:* though, since they cannot understand the purpose and provisions of a law, it is impossible that sanctions should effectually move them to obedience, or that their conduct should be guided by a regard to duties or obligations. We mean that they act in certain uniform modes, either in consequence of instincts (or causes which we cannot explain), or else in consequence of hints which they catch from experience and observation: and that, since their uniformity of action is an effect of the Divine pleasure, it closely resembles the uniformity of conduct which is wrought by the authors of laws in those who are obnoxious to the sanctions. . . .

. . . These metaphorical laws which govern the lower animals, and which govern (though less despotically) the human species itself, should not have been blended and confounded, by a grave writer upon jurisprudence, with laws properly so called. It is true that the instincts of the animal man, like many of his affections which are not instinctive, are amongst the causes of laws in the proper acceptation of the term. More especially, the laws regarding the relation of husband and wife, and the laws regarding the relation of parent and child, are mainly caused by the instincts . . . But nothing can be more absurd than the ranking with laws themselves the causes which lead to their existence. And if human instincts are laws because they are causes of laws, there is scarcely a faculty or affection belonging to the human mind, and scarcely a class of objects presented by the outward world, that must not be esteemed a law and an appropriate subject of jurisprudence . . . The *jus naturale* of the classical jurists generally . . . is equivalent to the *natural law* of modern writers upon jurisprudence . . . It means those positive laws, and those rules of positive morality, which are not peculiar or appropriate to any nation or age, but obtain, or are thought to obtain, in all nations and ages: and which, by reason of their obtaining in all nations and ages, are supposed to be formed or fashioned on the law of God or Nature as known by the moral sense . . . And the law of nature, as thus understood, is not intrinsically absurd. For as some of the dictates of utility are always and everywhere the same, and are also so plain and glaring that they hardly admit of mistake, there are legal and moral rules which are nearly or quite *universal,* and the expediency of which must be seen by merely *natural* reason, or by reason without the lights of extensive experience and observation . . . The *jus naturale* . . . would be liable to little objection, if it were not supposed to be the offspring of a moral instinct or sense, or of innate practical principles. But, since it is closely allied . . . to that misleading and pernicious jargon, it ought to be expelled, with the *natural law* of the moderns, from the sciences of jurisprudence and morality. . . .

LECTURE VI

. . . The superiority which is styled sovereignty, and the independent political society which sovereignty implies, is distinguished from other superiority, and from other society, by the following marks or characters.—1. The *bulk* of the given society are in a *habit* of obedience or submission to a *determinate* and *common* superior . . . 2. That certain individual, or that certain body of individuals, is *not* in a habit of obedience to a determinate human superior. . . .

Unless habitual obedience be rendered by the *bulk* of its members, and be rendered by the bulk of its members to *one and the same* superior, the given society is either in a state of nature, or is split into two or more independent political societies. . . .

A natural society, a society in a state of nature, or a society independent but natural, is composed of persons who are connected by mutual intercourse, but are not members, sovereign or subject, of any society political. None of the persons who compose it lives in the positive state which is styled a state of subjection: or all the persons who compose it live in the negative state which is styled a state of independence.

Considered as entire communities, and considered in respect of one another, independent political societies live, it is commonly said, in a state of nature. And considered as entire communities, and as connected by mutual intercourse, independent political societies form, it is commonly said, a natural society. These expressions, however, are not perfectly apposite. Since all the members of each of the related societies are members of a society political, none of the related societies is strictly in a state of nature: nor can the larger society formed by their mutual intercourse be styled strictly a natural society . . . The sovereign and subject members of each of the related societies form a society political: but the sovereign portion of each of the related societies lives in the negative condition which is styled a state of independence.

Society formed by the intercourse of independent political societies, is the province of international law. . . .

. . . The law obtaining between nations is not positive law: for every positive law is set by a given sovereign to a person or persons in a state of subjection to its author . . . The law obtaining between nations is law (improperly so called) set by general opinion. The duties which it imposes are enforced by moral sanctions. . . .

. . . Sovereign power (according to Grotius) is perfectly or completely independent of other human power; insomuch that its acts cannot be annulled by any human will other than its own. But if perfect or complete independence be of the essence of sovereign power, there is not in fact the human power to which the epithet *sovereign* will apply with propriety. Every government, let it be never so powerful, renders occasional obedience to commands of other governments. Every government defers frequently to those opinions and sentiments which are styled international law. And every government defers habitually to the opinions and sentiments of its own subjects. If it be not in a habit of obedience to the commands of a determinate party, a government has all the independence which a government can possibly enjoy. . . .

. . . Exercise of sovereign powers through political subordinates or delegates, is rendered absolutely necessary, in every actual society, by innumerable causes. . . .

. . . Supreme power limited by positive law, is a flat contradiction in terms.

Nor would a political society escape from legal despotism, although the power of the sovereign were bounded by legal restraints. The power of the superior sovereign immediately imposing the restraints, or the power of some other sovereign superior to that superior, would still be absolutely free from the fetters of positive law. For unless the imagined restraints were ultimately imposed by a sovereign not in a state of subjection to a higher or superior sovereign, a series of sovereigns ascending to infinity would govern the imagined community. Which is impossible and absurd.

Monarchs and sovereign bodies have attempted to oblige themselves, or to oblige the successors to their sovereign powers. But in spite of the laws which sovereigns have imposed on themselves, or which they have imposed on the successors to their sovereign powers, the position that "sovereign power is incapable of legal limitation" will hold universally or without exception. . . .

As it regards the successors to the sovereign or supreme powers, a law of the kind amounts, at the most to a rule of positive morality. As it regards its immediate author, it is merely a law by a metaphor. For if we would speak with propriety, we cannot speak of a law set by a man to himself: though a man may adopt a principle as a guide to his own conduct, and may observe it as he would observe it if he were bound to observe it by a sanction. . . .

. . . I am led to consider the meanings of the epithet *unconstitutional*. . . .

1. In every, or almost every, independent political society, there are principles or maxims which the sovereign habitually observes, and which the bulk of the society, or the bulk of its influential members, regard with feelings of approbation. Not unfrequently, such maxims are expressly adopted, as well as habitually observed, by the sovereign or state. More commonly, they are not expressly adopted by the sovereign or state, but are simply imposed upon it by opinions prevalent in the community. Whether they are expressly adopted by the sovereign or state, or are simply imposed upon it by opinions prevalent in the community, it is bound or constrained to observe them by merely moral sanctions. Or (changing the phrase) in case it ventured to deviate from a maxim of the kind in question, it would not and could not incur a legal pain or penalty, but it probably would incur censure, and might chance to meet with resistance, from the generality or bulk of the governed.

Now, if a law or other act of a monarch or sovereign number conflict with a maxim of the kind to which I have adverted above, the law or other act may be called *unconstitutional.* . . .

2. The epithet *unconstitutional* as applied to conduct of a sovereign, and as used with the meaning which is more special and definite, imports that the conduct in question conflicts with *constitutional law.*

And here I would briefly remark, that I mean by the expression *constitutional law,* the positive morality, or the compound of positive morality and positive law, which fixes the constitution or structure of the given supreme government. I mean the positive morality, or the compound of positive morality and positive law, which determines the character of the person, or the respective characters of the persons, in whom, for the time being, the sovereignty shall reside: and . . . which determines moreover the mode wherein the sovereign powers shall be shared by the constituent members of the sovereign number or body. . . .

. . . An act of the British parliament vesting the sovereignty in the king, or vesting the sovereignty in the king and the upper or lower house, would essentially alter the structure of our present supreme government, and might therefore be styled with propriety an *unconstitutional* law. In case the imagined statute were also generally pernicious, and in case it offended moreover the generality or bulk of the nation, it might be styled *irreligious* and *immoral* as well as *unconstitutional.* But to call it *illegal* were absurd: for if the parliament for the time being be sovereign in the United Kingdom, it is the author, directly or circuitously, of all our positive law, and exclusively sets us the measure of legal justice and injustice. . . .

But if sovereign or supreme power be incapable of legal limitation, or if every supreme government be legally absolute, wherein (it may be asked) doth political liberty consist, and how do the supreme governments which are commonly deemed free, differ from the supreme governments which are commonly deemed despotic?

I answer, that political or civil liberty is the liberty from legal obligation, which is left or granted by a sovereign government to any of its own subjects: and that, since the power of the government is incapable of legal limitation, the government is legally free to abridge their political liberty, at its own pleasure or discretion . . . A government may be hindered by *positive morality* from abridging the political liberty which it leaves or grants to its subjects: and it is bound by the *law of God,* as known through the principle of utility, not to load them with legal duties which general utility condemns. . . .

Political or civil liberty has been erected into an idol, and extolled with extravagant praises by doting and fanatical worshippers. But political or civil liberty is not more worthy of eulogy than political or legal restraint. Political or civil liberty, like political or legal restraint, may be generally useful, or generally pernicious; and it is not as being liberty, but as conducing to the general good, that political or civil liberty is an object deserving applause.

. . . To say that political liberty ought to be its principal end, or to say that its principal end ought to be legal restraint, is to talk absurdly: for each is merely a mean to that furtherance of the common weal, which is the only ultimate object of good or beneficent sovereignty . . . I am legally free, for example, to move from place to place, in so far as I can move from place to place consistently with my legal obligations: but this my political liberty would be but a sorry liberty, unless my fellow-subjects were restrained by a political duty from assaulting and imprisoning my body. Through the ignorance or negligence of a sovereign government, some of the civil liberties which it leaves or grants to its subjects, may not be protected against their fellows by answering legal duties: and some of those civil liberties may perhaps be protected sufficiently by religious and moral obligations. But, speaking generally, a political or civil liberty is coupled with a legal right to it: and, consequently, political liberty is fostered by that very political restraint from which the devotees of the idol liberty are so fearfully and blindly averse. . . .

The rights which a government confers, and the duties which it lays on its subjects, ought to be conferred and imposed for the advancement of the common weal, or with a view to the aggregate happiness of all the members of the society. But in every political society, the government deviates, more or less, from that ethical principle or maxim. In conferring rights and imposing duties, it more or less disregards the common or general weal, and looks, with partial affection, to the peculiar and narrower interests of a portion or portions of the community.—Now the governments which deviate less from that ethical principle or maxim, are better than the governments which deviate more. . . .

. . . I proceed to the origin or causes of political government and society.

The proper purpose or end of a sovereign political government . . . is the greatest possible advancement of human happiness: Though, if it would duly . . . advance as far as is possible the weal or good of mankind, it commonly must labour directly and particularly to advance as far as is possible the weal of its own community. The good of the universal society formed by mankind, is the aggregate good of the particular societies . . . Though, then, the weal of mankind is the proper object of a government . . . it commonly ought to consult directly and particularly the weal of the particular community which the Deity has committed to its rule. If it truly adjust its conduct to the principle of general utility, it commonly will aim immediately at the particular and more precise, rather than the general and less determinate end.

It were easy to show, that the general and particular ends never or rarely conflict . . . An enlightened regard for the common happiness of nations, implies an enlightened patriotism; whilst the stupid and atrocious patriotism which looks exclusively to country, and would further the interests of country at the cost of all other communities, grossly misapprehends and frequently crosses the interests that are the object of its narrow concern. . . .

. . . Supposing that a given society were adequately instructed or enlightened, the habitual obedience to its government which was rendered by the bulk of the community, would exclusively arise from reasons bottomed in the principle of utility. If they thought the government perfect . . . this their conviction or opinion would be their motive to obey. If they deemed the government faulty, a fear that the evil of resistance might surpass the evil of obedience, would be their inducement to submit. . . .

Since every actual society is inadequately instructed or enlightened, the habitual obedience to its government which is rendered by the bulk of the community, is partly the consequence of custom . . . Or the habitual obedience to the government which is rendered by the bulk of the community, is partly the consequence of prejudices: meaning by "prejudices," opinions and sentiments which have no foundation whatever in the principle of general utility. . . .

But . . . it partly arises from a reason bottomed in the principle of utility. It partly arises from a perception, by the generality or bulk of the community, of the expediency of political government: or (changing the phrase) it partly arises from a preference, by the generality or bulk of the community, of any government to anarchy. . . .

The only general cause of the *permanence* of political governments, and the only general cause of the *origin* of political governments, are exactly or nearly alike. Though every government has arisen in part from specific or particular causes, almost every government must have arisen in part from the following general cause: namely, that the bulk of the natural society from which the political was formed, were desirous of escaping to a state of government, from a state of nature or anarchy. . . .

According to a current opinion (or according to a current expression), the permanence and origin of every government are owing to the people's *consent*. . . .

. . . If they like the government, they are determined to obey it habitually, or to *consent* to its continuance, by their special inclination or attachment. If they hate the government, they are determined to obey it habitually, or to *consent* to its continuance, by their dread of a violent revolution. . . .

The expression "that every government arises through the people's *consent*," is often uttered with the following meaning: That the bulk of a natural society about to become a political, or the inchoate subjects of an inchoate political government, *promise,* expressly or tacitly, to obey the future sovereign. The expression, however, as uttered with the meaning in question, confounds *consent* and *promise,* and therefore is grossly incorrect. That the inchoate subjects of every inchoate government *will* or *consent* to obey it, is one proposition: that they promise, expressly or tacitly, to render it obedience, is another proposition. . . .

The duties of the subjects towards the sovereign government, are partly religious, partly legal, and partly moral.

The religious duties of the subjects towards the sovereign government, are creatures of the Divine law as known through the principle of utility. If it thoroughly accomplish the purpose for which it ought to exist, or further the general weal to the greatest possible extent, the subjects are bound religiously to pay it habitual obedience. And, if the general good which probably would follow submission outweigh the general good which probably would follow resistance, the subjects are bound religiously to pay it habitual obedience, although it accomplish imperfectly its proper purpose or end.—The legal duties of the subjects towards the sovereign government, are creatures of positive laws which itself has imposed upon them, or which are incumbent upon them by its own authority and might.— The moral duties of the subjects towards the sovereign government, are creatures of positive morality. . . .

The duties of the sovereign government, towards the subjects, are partly religious and partly moral. If it lay under legal duties towards the subjects, it were not a supreme, but were merely a subordinate government.

Its religious duties towards the subjects, are creatures of the Divine law as known through the principle of utility . . . Its moral duties towards the subjects, are creatures of positive morality. . . .

. . . We account sufficiently for the origin of those obligations, when we simply refer them to those their obvious fountains. It seems to my understanding, that an ampler solution of their origin is not in the least requisite, and, indeed, is impossible. But there are many writers on political government and society, who are not content to account for their origin, by simply referring them to those their manifest sources . . . And, to find that ampler solution which they believe requisite, those writers resort to the hypothesis of the *original covenant* or *contract,* or the *fundamental civil pact.*

. . . The purport or effect of the hypothesis . . . may be stated generally thus:

To the formation of every society political and independent . . . all its future members then in being are joint or concurring parties: for all are parties to an agreement in which it then originates, and which is also the basis whereon it afterwards rests. As being the necessary source of the independent political society . . . this agreement of all is styled the *original covenant* . . . There are three several stages: . . . 1. The future members of the community just about to be created, jointly resolve to unite themselves into an independent political society: signifying and determining withal the paramount purpose of their union . . . To writers who admit the system which I style the theory of utility, this purpose or end is the advancement of human happiness. To a multitude of writers who have flourished and flourish in Germany, the following is the truly magnificent though somewhat mysterious object of political government and society: namely, the extension over the earth, or over its human inhabitants, of the empire of right or justice . . . It would seem that this right or justice is not a creature of law: that it was anterior to every law; exists independently of every law; and is the measure or test of all law and morality. Consequently, it is not the right or justice which is a creature of the law of God, and to which the name of "justice" is often applied emphatically. It rather is a something, perfectly self-existent, to which his law conforms, or to which his law should conform. I, therefore, cannot understand it, and will not affect to explain it. Merely guessing at what it may be . . . I take it for general utility darkly conceived and expressed . . . 2. Having resolved to unite themselves into an independent political society, all the members of the inchoate community jointly determine the constitution of its sovereign political government . . . 3. The process of forming the independent political society, or the process of forming its supreme political government, is completed by promises given and accepted: namely, by a promise of the inchoate sovereign to the inchoate subjects, by promises of the latter to the former, and by a promise of each of the latter to all and each of the rest. . . .

. . . I now will suggest shortly a few of the conclusive objections to which the hypothesis is open.

1. To account for the duties of subjects towards their sovereign government, or for those of the sovereign government towards its subjects . . . is the scope of every writer who supposes an original covenant.—But, to account for the duties . . . we need not resort to the hypothesis of a fundamental civil pact. We sufficiently account for the origin of those respective obligations, when we refer them simply . . . to their apparent and obvious fountains: namely, the law of God, positive law, and positive morality.—Besides, although the formation of an independent political society were really preceded by a fundamental civil pact, scarce any of the duties lying thereafter on the subjects, or . . . on the sovereign, would be engendered or influenced by that foregoing convention. . . .

. . . If the sovereign government were bound *legally* by the fundamental civil pact, the legal duty lying on the government were the creature of a positive law: that is to say, the legal duty lying on the government were the creature of a positive law annexing the duty to the pact. And, seeing that a law set by the government to itself were merely a

law through a metaphor, the positive law annexing the duty to the pact would be set to the sovereign government by another and superior sovereign. Consequently, the sovereign government legally bound by the pact would be in a state of subjection . . . If they were bound legally to keep the original covenant, without a positive law set by their own sovereign, the subjects would be bound legally to keep the original covenant, through a positive law set by another sovereign: that is to say, they would be in a state of subjection to their own sovereign government, and also to a sovereign government conferring rights upon their own.

. . . If the sovereign or subjects were bound *religiously* by the fundamental civil pact, the religious duty lying on the sovereign, or the religious duty lying on the subjects, would properly proceed from the Divine law, and not from the pact itself. . . .

. . . Whatever be the nature of the index to the law of God, the sovereign would be bound religiously, without an original covenant, to govern to that absolute end: whilst the subjects would be bound religiously, without an original covenant, to render to the sovereign the obedience which the accomplishment of the end might require. Consequently . . . the original covenant would not oblige religiously either of the two parties. . . .

If the sovereign were bound *morally* to keep the original covenant, the sovereign would be bound by opinions current amongst the subjects, to govern to the absolute end at which its authors had aimed: And if the subjects were bound *morally* to keep the original covenant, the subjects would be bound severally by opinions of the community at large, to render to the sovereign the obedience which the accomplishment of the end might require. But the moral obligations thus incumbent on the sovereign, with the moral obligations thus incumbent on the subjects, would not be engendered or affected by the original covenant. . . .

We may, if we like, imagine and assume, that the fancied original covenant was conceived and constructed by its authors, with some particularity and precision: that, having determined the absolute end of their union, it specified some of the ends positive or negative, or some of the means or modes positive or negative, through which the sovereign government should rule to that absolute end. The founders, for example, of the independent political society . . . might have adverted specially to the monstrous and palpable mischiefs of *ex post facto* legislation: and therefore the fancied covenant might have determined specially, that the sovereign government about to be formed should forbear from legislation of the kind. . . .

. . . Speaking generally, the proper subordinate ends of a sovereign political government (let those ends or means be what they may) may be imagined in forms, or may be stated in expressions, which are neither extremely abstract, nor extremely vague. Consequently, if the government ventured to deviate from any of the subordinate ends to which those uniform opinions were decidedly favourable, the bulk or generality of the subjects would probably unite in resenting, and even in resisting its measures: for if they tried its measures by one and the same standard, and if that standard or test were determinate and not dubious, their respective opinions concerning its measures would exactly or nearly tally. Consequently, a fear of encountering an effectual resistance, in case it should venture to deviate from any of those ends, would constantly hold the government to all the subordinate ends which the uniform opinions of the mass decidedly favoured. . . .

. . . And here (it might be argued) the sovereign would be bound morally to rule to those same ends, through the fundamental pact, or in consequence of the fundamental pact . . . It will, however, appear, on a moment's reflection, that the opinions of the generality of the subjects, concerning those same ends, would not be engendered by, but rather would have engendered the covenant. . . .

The following (I think) is the only, or nearly the only case, wherein an original covenant, as being a covenant or pact, might generate or influence any of the duties lying on the sovereign or subjects.

It might be believed by the bulk of the subjects, that an agreement or convention . . . has that mysterious efficacy which is expressly or tacitly ascribed to it by those who resort to the hypothesis of a fundamental civil pact . . . Now, if the mass of the subjects potently believed these positions, the duties of the government towards its subjects, which the positive morality of the community imposed upon it would be engendered or affected by the original covenant. . . .

If the covenant of the founders of the community did not affect the opinions of its following members, the covenant would be simply useless.

If the covenant of the founders of the community did affect the opinions of its following members, the covenant probably would be positively pernicious. For the opinions of the following members would probably be affected by the covenant as being a covenant or pact made by the founders. They probably would impute to the subordinate end specified by the original covenant, a worth extrinsic and arbitrary, or independent of their intrinsic merits . . . They probably would respect the specified ends, or probably would partly respect them, because the venerable founders of the independent political society (by the venerable covenant or pact which was the basis of the social fabric) had determined that those same ends were some of the ends or means through which the weal of the community might be furthered by its sovereign government. Now the venerable age or times wherein the community was founded, would probably be less enlightened (notwithstanding its claims to veneration) than any of the ensuing and degenerate ages through which the community might endure. . . .

2. . . . It will appear from the following strictures, that the hypothesis of the fundamental pact is not only a fiction, but is a fiction approaching to an impossibility. . . .

The conventions enforced by positive law

or morality, are enforced legally or morally for various reasons. But of the various reasons for enforcing any convention, the following is always one.—Sanctions apart, a convention *naturally* raises in the mind of the promisee, (or a convention *tends* to raise in the mind of the promisee,) an *expectation* that its object will be accomplished: and to the expectation naturally raised by the convention, he as naturally shapes his conduct. Now, as much of the business of human life turns or moves upon conventions, frequent disappointments of those expectations which conventions naturally excite, would render human society a scene of baffled hopes, and of thwarted projects and labours. To prevent disappointments of such expectations, is therefore a main object of the legal and moral rules whose direct and appropriate purpose is the enforcement of pacts or agreements. . . .

. . . An original covenant properly so called, or aught resembling the idea of a proper original covenant, could hardly precede the formation of an independent political society. . . .

. . . The promise of the sovereign to the subjects would not be a covenant properly, unless the subjects *accepted* it. But the subjects could hardly accept it, unless they apprehended its object. Unless they apprehended its object, it hardly could raise in their minds any determinate expectation: and unless it raised in their minds a determinate expectation, they hardly could signify virtually any determinate expectation, or could hardly accept virtually the proffered promise . . . We know that the great majority, in any actual community, have no determinate notions concerning the absolute end to which their sovereign government ought to rule: that they have no determinate notions concerning the ends or means through which it should aim at the accomplishment of that its paramount purpose. . . .

If you would suppose an original covenant which as a mere hypothesis will hold water, you must suppose that the society about to be formed is composed entirely of adult members: that all these adult members are

persons of sane mind, and even of much sagacity and much judgment: and that being very sagacious and very judicious, they also are perfectly familiar, or at least are passably acquainted, with political and ethical science. . . .

. . . There is no historical evidence, that the hypothesis has ever been realised: that the formation of any society political and independent has actually been preceded by a proper original covenant, or by aught approaching to the idea.

In a few societies political and independent, (as for example, in the Anglo-American States,) the sovereign political government has been determined at once, and agreeably to a scheme or plan. But, even in these societies, the parties who determined the constitution (either as scheming or planning, or as simply voting or adopting it) were merely a slender portion of the whole of the independent community, and were virtually sovereign therein before the constitution was determined: insomuch that the constitution was not constructed by the whole of an inchoate community, but rather was constructed by a fraction of a community already consummate or complete . . . In most societies political and independent, the constitution of the supreme government has *grown*. By which fustian but current phrase, I intend not to intimate that it hath come of itself, or is a marvellous something fashioned without hands. For though we say of governments which we mean to praise, "that they are governments of laws, and not governments of men," all human governments are governments of men: and, without men to make them, and without men to enforce them, human laws were just nothing at all, or were merely idle words scribbled on paper or parchment. I intend to intimate, by the phrase in question, that the constitution of the supreme government has not been determined at once, or agreeably to a scheme or plan: that positive moral rules of succcessive generations of the community (and, perhaps, positive laws made by its successive sovereigns) have determined the constitution, with more or less of exactness, slowly and unsystematically. Consequently, the supreme government was not constituted by the original members of the society: Its constitution has been the work of a long series of authors, comprising the original members and many generations of their followers. And the same may be said of most of the ethical maxims which opinions current with the subjects constrain the sovereign to observe. The original sovereign government could not have promised its subjects to govern by those maxims. For the current opinions which actually enforce those maxims, are not coeval with the independent political society, but rather have arisen insensibly since the society was formed. . . .

15

John Stuart Mill

1806–1873

James Mill met Jeremy Bentham and became his disciple when his first child, John Stuart, was two. Perhaps Bentham, who had been a child scholar, inspired the early start of John Stuart's studies. At three he was at work on Greek, and had read many classics before he was eight. His father (a scholarly preacher turned agnostic) was his teacher. John worked in his father's study, and the pair often took long conversational walks. Never once in his autobiography did Mill mention his mother. He applauded his training as an example of the reach of education pursued with fervor. He said he was not crammed with knowledge, but was encouraged to work out answers to his own questions as they arose. When he was eight his younger sisters became his pupils. He read proof for his father's well-thought-of History of India when he was twelve. His father guided him particularly to philosophy and economics. For fun he read history and science. Apart from walking, he worked at nothing but study and talk. When he was fourteen he went to France and spent a year in Bentham's brother's house. There he learned French, studied chemistry and mathematics. There he also became an amateur botanist—a hobby that engrossed him in his old age.

At fifteen he came back to England and started reading law under John Austin, but gave up within a year for a job alongside his father in India House. When his father died, twenty-year-old Mill was put in charge of the East India Company's relations with native states. At forty he was made chief examiner of the India House Office and be-

came an important force in the solution of practical problems of government of the subcontinent. Two years later the East India Company's powers were revoked and government of India became a public function. Mill was asked to join the diplomatic service as an India expert, but he refused and retired with a good pension. His work at India House kept him out of active politics, but it interfered little with his scholarly growth. At one time he did not only his own work, but also that of an ailing fellow, and still managed a full literary life.

During his youth Mill liked organized debate; in it he found both clarification of his ideas and intellectual companionship. Much of his time was spent in writing for liberal periodicals. At nineteen he edited Bentham's *Rationale of Judicial Evidence,* a job which included filling gaps, resolving contradictions, and reducing over-generalizations; it is said that this editorial job is the best done on any of Bentham's works. His interest in logic and social science ripened in his twenties, and his writings on those subjects then began to flow.

Mental depression gripped Mill in his early twenties. He thought his gloom was the aftermath of an education too much aimed at developing powers of cold analysis. He decided to change his personality—to pursue ends for themselves, to pay more attention to his emotions, to thrill to appreciation of the arts. In his *Autobiography* he tells of joy got from Weber's music and Wordsworth's poetry. His intellectualism would not be downed; he worried about the small number of musical themes that could be composed in an eight-note scale; he found Byron's poetry too dramatically sombre to relieve his gloom. Mill came out of this period emancipated from the tight confines of his father's and Bentham's philosophy. He also came out of it with a facial tic which stayed with him for the rest of his life.

When Mill was twenty-five he met a twenty-three-year-old matron, Mrs. Taylor, wife of a drysalter and wholesale druggist. Instant attachment kept them much in each other's company. She was an intellectual; her plodding husband tolerated her constant platonic association with Mill. But they were too much together for twenty years to escape gossip. When Mr. Taylor died, the pair married. Their relationship had long offended Mill's family; the marriage worked complete estrangement. Most of their short married life was spent in France in search of better health for Mrs. Mill. Seven years after the marriage she died at Avignon of tuberculosis caught from Mill. Mill reported that she was virtually co-author of all of his work; he warmly and pathetically dedicated his famous essay, *On Liberty,* to her and acknowledged her as a collaborator.

Though philosophy and letters were Mill's main interest in his mature years, he kept abreast of the current scene. He was a supporter of the North in the Civil War—insisting that abolition of slavery was the critical issue, and discounting distracting arguments on side issues. He was strong for women's suffrage, and, with two powerful women, was one incorporator of the first organization to work for it.

At fifty-nine he stood for Parliament. He refused to campaign and would pay no politician to campaign for him. Reluctantly he attended a few political meetings and answered questions put to him. His reputation elected him. He was an active M.P. and often took part in debates—mostly on measures proposed by others. One idea which he espoused was that the national debt ought to be paid off before English coal was exhausted. He spoke deliberately and in beautiful phrases, but he paused annoyingly in mid-sentence—he was no spellbinder. Nor

was he much of a politician; he took unpopular stands without a qualm. He was defeated when he first stood for re-election.

Avignon and his wife's grave drew him back to France in his last years. He lived with his step-daughter—whom he admired almost as much as his wife. She, like his wife, took an active part in his work. His Avignon cottage was filled with books and newspapers. There he played the piano, read and wrote, walked and botanized. He loved the countryside and left an unfinished study of the flora of the Avignon locality. He died at sixty-seven.

Mill's social and economic views were extreme. He had no faith in common men around him—they were too uneducated and shortsighted for democracy. At a political meeting when he was standing for Parliament a heckler asked, "Did you not once say that the working classes are generally liars?" His answer was a candid, "I did!" He feared for minorities and nonconformists in democracy, and to give them a voice he supported the Hare system of preferential voting for legislators. He had no respect for the idea that the institution of private property was sacred, and hoped for a socialistic economy which would supply human wants evenhandedly and without privilege.

Mill's best known and perhaps most influential political work is his essay, *On Liberty* (1859). Its style and respect for intellectual freedom make it required reading. More central to his thinking on law, however, is his essay called *Utilitarianism,* (1863). Excerpts from both these works follow.

UTILITARIANISM *

CHAPTER I

General Remarks

There are few circumstances among those which make up the present condition of human knowledge, more unlike what might have been expected, or more significant of

* From Number 482A. Everyman's Library. Reprinted by permission of E. P. Dutton & Co., Inc.

the backward state in which speculation on the most important subjects still lingers, than the little progress which has been made in the decision of the controversy respecting the criterion of right and wrong. . . .

. . . Though in science the particular truths precede the general theory, the contrary might be expected to be the case with a practical art, such as morals or legislation. All action is for the sake of some end, and rules of action, it seems natural to suppose, must take their whole character and colour from the end to which they are subservient. When we engage in a pursuit, a clear and precise conception of what we are pursuing would seem to be the first thing we need, instead of the last we are to look forward to. A test of right and wrong must be the means, one would think, of ascertaining what is right or wrong, and not a consequence of having already ascertained it.

The difficulty is not avoided by having recourse to the popular theory of a natural faculty, a sense or instinct, informing us of right and wrong. For—besides that the existence of such a moral instinct is itself one of the matters in dispute—those believers in it who have any pretensions to philosophy, have been obliged to abandon the idea that it discerns what is right or wrong in the particular case in hand, as our other senses discern the sight or sound actually present. Our moral faculty, according to all those of its interpreters who are entitled to the name of thinkers, supplies us only with the general principles of moral judgments; it is a branch of our reason, not of our sensitive faculty; and must be looked to for the abstract doctrines of morality, not for perception of it in the concrete. The intuitive, no less than what may be termed the inductive, school of ethics, insists on the necessity of general laws . . . According to the one opinion, the principles of morals are evident *a priori,* requiring nothing to command assent, except that the meaning of the terms be understood. According to the other doctrine, right and wrong, as well as truth and falsehood, are questions of observation and experience. But both hold equally that morality must

be deduced from principles; and the intuitive school affirm as strongly as the inductive, that there is a science of morals. Yet they seldom attempt to make out a list of the *a priori* principles which are to serve as the premises of the science; still more rarely do they make any effort to reduce those various principles to one first principle, or common ground of obligation . . . Yet to support their pretensions there ought either to be some one fundamental principle or law, at the root of all morality, or if there be several, there should be a determinate order of precedence among them. . . .

. . . Although the non-existence of an acknowledged first principle has made ethics not so much a guide as a consecration of men's actual sentiments, still, as men's sentiments, both of favour and of aversion, are greatly influenced by what they suppose to be the effects of things upon their happiness, the principle of utility, or as Bentham latterly called it, the greatest happiness principle, has had a large share in forming the moral doctrines even of those who most scornfully reject its authority. Nor is there any school of thought which refuses to admit that the influence of actions on happiness is a most material and even predominant consideration in many of the details of morals, however unwilling to acknowledge it as the fundamental principle of morality, and the source of moral obligation. I might go much further, and say that to all those *a priori* moralists who deem it necessary to argue at all, utilitarian arguments are indispensable. It is not my present purpose to criticise these thinkers; but I cannot help referring, for illustration, to a systematic treatise by one of the most illustrious of them, the *Metaphysics of Ethics,* by Kant. This remarkable man, whose system of thought will long remain one of the landmarks in the history of philosophical speculation, does, in the treatise in question, lay down a universal first principle as the origin and ground of moral obligation; it is this:—"So act, that the rule on which thou actest would admit of being adopted as a law by all rational beings." But when he begins to deduce from this precept any of the actual duties of morality, he fails, almost grotesquely, to show that there would be any contradiction, any logical (not to say physical) impossibility, in the adoption by all rational beings of the most outrageously immoral rules of conduct. All he shows is that the *consequences* of their universal adoption would be such as no one would choose to incur.

On the present occasion, I shall, without further discussion of the other theories, attempt to contribute something towards the understanding and appreciation of the Utilitarian or Happiness theory, and towards such proof as it is susceptible of. It is evident that this cannot be proof in the ordinary and popular meaning of the term. Questions of ultimate ends are not amenable to direct proof. Whatever can be proved to be good, must be so by being shown to be a means to something admitted to be good without proof. The medical art is proved to be good by its conducing to health; but how is it possible to prove that health is good? . . . We are not, however, to infer that its acceptance or rejection must depend on blind impulse, or arbitrary choice. There is a larger meaning of the word proof, in which this question is as amenable to it as any other of the disputed questions of philosophy. The subject is within the cognisance of the rational faculty; and neither does that faculty deal with it solely in the way of intuition. Considerations may be presented capable of determining the intellect either to give or withhold its assent to the doctrine; and this is equivalent to proof.

We shall examine presently of what nature are these considerations; in what manner they apply to the case, and what rational grounds, therefore, can be given for accepting or rejecting the utilitarian formula. . . .

CHAPTER II

What Utilitarianism Is

. . . The creed which accepts as the foundation of morals, Utility, or the Greatest Happiness Principle, holds that actions are right in proportion as they tend to promote happiness, wrong as they tend to produce the reverse of happiness. By happiness is intended pleasure, and the absence of pain; by unhappiness, pain, and the privation of pleasure . . . Pleasure, and freedom from pain, are the only things desirable as ends; and . . . all desirable things (which are as numerous in the utilitarian as in any other scheme) are desirable either for the pleasure inherent in themselves, or as means to the promotion of pleasure and the prevention of pain. . . .

. . . As between his own happiness and that of others, utilitarianism requires him to be as strictly impartial as a disinterested and benevolent spectator. In the golden rule of Jesus of Nazareth, we read the complete spirit of the ethics of utility. To do as you would be done by, and to love your neighbour as yourself, constitute the ideal perfection of utilitarian morality. As the means of making the nearest approach to this ideal, utility would enjoin, first, that laws and social arrangements should place the happiness, or (as speaking practically it may be called) the interest, of every individual, as nearly as possible in harmony with the interest of the whole; and secondly, that education and opinion, which have so vast a power over human character, should so use that power as to establish in the mind of every individual an indissoluble association between his own happiness and the good of the whole; especially between his own happiness and the practice of such modes of conduct, negative and positive, as regard for the universal happiness prescribes; so that not only he may be unable to conceive the possibility of happiness to himself, consistently with conduct opposed to the general good, but also that a direct impulse to promote the general good may be in every individual one of the habitual motives of action, and the sentiments connected therewith may fill a large and prominent place in every human being's sentient existence. . . .

. . . The great majority of good actions are intended not for the benefit of the world, but for that of individuals, of which the good of the world is made up and the thoughts of the most virtuous man need not on these occasions travel beyond the particular persons concerned, except so far as is necessary to assure himself that in benefiting them he is not violating the rights, that is, the legitimate and authorised expectations, of any one else. The multiplication of happiness is, according to the utilitarian ethics, the object of virtue: the occasions on which any person (except one in a thousand) has it in his power to do this on an extended scale, . . . are but exceptional; and on these occasions alone is he called on to consider public utility; in every other case, private utility, the interest or happiness of some few persons, is all he has to attend to. . . .

. . . Among utilitarians as among adherents of other systems, there is every imaginable degree of rigidity and of laxity in the application of their standard: some are even puritanically rigorous, while others are as indulgent as can possibly be desired by sinner or by sentimentalist. But on the whole, a doctrine which brings prominently forward the interest that mankind have in the repression and prevention of conduct which violates the moral law, is likely to be inferior to no other in turning the sanctions of opinion against such violations. It is true, the question, What does violate the moral law? is one on which those who recognise different standards of morality are likely now and then to differ. But difference of opinion on moral questions was not first introduced into the world by utilitarianism, while that doctrine does supply, if not always an easy, at all events a tangible and intelligible mode of deciding such differences. . . .

. . . If it be a true belief that God desires, above all things, the happiness of his creatures, and that this was his purpose in their creation, utility is not only not a godless doctrine, but more profoundly religious than any other. If it be meant that utilitarianism does not recognize the revealed will of God as the supreme law of morals, I answer, that a utilitarian who believes in the perfect goodness and wisdom of God, necessarily believes that whatever God has thought fit to reveal on the subject of morals, must fulfil the requirements of utility in a supreme degree. But others besides utilitarians have been of opinion that the Christian revelation was intended, and is fitted, to inform the hearts and minds of mankind with a spirit which should enable them to find for themselves what is right, and incline them to do it when found, rather than to tell them, except in a very general way, what it is; and that we need a doctrine of ethics, carefully followed out, to *interpret* to us the will of God. Whether this opinion is correct or not, it is superfluous here to discuss; since whatever aid religion either natural or revealed, can afford to ethical investigation, is as open to the utilitarian moralist as to any other. He can use it as the testimony of God to the usefulness or hurtfulness of any given course of action, by as good a right as others can use it for the indication of a transcendental law, having no connection with usefulness or with happiness.

Again, Utility is often summarily stigmatised as an immoral doctrine by giving it the name of Expediency, and taking advantage of the popular use of that term to contrast it with Principle. But the Expedient, in the sense in which it is opposed to the Right, generally means that which is expedient for the particular interest of the agent himself; as when a minister sacrifices the interests of his country to keep himself in place. When it means anything better than this, it means that which is expedient for some immediate object, some temporary purpose, but which violates a rule whose observance is expedient in a much higher degree. The Expedient, in this sense, instead of being the same thing with the useful, is a branch of the hurtful. . . .

Again, defenders of utility often find themselves called upon to reply to such objections as this—that there is not time, previous to action, for calculating and weighing the effects of any line of conduct on the general happiness. This is exactly as if any one were to say that it is impossible to guide our conduct by Christianity, because there is not time, on every occasion on which anything has to be done, to read through the Old and New Testaments . . . People talk as if the commencement of . . . experience had hitherto been put off, and as if at the moment when some man feels tempted to meddle with the property or life of another, he had to begin considering for the first time whether murder and theft are injurious to human happiness . . . It is truly a whimsical supposition that, if mankind were agreed in considering utility to be the test of morality, they would remain without any agreement as to what *is* useful, and would take no measures for having their notions on the subject taught to the young, and enforced by law and opinion . . . That mankind have still much to learn as to the effects of actions on the general happiness, I admit, or rather, earnestly maintain. The corollaries from the principle of utility, like the precepts of every practical art, admit of indefinite improvement, and, in a progressive state of the human mind, their improvement is perpetually going on. But to consider the rules of morality as improvable, is one thing; to pass over the intermediate generalisations entirely, and endeavour to test each individual action directly by the first principle, is another. It is a strange notion that the acknowledgment of a first principle is inconsistent with the admission of secondary ones. To inform a traveller respecting the place of his ultimate destination, is not to forbid the use of landmarks and direction-posts on the way. . . .

. . . We are told that a utilitarian will be apt to make his own particular case an exception to moral rules, and, when under temptation, will see a utility in the breach of a rule, greater than he will see in its observance. But is utility the only creed which is able to furnish us with excuses for evil doing, and means of cheating our own conscience? They are afforded in abundance by all doctrines which recognise as a fact in morals the existence of conflicting considerations; which all doctrines do, that have been believed by sane persons. It is not the fault of any creed, but of the complicated nature of human affairs, that rules of conduct can-

not be so framed as to require no exceptions, and that hardly any kind of action can safely be laid down as either always obligatory or always condemnable. There is no ethical creed which does not temper the rigidity of its laws, by giving a certain latitude, under the moral responsibility of the agent, for accommodation to peculiarities of circumstances; and under every creed, at the opening thus made, self-deception and dishonest casuistry get in. There exists no moral system under which there do not arise unequivocal cases of conflicting obligation. These are the real difficulties, the knotty points both in the theory of ethics, and in the conscientious guidance of personal conduct. They are overcome practically, with greater or with less success, according to the intellect and virtue of the individual; but it can hardly be pretended that any one will be the less qualified for dealing with them, from possessing an ultimate standard to which conflicting rights and duties can be referred. If utility is the ultimate source of moral obligations, utility may be invoked to decide between them when their demands are incompatible. Though the application of the standard may be difficult, it is better than none at all: while in other systems, the moral laws all claiming independent authority, there is no common umpire entitled to interfere between them; their claims to precedence one over another rest on little better than sophistry, and unless determined, as they generally are, by the unacknowledged influence of considerations of utility, afford a free scope for the action of personal desires and partialities. . . .

CHAPTER III

Of the Ultimate Sanction of the Principle of Utility

. . . The social state is at once so natural, so necessary, and so habitual to man, that, except in some unusual circumstances or by an effort of voluntary abstraction, he never conceives himself otherwise than as a member of a body; and this association is riveted more and more, as mankind are further removed from the state of savage independence. Any condition, therefore, which is essential to a state of society, becomes more and more an inseparable part of every person's conception of the state of things which he is born into, and which is the destiny of a human being. Now, society between human beings, except in the relation of master and slave, is manifestly impossible on any other footing than that the interests of all are to be consulted. Society between equals can only exist on the understanding that the interests of all are to be regarded equally. And since in all states of civilization, every person, except an absolute monarch, has equals, every one is obliged to live on these terms with somebody; and in every age some advance is made towards a state in which it will be impossible to live permanently on other terms with anybody. In this way people grow up unable to conceive as possible to them a state of total disregard of other people's interests. They are under a necessity of conceiving themselves as at least abstaining from all the grosser injuries, and (if only for their own protection) living in a state of constant protest against them. They are also familiar with the fact of co-operating with others, and proposing to themselves a collective, not an individual interest as the aim (at least for the time being) of their actions. So long as they are co-operating, their ends are identified with those of others; there is at least a temporary feeling that the interests of others are their own interests. Not only does all strengthening of social ties, and all healthy growth of society, give to each individual a stronger personal interest in practically consulting the welfare of others; it also leads him to identify his *feelings* more and more with their good, or at least with an even greater degree of practical consideration for it. He comes, as though instinctively, to be conscious of himself as a being who *of course* pays regard to others . . . This mode of conceiving ourselves and human life, as civilisation goes on, is felt to be more and more natural. Every step in political improvement renders it more so, by removing the sources of opposition of interest, and levelling those inequalities of legal privilege between individuals or classes, owing to which there are large portions of mankind whose happiness it is still practicable to disregard. . . .

CHAPTER V

On the Connection Between Justice and Utility

In all ages of speculation, one of the strongest obstacles to the reception of the doctrine that Utility or Happiness is the criterion of right and wrong, has been drawn from the idea of Justice. The powerful sentiment, and apparently clear perception, which that word recalls with a rapidity and certainty resembling an instinct, have seemed to the majority of thinkers to point to an inherent quality in things; to show that the Just must have an existence in Nature as something absolute, generically distinct from every variety of the Expedient . . . .

In the case of this, as of our other moral sentiments, there is no necessary connection between the question of its origin, and that of its binding force. That a feeling is bestowed on us by Nature, does not necessarily legitimate all its promptings . . . Mankind are always predisposed to believe that any subjective feeling, not otherwise accounted for, is a revelation of some objective reality. Our present object is to determine whether the reality, to which the feeling of justice corresponds, is one which needs any such special revelation . . . Inasmuch as the subjective mental feeling of Justice is different from that which commonly attaches to simple expediency, and, except in the extreme cases of the latter, is far more imperative in its demands, people find it difficult to see, in Justice, only a particular kind or branch of general utility, and think that its superior binding force requires a totally different origin.

To throw light upon this question, it is necessary to attempt to ascertain what is the distinguishing character of justice, or of injustice: what is the quality, or whether there is any quality, attributed in common to all modes of conduct designated as unjust (for justice, like many other moral attributes, is best defined by its opposite), and distinguishing them from such modes of conduct as are disapproved, but without having that particular epithet of disapprobation applied to them. If in everything which men are accustomed to characterise as just or unjust, some one common attribute or collection of attributes is always present, we may judge whether this particular attribute or combination of attributes would be capable of gathering round it a sentiment of that peculiar character and intensity by virtue of the general laws of our emotional constitution, or whether the sentiment is inexplicable, and requires to be regarded as a special provision of Nature. . . .

In the first place, it is mostly considered unjust to deprive any one of his personal liberty, his property, or any other thing which belongs to him by law. Here, therefore, is one instance of the application of the terms just and unjust in a perfectly definite sense, namely, that it is just to respect, unjust to violate, the *legal rights* of any one. But this judgment admits of several exceptions, arising from the other forms in which the notions of justice and injustice present themselves. . . .

Secondly; the legal rights of which he is deprived, may be rights which *ought* not to have belonged to him; in other words, the law which confers on him these rights, may be a bad law. When it is so, or when (which is the same thing for our purpose) it is supposed to be so, opinions will differ as to the justice or injustice of infringing it. Some maintain that no law, however bad, ought to be disobeyed by an individual citizen; that his opposition to it, if shown at all, should only be shown in endeavouring to get it altered by competent authority. This opinion (which condemns many of the most illustrious benefactors of mankind, and would often protect pernicious institutions against the only weapons which, in the state of things existing at the time, have any chance of succeeding against them) is defended, by those who hold it, on grounds of expediency; principally on that of the importance, to the common interest of mankind, of maintaining inviolate the sentiment of submission to law. Other persons, again, hold the directly contrary opinion, that any law, judged to be bad, may blamelessly be disobeyed, even though it be not judged to be unjust, but only inexpedient; while others would confine the licence of disobedience to the case of unjust laws: but again, some say, that all laws which are inexpedient are unjust; since every law imposes some restriction on the natural liberty of mankind, which restriction is an injustice, unless legitimated by tending to their good. Among these diversities of opinion, it seems to be universally admitted that there may be unjust laws, and that law, consequently, is not the ultimate criterion of justice . . . We may say, therefore, that a second case of injustice consists in taking or withholding from any person that to which he has a *moral right.*

Thirdly, it is universally considered just that each person should obtain that (whether good or evil) which he *deserves;* and unjust that he should obtain a good, or be made to undergo an evil, which he does not deserve . . . Speaking in a general way, a person is understood to deserve good if he does right, evil if he does wrong; and in a more particular sense, to deserve good from those to whom he does or has done good, and evil from those to whom he does or has done evil. . . .

Fourthly, it is confessedly unjust to *break faith* with any one: to violate an engagement, either express or implied, or disappoint expectations raised by our own conduct, at least if we have raised those expectations knowingly and voluntarily. Like the other obligations of justice already spoken of, this one is not regarded as absolute. . . .

Fifthly, it is, by universal admission, inconsistent with justice to be *partial;* to show favour or preference to one person over another, in matters to which favour and preference do not properly apply . . . Favour and preference are not always censurable, and indeed the cases in which they are condemned are rather the exception than the rule. A person would more likely to be blamed than applauded for giving his family or friends no superiority in good offices over strangers, when he could do so without violating any other duty; and no one thinks it unjust to seek one person in preference to another as a friend, connection, or companion. Impartiality where rights are concerned is of course obligatory, but this is involved in the more general obligation of giving to every one his right. A tribunal, for example, must be impartial, because it is bound to award, without regard to any other consideration, a disputed object to the one of two parties who has the right to it . . . Impartiality, in short, as an obligation of justice, may be said to mean, being exclusively influenced by the considerations which it is supposed ought to influence the particular case in hand; and resisting the solicitation of any motives which prompt to conduct different from what those considerations would dictate.

Nearly allied to the idea of impartiality is that of *equality;* which often enters as a component part both into the conception of justice and into the practice of it, and, in the eyes of many persons, constitutes its essence. But in this, still more than in any other case, the notion of justice varies in different persons, and always conforms in its variations to their notion of utility. Each person maintains that equality is the dictate of justice, except where he thinks that expediency requires inequality. The justice of giving equal protection to the rights of all, is maintained by those who support the most outrageous inequality in the rights themselves. Even in slave countries it is theoretically admitted that the rights of the slave, such as they are, ought to be as sacred as those of the master; and that a tribunal which fails to enforce them with equal strictness is wanting in justice; while, at the same time, institutions which leave to the slave scarcely any rights to enforce, are not deemed unjust,

because they are not deemed inexpedient. Those who think that utility requires distinctions of rank, do not consider it unjust that riches and social privileges should be unequally dispensed; but those who think this inequality inexpedient, think it unjust also. Whoever thinks that government is necessary, sees no injustice in as much inequality as is constituted by giving to the magistrate powers not granted to other people. Even among those who hold levelling doctrines, there are as many questions of justice as there are differences of opinion about expediency. Some Communists consider it unjust that the produce of the labour of the community should be shared on any other principle than that of exact equality; others think it just that those should receive most whose wants are greatest; while others hold that those who work harder, or who produce more, or whose services are more valuable to the community, may justly claim a larger quota in the division of the produce. And the sense of natural justice may be plausibly appealed to in behalf of every one of these opinions.

Among so many diverse applications of the term Justice, which yet is not regarded as ambiguous, it is a matter of some difficulty to seize the mental link which holds them together, and on which the moral sentiment adhering to the term essentially depends. Perhaps, in this embarrassment, some help may be derived from the history of the word, as indicated by its etymology.

In most, if not in all, languages, the etymology of the word which corresponds to Just, points distinctly to an origin connected with the ordinances of law. *Justum* is a form of *jussum,* that which has been ordered . . . *Recht,* from which came *right* and *righteous,* is synonymous with law . . . The primitive element in the formation of the notion of justice, was conformity to law. It constituted the entire idea among the Hebrews, up to the birth of Christianity; as might be expected in the case of a people whose laws attempted to embrace all subjects on which precepts were required, and who believed those laws to be a direct emanation from the Supreme Being. But other nations, and in particular the Greeks and Romans, who knew that their laws had been made originally, and still continued to be made, by men, were not afraid to admit that those men might make bad laws . . . Hence the sentiment of injustice came to be attached, not to all violations of law, but only to violations of such laws as *ought* to exist . . . In this manner the idea of law and of its injunctions was still predominant in the notion of justice, even when the laws actually in force ceased to be accepted as the standard of it.

It is true that mankind consider the idea of justice and its obligations as applicable to many things which neither are, nor is it desired that they should be, regulated by law. Nobody desires that laws should interfere with the whole detail of private life; yet every one allows that in all daily conduct a person may and does show himself to be either just or unjust. But even here, the idea of the breach of what ought to be law, still lingers in a modified shape. It would always give us pleasure, and chime in with our feelings of fitness, that acts which we deem unjust should be punished, though we do not always think it expedient that this should be done by the tribunals . . . We consider the impunity given to injustice as an evil, and strive to make amends for it by bringing a strong expression of our own and the public disapprobation to bear upon the offender. Thus the idea of legal constraint is still the generating idea of the notion of justice, though undergoing several transformations before that notion, as it exists in an advanced state of society, becomes complete.

The above is, I think, a true account, as far as it goes, of the origin and progressive growth of the idea of justice. But we must observe, that it contains, as yet, nothing to distinguish that obligation from moral obligation in general. For the truth is, that the idea of penal sanction, which is the essence of law, enters not only into the conception of injustice, but into that of any kind of wrong. We do not call anything wrong, unless we mean to imply that a person ought to be punished in some way or other for doing it; if not by law, by the opinion of his fellow-creatures; if not by opinion, by the reproaches of his own conscience. This seems the real turning point of the distinction between morality and simple expediency. It is a part of the notion of Duty in every one of its forms, that a person may rightfully be compelled to fulfil it. Duty is a thing which may be *exacted* from a person, as one exacts a debt. Unless we think that it may be exacted from him, we do not call it his duty. Reasons of prudence, or the interest of other people, may militate against actually exacting it; but the person himself, it is clearly understood, would not be entitled to complain. There are other things, on the contrary, which we wish that people should do, which we like or admire them for doing, perhaps dislike or despise them for not doing, but yet admit that they are not bound to do; it is not a case of moral obligation . . . I think there is no doubt that this distinction lies at the bottom of the notions of right and wrong; that we call any conduct wrong, or employ, instead, some other term of dislike or disparagement, according as we think that the person ought, or ought not, to be punished for it; and we say, it would be right to do so and so, or merely that it would be desirable or laudable, according as we would wish to see the person whom it concerns, compelled, or only persuaded and exhorted, to act in that manner.

This, therefore, being the characteristic difference which marks off, not justice, but morality in general, from the remaining provinces of Expediency and Worthiness; the character is still to be sought which distinguishes justice from other branches of morality. Now it is known that ethical writers divide moral duties into two classes, denoted by the ill-chosen expressions, duties of perfect and of imperfect obligation; the latter being those in which, though the act is obligatory, the particular occasions of performing it are left to our choice; as in the case of charity or beneficence, which we are indeed bound to practise, but not towards any definite person, nor at any prescribed time. In the more precise language of philosophic jurists, duties of perfect obligation are those duties in virtue of which a correlative *right* resides in some person or persons; duties of imperfect obligation are those moral obligations which do not give birth to any right. I think it will be found that this distinction exactly coincides with that which exists between justice and the other obligations of morality. In our survey of the various popular acceptations of justice, the term appeared generally to involve the idea of a personal right . . . Whether the injustice consists in depriving a person of a possession, or in breaking faith with him, or in treating him worse than he deserves, or worse than other people who have no greater claims, in each case the supposition implies two things—a wrong done, and some assignable person who is wronged. Injustice may also be done by treating a person better than others; but the wrong in this case is to his competitors, who are also assignable persons . . . Whoever does not place the distinction between justice and morality in general, where we have now placed it, will be found to make no distinction between them at all, but to merge all morality in justice. . . .

. . . We are ready to enter on the inquiry, whether the feeling, which accompanies the idea, is attached to it by a special dispensation of nature, or whether it could have grown up, by any known laws, out of the idea itself; and in particular, whether it can have originated in considerations of general expediency.

I conceive that the sentiment itself does not arise from anything which would commonly, or correctly, be termed an idea of expediency; but that though the sentiment does not, whatever is moral in it does.

We have seen that the two essential ingredients in the sentiment of justice are, the desire to punish a person who has done harm, and the knowledge or belief that there is some definite individual or individuals to whom harm has been done.

. . . The desire to punish a person who has done harm to some individual is a spontaneous outgrowth from two sentiments, both in the highest degree natural, and which either are or resemble instincts; the impulse of self-defence, and the feeling of sympathy.

It is natural to resent, and to repel or retaliate, any harm done or attempted against ourselves, or against those with whom we sympathise. The origin of this sentiment it is not necessary here to discuss. Whether it be an instinct or a result of intelligence, it is, we know, common to all animal nature; for every animal tries to hurt those who have hurt, or who it thinks are about to hurt, itself or its young. Human beings, on this point, only differ from other animals in two particulars. First, in being capable of sympathising, not solely with their offspring, or, like some of the more noble animals, with some superior animal who is kind to them, but with all human, and even with all sentient, beings. Secondly, in having a more developed intelligence, which gives a wider range to the whole of their sentiments, whether self-regarding or sympathetic. By virtue of his superior intelligence, even apart from his superior range of sympathy, a human being is capable of apprehending a community of interest between himself and the human society of which he forms a part, such that any conduct which threatens the security of the society generally, is threatening to his own, and calls forth his instinct (if instinct it be) of self-defence. The same superiority of intelligence, joined to the power of sympathising with human beings generally, enables him to attach himself to the collective idea of his tribe, his country, or mankind, in such a manner that any act hurtful to them, raises his instinct of sympathy, and urges him to resistance.

The sentiment of justice, in that one of its elements which consists of the desire to punish, is thus, I conceive, the natural feeling of retaliation or vengeance, rendered by intellect and sympathy applicable to those injuries, that is, to those hurts, which wound us through, or in common with, society at large. This sentiment, in itself, has nothing moral in it; what is moral is, the exclusive subordination of it to the social sympathies, so as to wait on and obey their call. For the natural feeling would make us resent indiscriminately whatever any one does that is disagreeable to us; but when moralised by the social feeling, it only acts in the directions conformable to the general good: just persons resenting a hurt to society, though not otherwise a hurt to themselves, and not resenting a hurt to themselves, however painful, unless it be of the kind which society has a common interest with them in the repression of.

It is no objection against this doctrine to say, that when we feel our sentiment of justice outraged, we are not thinking of society at large, or of any collective interest, but only of the individual case. It is common enough certainly, though the reverse of commendable, to feel resentment merely because we have suffered pain; but a person whose resentment is really a moral feeling, that is, who considers whether an act is blamable before he allows himself to resent it—such a person, though he may not say expressly to himself that he is standing up for the interest of society, certainly does feel that he is asserting a rule which is for the benefit of others as well as for his own. If he is not feeling this—if he is regarding the act solely as it affects him individually—he is not consciously just; he is not concerning himself about the justice of his actions. This is admitted even by anti-utilitarian moralists. When Kant (as before remarked) propounds as the fundamental principle of morals, "So act, that thy rule of conduct might be adopted as a law by all rational beings," he virtually acknowledges that the interest of mankind collectively, or at least of mankind indiscriminately, must be in the mind of the agent when conscientiously deciding on the morality of the act . . . To give any meaning to Kant's principle, the sense put upon it must be, that we ought to shape our conduct by a rule which all rational beings might adopt *with benefit to their collective interest*. . . .

I have, throughout, treated the idea of a *right* residing in the injured person, and violated by the injury, not as a separate element in the composition of the idea and sentiment, but as one of the forms in which the other two elements clothe themselves. These elements are, a hurt to some assignable person or persons on the one hand, and a demand for punishment on the other. An examination of our own minds, I think, will show, that these two things include all that we mean when we speak of violation of a right. When we call anything a person's right, we mean that he has a valid claim on Society to protect him in the possession of it, either by the force of law, or by that of education and opinion . . . Thus, a person is said to have a right to what he can earn in fair professional competition; because society ought not to allow any other person to hinder him from endeavouring to earn in that manner as much as he can. But he has not a right to three hundred a-year, though he may happen to be earning it; because society is not called on to provide that he shall earn that sum. On the contrary, if he owns ten thousand pounds three per cent, stock, he *has* a right to three hundred a-year; because society has come under an obligation to provide him with an income of that amount.

To have a right, then, is, I conceive, to have something which society ought to defend me in the possession of. If the objector goes on to ask, why it ought? I can give him no other reason than general utility. If that expression does not seem to convey a sufficient feeling of the strength of the obligation, not to account for the peculiar energy of the feeling, it is because there goes to the composition of the sentiment, not a rational only, but also an animal element, the thirst for retaliation; and this thirst derives its intensity, as well as its moral justification, from the extraordinarily important and impressive kind of utility which is concerned. The interest involved is that of security, to every one's feelings the most vital of all interests. All other earthly benefits are needed by one person, not needed by another; and many of them can, if necessary, be cheerfully foregone, or replaced by something else; but security no human being can possibly do without . . . Now this most indispensable of all necessaries, after physical nutriment, cannot be had, unless the machinery for providing it is kept unintermittedly in active play. Our notion, therefore, of the claim we have on our fellow-creatures to join in making safe for us the very groundwork of our existence, gathers feelings around it so much more intense than those concerned in any of the more common cases of utility, that the difference in degree (as is often the case in psychology) becomes a real difference in kind. The claim assumes that character of absoluteness, that apparent infinity, and incommensurability with all other considerations, which constitute the distinction between the feeling of right and wrong and that of ordinary expediency and inexpediency. The feelings concerned are so powerful, and we count so positively on finding a responsive feeling in others (all being alike interested), that *ought* and *should* grow into *must,* and recognised indispensability becomes a moral necessity, analogous to physical, and often not inferior to it in binding force. . . .

We are continually informed that Utility is an uncertain standard, which every different person interprets differently, and that there is no safety but in the immutable, ineffaceable, and unmistakeable dictates of Justice, which carry their evidence in themselves, and are independent of the fluctuations of opinion. One would suppose from this that on questions of justice there could be no controversy . . . So far is this from being the fact, that there is as much difference of opinion, and as much discussion, about what is just, as about what is useful to society. Not only have different nations and individuals different notions of justice, but in the mind of one and of the same individual, justice is not some one rule, principle, or maxim, but many, which do not always coincide in their dictates, and in choosing between which, he is guided either by some extraneous standard, or by his own personal predilections.

For instance, there are some who say, that it is unjust to punish any one for the sake of example to others; that punishment is just, only when intended for the good of the sufferer himself. Others maintain the extreme reverse, contending that to punish persons who have attained years of discretion, for their own benefit, is despotism and injustice, since if the matter at issue is solely their own good, no one has a right to control their own judgment of it; but that they may justly be punished to prevent evil to others, this being the exercise of the legitimate right of self-defence. Mr. Owen, again, affirms that it is unjust to punish at all; for the criminal did not make his own character; his education, and the circumstances which surrounded him, have made him a criminal, and for these he is not responsible. All these opinions are extremely plausible; and so long as the question is argued as one of justice simply, without going down to the principles which lie under justice and are the source of its authority, I am unable to see how any of these reasoners can be refuted. For in truth every one of the three builds upon rules of justice confessedly true. The first appeals to the acknowledged injustice of singling out an individual, and making him a sacrifice, without his consent, for other people's benefit. The second relies on the acknowledged justice of self-defence, and the admitted injustice of forcing one person to conform to another's notions of what constitutes his good. The Owenite invokes the admitted principle, that it is unjust to punish any one for what he cannot help. Each is triumphant so long as he is not compelled to take into consideration any other maxims of justice than the one he has selected; but as soon as their several maxims are brought face to face, each disputant seems to have exactly as much to say for himself as the others. No one of them can carry out his own notion of justice without trampling upon another equally binding. These are difficulties; they have always been felt to be such; and many devices have been invented to turn rather than to overcome them. As a refuge from the last of the three, men imagined what they called the freedom of the will; fancying that they could not justify punishing a man whose will is in a thoroughly hateful state, unless it be supposed to have come into that state through no influence of anterior circumstances. To escape from the other difficulties, a favourite contrivance has been the fiction of a contract, whereby at some unknown period all the members of society engaged to obey the laws, and consented to be punished for any disobedience to them; thereby giving to their legislators the right, which it is assumed they would not otherwise have had, of punishing them, either for their own good or for that of society. This happy thought was considered to get rid of the whole difficulty, and to legitimate the infliction of punishment, in virtue of another received maxim of justice, *Volenti non fit injuria;* that is not unjust which is done with the consent of the person who is supposed to be hurt by it. I need hardly remark, that even if the consent were not a mere fiction, this maxim is not superior in authority to the others which it is brought in to supersede. It is, on the contrary, an instructive specimen of the loose and irregular manner in which supposed principles of justice grow up. This particular one evidently came into use as a help to the coarse exigencies of courts of law, which are sometimes obliged to be content with very uncertain presumptions, on account of the greater evils which would often arise from any attempt on their part to cut finer. But even courts of law are not able to adhere consistently to the maxim, for they allow voluntary engagements to be set aside on the ground of fraud, and sometimes on that of mere mistake or misinformation.

Again, when the legitimacy of inflicting punishment is admitted, how many conflicting conceptions of justice come to light in discussing the proper apportionment of punishments to offences. No rule on the subject recommends itself so strongly to the primitive and spontaneous sentiment of justice, as the *lex talionis,* an eye for an eye and a tooth for a tooth. Though this principle of the Jewish and of the Mahomedan law has been generally abandoned in Europe as a practical maxim, there is, I suspect, in most minds, a secret hankering after it; and when retribution accidentally falls on an offender in that precise shape, the general feeling of satisfaction evinced bears witness how natural is the sentiment to which this repayment in kind is acceptable. With many, the test of justice in penal infliction is that the punishment should be proportioned to the offence; meaning that it should be exactly measured by the moral guilt of the culprit (whatever be their standard for measuring moral guilt): the consideration, what amount of punishment is necessary to deter from the offence, having nothing to do with the question of justice, in their estimation: while there are others to whom that consideration is all in all; who maintain that it is not just, at least for man, to inflict on a fellow-creature, whatever may be his offences, any amount of suffering beyond the least that will suffice to prevent him from repeating, and others from imitating, his misconduct.

To take another example from a subject already once referred to: In a co-operative industrial association, is it just or not that talent or skill should give a title to superior remuneration? On the negative side of the question it is argued, that whoever does the best he can, deserves equally well, and ought not in justice to be put in a position of inferiority for no fault of his own; that superior abilities have already advantages more than enough, in the admiration they excite, the personal influence they command, and the internal sources of satisfaction attending them, without adding to these a superior share of the world's goods; and that society is bound in justice rather to make compensation to the less favoured, for this unmerited inequality of advantages, than to aggravate it. On the contrary side it is contended that society receives more from the more efficient labourer; that his services being more useful, society owes him a larger return for them; that a greater share of the joint result is actually his work, and not to allow his claim to it is a kind of robbery; that if he is only to receive as much as others, he can only be justly required to produce as much, and to give a smaller amount of time and exertion, proportioned to his superior efficiency. Who shall decide between these appeals to conflicting principles of justice? Justice has in this case two sides to it, which it is impossible to bring into harmony, and the two disputants have chosen opposite sides; the one looks to what it is just that the individual should receive, the other to what it is just that the community should give. Each, from his own point of view, is unanswerable; and any choice between them, on grounds of justice, must be perfectly arbitrary. Social utility alone can decide the preference.

How many, again, and how irreconcilable, are the standards of justice to which reference is made in discussing the repartition of taxation. One opinion is, that payment to the State should be in numerical proportion to pecuniary means. Others think that justice dictates what they term graduated taxation; taking a higher percentage from those who have more to spare. In point of natural justice a strong case might be made for disregarding means altogether, and taking the same absolute sum (whenever it could be got) from every one: as the subscribers to a mess, or to a club, all pay the same sum for the same privileges, whether they can all equally afford it or not. Since the protection (it might be said) of law and government is afforded to, and is equally required by all, there is no injustice in making all buy it at the same price. It is reckoned justice, not injustice, that a dealer should charge to all customers the same price for the same article, not a price varying according to their means of payment. This doctrine, as applied to taxation, finds no advocates, because it conflicts so strongly with man's feelings of humanity and of social expediency; but the principle of justice which it invokes is as true and binding as those which can be appealed to against it. Accordingly it exerts a tacit influence on the line of defence employed for other modes of assessing taxation. People feel obliged to argue that the State

does more for the rich than for the poor, as a justification for its taking more from them: though this is in reality not true, for the rich would be far better able to protect themselves, in the absence of law or government, than the poor, and indeed would probably be successful in converting the poor into their slaves. Others, again, so far defer to the same conception of justice, as to maintain that all should pay an equal capitation tax for the protection of their persons (these being of equal value to all), and an unequal tax for the protection of their property, which is unequal. To this others reply, that the all of one man is as valuable to him as the all of another. From these confusions there is no other mode of extrication than the utilitarian.

Is, then, the difference between the Just and the Expedient a merely imaginary distinction? Have mankind been under a delusion in thinking that justice is a more sacred thing than policy, and that the latter ought only to be listened to after the former has been satisfied? By no means. The exposition we have given of the nature and origin of the sentiment, recognises a real distinction; and no one of those who profess the most sublime contempt for the consequences of actions as an element in their morality, attaches more importance to the distinction than I do. While I dispute the pretensions of any theory which sets up an imaginary standard of justice not grounded on utility, I account the justice which is grounded on utility to be the chief part, and incomparably the most sacred and binding part of all morality. Justice is a name for certain classes of moral rules, which concern the essentials of human well-being more nearly, and are therefore of more absolute obligation, than any other rules for the guidance of life; and the notion which we have found to be of the essence of the idea of justice, that of a right residing in an individual, implies and testifies to this more binding obligation.

The moral rules which forbid mankind to hurt one another (in which we must never forget to include wrongful interference with each other's freedom) are more vital to human well-being than any maxims, however important, which only point out the best mode of managing some department of human affairs. . . .

. . . Good for good is also one of the dictates of justice; and this, though its social utility is evident, and though it carries with it a natural human feeling, has not at first sight that obvious connection with hurt or injury, which, existing in the most elementary cases of just and unjust, is the source of the characteristic intensity of the sentiment. But the connection, though less obvious, is not less real. He who accepts benefits, and denies a return of them when needed, inflicts a real hurt, by disappointing one of the most natural and reasonable of expectations, and one which he must at least tacitly have encouraged, otherwise the benefits would seldom have been conferred. The important rank, among human evils and wrongs, of the disappointment of expectation, is shown in the fact that it constitutes the principal criminality of two such highly immoral acts as a breach of friendship and a breach of promise. Few hurts which human beings can sustain are greater, and none wound more, than when that on which they habitually and with full assurance relied, fails them in the hour of need; and few wrongs are greater than this mere withholding of good; none excite more resentment, either in the person suffering, or in a sympathising spectator. The principle, therefore, of giving to each what they deserve, that is, good for good as well as evil for evil, is not only included within the idea of Justice as we have defined it, but is a proper object of that intensity of sentiment, which places the Just, in human estimation, above the simply Expedient.

Most of the maxims of justice current in the world, and commonly appealed to in its transactions, are simply instrumental to carrying into effect the principles of justice which we have now spoken of. That a person is only responsible for what he has done voluntarily, or could voluntarily have avoided; that it is unjust to condemn any person unheard; that the punishment ought to be proportioned to the offence, and the like, are maxims intended to prevent the just principle of evil for evil from being perverted to the infliction of evil without that justification. The greater part of these common maxims have come into use from the practice of courts of justice, which have been naturally led to a more complete recognition and elaboration than was likely to suggest itself to others, of the rules necessary to enable them to fulfil their double function, of inflicting punishment when due, and of awarding to each person his right.

That first of judicial virtues, impartiality, is an obligation of justice, partly for the reason last mentioned; as being a necessary condition of the fulfilment of the other obligations of justice. But this is not the only source of the exalted rank, among human obligations, of those maxims of equality and impartiality, which, both in popular estimation and in that of the most enlightened, are included among the precepts of justice. In one point of view, they may be considered as corollaries from the principles already laid down. If it is a duty to do to each according to his deserts, returning good for good as well as repressing evil by evil, it necessarily follows that we should treat all equally well (when no higher duty forbids) who have deserved equally well of *us,* and that society should treat all equally well who have deserved equally well of *it,* that is, who have deserved equally well absolutely. This is the highest abstract standard of social and distributive justice; towards which all institutions, and the efforts of all virtuous citizens, should be made in the utmost possible degree to converge. But this great moral duty rests upon a still deeper foundation, being a direct emanation from the first principle of morals, and not a mere logical corollary from secondary or derivative doctrines. It is involved in the very meaning of Utility, or the Greatest Happiness Principle. That principle is a mere form of words without rational signification, unless one person's happiness, supposed equal in degree (with the proper allowance made for kind), is counted for exactly as much as another's . . . The equal claim of everybody to happiness in the estimation of the moralist and of the legislator, involves an equal claim to all the means of happiness, except in so far as the inevitable conditions of human life, and the general interest, in which that of every individual is included, set limits to the maxim; and those limits ought to be strictly construed. As every other maxim of justice, so this is by no means applied or held applicable universally; on the contrary, as I have already remarked, it bends to every person's ideas of social expediency. But in whatever case it is deemed applicable at all, it is held to be the dictate of justice. All persons are deemed to have a *right* to equality of treatment, except when some recognised social expediency requires the reverse. And hence all social inequalities which have ceased to be considered expedient, assume the character not of simple inexpediency, but of injustice, and appear so tyrannical, that people are apt to wonder how they ever could have been tolerated; forgetful that they themselves perhaps tolerate other inequalities under an equally mistaken notion of expediency, the correction of which would make that which they approve seem quite as monstrous as what they have at last learnt to condemn . . . .

It appears from what has been said, that justice is a name for certain moral requirements, which, regarded collectively, stand higher in the scale of social utility, and are therefore of more paramount obligation, than any others; though particular cases may occur in which some other social duty is so important, as to overrule any one of the general maxims of justice. Thus, to save a life, it may not only be allowable, but a duty, to steal, or take by force, the necessary food or medicine, or to kidnap, and compel to officiate, the only qualified medical practitioner. In such cases, as we do not call anything justice which is not a virtue, we usually say, not that justice must give away to some other moral principle, but that what is just in ordinary cases is, by reason of that other principle, not just in the particular case. By this useful accommodation of language, the character of indefeasibility attributed to

justice is kept up, and we are saved from the necessity of maintaining that there can be laudable injustice.

The considerations which have now been adduced resolve, I conceive, the only real difficulty in the utilitarian theory of morals. It has always been evident that all cases of justice are also cases of expediency: the difference is in the peculiar sentiment which attaches to the former, as contradistinguished from the latter. If this characteristic sentiment has been sufficiently accounted for; if there is no necessity to assume for it any peculiarity of origin; if it is simply the natural feeling of resentment, moralised by being made coextensive with the demands of social good; and if this feeling not only does but ought to exist in all classes of cases to which the idea of justice corresponds; that idea no longer presents itself as a stumbling-block to the utilitarian ethics. Justice remains the appropriate name for certain social utilities which are vastly more important, and therefore more absolute and imperative, than any others are as a class (though not more so than others may be in particular cases); and which, therefore, ought to be, as well as naturally are, guarded by a sentiment not only different in degree, but also in kind; distinguished from the milder feeling which attaches to the mere idea of promoting human pleasure or convenience, at once by the more definite nature of its commands, and by the sterner character of its sanctions.

ON LIBERTY *

The grand, leading principle, towards which every argument unfolded in these pages directly converges, is the absolute and essential importance of human development in its richest diversity.

WILHELM VON HUMBOLDT:
Sphere and Duties of Government

CHAPTER I

Introductory

The subject of this Essay is . . . Civil, or Social Liberty: the nature and limits of the

* From Number 482A. Everyman's Library. Reprinted by permission of E. P. Dutton & Co., Inc.

power which can be legitimately exercised by society over the individual. . . .

The struggle between Liberty and Authority is the most conspicuous feature in the portions of history with which we are earliest familiar . . . But in old times this contest was between subjects, or some classes of subjects, and the Government. By liberty, was meant protection against the tyranny of the political rulers. The rulers were conceived . . . as in a necessarily antagonistic position to the people whom they ruled. . . . Their power was regarded as necessary, but also as highly dangerous; as a weapon which they would attempt to use against their subjects, no less than against external enemies. To prevent the weaker members of the community from being preyed upon by innumerable vultures, it was needful that there should be an animal of prey stronger than the rest, commissioned to keep them down. But as the king of the vultures would be no less bent upon preying on the flock than any of the minor harpies, it was indispensable to be in a perpetual attitude of defence against his beak and claws. The aim, therefore, of patriots was to set limits to the power which the ruler should be suffered to exercise over the community; and this limitation was what they meant by liberty. It was attempted in two ways. First, by obtaining a recognition of certain immunities, called political liberties or rights, which it was to be regarded as a breach of duty in the ruler to infringe, and which if he did infringe, specific resistance, or general rebellion, was held to be justifiable. A second, and generally a later expedient, was the establishment of constitutional checks, by which the consent of the community, or of a body of some sort, supposed to represent its interests, was made a necessary condition to some of the more important acts of the governing power. To the first of these modes of limitation, the ruling power, in most European countries, was compelled, more or less, to submit. It was not so with the second; and, to attain this, or when already in some degree possessed, to attain it more completely, became everywhere the principal object of the lovers of liberty. . . .

A time, however, came, in the progress of human affairs, when men ceased to think it a necessity of nature that their governors should be an independent power, opposed in interest to themselves. It appeared to them much better that the various magistrates of the State should be their tenants or delegates, revocable at their pleasure. In that way alone, it seemed, could they have complete security that the powers of government would never be abused to their disadvantage . . . As the struggle proceeded for making the ruling power emanate from the periodical choice of the ruled, some persons began to think that too much importance had been attached to the limitation of the power itself . . . What was now wanted was, that the rulers should be identified with the people; that their interest and will should be the interest and will of the nation. The nation did not need to be protected against its own will . . . Let the rulers be effectually responsible to it, promptly removable by it, and it could afford to trust them with power of which it could itself dictate the use to be made. . . .

. . . The notion, that the people have no need to limit their power over themselves, might seem axiomatic, when popular government was a thing only dreamed about, or read of as having existed at some distant period of the past . . . In time, however, a democratic republic came to occupy a large portion of the earth's surface, and made itself felt as one of the most powerful members of the community of nations; and elective and responsible government became subject to the observations and criticisms which wait upon a great existing fact. It was now perceived that such phrases as "self-government," and "the power of the people over themselves," do not express the true state of the case. The "people" who exercise the power are not always the same people with those over whom it is exercised, and the "self-government" spoken of is not the government of each by himself, but of each by all the rest. The will of the people, moreover, practically means the will of the most numerous or the most active *part* of the people; the majority, or those who succeed in making themselves accepted as the majority; the people, consequently *may* desire to oppress a part of their number; and precautions are as much needed against this as against any other abuse of power. The limitation, therefore, of the power of government over individuals loses none of its importance when the holders of power are regularly accountable to the community, that is, to the strongest party therein . . . In political speculations "the tyranny of the majority" is now generally included among the evils against which society requires to be on its guard.

Like other tyrannies, the tyranny of the majority was at first, and is still vulgarly, held in dread, chiefly as operating through the acts of the public authorities. But reflecting persons perceived that when society is itself the tyrant—society collectively over the separate individuals who compose it—its means of tyrannising are not restricted to the acts which it may do by the hands of its political functionaries. Society can and does execute its own mandates: and if it issues wrong mandates instead of right, or any mandates at all in things with which it ought not to meddle, it practises a social tyranny more formidable than many kinds of political oppression, since, though not usually upheld by such extreme penalties, it leaves fewer means of escape, penetrating much more deeply into the details of life, and enslaving the soul itself. . . .

. . . The practical question, where to place the limit—how to make the fitting adjustment between individual independence and social control—is a subject on which nearly everything remains to be done. All that makes existence valuable to any one, depends on the enforcement of restraints upon the actions of other people. Some rules of conduct, therefore, must be imposed, by law in the first place, and by opinion on many things which are not fit subjects for the operation of law. What these rules should be is the principal question in human affairs; but if we except a few of the most obvious cases, it is one of those which least progress has

been made in resolving. No two ages, and scarcely any two countries, have decided it alike; and the decision of one age or country is a wonder to another. Yet the people of any given age and country no more suspect any difficulty in it, than if it were a subject on which mankind had always been agreed. The rules which obtain among themselves appear to them self-evident and self-justifying. This all but universal illusion is one of the examples of the magical influence of custom. . . . Wherever there is an ascendant class, a large portion of the morality of the country emanates from its class interests, and its feelings of class superiority. The morality between Spartans and Helots, between planters and negroes, between princes and subjects, between nobles and roturiers, between men and women, has been for the most part the creation of these class interests and feelings: and the sentiments thus generated react in turn upon the moral feelings of the members of the ascendant class, in their relations among themselves. . . . Among so many baser influences, the general and obvious interests of society have of course had a share, and a large one, in the direction of the moral sentiments: less, however, as a matter of reason, and on their own account, than as a consequence of the sympathies and antipathies which grew out of them: and sympathies and antipathies which had little or nothing to do with the interests of society, have made themselves felt in the establishment of moralities with quite as great force.

. . . In general, those who have been in advance of society in thought and feeling, have left this condition of things unassailed in principle, however they may have come into conflict with it in some of its details. They have occupied themselves rather in inquiring what things society ought to like or dislike, than in questioning whether its likings or dislikings should be a law to individuals. They preferred endeavouring to alter the feelings of mankind on the particular points on which they were themselves heretical, rather than make common cause in defence of freedom, with heretics generally. The only case in which the higher ground has been taken on principle and maintained with consistency, by any but an individual here and there, is that of religious belief. . . . Those who first broke the yoke of what called itself the Universal Church, were in general as little willing to permit differences of religious opinion as that church itself. But when the heat of the conflict was over, without giving a complete victory to any party, and each church or sect was reduced to limit its hopes to retaining possession of the ground it already occupied; minorities, seeing that they had no chance of becoming majorities, were under the necessity of pleading to those whom they could not convert, for permission to differ. It is accordingly on this battle field, almost solely, that the rights of the individual against society have been asserted on broad grounds of principle, and the claim of society to exercise authority over dissentients openly controverted . . . In the minds of almost all religious persons, even in the most tolerant countries, the duty of toleration is admitted with tacit reserves. One person will bear with dissent in matters of church government, but not of dogma; another can tolerate anybody, short of a Papist or a Unitarian; another every one who believes in revealed religion; a few extend their charity a little further, but stop at the belief in a God and in a future state. . . .

. . . There is, in fact, no recognised principle by which the propriety or impropriety of government interference is customarily tested. People decide according to their personal preferences. Some, whenever they see any good to be done, or evil to be remedied, would willingly instigate the government to undertake the business; while others prefer to bear almost any amount of social evil, rather than add one to the departments of human interest amenable to governmental control. And men range themselves on one or the other side in any particular case, according to this general direction of their sentiments; or according to the degree of interest which they feel in the particular thing which it is proposed that the government should do, or according to the belief they entertain that the government would, or would not, do it in the manner they prefer; but very rarely on account of any opinion to which they consistently adhere, as to what things are fit to be done by a government. And it seems to me that in consequence of this absence of rule or principle, one side is at present as often wrong as the other; the interference of government is, with about equal frequency, improperly invoked and improperly condemned.

The object of this Essay is to assert one very simple principle, as entitled to govern absolutely the dealings of society with the individual in the way of compulsion and control, whether the means used be physical force in the form of legal penalties, or the moral coercion of public opinion. That principle is, that the sole end for which mankind are warranted, individually or collectively, in interfering with the liberty of action of any of their number, is self-protection. That the only purpose for which power can be rightfully exercised over any member of a civilised community, against his will, is to prevent harm to others. His own good, either physical or moral, is not a sufficient warrant. He cannot rightfully be compelled to do or forbear because it will be better for him to do so, because it will make him happier, because, in the opinions of others, to do so would be wise, or even right. These are good reasons for remonstrating with him, or reasoning with him, or persuading him, or entreating him, but not for compelling him, or visiting him with any evil in case he do otherwise. . . .

It is, perhaps hardly necessary to say that this doctrine is meant to apply only to human beings in the maturity of their faculties. . . . For the same reason, we may leave out of consideration those backward states of society in which the race itself may be considered as in its nonage. . . . Despotism is a legitimate mode of government in dealing with barbarians, provided the end be their improvement, and the means justified by actually effecting that end. Liberty, as a principle, has no application to any state of things anterior to the time when mankind have become capable of being improved by free and equal discussion. . . .

. . . I regard utility as the ultimate appeal on all ethical questions; but it must be utility in the largest sense, grounded on the permanent interests of a man as a progressive being. Those interests, I contend, authorize the subjection of individual spontaneity to external control, only in respect to those actions of each, which concern the interest of other people . . . There are . . . many positive acts for the benefit of others, which he may rightfully be compelled to perform; such as to give evidence in a court of justice; to bear his fair share in the common defence, or in any other joint work necessary to the interest of the society of which he enjoys the protection; and to perform certain acts of individual beneficence, such as saving a fellow-creature's life, or interposing to protect the defenceless against ill-usage, things which whenever it is obviously a man's duty to do, he may rightfully be made responsible to society for not doing. . . .

But there is a sphere of action in which society, as distinguished from the individual, has, if any, only an indirect interest; comprehending all that portion of a person's life and conduct which affects only himself, or if it also affects others, only with their free, voluntary, and undeceived consent and participation. . . . This, then, is the appropriate region of human liberty. It comprises, first, the inward domain of consciousness; demanding liberty of conscience in the most comprehensive sense; liberty of thought and feeling; absolute freedom of opinion and sentiment on all subjects, practical or speculative, scientific, moral, or theological. The liberty of expressing and publishing opinions may seem to fall under a different principle, since it belongs to that part of the conduct of an individual which concerns other people; but, being almost of as much importance as the liberty of thought itself, and resting in great part on the same reasons, is practically inseparable from it. Secondly, the principle requires liberty of tastes

and pursuits; of framing the plan of our life to suit our own character; of doing as we like, subject to such consequences as may follow: without impediment from our fellow-creatures, so long as what we do does not harm them, even though they should think our conduct foolish, perverse, or wrong. Thirdly, from this liberty of each individual, follows the liberty, within the same limits, of combination among individuals; freedom to unite, for any purpose not involving harm to others: the persons combining being supposed to be of full age, and not forced or deceived. . . .

Though this doctrine is anything but new, and, to some persons, may have the air of a truism, there is no doctrine which stands more directly opposed to the general tendency of existing opinion and practice. Society has expended fully as much effort in the attempt (according to its lights) to compel people to conform to its notions of personal as of social excellence. . . .

CHAPTER II

Of the Liberty of Thought and Discussion

The time, it is to be hoped, is gone by, when any defence would be necessary of the "liberty of the press" as one of the securities against corrupt or tyrannical government . . . Speaking generally, it is not, in constitutional countries, to be apprehended, that the government, whether completely responsible to the people or not, will often attempt to control the expression of opinion, except when in doing so it makes itself the organ of the general intolerance of the public . . . I deny the right of the people to exercise such coercion, either by themselves or by their government . . . It is as noxious, or more noxious, when exerted in accordance with public opinion, than when in opposition to it. If all mankind minus one were of one opinion, and only one person were of the contrary opinion, mankind would be no more justified in silencing that one person, than he, if he had the power, would be justified in silencing mankind . . . The peculiar evil of silencing the expression of an opinion is, that it is robbing the human race; posterity as well as the existing generation; those who dissent from the opinion, still more than those who hold it. If the opinion is right, they are deprived of the opportunity of exchanging error for truth: if wrong, they lose, what is almost as great a benefit, the clearer perception and livelier impression of truth, produced by its collision with error. . . .

First: the opinion which it is attempted to suppress by authority may possibly be true. Those who desire to suppress it, of course deny its truth; but they are not infallible. They have no authority to decide the question for all mankind, and exclude every other person from the means of judging. . . .

. . . While every one well knows himself to be fallible, few think it necessary to take any precautions against their own fallibility . . . In proportion to a man's want of confidence in his own solitary judgment, does he usually repose, with implicit trust, on the infallibility of "the world" in general. And the world, to each individual, means the part of it with which he comes in contact . . . Nor is his faith in this collective authority at all shaken by his being aware that other ages, countries, sects, churches, classes, and parties have thought, and even now think, the exact reverse . . . It never troubles him that mere accident has decided which of these numerous worlds is the object of his reliance, and that the same causes which make him a Churchman in London, would have made him a Buddhist or a Confucian in Pekin. . . .

The objection likely to be made to this argument would probably take some such form as the following. . . . Judgment is given to men that they may use it. Because it may be used erroneously, are men to be told that they ought not to use it at all? To prohibit what they think pernicious, is not claiming exemption from error, but fulfilling the duty incumbent on them, although fallible, of acting on their conscientious conviction . . . It is the duty of governments, and of individuals, to form the truest opinions they can; to form carefully, and never impose them

upon others unless they are quite sure of being right. But when they are sure (such reasoners may say), it is not conscientiousness but cowardice to shrink from acting on their opinions, and allow doctrines which they honestly think dangerous to the welfare of mankind, either in this life or in another, to be scattered abroad without restraint, because other people, in less enlightened times, have persecuted opinions now believed to be true . . . We may, and must, assume our opinion to be true for the guidance of our own conduct: and it is assuming no more when we forbid bad men to pervert society by the propagation of opinions which we regard as false and pernicious.

I answer, that it is assuming very much more. There is the greatest difference between presuming an opinion to be true, because, with every opportunity for contesting it, it has not been refuted, and assuming its truth for the purpose of not permitting its refutation. Complete liberty of contradicting and disproving our opinion is the very condition which justifies us in assuming its truth for purposes of action; and on no other terms can a being with human faculties have any rational assurance of being right.

. . . Why is it, . . . that there is on the whole a preponderance among mankind of rational opinions and rational conduct? If there really is this preponderance—which there must be unless human affairs are, and have always been, in an almost desperate state—it is owing to a quality of the human mind, the source of everything respectable in man either as an intellectual or as a moral being, namely, that his errors are corrigible. He is capable of rectifying his mistakes, by discussion and experience, not by experience alone. There must be discussion, to show how experience is to be interpreted. Wrong opinions and practices gradually yield to fact and argument; but facts and arguments, to produce any effect on the mind, must be brought before it. Very few facts are able to tell their own story without comments to bring out their meaning. . . .

. . . If even the Newtonian philosophy were not permitted to be questioned, mankind could not feel as complete assurance of its truth as they now do. . . .

Strange it is, that men should admit the validity of the arguments for free discussion, but object to their being "pushed to an extreme"; not seeing that unless the reasons are good for an extreme case, they are not good for any case. . . . To call any proposition certain, while there is any one who would deny its certainty if permitted, but who is not permitted, is to assume that we ourselves, and those who agree with us, are the judges of certainty, and judges without hearing the other side.

. . . There are, it is alleged, certain beliefs so useful, not to say indispensable, to well-being that it is as much the duty of governments to uphold those beliefs, as to protect any other of the interests of society . . . It is also often argued, and still oftener thought, that none but bad men would desire to weaken these salutary beliefs; and there can be nothing wrong, it is thought, in restraining bad men, and prohibiting what only such men would wish to practice. This mode of thinking makes the justification of restraints on discussion not a question of the truth of doctrines, but of their usefulness; and flatters itself by that means to escape the responsibility of claiming to be an infallible judge of opinions . . . The usefulness of an opinion is itself matter of opinion: as disputable, as open to discussion, and requiring discussion as much as the opinion itself. There is the same need of an infallible judge of opinions to decide an opinion to be noxious, as to decide it to be false, unless the opinion condemned has full opportunity of defending itself. And it will not do to say that the heretic may be allowed to maintain the utility or harmlessness of his opinion, though forbidden to maintain its truth. The truth of an opinion is part of its utility. If we would know whether or not it is desirable that a proposition should be believed, is it possible to exclude the consideration of whether or not it is true? . . . In point of fact, when law or public feeling do not permit the truth of an opinion to be disputed, they are just as little tolerant of a denial of its use-

fulness. The utmost they allow is an extenuation of its absolute necessity, or of the positive guilt of rejecting it. . . .

. . . If ever any one, possessed of power, had grounds for thinking himself the best and most enlightened among his contemporaries, it was the Emperor Marcus Aurelius. . . . The few failings which are attributed to him were all on the side of indulgence: while his writings, the highest ethical product of the ancient mind, differ scarcely perceptibly, if they differ at all, from the most characteristic teachings of Christ . . . Existing society he knew to be in a deplorable state. But such as it was, he saw, or thought he saw, that it was held together, and prevented from being worse, by belief and reverence of the received divinities . . . The new religion openly aimed at dissolving these ties: unless, therefore, it was his duty to adopt that religion, it seemed to be his duty to put it down. . . . No one plea which can be urged for punishing anti-Christian teaching was wanting to Marcus Aurelius for punishing, as he did, the propagation of Christianity. No Christian more firmly believes that Atheism is false, and tends to the dissolution of society, than Marcus Aurelius believed the same things of Christianity. . . .

Aware of the impossibility of defending the use of punishment for restraining irreligious opinions by any argument which will not justify Marcus Antoninus, the enemies of religious freedom, when hard pressed, occasionally accept this consequence, and say, with Dr. Johnson, that the persecutors of Christianity were in the right; that persecution is an ordeal through which truth ought to pass, and always passes successfully, legal penalties being, in the end, powerless against truth, though sometimes beneficially effective against mischievous errors. . . .

A theory which maintains that truth may justifiably be persecuted because persecution cannot possibly do it any harm, cannot be charged with being intentionally hostile to the reception of new truths; but we cannot commend the generosity of its dealing with the persons to whom mankind are indebted for them. To discover to the world something which deeply concerns it, and of which it was previously ignorant; to prove to it that it had been mistaken on some vital point of temporal or spiritual interest, is as important a service as a human being can render to his fellow-creatures . . . That the authors of such splendid benefits should be requited by martyrdom; that their reward should be to be dealt with as the vilest of criminals, is not, upon this theory, a deplorable error and misfortune, for which humanity should mourn in sackcloth and ashes, but the normal and justifiable state of things. . . .

But, indeed, the dictum that truth always triumphs over persecution is one of those pleasant falsehoods which men repeat after one another till they pass into commonplaces, but which all experience refutes. History teems with instances of truth put down by persecution. If not suppressed forever, it may be thrown back for centuries . . . It is a piece of idle sentimentality that truth, merely as truth, has any inherent power denied to error of prevailing against the dungeon and the stake . . . The real advantage which truth has consists in this, that when an opinion is true, it may be extinguished once, twice, or many times, but in the course of ages there will generally be found persons to rediscover it, until some one of its reappearances falls on a time when from favourable circumstances it escapes persecution until it has made such head as to withstand all subsequent attempts to suppress it. . . .

. . . For a long time past, the chief mischief of the legal penalties is that they strengthen the social stigma. It is that stigma which is really effective, and so effective is it, that the profession of opinions which are under the ban of society is much less common in England than is, in many other countries, the avowal of those which incur risk of judicial punishment. In respect to all persons but those whose pecuniary circumstances make them independent of the good will of other people, opinion, on this subject, is as efficacious as law; men might as well be imprisoned, as excluded from the means of earning their bread. Those whose bread is already secured, and who desire no favours from men in power, or from bodies of men, or from the public, have nothing to fear from the open avowal of any opinions, but to be ill-thought of and ill-spoken of, and this it ought not to require a very heroic mould to enable them to bear. There is no room for any appeal *ad misericordiam* in behalf of such persons. But though we do not now inflict so much evil on those who think differently from us as it was formerly our custom to do, it may be that we do ourselves as much evil as ever by our treatment of them . . . A state of things in which a large portion of the most active and inquiring intellects find it advisable to keep the general principles and grounds of their convictions within their own breasts, and attempt, in what they address to the public, to fit as much as they can of their own conclusions to premises which they have internally renounced, cannot send forth the open, fearless characters, and logical, consistent intellects who once adorned the thinking world. The sort of men who can be looked for under it, are either mere conformers to commonplace, or timeservers for truth, whose arguments on all great subjects are meant for their hearers, and are not those which have convinced themselves. . . .

Those in whose eyes this reticence on the part of heretics is no evil should consider, in the first place, that in consequence of it there is never any fair and thorough discussion of heretical opinions; and that such of them as could not stand such a discussion, though they may be prevented from spreading, do not disappear. But it is not the minds of heretics that are deteriorated most by the ban placed on all inquiry which does not end in the orthodox conclusions. The greatest harm done is to those who are not heretics, and whose whole mental development is cramped, and their reason cowed, by the fear of heresy. Who can compute what the world loses in the multitude of promising intellects combined with timid characters, who dare not follow out any bold, vigorous, independent train of thought, lest it should land them in something which would admit of being considered irreligious or immoral? . . . Not that it is solely, or chiefly, to form great thinkers, that freedom of thinking is required. On the contrary, it is as much and even more indispensable to enable average human beings to attain the mental stature which they are capable of. There have been, and may again be, great individual thinkers in a general atmosphere of mental slavery. But there never has been, nor ever will be, in that atmosphere an intellectually active people. Where any people has made a temporary approach to such a character, it has been because the dread of heterodox speculation was for a time suspended. . . .

. . . However unwillingly a person who has a strong opinion may admit the possibility that his opinion may be false, he ought to be moved by the consideration that, however true it may be, if it is not fully, frequently, and fearlessly discussed, it will be held as a dead dogma, not a living truth.

There is a class of persons (happily not quite so numerous as formerly) who think it enough if a person assents undoubtingly to what they think true, though he has no knowledge whatever of the grounds of the opinion, and could not make a tenable defence of it against the most superficial objections. Such persons, if they can once get their creed taught from authority, naturally think that no good, and some harm, comes of its being allowed to be questioned. Where their influence prevails, they make it nearly impossible for the received opinion to be rejected wisely and considerately, though it may still be rejected rashly and ignorantly; for to shut out discussion entirely is seldom possible, and when it once gets in, beliefs not grounded on conviction are apt to give way before the slightest semblance of an argument. Waiving, however, this possibility—assuming that the true opinion abides in the mind, but abides as a prejudice, a belief independent of, and proof against, argument —this is not the way in which truth ought to be held by a rational being. This is not knowing the truth. . . .

. . . But, some one may say, "Let them be *taught* the grounds of their opinions. It does

not follow that opinions must be merely parroted because they are never heard controverted." . . . On every subject on which difference of opinion is possible, the truth depends on a balance to be struck between two sets of conflicting reasons . . . It has to be shown why that other theory cannot be the true one: and until this is shown, and until we know how it is shown, we do not understand the grounds of our opinion . . . He who knows only his own side of the case, knows little of that. His reasons may be good, and no one may have been able to refute them. But if he is equally unable to refute the reasons on the opposite side; if he does not so much as know what they are, he has no ground for preferring either opinion . . . Nor is it enough that he should hear the arguments of adversaries from his own teachers, presented as they state them, and accompanied by what they offer as refutations . . . He must be able to hear them from persons who actually believe them; who defend them in earnest, and do their very utmost for them. He must know them in their most plausible and persuasive form; he must feel the whole force of the difficulty which the true view of the subject has to encounter and dispose of; else he will never really possess himself of the portion of truth which meets and removes that difficulty . . . So essential is this discipline to a real understanding of moral and human subjects, that if opponents of all important truths do not exist, it is indispensable to imagine them, and supply them with the strongest arguments which the most skilful devil's advocate can conjure up. . . .

. . . We have hitherto considered only two possibilities: that the received opinion may be false, and some other opinion, consequently, true; or that, the received opinion being true, a conflict with the opposite error is essential to a clear apprehension and deep feeling of its truth. But there is a commoner case than either of these; when the conflicting doctrines, instead of being one true and the other false, share the truth between them . . . Every opinion which embodies somewhat of the portion of truth which the common opinion omits, ought to be considered precious, with whatever amount of error and confusion that truth may be blended. No sober judge of human affairs will feel bound to be indignant because those who force on our notice truths which we should otherwise have overlooked, overlook some of those which we see. Rather, he will think that so long as popular truth is one-sided, it is more desirable than otherwise that unpopular truth should have one-sided assertors too; such being usually the most energetic, and the most likely to compel reluctant attention to the fragment of wisdom which they proclaim as if it were the whole.

Thus, in the eighteenth century, when nearly all the instructed, and all those of the uninstructed who were led by them, were lost in admiration of what is called civilisation, and of the marvels of modern science, literature, and philosophy, and while greatly overrating the amount of unlikeness between the men of modern and those of ancient times, indulged the belief that the whole of the difference was in their own favour; with what a salutary shock did the paradoxes of Rousseau explode like bombshells in the midst, dislocating the compact mass of one-sided opinion, and forcing its elements to recombine in a better form and with additional ingredients. . . .

. . . Unless opinions favourable to democracy and to aristocracy, to property and to equality, to co-operation and to competition, to luxury and to abstinence, to sociality and individuality, to liberty and discipline, and all the other standing antagonisms of practical life, are expressed with equal freedom, and enforced and defended with equal talent and energy, there is no chance of both elements obtaining their due; one scale is sure to go up, and the other down . . . On any of the great open questions just enumerated, if either of the two opinions has a better claim than the other, not merely to be tolerated, but to be encouraged and countenanced, it is the one which happens at the particular time and place to be in a minority. That is the opinion which, for the time being, represents the neglected interests, the side of

human well-being which is in danger of obtaining less than its share. . . .

Before quitting the subject of freedom of opinion, it is fit to take some notice of those who say that the free expression of all opinions should be permitted, on condition that the manner be temperate, and do not pass the bounds of fair discussion. Much might be said on the impossibility of fixing where these supposed bounds are to be placed . . . Undoubtedly the manner of asserting an opinion, even though it be a true one, may be very objectionable, and may justly incur severe censure. But the principal offences of the kind are such as it is mostly impossible, unless by accidental self-betrayal, to bring home to conviction. The gravest of them is, to argue sophistically, to suppress facts or arguments, to misstate the elements of the case, or misrepresent the opposite opinion. But all this, even to the most aggravated degree, is so continually done in perfect good faith, by persons who are not considered, and in many other respects may not deserve to be considered, ignorant or incompetent, that it is rarely possible, on adequate grounds, conscientiously to stamp the misrepresentation as morally culpable; and still less could law presume to interfere with this kind of controversial misconduct. With regard to what is commonly meant by intemperate discussion, namely invective, sarcasm, personality, and the like, the denunciation of these weapons would deserve more sympathy if it were ever proposed to interdict them equally to both sides; but it is only desired to restrain the employment of them against the prevailing opinion: against the unprevailing they may not only be used without general disapproval, but will be likely to obtain for him who uses them the praise of honest zeal and righteous indignation. Yet whatever mischief arises from their use is greatest when they are employed against the comparatively defenceless; and whatever unfair advantage can be derived by any opinion from this mode of asserting it, accrues almost exclusively to received opinions. The worst offence of this kind which can be committed by a polemic is to stigmatise those who hold the contrary opinion as bad and immoral men. To calummy of this sort, those who hold any unpopular opinion are peculiarly exposed, because they are in general few and uninfluential, and nobody but themselves feels much interested in seeing justice done them; but this weapon is, from the nature of the case, denied to those who attack a prevailing opinion: they can neither use it with safety to themselves, nor, if they could, would it do anything but recoil on their own cause. In general, opinions contrary to those commonly received can only obtain a hearing by studied moderation of language, and the most cautious avoidance of unnecessary offence, from which they hardly ever deviate even in a slight degree without losing ground . . . .

CHAPTER III

Of Individuality, as One of the Elements of Well-Being

. . . Let us next examine whether the same reasons do not require that men should be free to act upon their opinions—to carry these out in their lives, without hindrance, either physical or moral, from their fellowmen, so long as it is at their own risk and peril. This last proviso is of course indispensable. No one pretends that actions should be as free as opinions. On the contrary, even opinions lose their immunity when the circumstances in which they are expressed are such as to constitute their expression a positive instigation to some mischievous act. An opinion that corn-dealers are starvers of the poor, or that private property is robbery, ought to be unmolested when simply circulated through the press, but may justly incur punishment when delivered orally to an excited mob assembled before the house of a corn-dealer, or when handed about among the same mob in the form of a placard . . . The liberty of the individual must be thus far limited; he must not make himself a nuisance to other people. But if he refrains from molesting others in what concerns them, and merely acts according to his own inclination and judgment in things which concern himself, the same reasons which show that opinion should be free, prove also that he should be allowed, without molestation, to carry his opinions into practice at his own cost . . . As it is useful that while mankind are imperfect there should be different opinions, so it is that there should be different experiments of living; that free scope should be given to varieties of character, short of injury to others; and that the worth of different modes of life should be proved practically, when any one thinks fit to try them. . . .

. . . If it were felt that the free development of individuality is one of the leading essentials of well-being; that it is not only a co-ordinate element with all that is designated by the terms civilisation, instruction, education, culture, but is itself a necessary part and condition of all those things; there would be no danger that liberty should be undervalued . . . But the evil is, that individual spontaneity is hardly recognised by the common modes of thinking as having any intrinsic worth, or deserving any regard on its own account. The majority, being satisfied with the ways of mankind as they now are (for it is they who make them what they are), cannot comprehend why those ways should not be good enough for everybody; and what is more, spontaneity forms no part of the ideal of the majority of moral and social reformers, but is rather looked on with jealousy, as a troublesome and perhaps rebellious obstruction to the general acceptance of what these reformers, in their own judgment, think would be best for mankind. . . .

. . . No one's idea of excellence in conduct is that people should do absolutely nothing but copy one another . . . On the other hand, it would be absurd to pretend that people ought to live as if nothing whatever had been known in the world before they came into it; as if experience had as yet done nothing towards showing that one mode of existence, or of conduct, is preferable to another. Nobody denies that people should be so taught and trained in youth as to know and benefit by the ascertained results of human experience. But it is the privilege and proper condition of a human being, arrived at the maturity of his faculties, to use and interpret experience in his own way. It is for him to find out what part of recorded experience is properly applicable to his own circumstances and character . . . Customs are made for customary circumstances and customary characters; and his circumstances or his character may be uncustomary. . . .

. . . It really is of importance, not only what men do, but also what manner of men they are that do it. Among the works of man, which human life is rightly employed in perfecting and beautifying, the first in importance surely is man himself. Supposing it were possible to get houses built, corn grown, battles fought, causes tried, and even churches erected and prayers said, by machinery—by automatons in human form—it would be a considerable loss to exchange for these automatons even the men and women who at present inhabit the more civilised parts of the world, and who assuredly are but starved specimens of what nature can and will produce. Human nature is not a machine to be built after a model, and set to do exactly the work prescribed for it, but a tree, which requires to grow and develop itself on all sides, according to the tendency of the inward forces which make it a living thing.

. . . To a certain extent it is admitted that our understanding should be our own: but there is not the same willingness to admit that our desires and impulses should be our own likewise; or that to possess impulses of our own, and of any strength, is anything but a peril and a snare. Yet desires and impulses are as much a part of a perfect human being as beliefs and restraints . . . Strong impulses are but another name for energy. Energy may be turned to bad uses; but more good may always be made of an energetic nature, than of an indolent and impassive one. Those who have most natural feeling are always those whose cultivated feelings may be made the strongest.

The same strong susceptibilities which make the personal impulses vivid and powerful, are also the source from whence are generated the most passionate love of virtue, and the sternest self-control. It is through the cultivation of these that society both does its duty and protects its interests: not by rejecting the stuff of which heroes are made, because it knows not how to make them. . . .

In some early states of society, these forces might be, and were, too much ahead of the power which society then possessed of disciplining and controlling them. There has been a time when the element of spontaneity and individuality was in excess, and the social principle had a hard struggle with it. The difficulty then was to induce men of strong bodies or minds to pay obedience to any rules which required them to control their impulses. To overcome this difficulty, law and discipline, like the Popes struggling against the Emperors, asserted a power over the whole man, claiming to control all his life in order to control his character—which society had not found any other sufficient means of binding. But society has now fairly got the better of individuality; and the danger which threatens human nature is not the excess, but the deficiency, of personal impulses and preferences . . . Not only in what concerns others, but in what concerns only themselves, the individual or the family do not ask themselves—what do I prefer? or, what would suit my character and disposition? or, what would allow the best and highest in me to have fair play, and enable it to grow and thrive? They ask themselves, what is suitable to my position? what is usually done by persons of my station and pecuniary circumstances? or (worse still) what is usually done by persons of a station and circumstances superior to mine? . . .

. . . In proportion to the development of his individuality, each person becomes more valuable to himself, and is therefore capable of being more valuable to others . . . To be held to rigid rules of justice for the sake of others, develops the feelings and capacities which have the good of others for their object. But to be restrained in things not affecting their good, by their mere displeasure, develops nothing valuable, except such force of character as may unfold itself in resisting the restraint. If acquiesced in, it dulls and blunts the whole nature . . . Even despotism does not produce its worst effects, so long as individuality exists under it; and whatever crushes individuality is despotism, by whatever name it may be called, and whether it professes to be enforcing the will of God or the injunctions of men. . . .

. . . There is always need of persons not only to discover new truths, and point out when what were once truths are true no longer, but also to commence new practices, and set the example of more enlightened conduct, and better taste and sense in human life. . . . It is true that this benefit is not capable of being rendered by everybody alike: there are but few persons, in comparison with the whole of mankind, whose experiments, if adopted by others, would be likely to be any improvement on established practice. But these few are the salt of the earth; without them, human life would become a stagnant pool. Not only is it they who introduce good things which did not before exist; it is they who keep the life in those which already exist. . . . There is only too great a tendency in the best beliefs and practices to degenerate into the mechanical; and unless there were a succession of persons whose ever-recurring originality prevents the grounds of those beliefs and practices from becoming merely traditional, such dead matter would not resist the smallest shock from anything really alive, and there would be no reason why civilisation should not die out, as in the Byzantine Empire. . . .

. . . In ancient history, in the Middle Ages, and in a diminishing degree through the long transition from feudality to the present time, the individual was a power in himself; and if he had either great talents or a high social position, he was a considerable power. At present individuals are lost in the crowd. In politics it is almost a triviality to say that public opinion now rules the world. The only power deserving the name is that of masses, and of governments while they make themselves the organ of the tendencies and instincts of masses. This is as true in the moral and social relations of private life as in public transactions. Those whose opinions go by the name of public opinion are not always the same sort of public: in America they are the whole white population; in England, chiefly the middle class. But they are always a mass, that is to say, collective mediocrity. And what is a still greater novelty, the mass do not now take their opinions from dignitaries in Church or State, from ostensible leaders, or from books. Their thinking is done for them by men much like themselves, addressing them or speaking in their name, on the spur of the moment, through the newspapers. I am not complaining of all this. I do not assert that anything better is compatible, as a general rule, with the present low state of the human mind. But that does not hinder the government of mediocrity from being mediocre government . . . The initiation of all wise or noble things comes and must come from individuals; generally at first from some one individual . . . It is in these circumstances most especially, that exceptional individuals, instead of being deterred, should be encouraged in acting differently from the mass. In other times there was no advantage in their doing so, unless they acted not only differently but better. In this age, the mere example of non-conformity, the mere refusal to bend the knee to custom, is itself a service . . . That so few now dare to be eccentric marks the chief danger of the time.

. . . Nowhere (except in some monastic institutions) is diversity of taste entirely unrecognised; a person may, without blame, either like or dislike rowing, or smoking, or music, or athletic exercises, or chess, or cards, or study, because both those who like each of these things, and those who dislike them, are too numerous to be put down. But the man, and still more the woman, who can be accused either of doing "what nobody does," or of not doing "what everybody does," is the subject of as much depreciatory remark as if he or she had committed some grave moral delinquency . . . Whoever allow themselves much of that indulgence, incur the risk of something worse than disparaging speeches—they are in peril of a commission *de lunatico,* and of having their property taken from them and given to their relations. . . .

. . . In a passage already quoted from Wilhelm von Humboldt, he points out two things as necessary conditions of human development, because necessary to render people unlike one another; namely, freedom, and variety of situations. The second of these two conditions is in this country every day diminishing . . . Formerly, different ranks, different neighbourhoods, different trades and professions, lived in what might be called different worlds . . . They now read the same things, listen to the same things, see the same things, go to the same places, have their hopes and fears directed to the same objects, have the same rights and liberties, and the same means of asserting them . . . And the assimilation is still proceeding. All the political changes of the age promote it, since they all tend to raise the low and to lower the high. Every extension of education promotes it, because education brings people under common influences, and gives them access to the general stock of facts and sentiments. Improvement in the means of communication promotes it, by bringing the inhabitants of distant places into personal contact, and keeping up a rapid flow of changes of residence between one place and another. . . .

The combination of all these causes forms so great a mass of influences hostile to individuality, that it is not easy to see how it can stand its ground. It will do so with increasing difficulty, unless the intelligent part of the public can be made to feel its value . . . .

CHAPTER IV

Of the Limits to the Authority of Society Over the Individual

. . . To individuality should belong the part of life in which it is chiefly the individual that is interested; to society, the part which chiefly interests society.

Though society is not founded on a contract, and though no good purpose is answered by inventing a contract in order to deduce social obligations from it, every one who receives the protection of society owes a return for the benefit, and the fact of living in society renders it indispensable that each should be bound to observe a certain line of conduct towards the rest. This conduct consists, first, in not injuring the interests of one another; or rather certain interests, which, either by express legal provision, or by tacit understanding, ought to be considered as rights; and secondly, in each person's bearing his share (to be fixed on some equitable principle) of the labours and sacrifices incurred for defending the society or its members from injury and molestation. These conditions society is justified in enforcing, at all costs to those who endeavour to withhold fulfilment. Nor is this all that society may do. The acts of an individual may be hurtful to others, or wanting in due consideration for their welfare, without going to the length of violating any of their constituted rights. The offender may then be justly punished by opinion, though not by law. As soon as any part of a person's conduct affects prejudicially the interests of others, society has jurisdiction over it, and the question whether the general welfare will or will not be promoted by interfering with it, becomes open to discussion. But there is no room for entertaining any such question when a person's conduct affects the interests of no persons besides himself, or needs not affect them unless they like (all the persons concerned being of full age, and the ordinary amount of understanding). In all such cases, there should be perfect freedom, legal and social, to do the action and stand the consequences.

It would be a great misunderstanding of this doctrine to suppose that it is one of selfish indifference, which pretends that human beings have no business with each other's conduct in life, and that they should not concern themselves about the well-doing or well-being of one another, unless their own interest is involved. Instead of any diminution, there is need of a great increase of disinterested exertion to promote the good of others. But disinterested benevolence can find other instruments to persuade people to their good than whips and scourges, either of the literal or the metaphorical sort. . . .

I do not mean that the feelings with which a person is regarded by others ought not to be in any way affected by his self-regarding qualities or deficiencies. This is neither possible nor desirable . . . Though doing no wrong to any one, a person may so act as to compel us to judge him, and feel to him, as a fool, or as a being of an inferior order: and since this judgment and feeling are a fact which he would prefer to avoid, it is doing him a service to warn him of it beforehand, as of any other disagreeable consequence to which he exposes himself . . . We have a right, also, in various ways, to act upon our unfavourable opinion of any one, not to the oppression of his individuality, but in the exercise of ours. We are not bound, for example, to seek his society . . . We have a right, and it may be our duty, to caution others against him, if we think his example or conversation likely to have a pernicious effect on those with whom he associates. . . .

. . . Acts injurious to others require a totally different treatment. Encroachment on their rights; infliction on them of any loss or damage not justified by his own rights; falsehood or duplicity in dealing with them; unfair or ungenerous use of advantages over them; even selfish abstinence from defending them against injury—these are fit objects of moral reprobation, and, in grave cases, of moral retribution and punishment. And not only these acts, but the dispositions which lead to them, are properly immoral, and fit subjects of disapprobation which may rise to abhorrence. . . .

The distinction between the loss of consideration which a person may rightly incur by defect of prudence or of personal dignity, and the reprobation which is due to him for an offence against the rights of others, is not a merely nominal distinction. It makes a vast difference both in our feelings and in our conduct towards him whether he displeases us in things in which we think we have a right to control him, or in things in which we know that we have not. If he displeases us, we may express our distaste, and we may stand aloof . . . He may be to us an object of pity, perhaps of dislike, but not of anger or resentment; we shall not treat him like an enemy of society . . . It is far otherwise if he has infringed the rules necessary for the protection of his fellow-creatures, individually or collectively. The evil consequences of his acts do not then fall on himself, but on others; and society, as the protector of all its members, must retaliate on him; must inflict pain on him for the express purpose of punishment, and must take care that it be sufficiently severe. . . .

The distinction here pointed out between the part of a person's life which concerns only himself, and that which concerns others, many persons will refuse to admit . . . If he injures his property, he does harm to those who directly or indirectly derived support from it, and usually diminishes, by a greater or less amount, the general resources of the community. If he deteriorates his bodily or mental faculties, he not only brings evil upon all who depended on him for any portion of their happiness, but disqualifies himself for rendering the services which he owes to his fellow-creatures generally. . . Finally, if by his vices or follies a person does no direct harm to others, he is nevertheless (it may be said) injurious by his example; and ought to be compelled to control himself, for the sake of those whom the sight or knowledge of his conduct might corrupt or mislead.

And even (it will be added) if the consequences of misconduct could be confined to the vicious or thoughtless individual, ought society to abandon to their own guidance those who are manifestly unfit for it? If protection against themselves is confessedly due to children and persons under age, is not society equally bound to afford it to persons of mature years who are equally incapable of self-government? If gambling, or drunkenness, or incontinence, or idleness, or uncleanliness, are as injurious to happiness, and as great a hindrance to improvement, as many or most of the acts prohibited by law, why (it may be asked) should not law, so far as is consistent with practicability and social convenience, endeavour to repress these also? And as a supplement to the unavoidable imperfections of law, ought not opinion at least to organise a powerful police against these vices, and visit rigidly with social penalties those who are known to practise them? There is no question here (it may be said) about restricting individuality, or impeding the trial of new and original experiments in living. The only things it is sought to prevent are things which have been tried and condemned from the beginning of the world until now; things which experience has shown not to be useful or suitable to any person's individuality. . . .

I fully admit that the mischief which a person does to himself may seriously affect, both through their sympathies and their interests, those nearly connected with him and, in a minor degree, society at large. When, by conduct of this sort, a person is led to violate a distinct and assignable obligation to any other person or persons, the case is taken out of the self-regarding class, and becomes amenable to moral disapprobation in the proper sense of the term. If, for example, a man, through intemperance or extravagance, becomes unable to pay his debts, or, having undertaken the moral responsibility of a family, becomes from the same cause incapable of supporting or educating them, he is deservedly reprobated, and might be justly punished; but it is for the breach of duty to his family or creditors, not for the extravagance. If the resources which ought to have been devoted to them, had been diverted from them for the most prudent investment, the moral culpability would have been the same . . . Again, in the frequent case of a man who causes grief to his family by addiction to bad habits, he deserves reproach for his unkindness or ingratitude; but so he may for cultivating habits not in themselves vicious, if they are painful to those with whom he passes his life, or who from personal ties are dependent on him for their comfort. . . . In like manner, when a person disables himself, by conduct purely self-regarding, from the performance of some definite duty incumbent on him to the public, he is guilty of a social offence. No person ought to be punished simply for being drunk; but a soldier or a policeman should be punished for being drunk on duty. Whenever, in short, there is a definite damage, or a definite risk of damage, either to an individual or to the public, the case is taken out of the province of liberty, and placed in that of morality or law.

But with regard to the merely contingent, or, as it may be called, constructive injury which a person causes to society, by conduct which neither violates any specific duty to the public, nor occasions perceptible hurt to any assignable individual except himself; the inconvenience is one which society can afford to bear, for the sake of the greater good of human freedom. . . .

Under the name of preventing intemperance, the people of one English colony, and of nearly half the United States, have been interdicted by law from making any use whatever of fermented drinks, except for medical purposes . . . An attempt has notwithstanding been commenced, and is prosecuted with considerable zeal by many of the professed philanthropists, to agitate for a similar law in this country. The association, or "Alliance" as it terms itself, which has been formed for this purpose, has acquired some notoriety through the publicity given to a correspondence between its secretary and one of the very few English public men who hold that a politician's opinions ought to be founded on principles . . . The secretary . . . says, "I claim, as a citizen, a right to legislate whenever my social rights are invaded by the social act of another." And now for the definition of these "social rights." "If anything invades my social rights, certainly the traffic in strong drink does. It destroys my primary right of security, by constantly creating and stimulating social disorder. It invades my right of equality, by deriving a profit from the creation of a misery I am taxed to support. It impedes my right to free moral and intellectual development, by surrounding my path with dangers, and by weakening and demoralising society, from which I have a right to claim mutual aid and intercourse." A theory of "social rights" the like of which probably never before found its way into distinct language: being nothing short of this—that it is the absolute social right of every individual, that every other individual shall act in every respect exactly as he ought; that whosoever fails thereof in the smallest particular violates my social right, and entitles me to demand from the legislature the removal of the grievance. So monstrous a principle is far more dangerous than any single interference with liberty; there is no violation of liberty which it would not justify; it acknowledges no right to any freedom whatever, except perhaps to that of holding opinions in secret, without ever disclosing them: for, the moment an opinion which I consider noxious passes any one's lips, it invades all the "social rights" attributed to me by the Alliance. The doctrine ascribes to all mankind a vested interest in each other's moral, intellectual, and even physical perfection, to be defined by each claimant according to his own standard. . . .

I cannot refrain from adding to these examples of the little account commonly made of human liberty, the language of downright persecution which breaks out from the press of this country whenever it feels called on to notice the remarkable phenomenon of Mormonism . . . Many in this country openly declare that it would be right (only that it is not convenient) to send an expedition against them, and compel them by force to conform to the opinions of other people. The article of the Mormonite doctrine which is the chief provocative to the antipathy which thus breaks through the ordinary restraints of religious tolerance, is its sanction of polygamy; which, though permitted to Mahomedans, and Hindoos, and Chinese, seems to excite unquenchable animosity when practised by persons who speak English and profess to be a kind of Christians. No one has a deeper disapprobation than I have of this Mormon institution . . . Still, it must be remembered that this relation is as much voluntary on the part of the women concerned in it, and who may be deemed the sufferers by it, as is the case with any other form of the marriage institution . . . Other countries are not asked to recognise such unions, or release any portion of their inhabitants from their own laws on the score of Mormonite opinions. But when the dissentients have conceded to the hostile sentiments of others far more than could justly be demanded; when they have left the countries to which their doctrines were unacceptable, and established themselves in a remote corner of the earth, which they have been the first to render habitable to human beings; it is difficult to see on what principles but those of tyranny they can be prevented from living there under what laws they please, provided they commit no aggression on other nations, and allow perfect freedom of departure to those who are dissatisfied with their ways . . . I am not aware that any community has a right to force another to be civilised. So long as the sufferers by the bad law do not invoke assistance from other communities, I cannot admit that persons entirely unconnected with them ought to step in and require that a condition of things with which all who are directly interested appear to be satisfied, should be put an end to because it is a scandal to persons some thousands of miles distant, who have no part or concern in it . . . If civilisation has got the better of barbarism when barbarism had the world to itself, it is too much to profess to be afraid lest barbarism, after having been fairly got under, should revive and conquer civilisation. . . .

16

Rudolf von Ihering

1818–1892

The direct line of paternal ancestors of Rudolf von Ihering was a long string of lawyers and administrators. No career other than law was considered by him. Like Savigny he followed the German fad of going to several universities; at twenty-four a doctor's degree in law was conferred on him by Berlin University. After three years as a tutor he got his first professorship. He taught at half a dozen German law schools, spending sixteen of his middle years at Giessen and twenty of his later years at Gottingen. During his short stay at the University of Vienna the Emperor of Austria ennobled him. One biographer says of Ihering, "The power of his personality is attested by the fact of his great popularity. His lectures were always crowded with listeners; and his home was the shrine at which the devoted from all quarters of the world worshipped."

The bulk of Ihering's writings is mountainous—more than twenty volumes on Roman and German law, and jurisprudence. He has been called "the most encyclopedic mind in German law in the Nineteenth Century." His two best known jurisprudential books are *The Struggle for Law* (1872) and *Law as a Means to an End* (1877-82), the first volume of which was published when he was 59 and the second when he was 64; Excerpts which follow are from volume I.

In his middle years Ihering was much moved by the Schleswig-Holstein question—an on-going, complicated territorial dispute between German and Danish powers. He became a member of a committee of political agitators ready for armed action in the disputed territory if German princes threatened to compromise German honor. He was criticized for his connection with Prussian troops moving toward the disputed territory. He was won over to Bismark's devious and complicated program for Schleswig-Holstein, and became a Bismark partisan in other power moves. Ihering took great joy in Germany's unification and rise, and his letters written in 1870 glowed with national pride and patriotism. Internal politics seldom held his interest—though at fifty-nine he did run for a seat in the German Parliament and was roundly trounced. He was a monarchist, and yet a moderate liberal who developed socialistic tendencies.

Ihering was gusty. Fond of eating and drinking, he basked in social life and had an eye for handsome women. He liked travel and spent most of his holidays in Italy and the Alps. He treasured literature and knew his Shakespeare, Dante, and Goethe. He played piano well enough to entertain himself and friends. He was a self-centered man —wise enough to change his mind, but seldom willing to give in gracefully to an opponent. He was not used to having his views challenged.

His jurisprudence was much influenced by the English Utilitarians and classical economic thought. He saw economic man motivated by his desires and opportunities in the trading and subsisting world. But his vision was wider and included non-economic values built on softened Kantian ethics. He saw forces other than law supporting and supplanting legal commands. Both widened social dimensions and deepened social responsibilities were taught to the nineteenth century by Rudolf von Ihering.

LAW
AS A MEANS TO AN END *

Part I

THE CONCEPT OF PURPOSE

CHAPTER III

Egoism in the Service of Altruistic Purposes

§1. *Coincidence of Purposes.* How can the world exist under a regime of egoism, which desires nothing for the world, but everything for itself alone? . . . The world exists by taking egoism into its service, by paying it the reward which it desires . . .

§2. *Nature* . . . The self-preservation and propagation of the individual are . . . necessary conditions for the attainment of nature's purpose. How does she attain this purpose? By interesting egoism in it. This she accomplishes by offering the latter a premium in case it does what it should, *viz.*, pleasure, and by threatening punishment if it does not do what it should, or does what it should not, *viz.*, pain . . . .

. . . If there is anything which confirms me in the belief of purpose in nature, it is the use she makes of pain and pleasure. Imagine them absent or interchanged, associate pain with nourishment and pleasure with death, and the human race would disappear in the first generation . . . .

§3. *Commerce.* Nature herself has shown man the way he must follow in order to gain another for his purposes: it is that of *connecting one's own purpose with the other man's interest.* Upon this principle rests all our human life: the State, society, commerce, and intercourse. The co-operation of a number of people for the same purpose is brought about only by the converging of all

* Translated by Isaac Husik, copyright 1913, Boston Book Co. Reprinted by permission of The Macmillan Co.

the interests upon the same point. No one perhaps has in view the purpose as such, but every one has his own interest in view, a subjective purpose which is quite different from the general objective one, but the coincidence of their interests with the general purpose brings it about that every one in taking pains for himself at the same time becomes active for the general purpose.

Where such an interest is not present originally, it must be created artificially . . . The extension of my factory requires the cession of a piece of land on the part of my neighbor . . . By means of my offer of purchase I create artificially in the person of my neighbor an interest in the realization of my purpose, provided I offer him an amount such that his interest in relinquishing his claim to the land is greater than in retaining it . . . .

. . . The purposes of social life also can be attained only by moving the other side with a lever of interest, except that the interest here is of a different nature from that which is employed in commercial life. Here it is the interest of entertainment, distraction, pleasure, vanity, ambition, social consideration, etc. . . .

§4. *Organized and Unorganized Purposes.* . . .

I. *Unorganized Purposes.* 1. *Science.* Science unites all its members into an invisible community. They all exert their powers for the purposes of science, and the total result of the co-operation of all its disciples consists in the preservation, extension, and increase of science . . .

. . . In science it is the purely self-regarding interest of the individual that produces the activity, except that the interest in science is incomparably more complex; consisting as it does in the inner satisfaction which it yields, the feeling of duty, of ambition, of vanity; the living it offers; and after the failure of all other motives besides, that of mere habit; to be secure from the dread of *ennui.* He who does not in some way find his advantage in science, will not work for it, any more than will a laborer whom the pay does not attract. . . .

II. *Organized Purposes.* Organized purposes are so extensively represented in our modern world as to make it scarcely necessary to cite examples . . . Let me select from their number an example which will be especially instructive from our point of view —the formation of a joint-stock company for the purposes of building a railway. Of all the shareholders, no single one perhaps is interested in the objective purpose of the railway, *viz.,* the opening of a new route of communication . . . Of the shareholders one has in view the permanent investment of his capital; the other buys shares only to sell them again immediately; the third, a wealthy proprietor of landed estate, or manufacturer, buys in the interest of facilitating the realization on his products or manufactures . . . Everyone has his special interest in view, no one thinks of the purpose, and yet the same is perhaps furthered in this way more surely and quickly than if it had been pursued by the government directly.

§5. *The State and the Law.* The organization of purpose attains its highest point in the State. . . .

. . . The law itself, even though it carries necessity on its banner, must after all appeal to interest . . . The criminal is not concerned about the purpose of the State or of society, he is guided in his deed solely by his own purpose, by his lust, his greed or other viciousness, in short, his interest. But it is exactly this interest of his with regard to which the State calculates what means for protecting itself against him it has, by punishment . . . If the instrument so often fails of its purpose despite the fact that the punishment is made severe enough, this is due in most instances to the fact that the threat of punishment is after all no more than a threat, the psychological effect of which in every case depends upon the criminal's calculation of the chances of his discovery.

But not every law carries punishment with it. The law which commands the debtor to pay his debt, or the possessor of an article belonging to another to return it to its owner, threatens no punishment . . . Other disadvantages await them (legal costs). If

despite this prospect so many legal actions are preferred by those who know that they are in the wrong, the reason is . . . the hope that for lack of evidence the law will not succeed in reaching them.

But although in this case the law to a certain extent still finds in interest an ally, there is a point where the possibility of such alliance ceases, and where direct compulsion alone can accomplish the thing desired. Interest will not determine the accused or the condemned to betake himself to the inquest chamber or the house of correction, or to mount the scaffold—direct compulsion is necessary. . . .

CHAPTER IV

The Problem of Self-Denial

§3. *Self-regarding and Non-self-regarding Acts* . . . That which does refer to the agent himself in an act of self-denial is solely the feeling of having helped another in need, of having caused him joy . . . He is content with a minimum part thereof, and in this very height of unpretentiousness lies the beauty, the sublimity of self-denial. . . .

Reward there is after all, the egoist will exclaim . . . The reward which the hero obtains who, in order not to let the battleship or the fort fall into the hands of the enemy, is blown up with it, would very likely offer small temptations for him: a few minutes or seconds of inner satisfaction purchased at the expense of one's whole life—in truth a dearly bought pleasure, the egoist would think! . . . But the egoist calculates too well for this; self-denial is a luxury for him which he cannot afford, and in his heart of hearts he regards it as folly when he meets it in others, or tries to adjust it to his own standpoint by introducing ignoble and egoistic motives. That such motives as vanity, expectation of gratitude, appreciation, etc., *may* enter is just as incontrovertible as it is undoubted that they *need* not. . . .

§6. *The Different Species of Self-assertion.* The purposes of human existence in general fall into two large groups; those of the individual, and those of the community (society). This contrast we place as the basis of our presentation. This does not mean that in the manner of those holding the theory of the Law of Nature we wish to isolate the individual, separating him artificially from his historical connection with society, and then to present over against such merely theoretical being-for-himself of an individual, his actual life in society and being-for-others. We consider the individual in the position which he actually holds in the real world, but in picturing his life to ourselves we separate from it those purposes by which he holds in view solely himself, and not society, *i.e.,* any other person or a higher purpose. These purposes, which proceed from the agent and return to him, we designate, as is well known, by the term *egoistic. . . .*

. . . The activity of the individual for these purposes of society is fittingly designated by the term *social.* The motives which prompt such social action by the individual are of two kinds. The first is egoism . . . The means by which the State and society gain the mastery over this motive are reward and punishment. The second motive is that which contains in itself the solution of our problem of self-denial. It is the feeling on the part of the agent of the ethical destiny of his being, *i.e.,* his feeling that existence was given to him not merely for himself, but also for the service of humanity . . . .

CHAPTER V

The Purposes of Egoistical Self-Assertion

§1. *Physical Self-assertion* . . . The physical self-preservation of the animal is with few exceptions calculated for the next moment . . . In man, on the contrary, it . . . is not exhausted, as in the case of the animal, in a concern for the present, but in the present it is already thoughtful of the future, especially in the way of securing his future means of subsistence. . . .

§2. *Economic Self-assertion* . . . Securing the future life becomes securing one's future life in comfort; procuring the necessary and

indispensable prepares the ground for what is dispensable but agreeable . . . Everywhere property takes its stand by the side of culture, ever informing of new wants and purposes. . . .

§4. *Right and Duty.* The purpose of life's maintenance produced property—for without property there is no secure future for existence; the purpose of the two conjoined leads to Law—without law there is no securing life and property.

. . . To have a right means, there is something *for us,* and the power of the State recognizes this and protects us. Now that which exists for us may be,

(1) *Ourselves.* The legal expression for this is the right of *personality.* The ethical ground of this concept is the principle, man is an *end in himself. . . .*

That which exists for us may be,

(2) *A Thing.* The expression which designates this relation of the thing to our purposes is the right to the thing, or ownership in the widest sense.

That which exists for us may be,

(3) *A Person.* He may exist for us either as a personality in its entirety,—with reciprocal relations (the legal relations of the *family*), or in reference to particular acts (right "in personam").

That which exists for us may be finally,

(4) *The State.* The legal expression for this subserviency of the State to our purposes is *citizenship.*

Opposed to Right is *Duty.* The former tells us that there is something for us, the latter that *we are for another,* but not in the sense that the entire purpose of our being is exhausted in it—in that case the relation would be slavery—but in the sense that this subserviency forms only a particular incident in the purpose of our being.

Accordingly, the position of a person in the world depends upon three conditions, the two from which he derives his right, and a third upon which the world bases his duty to it:

(1) *I exist for myself;*

(2) *The world exists for me;*

(3) *I exist for the world.*

Upon these three concise statements rests the entire scheme of law, and not merely that of law, but the whole ethical world-order. . . .

§6. *Exchange* . . . Exchange as a form of commerce has . . . as its object the directing of every thing where it will do that for which it was intended . . . Every thing finds its right owner; the anvil finds the blacksmith, the fiddle the musician, the worn coat the poor man, a Raphael the picture gallery. . . .

§7. *Contract.* The form of exchange is the *contract* . . . With the delivery of the object sold in return for the price agreed upon, both the buyer and the seller attain what they intend. . . .

But the interests which now meet may subsequently diverge . . . Now if the law did not step in with its constraining power, the law which upholds a contract once concluded, the former understanding would not come to execution on account of the want of present agreement of interests. The recognition of the binding force of contracts, considered from the standpoint of the idea of purpose, means nothing else than securing the original purpose against the prejudicial influence of a later shifting of interest, or of a change of judgment touching his interest on the part of one of the parties. . . .

CHAPTER VI

Life Through and for Others, or Society

§1. *Social Form of Human Existence* . . . There is no human life which exists merely for itself . . . Even if he is the most insignificant laborer, he takes part in one of its problems, and even if he does not work at all, he helps along in his every day speech, for by doing this he helps to keep alive the words of the language handed down to him, and transmits them in his turn. . . .

§5. *Social Life as a Law of Culture* . . . All that I have said so far of individuals holds true also of nations. These also exist not merely for themselves, but for the other nations, for humanity . . . .

§6. *Concept of Society* . . . A society ("societas") in the juristic sense is a union of a number of persons who have combined for the prosecution of a common purpose, and hence every one of them in acting for the purpose of the society at the same time acts for himself. A society in this juristic sense presupposes a *contract,* directed to its construction and regulation—the social contract. But actual society, namely, co-operation for common purposes, is found repeatedly in life without this form. Our whole life, our whole intercourse, is in this actual nonjuristic sense a society, *i.e.,* a working together for common purposes, in which everyone in acting for others acts also for himself, and in acting for himself acts also for others. . . .

§7. *Society and State.* It follows from this that the concept of society partly coincides with that of the State. . . . Commerce and trade, agriculture, manufacture and industry, art and science, the usage of the home and the customs of life, organize themselves essentially. Only occasionally does the State interfere with its law, so far as it is absolutely necessary to secure against violation the order which these interests have evolved independently.

§8. *Problem of Social Movement.* But geographically, too, the sphere of society does not coincide with that of the State; the latter ends with the boundary posts of its territory, the former extends over the whole earth . . . .

CHAPTER VII

Social Mechanics, or the Levers of Social Movement

Social Mechanics . . . The machine *must* obey the master; the laws of mechanics enable him to *compel* it. But the force which moves the wheelwork of human society is the human *will;* that force which, in contrast to the forces of nature, boasts of its freedom; but the will in that function is the will of thousands and millions of individuals, the struggle of interests, of the opposition of efforts, egoism, self-will, insubordination, inertia, weakness, wickedness, crime. There is no greater miracle in the world than the disciplining and training of the human will, whose actual realization in its widest scope we embrace in the word society.

The sum of impulses and powers which accomplish this work I call *social mechanics*. . . .

. . . This social mechanics is identical with the principle of leverage, by means of which society sets the will in motion for her purposes, or in short, *the principle of the levers of social motion.*

There are *four* such levers. Two of them have egoism as their motive and presupposition; I call them the *lower* or *egoistic* social levers; they are *reward* and *coercion* . . . Opposed to these are two other impulses which have not egoism as their motive and presupposition . . . I call them the *higher* or . . . the *moral* or *ethical* levers of social motion. They are the *Feeling of Duty* and of *Love;* the former the prose, the latter the poetry of the moral spirit . . .

Commerce. Commerce is the organization of the assured satisfaction of human wants, which is based upon the lever of reward . . . .

Want is the band with which nature draws man into society, the means by which she realizes the two principles of all morality and culture, "Everybody exists for the world," and "the world exists for everybody. . . ."

§4. *Equivalent.* The concepts remuneration and equivalent do not coincide. . . .

. . . The conception from which the law starts is that each of the two parties has in mind his own advantage, each one endeavors to use the disadvantage of the other man's position in his own favor. This disadvantage may rise to a position of actual duress, when the highest degree of want on the one side coincides with the exclusive possibility of satisfying it on the other . . . The drowning man will promise a fortune, if necessary, for a rope. . . .

Is this, then, the fruit of egoism, which has been so glorified by us, namely, pitiless exploitation of another's need! . . . Must we not confess that society needs a fixed principle by which to be guided in order that egoism, which is insatiable by nature, may have imposed upon it from outside the restraint which it does not bear within itself?

. . . Equivalent is the realization of the *idea of justice* in the domain of *commerce.* For justice, simply and intelligibly expressed, is nothing else than that which suits *all,* where *all* can subsist. Accordingly, to enforce as much as possible the principle of equivalence in all relations is one of the chief problems in the life of commerce.

How does society solve it? Does it solve it by law? If it is true that it is a problem of justice, then it seems inevitably a legal problem; for what justice demands must be realized by law . . . When it is made out that the interest of *all* demands a certain order, we must still consider first whether the interest is not strong enough to establish the order by itself. In this case there is no need of a law—no law finds it necessary to prescribe marriage and to forbid suicide.

Now, does commerce possess the means to realize the idea of equivalent out of its own power? On the whole, this must evidently be the case; no law prescribes the prices for the laborer, manufacturer, shop-keeper, etc., and yet they observe a price . . . Egoism forms in this case its own corrective . . .—*competition is the social self-adjustment of egoism.*

But no matter how true this may be on the whole, there may be special cases or peculiar relations in which competition is temporarily or even permanently excluded. The only innkeeper, physician, apothecary in the place has no competition to be concerned about . . . .

. . . When the dangers which egoism threatens assume a serious aspect there is nothing left to society but the means whereby it always tries to ward off the dangerous excesses of egoism, *viz., the law* . . . There will be need of more numerous and bitter experiences before people will become aware again what dangers to society individual egoism, freed from all bonds, carries with it, and why the past has found it necessary to put a check upon it . . . That the wolves cry for freedom is easy to understand. But when the sheep, as has often been the case in this question, join in the cry, they only show thereby that they are sheep. . . .

. . . Society has the right to check the excesses of the selfish motive when these become dangerous to the success of society . . . Justice is above *freedom*. The individual exists not only for himself, but also for the world—therefore *freedom,* that which is expedient for the individual, must be subordinated to *justice,* which is for the advantage of all. . . .

§5. *Organization of Work in the Form of a Vocation, Business or Trade* . . . He who takes up a definite business declares thereby publicly his fitness and inclination for all services connected with it. The public receives the assurance that every one who needs him can count on him, and he gives every one the authority to call upon him. His own interest, to be sure, and the spur of competition guarantee as a rule his readiness; but both motives may fail sometimes, and what then? . . . Has the innkeeper a right to refuse the stranger; the shopkeeper, baker, butcher to refuse the customer; the apothecary, the physician to refuse the patient; the lawyer the client? Every true man of business has the feeling that he has *not* the right . . . Why? . . . Because by the adoption of his particular vocation he has given society an assurance, which he is not making good. . . .

. . . A vocation is *the organization* of reward. The organization of reward consists in its promotion from the vacillating and accidental character of a rate measured according to purely individual estimate to the uniformity and certainty of a universal standard of value. In other words, it is the advance from a purely individual standard of measurement to the realization of the *idea of equivalent.* The influence which the vocation exerts in this respect is twofold; it *determines* the amount of the equivalent, and it *secures* the practical maintenance of the same. It accomplishes the former by fixing, on the basis of constantly repeated experience, the measure and the costs of the work necessary to produce the service. Only

he is able to do this who has devoted his whole power and his whole life to the problem. He alone knows what work costs; and the possible errors in his experience, which may be due to the influence of special individual factors, are rectified by the experience of all the other people. . . .

As the branch of industry *determines* the right amount of the equivalent, so it *secures* the actual maintenance of the same. . . .

Accordingly the vocation may be designated the regulator of compensation. The compensation which it fixes is in the long run always the right one, *i.e.,* an amount which corresponds to the service, and hence fair and just for both parties. Society has the most vital interest in preventing remuneration from being reduced below its proper measure, for a just price is the condition of a just work. The vocation itself must suffer when it does not get its right. Therefore he who lowers the prices below this measure is not a benefactor of society, but an enemy thereof . . . Every branch of industry has developed by experience an equilibrium between burdens and advantages, duties and rights. He who appropriates the advantages alone, without taking upon him the duties of the vocation, disturbs this equilibrium and endangers the branch of industry; he is a social freebooter whom society has all reason to suppress. . . .

§7. *Ideal Reward and Its Combination with Economic Reward* . . . The use which society makes of reward nowadays is far behind that of punishment; she has taken in this respect, in comparison with antiquity, a considerable step backward . . . Whether it is reward or punishment (the function of both being simply the realization of the idea of justice) that errs, *i.e.,* misses the right man and finds the wrong one, is equally incompatible with the idea of justice.

But it is not the personal representative of sovereignty alone who rewards social merit; there is an impersonal power besides, *viz.,* public opinion . . . The laurel around Dante's temples is ever green and will never fade; one leaf of it outweighs wagon loads of grand crosses.

The species of reward which I have considered just now I designate as *ideal* reward. I call it ideal in contradistinction to material reward (money), which bears its value in itself, whereas the ideal value depends solely upon the ideas which are associated with it. . . .

I distinguish two kinds of ideal remuneration: *external* and *internal*. By the first I understand the reward which is paid by society or the power of the State: fame, recognition, honor; by the second I denote that satisfaction which a work itself affords; such is the delight in intellectual work *per se*, the charm of proving one's power, the joy of discovery, the pleasure in creating, the consciousness of having done a service to the world, of having utilized one's faculties for the welfare of humanity. . . .

§8. . . . *Association* . . . The problem which I have so far tried to solve consisted in demonstrating the apparatus of which society makes use, by means of the lever of egoism, to satisfy its need; not, however, as a given and ready-made system, but as a process gradually developing under the influence of the idea of purpose. Having arrived at this point, I will finally attempt to convey an idea of the social problems which commerce realizes in its sphere more or less perfectly. They are the following:—

(1) *Independence of the Person.*
(2) *Equality of the Person.*
(3) *The Idea of Justice.*

(1) *The Independence of the Person.* Independence does not mean so much, as is commonly supposed, to have as few needs as possible . . . but rather to be able to satisfy one's needs. In so far as commerce makes this possible, the service which it thereby renders to human society may be designated as the establishment of human independence . . . In a civilized land the wage of the most insignificant laborer is sufficient to procure for him the labor products of thousands of men. . . .

The phenomenon here presented is based upon three institutions which we owe to the perfection of our present system of commerce, *viz.*, the division of labor, the undertaking of work for an indefinite number of future customers, and the extension of trade over the whole earth. . . .

(2) *The Principle of Equality of the Person.* Commerce knows no respect of persons . . . it regards the money alone. This complete impartiality of the intercourse of exchange toward persons . . . is socially of truly inestimable value; for it gives every man, whoever he may be, provided he has the money, the certainty of satisfying his wants, the opportunity of living in accordance with the cultural conditions of his time . . . A man may be good for nothing else; people may avoid his company and contact with him, but he is always good enough to do business with . . . .

(3) *The Idea of Justice.* The idea of justice is the equality which is demanded and measured by the interests of society between a deed and its consequences for the doer, *i.e.*, between an *evil* deed and *punishment*, and a *good* deed and its *reward*. This is nowhere realized in the latter direction to the same extent as in the sphere of commerce. In business intercourse each party receives on an average, by means of the consideration, as much in return as he has given . . . The equivalent may therefore be defined as *the realization of the idea of justice in the economic sphere.* The fixing of punishment is something arbitrary and the effect of a positive determination by the State. The standard which the State applies in awarding punishment is highly elastic and unreliable. The fixing of the equivalent, on the other hand, is the result of the most careful investigations and experiences, constantly renewed by all those interested. Reward is as sensitive as the mercury in a barometer; it rises and falls at the slightest changes in the economic atmosphere. If I ask myself where the idea of justice is *most perfectly* realized in our social institutions, the answer is: in business. If I ask where it is realized the *earliest,* the answer is again: in business. Business and its remuneration found their suitable form earlier than did the State and its punishments. If I ask finally where it is realized *most uniformly* in the whole world, I get the answer a third time: in business.

Law and punishment may have a different form on this or that side of the frontier line, but prices and compensations know no State boundaries; although, to be sure, positive regulations of the State, by duties and taxes, may prevent their complete equalization in different States . . . .

CHAPTER VIII

Social Mechanics, or the Levers of Social Motion

2. Egoistic-Coercion

. . . Coercion organized makes the State and Law. . . .

. . . In addition to *political* coercion, there is still another, unorganized, which historically everywhere preceded the other, and asserted itself everywhere along with it. I call this the *social*. Political coercion has for its object the realization of *law*, social coercion has for its object the realization of morality. . . .

It is without doubt a great advance of modern philosophy of law as distinguished from the earlier Law of Nature that it has recognized and forcibly emphasized the dependence of law upon the State. But it goes too far when, as Hegel in particular does, it denies the scientific interest of the conditions before the State came into existence. . . .

. . . It stands to the credit of the advocates of the Law of Nature that they were not satisfied with the mere facts of the law and the State but raised the question, whence are the two? But the manner in which they solved the problem, in making the historical State originate in a contract, was a mistaken one. This is a pure construction without regard to actual history. . . .

§2. *Man—Self-control of Force.* Life of the stronger at the expense of the weaker, annihilation of the latter in conflict with the former,—such is the form of life in the animal world; assured existence also of the weakest and the poorest by the side of the strongest and mightiest,—such is the form of life in the human world. And yet man historically found no other point of departure

than the animal; but nature equipped him in such a way that he was not only able, but compelled, to raise himself to the higher stage in the course of history. . . .

. . . In slavery for the first time is solved the problem of the co-existence of the powerful and the weak. . . .

. . . What determined the strong man, before the opponent lay as a slave at his feet, to place his sword in its sheath and offer him fair terms? . . . It was no other humanity than that which induced him to spare the life of the subdued enemy, *viz.,* his own interest. The prospect of probable or perhaps certain victory if he continued the fight was obscured by a regard for the price at which it must be bought . . . Thus: is it more advantageous to buy more at a high price, or less at a fair price? . . . If he possesses enough self-control to give a hearing to his intelligent consideration instead of his passion, he will prefer in his own interest not to arouse his opponent to a desperate struggle by proposing unacceptable terms, with further prospects of exertions and sacrifices on his own part, which stand in no true relation to the profit that is aimed at. . . .

. . . Force thus sets a limit to itself, which it desires to respect; it recognizes a norm to which it intends to subordinate itself, and this norm approved by itself is *Law* . . . The law has been placed in the world once for all, and this fact can never be undone again. It has laid down a rule for its conduct, and set up a standard by which to judge it, unknown before. . . .

The process which we have here outlined gives the impression of an *a priori* construction, but in reality it is derived from a consideration of history . . . The process has equal significance for the development of law in the interior of States; it makes public law as well as private. Whoever will trace the legal fabric of a people to its ultimate origins will reach innumerable cases where the force of the stronger has laid down the law for the weaker. . . .

. . . Force arrives at law not as at something foreign to it, which it must borrow from the outside, from the feeling of law;

neither does it arrive at law as to something superior to which it must subordinate itself with a feeling of its own inferiority. Force produces law immediately out of itself, and as a measure of itself, *law evolving as the politics of force* . . . Law is not the highest thing in the world, not an end in itself; but merely a means to an end, the final end being the existence of society. . . .

. . . Law without force is an empty name, a thing without reality, for it is force, in realizing the norms of law, that makes law what it is and ought to be . . . The despots and inhuman tyrants . . . have done just as much for educating mankind in law as the wise lawgivers . . . the former had to come first in order that the latter might appear . . . It accustomed the will to subordinate itself and recognize a superior over it. Not until it had learned this did the time come for law to take the place of force; for earlier, law would have had no prospects of success . . . If we conceive the people in that stage as equipped with our modern feeling for right and humanity, it would indeed be a riddle to us to understand how they could allow such cruel deeds as history reports of their rulers in inexhaustible plenty. But the riddle is solved by the fact that the ethical standard for judging these things, with which we quite unhistorically equip them, was quite a foreign thing to them. . . .

§3. *Propulsive Coercion in Law—Person, Property.* The first relation in which the purpose of human existence postulates force is personality. When its existence and life are threatened by foreign attack, it defends itself and repels violence with violence (*propulsive* coercion). Nature herself, in giving man life and implanting in him the impulse of self-preservation, requires this conflict . . . Necessary defence is both a right and a duty; a right in so far as the subject exists for himself, a duty in so far as he exists for the world. . . .

But the self-protection of the person embraces not merely what he *is* but also what he *has,* for having is extended being. . . .

§4. *Compulsive Coercion—The Family* . . . The master of the house . . . must have the authority . . . and nature herself has indicated this position for him in its essential outlines—in relation to his wife, by the superiority of his physical strength and by the greater amount of work which falls to his share—in relation to the children, by the helplessness and dependence in which they are for years,—the influence of which, even after they are grown up, remains. . . .

Thus nature herself has determined the family relation to be one of superiority and subordination; and in making every man . . . pass through the latter relation, has provided that no one shall enter society who has not already learned this lesson of superiority and subordination upon which relation the existence of the State depends . . . .

§5. *Compulsive Coercion—Contract.* Not every contract requires compulsive coercion for its security; a contract of sale or exchange which is at once carried out affords no room for it, since it leaves nothing to be gotten by coercion . . . Certain contracts necessarily presuppose the postponement of the performance on the one side. . . .

Promise denotes a very great progress. . . .

But in order that the word shall take the place of the act, there must be security that it will be exchanged for the act at the proper time . . . The guarantee for such fulfilment depends upon coercion. . . .

The binding force of a promise is not a thing that comes to it from the outside; it is inevitably posited in the practical function of it. If a promise were not binding, loan would be as good as useless in business intercourse; only a friend would then be able to get a loan. . . .

In view of this practical indispensableness of the binding force of contracts it is scarcely conceivable how the doctrine of the Law of Nature could have considered it so difficult a problem . . . The question became a problem only because the element of purpose in it, *i.e.,* the function of promise in business, was altogether left out of sight, and the attempt was made to answer the question merely from reasoning on the nature of the will . . . The middle ages recognized contracts as valid which we today simply reject, and the same relation will always be repeated. To answer the question of the binding force of contracts by an abstract formula is no better than to do the same in reference to the question of the best form of government. Rights of contract and forms of government are facts of history, which can only be comprehended in their relation to history, *i.e.* to the conditions and needs of the time when they arose. By abandoning the firm ground of history and undertaking to answer the question from the nature of the subjective will, abstracted from society and history, the doctrine of the Law of Nature deprived itself of all prospect of solution. . . .

§6. *The Self-regulation of Coercion.—Partnership* . . . The whole question of the social organization of coercion is connected with the problem of *bringing the preponderance of force on the side of right.* . . .

He who does not regard his power as sufficient for maintaining his right against violent injury or deforcement, will look around for help, whether it be in the moment of danger when the right is threatened, or as soon as it is established. Both forms of protection take shape daily before our eyes in international intercourse; in the first case by *alliance,* in the second by *guarantee* . . . Both of them contain the first beginnings of the realization of the problem of right; which is, to create a preponderance on the side of right. But only the first beginnings, for the success of either is ever highly problematical. The one who menaces can look around for allies just as well as the one threatened; he who finds the most is the strongest, and it is not right but accident that decides the matter. Guarantee goes a step higher. But its value, too, as the experience of international law has at all times shown, is highly problematical; for who will guarantee the guarantor? . . .

These are the facts regarded externally. The case is quite different when looked at from within; and here, indeed, we finally come upon the vital point in the whole organization of right. This consists in the preponderance of the *common* interests of *all* over the *particular* interests of one *individ-*

ual; *all* join for the common interests, only the *individual* stands for the particular interest. But the power of all is, the forces being equal, superior to that of the individual; and the more so the greater their number. . . .

The form in private law of a combination of several persons for the pursuit of the same common interest is *partnership,* and although in other respects the State is very different from partnership, the formula in reference to regulating force by interest is quite the same in both . . . Conceptually as well as historically, partnership forms the transition from the unregulated form of force in the individual to its regulation by the State . . . In partnership all partners present a united front against the one who pursues his own interests at the expense of these common interests assigned by the contract, or who refuses to carry out the duties undertaken by him in the contract . . . Partnership may therefore be designated as the mechanism of the *self-regulation of force according to the measure of right.* . . .

The solution of the problem to which our entire investigation has till now been devoted depends then upon the fact . . . that society is stronger than the individual; and that therefore where it is obliged to summon its power in order to assert its right against the individual, the preponderance is always found on its side, *i.e.,* on the side of right.

. . . A comparison of private society with political will show the relative similarity of the two. The fundamental features of both are exactly alike, as follows:

1. Community of purpose.

2. The presence of norms, which regulate its pursuit; in the one, in the form of a contract, the "lex privata," in the other in the form of a law, the "lex publica."

3. In their content: their legal status, the rights and duties of the whole as well as of the individuals.

4. Realization of these norms against the resistant will of the individual by means of coercion.

5. Administration: the free pursuit of the purpose with the means at the disposal of society within the limits set by the above

norms, and all that is connected therewith, namely, the creation of a special organ for administrative purposes when the number of members is large (board of management, government). Belonging to this is the distinction between those *by* whom and those *for* whom the administration is carried on (functionaries, officials—shareholders, citizens, subjects). Also the danger thence arising of applying the common means in opposition to the interests of the society and in favor of its administrators; a danger to be feared no less in political society than in private. Furthermore, and as a means of protection against this danger, the control of the administrators by the society itself (general assembly; assembly of the estates of the realm). . . .

§7. *Public Association* . . . Associations animated by the right spirit rather zealously endeavor to gain new members; every association seeks to expand, to grow as far as possible in power, prestige and influence. *Exclusion* is the essence of partnership, *expansion* is the essence of association. This impulse of expansion is common to all associations, the most important as well as the least important. State and Church, political, ecclesiastical, scientific, social—the State conquers, the Church makes propaganda, associations solicit members. . . .

Association belongs to public law, or, more correctly, it is altogether coincident with it, just as private law coincides with the individual. It is arbitrary in my opinion to limit the concept of public law to the State and the Church . . . Not only was the State's original content in the beginning of history relatively modest, and limited essentially to the maintenance of security within and without, but also . . . the living needs of society constantly produced new objects, in addition to those which the State had already absorbed. These new purposes, being foreign to the State, led a separate and independent existence in the form of associations until they had attained the necessary degree of maturity; and then they burst the covering in which they had existed hitherto and emptied their entire content into that form which it

would seem was intended to take up everything within itself, *viz.,* the State. What was instruction formerly? *A private affair.* What was it next? *The business of association.* What is it now? *The business of the State.* What was the care of the poor formerly? *A private matter.* What was it next? *The business of association.* What is it now? *The business of the State.* . . .

§8. *The State. Separation from Society* . . . In the State, right for the first time finds what it was looking for: mastery over force. But it attains its goal only *within the State;* for on the outside, in the conflict of States among themselves, might stands opposed to right. . . .

. . . The State is society as the bearer of the regulated and disciplined coercive force. The sum total of principles according to which it thus functions by a discipline of coercion, is *Law* . . .

. . . In order to be able to coerce, society takes the form of the State; the State is that form which the regulated and assured exercise of social coercive force takes. . . . But yet the State remains behind society; for the latter is universal, the former particularistic. The State only solves those problems which arise for it within limited geographical bounds. . . .

The organization of social coercive force embraces two sides; the establishment of the external mechanism of force, and the setting up of principles to regulate its use. The form of solution of the first problem is the *State force,* that of the second is the *Law.* . . .

§9. *State Force.*

. . . If the question of power in the State were decided by mere numbers, the predominance of power would necessarily go over to the side of the majority, and then the force of the State would always be powerless against the majority. But the experience of all times has shown that the force of the State may have the entire population against it, and yet be in a position to maintain its own power. Numbers alone, therefore, do not decide the matter, else the force in the State would always be with the majority of the given moment, and the political power would be in a constant state of fluctuation and vacillation. Happily, however, the matter is different. The firmness of the State depends upon the fact that the influence of the numerical element on the question of power is counteracted by two other factors: the organization of power in the hands of the State force, and the moral power which the idea of the State exerts . . . .

The State is the only competent as well as the sole owner of social coercive force—the right to coerce forms the *absolute monopoly* of the State. Every association that wishes to realize its claims upon its members by means of mechanical coercion is dependent upon the co-operation of the State, and the State has it in its power to fix the conditions under which it will grant such aid. But this means in other words that the State is the only source of law, for norms which cannot be enforced by him who lays them down are not *legal rules.* . . .

§10. *The Law—Its Dependence upon Coercion.* The current definition of law is as follows: law is the sum of the *compulsory rules* in force in a State, and in my opinion it has therewith hit the truth. . . .

In so far, however, as the Church, without the help of the external power of the State, is able to realize the commandments which it imposes upon its members by the moral lever of the religious feeling, we can say that these rules, although they are devoid of external coercion and hence are not legal norms, nevertheless practically exercise the *function* of legal rules. But if we should want to call these rules law for this reason, we could do the same with every other association, even one that is forbidden by the State; and we should then have to speak of law in a robber band. The jurist who does not want to lose all firm ground under his feet must not speak of law in such a case. . . .

. . . The criterion of the organization of coercion for the realization of law fails entirely in *International Law,* and in another division, namely in *Public Law,* it fails at least in so far as concerns the duties of the monarch within an absolute or constitutional monarchy. . . .

What attitude must the theory of law take up in relation to these facts? It may pursue three different courses. The first consists in completely denying to international law and the above-mentioned regulations of public law the character of *legal rules,* for the very reason that they cannot be enforced, and allowing them only that of *moral* precepts and duties. . . .

. . . A second view . . . lets the element of enforceability fall in the concept of law. . . .

The *third* course, which I regard as the only correct one, consists in holding firmly to coercion as an essential requirement of law, but with this must be combined the knowledge that the *organization* of it in those two cases meets with obstructions which cannot be overcome . . . .

§11. *The Law—The Element of Norm* . . . A norm is . . . a *rule* according to which we should direct ourselves . . . Every norm is an *imperative (positive—command, negative—prohibition).* An imperative has meaning only in the mouth of him who has the power to impose such limitation upon another's will . . . According as the imperative merely designates conduct in a particular case, or a type of conduct for all cases of a certain kind, we distinguish *concrete* and *abstract* imperatives. The latter coincide with norm. . . .

The ethical world-order contains three classes of such abstract imperatives: of law, of morality, and of ethics. What is common to them is the social purpose; all three have society as the subject of their purpose, and not the individual . . . .

. . . There are imperatives which are directed exclusively to the authorities. The regulations which govern the organization, the management and the jurisdiction of the authorities, have nothing to do with the private person. . . .

Over against these purely *internal* coercive norms, as I shall call them, are the *external,* the effectiveness of which shows itself passively in the private person, who is held to their observance on the appeal of another private person, or on the initiative of **the**

State force itself by a threat of coercion or of punishment. . . .

But there are doubtless many legal regulations which direct no imperatives at the private person, either in respect to their form or content, and yet they are intended to be applied to him by the judge. I name as an example, in civil law, the propositions having to do with the development of legal concepts; the regulations of the age of majority; concerning the influence of error on acts in the law; concerning the interpretation of laws and acts in the law; in criminal law, the regulations concerning criminal responsibility, and state of necessity. Where is coercion here, which is to constitute the criterion of all legal norms? . . .

. . . The imperative shows itself here also; it asserts itself in the person of the judge, who is expected to apply all these norms. . . .

If we repeat from this standpoint of our consideration of the State and of law the above question: To whom are the imperatives of the State directed? The answer can only be: to the organs which are entrusted with the management of coercion . . . Every legal rule, every political imperative is characterized by the fact that some bearer of political force is entrusted with its practical realization. Coercion against the private person, though it belongs to it, is an unsafe criterion of law. . . .

. . . Observance of the same on the part of the people . . . must be designated from this purely *formal-juristic* point of view (not from the *teleological*) merely as *secondary* in comparison with the other as *primary*. All legal imperatives without exception are directed in the *first* instance to the authorities . . . In reference to the *purpose* of such norms we may say that they aim at the private person; the above statement that in *form* they are directed solely to the organs of the State force is not invalidated thereby. . . .

. . . The despot, *i.e.*, the master of slaves . . . has not the object of putting a limit upon himself by means of the norms which he issues; he rather reserves to himself the privilege to disregard them in every case where they prove inconvenient to him. Can we speak of *law* at all in such a condition? In so far as we understand by law merely a sum of compulsory norms, yes. In so far as we apply the standard of that which the law can and should be, *viz.*, the assured order of civil society, no. But the germs of the law in the latter sense are after all already present here also. . . .

These are first *order*, *i.e.*, uniformity of social action. It may be interrupted, it is true, at any time by arbitrary acts, but so far as this does not happen, there is already order. . . .

The other element of law is *equality*. It is posited in principle in the norm as such; for every abstract proposition is based upon the affirmation of the equality of the concrete; and no matter how arbitrarily the law of the despot may shape the particular categories for which he issues his regulations, within a particular category he proclaims in principle, by means of every law, the theory of equality . . . This is the point where the moral element of the legal norm makes itself felt for the first time in the shape of fear of open contradiction with itself . . . At the moment when force invites the law to announce its commands, it opens its own house up to the law, and there at once commences a reaction of law upon force . . . Whilst at first merely a scullion in the house of force it becomes in the course of time the major-domo. . . .

. . . We have adopted above the current definition of law which designates it as the sum of the valid coercive norms in a State. . . .

Law, therefore, in this full sense of the word, means the *bilaterally* binding force of the statute; self-subordination on the part of the State authority to the laws issued by it. . . .

. . . We speak not only of arbitrary decisions of the judge and arbitrary acts of the government where we apply the standard of positive law, but also of arbitrary laws. But the legislating authority does not stand like the judge and the executive power *under* the law, but *above* it. Every law which it issues, no matter what its content, is in the juristic sense a perfectly legal act . . . But just as the father is bound morally, though not legally, to use the power entrusted to him in accordance with the meaning of the paternal relation, so is the legislator bound to use his power in the interests of society....

... We use the expression arbitrary of those legal determinations which imply that the legislator, according to our opinion, has set himself in opposition to the general principles of law. In this case we raise the charge against him that he has disregarded the norms which we consider as binding upon him. We also use the expression *unjust* as meaning the same thing....

... Justice and arbitrariness are correlates. The former denotes that the person who has the authority and the power to establish order in the circle of his subordinates agrees to be subjected by the norms to which we regard him as bound, the latter that he does not.

... This obligation may be of two kinds, *legal* and *moral*. For the judge it is of the former kind, for the legislator of the latter; the former stands beneath the law, the latter above it; the former is directed by justice ("rechtlich") to apply the law, and he is just ("gerecht") if he does it. He is not responsible for the injustices of the law itself; these fall to the account of the legislator. For the latter, who must set up the law for the first time, the standard of justice cannot be derived from the law itself; he must first seek and find justice in order to realize it in the law. It is desirable to express in language this bifurcation of the concept of justice; and the nearest expression that offers itself is that of *judicial* and *legislative* justice ... The most appropriate designation would be *formal* and *material* justice....

The practical aim of justice is the establishment of *equality*. The aim of material justice is to establish *internal* equality, *i.e.,* equilibrium between merit and reward, and between punishment and guilt. The aim of formal justice is to establish *external* equality, *i.e., uniformity* in the application of the norm to all cases when it is once established....

... What is there so great in equality that we measure the highest concept of right—for this is what justice is—by it? ... The desire for equality seems to have its ultimate ground in an ugly trait of the human heart; in ill-will and envy. No one shall be better or less badly off than I....

But the reason we want equality in law is not because it is something worth striving after in itself ... Our reason for wanting it is because it is the condition of the *welfare* of society....

The Roman jurists recognize the principle of equality expressly as the leading point of view as the principle of organization of the "societas" ... A society which desires to flourish must be sure of the complete devotion of the particular member to the purposes of the society; and in order to have this it must grant him the full equivalent for his co-operation. If it does not do so, it endangers its own purpose. The interest of the injured member in the carrying out of the common purpose becomes weakened, his zeal and energy are impaired, one of the springs of the machine refuses to work, and finally, the machine itself comes to a standstill....

It is therefore the practical interest in the continuance and success of society which dictates the principle of equality in this sense, and not the *a priori* categorical imperative of an equality to be realized in all human relations. If experience showed that society could exist better with inequality, such would deserve the preference ... The determining standpoint in this matter is not that of the individual, but of society. From the former we arrive at an external, mechanical equality which measures all by the same standard—small and great, rich and poor, children and adults, wise and foolish; and which, by treating the unequal as equal, in reality brings about the greatest inequality ... This is the basis of the concept of true justice. The equality which it endeavors to attain is the equality of the law itself; the equilibrium between the determinations of the law and circumstances ... That law is unjust which imposes the same burdens upon the poor as upon the rich; for it then ignores the difference in the ability to perform. The law is unjust which inflicts the same punishment for a light offence as for a heavy one; for it then disregards the proportion between crime and punishment. The law is unjust which treats the person of unsound mind like him of sound mind; for it pays no regard to the nature of guilt. . . .

Punishment in the hands of the State is a two-edged sword. If it is improperly used, it turns its edge against the State itself and injures it along with the offender. With every offender which it condemns it deprives itself of one of its members; every time it confines one in prison or in a house of correction it cripples his energy. The recognition of the worth of human life and human strength has an eminently practical significance for criminal law. . . .

1. *The Motive.* What motive can induce the authorities to subordinate themselves to the law? The same motive which suffices to determine a person to self-control, *viz.,* self-interest. Self-control pays itself . . . Where the State authorities obey the orders of their own prescription, there alone are the orders secure of their proper effect. Where the law is supreme, there alone the national well-being prospers, commerce and industry flourish, and the innate spiritual and moral force of the people unfolds in its full strength. *Law is the intelligent policy of power;* not the short-sighted policy of the moment, and momentary interest, but that far-sighted policy which looks into the future and weighs the end. . . .

2. *The Guarantees.* There are two, one internal, the other external; one is the *feeling of right,* the other the *administration of justice.*

. . . The sense of right cannot develop in the State's subjects if the authorities themselves tread under foot the law which they issue—respect for law cannot win its way below where it is wanting above. . . .

. . . I designate the fear which the State authorities have of the reaction of the nation's sense of right as the ultimate guarantee of the security of the law, and I do not fail to see either that when once the sense of right has attained to its full influence among the people, it will not fail to exert its purely moral influence upon the powers of the State also.

. . . A lame sense of right in the nation means an insecure law; a healthy and strong sense of right means a secure law. The security of the law is everywhere the work and the merit of the people itself. . . .

. . . It must not be said that this is an argument in a circle; that the law is made the condition of the national character, and this again the condition of the law; for there is the same reciprocal influence here as in art. The people make art, but art in turn makes the people; the people make the law, but the law in turn makes the people. . . .

To the sense of right as the inner guarantee of the secured existence of the law I opposed above the *administration of justice* as the *outer* guarantee. The peculiar character of the administration of justice in contradistinction to the other tasks and branches of the State's activities, is based upon two factors; the *inner* peculiarity of the *purpose,* and the *outer* peculiarity of the *means* and *forms* by which it is carried out. In respect to the former, the distinction of the administration of justice from the other branches of the State's activities consists in the fact that its intention is *exclusively to realize the law,* —its motto is *the law and nothing but the law* . . . The judge must in a certain sense be nothing else than the law become alive in his person and endowed with speech. If justice could descend from heaven and take a pencil in its hands to write down the law with such definiteness, precision and detail that its application should become a work of mechanical routine, nothing more perfect could be conceived for the administration of justice; and the kingdom of justice would be complete upon earth. For absolute equality and the strict dependence of the judicial sentence upon it are so far from being incompatible with the idea of justice that on the contrary they form its highest aim. . . .

Upon this contrast of the two ideas, of the *constrained* character of *justice* and the *freedom* of *adaptability to an end,* is based the inner distinction between the administration of justice, and the executive function of the government. . . .

. . . The separation of the judicial as a separate branch of State activity means the retirement of the law into itself for the purpose of solving its problems with security and completeness. . . .

. . . By separating the judicial function, the State authority recognizes in principle that the law is a distinct problem, and that the considerations determining its solution are different from all those other problems which the State reserves for itself. In handing over the administration of justice to the judge they actually declare before all the people that they wish to renounce that privilege. The establishment of the judicial office signifies *self-limitation in principle* on the part of the State authorities in reference to that portion of the law which is handed over to the administration of the judge. It means empowering the judge to find the law independently of them and in accordance altogether with his own convictions, and the assurance of the binding force of the sentence handed down by him. . . .

3. *The Limits of the Subordination of the Government to the Law.* By the law the government ties its own hands. How far should the government do this? Absolutely? In this case every man would have to obey the law only. The government would have no right to command or forbid anything which was not provided for in the law. The law of the State would thus be placed on the same line as the law of nature. As in nature so in the State, the law would be the only power which moves every thing. . . .

This would be the just State, as it seems, as perfect as one can think it. Only one quality would be missing—*vitality*. Such a State would not be able to exist a month. In order to be able to do so, it would have to be what it is not, clock-work . . . Society would give herself up with bound hands to rigid necessity, standing helpless in the presence of all circumstances and requirements of life which were not provided for in the law . . . It is a wrong belief that the interest of the security of right and of political freedom requires the greatest possible limitation of the government by the law. . . .

. . . There will always be the possibility of unusual cases in which the government finds itself placed before the alternative of sacrificing either the law or the welfare of society. What shall be the choice? . . .

. . . The law is not an end in itself, but only a means to an end. The end of the State as well as of the law is the establishment and security of the conditions of social life. Law exists for the sake of society, not society for the sake of law. . . .

At the same time, however, the open violation of the laws is a deplorable proceeding which legislation must spare the government as far as possible. It can be done by bringing the right of inevitable necessity itself under the form of law, as is done more or less in all modern laws and State constitutions. . . .

. . . It is possible that the comprehensive catalogue of crimes which legislation has drawn up on the basis of long experiences appears defective in a particular case. Refined wickedness may invent new crimes which are not provided for by law . . . Shall justice declare itself powerless before such a fiend . . . The answer of the jurist is, Yes . . . The unsophisticated sense of right of the people demands punishment here also, and I agree with them completely . . . The highest aim of law is not to keep away arbitrariness but to realize justice . . . It is a question of finding a form which will afford a guarantee that the release of the judge from the positive law will be to the advantage of justice alone and not also of arbitrariness. For this purpose there is need of establishing a highest court of justice *above* the law, which will, by the manner in which it is constituted, exclude in advance all apprehension that it might become some day an instrument in the hands of an arbitrary government.

. . . In Scotland a court of justice of this kind exists. But even if it did not exist anywhere, for me it is not a question of what *is*, but of what *should* be. . . .

In the form just outlined, the higher judge, placed superior to the one who abjudicates strictly according to the written law, removes the imperfections of the law in the spirit of the legislator, by deciding the particular case as the legislator would have decided it when he issued the law . . . I am not defending individualization of criminal administration in general (this is found also in the despot, who pays attention to no law), but individualization by a *judicial* authority. . . .

. . . The security of the formal justice of the judge stands higher with us than the advantages of an uncertain material justice, behind which arbitrariness could conceal itself only too easily. . . .

§12. *The Purpose of the Law.—The Conditions of Social Life* . . . Belief and superstition, barbarism and culture, vengeance and love, cruelty and humanity—what else shall I name?—all these have found a willing reception in the law. Unresistingly it seems to yield to all influences which are powerful enough to make it serviceable to them, without having a fixed support of its own. Contradiction, external change, seems to constitute the essential content of the law. . . .

. . . The content of the will may be different in one condition from what it is in another, and yet be right, *i.e.,* appropriate to the purpose, in both. . . .

. . . The law cannot always make the same regulations, it must likewise adapt them to the conditions of the people, to their degree of civilization, to the needs of the time. . . . A universal law for all nations and times stands on the same line with a universal remedy for all sick people. . . .

. . . Certain legal principles are found among all peoples; murder and robbery are everywhere forbidden . . . Consequently, in these cases, one may urge, we actually have absolute truth. . . .

Now a science which, like the science of law, has the purposive as its object, may indeed separate all those institutions which have stood the test of history in this way from the others which can boast only a limited (temporal or spatial) usefulness, and combine them in a separate class, as the Romans did with "jus gentium" and "naturalis ratio" . . . But it must not forget that

here too it has to do not with the true but with the useful. . . .

. . . The entire law is simply one creation of purpose, except that most of the particular creative acts reach back into such a distant past that humanity has lost remembrance of them. . . .

Now what is the purpose of law? . . . I define law in reference to its content as the form of the *security of the conditions of social life,* procured by the power of the State. . . .

The purpose of the criminal law is no different from that of any law, *viz.,* the security of the conditions of social life. But the manner in which it pursues this purpose is peculiar. It makes use of *punishment.* Why? Is it because all disregard of law is a revolt against the authority of the State and therefore deserves punishment? In that case every violation of law should be punished; the refusal of the seller to fulfil his contract, of the debtor to pay his debt, and innumerable other cases; and then there would be only one kind of punishment, *viz.,* for disregard of the law, and only one kind of crime, *viz.,* the insubordination of the subject to the commands or prohibitions of the government.

Wherein lies the reason of the fact that whereas the law punishes certain acts which are in opposition to it, it leaves others unpunished? . . . Society can no more exist if contracts of sale are not carried out, and loans are not repaid, than if one man kills or robs the other. Why punishment in the one case and not in the other?

Self-preservation also, and reproduction and work are conditions of social life. Why does not society secure these by law? The answer is, because it has no need of doing so. The same consideration which causes society to take refuge in the law at all, namely the recognition that it needs it, guides it also in reference to the criminal law. Where the other means are sufficient for the realization of the law, the application of punishment would be an irresponsible measure, because society itself would be the sufferer by it. The question for what cases legislation shall fix a penalty is purely a question of social politics. . . .

. . . Germany once had a large export trade in linen. Now the German linen industry in foreign markets has been crowded out almost everywhere, and rightly so. The thousands of dollars which dishonest weavers or manufacturers gained by the mixture of cotton have lost the German nation millions, quite apart from the injury done to our good name abroad. If these falsifiers had been threatened in good time with the penalty of imprisonment, we should be better off . . . We shall probably have to have many bitter experiences yet before we . . . free ourselves from the academic prejudice that the sphere of contracts is a privileged wrestling ground for civil injustice, which is regarded in principle as inaccessible to punishment. . . .

The criminal law shows us everywhere a gradation of punishment according to the nature of the crime. . . .

The higher a good stands, the more thought we take to make it secure. Society does the same thing with its conditions of life (I shall call them social goods) in so far as the legal protection is concerned which it summons for their security. The higher the good, the higher the punishment. *The list of penalties gives the standard of values for social goods. . . .*

In addition to the *objective* element of the threatened *good* on the part of society, there is the *subjective* element, on the part of the criminal, arising from his disposition and the manner in which the crime was carried out, which constitutes him a *danger* to society. Not every criminal who commits the same crime endangers society in the same degree. Society has more to fear from the relapsing or habitual criminal than from the novice in crime; it has more to fear from a conspiracy or band than from a single individual. Cunning threatens greater dangers than passion; design than negligence. . . .

. . . We have . . . been led to the exhaustive definition of law with which we now close our whole investigation.

Law is the sum of the conditions of social life in the widest sense of the term, as secured by the power of the State through the means of external compulsion.

. . . Society is nothing more than the sum of the individuals; and even though, in order to present the significance of law as a part of the whole order of human things, we may look away from the individual and substitute the community for it, still it is after all the individual upon whom the law exerts its activity; it is for his benefit, and it is upon him that its limitations are laid. Is the individual reimbursed for the limitations to which he submits in the interest of society, by the advantages which the latter offers him? . . .

§13. *The Pressure of the Law upon the Individual* . . . Society becomes ever more covetous and pretentious. Every satisfied desire bears the germ of a new one. But every new purpose which is added on the list of social purposes to those already existing magnifies, with the measure of labor power and money which it requires, the contribution demanded of the individual. . . .

. . . The administrators of the public revenue have solved the problem of making all persons and things tributary to the purposes of society. . . .

In taxes you see what society costs you in cash money. But there are besides the personal services which it requires of you, *viz.,* the duty (in Germany) of military service, which costs you a few years of your life, and if there is a war, may cost you your life or your limbs. . . .

Now, you will say, I have finally done with society. What remains now belongs to me alone. Society can not interfere in the sphere of my private rights; here her empire ends and mine begins. Here is the point where I can say to her, so far and no further. . . .

If the idea that a right exists exclusively for the person entitled is to be verified in any institution of private law it could only be *property,* and this is as a matter of fact the prevailing conception. . . .

It is . . . not true that property involves in its "idea" the absolute power of disposition

. . . The "idea" of property cannot contain anything which is in contradiction with the "idea" of society. This standpoint is a last remnant of that unhealthy conception of the Law of Nature which isolated the individual as a being all apart. It needs no proof to show where it would lead to if an owner could retire to his property as to an inaccessible fortress. The resistance of a single person would prevent the construction of a public road or a railway; the laying out of fortifications—works upon which may depend the well-being of thousands the prosperity of an entire province, perhaps the safety of the State . . . The principle of the inviolability of property means the delivery of society into the hands of ignorance, obstinacy and spite. . . .

. . . There will come a time when property will bear another form than it does at present; when society will no more recognize the alleged right of the individual to gather together as much as possible of the goods of this world . . . Private property and the right of inheritance will always remain, and the socialistic and communistic ideas directed to its removal I regard as vain folly. But we must have little confidence in the skill of our financial artists if we think they cannot succeed, through increased taxes . . . in exerting a pressure upon private property which will prevent an excess of its accumulation at single points . . . This will bring about a distribution of the goods of this world more in accord with the interests of society, *i.e., more just* than has been and must be affected under the influence of a theory of property which, if it is to be called by its right name, is the *insatiability and voraciousness of egoism.* . . .

I have drawn up the account of the individual, as I have promised. It says, you have nothing for yourself alone, everywhere society or, as the respresentative of its interests, the law, stands by your side. Everywhere society is your partner, desiring a share in all that you have; in yourself, in your labor power, in your body, in your children, in your fortune. Law is the realized partnership of the individual and society. . . .

. . . John Stuart Mill undertook in his work on *Liberty* to assign the law its limits. . . .

The formula which Mill sets up for the attitude of the law toward the individual is . . . as follows: "The sole end for which mankind are warranted, individually or collectively, in interfering with the liberty of action of any of their number, is self-protection . . . The only purpose for which power can be rightfully exercised over any member of a civilized community, against his will, is to prevent harm to others. His own good, either physical or moral, is not a sufficient warrant . . . In the part which merely concerns himself, his independence is, of right, absolute." . . .

But all acts of sufficient meaning to make it worth our while raising this question at all extend in their effects to others. . . . I know of no example of a legal rule which has as its purpose to force an individual against his own will in his *own* interest for his good. Where it appears to do so, it is always in the interest of society. . . .

Has legislation a right to fix the maximum hours of labor? Has it the right, according to the theory of freedom, to prevent the laborer if he wishes to shorten his life by excessive labor? Mill also agrees with this legal measure, the introduction of which will always redound to the credit of the enlightened and practical sense of his countrymen. He approves of the provisions for the protection of the health of the workmen and for their safety in dangerous works. But the reason he assigns,—"the principle of individual liberty is not involved here"—is again of such a nature that his whole theory can be lifted by it out of its hinges. For if the prohibition to work as much and as little as I please does not constitute an interference with my personal freedom, where does such interference begin? . . .

§14. *The Benefit of the State* . . . The *demands* which the State makes upon the individual we could designate as the demands of the *law,* because they bear the form of law, but we cannot do this in reference to the *benefits* of the State, for they do not coincide with those of the law, they extend far beyond it.

He who wishes to settle his account with the State must be careful to keep the following two questions distinct from each other. One is, do I get a corresponding equivalent for my contribution ... The other is, do not others get more than their due in proportion to me; does the distribution of the advantages of political community to all the members correspond to the principles of justice? ...

The following investigation has to do exclusively with the first question, which alone permits of abstract treatment; whereas the second can be answered only in reference to given historical conditions. Only so much must be quite generally admitted for the second question also, *viz.,* that there have not been wanting examples in history of the kind of social injustice which favors one class of the population at the expense of the other. ...

Although it is true that justice is the vital principle of society and hence the highest purpose which it has to realize, still it would be mistaken to refuse to recognize that there may be situations in the life of nations when social injustice may have a temporary and relative justification and necessity ... Better slavery than slaughter of the enemy; better a society established on the basis of inequality of rights than bare force and lawlessness. ...

I shall now return to the *first* question. ...

What does the State give me? ...

The *first* thing the State gives me is protection against injury from without. ...

The *second* good is protection within the State, namely, law. ...

The *third* good which the State gives to its members consists in all those public arrangements and plans which it brings to life in the interest of society. There seems to be a certain amount of opposition in reference to these. What benefit does the peasant derive from universities, libraries, museums? And yet he must contribute his share, be it ever so small. But if he charges these institutions to the scholar, the latter charges him with those devoted to *his* interests and for which the scholar must pay his contribution. And then, how insignificant are these contributions, and how valuable they prove ultimately for the whole of society, and hence also for him! ...

§15. *Solidarity of the Interests of Society and the Individual* ... The State is the individual himself ... The State he has in common with all other citizens ... If the State were myself, the individual will reply, it would not have to compel me to do all that it requires of me, for I care for myself for the sake of my own interest, and do not have to be compelled.

When the child is forced by the teacher to learn, is it done for the sake of the child or the teacher? And yet the child must be compelled. Why? Because he is still a child. If he were grown up, he would do from his own impulse what he requires compulsion to do now. So the State compels you to do that which, if you had the true insight, you would do of your own accord. ...

Upon the presence or absence of this insight is based the political maturity and immaturity of nations ... True politics defined in a word is *far-sightedness.* ...

Law may be defined as the union of the intelligent and far-sighted against the near-sighted. The former must force the latter to that which their own interest prompts. Not for their own sake, to make them happy against their will, but in the interest of the whole. ...

The result with which the discussion closes is *the social indispensability of coercion.*

But however indispensable it may be, it is also at the same time *insufficient.* If it should attain its purpose completely, there would have to be no crimes ... What keeps a man from committing an injustice where he knows that he will not be found out and need not therefore fear compulsion? ... The two egoistic levers of which society makes use to make the individual serviceable to its purposes, are not the only ones. There is still another, which appeals not to the lower egoism, but to something higher in man—*morality.*

17

Oliver Wendell Holmes, Jr.
1841–1935

Wendell Holmes was a lanky, quiet son of a small, cocky New England doctor. Oliver, Sr. was a Harvard professor of anatomy, a practitioner whose wit often repelled paying patients, and a distinguished (but sometimes too-precious) poet and essayist.

When Wendell was ready for secondary school Dr. Holmes sent him to a schoolmaster named Dixwell who had just left public Boston Latin School to open his own small and expensive private school. Latin School was well thought of, but Dr. Holmes did not approve the frequent use of the strap on its students. Dixwell's pupils were exposed mainly to Latin and Greek; mathematics was grudgingly taught, and his students got a smattering of French, but no modern history, no science, and, of course, no social studies. Wendell's marks were unexceptional.

At sixteen the young Bostonian aristocrat entered Harvard—without, of course, considering other alternatives. He continued to live at home and commuted between Boston and Cambridge by horse-car. The four hundred Harvard students were closely supervised, and subjected mostly to rote memory of the classics. The biologic scientists were making a vigorous beginning, but were not yet much recognized. Wendell's mind, nevertheless, ranged and he cultivated many interests on his own. He was in the top third of his class, and his third year average was good enough to get him into Phi Beta Kappa. He took no part in formal athletics, but enjoyed long rambling walks, and went to skating parties followed by much beer and many oysters. He wrote for Harvard undergraduate publications on literature, philos-

ophy, and art. One of these pieces presaged his skepticism; in it he adjured his fellows to read books for their ideas, rather than their authors.

Holmes' youth was a time of mounting tension over slavery. Wendell at twelve read *Uncle Tom's Cabin* hot off the press. Fugitive slaves were captured, imprisoned, tried, and rioted-over within blocks of the Holmes house during Wendell's teens. In April of 1861, Confederate forces bombarded Ft. Sumter. Twelve days later Wendell Holmes, then a Harvard senior, enlisted in the Union Army. His company was stationed in Cambridge long enough for him to graduate two months later and recite as class poet in the closing exercises. It is said that he learned of his lieutenant's commission, which came through just before his regiment went south, "as he was walking down Beacon Hill with Hobbes' *Leviathan* in his hand." He had a full dose of war, glamorous, boring, harrowing, sickening, and dangerous. He was wounded three times—each time miraculously barely escaping death or serious maiming. After each wound he was invalided back to Cambridge for convalescence. When his third wound healed he was made an aide to Brigadier General Wright, who defended the District of Columbia against a thrust of Jubal Early's forces. Lincoln came to Ft. Stevens to watch the battle. When Lincoln exposed himself to fire on a dangerous vantage point, Holmes spoke the only words he ever said to Lincoln: "Get down you fool." In July of 1864 Holmes' three-year enlistment expired and he was mustered out as a Lieutenant Colonel. Lee's surrender in

418

April of 1865 out-moded his plan to re-enlist.

Soon after he was discharged, twenty-three year old Holmes, over his father's mild objection, enrolled in Harvard Law School, not yet come to the greatness it was soon to achieve under Langdell. Three elderly practicing lawyers gave dogmatic lectures. There were virtually no entrance requirements. After eighteen months of attendance students got degrees without taking examinations. Holmes supplemented this dry training with afternoon clerking in a law office where theory was translated into more meaningful action.

In this post-war school period Holmes' third-floor room in his father's house was often the site of lively evening bull sessions with William James, Charles Pierce, John Chipman Gray, and a dozen other brilliant young men. Talk on round and important topics was seasoned with whiskey and rolled through blue pipe smoke.

Holmes was admitted to the bar in 1866, and though he worked hard and learned the routine of general practice, he participated in no outstanding litigation and made little money in the next several years. Practice bored him; his real enthusiasm for law was as a student of its larger aspects. His first important legal writing was a new edition of Kent's, *Commentaries on American Law,* which had not been brought down to date for twenty-five years. The apprentice lawyer could work on the *Commentaries* only at night; his absorption grew, and he became more and more sharp tempered as his writing drained his energies. He was obsessed with fear he would lose the manuscript, and carried it with him wherever he went. Fortunately an older adviser insisted that Holmes abandon attempt at perfection and finish up the job. In 1870 his legal scholarship was recognized when he was made a lecturer on constitutional law at the Harvard Law School (probably at the behest of young President Charles Eliot, who liked Holmes' scientific, skeptical outlook). This was no professorship; it was only an ill-paid toe-hold on teaching. The next summer Holmes wrote *Codes and the Arrangement of Law*

for the American Law Review; it was so well received that he was made editor of the Review—for which he wrote much in the next three years.

At thirty Holmes was still not financially independent. Nevertheless he married his old school-master's daughter, Fanny Dixwell, and brought her to live in his father's house. A year later he was taken into a law firm and began to earn money enough for bed and board. The couple moved into rooms over a drug store, taking most meals out. Dinner was usually at the Parker House where they often met friends, opened a bottle of wine, and had a gay time.

Holmes was invited to deliver a series of twelve lectures at Lowell Institute in the winter of 1880-81. As he prepared for them his ideas unified and took significant form. These lectures were afterwards published in book form and called *The Common Law—* Holmes' best known systematic work. He left the analytical traditions to look at law institutionally. He saw law as embodying "the story of a nation's development" and said at the outset of his lectures, "The life of the law has not been logic, it has been experience. The felt necessities of the time, the prevalent moral and political theories, intuitions of public policy, avowed or unconscious, even the prejudices which judges share with their fellow men, have a good deal more to do than the syllogism in determining the rules by which men should be governed." His book was well reviewed, and his lectures were well received by an audience that included the newly vitalized Harvard Law faculty and Harvard's President Eliot. It was a fortunate time to make a good impression, for shortly afterward a Harvard graduate endowed a new chair of law, and it was given to Holmes. He taught well and with enjoyment in the autumn of 1882. At the law school he first came to know Brandeis, who was then a young lecturer.

When Holmes accepted Harvard's call he specified he was to be free to take a judicial appointment if and when one was tendered. An offer came sooner than either he or Eliot expected. At turn of the year he accepted a place on the Massachusetts Supreme Court. He was then forty-two and for the first time, made a good living. On his six thousand dollar salary he could afford a comfortable home; he and Fanny left their suite of rooms for a Beacon Hill house staffed with two servants.

Deaths in the family left Dr. Holmes alone in his big house, and after enjoying only six years in their own home, Fanny and Wendell moved in to take care of him. Wendell Holmes had lived too long in the shadow of the Doctor, irked by his chattering, galled by his egotism, revolted by his literary exposure of family privacy. Wendell made himself get along with his father in the old Doctor's last five years, but he stayed out of the doctor's way as much as he could. Wendell and Fanny stayed on in the old Holmes house after the Doctor's death, expansively and in comfort. But Fanny's health and confidence seemed to fail. The Judge increasingly went about in Boston society without her. His social triumphs became greater and greater.

In 1899 Holmes, then forty-eight, was elevated to Chief Justice of Massachusetts. He had written more than a thousand opinions. Many were routine. A few were dissents. All were well written and showed judicial restraint, especially when constitutionality of statutes was attacked. He was thought of as a liberal because he dissented both when the court enjoined peaceful picketing and when the court gave an opinion that a proposal to enable towns to deal in coal and wood was unconstitutional. Actually, he was an aristocrat who did not share middle-class commercial views and who believed that courts should not impose their economic and social theories on the people.

Holmes' reputation for being a liberal and his Massachusetts residence drew Theodore Roosevelt's attention to him when Justice Gray retired from the United States Supreme Court in 1902. Theodore Roosevelt, thinking Holmes' politics to be much like his own, offered him the appointment. Wendell hesitated, but Fanny had no doubts, and he accepted. Fanny's social importance as a Supreme Court Justice's wife, rekindled her

confidence. The two of them were immediate social successes in Washington and made a great hit at the White House. Soon Roosevelt was disappointed with Holmes and turned cool to him. The first big trust-busting case that Theodore Roosevelt's administration brought before the Supreme Court was the *Northern Securities Case.* Holmes wrote the dissenting opinion disagreeing with the majority's holding that a railroad combination had run afoul of the Sherman Anti-Trust Act. This was the first in a long series of great dissents. Holmes often differed from his brethren, showing two main traits: (1) a toleration for legislative social experiment even though he thought it unwise and (2) intolerance of invasions of civil rights, especially the right of free speech.

One Holmes innovation was hiring bright young law school graduates as his clerks. He took a new one each year from the graduating class of Harvard Law School. Many of these young lawyers grew to tower tall in the practice and in public service. Nowadays most of the judiciary follow his example and recruit their clerks from ranks of high standing recent graduates.

In 1921 Taft succeeded White as Chief Justice. Taft looked on Holmes with little respect and did not make his life especially pleasant. Taft thought Holmes too old to be on the bench and always referred to him as "the old gentleman"; on occasions Taft insinuated that Holmes' presence on the court gave Brandeis two votes. But Holmes stayed vigorous and unmovable and was still serving on the court two years after Taft's death. The story is told that on Holmes' eighty-seventh birthday (when he became the oldest man ever to sit on the court) a Washington inquiring reporter set out to ask the man in the street whether he knew who Holmes was. He put his question to a man in overalls who was reading a sports page in Capitol Square. The man replied, "Holmes? Oh, sure. He's the young guy on the Supreme Court who always disagrees with the old guys."

In 1929 Fanny died, and Holmes' friends feared for him. But he made a pretty good adjustment and managed six more fairly good years before he died—two days before he was ninety-four. He stayed on the court until he was ninety-one. In the last months of 1931 he did not always pay the attention he should. On January 11, 1932 he faltered when trying to read an opinion from the bench. When court rose that afternoon, he put on his hat and coat, walked to the clerk's desk and said, "I won't be down tomorrow." That night he sent his resignation to the President.

Materials that follow are *The Path of the Law,* a talk to students at Boston University Law School given in 1897, and *Natural Law,* a law review note published first in 1918. Both are unabridged.

THE PATH OF THE LAW *

When we study law we are not studying a mystery but a well-known profession. We are studying what we shall want in order to appear before judges, or to advise people in such a way as to keep them out of court. The reason why it is a profession, why people will pay lawyers to argue for them or to advise them, is that in societies like ours the command of the public force is intrusted to the judges in certain cases, and the whole power of the state will be put forth, if necessary, to carry out their judgments and decrees. People want to know under what circumstances and how far they will run the risk of coming against what is so much stronger than themselves, and hence it becomes a business to find out when this danger is to be feared. The object of our study, then, is prediction, the prediction of the incidence of the public force through the instrumentality of the courts.

The means of the study are a body of reports, of treatises, and of statutes, in this country and in England, extending back for six hundred years, and now increasing annually by hundreds. In these sibylline leaves are gathered the scattered prophecies of the past upon the cases in which the axe will

* From 10 Harvard Law Review 457. Reprinted by permission of The Harvard Law Review.

fall. These are what properly have been called the oracles of the law. Far the most important and pretty nearly the whole meaning of every new effort of legal thought is to make these prophecies more precise, and to generalize them into a thoroughly connected system. The process is one, from a lawyer's statement of a case, eliminating as it does all the dramatic elements with which his client's story has clothed it, and retaining only the facts of legal import, up to the final analyses and abstract universals of theoretic jurisprudence. The reason why a lawyer does not mention that his client wore a white hat when he made a contract, while Mrs. Quickly would be sure to dwell upon it along with the parcel gilt goblet and the sea-coal fire, is that he foresees that the public force will act in the same way whatever his client had upon his head. It is to make the prophecies easier to be remembered and to be understood that the teachings of the decisions of the past are put into general propositions and gathered into text-books, or that statutes are passed in a general form. The primary rights and duties with which jurisprudence busies itself again are nothing but prophecies. One of the many evil effects of the confusion between legal and moral ideas, about which I shall have something to say in a moment, is that theory is apt to get the cart before the horse, and to consider the right or the duty as something existing apart from and independent of the consequences of its breach, to which certain sanctions are added afterward. But, as I shall try to show, a legal duty so called is nothing but a prediction that if a man does or omits certain things he will be made to suffer in this or that way by judgment of the court; and so of a legal right.

The number of our predictions when generalized and reduced to a system is not unmanageably large. They present themselves as a finite body of dogma which may be mastered within a reasonable time. It is a great mistake to be frightened by the ever-increasing number of reports. The reports of a given jurisdiction in the course of a generation take up pretty much the whole body of the law, and restate it from the present point of view. We could reconstruct the corpus from them if all that went before were burned. The use of the earlier reports is mainly historical, a use about which I shall have something to say before I have finished.

I wish, if I can, to lay down some first principles for the study of this body of dogma or systematized prediction which we call the law, for men who want to use it as the instrument of their business to enable them to prophesy in their turn, and, as bearing upon the study, I wish to point out an ideal which as yet our law has not attained.

The first thing for a business-like understanding of the matter is to understand its limits, and therefore I think it desirable at once to point out and dispel a confusion between morality and law, which sometimes rises to the height of conscious theory, and more often and indeed constantly is making trouble in detail without reaching the point of consciousness. You can see very plainly that a bad man has as much reason as a good one for wishing to avoid an encounter with the public force, and therefore you can see the practical importance of the distinction between morality and law. A man who cares nothing for an ethical rule which is believed and practised by his neighbors is likely nevertheless to care a good deal to avoid being made to pay money, and will want to keep out of jail if he can.

I take it for granted that no hearer of mine will misinterpret what I have to say as the language of cynicism. The law is the witness and external deposit of our moral life. Its history is the history of the moral development of the race. The practice of it, in spite of popular jests, tends to make good citizens and good men. When I emphasize the difference between law and morals I do so with reference to a single end, that of learning and understanding the law. For that purpose you must definitely master its specific marks, and it is for that I ask you for the moment to imagine yourselves indifferent to other and greater things.

I do not say that there is not a wider point of view from which the distinction between law and morals becomes of secondary or no importance, as all mathematical distinctions vanish in presence of the infinite. But I do say that that distinction is of the first importance for the object which we are here to consider—a right study and mastery of the law as a business with well understood limits, a body of dogma enclosed within definite lines. I have just shown the practical reason for saying so. If you want to know the law and nothing else, you must look at it as a bad man, who cares only for the material consequences which such knowledge enables him to predict, not as a good one, who finds his reasons for conduct, whether inside the law or outside of it, in the vaguer sanctions of conscience. The theoretical importance of the distinction is no less, if you would reason on your subject aright. The law is full of phraseology drawn from morals, and by the mere force of language continually invites us to pass from one domain to the other without perceiving it, as we are sure to do unless we have the boundary constantly before our minds. The law talks about rights, and duties, and malice, and intent, and negligence, and so forth, and nothing is easier, or, I may say, more common in legal reasoning, than to take these words in their moral sense, at some stage of the argument, and so to drop into fallacy. For instance, when we speak of the rights of man in a moral sense, we mean to mark the limits of interference with individual freedom which we think are prescribed by conscience, or by our ideal, however reached. Yet it is certain that many laws have been enforced in the past, and it is likely that some are enforced now, which are condemned by the most enlightened opinion of the time, or which at all events pass the limit of interference as many consciences would draw it. Manifestly, therefore, nothing but confusion of thought can result from assuming that the rights of man in a moral sense are equally rights in the sense of the Constitution and the law. No doubt simple and extreme cases can be put of imaginable laws which the statute-making power would not dare to enact, even in the absence of written constitutional prohibitions, because the community would rise in rebellion and fight; and this gives some plausibility to the proposition that the law, if not a part of morality, is limited by it. But this limit of power is not coextensive with any system of morals. For the most part it falls far within the lines of any such system, and in some cases may extend beyond them, for reasons drawn from the habits of a particular people at a particular time. I once heard the late Professor Agassiz say that a German population would rise if you added two cents to the price of a glass of beer. A statute in such a case would be empty words, not because it was wrong, but because it could not be enforced. No one will deny that wrong statutes can be and are enforced, and we should not all agree as to which were the wrong ones.

The confusion with which I am dealing besets confessedly legal conceptions. Take the fundamental question, What constitutes the law? You will find some text writers telling you that it is something different from what is decided by the courts of Massachusetts or England, that it is a system of reason, that it is a deduction from principles of ethics or admitted axioms or what not, which may or may not coincide with the decisions. But if we take the view of our friend the bad man we shall find that he does not care two straws for the axioms or deductions, but that he does want to know what the Massachusetts or English courts are likely to do in fact. I am much of his mind. The prophecies of what the courts will do in fact, and nothing more pretentious, are what I mean by the law.

Take again a notion which as popularly understood is the widest conception which the law contains—the notion of legal duty, to which already I have referred. We fill the word with all the content which we draw from morals. But what does it mean to a bad man? Mainly, and in the first place, a prophecy that if he does certain things he will be subjected to disagreeable consequences by way of imprisonment or compulsory payment of money. But from his point of view, what is the difference between being fined and being taxed a certain sum for doing a certain thing? That his point of view is the test of legal principles is shown by the many discussions which have arisen in the courts on the very question whether a given statutory liability is a penalty or a tax. On the answer to this question depends the decision whether conduct is legally wrong or right, and also whether a man is under compulsion or free. Leaving the criminal law on one side, what is the difference between the liability under the mill acts or statutes authorizing a taking by eminent domain and the liability for what we call a wrongful conversion of property where restoration is out of the question. In both cases the party taking another man's property has to pay its fair value as assessed by a jury, and no more. What significance is there in calling one taking right and another wrong from the point of view of the law? It does not matter, so far as the given consequence, the compulsory payment, is concerned, whether the act to which it is attached is described in terms of praise or in terms of blame, or whether the law purports to prohibit it or to allow it. If it matters at all, still speaking from the bad man's point of view, it must be because in one case and not in the other some further disadvantages, or at least some further consequences, are attached to the act by the law. The only other disadvantages thus attached to it which I ever have been able to think of are to be found in two somewhat insignificant legal doctrines, both of which might be abolished without disturbance. One is, that a contract to do a prohibited act is unlawful, and the other, that, if one of two or more joint wrongdoers has to pay all the damages, he cannot recover contribution from his fellows. And that I believe is all. You see how the vague circumference of the notion of duty shrinks and at the same time grows more precise when we wash it with cynical acid and expel everything except the object of our study, the operations of the law.

Nowhere is the confusion between legal and moral ideas more manifest than in the law of contract. Among other things, here again the so called primary rights and duties are invested with a mystic significance beyond what can be assigned and explained. The duty to keep a contract at common law means a prediction that you must pay damages if you do not keep it—and nothing else. If you commit a tort, you are liable to pay a compensatory sum. If you commit a contract, you are liable to pay a compensatory sum unless the promised event comes to pass, and that is all the difference. But such a mode of looking at the matter stinks in the nostrils of those who think it advantageous to get as much ethics into the law as they can. It was good enough for Lord Coke, however, and here, as in many other cases, I am content to abide with him. In *Bromage v. Genning*,[1] [1 Roll. Rep. 368] a prohibition was sought in the King's Bench against a suit in the marches of Wales for the specific performance of a covenant to grant a lease, and Coke said that it would subvert the intention of the covenantor, since he intends it to be at his election either to lose the damages or to make the lease. Sergeant Harris for the plaintiff confessed that he moved the matter against his conscience, and a prohibition was granted. This goes further than we should go now, but it shows what I venture to say has been the common law point of view from the beginning, although Mr. Harriman, in his very able little book upon Contracts has been misled, as I humbly think, to a different conclusion.

I have spoken only of the common law, because there are some cases in which a logical justification can be found for speaking of civil liabilities as imposing duties in an intelligible sense. These are the relatively few in which equity will grant an injunction, and will enforce it by putting the defendant in prison or otherwise punishing him unless he complies with the order of the court. But I hardly think it advisable to shape general theory from the exception, and I think it would be better to cease troubling ourselves about primary rights and sanctions altogether, than to describe our prophecies concerning the liabilities commonly imposed by the law in those inappropriate terms.

I mentioned, as other examples of the use by the law of words drawn from morals, malice, intent, and negligence. It is enough to take malice as it is used in the law of civil liability for wrongs—what we lawyers call the law of torts—to show that it means something different in law from what it means in morals, and also to show how the difference has been obscured by giving to principles which have little or nothing to do with each other the same name. Three hundred years ago a parson preached a sermon and told a story out of Fox's *Book of Martyrs* of a man who had assisted at the torture of one of the saints, and afterward died, suffering compensatory inward torment. It happened that Fox was wrong. The man was alive and chanced to hear the sermon, and thereupon he sued the parson. Chief Justice Wray instructed the jury that the defendant was not liable, because the story was told innocently, without malice. He took malice in the moral sense, as importing a malevolent motive. But nowadays no one doubts that a man may be liable, without any malevolent motive at all, for false statements manifestly calculated to inflict temporal damage. In stating the case in pleading, we still should call the defendant's conduct malicious; but, in my opinion at least, the word means nothing about motives, or even about the defendant's attitude toward the future, but only signifies that the tendency of his conduct under the known circumstances was very plainly to cause the plaintiff temporal harm.[2] [2 See *Hanson v. Globe Newspaper Co.,* 159 Mass. 293, 302.]

In the law of contract the use of moral phraseology has led to equal confusion, as I have shown in part already, but only in part. Morals deal with the actual internal state of the individual's mind, what he actually intends. From the time of the Romans down to now, this mode of dealing has affected the language of the law as to contract, and the language used has reacted upon the thought. We talk about a contract as a meeting of the minds of the parties, and thence it is inferred in various cases that there is no contract because their minds have not met; that is, because they have intended different things or because one party has not known of the assent of the other. Yet nothing is more certain than that parties may be bound by a contract to things which neither of them intended, and when one does not know of the other's assent. Suppose a contract is executed in due form and in writing to deliver a lecture, mentioning no time. One of the parties thinks that the promise will be construed to mean at once, within a week. The other thinks that it means when he is ready. The court says that it means within a reasonable time. The parties are bound by the contract as it is interpreted by the court, yet neither of them meant what the court declares that they have said. In my opinion no one will understand the true theory of contract or be able even to discuss some fundamental questions intelligently until he has understood that all contracts are formal, that the making of a contract depends not on the agreement of two minds in one intention, but on the agreement of two sets of external signs—not on the parties' having *meant* the same thing but on their having *said* the same thing. Furthermore, as the signs may be addressed to one sense or another—to sight or to hearing—on the nature of the sign will depend the moment when the contract is made. If the sign is tangible, for instance, a letter, the contract is made when the letter of acceptance is delivered. If it is necessary that the minds of the parties meet, there will be no contract until the acceptance can be read—none, for example, if the acceptance be snatched from the hand of the offerer by a third person.

This is not the time to work out a theory in detail, or to answer many obvious doubts and questions which are suggested by these general views. I know of none which are not easy to answer, but what I am trying to do now is only by a series of hints to throw some light on the narrow path of legal doctrine, and upon two pitfalls which, as it seems to me, lie perilously near to it. Of the first of these I have said enough. I hope that my illustrations have shown the danger, both to speculation and to practice, of confounding morality with law, and the trap which legal language lays for us on that side of our way. For my own part, I often doubt whether it would not be a gain if every word of moral significance could be banished from the law altogether, and other words adopted which should convey legal ideas uncolored by anything outside the law. We should lose the fossil records of a good deal of history and the majesty got from ethical associations, but by ridding ourselves of an unnecessary confusion we should gain very much in the clearness of our thought.

So much for the limits of the law. The next thing which I wish to consider is what are the forces which determine its content and its growth. You may assume, with Hobbes and Bentham and Austin, that all law emanates from the sovereign, even when the first human beings to enunciate it are the judges, or you may think that law is the voice of the Zeitgeist, or what you like. It is all one to my present purpose. Even if every decision required the sanction of an emperor with despotic power and a whimsical turn of mind, we should be interested none the less, still with a view to prediction, in discovering some order, some rational explanation, and some principle of growth for the rules which he laid down. In every system there are such explanations and principles to be found. It is with regard to them that a second fallacy comes in, which I think it important to expose.

The fallacy to which I refer is the notion that the only force at work in the development of the law is logic. In the broadest sense, indeed, that notion would be true. The postulate on which we think about the universe is that there is a fixed quantitative relation between every phenomenon and its antecedents and consequents. If there is such a thing as a phenomenon without these fixed quantitative relations, it is a miracle. It is outside the law of cause and effect, and as such transcends our power of thought, or at least is something to or from which we cannot reason. The condition of our thinking about the universe is that it is capable of being thought about rationally, or, in other words, that every part of it is effect and cause in the same sense in which those parts are with which we are most familiar. So in the broadest sense it is true that the law is a logical development, like everything else. The danger of which I speak is not the admission that the principles governing other phenomena also govern the law, but the notion that a given system, ours, for instance, can be worked out like mathematics from some general axioms of conduct. This is the natural error of the schools, but it is not confined to them. I once heard a very eminent judge say that he never let a decision go until he was absolutely sure that it was right. So judicial dissent often is blamed, as if it meant simply that one side or the other were not doing their sums right, and, if they would take more trouble, agreement inevitably would come.

This mode of thinking is entirely natural. The training of lawyers is a training in logic. The processes of analogy, discrimination, and deduction are those in which they are most at home. The language of judicial decision is mainly the language of logic. And the logical method and form flatter that longing for certainty and for repose which is in every human mind. But certainty generally is illusion, and repose is not the destiny of man. Behind the logical form lies a judgment as to the relative worth and importance of competing legislative grounds, often an inarticulate and unconscious judgment, it is true, and yet the very root and nerve of the whole proceeding. You can give any conclusion a logical form. You always can imply a condition in a contract. But why do you imply it? It is because of some belief as to the practice of the community or of a class, or because of some opinion as to policy, or, in short, because of some attitude of yours upon a matter not capable of exact quantitative measurement, and therefore not capable of founding exact logical conclusions. Such matters really are battle grounds where the means do not exist for determinations that shall be good for all time, and where the decision can do no more than embody the preference of a given body in a given time and place. We do not realize how large a part of our law is open to reconsideration upon a slight change in the habit of the public mind. No concrete proposition is self evident, no matter how ready we may be to accept it, not even Mr. Herbert Spencer's "Every man has a right to do what he wills, provided he interferes not with a like right on the part of his neighbors."

Why is a false and injurious statement privileged, if it is made honestly in giving information about a servant. It is because it has been thought more important that information should be given freely, than that a man should be protected from what under other circumstances would be an actionable wrong. Why is a man at liberty to set up a business which he knows will ruin his neighbor? It is because the public good is supposed to be best subserved be free competition. Obviously such judgments of relative importance may vary in different times and places. Why does a judge instruct a jury that an employer is not liable to an employee for an injury received in the course of his employment unless he is negligent, and why do the jury generally find for the plaintiff if the case is allowed to go to them? It is because the traditional policy of our law is to confine liability to cases where a prudent man might have foreseen the injury, or at least the danger, while the inclination of a very large part of the community is to make certain classes of persons insure the safety of those with whom they deal. Since the last words were written, I have seen the requirement of such insurance put forth as part of the programme of one of the best known labor organizations. There is a concealed, half conscious battle on the question of legislative policy, and if any one thinks that it can be settled deductively, or once for all, I only can say that I think he is theoretically wrong, and that I am certain that his conclusion will not be accepted in practice *semper ubique et ab omnibus.*

Indeed, I think that even now our theory upon this matter is open to reconsideration, although I am not prepared to say how I should decide if a reconsideration were proposed. Our law of torts comes from the old days of isolated, ungeneralized wrongs, assaults, slanders, and the like, where the damages might be taken to lie where they fell by legal judgment. But the torts with which our courts are kept busy to-day are mainly the incidents of certain well known businesses. They are injuries to person or property by railroads, factories, and the like. The liability for them is estimated, and sooner or later goes into the price paid by the public. The public really pays the damages, and the question of liability, if pressed far enough, is really the question how far it is desirable that the public should insure the safety of those whose work it uses. It might be said that in such cases the chance of a jury finding for the defendant is merely a chance, once in a while rather arbitrarily interrupting the regular course of recovery, most likely in the case of an unusually conscientious plaintiff, and therefore better done away with. On the other hand, the economic value even of a life to the community can be estimated, and no recovery, it may be said, ought to go beyond that amount. It is conceivable that some day in certain cases we may find ourselves imitating, on a higher plane, the tariff for life and limb which we see in the *Leges Barbarorum.*

I think that the judges themselves have failed adequately to recognize their duty of weighing considerations of social advantage. The duty is inevitable, and the result of the often proclaimed judicial aversion to deal with such considerations is simply to leave the very ground and foundation of judgments inarticulate, and often unconscious, as I have said. When socialism first began to be talked about, the comfortable classes of the community were a good deal frightened. I suspect that this fear has influenced judicial action both here and in England, yet it is certain that it is not a conscious factor in the decisions to which I refer. I think that something similar has led people who no longer hope to control the legislatures to look to the courts as expounders of the Constitutions, and that in some courts new principles have been discovered outside the bodies of those instruments, which may be generalized into acceptance of the economic doctrines which prevailed about fifty years ago, and a wholesale prohibition of what a tribunal of lawyers does not think about right. I cannot but believe that if the training of lawyers led them habitually to consider more definitely and explicitly the social advantage on which the rule they lay down must be justified, they sometimes would hesitate where now they are confident, and see that really they were taking sides upon debatable and often burning questions.

So much for the fallacy of logical form. Now let us consider the present condition of the law as a subject for study, and the ideal toward which it tends. We still are far from the point of view which I desire to see reached. No one has reached it or can reach it as yet. We are only at the beginning of a philosophical reaction, and of a reconsideration of the worth of doctrines which for the most part still are taken for granted without any deliberate, conscious, and systematic questioning of their grounds. The development of our law has gone on for nearly a thousand years, like the development of a plant, each generation taking the inevitable next step, mind, like matter, simply obeying a law of spontaneous growth. It is perfectly natural and right that it should have been so. Imitation is a necessity of human nature, as has been illustrated by a remarkable French writer, M. Tarde, in an admirable book, *Les Lois de l'Imitation.* Most of the things we do, we do for no better reason than that our fathers have done them or that our neighbors do them, and the same is true of a larger part than we suspect of what we think. The reason is a good one, because our short life gives us no time for a better, but it is not the best. It does not follow, because we all are compelled to take on faith at second hand most of the rules on which we base our action and our thought, that each of us may not try to set some corner of his world in the order of reason, or that all of us collectively should not aspire to carry reason as far as it will go throughout the whole domain. In regard to the law, it is true, no doubt, that an evolutionist will hesitate to affirm universal validity for his social ideals, or for the principles which he thinks should be embodied in legislation. He is content if he can prove them best for here and now. He may be ready to admit that he knows nothing about an absolute best in the cosmos, and even that he knows next to nothing about a permanent best for men. Still it is true that a body of law is more rational and more civilized when every rule it contains is referred articulately and definitely to an end which it subserves, and when the grounds for desiring that end are stated or are ready to be stated in words.

At present, in very many cases, if we want to know why a rule of law has taken its particular shape, and more or less if we want to know why it exists at all, we go to tradition. We follow it into the Year Books, and perhaps beyond them to the customs of the Salian Franks, and somewhere in the past, in the German forests, in the needs of Norman kings, in the assumptions of a dominant class, in the absence of generalized ideas, we find out the practical motive for what now best is justified by the mere fact of its acceptance and that men are accustomed to it. The rational study of law is still to a large extent the study of history. History must be a part of the study, because without it we cannot know the precise scope of rules which it is our business to know. It is a part of the rational study, because it is the first step toward an enlightened scepticism, that is, towards a deliberate reconsideration of the worth of those rules. When you get the dragon out of his cave on to the plain and in the daylight, you can count his teeth and claws, and see just what is his strength. But to get him out is only the first step. The next is either to kill him, or to tame him and make him a useful animal. For the rational study of the law the black-letter man may be the man of the present, but the man of the future is the man of statistics and the master of economics. It is revolting to have no better reason for a rule of law than that so it was laid down in the time of Henry IV. It is still more revolting if the grounds upon which it was laid down have vanished long since, and the rule simply persists from blind imitation of the past. I am thinking of the technical rule as to trespass *ab initio*, as it is called, which I attempted to explain in a recent Massachusetts case.[3] [3 *Commonwealth v. Rubin*, 165 Mass. 453.]

Let me take an illustration, which can be stated in a few words, to show how the social end which is aimed at by a rule of law is obscured and only partially attained in consequence of the fact that the rule owes its form to a gradual historical development, instead of being reshaped as a whole, with conscious articulate reference to the end in view. We think it desirable to prevent one man's property being misappropriated by another, and so we make larceny a crime. The evil is the same whether the misappropriation is made by a man into whose hands the owner has put the property, or by one who wrongfully takes it away. But primitive law in its weaknesss did not get much beyond an effort to prevent violence, and very naturally made a wrongful taking, a trespass, part of its definition of the crime. In modern times the judges enlarged the definition a little by holding that, if the wrongdoer gets possession by a trick or device, the crime is committed. This really was giving up the requirement of a trespass, and it would have been more logical, as well as truer to the present object of the law, to abandon the requirement altogether. That, however, would have seemed too bold, and was left to statute. Statutes were passed making embezzlement a crime. But the force of tradition caused the crime of embezzlement to be regarded as so far distinct from larceny that to this day, in some jurisdictions at least, a slip corner is kept open for thieves to contend, if indicted for larceny, that they should have been indicted for embezzlement, and if indicted for embezzlement, that they should have been indicted for larceny, and to escape on that ground.

Far more fundamental questions still await a better answer than that we do as our fathers have done. What have we better than a blind guess to show that the criminal law in its present form does more good than harm? I do not stop to refer to the effect which it has had in degrading prisoners and in plunging them further into crime, or to the question whether fine and imprisonment do not fall more heavily on a criminal's wife and children than on himself. I have in mind more far-reaching questions. Does punishment deter? Do we deal with criminals on proper principles? A modern school of continental criminalists plumes itself on the formula, first suggested, it is said, by Gall, that we must consider the criminal rather than the crime. The formula does not carry us very far, but the inquiries which have been started look toward an answer of my questions based on science for the first time. If the typical criminal is a degenerate, bound to swindle or to murder by as deep-seated an organic necessity as that which makes the rattlesnake bite, it is idle to talk of deterring him by the classical method of imprisonment. He must be got rid of; he cannot be improved, or frightened out of his structural reaction. If, on the other hand, crime, like normal human conduct, is mainly a matter of imitation, punishment fairly may be expected to help to keep it out of fashion. The study of criminals has been thought by some well known men of science to sustain the former hypothesis. The statistics of the relative increase of crime in crowded places like large cities, where example has the greatest chance to work, and in less populated parts, where the contagion spreads more slowly, have been used with great force in favor of the latter view. But there is weighty authority for the belief that, however this may be, "not the nature of the crime, but the dangerousness of the criminal, constitutes the only reasonable legal criterion to guide the inevitable social reaction against the criminal." [4] [4 Havelock Ellis, *The Criminal*, 41, citing Garofalo. See also Ferri, *Sociologie Criminelle, passim.* Compare Tarde, *La Philosophie Penale.*]

The impediments to rational generalization, which I illustrated from the law of larceny, are shown in the other branches of the law, as well as in that of crime. Take the law of tort or civil liability for damages apart from contract and the like. Is there any general theory of such liability, or are the cases in which it exists simply to be enumerated, and to be explained each on its special ground, as is easy to believe from the fact that the right of action for certain well known classes of wrongs like trespass or slander has its special history for each class? I think that there is a general theory to be discovered, although resting in tendency rather than established and accepted. I think that the law regards the infliction of temporal damage by a responsible person as actionable, if under the circumstances known to him the danger of his act is manifest according to common experience, or according to his own experience if it is more than common, except in cases where upon special grounds of policy the law refuses to protect the plaintiff or grants a privilege to the defendant.[5] [5 An example of the law's refusing to protect the plaintiff is when he is interrupted by a stranger in the use of a valuable way, which he has travelled adversely for a week less than the period of prescription. A week later he will have gained a right, but now he is only a trespasser. Example of privilege I have given already. One of the best is competition in business.] I think that commonly malice, intent, and negligence mean only that the danger was manifest to a greater or less degree, under the circumstances known to the actor, although in some cases of privilege malice may mean an actual malevolent motive, and such a motive may take away a permission knowingly to inflict harm, which otherwise would be granted on this or that ground of dominant public good. But when I stated my view to a very eminent English judge the other day, he said: "You are discussing what the law ought to be; as the law is, you must show a right. A man is not liable for negligence unless he is subject to a duty." If our difference was more than a difference in words, or with regard to the proportion between the exceptions and the rule, then, in his opinion, liability for an act cannot be referred to the manifest tendency of the act to cause temporal damage in general as a sufficient explanation, but must be referred to the special nature of the damage, or must be derived from some special circumstances outside of the tendency of the act, for which no generalized explanation exists. I think that such a view is wrong, but it is familiar, and I dare say generally is accepted in England.

Everywhere the basis of principle is tradition, to such an extent that we even are in danger of making the role of history more important than it is. The other day Professor Ames wrote a learned article to show, among other things, that the common law did not recognize the defence of fraud in actions upon specialties, and the moral might seem to be that the personal character of that defence is due to its equitable origin. But if, as I have said, all contracts are formal, the difference is not merely historical, but theoretic, between defects of form which prevent a contract from being made, and mistaken motives which manifestly could not be considered in any system that we should call rational except against one who was privy to those motives. It is not confined to specialties, but is of universal application. I ought to add that I do not suppose that Mr. Ames would disagree with what I suggest.

However, if we consider the law of contract, we find it full of history. The distinctions between debt, covenant, and assumpsit are merely historical. The classification of certain obligations to pay money, imposed by the law irrespective of any bargain as quasi contracts, is merely historical. The doctrine of consideration is merely historical. The effect given to a seal is to be explained by history alone. Consideration is a mere form. Is it a useful form? If so, why should it not be required in all contracts? A seal is a mere form, and is vanishing in the scroll and in enactments that a consideration must be given, seal or no seal. Why should any merely historical distinction be allowed to affect the rights and obligations of business men?

Since I wrote this discourse I have come on a very good example of the way in which tradition not only overrides rational policy, but overrides it after first having been misunderstood and having been given a new and broader scope than it had when it had a meaning. It is the settled law of England that a material alteration of a written contract by a party avoids it as against him. The doctrine is contrary to the general tendency of the law. We do not tell a jury that if a man ever has lied in one particular he is to be presumed to lie in all. Even if a man has tried to defraud, it seems no sufficient reason for preventing him from proving the truth. Objections of like nature in general go to the weight, not to the admissibility, of evidence. Moreover, this rule is irrespective of fraud, and is not confined to evidence. It is not merely that you cannot use the writing, but that the contract is at an end. What does this mean? The existence of a written contract depends on the fact that the offerer and offeree have interchanged their written expressions, not on the continued existence of those expressions. But in the case of a bond, the primitive notion was different. The contract was inseparable from the parchment. If a stranger destroyed it, or tore off the seal, or altered it, the obligee could not recover, however free from fault, because the defendant's contract, that is, the actual tangible bond which he had sealed, could not be produced in the form in which it bound him. About a hundred years ago Lord Kenyon undertook to use his reason on this tradition, as he sometimes did to the detriment of the law, and, not understanding it, said he could see no reason why what was true of a bond should not be true of other contracts. His decision happened to be right, as it concerned a promissory note, where again the common law regarded the contract as inseparable from the paper on which it was written, but the reasoning was general, and soon was extended to other written contracts, and various absurd and unreal grounds of policy were invented to account for the enlarged rule.

I trust that no one will understand me to be speaking with disrespect of the law, because I criticise it so freely. I venerate the law, and especially our system of law, as one of the vastest products of the human mind. No one knows better than I do the countless number of great intellects that have spent themselves in making some addition or improvement, the greatest of which is trifling when compared with the mighty whole. It has the final title to respect that it exists, that it is not a Hegelian dream, but a part of the lives of men. But one may criticise even what one reveres. Law is the business to which my life is devoted, and I should show less than devotion if I did not do what in me lies to improve it, and, when I perceive what seems to me the ideal of its future, if I hesitated to point it out and to press toward it with all my heart.

Perhaps I have said enough to show the part which the study of history necessarily plays in the intelligent study of the law as it is to-day. In the teaching of this school and at Cambridge it is in no danger of being undervalued. Mr. Bigelow here and Mr. Ames and Mr. Thayer there have made important contributions which will not be forgotten, and in England the recent history of early English law by Sir Frederick Pollock and Mr. Maitland has lent the subject an almost deceptive charm. We must beware of the pitfall of antiquarianism, and must remember that for our purposes our only interest in the past is for the light it throws upon the present. I look forward to a time when the part played by history in the explanation of dogma shall be very small, and instead of ingenious research we shall spend our energy on a study of the ends sought to be attained and the reasons for desiring them. As a step toward that ideal it seems to me that every lawyer ought to seek an understanding of economics. The present divorce between the schools of political economy and law seems to me an evidence of

how much progress in philosophical study still remains to be made. In the present state of political economy, indeed, we come again upon history on a larger scale, but there we are called on to consider and weigh the ends of legislation, the means of attaining them, and the cost. We learn that for everything we have we give up something else, and we are taught to set the advantage we gain against the other advantage we lose, and to know what we are doing when we elect.

There is another study which sometimes is undervalued by the practical minded, for which I wish to say a good word, although I think a good deal of pretty poor stuff goes under that name. I mean the study of what is called jurisprudence. Jurisprudence, as I look at it, is simply law in its most generalized part. Every effort to reduce a case to a rule is an effort of jurisprudence, although the name as used in English is confined to the broadest rules and most fundamental conceptions. One mark of a great lawyer is that he sees the application of the broadest rules. There is a story of a Vermont justice of the peace before whom a suit was brought by one farmer against another for breaking a churn. The justice took time to consider, and then said that he had looked through the statutes and could find nothing about churns, and gave judgment for the defendant. The same state of mind is shown in all our common digests and textbooks. Applications of rudimentary rules of contract or tort are tucked away under the head of Railroads or Telegraphs or go to swell treatises on historical subdivisions, such as Shipping or Equity, or are gathered under an arbitrary title which is thought likely to appeal to the practical mind, such as Mercantile Law. If a man goes into law it pays to be a master of it, and to be a master of it means to look straight through all the dramatic incidents and to discern the true basis for prophecy. Therefore, it is well to have an accurate notion of what you mean by law, by a right, by a duty, by malice, intent, and negligence, by ownership, by possession, and so forth. I have in my mind cases in which the highest courts seem to me to have floundered because they had no clear ideas on some of these themes. I have illustrated their importance already. If a further illustration is wished, it may be found by reading the Appendix to Sir James Stephen's *Criminal Law* on the subject of possession, and then turning to Pollock and Wright's enlightened book. Sir James Stephen is not the only writer whose attempts to analyze legal ideas have been confused by striving for a useless quintessence of all systems, instead of an accurate anatomy of one. The trouble with Austin was that he did not know enough English law. But still it is a practical advantage to master Austin, and his predecessors, Hobbes and Bentham, and his worthy successors, Holland and Pollock. Sir Frederick Pollock's recent little book is touched with the felicity which marks all his works, and is wholly free from the perverting influence of Roman models.

The advice of the elders to young men is very apt to be as unreal as a list of the hundred best books. At least in my day I had my share of such counsels, and high among the unrealities I place the recommendation to study the Roman law. I assume that such advice means more than collecting a few Latin maxims with which to ornament the discourse—the purpose for which Lord Coke recommended Bracton. If that is all that is wanted, the title *De Regulis Juris Antiqui* can be read in an hour. I assume that, if it is well to study the Roman Law, it is well to study it as a working system. That means mastering a set of technicalities more difficult and less understood than our own, and studying another course of history by which even more than our own the Roman law must be explained. If any one doubts me, let him read Keller's *Der Romische Civil Process und die Actionen,* a treatise on the praetor's edict, Muirhead's most interesting *Historical Introduction to the Private Law of Rome,* and, to give him the best chance, Sohm's admirable *Institutes.* No. The way to gain a liberal view of your subject is not to read something else, but to get to the bottom of the subject itself. The means of doing that are, in the first place, to follow the existing body of dogma into its highest generalizations by the help of jurisprudence; next, to discover from history how it has come to be what it is; and, finally, so far as you can, to consider the ends which the several rules seek to accomplish, the reasons why those ends are desired, what is given up to gain them, and whether they are worth the price.

We have too little theory in the law rather than too much, especially on this final branch of study. When I was speaking of history, I mentioned larceny as an example to show how the law suffered from not having embodied in a clear form a rule which will accomplish its manifest purpose. In that case the trouble was due to the survival of forms coming from a time when a more limited purpose was entertained. Let me now give an example to show the practical importance, for the decision of actual cases, of understanding the reasons of the law, by taking an example from rules which, so far as I know, never have been explained or theorized about in any adequate way. I refer to statutes of limitation and the law of prescription. The end of such rules is obvious, but what is the justification for depriving a man of his rights, a pure evil as far as it goes, in consequence of the lapse of time? Sometimes the loss of evidence is referred to, but that is a secondary matter. Sometimes the desirability of peace, but why is peace more desirable after twenty years than before? It is increasingly likely to come without the aid of legislation. Sometimes it is said that, if a man neglects to enforce his rights, he cannot complain if, after a while, the law follows his example. Now if this is all that can be said about it, you probably will decide a case I am going to put, for the plaintiff; if you take the view which I shall suggest, you possibly will decide it for the defendant. A man is sued for trespass upon land, and justifies under a right of way. He proves that he has used the way openly and adversely for twenty years, but it turns out that the plaintiff had granted a license to a person whom he reasonably supposed to be the defendant's agent, although not so in fact, and therefore had assumed that the use of the way was permissive, in which case no right would be gained. Has the defendant gained a right or not? If his gaining it stands on the fault and neglect of the landowner in the ordinary sense, as seems commonly to be supposed, there has been no such neglect, and the right of way has not been acquired. But if I were the defendant's counsel, I should suggest that the foundation of the acquisition of rights by lapse of time is to be looked for in the position of the person who gains them, not in that of the loser. Sir Henry Maine has made it fashionable to connect the archaic notion of property with prescription. But the connection is further back than the first recorded history. It is in the nature of man's mind. A thing which you have enjoyed and used as your own for a long time, whether property or an opinion, takes root in your being and cannot be torn away without your resenting the act and trying to defend yourself, however you came by it. The law can ask no better justification than the deepest instincts of man. It is only by way of reply to the suggestion that you are disappointing the former owner, that you refer to his neglect having allowed the gradual dissociation between himself and what he claims, and the gradual association of it with another. If he knows that another is doing acts which on their face show that he is on the way toward establishing such an association, I should argue that in justice to that other he was bound at his peril to find out whether the other was acting under his permission, to see that he was warned, and if necessary, stopped.

I have been speaking about the study of the law, and I have said next to nothing of what commonly is talked about in that connection—text-books and the case system, and all the machinery with which a student comes most immediately in contact. Nor shall I say anything about them. Theory is my subject, not practical details. The modes of teaching have been improved since my time, no doubt, but ability and industry will master the raw material with any mode. Theory is the most important part of the dogma of the law, as the architect is the most important man who takes part in the building of a house. The most important improvements of the last twenty-five years are improvements in theory. It is not to be feared as unpractical, for, to the competent, it simply means going to the bottom of the subject. For the incompetent, it sometimes is true, as has been said, that an interest in general ideas means an absence of particular knowledge. I remember in army days reading of a youth who, being examined for the lowest grade and being asked a question about squadron drill, answered that he never had considered the evolutions of less than ten thousand men. But the weak and foolish must be left to their folly. The danger is that the able and practical minded should look with indifference or distrust upon ideas the connection of which with their business is remote. I heard a story, the other day, of a man who had a valet to whom he paid high wages, subject to deduction for faults. One of his deductions was, "For lack of imagination, five dollars." The lack is not confined to valets. The object of ambition, power, generally presents itself nowadays in the form of money alone. Money is the most immediate form, and is a proper object of desire. "The fortune," said Rachel, "is the measure of the intelligence." That is a good text to waken people out of a fool's paradise. But, as Hegel says,[6] [6 *Phil. des Rechts,* § 190.] "It is in the end not the appetite, but the opinion, which has to be satisfied." To an imagination of any scope the most far-reaching form of power is not money, it is the command of ideas. If you want great examples, read Mr. Leslie Stephen's *History of English Thought in the Eighteenth Century,* and see how a hundred years after his death the abstract speculations of Descartes had become a practical force controlling the conduct of men. Read the works of the great German jurists, and see how much more the world is governed to-day by Kant than by Bonaparte. We cannot all be

Descartes or Kant, but we all want happiness. And happiness, I am sure from having known many successful men, cannot be won simply by being counsel for great corporations and having an income of fifty thousand dollars. An intellect great enough to win the prize needs other food besides success. The remoter and more general aspects of the law are those which give it universal interest. It is through them that you not only become a great master in your calling, but connect your subject with the universe and catch an echo of the infinite, a glimpse of its unfathomable process, a hint of the universal law.

NATURAL LAW *

It is not enough for the knight of romance that you agree that his lady is a very nice girl—if you do not admit that she is the best that God ever made or will make, you must fight. There is in all men a demand for the superlative, so much so that the poor devil who has no other way of reaching it attains it by getting drunk. It seems to me that this demand is at the bottom of the philosopher's effort to prove that truth is absolute and of the jurist's search for criteria of universal validity which he collects under the head of natural law.

I used to say, when I was young, that truth was the majority vote of that nation that could lick all others. Certainly we may expect that the received opinion about the present war will depend a good deal upon which side wins (I hope with all my soul it will be mine), and I think that the statement was correct in so far as it implied that our test of truth is a reference to either a present or an imagined future majority in favor of our view. If, as I have suggested elsewhere, the truth may be defined as the system of my (intellectual) limitations, what gives it objectivity is the fact that I find my fellow man to a greater or less extent (never wholly) subject to the same *Can't Helps*. If I think that I am sitting at a table I find that the other

* From 32 Harvard Law Review 40 (1918). Reprinted by permission of The Harvard Law Review

persons present agree with me; so if I say that the sum of the angles of a triangle is equal to two right angles. If I am in a minority of one they send for a doctor or lock me up; and I am so far able to transcend the to me convincing testimony of my senses or my reason as to recognize that if I am alone probably something is wrong with my works.

Certitude is not the test of certainty. We have been cock-sure of many things that were not so. If I may quote myself again, property, friendship, and truth have a common root in time. One can not be wrenched from the rocky crevices into which one has grown for many years without feeling that one is attacked in one's life. What we most love and revere generally is determined by early associations. I love granite rocks and barberry bushes, no doubt because with them were my earliest joys that reach back through the past eternity of my life. But while one's experience thus makes certain preferences dogmatic for oneself, recognition of how they came to be so leaves one able to see that others, poor souls, may be equally dogmatic about something else. And this again means scepticism. Not that one's belief or love does not remain. Not that we would not fight and die for it if important—we all, whether we know it or not, are fighting to make the kind of a world that we should like—but that we have learned to recognize that others will fight and die to make a different world, with equal sincerity or belief. Deep-seated preferences can not be argued about—you can not argue a man into liking a glass of beer—and therefore, when differences are sufficiently far reaching, we try to kill the other man rather than let him have his way. But that is perfectly consistent with admitting that, so far as appears, his grounds are just as good as ours.

The jurists who believe in natural law seem to me to be in that naive state of mind that accepts what has been familiar and accepted by them and their neighbors as something that must be accepted by all men everywhere. No doubt it is true that, so far as we can see ahead, some arrangements and the rudiments of familiar institutions seem to be necessary elements in any society that may spring from our own and that would seem to us to be civilized—some form of permanent association between the sexes—some residue of property individually owned—some mode of binding oneself to specified future conduct—at the bottom of all, some protection for the person. But without speculating whether a group is imaginable in which all but the last of these might disappear and the last be subject to qualifications that most of us would abhor, the question remains as to the *Ought* of natural law.

It is true that beliefs and wishes have a transcendental basis in the sense that their foundation is arbitrary. You can not help entertaining and feeling them, and there is an end of it. As an arbitrary fact people wish to live, and we say with various degrees of certainty that they can do so only on certain conditions. To do it they must eat and drink. That necessity is absolute. It is a necessity of less degree but practically general that they should live in society. If they live in society, so far as we can see, there are further conditions. Reason working on experience does tell us, no doubt, that if our wish to live continues, we can do it only on those terms. But that seems to me the whole of the matter. I see no *a priori* duty to live with others and in that way, but simply a statement of what I must do if I wish to remain alive. If I do live with others they tell me that I must do and abstain from doing various things or they will put the screws on to me. I believe that they will, and being of the same mind as to their conduct I not only accept the rules but come in time to accept them with sympathy and emotional affirmation and begin to talk about duties and rights. But for legal purposes a right is only the hypostasis of a prophecy—the imagination of a substance supporting the fact that the public force will be brought to bear upon those who do things said to contravene it—just as we talk of the force of gravitation accounting for the conduct of bodies in space. One phrase adds no more than the other to what we know without it. No doubt behind these legal rights is the fighting will

of the subject to maintain them, and the spread of his emotions to the general rules by which they are maintained; but that does not seem to me the same thing as the supposed *a priori* discernment of a duty or the assertion of a preexisting right. A dog will fight for his bone.

The most fundamental of the supposed preexisting rights—the right to life—is sacrificed without a scruple not only in war, but whenever the interest of society, that is, of the predominant power in the community, is thought to demand it. Whether that interest is the interest of mankind in the long run no one can tell, and as, in any event, to those who do not think with Kant and Hegel it is only an interest, the sanctity disappears. I remember a very tenderhearted judge being of opinion that closing a hatch to stop a fire and the destruction of a cargo was justified even if it was known that doing so would stifle a man below. It is idle to illustrate further, because to those who agree with me I am uttering commonplaces and to those who disagree I am ignoring the necessary foundations of thought. The *a priori* men generally call the dissentients superficial. But I do agree with them in believing that one's attitude on these matters is closely connected with one's general attitude toward the universe. Proximately, as has been suggested, it is determined largely by early associations and temperament, coupled with the desire to have an absolute guide. Men to a great extent believe what they want to—although I see in that no basis for a philosophy that tells us what we should want to want.

Now when we come to our attitude toward the universe I do not see any rational ground for demanding the superlative—for being dissatisfied unless we are assured that our truth is cosmic truth, if there is such a thing—that the ultimates of a little creature on this little earth are the last word of the unimaginable whole. If a man sees no reason for believing that significance, consciousness and ideals are more than marks of the finite, that does not justify what has been familiar in French sceptics; getting upon a pedestal and professing to look with haughty scorn upon a world in ruins. The real conclusion is that the part can not swallow the whole—that our categories are not, or may not be, adequate to formulate what we cannot know. If we believe that we come out of the universe, not it out of us, we must admit that we do not know what we are talking about when we speak of brute matter. We do know that a certain complex of energies can wag its tail and another can make syllogisms. These are among the powers of the unknown, and if, as may be, it has still greater powers that we can not understand, as Fabre in his studies of instinct would have us believe, studies that gave Bergson one of the strongest strands for his philosophy and enabled Maeterlinck to make us fancy for a moment that we heard a clang from behind phenomena—if this be true, why should we not be content? Why should we employ the energy that is furnished to us by the cosmos to defy it and shake our fist at the sky? It seems to me silly.

That the universe has in it more than we understand, that the private soldiers have not been told the plan of campaign, or even that there is one, rather than some vaster unthinkable to which every predicate is an impertinence, has no bearing upon our conduct. We still shall fight—all of us because we want to live, some, at least, because we want to realize our spontaneity and prove our powers, for the joy of it, and we may leave to the unknown the supposed final valuation of that which in any event has value to us. It is enough for us that the universe has produced us and has within it, as less than it, all that we believe and love. If we think of our existence not as that of a little god outside, but as that of a ganglion within, we have the infinite behind us. It gives us our only but our adequate significance. A grain of sand has the same, but what competent person supposes that he understands a grain of sand? That is as much beyond our grasp as man. If our imagination is strong enough to accept the vision of ourselves as parts inseverable from the rest, and to extend our final interest beyond the boundary of our skins, it justifies the sacrifice even of our lives for ends outside of ourselves. The motive, to be sure, is the common wants and ideals that we find in man. Philosophy does not furnish motives, but it shows men that they are not fools for doing what they already want to do. It opens to the forlorn hopes on which we throw ourselves away, the vista of the farthest stretch of human thought, the chords of a harmony that breathes from the unknown.

18

Eugen Ehrlich

1862–1922

Little biographical material is available on Eugen Ehrlich, who is an important founder of sociological jurisprudence. The following facts are gleaned mostly from Professor Edwin Patterson's note on him in the *Encyclopedia of Social Science:*

Ehrlich came from Chernovtsy which is now in the Ukraine, U.S.S.R., but which was then Czernowitz, capital of the Austro-Hungarian province of Bucovina. His father was a lawyer. He went to law school in Vienna and after graduation stayed on as a tutor. He was appointed Professor of Law at Czernowitz University at the age of thirty-five.

Ehrlich's European reputation suffered from his quarrelsome disposition and unreliability of his technical legal writing. World War I set back his American influence.

One of his unique activities was his "seminar of living law," whose student-members conducted personal interviews which were primitive forerunners of modern "scientific polls." One study showed, for example, that family customs varied greatly in Romanian racial groups and departed widely from sovereign codified law.

Ehrlich was a leader in the free law movement. He saw judicial opinions as rationalizations of decisions reached by intuitive balancing of interests, and thought judicial intuition too valuable to check.

Ehrlich wrote extensively. His most important work is *Principles of the Sociology of Law*, (excerpts from which follow this note) published first in 1913.

FUNDAMENTAL PRINCIPLES OF THE SOCIOLOGY OF LAW *

Foreword

It is often said that a book must be written in a manner that permits of summing up its content in a single sentence. If the present volume were to be subjected to this test, the sentence might be the following: At the present as well as at any other time, the center of gravity of legal development lies not in legislation, nor in juristic science, nor in judicial decision, but in society itself. This sentence, perhaps, contains the substance of every attempt to state the fundamental principles of the sociology of law.

THE AUTHOR

Paris, on Christmas Day, 1912

I

The Practical Concept of Law

. . . In jurisprudence the distinction between the theoretical science of law and the practical science of law . . . is being made only just now, and, for the time being, the greater number of those that are working in this field are not aware that it is being made. This distinction, however, is the basis of an independent science of law, whose purpose

* Reprinted by permission of publisher, from Translation by W. L. Moll, Cambridge, Mass.; Harvard University Press. Copyright 1936 by the President and Fellows of Harvard College.

is not to subserve practical ends but to serve pure knowledge, which is concerned not with words but with facts . . . The new science of law will bring about much enlightenment as to the nature of law and of legal institutions that has hitherto been withheld from us, and doubtless it will also yield results that are of practical usefulness. . . .

It is the tragic fate of juristic science that, though at the present time it is an exclusively practical science of law, it is at the same time the only science of law in existence. The result of this situation is that its teaching on the subject of law and legal relations is, as to tendency, subject matter, and method, only that which the practical science of law can give. Indeed it is as if mineralogy and chemistry could teach us no more about iron than that which has been discovered for the purposes of structural-iron engineering. . . .

. . . The important thing is not the definitions that are found in the introductory chapters of handbooks or monographs, but the concept of law with which juristic science actually works; for concepts are not merely external ornamentation, but implements for the erection of a structure of scientific thought.

From the point of view of the judge, the law is a rule according to which the judge must decide the legal disputes that are brought before him. According to the definition which is current in juristic science . . . the law is a rule of human conduct. The rule of human conduct and the rule according to which the judges decide legal disputes may be two quite distinct things; for men do not always act according to the rules that will be applied in settling their disputes. No doubt the legal historian conceives of law as a rule of human conduct; he states the rules according to which, in antiquity or in the Middle Ages, marriages were entered into, husband and wife, parents and children lived together in the family; he tells whether property was held individually or in common, whether the soil was tilled by the owner or by a lessee paying rent or by a serf rendering services; how contracts were entered into, and how property descended. One would hear the same thing if one should ask a traveler returning from foreign lands to give an account of the law of the peoples he has become acquainted with. He will tell of marriage customs, of family life, of the manner of entering into contracts; but he will have little to say about the rules according to which law-suits are being decided.

This concept of law, which the jurist adopts quite instinctively when he is studying the law of a foreign nation or of remote times for a purely scientific purpose, he will give up at once when he turns to the positive law of his own country and of his own time. Without his becoming aware of it, secretly as it were, the rule according to which men act becomes the rule according to which their acts are being adjudged by courts and other tribunals. The latter, indeed, is also a rule of conduct, but it is such for but a small part of the people, i.e. for the authorities, entrusted with the application of the law; but not like the former, for the generality of the people . . . It is true, jurists look upon these rules as rules of conduct as well, but they arrive at this view by a jump in their thinking. They mean to say that the rules according to which courts decide are the rules according to which men ought to regulate their conduct. To this is added a vague notion that in the course of time men will actually regulate their conduct in accordance with the rules according to which the courts render their decisions . . . No one denies that judicial decisions influence the conduct of men, but we must first of all inquire to what extent this is true and upon what circumstances it depends . . . .

. . . A juristic science which conceives of law as a rule of conduct could not consistently have laid down a principle that men are bound by the law even though they do not know it; for one cannot act according to a rule that one does not know. On the contrary, it ought to have discussed the question how much of a given legal material is known as a rule of conduct and is followed as such, and, at most, what can be done to make it known. . . .

. . . No scientifically trained jurist doubts that a considerable part of the law of the past was not created by the state, and that even today it is derived to a great extent from other sources . . . .

. . . Even the believers in the doctrine of the omnipotence of the state have not very often seriously thought that the state can make rules to regulate the whole field of human conduct . . . If juristic science today is devoted exclusively to state law, the reason for this must be sought in the fact that the state, in the course of historical development, has come to believe that it is able to add to the monopoly of the administration of law, which it acquired long ago, a monopoly of the creation of law. And I do not doubt, therefore, that the modern free-finding-of-law movement marks not only an advance in scientific insight, but also an actual shift in the relation of the state and society—a shift which has taken place long ago in other spheres.

Where the judge renders his decisions chiefly according to custom . . . the idea, self-evidently, does not enter the head of anyone to derive the law as such from the state . . . It is only after the state has grown extremely powerful, and has begun to tend toward an absolute form of government, that the thought begins to germinate, and the impulse awakens, to make the state the authoritative, and in the course of time the sole, source of law. . . .

. . . There never was a time when the law promulgated by the state in statutory form was the only law, even for the courts and other tribunals, and there has always been an undercurrent, therefore, which strove to secure proper recognition for law that was not promulgated by the state. This undercurrent forced its way to the surface at two different periods: in the writings of the teachers of the law of nature school in the seventeenth and eighteenth centuries, and again in the writings of Savigny and Puchta, the founders of the Historical School. . . .

Neither of these schools has fully followed out its ideas . . . In spite of their radicalism, the teachers of the law of nature . . . never dared to assert, with any show of firmness at least, that a judge can ever be under a duty to apply a rule of law that has not, tacitly at least, been approved by the state. Accordingly the law of nature is, in fact, suspended in mid-air. . . .

Savigny and Puchta perhaps were the first to conceive, vaguely at least, the idea of a science of law the exclusive object of which is to promote knowledge . . . Far in advance of their time, they turned away from the insignificant figure of the personal legislator and directed their attention to the great elemental forces that are at work in the creation of law . . . Nevertheless the task of creating a science of law proved too great even for them. They made a beginning, but were unable to carry it out.

The founders of the Historical School never attempted actually to apply in their dogmatic works the methodological principles which they professed in theory . . . They do indeed insist that the law develops in the popular legal consciousness, but barring the much decried method of legislation, they cannot tell us how new law is received into the body of already existing positive law. . . .

. . . The ultimate inference which is drawn by the exponents of this school is the doctrine of the perfection and completeness of the legal system. When the Historical School makes this assertion, it reverses itself just as the Law of Nature School did when it demanded legislation by the state. . . .

In the light of these considerations, it is possible to understand the view, which still prevails at the present time, that the law is a compulsory order, that it is an essential element of the law to recognize enforceable claims and to impose enforceable duties. First of all we must arrive at a clear understanding of what is meant by compulsion . . . It can . . . mean only such compulsion as is considered characteristic of law; i.e. only such psychological compulsion as is exercised by threat of penalty or of compulsory execution. That these two kinds of compulsion have been considered essential characteristics of law can be explained only by the fact that law has always been believed to be the rule to be applied by the judge . . . To a person, however, whose conception of law is that of a rule of conduct, compulsion by threat of penalty as well as of compulsory execution becomes a secondary matter. To him, the scene of all human life is not the court room. It is quite obvious that a man lives in innumerable legal relations, and that, with few exceptions, he quite voluntarily performs the duties incumbent upon him because of these relations. One performs one's duties as father or son, as husband or wife, does not interfere with one's neighbor's enjoyment of his property, pays one's debts, delivers that which one has sold, and renders to one's employer the performance to render which one has obliged oneself. The jurist, of course, is ready with the objection that all men perform their duties only because they know that the courts could eventually compel them to perform them. If he should take the pains, to which, indeed, he is not accustomed, to observe what men do and leave undone, he would soon be convinced of the fact that, as a rule, the thought of compulsion by the courts does not even enter the minds of men . . . The jurist ought to be the last person of all to overlook the fact that that which men do or leave undone as a legal duty in this sense often is something quite different from, occasionally is much more than, that which the authorities could ever compel them to do or leave undone. . . .

. . . I will emphasize but one point—a point which has been neglected hitherto, i.e. the great number of situations in private law for which no effective legal sanction has been provided . . . Would an employer sue a servant girl for not tidying the house? What would a suit of this kind avail him? The claim for damages would not afford relief, for no matter how much importance he may have attached to his right at the moment, in the end he will not be able to prove damage that is worth mentioning . . . The order of human society is based upon the fact that, in general, legal duties are being performed, not upon the fact that failure to perform gives rise to a cause of action.

. . . It is not an essential element of the concept of law that it be created by the state, nor that it constitute the basis for the decisions of the courts or other tribunals, nor that it be the basis of a legal compulsion consequent upon such a decision. A fourth element remains, and that will have to be the point of departure, i.e. the law is an ordering. . . .

II

The Inner Order of the Social Associations

. . . Society is the sum total of the human associations that have mutual relations with one another. And these associations that constitute human society are very heterogeneous. . . .

From these various kinds of groups of human beings, we must select, first of all, a certain kind of organized association, which we shall hereafter designate as the primitive (genetic) association . . . The clan and the family are its original forms . . . It is self-evident that, from the moment in which men begin to form associations, increased capacity for association with others becomes a weapon in the struggle for existence. It effects the gradual exclusion and extinction of those in whom self-seeking and predatory instincts predominate, and the survival of those that have capacity for socialization, who henceforth are the stronger because they can avail themselves of the strength of the whole association. . . . Out of the union of genetic associations, clans, families, house communities, grows the tribe, and, in course of time, the nation.

. . . Among the peoples of the highest degree of civilization, a man becomes a member of an almost incalculable number of associations of the most diverse kinds; his life becomes richer, more varied, more complex. And in consequence, the once powerful genetic associations languish and, in part, fall into decay. Only . . . the family . . . has been able to maintain itself in full vigor down to our day. . . .

. . . One hundred years ago, a man's occupation or his profession, his religious fellowship, his political affiliations, and his social connections, were determined to a much greater extent than they are today, by his descent, i.e. by the genetic association to which he belonged. All these things were determined by free choice to a much lesser extent than they are today.

Though we know very little of the law of the early times . . . there can be no doubt that of what today is mostly, and sometimes even exclusively, called law, i.e. of the fixed rule of law, formulated in words, which issues from a power superior to the individual, and which is imposed upon the latter from without, only a few negligible traces can be found among them. Their law is chiefly the order of the clans, families, houses. It determines the prerequisites and the consequences of a valid marriage, the mutual relation of the spouses, of parents and children, and the mutual relations of the other members of the clan, family, and household. Each association creates this order for itself quite independently . . . And if the orders in associations of the same kind differ very little from each other, this must be attributed to the similarity of the conditions of life; often to borrowing; but by no means to a uniform order in some manner prescribed for them from without. . . .

As soon as ownership of land becomes established, law arises concerning it, but without any general rules of law. Each settlement creates its own land law; each landlord imposes it independently upon his villeins; each royal grant, quite independently of all others, makes provision for the legal status of the estate it grants. There are concrete legal relations in the various communes, settlements, and manors, but no law of ownership in land. . . .

The same holds true for the contract. The law of contracts is based solely upon the content of the contracts that are being entered

into. There are no general legal propositions governing contracts . . . Where the contract is silent, there is no law; and the literal, narrow interpretation of contracts, which is so characteristic of the older law, is not based upon formalism, which is usually imputed to primitive times, but which in reality is quite foreign to them, but upon the fact that, outside of the language of the contract, there is nothing to stand on. . . .

The earliest state is based exclusively upon the agreement entered into by the noble clans that found it; and over and above this agreement there is nothing that might determine the position, rights, and duties of the individual organs of the state . . . If the king can rely upon his retainers, his power may be very great; if not, he must, in matters of important governmental action, secure the consent of the influential men among the people, possibly of all the people. Accordingly the council of the elders and the popular assembly are not constitutional institutions, but merely means employed by the king to enforce his will. . . .

. . . Within the feudal state, the clan, the family, the house continued . . . New local associations arose, which took over a considerable number of social functions. Among the local associations, the city soon became very important . . . Within the walls of the city, a vast number of social associations, which were unknown elsewhere, and an active legal life developed. Here for the first time fully developed legal institutions were expressed in a number of legal propositions: the law of real property, of pledge, of contract, of inheritance.

But these legal propositions constitute an infinitesimal part of the legal order. In the feudal state as well as elsewhere, the great bulk of the legal order is not based upon the legal propositions, but upon the inner order of the social associations . . . If one would obtain a knowledge of the law of mediaeval society, one must not confine oneself to a study of the legal propositions, but must study it in the deeds of grant, the charters, the land registers, the records of the guilds, the city books, the regulations of the guilds. . . .

. . . The idea that the law is nothing but a body of legal propositions dominates legal thinking today.

This idea, however, contains so many contradictory elements that it refutes itself . . . Every judge, every administrative official, knows that, comparatively speaking, he rarely renders a decision based solely on legal propositions. By far the greatest number of decisions are based upon documents, testimony of witnesses or experts, contracts, articles of association, last wills and testaments, and other declarations. In other words, in the language of jurists, in a much greater number of instances judgment is being rendered upon questions of fact than upon questions of law. . . .

This truth is hidden from the eye of the jurist by the fact that to him an adjudication upon a question of fact merely amounts to a subsumption of the ascertained facts under a legal proposition. But this is due solely to a juristic habit of thought. . . .

The inner order of the associations of human beings is not only the original, but also, down to the present time, the basic form of law. The legal proposition not only comes into being at a much later time, but is largely derived from the inner order of the associations. . . .

The inner order of the associations is determined by legal norms. Legal norms must not be confused with legal propositions. The legal proposition is the precise, universally binding formulation of the legal precept in a book of statutes or in a law book. The legal norm is the legal command, reduced to practice, as it obtains in a definite association, perhaps of very small size, even without any formulation in words . . . In the past centuries, all legal norms that were determinative of the inner order of the associations were based upon custom, upon contracts, and upon articles of association of corporations. In the main, this is the situation today.

III

The Social Associations and the Social Norms

A social association is a plurality of human beings who, in their relations with one another, recognize certain rules of conduct as binding, and, generally at least, actually regulate their conduct according to them. These rules are of various kinds and have various names: rules of law, of morals, of religion, of ethical custom, of honor, of decorum, of tact, of etiquette, of fashion . . . These rules are social facts, the resultants of the forces that are operative in society, and can no more be considered separate and apart from society, in which they are operative, than the motion of the waves can be computed without considering the element in which they move. . . .

The legal norm, therefore, is merely one of the rules of conduct, of the same nature as all other rules of conduct . . . The prevailing school of juristic science does not stress this fact, but, for practical reasons, emphasizes the antithesis between law and the other norms, especially the ethical norms, in order to urge upon the judge at every turn as impressively as possible that he must render his decisions solely according to law. . . .

Not all human associations are being regulated by legal norms, but manifestly only those associations are parts of the legal order whose order is based upon legal norms. The sociology of law deals exclusively with these; the others are the subject matter of other branches of sociology. Among the legal associations there are some that are readily recognizable by external criteria, i.e. those that jurists style juristic persons, corporations, institutions, foundations, and, first and foremost, the state. But even in public law, there are numerous legal associations that have no legal personality; such as administrative boards, public institutions, the people, the army, the various classes, ranks, and professions. Much more of this is to be found in private law.

In all legal associations the legal norm constitutes the backbone of the inner order;

it is the strongest support of their organization. By organization we mean that rule in the association which assigns to each member his relative position in the association (whether of domination or of subjection) and his function . . . But only those rules of law have a share in the creation of the legal order of the association that have actually become rules of conduct in the association, i.e. that are being recognized and followed by men, in a general way at least. Rules of law that have remained mere norms for decision, that become effective only in the very rare cases of legal controversy, do not take part in the ordering of the associations . . . It is always necessary therefore to ask not only how much of what has been promulgated by the lawgiver, proclaimed by the founder of a religion, or taught by the philosopher has been applied by the courts, preached from the pulpits, or taught in books or schools, but how much has actually been practiced and lived. . . .

The first and most important function of the sociological science of law, therefore, is to separate those portions of the law that regulate, order, and determine society from the mere norms for decision, and to demonstrate their organizing power. . . .

. . . There is no individual law. All law is social law . . . The law always sees in man solely a member of one of the countless associations in which life has placed him . . . Membership in the association occasionally, but by no means always, gives rise to individual rights and duties of the individual, but this is not its purpose, is not its essential content.

In the prevailing system of private law, however, the association is given very inadequate expression . . . In actual fact the entire private law is a law of associations. For the private law is preponderantly, and, apart from family law, exclusively, the law of economic life, and economic life goes on exclusively in associations.

Economic life comprises production of goods, exchange of goods, and consumption of goods. Accordingly the economic associations subserve these three functions. Just at this point, however, there is an enormous contrast betweeen the economic undertakings of today and those of a not far distant past. In antiquity and in the Middle Ages, the economically self-sufficing household of the free farmer and the *Oikenwirtschaft* (self-sufficing economic establishment) of the royal court and of the seigniorial manor were the prevailing forms. These manifestly were economic associations, and their legal order was apparent . . . At the present time . . . the production of goods takes place in the workshop; the exchange, in commerce; the consumption, in the home. And to this three-fold division the legal order of the economic associations of our day must conform. . . .

On the farm, which the farmer manages with the assistance of his wife and children, his men-servants and women-servants, he raises grain and tubers, cattle and sheep. This is the economic content of this association. Its juristic form is ownership, the real right of usufruct or of usufructuary lease in the farm, the family law which unites the members of the family, the contract of service which binds the men-servants and women-servants to the farm . . . The tradesman, together with his journeymen and apprentices, works in a rented workshop with his own materials and his own tools; the right of tenancy in the shop, the ownership of tools and materials, the contract for wages with the journeyman, and the contract of apprenticeship constitute both the juristic form and the economic content of the trade. The factories of a share company can throw goods on the market whose value amounts to millions of dollars. The share company with its board of directors and board of supervisors, its members and the meeting of the members, with an army of officers and employees, with its right of ownership, its relations of usufruct and ordinary lease in factories, machinery, sources of power, raw materials, and merchandise—all of these constitute the economic order of the manufacturing establishment, which is reflected in the contract of association, in a multitude of legal relations involving real rights, in countless contractual relations with employers and workmen, with ordinary and usufructuary lessors.

A discussion of the other economic associations, of the commercial establishment, of the bank, of the household as a community of consumers, leads to similar results. . . .

The family law within the family, the contract of service, of wages, and of employment in the factory, in the workshop, in the commercial establishment and in the bank, accomplish the same results everywhere that are accomplished in the corporation by the articles of association . . . i.e. they bring about the inner order of the group of human beings that has its being within these economic associations. This applies, however, not only to the contract of service, of wages, and of employment, but also to all other kinds of agreements, especially to the contract of barter, to contracts for supplying things for use . . . and to the contract for the extension of credit. The organizing power of all these contracts appears at once if one considers not merely, as is usually done for purely practical juristic purposes, the two parties that enter into the contract, but the whole group of persons who are brought into relation with one another by means of the regular exchange of goods arranged for by contract. . . .

. . . Not only the making of the contract, but also its content, is a result of social interrelations. In connection with any one of the ordinary contracts of daily life, it may suffice to raise the question which part of it is peculiar to this specific contract and which part is determined by the social order and by the organization of economic life and of commercial intercourse, in order to satisfy ourselves of the extent to which the latter elements preponderate. The fact that we are in a position today to satisfy our needs as to food, clothing, and housing by means of the everyday contracts of sale and lease and the contracts for work and labor, we owe to the other fact that in the community in which we live commerce and production of goods have been regulated sufficiently to make this manner of satisfying one's needs possible

. . . A person who has changed his residence will notice at once that he is making contracts of an entirely different nature from those that he made before . . . In England, as a rule, one does not rent an apartment but a whole house; one does not purchase one's daily supply of meat at the butcher's, but has it delivered weekly at one's residence. Accordingly rental contracts and contracts for the purchase of meat in England have a quite different content from those on the Continent . . . .

. . . Every social and economic change causes a change in the law, and it is impossible to change the legal bases of society and of economic life without bringing about a corresponding change in the law. If the changes in the law are arbitrary and of such a nature that the economic institutions cannot adapt themselves to them, the order of the latter is destroyed without compensation. The farmer is able to produce on his farm the goods that he requires in order to supply not only himself but also the other classes of society with raw materials only so long as the legal order guarantees to him, in a great measure at least, the returns of his labor. If therefore a class which is all-powerful in the state should force upon the farmer a legal order which compels him to give up all that he has harvested, the farm would be deserted . . . Even foreign conquerors, therefore, have been content with reducing the free farmers to a state of serfdom . . . .

. . . There is another part of the law, which does not directly regulate and order the associations, but only protects them against attacks . . . This applies to the law of procedure before the courts and other tribunals; for it is merely a part of the order of the tribunals which have been created for the protection of social institutions; it is without direct influence upon society. It applies also to penal law, for the latter creates no social institutions; it merely protects goods that are already in existence in society and institutions that have already been established. And, lastly, it applies also to all those provisions of the material private law that concern only the protection afforded by law;

like penal law, they create neither goods nor social institutions; they but regulate the already existing protection afforded by the courts and other tribunals. These norms did not come into being within the social associations themselves as the inner order of the latter, but arose in juristic law or in the law created by the state. All rights of monopoly, especially patent rights and copyrights, are created by the state. They consist in a command, addressed to all who are subjected to the will of the state, except the person who holds the right, to refrain from engaging in any activity in a certain sphere. Norms of similar nature have occasionally arisen in juristic law also.

And now we must point out the significance, but slightly considered hitherto, of the extra-legal norms for the inner ordering of the associations. The statement that legal institutions are based exclusively on legal norms is not true. Morality, religion, ethical custom, decorum, tact, even etiquette and fashion, do not order the extra-legal relations only; they also affect the legal sphere at every turn. Not a single one of the jural associations could maintain its existence solely by means of legal norms . . . .

. . . A family the members of which reciprocally insist upon their legal rights has already disintegrated in most cases as a social and economic association. If they appeal to the judge, they have arrived at the point where they part company. The prohibition of the abusive exercise of legal rights *(Chicane)* shows that even real rights may not be exercised without giving heed to certain extra-legal norms; and where land or dwellings adjoin, there is the further requirement of customary observance of the dictates of morality, ethical custom, decorum, tact, and etiquette. Contracts must be interpreted and performed according to the requirements of good faith and commercial custom. That is to say that many other things must be considered besides the rule of law and the meaning and language of the contract. Nevertheless life demands a great deal more than even the most liberal-minded jurist would concede on the basis of good faith and business custom.

There is perhaps no other contractual relation which is so thoroughly stripped of extra-legal content as is the contract of ordinary lease in a large city; nevertheless even in this relation the "good landlord" and "the desirable tenant" are valued highly . . . The organizing significance of the extra-legal norms appears with particular clearness in the contract for services and wages. On the part of the entrepreneur or of his authorized representative, a certain firm insistence upon his legal right, together with an instinct for morality, ethical custom, decorum, and tact constitutes the principal part of the aptitude which is usually called a talent for organization; if this is lacking, a contract is without value not only for him but also for the workmen and employees. On the other hand an entrepreneur could not work with people who recognize only the legal point of view. . . .

. . . It is true, the extra-legal norms are not being observed inviolably, but this is equally true of the legal norms. The order of the social machine is continually being interfered with. And though it does its work with much creaking and groaning, the important thing is that it shall continue to function. . . .

Let us for a moment compare our present-day society and its legal order with a socialistic society as various socialists have so often pictured it . . . In a socialistic society, as well as in our present-day society, there will be farms, mines, and factories, in which goods are being produced; there will be means of transportation like our railroads, steamboats, and vehicles, which deliver these goods at large magazines and storehouses where they will have to be stored, as is done in our warehouses and shops, until there is a demand for them; finally there will have to be smaller undertakings in which goods are being prepared for immediate consumption, as is being done today in the workshop of the mechanic and also in the kitchen and in housekeeping generally. In a socialistic society . . . above them all will hover an all-knowing and all-overseeing official body which makes an advance estimate of the total requirement, orders its production, directs the workman to the places where the work is to be done, and orders the products to be sent where they are needed. Our present-day society indeed has no official body of this kind. But the task which, in a socialistic society, is to be performed by this omnipotent board of superhuman stature is performed in our present-day society by the law acting automatically and with such simple instrumentalities as the family order, possession, contract, and the law and right of inheritance. The owners, as entrepreneurs, provide the establishments at which goods are being produced, the means of transportation, the warehouses, and the salerooms; they assemble the workers by means of contracts of service and wages, and secure the necessary capital by means of contracts for the extension of credit. The merchants estimate in advance how much merchandise the human race will require, and, by means of agreements of exchange, direct it to the places where it is needed. And they accomplish all of this, it is true, not without a considerable amount of error, friction, and opposition, but certainly with much less friction and expenditure of energy than the most efficient purely bureaucratic board could accomplish it. . . .

IV

*Social and State Sanction
of the Norms*

A doctrine which has a great vogue at the present time . . . seeks to explain the origin of the legal norms and, occasionally, also of the other social norms, especially those of morality, by the power of the dominant groups in society, which have established them, and are enforcing them in their own interest. But power over men can be maintained and exercised permanently only by uniting them in associations and prescribing rules of conduct for them within the association, i.e. by organizing them . . . Man always acts in his own interest . . . It is quite incorrect to say that the interests of the dominant groups in the associations conflict with those

of the whole association or with those of the other members. To a certain extent the interests of the dominant groups must coincide with the interest of the whole association, or at least with those of the majority of the members of the association; for if this were not so, the other members would not obey the norms established by the dominant group . . . The order of an association, abstractly considered, may be a poor one, may perhaps afford undue advantages to its leaders, may impose heavy burdens upon the others, but it is always better than no order at all. And the fact that there is no better order in existence is always a cogent proof that the association, in its given spiritual and moral condition, and in view of the economic supplies it has had at its disposal, has been unable to create a better order. . . .

Sanction is not a peculiarity of the legal norms. The norms of ethical custom, morality, religion, tact, decorum, etiquette, and fashion would be quite meaningless if they did not exercise a certain amount of coercion . . . There is no one to whom country, native land, religious communion, family, friends, social relations, political party, are mere words. Most people perhaps will set little store by one or the other of these, but doubtless there would be very few who do not cling with all their hearts and minds to one group at least. It is within his circle that each man seeks aid in distress, comfort in misfortune, moral support, social life, recognition, respect, honor . . . The importance of these associations is not limited to these moral, intangible considerations, for on them depends success in one's profession and business. On the other hand, one's profession and business draw one into a number of professional and business associations.

. . . It is impossible for the associations to offer something to each one of its members unless each individual is at the same time a giver. And in fact all these associations . . . make certain demands in exchange for that which they give; and the social norms which prevail in these communities are nothing more than the universally valid precipitate of the claims which the latter make upon the individual. He therefore who is in need of the support of the circle to which he belongs—as who is not?—does wisely if he conforms, at least in a general way, to its norms. He who refuses . . . will gradually be deserted, avoided, excluded. . . .

A man therefore conducts himself according to law, chiefly because this is made imperative by his social relations. In this respect the legal norm does not differ from the other norms . . . If the family law were abolished in its entirety, families would not bear an aspect much different from that which they bear today; for fortunately the family law requires state sanction only in rare instances. If the workman, the employee, the office-holder, the military officer, do not perform their contractural and official duties from a sense of duty, they do so because they wish to keep their positions, perhaps because they wish to rise to better ones . . . Penalty and levy of execution is the last thing that enters their minds. There are large mercantile houses which as a matter of principle, do not bring suit on a matter arising in their commercial relations, and as a rule do not permit themselves to be sued, but satisfy even an unfounded claim in full. They meet refusal of payment and frivolous demands by severing commercial relations. . . .

. . . If the law were without sanction, or to put it accurately, without the coercion effected by penalty and compulsory execution, would it really be merely a fire that does not burn as Jhering thinks? . . . If we exclude the cases in which appeal is made to the courts because the question of fact or of law is in dispute, in which it is not a matter of enforcing law and right by coercion but of showing what is law and right in the given case, it will appear that the coercive force of penalty and of compulsory execution, as mass phenomena at least—and only these are of moment here—is effective only in a very limited measure and in so far as, for some reason or other, the other sanctions of the social organizations fail to function.

As to penalty, its true significance is shown by penal statistics. It is true, penal offenses occur in all social circles. But if we disregard persons of inferior social value who are not amenable to social restraints; if we leave out of consideration a few misdeeds as to which social influences are less effective because these misdeeds as such do not affect social position (insult, duel, political crime, and, among a large part of the German peasantry, bodily injury); if we consider not individual cases, but the great bulk of the daily work done by the criminal courts, we shall see that criminal law is directed almost exclusively against those whom descent, economic distress, neglected education or moral degradation has excluded from the human associations. It is only in the case of these outcasts that the widest association, which includes even them, i.e. the state, steps in with its power to punish. The state as an organ of society protects society against those that are outside the pale of society. The measure of its success is shown by its experience extending over thousands of years. The conviction is steadily gaining ground that the only serious weapon against crime is the possibility of regaining the criminal for human society and thus again subjecting him to social restraint.

Is the situation otherwise in case of compulsory execution? . . . It is of social significance only in the case of obligations to pay money, i.e. in but a small fraction of legal life. At this point it may suffice to raise the question whether the agreements from which obligations to pay money arise are being entered into with an eye to compulsory execution . . . In a developed economic system a person may not safely be granted credit if the creditor has to take into consideration the possibility of the necessity of compulsory execution. Whether or not credit can safely be extended is determined in general by means of a thorough social and psychological investigation of the person who is asking for credit. . . .

. . . The gambler pays his unenforceable gambling debts under a merely social compulsion, and the average man is at least as sensitive to social sanction as the average gambler. Even unenforceable debts arising from stock-exchange differences are usually being paid, although in these cases the social and economic consequences of failure to do so are much less than in case of true business debts. The generally known ineffectiveness of the usury laws demonstrates that the persons from whom usury is being exacted can be compelled to pay even without compulsory execution. The reports of mercantile credit associations show that the well known purely economic means of coercion, to wit boycott and black list, are effective even where compulsory execution has remained altogether fruitless . . . Compulsory execution, like penalty, we may therefore say, exists only for those that have come down in the world and for those whom society has cast out. It is effective against the reckless borrower, the cheat, the bankrupt, and against him who has become insolvent through misfortune. However much of a burden these classes of borrowers may be on business life, they are too insignificant to warrant the statement that the value of the legal order depends upon the protection it affords against such elements.

. . . Before the judicial reform of the thirties of the last century, the benefits of the expensive and cumbersome English civil procedure did not extend far beyond the well-to-do upper crust of English society. This however did not prevent the English from becoming a rich and highly civilized nation . . . It is a more serious matter if the administration of criminal justice breaks down also. But Hungary, southern Italy, and Spain prove that a nation can survive centuries of brigandage. . . .

. . . The fact that the force of the social norms is so universally traced to the coercive power of the state requires explanation. Every false doctrine must, in the nature of things, be based on a correct observation of some sort or other . . . In the first place, the validity of only a part of the law is maintained by the coercive power of the state. This part is neither very great nor very important, but it is the part which is of greatest interest to the jurist; because the latter is not concerned until coercion becomes necessary.

In the second place there are doubtless many norms which most people would not observe if there were no sanction in the form of penalty or compulsory execution . . . The entire military system and the entire tax system of the modern state, that is to say, the very thing which customarily is considered the basis of the life of the state, could not exist for a single moment without coercion exercised by the state. All this however merely amounts to saying that the state and a considerable portion of society have consciously become antagonistic to each other. In consequence of this antagonism, the military and the tax system of the state have remained so unrelated to society that they have become state institutions exclusively. History will probably show that this is merely a transition stage. It was not the case in antiquity. . . .

. . . But that is not the whole story. To a considerable extent, this conception has been derived from a consideration not merely of law, but of social life as a whole. It is being observed that there is an enormous contrast in society between the rich and the poor; that the entire burden of the work of society rests upon the poor; that in exchange they receive little more than the bare necessaries of life . . . That this state of affairs is endured by those to whom it causes such losses can be understood only if one assumes that it is being forcibly maintained by the sovereign power of the state. This thought has been followed through to its logical conclusion in the socialist philosophy of history . . . The older economic order, it is contended, was sustained by the great majority, who found it to be to their advantage to do so; the later capitalistic order is being maintained exclusively by the state, which is a powerful, elaborate organization of those who have . . . the protection of the legal order, which is based on property, contract, and the law of inheritance. The socialists therefore quite consistently urge those who have not to oppose to the organization of those who have the organization of the masses in order to bring about a legal order which is more favorable to the latter.

If it were true that the legal order of the present day cannot be maintained without the help of the state and that the latter is nothing but an organization of the small and ever decreasing minority of those who have against the great mass of those who have not, the legal order and the state were condemned already. But the present inquiry has shown that the resources of the state for the protection of the legal order are, in actual fact, not being employed against the great masses of the people but only against the small minority of those who have been cast out, who are cut off from all social relations. There is no need for any exertion on the part of the state to subdue the great mass of the people; the latter submit to the legal order willingly because they realize that the legal order is their order, the order of the economic and social associations, of which each one of them is a member. It cannot be true therefore that a small minority makes use of these associations for the purpose of exploiting the great majority. To say that this can be done for a long period of time without eruptions of violence is to contradict all historical experience and all mass psychology. . . .

In fact, since the present legal order is at the same time an organization of production and exchange of goods it is not possible to abolish it without, at the same time, depriving the great majority as well as the small minorities of the means of subsistence. It is necessary, therefore, if civilization is to continue, that the existing legal order should not be abolished, unless it can at once be replaced by another, a socialistic order. That this can be accomplished at any time without further ado is no longer contended by anyone competent to judge, even a socialist. Intelligent socialists have long since been speaking only of a gradual development of the capitalistic economy into a socialistic one . . .

. . . With the great mass of men who throughout their whole lives permit themselves, without objection, to be fitted into the vast social mechanism, it is not a matter of conscious thinking, but of unconsciously habituating themselves to the emotions and thoughts of their surroundings, which are with them from the cradle to the grave. The most important norms function only through suggestion . . . They are being impressed upon his mind in his childhood; an "It is not done," "It is not proper," "Thus hath God commanded" follows him through his whole life. And he submits with a willingness which is the greater the more emphatically experience brings home to him the advantages of obedience and the disadvantages of disobedience. The advantages and disadvantages are not only social but also individual; for he who obeys a command is spared the arduous labor of doing his own thinking, and the still more arduous labor of making his own decision. Liberty and independence are ideals of the poet, the artist, and the thinker only. The average man is a Philistine, without much appreciation of these things. He loves that to which he has become habituated, the instinctive, and hates nothing more than intellectual exertion. That is the reason why women become enthusiastic over men of strong will. . . .

. . . The living law, even where it is created by the state, is preponderantly, as to its content, limited to an association . . . It is only as to the claim to life, liberty, and property that a different rule obtains at the present time; for this claim is being recognized, at least within the territory in which European civilization holds undisputed sway, as a valid claim of everyone, irrespective of nationality. This is a relatively modern achievement. As late as the sixteenth century, the life and the property of the alien were by no means secure in Europe. Even today it is not an indispensable element of civilization, as is shown by the history of colonies everywhere and by the fate of the Negroes in America . . . But with these temporal and local limitations, respect for the life, the liberty, and the property of every man is today not merely a norm for decision and a policy of the state, but has actually become a principle of the living law. . . .

VI

The Norms for Decision

Courts do not come into being as organs of the state but of society. Their function originally was merely to determine, upon authority given by clans or families which had entered into a close relationship with one another, whether a quarrel between the members of different associations could be composed by payment of a penalty or whether it could be expiated only in blood, and eventually to determine the amount of the penalty. It is not until a much later date that courts are being erected by the state for matters that directly concern the state, e.g. attempts on the life of the king, trading with the enemy, violation of the military order. At a later time, the state gains control also over the courts of the former class; but the distinction between administration of justice by the state and by society continues today in the distinction between the jurisdiction of criminal and of civil causes . . . Society has always had, and has kept to the present day, courts of its own that are independent of the state . . . The sociology of law, when it defines the term court, is concerned only with the question whether or not the institution involved performs the general functions of a court. Considered functionally, the court is a person or a group of persons who are not parties to the controversy and whose function is to establish peace by the opinion which they express about the subject matter of the controversy. This opinion has no binding force even when pronounced by a state court of primitive times; it is a mere opinion. He who refuses to submit may resort to self-help, to a feud, but he puts himself in the wrong, and loses the purely social advantage of having a just quarrel. . . .

. . . Courts, of whatsoever description they may be, must not render their judgments arbitrarily or without giving reasons, but must base them on general principles. The norms for decision upon which the latter are based invariably appear as the result of an inspiration of higher power and wisdom; nay, indeed, at a lower stage, as the result of an illumination by the godhead. . . .

. . . Every norm for decision therefore is based primarily upon . . . the usages, which assign to each individual his position and his function in the association, upon relations of domination and possession, contracts, articles of association, testamentary dispositions. In every quarrel the point involved is that a norm which is based on these facts has been violated, and in all litigation, in order to be able to render a decision, the judge must ascertain these facts either from his own knowledge or from the evidence. All these facts constitute the basis of the decision just as they have developed and taken shape in the concrete association before the quarrel arose.

In the past there has frequently been a toying, especially among exponents of the natural law theory, with the thought that the whole law must be susceptible of being summed up in a few clear propositions that are obvious to unaided human reason. They evidently had an idea, quite vague indeed, that the existing usages, relations of possession, contracts, articles of association, testamentary dispositions, were sufficient for the rendering of judicial decisions and required only a few additional rules to complement them. But he who adopts this view fails to see that the norm for decision is always something more than and distinct from the inner order of the association . . . A relation as to which there is a dispute is something different from the same relation at peace. That which before had been adaptable and flexible has become rigid, immovable; vague outlines have become clear and sharply drawn, and often a meaning must be read into the words that the parties had never been clearly conscious of. But the judge in a law-suit has duties to perform with reference to the relation submitted to him for decision which involve more than this relation, which have remained altogether foreign to the experience of the associations so long as they were left to themselves; and as to these duties he can learn nothing from the inner order of the associations. For such cases, he must have at his disposal norms for decision which are independent of this latter order.

We must consider chiefly the requirements of the administration of justice as such. Every social association is, to be accurate, a special case that cannot be duplicated anywhere in the world . . . The administration of justice cannot function where there is such a medley; for technical reasons, if for no others, it must reduce the same to simple formulae. This is done by means of universalization and reduction to unity. Social relations are judged according to the form of relations of this kind that prevails in a given locality, or the social relations of a whole country are judged indiscriminately by the form of these relations that prevails in a certain part of the country or in a certain social class. If it is customary in a given locality for the husband to have absolute power of disposition over the property of his wife, a disposition actually made by a husband is held binding on the wife with utter disregard of the question whether or not this was the custom in the given family . . . This results in general and unitary norms for decision, but not in a general and unitary living law; and individual as well as local differences may well continue to exist beneath the crust of external uniformity.

But the associations themselves require norms for decision for their own completion and perfection. In their normal state, they are supplied with norms for those situations only which the parties involved have anticipated; every new situation, which has not been anticipated, confronts them with the necessity of finding new rules of conduct. This indispensable task of completing the structure of the associations is usually performed from within . . . The difficulties created by such an unanticipated event . . . most frequently cause the parties to appeal to the judge. The judge cannot find the solution in the inner order of the association; for the latter has at this very juncture proved unable to create an order. He must have special norms for the decision of the case at hand. . . . When a quarrel or controversy arises,

the associations have usually got out of their established order into a state of disorder . . . Special norms are required, not for the peaceful relation but for the legal dispute. And these will often differ from the former even as to content. . . .

. . . An extreme measure of parental or marital authority may be proportionate to the distribution of power within a certain family or within the family in a certain class or locality; but it is in conflict with the general order of the family in the state and in society, which have impressed their stamp upon the prevailing norms of law of morality, of ethical custom, of etiquette. The state and society therefore will not tolerate it, and will attempt to bring about an order which is more in harmony with the views that prevail generally, at least when appeal is made to its courts for the settling of disputes. Every wage contract, however disadvantageous to the working-man, will reflect quite accurately the relation of power that obtained between the employer and the employe at the time the contract was made. But if the working class obtains a greater measure of influence in society, it will attempt to shape the wage contract according to its ideas; a movement will arise within society which will stigmatize one or the other provision of the contracts of wages as contrary to morality and decency, and which, perhaps, will attain power enough to influence even the norms for decision applicable to wage contracts.

The courts decide on the basis of their norms for decision whether a social norm has been transgressed or not. The prevailing juristic science takes for granted that it must be a legal norm that has been transgressed, that the object for which courts have been erected is not the protection of non-legal norms. But it is evident that this can apply only to the organs of the state for the administration of justice. And even as to these it is true only if we call every norm according to which a court renders a decision a legal norm. But if we do that, the question becomes a mere question of terminology. If we consider the inner content of the norms according to which the courts must render their decisions—and that is the only fair way to proceed—we shall be convinced that the non-legal norms play an important role even in the courts of the state.

. . . The Roman *prudentes* and the German *Schoffen* appeal without hesitation to morality, ethical custom and decorum; the English judge, who at the present time is perhaps the only heir of the traditions of the ancient judicial office, does the same thing. But all of these are bound by the ever recurring limitation that non-legal norms may be used only to eke out the positive law, to act as stop-gaps; the judge therefore is not authorized to disregard the legal norms in favor of the non-legal ones. The principal is extremely elastic, and occasionally the limitation which it imposes upon the discretion of the judges can scarcely be felt; nevertheless it is of very great importance. It imports that the bases of our social order that have been expressed in legal norms may not be disturbed by other social orderings and rules. It does not apply therefore when the state itself intervenes in the administration of justice. The Roman praetor, the king in the Frankish and in the German kingdom, the English chancellor, render decisions according to fairness or according to morals, i.e. according to non-legal norms, and occasionally even contrary to the established law. From these decisions, it is true, legal propositions subsequently evolve. Although the praetorian law and English equity grew chiefly out of norms of morality, ethical custom, and decorum, they became separate and distinct legal systems in the course of time. This however merely shows that the chief difference between law and non-legal norms of this kind is a matter of stability, certainty, and the general conviction as to their social importance, not of content.

. . . The principle that the courts must base their decisions exclusively upon the law was never more than a matter of seeming. The rule of law itself continually refers them to other social norms; it will tolerate no abuse of the law which violates morality,

ethical custom, or decorum; it forbids immoral contracts; commands performance of contracts according to good faith and the custom of everyday life; provides penalties for insults, for violation of the proprieties and for gross mischief . . . The fact that the judge was rigidly confined to the law in every respect has hitherto merely prevented the judges from openly making non-legal norms the bases of their decisions, but not from doing so in various, sometimes very transparent, disguises. . . .

All of this, of course, does not mean that the courts should, without more ado, render their decisions according to non-legal norms. All legal propositions are not suitable for norms for decisions; *a fortiori* all non-legal norms, taken indiscriminately, are still less so. To make a proper selection is a task of enormous difficulty . . . .

The norm for decision contains the general proposition on which the decision is based, and thereby sets up the pretension that it is a truth which is valid, not only for the specific case under discussion but for every like or similar case . . . .

This is the law of the stability of legal norms, which is of such vast importance for the creation of law. It is based, in the first place, on social psychology. Rendering contrary decisions in like or in similar cases would not be law and right, but arbitrariness or caprice. It is based also on a certain sound economic quality of thinking. The expenditure of intellectual labor which undoubtedly is always involved in seeking norms for decision can often be avoided by rendering a decision according to a norm which has already been found. Moreover there is a great social need of stable norms for decision, which make it possible in a limited measure to foresee and predict the decisions and thereby to put a man in position to make his arrangements accordingly.

The law of the stability of the norms for decision functions chiefly in time. The court will not, without good cause, depart from a norm which it has applied in the decision of a case as long as the norm is remembered, and often special measures are being taken to prevent its being forgotten. But it functions in space also; for the norms for decision which have been found by one court will readily be applied by other courts which exist in the same sphere of influence, if for no other reason, in order to avoid the labor incident to finding norms. . . .

The sovereignty of the state in the field of law, which is so significant for modern law, is based on the stability of the legal norms . . . The stability of the norms for decision receives a special significance because of the fact that it extends not merely to like or similar cases but also to cases that are only approximately similar. This makes it possible to apply a norm to cases as to which it is not a decision at all, on the sole ground that the latter are similar to the decided cases. Every such decision, indeed, is based on a new norm for decision, but the content of this new norm is merely this: that the existing norm is applicable to the case. The new norm has extended the sphere of application of the original norm and enriched its content; and every such extension and enrichment in turn functions according to the law of the stability of the norms for decision . . . Thanks to this law of stability, the norms acquire an extremely tenacious life and an enormous extensibility. Every reception of foreign law is an instance of the operation of the law of the stability of the norms. Many a norm which, possibly, the Roman *pontifices* have thought out, continues to function today. One might raise the question here: If it is true that the norms grow out of the situations themselves for the decision concerning which they are to constitute the basis, how does it come about that a norm can still be applicable so long after it was created and under a totally different social and economic order. . . ?

The answer is this: The norms, especially those that have been derived from Roman law, have become so general and so abstract, by the uninterrupted process of extension and of enrichment of their content in the course of the millennia, that they are adaptable to the most diverse situations. This shows however that after all the law of the stability of the norms is based on a superficial view of things. In actual fact it is not the same norm at all; it has remained unchanged in appearance only; it has received an entirely new inner content.

The great contrasts between the law of the past and the law of the present, the differences between the laws of the various countries and nations, are based on the facts of the law, in every instance, rather than on the legal norms. The usages, relations of domination and subjection, relations of possession, contracts, testamentary dispositions, change to a much greater extent than the norms, and react upon the latter even though the wording of the latter has remained unchanged. . . .

Nevertheless one must not assume that this pouring of a new content into the norms obviates all difficulties involved in the law of the stability of the norms. The bulk of the complaints about unsatisfactory laws amounts to this: that the norms, because of their stability, function in situations for which they were not created, and to which therefore they are not adapted. But the evil effects are limited considerably by the fact that these norms are not norms of conduct but of decision. If the stability of the Roman norms should actually compel us to live according to Roman law, e.g. in the enlarged family of the Romans with its *manus* marriage or its free marriage arbitrarily dissoluble, if it should actually compel us to adapt our system of landholding to the Roman *fundus*, the resulting situation would be unendurable. In actual fact, all that it comes to is that occasionally a law-suit is decided according to Roman law. The part of our daily life that appears in the courts is by far too insignificant to make it impossible for us to endure the most unjust decisions. Much though we may suffer under this state of affairs, we submit to the inevitable; for stability of the norms, as a basis for judicial decision and for juristic science, is inevitable. . . .

VII

The State and the Law

. . . Wherever the legal norm attracted the attention of the sociologist . . . it has always been found in the company of other social norms. Nevertheless there can be no doubt that there is an unmistakable difference between it and the non-legal norms. . . .

Difficult though it may be to draw the line with scientific exactitude between the legal norm and other kinds of norms, practically this difficulty exists but rarely. In general anyone will be in position to tell without hesitation whether a given norm is a legal norm or whether it belongs to the sphere of religion, ethical custom, morality, decorum, tact, fashion, or etiquette . . . The difference between the legal and the non-legal norm is a question not of social science but of social psychology. The various classes of norms release various overtones of feeling, and we react to the transgression of different norms with different feelings. Compare the feeling of revolt that follows a violation of law with the indignation at a violation of a law of morality, with the feeling of disgust occasioned by an indecency, with the disapproval of tactlessness, the ridiculousness of an offense against eitquette, and lastly with the critical feeling of superiority with which a votary of fashion looks down upon those who have not attained the heights which he has scaled. . . .

. . . Norms with apparently identical content, at different times, in different countries, in different classes and ranks of society, manifestly belong to different groups, and . . . they readily pass from one group to another. In the course of the millennia the prohibition of marriage outside of one's own rank has been a norm of law, of religion, of morality, of ethical custom, of decorum, and today, perhaps, it is merely a norm of tact, of etiquette, or even of fashion. . . .

. . . Though a norm of the same wording can indeed belong to two different groups, it has a different content in each case. The agreement in wording therefore is a purely external thing. The proposition, "Honor thy father and thy mother," can be considered a command of law, of morality, of religion, of ethical custom, of decorum, of tact, of etiquette, and of fashion. As a legal norm it commands a child to honor his parents by means of certain outward demonstrations; as a norm of morality, in general, by means of conduct evincing honor and respect. Religion, unless it simply repeats the command of morality, prescribes religious duties in addition, especially prayers for one's father and one's mother. Ethical custom demands that one show such respect for one's parents as is customary in good families. As a norm of decorum it forbids such omission of manifestations of respect as would be offensive to others; as a norm of tact it disapproves of much less serious offenses which might release a feeling of displeasure among those that happen to be present. Etiquette refers solely to deportment toward one's father and mother in society. If respectful demeanor toward one's parents were fashionable at a given time in fashionable circles, a person moving in these circles who should omit it would be guilty of an offense against fashion.

. . . A norm, whether it be a legal norm or a norm of some other kind, must be *recognized* in the sense that men actually regulate their conduct according to it. A system of law or of ethics that no one gives heed to is like a fashion that no one follows. Only we must bear in mind that what has been said about the rule of conduct must not be applied to the norm for decision; for courts may at any time draw forth a legal proposition which has been slumbering for centuries and make it the basis of their decisions. . . .

The sociological science of law, therefore, will not be able to state the difference between law and morals in a brief simple formula in the manner of the juristic science that has hitherto been current. Only a thorough examination of the psychic and social facts, which at the present time have not even been gathered, can shed light upon this difficult question. Though we are well aware of the great degree of caution made imperative by the present state of juristic science, we may perhaps be permitted to assume, at this time, the following essential characteristics of law. The legal norm regulates a matter which, at least in the opinion of the group within which it has its origin, is of great importance, of basic significance. The individual act which is commanded by the legal proposition may not be of great weight, as for instance in the case of statutes regulating foods, or concerning prevention of fires or infectious diseases of cattle, but we must always consider the consequences if violations of these statutes should assume the dimension of a mass phenomenon. Only matters of lesser significance are left to other social norms . . . The legal norm, as contrasted with the other norms, can always be stated in clear definite terms. It thereby gives a certain stability to the associations that are based on legal norms, whereas associations not based on legal norms, e.g. political parties, religious communions, groups of relatives, social relations, are characterized by a looseness, a lack of stability, until they assume a legal form. Norms of morality, too, of ethical custom, of decorum, often become legal norms as soon as they lose their universal character, and, couched in clear precise terms, assume basic significance for the legal order of society . . . In this way, equity arose in England, which is today a system of law as fully developed as the common law. It may well be possible therefore that the normal precept of good faith in contractual relations may, in the course of time, be compressed into a series of definite and clear legal propositions.

. . . In the case of legal norms, society devotes much more thought to the matter of formulating than in the case of norms of morals and of the other non-legal norms; in view of the importance it attaches to law it is anxious to have not merely a general direction, but a detailed precept. Everyone ought to be able to know from the mere wording of the legal norm how he is to regulate his conduct in a given case . . . A man without any inner sense of law knows how to perform his duties as a citizen of the state, knows that he must perform his contracts, respect the property right of others; but in order to be able to conduct himself correctly from the point of view of morals, religion, ethical custom, decorum, etiquette, and fashion, he requires a sense of morality, religion, ethical custom, decorum, tact, etiquette, and fashion. Without this sense, he cannot hit upon the correct thing. For this reason, when non-legal norms are involved, the center of gravity is inwardly within a man's self to a much greater extent than when legal norms are involved. . . .

VIII

The Creation of the Legal Proposition

. . . Every legal proposition which is to serve as the basis for judicial decisions is itself a norm for decision, formulated in words, and published in an authoritative manner, asserting claim to universal validity, but without reference to the case that may have occasioned it. The prevailing school of juristic science treats the judicial decision as a logical syllogism in which a legal proposition is the major premise; the matter litigated, the minor; and the judgment of the court, the conclusion. This idea presupposes that every judgment is preceded in time by a legal proposition. Historically this is quite incorrect. The judge who, in the beginnings of the administration of justice, awards a penalty to the plaintiff has found the existence of a concrete relation . . . and a violation thereof, and thereupon has independently found the norm fixing the penalty. Perhaps in each of these decisions the thought is germinating that in a similar situation, a like or a similar decision ought to be arrived at; but this germ at this time is buried deep in the subliminal consciousness of the judge. If we assume that the judge in primitive times protected possession or contract only because he had assumed the existence of a legal proposition according to which possession or contract ought to be protected by law, we are attributing our own conception to him. He thinks only of the concrete, not of the abstract . . . Nevertheless, in spite of the lack of legal propositions, the norm for decision was not a matter of pure caprice. The judge always drew it from the facts of the law, which had been established either on the basis of his own knowledge or of evidence, i.e. from usages, from relations of domination and of possession, from declarations of will, and, chiefly, from contracts. Given these facts, the norm was given; it was impossible to separate the question of fact from the question of law.

Today we have the identical situation when there is no legal proposition in existence for the case that is to be decided . . . .

But even where a legal proposition has been found which covers the instant case, the legal proposition does not yield the decision without more ado. The legal proposition is always couched in general terms; it can never be as concrete as the case itself . . . Here too the judge must ascertain the facts; here too he must decide independently whether the ascertained facts correspond to the definition[s] . . . contained in the legal proposition. Whether the judge answers this question in the affirmative or in the negative, the judgment is always rendered on the basis of a norm for decision which he has found independently . . . In such a case, the prevailing tendency in juristic science invariably assumes that we have a decision as to a question of law . . . But it is clear that in this case, as in the earlier cases, the question of fact, the ascertained facts, cannot be dissociated from the question of law, the norm for decision which the judge has found at this very moment. This concrete norm for decision, which the judge has deduced from the facts, is introduced between the legal proposition which contains the general norm for decision and the ascertainment of the facts by the judge.

. . . The more concrete the legal proposition, the more precisely the judicial norm of decision will be determined by the norm of the legal proposition; the more general the legal proposition, the more independently and the more freely the judicial norm will be found. But there are legal proposi-

tions which grant an unlimited discretion to the judge. Examples of this kind in private law are the legal propositions on . . . good faith, on unjust enrichment. In criminal law and in administrative law they also play an important part . . . The upshot of all this is that the difference between a decision according to a legal proposition and one not according to a legal proposition is a difference of degree merely. The judge is never delivered up to the legal proposition, bound hand and foot, without any will of his own, and the more general the legal proposition, the greater the freedom of the judge. . . .

It is possible that now and then legal propositions were thought out by jurists without reference to a definite decision . . . Of course these can be only very insignificant legal propositions. We can also say that a legal proposition is prior in time to the norms for decision where a statute regulates an institution in order to introduce it, particularly where the latter is imported from a foreign country, as, for instance, the statute concerning companies with limited liability . . . But apart from these exceptions the concrete, as is usual, is prior to the abstract; the norm for decision, to the legal proposition.

The creation of a legal proposition out of the norms for decision requires that further intellectual effort be applied to the latter; for we must extract from them that which is universally valid and state it in a proper manner. This intellectual labor, whosoever it may be that is able to do it, is called juristic science. The Historical School of jurisprudence has taken infinite pains to show how "customary law," or, to put it more accurately, legal propositions of "customary law," arise immediately in the popular consciousness. It is a vain endeavor . . . Legal propositions are created by jurists, preponderantly on the basis of norms for decision found in the judgments of courts. The judge therefore who, when he gives the reasons for his decision, states the norm for decision in the form in which it is to be binding in future cases, may be said to be engaged in juristic labor. Judge-made law is always merely a subdivision of juristic law. Juristic science is created by the writer or teacher . . . and he does this even where, as editor of a collection of decisions, he states the legal propositions that are derived from the decision in the form of a head note, or where, as editor of a statute, he adds them to the various sections in the form of annotations . . . Lastly the legislator who puts the norms for decision into statutory form is also engaged in scientific juristic labor . . . And every such legal proposition, wheresoever it may have had its origin, lays claim to universal validity . . . To be sure, as a rule, only the legislator has the power to make his will prevail. In the case of a judge or a writer the value of the performance is decisive of the success of his intellectual labor. If the legal proposition is good and practical, its chances of gaining recognition are as fair as the chances of a good and practical idea in any other sphere, perhaps as fair as the chances of a good and practical invention. . . .

. . . As daily experience shows, the success of a thought in every field of human activity does not depend exclusively upon its inner value but also upon certain outward circumstances, particularly upon the weight generally attached to the words of the person who has given utterance to the thought. This weight very often increases with the power of the author of the legal proposition in the state, his position, and his personal reputation. . . .

. . . Science can only know that which is, and cannot command what should be, . . . science therefore creates no norms, but merely investigates, presents, and teaches . . . The question is not whether new law arises from the knowledge of law, but whether the jurist, as a person versed in the law, claims the right to create new law. It is self-evident that this question can be answered historically only, and, the answer will be in the affirmative wherever juristic science is not content to be limited to making a most faithful and unprejudiced presentation of that which is law, but strives, over and above this, to create norms independently which shall

be binding upon the judges for all cases for which none can be found in the other sources of law. . . .

Great differences, indeed, appear in details. It is self-evident that the importance of science is in an inverse ratio to that of the statute and that of the judge; the higher the position of the judge the greater the jealousy with which he guards his independence; the more omnipotent and comprehensive legislation, the more limited the sphere it is willing to concede to the jurist. For this reason juristic science declines whenever a codification has been made and does not awaken to a new life until the people become aware of defects and gaps in the latter. . . .

. . . The power of the judge is not sufficient to overcome the enormous powers of resistance inherent in society which would rise up in opposition to an attempt to place society on a new foundation by means of a judicial pronouncement; and a judge requires knowledge of the world sufficient to be able correctly to estimate these powers of resistance as well as his own power. The judge has often, it is true, disregarded the law in the service of an unscrupulous sovereign power; occasionally, supported by the law, he has been able to offer successful resistance to a strong sovereign power; but he has never risked a combat with the state, society, and traditional law. Much less has juristic science, with its limited powers, ever done this. . . .

. . . It has happened twice in the history of law that a state official acted when it became necessary to end the sway of norms for decision that had become rigid and antiquated. The Roman praetor and the English chancellor fulfilled their historic mission by opposing an altogether new legal system to the traditional system. . . .

Norms for decision in statutory form, whether taken from juristic law or created by the legislator, are a precarious matter. It is much more difficult for the legislator to formulate a correct general rule than for the judge to decide an individual case; and it is a much more hazardous thing for him to posit an absolutely binding dogma for all time to come than it is for a jurist, who is proceeding scientifically, to enunciate propositions which are continually being examined and re-examined. The norm for decision Lecomes an entirely different thing when published in a statute from what it was before. Hitherto merely a presentation of what appears to be the proper rule, it now becomes a precept as to what ought to be the rule. It loses the pliability which had enabled it to adapt itself to every better insight and to every development . . . A method of procedure that is permissible where a legal doctrine is involved might not be permissible at all, or at least only with greater difficulty, when one is dealing with a statute. The legislator therefore ought to attempt to mould life according to his own ideas only where this is absolutely necessary; and where he can let life take care of itself, let him refrain from unnecessary interference. This doubtless was the leading, though unexpressed, thought in the fight which Savigny, for a time, waged against legislation, not merely against codification as is often mistakenly asserted today. Every superfluous statute is a bad statute.

Nevertheless it would be childish to give up altogether the thought of expressing juristic law in statutory form . . . In more advanced stages of development mankind is brought face to face with a number of problems of legal life that can be satisfactorily dealt with only by the state. . . .

. . . Statutes are indispensable for the purpose of getting rid of antiquated law and of quickly bringing about necessary innovations; for the rule that juristic science and administration of justice must not get into conflict with the law that has already been posited is an insuperable limitation upon their creative activity. . . .

IX

The Structure of the Legal Proposition

The immediate basis of the legal order of human society is the facts of the law: usage, relations of domination, relations of pos-

session, declarations of will, particularly in their most important forms, to wit: articles of association, contract, and testamentary disposition. From these facts the rules of conduct which determine the conduct of man in society derive. These facts alone, therefore, and not the legal propositions, according to which the courts render decisions, and according to which the administrative tribunals of the state proceed, are of authoritative significance for the legal order in human society. Nevertheless the legal propositions gain significance for the latter inasmuch as the decisions of the courts and the measures taken by the administrative agencies affect the facts of the law and thus bring about changes in the existing usages, relations of domination, relations of possesssion, articles of association, contracts, and testamentary dispositions; i.e., on this presupposition the decisions of the courts and the measures taken by the administrative agencies, which are based on the legal propositions, in turn produce norms which regulate the social conduct of human beings. New facts of the law therefore can be established . . . at least indirectly, by means of legal propositions. For this purpose however it is not sufficient that the legal proposition should have formal validity, or that it should be applied in isolated cases; for an isolated fact is not a social fact. It is necessary for this purpose that men regulate their conduct according to the legal proposition. . . .

. . . We must . . . distinguish three classes of legal propositions.

In the first place there are legal propositions that accord the protection of the courts and other tribunals to the facts of the law as they exist in society . . . Distinguished from legal propositions of this kind are those that negate existing facts of the law or that self-actively create facts of the law. On the basis of legal propositions courts and other state tribunals artificially create or dissolve associations, establish or abolish relations of domination, give, take away, or transfer possession, rescind articles of association, contracts, testamentary declarations of the will, or occasionally create them by compulsion.

Under this head are found chiefly the legal propositions that decree expropriation or forfeiture of things; that declare certain relations invalid, null, voidable, or punishable. . . .

A third species of legal propositions attaches legal consequences to facts of the law, quite independently of the norms that result from the usages, the relations of domination and of possession, and the dispositions created by these facts. . . .

. . . Accordingly the legal order which society self-actively creates for itself in the facts of the law, in the existing usages, relations of domination, and of possession, articles of association, contracts, testamentary dispositions, is brought face to face with a legal order which is created by means of legal propositions, and enforced solely by means of the activity of the courts and the other tribunals of the state. And norms, rules of conduct, flow from this second legal order no less than from the former, to the extent that it protects, gives form and shape to, modifies, or perhaps abolishes the facts of the law . . . The important thing for the norms of the second legal order is not the distribution of interests in the individual social associations, but the distribution in society as a whole, which comprises all the associations within a certain territory. The second legal order then is an order which has been imposed by society upon the associations. . . .

. . . Wherever there is no doubt as to where the power lies in a state, or where the voice of popular consciousness speaks in no uncertain tones, the task of the jurist is a merely technical one. The content of the legal proposition is given by society. His function is merely to provide the wording of it and to find the means whereby the interests which are to be secured can be secured most effectively. This technical function however must not be underrated. The clumsiness of procedure and the limited capacity for expression of the material law often cause enormous difficulty in this matter. They are the cause of all formalism in law. Formalism is not an admirable quality of law, but a technical defect which must be overcome . . . The present most unsatisfactory state of many legal institutions is attributable, in a measure, to the fact that we have not as yet been able to establish technically perfect legal propositions concerning them.

The decision as to the interests involved in a dispute is entrusted by the state to the jurist when it is clearly indicated neither by the general interest nor by the distribution of power in society as a whole. This situation may be brought about by various causes. In the first place very often the parties to the dispute are quite unaware of the great social interests involved in the decision; very often the latter are distributed among the various classes and ranks in such a manner as to place them above the struggles of class and rank; in many cases these social interests are too inconsiderable and insignificant to become involved in the dispute. Very often, too, the possessors of power, who are called upon to render the decision, are not at all involved in the conflict of interests. The most important cause however is the fact that the powers that are engaged in the struggle in behalf of the different interests counterbalance one another or that the influences that proceed from the groups that are most powerful politically, economically, or socially, are checked or thwarted by other social tendencies, which are based on religious, ethical, scientific, or other ideological convictions.

When the jurist is asked to draw the line between the conflicting interests independently, he is asked, by implication, to do it according to justice. This implies, in the first place, something negative. He is asked to arrive at a decision without any consideration of expediency and uninfluenced by the distribution of power. In recent times, it is true, it has often been said that justice, too, is a matter involving questions of power. If the writer means to say that the idea of justice, on which the decision is based, must have attained a certain power in the body social at the time when it influences the judicial finding of norms or the activity of the state, he is indeed stating a truth . . . But if he means to say that, under the cloak of justice, effect is always being given to the influence of political, social, or economic position, the statement is manifestly incorrect. A legal norm whose origin can be traced to such influences is usually stigmatized by that very fact as something unjust. Justice has always weighted the scales solely in favor of the weak and the persecuted. A just decision is a decision based on grounds which appeal to a disinterested person; it is a decision which is rendered by a person who is not involved in the conflict of interests, or which, even though it be rendered by a person involved in this conflict, nevertheless is such as a disinterested person would render or approve of. It is never based on taking advantage of a position of power. When a person who is in a position of power acts justly he acts against his own interest, at any rate against his immediate interest, prompted by religious, ethical, scientific, or other ideological considerations; perhaps merely by considerations of prudent policy. The parties of political and social justice . . . find their adherents chiefly among ideologists who are not personally interested in the political and social conflicts of interests. In this fact lies their strength and also their weakness.

But all of these are negative characteristics. Which are the positive characteristics of justice? The catch phrase about balancing of interests which is so successful at the present time is not an answer to this question; for the very question is: What is it that gives weight to the interests that are to be balanced? Manifestly it is not the balancing jurist, writer or teacher, judge or legislator, but society itself. The function of the jurist is merely to balance them. There are trends caused by the interests that flourish in society which ultimately influence even persons that are not involved in these conflicting interests. The judge who decides according to justice follows the tendency that he himself is dominated by. Justice therefore does not proceed from the individual, but arises in society.

The role of the person rendering the decision is of importance only inasmuch as, within certain limitations, he can select the solution which corresponds most nearly to his personal feelings. But in doing this, he cannot disregard the social basis of the decision . . . A judge who, in a decision which he renders, recognizes private property in means of production in spite of the fact that he is a socialist, or who admits the defense that the debt sued upon in a stock-exchange transaction is a gaming debt although in his opinion the setting-up of this plea is a breach of good faith, does not thereby contradict himself. In doing these things he is merely being guided by social tendencies against his own individual feeling in the matter. A rebellious slave, the government of a beleaguered city . . . can indeed proceed according to their individual feelings, but they can do so only because they have been removed from social influences by the force of circumstances. Justice is a power wielded over the minds of men by society.

It is the function of juristic science, in the first place, to record the trends of justice that are found in society, and to ascertain what they are, whence they come, and whither they lead; but it cannot possibly determine which of these is the only just one. In the forum of science, they are all equally valid. What men consider just depends upon the ideas they have concerning the end of human endeavor in this world of ours, but it is not the function of science to dictate the final ends of human endeavor on earth. That is the function of the founder of a religion, of the preacher, of the prophet, of the preacher of ethics, of the practical jurist, of the judge, of the politician . . . That a certain thing is just is no more scientifically demonstrable than is the beauty of a Gothic cathedral or of a Beethoven symphony to a person who is insensible to it. All of these are questions of the emotional life. Science can ascertain the effects of a legal proposition, but it cannot make these effects appear either desirable or loathsome to man. Justice is a social force, and it is always a question whether it is potent enough to influence the disinterested persons whose function it is to create juristic and statute law.

But although science can teach us nothing concerning the ends, once the end is determined, it can enlighten us as to the means to that end . . . Practical juristic science is concerned with the manner in which the ends may be attained that men are endeavoring to attain through law, but it must utilize the results of the sociology of law for this purpose. The legal proposition is not only the result, it is also a lever, of social development. . . .

. . . The highest aim of all science is to vouchsafe to us a glimpse of the future; the investigator gradually becomes a seer. As the physicist endeavors to determine the course of a cannon-ball in advance, so the disciples of the social sciences endeavor to calculate in advance the unifying regularities in the course of the future development of social happenings. . . .

. . . On the basis of the results of the steady progress of the science of sociology, juristic science will be in a correspondingly better position to tell the judge and the legislator when they are performing useful labors, and when, inasmuch as they are resisting the laws of development and failing to understand the effects of the legal propositions, they are bootlessly frittering social forces away. . . .

The sociologist, therefore, who on the basis of his scientific knowledge is endeavoring to draw a picture of the social order as it will exist in the future, and of a legal system that, even in the present, shall be adapted to the future, is by no means engaged in an unscientific undertaking . . . It is true, unfortunately, that in investigations of this kind very much that is untenable sails under the flag of science, but the blame for this must not be attributed to the subject but to the newness and incompleteness of this whole field of knowledge . . . All these matters that have been presented up to this point, the relation of the legal proposition to society and its being conditioned by the social development, were clearly discerned by the founders of the Historical School;

for what they call the legal consciousness of the people is but the trends of justice in society. It is true they were in error as to the scope of their doctrine, for the latter did not give an explanation of the law but only of the legal proposition; and not of every legal proposition, but only of the proposition that is based on justice. . . .

. . . If justice is to govern, the decisive factor must not be the wishes of one party or the other, but the question which of the conflicting interests are of greater importance to society, i.e. the interests of cattle-raising or of agriculture, of industry or of the sanitary condition of the neighborhood; of the owner of land or of the usufructuary; of the employer or of the employee; of commerce or of free exercise of one's powers; of increase of wealth in the hands of the propertied classes or of the welfare of the non-propertied classes. And he who is called upon to render a decision must take into account not only the present moment, but also the coming generations; not only the economic needs, but also the political, ethical, and cultural significance of cattle-raising and of agriculture, of industry and of public hygiene, of great landed estates and of rights of usufruct, of employer and of employee, of commerce and of free activity, of property and of the welfare of the non-propertied classes.

. . . To answer questions of this kind means to be able to read the signs of the development of the future in the society of today, to sense its needs in advance, and to determine its order in advance . . . Only an intellect equipped with the full armament of science can be called upon to perform this task. Meanwhile our sense of justice is merely one of those great indefinite divinings of hidden interrelations in the vast scheme of things, which, like religion, ethics, and perhaps art, lead mankind to distant unknown goals. In these paths the genius is the born leader of mankind . . . The genius is the more highly developed man in the midst of a human race that has remained far behind him; the man of the future, born, by a mysterious coincidence, into the present, who today thinks and feels as some day the whole race will think and feel. Therein lies his tragic fate, for he is lonely; and his sole compensation lies in this, that he shows the way to others . . . Though justice is based on social trends, it requires the personal activity of an individual to make it effective. In this it is most like art . . . And again like a work of art, which, though shaped out of social materials, nevertheless receives from the artist the stamp of his whole individual personality, justice owes to society only its rough content, but owes its individual form to the artist in justice who has created it. There is no such thing as one justice only, as there is no such thing as one beauty only, but in every work of justice there is justice, just as beauty speaks to mankind in every true work of art. Justice, as it has been given individual form in statutes, judicial decisions, works of literature, is, in its highest manifestations, the resultant of an inspired synthesis of opposites like every other grand creation of the human mind.

The mind of man is so manifold, the stratification of society is so variegated, that it is impossible to state the concept of justice in a single formula. Perhaps none has met with so much success as the formula which Bentham borrowed from Beccaria, to wit the greatest happiness of the greatest number. But it has never been "demonstrated," and it cannot be numbered among those truths that are evident without demonstration.

In the first place Bentham's formula will by no means convince everyone. Not the religious ascetic to whom earthly happiness in general appears as of no value whatever; not the member of the aristocracy according to whose ideas the "greatest number" has not been created for happiness but for labor and obedience; not the aesthete, to whom a Michelangelo or a Napoleon outweighs millions of the all-too-many; not the patriot, who is much more concerned with the power and greatness of his country than with the happiness of the individuals that constitute its citizens; not the energist, to whom striv-

ing and making his efforts effective is of much greater importance than happiness. This formula will gain adherents only among those who are convinced of it from the outset—those who consciously are democrats. It is a democratic catchword, and saying this we have said by implication that it expresses the thoughts and feelings of a small minority only. For democracy is an aristocratic thought . . . The plebeian is never a democrat. He demands equality only with those who are above him, never with those that are below him. There is something of the highest quality of nobility, a consciousness of enormous power, an unconquered defiance, in not only refraining from demanding privileges but also rejecting them when they are offered.

And what did all these democrats among aristocrats and aristocrats among democrats take the words "greatest number" to mean? To the Gracchi they were several hundred thousand proletarians among the Roman commonalty; to Ulrich von Hutten, the German order of knights, which certainly was not more numerous; to Bentham himself, the middle classes of the urban bourgeoisie; to Marx, the millions of the laboring classes. If one had demanded of the Gracchi that they should grant to the non-Italic peregrine equal rights with the citizens, or of Hutten that he should grant to the peasants equal rights with the knights of the Empire, they would have considered such a proposal most unjust. Bentham contented himself with the cold comfort that it is possible even for the lowest working-man to rise into the middle classes—perhaps for one among ten thousand. Is that the "greatest number"? The idea of offering some sort of assistance to factory workers by means of a very moderate social policy first occurred to Bentham's greatest disciple, John Stuart Mill. From the standpoint of pure arithmetic, Marx surely was right. But in his whole book there is not a single line on the question how the socialization of the means of production can be made to benefit those who are beyond the pale of society. And if one considers the population of the whole world, the latter surely are the "greatest number." . . .

And finally, what is the meaning of the "greatest happiness"? To Bentham and his disciples these words meant, in a general way, the economic well-being of the middle classes and the greatest possible scope for the free exercise of the powers of the individual. But is it not true that they who have the deepest insight into human nature have pointed out that the "greatest number" are happiest when they are led by strong men who forge their fates for them? When their individuality is merged in a community, or even when they serve a master who provides for the day, and in the evening protects them from privation and misery? Is it not true that a perhaps equally "great number" experience the greatest happiness when they live in contemplative laziness, at the expense of someone else, albeit suffering great privations withal? . . .

The prevailing school of jurisprudence, which sees in every legal proposition only the expression of the "will of the lawgiver," altogether fails to recognize the important part of society in its creation. The teachers of the Natural Law School, in their day, had a much deeper insight into the matter inasmuch as they endeavored to base the law upon the sense of justice, i.e. upon the social trends of justice; Savigny and Puchta with their doctrine of the popular consciousness of right and law as the basis of legal development merely restated thoughts of the natural law in terms of a social point of view. Bentham, by his principle of utility, with which Jhering's *Zweck im Rechte* coincides in the main, for the first time, in a comprehensive manner, directed attention to the general interest, which, it is true, he often enough confused with the interest of a single class, the bourgeois middle class. The materialistic interpretation of history went much further than the natural law doctrine, than the Historical School, than Bentham and Jhering. It pointed out to what extent the law, and therefore also the legal propositions, are a superstructure erected on the foundation of the economic order, and also to what extent

the legal propositions are being fashioned and created under the pressure of the distribution of power in society. But in doing this it became biassed, for it intentionally excluded from its consideration the element of human personality, the trends of justice as well as all non-economic influences which it always, and occasionally in an extremely arbitrary manner, traced back to economic ones, and usually, though quite unintentionally, all consideration of the general interest. The sociology of law must not overlook any of these things; it must consider everything that takes part in the creation of the legal proposition.

X

The Varying Content of the Concept of Justice

. . . Thus far then the whole law, which is based on justice, is nothing more than an expression of the existing facts of the law, an expression of social statics. In contrast to, and distinct from, this justice there is another justice, which is an expression of social dynamics. In the latter the idea prevails not only that the legal proposition is able to preserve the *status quo,* but that it is a means whereby society can order the relations within the various associations in its interest. The powerful impelling forces of this dynamics are individualism and collectivism. . . .

. . . The culmination of individualism is the principle that every man is an end unto himself and is not subject to any power that would use him for its own ends: neither to a domination that would subject him to the individual will of another nor to a domination that would subject him to the will of an association in which he does not serve himself but only the whole. The ideal of justice of individualism is the individual and his property, the individual who has an untrammeled power of disposition over his property, who recognizes no superior but the state, and is not bound by anything but the contracts he has freely entered into. Individualism therefore dissolves all relations of dependence established by custom, i.e., slavery, domination, and subjection, and abolishes, or at least weakens, the family law powers. . . . After the associations, into which the individuals appear to have been placed as members by society, have been dissolved and destroyed, the only connecting links that remain between the individual and society are ownership, contract, and the state, to which even individualism concedes the unlimited right to use the individual as a means to an end. Between the state and the individual are only those associations which the state creates as its institutions or endeavors to treat as such (commune, country, church), and those that the individual enters voluntarily either by joining or through contract (clubs, societies) . . . In general duties are imposed upon an individual by norms for decision only in a case where the individual has undertaken a duty contractually or has brought it upon himself through fault. . . .

The world-historical significance of individualism lies in this that it has done more than merely to create legal propositions . . . It has done away with the usages in the associations by abolishing the associations; it has changed them by changing the structure of the associations, especially by loosening the structure of the family and by bringing the state into an entirely new relation to the individual; and, in particular, it has given a deathblow to the power of domination in the family and in the ruling associations among civilized peoples. Through the establishment of liberty of property and the liberation of land from all burdens and charges, which followed in the train of liberty of property, it has utterly changed the relations of possession; through liberty of contract it has freed trade and commerce from untold fetters; and through liberty of industrial activity it has shifted the center of gravity in the acquisition of wealth to movable property. But the very greatness of the revolution most effectively bears witness to the fact that the legal propositions have brought about these effects solely through the elemental social forces, to which they in turn owed their very existence.

In the nineteenth century collectivism appeared as a reaction from individualism. Inasmuch as it found expression in socialism or communism it has no place in this discussion; for in this form it has had no influence upon the present-day development of law. Other, more moderate, forms of the idea . . . have come to be of great significance. . . .

. . . Individualism, even in the days of its greatest power and influence, was not able to prevent communities from coming into existence, and continuing to exist, in which at least certain claims of the members were satisfied by the whole body according to quite different principles . . . The individuals render services according to their powers and abilities, and receive according to their needs. . . .

The point of departure is the great inner contradiction with which individualism is afflicted. In spite of the endeavor to treat all men alike, it permits some of the greatest inequalities to remain, especially the inequality in wealth, which the equality before the law merely serves to accentuate . . . In contrast to socialism, the social movement that is based upon collectivism does not attempt to abolish the inequalities, but merely to mitigate them. Its aim is to counterbalance the advantage in fact which the rich enjoy by means of social institutions and legal propositions which impose limitations upon the rich and prevent them from availing themselves of these advantages in too great a measure . . . .

. . . Just as the old usury legislation tried to prevent the owner of money and consumable goods from availing himself of his ownership for the purpose of exploitation in the contract for the extension of credit, so the state today forbids the owner of the means of production to resort to certain kinds of exploitation in the contract of labor (limitation of the labor of women and children, of the working day . . .) It compels the owner of the means of production to permit the workman to receive a greater share of the fruits of his labor . . . It expends a part of the produce of the national economy for the benefit of the non-propertied classes (old age pensions, social insurance, state institutions for the public welfare. . . .) . . .

The social idea of justice therefore has not destroyed the individualistic idea of justice; it has fulfilled it. . . .

. . . There is much in the work of individualism that has called forth just criticism, nor have all the results of collectivism stood the test. It seems that we are again facing an individualistic tendency, which undoubtedly will be followed by a tendency of the opposite kind. Like the thread of a screw, these two ideas of justice alternately have been drawing the human race upward.

Among all of the ideas of justice that have been described until now there is not one that has failed to encounter an antagonist in the course of historical development who, in the deepest chest-tones of genuine conviction, would proclaim the opposite as that which alone is just. This affords a deep insight into the nature of justice . . . Often enough, at the same time, opposing principles are conceived to be just, sometimes in different strata of society, in circles that are remote from each other, but just as frequenty by people who are in a very close relationship to each other. Both the two parties to a law-suit are usually convinced of the justice of their cause, and perhaps they may well be; for each is appealing to a different idea of justice.

. . . Among the conflicting ideas of justice there always has been one that gained the victory at the time, and the victories were gained not because of historical accident but in accordance with an inner unifying regularity. As everywhere else in the universe, so also in society, the yesterday is contained in the today, and the today in the tomorrow . . . In order to become a legal proposition, the legal today and the legal tomorrow, born in society, must be given form and shape by a personality who thinks and senses what the future will bring. This is the basis of all practical juristic science, of all legislative policy, of all the systems of legal philosophy that have hitherto come into existence. It is true, we are in no better case than the herbalists of past centuries, to whom thousands of years of experience of the human race had given a vague idea of the virtues that are inherent in the various plants. The jurist and the legislator will gradually become more and more like the modern scientifically trained physician in proportion as sociology is able to trace and present the laws of the development of human society. At the present time there are a few modest beginnings in, and only in, the science of economics.

19

Jean Dabin

1889–

Jean Dabin is a Belgian, born and raised in the Flemish town of Liege. He practiced law after graduating from Liege University in 1911. His Alma Mater conferred a special doctorate of civil laws on him in 1920. He was a spirited young advocate; one of his friends says, "He did not always have towards the magistrates the naively reverential bearing of a young licentiate."

In 1922 he gave up practice when called to a chair at Catholic University in Louvain, Belgium—a school said by Professor Patterson to be "the principle center of Thomistic philosophy in Europe." Dabin has been exchange professor in several French Universities, including the University of Paris. He also spent a year in Switzerland's Lausanne University.

Dabin married a daughter of one of his Louvain colleagues, and has raised a large family. Three of his sons took religious orders. One of Dabin's brothers is also a Jesuit. He, himself, has been honored by the Roman Catholic Church with the papal decoration of the cross of St. Sylvester.

Early morning on school days he walks to school briskly, twirling his cane. The distance is considerable. He likes to teach the first class period of the day. He is a popular teacher whose courses are well attended. One of his friends characterizes him as lively and impulsive, a man of great enthusiasm and complete independence of spirit. His stature has been recognized by honorary degrees, membership in the Belgian Royal Academy, and other continental honorary societies, and decoration by the Belgian Crown. Dabin's many and important writings date back to

his graduate student days. His *General Theory of Law* (excerpts from which follow) was first published in French in 1944. Dabin shares with Jacques Maritain leadership in contemporary neo-Scholastic legal and political philosophy.

GENERAL THEORY OF LAW *

Part One

THE CONCEPT OF LAW

Introduction

3. *Adopting the Idea of "the Rule"; Philological Considerations.* The only method that will stand up under criticism is to set up at the very beginning the idea of the law as order, regulation, norm, or rule of conduct. No matter how the idea of the "rule" may be conceived—as a simple mental representation or as an objective reality . . . there is no doubt that the law exists as a certain rule of conduct. . . .

5. *As Usually Understood, the Rule Called "Law" Bears Upon Relationships Between Men.* But if the law is primarily a rule of conduct, it may at once be more precisely said, since the living usage of words has so decided, that the rule of conduct called "law," taken in its specific sense, is limited to relationships between men; that it does

* Reprinted by permission of publishers, from Translation by K. Wilk, The Legal Philosophies of Lask, Radbruch and Dabin; Cambridge, Mass., Harvard University Press, copyright 1950 by the President and Fellows of Harvard College.

not, or at least not directly concern either duties of man toward God or duties of man toward himself . . . However, the legal rule is not the only rule to govern relationships between men. Other kinds of rules, more or less closely related, or at any rate bearing other names, intervene with some competence in the same field. . . .

6. *Defining the Legal Rule* . . . This distinctive principle will be found only if the idea of law is approached from the idea of the organized group, especially of society. The law is a social rule not merely in that it presupposes a social environment, but in that it exists only in and by society, as the rule of that society . . . The law may be defined as follows: The sum total of the rules of conduct laid down, or at least consecrated, by civil society, under the sanction of public compulsion, with a view to realizing in the relationships between men a certain order— the order postulated by the end of the civil society and by the maintenance of the civil society as an instrument devoted to that end. . . .

CHAPTER I

Formal Definition of the Legal Rule

Section 1. The Law as the Rule of Civil Society

8. *Law Implies Societal Life* . . . The legal rule . . . comes into existence only on condition that men form a group, not solely by sharing certain common physical, psychological, or social traits producing mere solidarity (such as men of one nation or one social class), but on the basis of a veritable society, implying a specific social end, organization, and hierarchy . . . The legal rule, then, is the rule that governs the relationships between men thus grouped in organic, organized fashion.

9. *Why Societal Life Requires Law* . . . To speak of a legal relation is to speak of a societal relation: There is law, in the specific sense of a rule distinct from morals and manners, only where there is an organized society. The reciprocal statement, by the way,

is equally true . . . Every organized society calls forth a legal rule. First, in order to constitute itself to subsist, and to function. For the society exists only due to the human individuals of whom it is composed. They must therefore be kept in allegiance and under obligations inherent in the social state by a rule that determines and sanctions their status as members. Again, the society operates only by the action of individuals, called its "functionaries," officials and subordinates of all grades and employments up to the directing personnel, individuals who in turn are bound by a norm, that of social "service." Finally, as each society must obtain from its members not only some contribution to its existence through obligations properly social, but also some collaboration towards its ends, in larger or smaller measure as 'he case may be, it is important that there be a rule defining and guaranteeing that collaboration . . . .

12. *Distinct and Eminent Place of the Law of Civil Society* . . . The law of the civil society is competent to order all activities of the subjects within its territory, including the legal and non-legal activities of the particular groups. In that sense, the civil society is sovereign, it is the commander-in-chief of the individuals and groups, and hence its law, inasmuch as it is supreme, is the sole true law. . . .

13. *The Law of the Civil Society Is Nonetheless a Societal Law* . . . The end of the civil society or the state is general and human. It is man at whose perfectioning this society aims. By way of a certain public good, embracing within its radiation the universality of human needs, moral and economic, individual and social, the civil society seeks to provide for each and all of its members the good life in all spheres of the temporal order. Now one of the first conditions as well as one of the ends of the public good is that within the total community there should prevail a certain order in the relationships between the individuals and the groups, an order which the law, fixed by the civil society, undertakes to realize. But if that is so, how can it be imagined that

law could be defined without any reference to morals, which constitute the fundamental human discipline? How could the place of everyone in the society which is the state be marked without appealing to the principles that govern the rights and duties of man? It is not surprising therefore that the law of the state, which is to order private relations, often takes over as its own, precepts that have already been laid down by morals, especially social morals.

Let there be no mistake, however: The rule thus taken over from morals becomes a societal rule in every respect and not from a formal viewpoint alone. If it becomes a part of the law, if it is laid down and imposed under threat of compulsion, it is not at all by reason of its own value, even if that be absolute, but solely because the end of the state demands it. It matters little that that end is general and human (which justifies the connection of politics and morals); for all that it remains no less a specific end, and consequently the rule inspired by that end preserves its societal character.

14. *The Other Rules of Social Life (Morals, Manners) Are Not Societal.* It will perhaps be objected that all rules whatever that govern relationships between men are equally derived from society and are equally social. . . .

. . . It is very well for the moral rule (under the sociological interpretation) and the rule of social manners (indisputably) to proceed from society or, more exactly, from the social environment by way of repetition of the same attitudes, the same gestures (this is the social fact of custom): Still they have no institutional or societal character, they pursue no institutional or societal end, they do not subserve the institution or society as group laws . . . What gives a rule its legal character is that it is consecrated and sanctioned, not in an inorganic fashion by the public in the group, but by the group itself as a body—especially, the state—in the conviction that the rule is required for the good of the group and the attainment of its specific end. The social interest being at stake, social discipline enters the field, and with it

the organization of the group in the persons of its responsible authorities: Chiefs, functionaries, and judges, the dispensers and guarantors of discipline. . . .

15. *Customary Law Has Societal Character.* Even in making the assumption of a customary legal rule, the societal idea, especially the consideration of the social end, is the determining and distinctive element. The idea acts first upon the public of the group, which sees the social interest involved and calls for law to intervene; then, thanks to the public, it acts upon the social organization, which institutes the means of execution, the procedures of law and compulsion . . . Nor is there anything to prevent a custom that originally is a moral one or one of manners from attaining the rank of a legal custom: This phenomenon will be brought about precisely when in the public . . . there germinates the idea that the effective practice of these morals or these manners touches in some manner upon the life of the group or its social ideal . . . Moral or social conformity thus comes to generate the juridical rule.

Section 2. Power as the Source of the Legal Rule

16. *Power Alone Is Qualified To Lay Down the Legal Rule.* If law is not simply the rule of social life but the rule of civil society, it could only be laid down by the power, or at least with the approval and consecration of the power, which is qualified to act in the name of the civil society, to wit, public authority. We have here a condition that goes not to the efficacy or the validity of the law but to its very existence.

. . . In saying this, we do not adopt a "dogmatic" or authoritarian conception of the law; we merely recognize the organic and, in this sense, social character of the legal rule. Nothing prevents the authority in the state from being organized in a democratic fashion and exercised directly or indirectly by the nation itself . . . In fact, whatever may be the regime of the government or the way of establishing the legal rule—

statute, custom, case law—a great many people without official capacity collaborate in or contribute to the formation of the law ... The law develops slowly by largely collective work, in which it is quite difficult to discover rights of authorship. ...

However, law exists only from that moment when the state itself, by its organs, has erected it as a law of the state. ...

17. *The Courts, Creating Case Law, Constitute Power.*

... No matter how independent and, in this sense, sovereign they may be, the courts instituted by the state to administer justice in the name of the state are evidently depositaries of a part of public authority. From another aspect, the law they apply is very much the law of the state, whether they find it formulated in statutes or, in the absence of statutes, have to work it out themselves. For it is all very well to claim to separate the judicial power from the other powers of the state, the legislative and the executive, under the pretext that the latter two would represent political power while the power of the judge would be of exclusively legal nature. First, it is a mistake to oppose law—the law of the state—to politics: Law, the rule of the political society, is necessarily subordinate to the ends of politics. Further, to the extent that the courts have to work out the law, they have to do so very much as the business of the state and for its ends, which is a political task. Finally, it is illogical to regard as nonpolitical the judicial power when the latter, in the absence of a statutory rule, is allowed to supplement the legislative power, which is eminently political. ...

20. *The Rules Laid Down By Private Individuals Do Not Constitute Law.* On the other hand, the rules stemming from the wills of private individuals by way of private legal transactions fall outside of the category of the legal rule (in the sense of the law of the state), not only because their obligating force is limited to the parties of the case, but also because the private will of itself is not competent to lay down rules on the state level. This is true both for individual private acts (unilateral acts or contracts, for valuable consideration or by way of gift, among living parties or upon death) and for collective acts incorporating economic or other groups, whatever they may be, which may have a genuine regulatory power over their members. ...

21. *Transformation of Rules of Private Parties Into Law of the State.* However, modern law knows cases of the transformation of private rules into law of the state; such as, in the field of industrial relations, the extension to an entire craft or industry, by means of state approval, of stipulations inserted in collective bargaining agreements. Apparently, the issue is only one as to whom they cover: An agreement brings into effect rights and obligations with regard to persons who have not been parties to it at all. ...

Section 3. Law and Public Compulsion

22. *As Regards Its Execution, Law Is Guaranteed by the State.* The rule of the social discipline of the state, which is laid down and promulgated by the state, is also guaranteed by the state, in the sense that the state institutes certain means designed to realize its rule effectively and to carry out what that rule prescribes as exactly as possible.

... The life of the law is in its being carried out: Law that is in no way active is dead law ... If the law wants to succeed, if it wants to live, it should be fashioned so as to get itself obeyed, morally by a certain adaptation to common opinion, materially by a complex of measures of execution that may go as far as the use of compulsion.

23. *Law That Is Not Obeyed Does Not Lose Its Validity as Law* ... There are those who define the law, at least as positive law, by speaking of "law generally obeyed." ... But the validity of a rule must not be confounded with its efficacy ... If the contrary were true, the subjects of a law would be promoted to masters of that law, which would mean not only anarchy but the overthrow of the order ... It is quite another question to know if it

is good to lay down or maintain a rule that would only receive disobedience. . . .

26. *In General, the Law Is Obeyed.* Ordinarily, obedience to the law comes about spontaneously, without state intervention . . . Law on the whole is doubtless obeyed more often than it is disobeyed. And that is fortunate, for otherwise no compulsion would stand the test: The measures of enforcement would be paralyzed under the avalanche of infractions. This is the partial truth involved in the saying: Positive law (in the sense of "real," "realized" law) is the law generally obeyed. . . .

33. *Legal Compulsion as the Monopoly of the State.* Instituted for the ends of protecting the rule of the law of the state, compulsion, and especially the right to punish, belongs only to the state and its competent organs. In this sense, compulsion is, and cannot but be, public. It would be the reign of war and of anarchy if every citizen . . . had the right to employ force in order to guarantee the execution of the laws laid down by public power, even under the pretext that those laws would consecrate their own personal interests. . . . Historically, it was one of the first tasks of the state in its formative stage to substitute its justice and its compulsion for private justice and compulsion and gradually to monopolize the coercive power . . . .

34. *Special Cases of Private Compulsion.* It does happen, however, that private individuals find each other recognizing a certain right to use material pressure—physical or economic force—in order to safeguard the rights they hold by the rule of social discipline (private compulsion). The classical case is that of legitimate self-defense . . . But the question there is less one of compulsion tending to prevent the violation of the rule guaranteeing human life or property than one of instinctive defense of the essential goods that life and property are for everyone. In any case, the right of legitimate self-defense plays a subsidiary part: It is admitted only in the case of necessity, given the inability to have recourse to public force . . . Do we have to point also to the boycott and the blacklist? In cases where they are used legitimately, they represent the exercise of a right of contractual freedom that is no longer put at the service of other rights or of a law, but of mere interests in the field of the competition of life, so that the process no longer offers any analogy to the idea of legal compulsion.

35. *Disciplinary Power of Private Bodies* . . . The inferior and subordinate groups may well enjoy what is called "disciplinary" power, authorizing the application of so-called disciplinary penalties on the part of the group against members who have offended against the rule of its internal law. But that disciplinary penal power differs from the power of the state in extent and character. Not only is it limited as to the kind of offenses and the kind of penalties; but even where the authority of the group is competent to step in, there is always reserved an appeal to the state as the judge of last resort. Thus, controversies between husband and wife, parents and children, even in the field subject to the exercise of marital or parental authority, are susceptible to judgment by the state. . . .

CHAPTER II

Characteristics of the Legal Rule

* * *

Section 1. The Law as a Preceptive, Categorical Rule of Conduct

42. *The Two Constitutive Elements of Every Rule: Hypothesis and Solution.* Analyzed in its logical structure, the legal rule, consists of two parts, of which one indicates a hypothesis, the other (in a word that prejudges nothing) a [consequent] solution. The hypothesis states the conditions of the application of the rule, which by the way are defined in the abstract: Such and such a situation existing, such and such a solution shall or ought to follow . . . Take the rule: The minor lacks legal capacity. The hypothesis is: If a person is a minor; the solution: He lacks legal capacity. Again, it matters little whether the hypothe-

sis consists in a pure state of facts, a state of law, or a mixed state of facts and law. Take the rule: The spouse (or: The owner, the creditor, the heir, the state, the Belgian citizen) has such and such a right (or obligation). The quality of spouse (or owner, creditor, etc.), which forms the hypothesis of the rule, is a state of law, which again may derive sometimes from facts pure and simple and sometimes from legal transactions. . . .

43. *The Legal Solution Is a Norm* . . . Differing from the scientific solution, which is a statement of fact . . . the juridical solution is a norm, an order; that is, it belongs to the category of principles directing conduct . . . It *indicates* to everybody what is "to be done," and at the same time it *prescribes* what it indicates. In this respect, the legal laws are in no way comparable to the laws of nature . . . Man alone, who is spirit, is subject to laws put before his will and dictating his conduct. . . .

47. *The Legal Rule Imposes a Precept and not Advice.* . . .

The Law commands. Perhaps the authority would get a better response if it used advice rather than precept. That is a matter of national psychology; and there are in fact circumstances where the state, not daring to command, advises or, again, recommends and suggests. . . .

48. *A Precept Underlies the Disposing and the Permissive Rules* . . .

. . . But there are cases where the imperative remains implied in the legal solution. Take the so-called "disposing" rules. By assumption, they neither command nor prohibit any act; they define interests and rights, capacities and competencies; they determine the conditions on which a certain legal effect begins or the legal effects of a certain situation. Still more generally, they resolve a question concerning the relations among people—in short, they "dispose." For instance, the possessor in good faith of a movable shall be its owner; one's domicile shall be at the place of one's principal establishment. . . .

Yet every "disposition" involves an injunc-

tion to everyone—parties, third parties, officials administering the law—to respect the legal regulation. . . .

52. *The Legal Imperative Is Categorical and Not Conditioned or Technical.* But here is a further distinction: The imperative of the law is categorical.

Apparently this goes without saying, and it may be asked how an imperative could be anything but categorical. But, rightly or wrongly, since Kant one opposes to the straight, so-called categorical imperative a merely conditional, so-called hypothetical, imperative. Now the legal imperative has nothing conditional about it . . . Once the hypothesis is realized, the command is binding categorically, independently of any condition whatever. . . .

The so-called hypothetical or conditional imperative, on the contrary, is binding only in relation to a certain result of a technical nature; hence its synonymous name, "technical imperative." If one wants to arrive at the result . . . then one must take the means to it. By this token, the means is obligatory and in that sense commanded. . . .

Never is the legal rule, with regard to its subjects, technical in this manner. Assuredly, any rule whatever, the moral rule and the legal rule as well as the technical, exists only in relation to an end. But there is this capital difference that the technical rule serves the end of a work—a technical, special work, reserved in principle to the technicians, whereas the moral rule and the legal rule serve the end of order—a human order, valid for all men by reason of their quality as men. The human order which is envisaged by morals is the essential human order: that of perfecting man in his moral, spiritual being. Consequently, the rules of end and means translating the conditions of this perfection to which man is called necessarily have categorical character. The same goes for law. . . .

53. *The Sanction Does Not Transform the Categorical into the Hypothetical.* The sanction, penal or otherwise, which accompanies the legal rule, changes nothing in this analy-

sis. The sanction is decreed not in order to confer upon the subject an option between the disposition made by the rule and the sanction . . . Far from transforming the categorical imperative of the rule into a hypothetical imperative ("Observe the rule if you want to escape the sanction; nevertheless, if you prefer the sanction, you have the right not to observe the rule"), the role of the sanction is to come to the aid of the categorical imperative so as to bring about its realization in conduct as far as possible. . . .

55. *The Categorical Imperative of the Law Is Binding in the External and the Internal Forums.* To affirm the categorical character of the legal imperative is not the same as going into the question, in what manner that imperative is binding: in the internal forum, i.e., before the tribunal of conscience, or in the external forum, i.e., before a human tribunal armed with compulsion. . . .

. . . Outside of any thought of reference from morals to law, there is, in principle, ground for acknowledging that the legal rule is valid in the internal forum. The ground is that, as far as the state, a necessary and universal society, is concerned, the societal order is a human order wanted by nature, whence it follows that the rules set forth in the name of this natural human order oblige the subject in his conscience. Man would not be fully man were he not a subject member of society, respecting his obligations as a member, first among which ranks obedience to the rules and orders decreed in the name of the society by competent authority. Morals, then, enjoins upon the citizens to obey the legal rule and makes this a duty of conscience, at least whenever under the circumstances obedience is required for the realization of the ends the legislator has set for himself. Let us add that the duty in conscience to obey a law does not at all imply the duty to find it good, adequate or opportune; else how could the law progress? Equally we reserve the case of unjust laws, which are so by being contrary to the moral rule, for what is immoral could not bind the conscience.

Section 2. The Law as a General Rule

56. *The Thesis of the Advocates of the Individual Legal Rule . . .*

Until recently, the legal rule was always defined as general and abstract, addressed to the subjects in general, private individuals or officials, or to abstractly determined categories among them . . . But there is a certain trend of recent date among writers who see no inconvenience in admitting a category of purely individual rules. . . .

Evidently, every general rule is called upon to particularize itself in its application to individuals who are part of the envisaged "generality": The precept laid down for all is valid for everyone in particular, and the application of the general precept is necessarily individual. However, by a general rule we understand a rule established in the abstract, outside of any consideration of a particular individual and of an individual case. . . .

57. *Criticism of the Above Thesis.* But this analysis does not seem exact. That there exist individual legal situations—rights, powers, obligations, and functions—flowing from sources other than the general legal rule, is incontestable and uncontested; the administrative decision, the judgment, the contract, are sources of such situations. It does not follow that the administrative decision, the judgment, the contract, are legal rules. No doubt the administrative decision, the judgment, the contract, imply a command, an individual imperative, valid for the determined individuals, the addressees or contracting parties. But in themselves they constitute orders or sentences, and not rules, norms, or laws, because the legal rule, the norm, the law, called upon to govern many cases, implies generality . . . In the social discipline, above all, it is impossible for the authority to assign to everyone his line of conduct. And this impossibility suffices to justify the principle of the generality of the legal rule.

Again, in the actual state of political organization, the pretended individual legal rules merely put into effect a general rule.

If the administrative decision is binding upon the subject, this is so not by its own force but because it is rendered in execution of a rule of public law commanding the administrator to make the decision he has made (without, however, denying him a certain power of appraising discretion). If the losing litigant is bound to comply with the judgment, this is by virtue not of the imperative of the judge but of the imperative of a law on which the mission of the judge and the authority of his judgment are founded. If the contract engenders individual precepts for the parties or adherents to the agreement, it is because the legal rule attaches such effects to the conclusion of contracts . . . .

CHAPTER III

The Subject Matter of the Law

* * *

*Section 1. Exclusion of Inner Acts:
Duties Towards God and Duties
Towards Oneself*

65. *The Inner Acts Are Subject to Morals.* The law regulates the relations of men with men; this means that inner acts escape the realm of the law altogether. By inner acts we understand the multitude of psychological processes, of intelligence, will, sensibility, which remain confined to the inner man without being necessarily translated outward by conduct of commission or abstention. . . .

67. *Application of This Idea; the "Pedagogical Function" of the Laws.* Such are the reasons why the penal legislator thinks of punishing an attempt to commit a crime only if it be manifested by beginning its execution: As long as the crime lives only in thoughts the law keeps out and cannot but keep out, however morally illicit the criminal thought may be. Such again are the reasons why the legislator dealing with legal transactions—of private or of public law—

prescribes legal effects only for the expressed will. . . .

. . . The state makes use of the prestige of a formal law to inculcate in its people precepts which, despite its intervention, are and remain moral precepts. On the one hand, not every measure nor even every rule laid down by a law is necessarily of a legal character . . . The authority has the right to employ any honest means to attain the ends falling within its mission: If there are reasons to believe that the proclamation of a moral precept by the civil law would be such as to favor the practicing of that precept, technical distinctions could not check such a policy, especially since the mass of the people, which cares nothing about jurisdictional divisions, might be shocked by certain cases of silence of the law.

68. *In What Sense the Law Is Concerned with Intentions.* Still it is true that the law in all its branches is preoccupied with intentions . . . It is intention that qualifies the criminal infraction; that marks the difference between good and bad faith, voluntary and involuntary fault; that governs the interpretation of legal acts or transactions, private and public, including the statutes . . . The question in this case is no more one of pure intentions forming the subject matter for precepts of command or prohibition. It is one of outward acts—nonlegal or legal— which the jurist tries to connect with the intentions that accompany or explain them . . . Only in the light of the idea do the acts take on moral and even social significance (since society is composed of men). In fact, society is not indifferent to whether the intentions accompanying or explaining acts are innocent or malicious, social or antisocial, and hence the necessity to treat the acts accordingly, to diversify and shade the dispositions of the rules according to the intentions. . . .

69. *Of the Prudence Required in the Search for Intention.* However, prudence is called for . . . In practice the working conditions of the organs of application of the law

—administrative officials and judges—rarely permit a resort to the slow and nice methods of rigorously scientific analysis . . . Where the intention must normally remain indiscernible, it is preferable altogether to renounce speculative and often deceptive research and to stick instead to the materiality of facts—gestures, words, writings.

. . . Goods and documents call for rapid and unhampered circulation. Hence the renascence of formalism—a purely utilitarian formalism without symbolic value—which characterizes some parts of the commercial law of today. . . .

70. *The Relations of Man with God Are as Such Outside the Competence of the Law* . . .

. . . The civil society as such has no competence in religious matters . . . That task belongs strictly to the church and, for those who reject any church, to the individual conscience.

71. *Exceptions: Incidence of the Spiritual upon the Temporal.* However, account must be taken of the echo of religion, its principles, its worship, its institutions, at the level of temporal civil life . . . It will . . . be for the civil authority to proclaim the rule of freedom of worship and to safeguard it. . . .

. . . If the state deems it opportune it will lay down rules to prohibit certain acts or attitudes showing ostentatious contempt with regard to religion, e.g., blasphemy, sacrilege, parody of worship. Indeed, acts of that kind have nothing in common with the freedom, guaranteed as such, of sincere anti-religious propaganda . . . Finally, without having to assume the case where the state itself professes a natural or positive religion (case of a state religion), one could quite well understand that the state, acknowledging a practical value of the religious idea by reason of its social benefits, would favor religion, and that this policy would be translated into appropriate rules of public and private law (e.g., compulsory religious instruction in schools, privileges for the clergy, subsides for institutes and works). . . .

Part Two

THE LEGAL METHOD

CHAPTER I

Is the Law "Given" or "Construed," the Subject of a Science or of a Technique?

Section 1. State of the Problem and Present Theories

98. *Explanation of the Terms "Given" and "Construed."* . . .

A thing is given when it exists as an object outside of any productive intervention of man: Such as God, nature, human beings and their relations, the contingent facts of history. A thing is construed when, taken by itself, it has its cause in the efficient activity of man: Such as a house, a poem, a syllogism, the state . . . Now, with regard to the "given," to whatever category it may belong —physical, metaphysical, or historical—the attitude of man is that of knowledge, of science; with regard to the "construed," man, who by definition is the constructor, is operative and, in this sense, makes a work of art or of technology. On the one hand, the attitude of investigation or reception; on the other, creative operation. . . .

101. *In Its Historical Existence, the Law Is "Given."* In its historical existence, the law is obviously "given," an object of science . . . This given law, if it is in force, will no doubt require application to special cases, which belongs to a certain art rather than to science. But with a reservation for application to special cases, the historically given law, in force or not, does present itself as a reality, susceptive of a properly scientific, speculative knowledge. Again, the law of a country or of a group of countries or, if that is possible, of the entire world may be studied not as static, at an arrested moment of time, but in its evolution in the course of the ages. This is the viewpoint proper to the historian. Finally the law may be studied from a strictly sociological viewpoint, in its relations with the social life either of a coun-

try or an epoch or in general. Anyway, the activity is one of science. . . .

102. *But What about Law in Its Essence?* But outside of the "existential" law—present, past, future, or merely possible—there is law pure and simple, denuded of any form of concrete existence. It is in relation to the law as thus understood, in the state of essence, that our question is raised. In it one at once discerns the interest in an exact appraisal of the lawyer's mission. If the law is "given," at least for the jurist, it will be enough to gather the "given" thing in the reality that supplies it . . . The search always sets itself only one aim: To find out the law where it is, as something given. An appeasing doctrine! The jurist is a man of science: His conclusions have the objectivity and certainty of science . . . Contrariwise, if the law is construed, the door is open to the arbitrary subjectivism of the author of the rule. Even if the construction should be subjected to principles, the solutions evolved in applying them could only be vacillating, disputable and disputed.

But whatever may be the security—real or fancied—which one expects from a "scientific" conception of the law, it is impossible to found security upon error. The law will be even more arbitrary, or in any case more tyrannical, if it presents itself in the name of something given that would lack objective reality. . . .

103. *Attitude of Legal Positivism, and Criticism.* A whole juristic school adopts an attitude of indifference to the problem, on the stated ground that it would transcend the jurist's sphere of competence. According to them, the science of law would have only the historically given law as its subject, which the jurist as such would only have to outline in scientific form . . . As for the critique of that law or the search for some principle dominating the positive elaboration, that work, which is not indeed denied to be legitimate, would be "metajuridical," belonging to disciplines other than the law: Political science, sociology, philosophy . . . But even admitting that legal science could be immured in the pure exposition of the law, a non-suit for lack of jurisdiction is not a solution. With Legal science defaulting after pleading lack of jurisdiction, another discipline will have to take charge of the problem, which may be, if one likes, the discipline of legal philosophy.

104. *Everybody Recognizes that in Some Part the Law Is "Construed."* A first point admits of no discussion: Up to a certain point, more or less considerable according to varying opinions, the law is construed. Thus Savigny, the great master of the historical school, recognized the existence of a scientific elaboration of the law by the jurists, which he called "legal technique" and which he distinguished from the spontaneous creation of the law in the heart of the people . . . Among the adherents of natural law, none denies that it requires practical realization, which constitutes precisely the original resort of the positive law: The whole system is built upon the logical opposition between an element of law given by nature and a positive element issuing from the will of man. . . .

Section 2. Examination of the Theories of the "Given"

. . . Contrary to prevailing opinion, we would here take the part of the theory of *total* "construction" and try to prove it. . . .

112. *Critique of the Doctrines of the Popular "Given."* As for the variously shaded theories deriving the "given" from the people, it is easy to reply that the people as such are not qualified in legal matters, any more than in any other matters whatsoever—philosophical, scientific, technical—to decide what is or what ought to be: The true, the good, the just, the useful. Suppose the people have a certain opinion on a point of law, there is nothing to indicate that that opinion would be adequate to juridical truth and that the jurist would therefore be under a duty to accept it as the unobjectionable "given" of the legal regulation. The law is not a matter of the will, of masses or numbers; it is a matter of reason. . . .

113. *Critique of the Doctrines of Force.*

The law, say the "realistic" thinkers, is nothing else than the will of the stronger, and assuming competing forces, the solution will be given by the equilibrium of the forces . . . But, once again, force may well impose upon the legislator any legal "given," whatever pleases the interests or passions which it serves. By no means does it follow that force is qualified to "give" to the jurist whatever there is that is valid. Truth to tell, it "gives" nothing, the concept of the "given" implying, after all, the idea of a solution endowed with a virtue of its own. Now force is content to dictate the solution: Force creates it. Hence there is no more room for asking if the law includes a part of the "given"; the distinction no longer makes sense. The law, synonymous with force, is neither "given" nor "construed": It is traced back to an arbitrary pure fact.

114. *As for Natural Law, the Question Arises Only with Regard to Juridical Natural Law.* If the "given" of the law could not reside in facts—the facts of common consciousness or the facts of power—does one have to discover that "given" in the "fund of moral and economic verities," "commanding certain directions" which "center upon the supreme idea of the objective just," in short, in natural law?

Let us at the outset dissipate an equivocality which risks vitiating the entire discussion. It is certainly legitimate to attribute validity to the notions of natural law and justice in order then to deduce therefrom the rules destined to govern the conduct of man toward others, on the plane of strictly interindividual relationships as well as on the property social plane (family, state, and other groupings). But the question in that case is one of the fundamental human rule, that is, the moral rule . . . But the legal rule is something different from the moral rule. The former is the concrete rule laid down by the state-society for its subjects from the viewpoint of its own discipline. . . .

The question then is, on the specific level of this kind of rule, whether natural law and justice, which indeed constitute the "given" of the moral rule *ad alterum,* will serve equally as the "given" of the legal rule. If the answer is in the affirmative it would have to be admitted that the two rules start from the same "given" and, as the moral rule comes first, that the "given" of the legal rule is nothing else than that of the moral rule. Between the two systems no other differences would subsist than those which result from the diversity of positive determinations. . . .

115. *Nature Furnishes the Jurist with No Juridical "Given," No Necessary Rule.* Legal experience as it comes from the general practice of legislation, case law, and customs, does not confirm that conclusion. Indeed, it is seen that in certain cases the legal rule does take up the initial "given" of natural law and justice, save for subjecting it to certain adjustments; that in other cases it discards or modifies it, and not only in the details of determination, but also in a much more radical manner by reversing the directive, as for instance when the law lets itself be guided above all by preoccupation with security . . . What is this but to say that the jurist has to consult not solely natural law and justice, that he maintains a certain freedom of choice with regard to them?

Hence the mandatory "given" becomes optional, that is to say, it ceases to be given. . . .

The same criticism applies to another frequently used formula which calls natural law and justice the inspirational sources of the positive law. To be inspired by a model is not necessarily to copy it. On the contrary, that is to preserve freedom to take it as it is, to modify it, or not to take it at all, according to the circumstances.

Will it be said that even where he appears to be discarding natural law and justice in order to create an exception, the jurist does not cease to conform to natural law and justice, which he translates in his own way, taking account of the needs and requirements proper to the legal order? Notwithstanding its success, this formula badly disguises a false conclusion. To apply an exception to a principle is not to translate it, to be inspired by it, or even to adopt it; it is jolly well to contradict it, at least in the case under contemplation. The principle remains safe; but it is illogical to suggest that in decreeing the exception one continues to apply the principle. Further, if the legal order has its own needs and requirements, capable of influencing the content of its rules to the point of dictating exceptions to the "given" of the principles of natural law and justice, that proves that the legal rule, unlike the moral rule, is not subjected to, nor determined purely by, this "given," that it obeys other laws. . . .

Section 3. The Law is "Prudence" and Consequently Construed

* * *

124. *The Operations of the Jurist Belong to Practical Reason, Especially to Prudence.* Is this to say that the operations of the jurist in construing the law . . . may not be acts of reason? Not at all; but they are acts of practical reason. Tending toward a certain end of practical order, to wit, the good organization of social relationships, the elaboration of the law depends not on speculative understanding, scientific or philosophic, but on judgment. More precisely, as the good organization of social relationships touches upon the good of human life in general, the action ordered to that end belongs essentially to prudence, at least for the substance of the rule if not for its external "make-up." If, according to the ancient definition, the subject matter of prudence is the discernment and effective realization of means most appropriate to ends in the field of moral things the task of the jurist is that of adapting to the end of the legal system the means which constitutes the legal rule. . . .

. . . Prudential reason is not confined to the disposition of single cases, to professional consultation or the decision of a lawsuit. There is the prudence of legal counsel (the Roman "prudent") and the prudence of the judge, the latter providing the origin for the [French] technical term of *jurisprudence* to designate the work of legal creation and interpretation done by the courts. But there is also a *legislative* prudence, concerning the particular action of elaboration of the general rules designed to govern individual cases. This legislative prudence will guide the operations of all those who, in whatever capacity, collaborate in the building of the law, it will permit them to judge concretely of means and ends, their value and their opportunity with regard to the ultimate purpose of the legal order. . . .

125. *To Say "Prudent" Is Not to Say "Arbitrary."* From saying that the law is "construed" wholly and down to its foundations it does not follow that construction can take place in an arbitrary fashion or even with the freedom of artistic creation, precisely because it is a work of prudential reason . . . No doubt there remains room in the concrete work of elaboration for a certain proportion of arbitrary will. But the margin is enclosed within relatively narrow limits. . . .

126. *The Factual Presuppositions of the Jurist's Legal Rule.* The jurist does not draw his rule *ex nihilo* and he does not build it up in a vacuum. Like any rule whatsoever the law is based upon facts. By "facts," in the widest sense, we understand all realities whatsoever . . . capable of interesting the jurist in elaborating his own system. . . .

. . . In this sense it is exact to say unqualifiedly: *Ex facto oritur jus;* the facts are sources of law, generative elements of legal rules and solutions. For instance, that paternity is not susceptible of being established directly, at least in the present state of science; that material things are divided into movables and immovables; that man is endowed with personality; that he has an instinct of sociability; that in the ranks of society there are individuals of feeble mind, and of various kinds—these are inescapable facts, for the jurist as for everybody, which entail consequences in the field of the legal discipline. . . .

. . . Whether he adapts himself to them or approves them, or again claims to rectify, to correct or repress them, they *are,* and by that token they count. . . .

127. *Moral or Technical Precepts and Ex-*

isting Law as Presupposed Facts. Nor is this all. The facts composing the "given" that precedes the law embrace not merely the facts pure and simple which are objects of speculative science. They also embrace all the rules of action . . . There exists a mass of techniques, belonging to the most varied fields: The techniques of business, of banking, of insurance; the techniques of building machines, tools and apparatus; the techniques of ocean navigation and of air navigation; medical and surgical technique; techniques of aesthetic, scientific, literary work, and of legislative work, too, etc. For the jurist, the rules, procedures, and prescriptions of the different arts or techniques are obviously given as facts. In so far as the law is concerned with technical fields the jurist is consequently bound by the "given" of the technique which will provide him with the basic elements of his construction.

The same remark applies to rules of nontechnical human activity: The rule of morals or the rule of already established law (facts of the Ought) . . . What is . . . "construed" by the moralist becomes "given" for the jurist. The same holds for existing law in relation to the work of elaboration of a new rule: For the construing jurist, the existing law, which is itself in its entirety "construed," becomes a legal "given" inasmuch as it is a historical reality. And it is quite certain that the jurist, in making his rule, could not detach himself from this historical legal "given," whether he wishes to complete or perfect, or even to reform or reverse, the existing law.

But take care to note: These latter "given" factors remain prelegal . . . Though they may very closely touch the elaboration of the law—which precludes their being called "metajuridical"—yet they do not constitute the legal "given" of the rule to be construed . . . The jurist receives morals and moral solutions as "given" at their specific place and level, inasmuch as they are a moral "given." He does not have to receive them as a legal "given," that is, as a completely prepared "given" of his own rule. On this new level, he will make such use of them as is pre-

scribed by the rule of prudence related to his special work, the work of the law to be elaborated. Sometimes, then, prudence will dictate that one sanction the moral "given," sometimes it will command a different attitude: A refusal to intervene or a new arrangement of the moral "given." . . .

129. *The "Given" of the Method of Elaboration of the Law.* But what is given above all, outside of the precedent facts, is a method of elaboration of the law, consisting of certain principles evolved by philosophical reflection or legal philosophy. Different from the *solutions,* which in every case are determined by (legislative juridical) prudence, the *method* is given by science, a science turned toward action since we are concerned with elaborating the law, but a science made up of general, universal principles, which prudence has, precisely, to apply to particular cases. By definition, the principles of that science bind the construing jurist in a necessary, absolute fashion, with no possible derogation of any sort. In the absence of a juridical natural law, there thus exists a *natural legal method,* representing the permanent and invariable principles that preside over the elaboration of the law. This method the legislator must follow; this method, too, the judge must follow to the extent that he has to "act as a legislator." . . .

What, then, are the laws of legal elaboration? This will be studied systematically in the following chapter . . . .

CHAPTER II

The Guiding Principles of the Elaboration of the Law

INTRODUCTION

* * *

132. *The Instrumental Character of the Legal Rule Differentiates It from the Moral Rule.* Let us note this at once: The instrumental character of the law expresses a fundamental difference between law and morals . . . It would be wrong to present the moral rule, even the positive moral rule laid down by an external authority, as a mere means

with a view to an end, "a technique of obtaining our full beatitude," as one author puts it. In reality, the moral law, natural or positive, confines itself to translating the requests of the one and only morality, and it translates them as true, without preoccupation with extrinsic finality . . . Morals truly *pursues* no result, no good, not even the moral good: It *fuses* with the moral good, expressing its requirements and conveniences.

The legal rule on the contrary exists in view of a distinct and superior end, which it could quite well fail to attain, which could be attained also in other ways, so that a question may always be raised as to the utility of its provisions or even of its intervention at all in the particular case. . . . The law is utilitarian, morals is not. The legal rule is subordinate to a system which has itself the value of an instrument: The system of the temporal public good, the state's end and reason of being . . . .

SUBDIVISION I

The End of the Legal Ordinance: The Temporal Public Good

134. *"Lex est Ordinatio ad Bonum Commune."* If law is consubstantial with the idea of society, the end of the legal rule could only be the end of the society itself, to wit, the common good. . . .

. . . Inasmuch as politics is the science and art of the public good, the legal rule is at the service of politics, and the prudence that presides over the elaboration of the law, or legislative prudence, is a part of political prudence.

Section 1. Concept and Characteristics of the Temporal Public Good

137. *The Constitutive Elements of the Public Good: Order, Coordination, Aid* . . . The public good presupposes, in the first place, the establishment and maintenance of a certain order in society, generating security and confidence. How would the activities and the very life of the public be possible if the social surroundings were at the prey of violence, brutal or insidious (in the form of abuse of power), of faithlessness, and of fraud? . . . It will attain this, particularly, by the organization of a police force charged with preventing and repressing disorder, by the establishment of tribunals charged with adjudging controversies, and by the promulgation of fixed rules in the public and private fields. . . .

The liberal school claimed to keep to this stage of negative intervention, refusing to admit that the freedom of the individuals in their so-called private activities could ever be touched in any manner whatever by the state, whether in the form of regulations or in that of subsidies. But one has become aware that in a complex civilization the public good has other enemies than external disorder, to wit, the dispersion of efforts in unregulated competition. On reflection, the life of men, of each man in particular and of humanity in general, can be traced to a perpetual exchange of services, subject to the law of productivity and of equilibrium. Now dispersion prevents productivity and causes a disequilibrium. Hence the necessity of a certain reasoned coordination, a certain adjustment, which is in the interest of the mass of exchanges and therefore within the competence of the state which is set up over the common interest.

Finally, private individuals or subordinate groups are often in need of more concrete aid open to all "commoners" once they fulfill its conditions. . . . If a "service" has the characteristic of necessity or urgency with regard to the public good, the state will even be qualified to assume its management so as to replace impotent or insufficient private initiative. . . .

138. *The Public Good Covers All Human Values of the Temporal Order.* With respect to its content, the public good from its own angle embraces the totality of values of human interest . . . There is but one exception: The religious good, considered under the peculiarly religious aspect, falls within the competence of another society, equally pub-

lic within its sphere, the religious society . . . To the extent, however, to which religion merges with the temporal, the state regains its competence to maintain a temporal environment favorable to the specifically religious public and private good. . . .

140. *Political and Other Values of the Temporal Order.* To preach "separations" or simply distinctions between politics on the one hand and economics, morality, culture, health, etc., on the other, on the pretended ground that these matters are of a private order and therefore do not fall under politics, is to make a great mistake. First, economics, morality, culture, health are not exclusively of a private order . . . Furthermore, the separation or distinction between the political order and other supposed parallel orders destroys the very concept of politics by abolishing its reason for being. Politics in effect has no other reason for being than from the angle of the public good to govern or, if you will, serve the external human activities that are exerted according to their own objectives, economic, moral, sanitary, cultural. . . .

What is exact—it has already been noted —is that the state does not have to take charge . . . of these different sectors in such a way as to dispossess the individuals and groups thereof, precisely because its role in principle is only to guide and motivate and not to manage . . . .

141. *Need for a Philosophy of Values to Discern the Requirements of the Public Good.* However, the spheres of human values which the public good covers are not of equal rank, and thus the state will have to take sides . . . Values are often antagonistic. Who will deny that too exclusive preoccupation with material wealth, health, or physical strength conflicts with the true good of the human person?—that excessive care for the collective values runs the risk of compromising the legitimate prerogatives of individuals? . . .

142. *Our Philosophy of Values.* The answer, inspired by reason and conforming to Christian traditions, may be summarized in three points: Primacy of the spirit over mat-

ter (and by "spirit" we understand not only the intellectual values but above all the moral values: Virtue and character); prevalence of the individual human person over every collectivity; subordination of the state-society to society pure and simple. . . .

143. *Primarily Moral Character of the Notion of the Public Good* . . . Despite its intermediary character, the public good is not a merely technical thing because on all levels it is closely related to a certain conception of human ends. This is not to say that it knows no peculiarly technical solutions. For there are many techniques among the matters to which it applies, such as automobile traffic, organization of markets, factories; and even in moral matters the corresponding measures of public good may take on a technical character, as in the fight against prostitution, drunkenness, gambling, and other manifestations of public immorality. . . .

144. *Relativity of the Applications of the Idea of the Public Good* . . .

It is impossible to say in advance, relying upon scientific conclusions, that the public good requires such and such a form of economic organization or of political regime, valuable in themselves, always and everywhere, without regard to contingencies. . . .

Section 2. The Temporal Public Good as Norm of the Positive Content of the Law

146. *The Norm of the Public Good Governs All Branches of the Law.* The norm of the public good dominates all branches of the law, private and public, municipal and international. This is an obvious truth for public and administrative law . . . .

147. *Private Law and the Public Good.* What is important to emphasize, however, is that despite appearances the norm of the public good also presides over the elaboration of . . . private law . . . The law that is called private is private as to the sphere of relationships it governs; it is public, or rather . . . it is social, not only as to its

function but also as to its content. This means, no doubt, that in the regulation of private relationships the law that is called private will safeguard "public policy and public morals." . . . ; that, moreover, it will guard the interest of third parties . . . ; but still more, that in determining the respective rights and obligations, the legal rule will be conceived with less regard to the rights of the immediate parties than to the good of the entire community . . . .

148. *The Social Conception of Private Law and the Concern with Individual Rights* . . . Historical experience accords with social philosophy in testifying that the public good cannot be realized, cannot be conceived, without having respect for the individual right, or by abolishing the limits between "mine" and "thine." One does not in this way come back to individualism: It remains true that the measure of the individual right or, more exactly, of the protection assured it by the law, is the public good, not the right of the individual. And this thesis is not without practical consequences, as will be seen from the following examples.

149. *The Example of Rent Legislation.* All Western [European] countries after the World War of 1914-1918 and without interruption since then have known "rent legislation," extending leases and limiting the amount of rent. On account of the critical shortage of living quarters it was necessary to protect tenants of modest means (or business men) from being put out on the street at the expiration of their leases, a situation which would have entailed both iniquities and social disturbances . . . On all the evidence, this legislation sacrificed the right of the landlord to that of the tenant: From the viewpoint of commutative justice, on the level of "mine" and "thine," the equilibrium was broken . . . In the minds of some people rent legislation took on the meaning of an attack upon property or quite bluntly, an election maneuver. . . .

Yet objectively the solution was justified, at least in its principle, as a measure commanded by the public good under the circumstances . . . Social justice may require the citizens to give up certain things not only for the profit of the state under the perspective of public law, but also under the perspective of private law for the profit of other citizens or other social categories, when these particular sacrifices are indispensable for the good of the whole community.

150. *The Objection of "Legislation of Circumstance."* Will this example be rejected as legislation "of circumstance," . . ? The objection would not be pertinent. Continually the law has to do with situations that are sometimes conforming and sometimes contrary to normality . . . It is always the public good upon which either the principle or the exception is founded. In normal, i.e., calm, times, the public good will be likely to coincide with the consecration of commutative justice. In abnormal, i.e., troubled, times . . . the public good will suggest such more or less grave derogations from the rule of commutative justice.

151. *Examples from the Ordinary Law of Private Institutions: Prescription.* Does one nonetheless want to argue from a starting point in normal times? . . . The true reason of prescription lies in certain necessities or conveniences of social life. It matters for the public good that at the end of a certain time accounts should be cleared (liberating prescription or limitation of debts), unused rights in real property detached from ownership should disappear (extinctive prescription of usufructs and servitudes), illegitimate acquisitions of property should become regularized notwithstanding their original defects (case of acquisitive prescription of ownership and real rights). Yet these results contradict the individual right, since they operate so as to transfer value without compensation . . . The assured right of the owner is nevertheless immolated to the public good of security in society.

Will it be said that in fact the normal function of prescription is to clarify normal situations by relieving the beneficiary of an often difficult proof? Incontestably so. But the exactness of the remark does not permit us to neglect the cases, even though they are exceptional, where prescription implements injustice precisely because the law of prescription has stability and not justice in mind. . . .

Section 3. The Temporal Public Good as Norm of the Negative Content of the Law

156. *The Public Good Often Demands Abstention of the Jurist* . . . The "prudent" man does not think exclusively of justice; he seeks what is realizable; failing to obtain the best, he contents himself with less, which is sometimes the lesser evil . . . .

157. *The Dilemma: Freedom or Legal Rule* . . .

The dilemma is thus not one between freedom on the one hand and the public good on the other; it is one between freedom and the rule, both possible instruments in the service of the public good. Freedom has its perils: Disorder or injustice, which are precisely the reason of being of the rule; but the rule in turn is not without inconveniences . . . Spontaneous enthusiasm is controlled, contained, broken. The excess of discipline kills the spirit of initiative . . . From another aspect, discipline laid down in advance always errs through generality, which prevents it from adapting itself to the particularities of cases, while freedom, mobile and supple, knows how to invent exactly adjusted solutions. Lastly, let us not forget that the rule issuing from the will offers this superiority over the imposed rule, that it adds to the abstract force of the obligation the stimulus of personal engagement, which doubles its effective value. . . .

160. *The Psychology of the Subjects: Cases Where the Public Good Is Satisfied Without the Intervention of a Law* . . . Account must also be taken, to a large extent, of the psychology of the subjects.

Suppose, first, that ordinarily they spontaneously execute the order deduced from the public good. The result is here obtained without the rule having to show itself. Now if the legislator makes the claim to intervene, if only to support with a sanction the prin-

ciple already practiced in fact, the effect of his step could be radically different from what he had thought. Instead of confirming the subjects in their attitude, it may cause a turnabout dictated by a feeling of reaction against meddling that is deemed intolerable. . . .

161. *The Same: Cases Where the Order of the Public Good Would Meet with Resistance.* Provision must be made for the converse assumption: The people do not understand the requirements of the public good; they do not practice them and are not disposed to accept them. . . .

The dosage of legal requirements does, however, involve degrees. From the legislator's inability to prescribe the maximum, on account of the state of opinion, it does not follow that he ought to prescribe nothing at all. He will prescribe the minimum, or, more exactly, the maximum of what opinion is able to support. For example, divorce once having entered into the mores, the legislator will not necessarily go so far as to exclude it. Working with the fire, he will only take care to hinder its abuse and even its use by a series of precautions tending to restrain and sterilize the undesirable solution.

164. *Public Good and Public Opinion as Factors of the Elaboration of the Law.* . . . Opinion as such is no generator of law because it does not create the requirements of the public good nor the consequences they involve with regard to the law. But if the requirements of the public good are objective, the conception, true or false, which opinion may form of these same requirements in turn constitutes a fact endowed with objective reality. And that fact is of interest to the law in so far as the state of opinion is a factor in the realization of the rule. While a rule in accord with popular feeling is ordinarily assured of success, a rule disavowed by opinion is almost condemned to failure. Now the failure of the rule, signifying disobedience of the subjects, not only damages the law but also affects the public good itself, so that an alternative is raised: Either abstention of the rule, renouncing the benefit it ought theoretically to procure, or

inefficacious intervention with its fatal consequences for the prestige of the authority.

In reality, it is true, the dilemma rarely takes so trenchant a form. The failure of a rule is never complete; or even if complete, it does not always entail loss of the prestige of authority. The necessity of a choice remains, the more so as, outside of practical efficiency, the truth of a rule, the ideal it translates, also has its peculiarly social interest. In the eyes of righteous people, and even of others, the silence of the law, passing for indifference or complicity, is capable of engendering a scandal at least as damaging to the prestige of the authority as the lack of success . . . Opinion, in fact, conditions the elaboration of the law . . . Before a legal requirement of a nature to shock opinion can be established in an efficacious manner, it will be appropriate to await the conversion or neutralization of such opinion. Normally, the social action of education, exerted together by the state and by private initiative, will precede properly legal action.

. . . Often the alleged opinion is only that of a minority of writers whose theses find no echo in the public, or still again, the pretended opinion is divided into hostile currents and counter-currents. Nothing then prohibits the authority from taking advantage thereof, and by a bold decision, dictating the solutions it deems well founded. Its very intervention will often have the effect of rallying the indifferent, the undecided, and even some from the opponents. . . .

SUBDIVISION II

The Means: The Technical Equipment of the Law

Section 1. The Definition, or Legal Conceptualism

168. *Inconveniences of an Insufficiently Defined Law* . . . An undefined or insufficiently defined law is not at all practicable in that its application will occasion hesitations and controversies which generate inse-

curity. . . . Speaking socially, the total absence of any rule where one is necessary, or a rule imperfect in the substance of its disposition, is often preferable to an uncertain rule. Those solutions have at least the merit of clarity, and at worst certain arrangements will permit paring them down, while uncertainty adds to the disorder of conduct a more monstrous disorder, to wit, the disorder in the very ordinance that pretends to make order rule.

169. *Lack of Definition on the Part of the Formal Sources of the Law.* A lack of definition of the law may be found, first, in the formal sources, the assumption being that the existence of the rule is in doubt . . . It is the great advantage of the system of statutory sources to do away with these perplexities. On the one hand, the statute by the sole fact that it is the rule enacted by the authority in the state is necessarily preeminent over the other sources, at least in principle; on the other hand, the statute is born at a precise moment in time, it is published and easy to prove. True, there remain the difficulties of interpretation. But the doubt in this case bears upon the content of the rule and no longer upon its existence, an assuredly lesser evil which by the way is inevitable and common to all sources . . . Now case law, which proceeds by successive stages and by the haphazard bringing of suits, remains uncertain for a rather long time while its often laborious formation is continuing. As for custom, issuing from habitual usage recognized as law, the difficulty is to discover it in both of its elements, the *usus* and the *opinio juris.* . . .

171. *The Lack of Precision of the Law in Its Formal Content.* The insufficiency of definition may be found, further, in the very context of the law . . . Its terms are indecisive, to the point where it escapes easy and sure management. . . .

. . . Such would be the rule that would place under the clearly determined regime of guardianship individuals "incapable of managing their affairs by themselves" (how is that incapacity to be defined or discerned in practice without too much risk of error for each individual?), or again the rule that would condemn to a clearly determined penalty of imprisonment individuals guilty of "acts contrary to public peace" (how is the "contrariety to public peace" to be defined or discerned in practice without too much risk of error for each act?). . . .

175. *Special Difficulty of Definition of Qualitative Values.* A great many things are better understood by not being defined; such are the values of the spiritual and moral order, which are of a qualitative kind. In the more or less concrete evaluation, feeling decides there with more penetration and refinement than the logical reason armed with its always crude categories . . . Rules which rely upon the sole appraisal of the interpreter, whether subject or judge, are not without danger. Intelligence, guided and in a certain manner bound by the categories, takes less risk of going astray than judgment, which is always more or less subjective, especially in certain periods in the life of peoples when the justness of feeling is even more "off its axis" than the logic of minds.

Take the repression of obscene shows, an incontestable cause of public immorality. How make the distinction between the show which is obscene and that which is not? A question of fact, no doubt, rather than of definition. But what will the feeling of the judge be? One tribunal will show itself indulgent, another one, rigorous; without a criterion that can be grasped, precision is impossible. The problem—of political prudence—then is to find out where the lesser evil lies . . . This is by no means to say, though, that the obstacle is insurmountable. The jurist has the duty unceasingly to perfect his instruments and in the light of science and experience to search for the formula adhering as closely as possible to truth while providing the maximum of practicability. . . .

179. *But Not All Matters Lend Themselves Equally to Broad Definitions: The Penal Law* . . . There are those matters where the need for security prevails over the considerations of truth and expediency, as in every case where the law provides for penalties, forfeitures, or other measures punitive in character. In a society respectful of the rights of man, it would be intolerable to have the most precious human goods—life, honor, liberty—depend upon the free appraisal of one or several men, even if these be qualified public functionaries such as the judge or administrator. . . .

180. *The Jurist Does Not Cease to Search for the Strict Definition.* Precision in the law answers to so natural a tendency that even in matters subject to the regime of directives, judges and lawyers exert themselves to banish the vagueness of concepts by introducing notes of specification. So a division of labor is established at the end between the statute which from above formulates the "directive" and the other sources, closer to the concrete, which with lesser, and also variable, authority set forth its applications in detail . . . The human mind, as much as social life, thirsts for precision. If the rule does not provide it, the mind creates it; the directive evolves into a rule.

181. *Cases Where the Law is Obliged to Renounce All Definition.* There are, however, matters where the law is constrained to renounce any definition whatever and, for that reason, any intervention: That is, when the very science of these matters speaks reservedly . . . A typical case is that of medical fault: Despite the general competence to judge any fault whatsoever in no matter what field, which the statute grants the courts, they ordinarily refuse to pronounce upon the fault committed by physicians and surgeons, at least where it is properly medical or surgical, relating to the very technique of the medical or surgical art. Medical science is not always in agreement as to the value and expediency of a treatment or a surgical operation . . . How then should the legislator or the judge take sides on the questions disputed among scholars in the field? Simple prudence prohibits the jurisprudent from venturing into regions where the science—which by hypothesis is alone competent—hesitates to make its pronouncement . . . .

182. . . . Whatever one may do or want to do, the legal definition will always remain more or less approximate, expeditious, and summary. To grasp the phenomena in their logical or historical entirety and continuity, and *a fortiori* to penetrate into the essence of things is not, and never will be, the forte of the jurist, because his task is not to establish scientifically correct definitions but to elaborate applicable rules, and the practicability of the law seeks relatively simple, manageable definitions.

Section 3. The Concentration of Legal Matter

190. *Preserving a Just Measure in Evaluating "Practicability."* . . . It must not be forgotten that the impracticability of today can disappear tomorrow or find its remedy, thanks to the progress of science in the definition of its concepts, to the perfecting of the technique of proofs, to a more logical distribution of the subject matter of the law. Thus, for instance, the uncertainty in the field of medical fault may give way to surer appraisals; resort to statistical procedures may lead to a more exact measurement of social facts; the discovery of the so-called "blood-group test" has permitted us to circumscribe, if not to eliminate, the mystery of paternity; the system of organic laws and codifications diminishes the inconveniences of the multiplicity of rules, etc.

Conclusions on the Legal Method and Corollaries

Section 2. Relative Certainty and Variability of the Law

196. *The Different Causes of Variation of the Law* . . .
The law is called upon to undergo change, first, by reason of the variations in the subject matter of regulation . . . Every rule no doubt imposes its form upon a pre-existent matter; but the latter reacts upon the form inasmuch as the rule is bound to impress upon the matter the form appropriate thereto. . . .

The second cause of variation lies in the public good . . . the requirements of which are changeable in space and in time. While one may discover common principles of the common good, of a philosophical, scientific, or technical order, valid for any society, whatever may be its historical physiognomy (climate, soil, the physical, intellectual, and moral aptitudes of its members) . . . different political groups have their particular traits, which necessarily influence the applications. Thus, the requirements of the public good are not the same in rudimentary societies as in those of refined civilization. Again, in a society of the agricultural type, the public good of agriculture represents a more considerable value within the total public good than does the industrial public good, and vice versa . . . .

Essentially variable, too, are the reactions of public opinion with regard to the rules: Favorable in a certain environment and in a certain epoch, hostile elsewhere or in other times. . . .

197. *The So-Called "Conservative Function" of the Law.* Such are the reasons why the law, the so-called positive law, is not always and everywhere the same: The subject matter changes, the public good and the relationship between the law and the public good change, public opinion is modified. No part or branch of the law escapes this rule, not even the most fundamental provisions of public or private law, though admittedly the foundations are ordinarily of greater stability than the superstructures. So when social changes or, *a fortiori*, social upheavals occur, the law is logically and normally obliged, if not to be taken in tow by the movement, at least to revise its attitude in the light of the new fact. That is why it is inexact or at the very least equivocal to speak of a "conservative function of the law." The law has neither to conserve itself, in the sense of maintaining the legal status quo, nor to fight against life, once the change (supposing that it depends on the

will of men) offers nothing socially reprehensible. It would be better on the contrary to speak of a duty of adaptation and thus of renewal of the law.

It is true, the organs authorized to interpret and apply the laws do not always have the competence to modify it, to the ends of readaptation. In this sense, their mission is to conserve the rules of enacted law and to maintain them against deformations as well as against violations pure and simple. But, to begin with, the maintenance of enacted statutory rules does not necessarily involve the stagnation of the whole law. The readaptation may be the work of other modes of expressing the law than statutory enactment. Above all, it is for the legislator himself to reform his statute, to improve it where it is imperfect, to bring it up to date where it lags behind life . . .

198. *Necessity of Prudence in Change.* At the outset, prudence commands one to conserve what one has gotten as long as one is not sure of the value of what one will get. Any change, concerning the future, involves an unknown: What will be the real effect of the new law? Better or worse than the old? The most probable calculations may be destroyed by the intrusion of the famous "imponderables." . . .

. . . Any change in the laws, even when justified in itself, provokes a crisis and consequently an evil: Juridical habits are disturbed; business arrangements are frustrated; more or less respectable, and in any event vested, interests are affronted . . . If the disadvantages outweigh the advantages, one will have to stick to the status quo, notwithstanding its insufficiency or shortcomings. Although perfection is the ideal to be attained, it is not always expedient to try to realize it . . . Often in practice the better is the enemy of the good. That is why the laws will be changed only in case of "very grave and absolutely obvious utility" or of "extreme necessity" in order to abolish a manifest injustice or any injurious rule. Even on this assumption, prudence may advise certain arrangements, certain temporiza-

tions or "transitional measures," so as to attenuate the brusqueness of the shock and to get our minds used to the novelty.

Part Three

NATURAL LAW, JUSTICE, AND THE LEGAL RULE

Introduction

199. *Statement of the Problem* . . . What place do the concepts of natural law and justice occupy within the "complex" of the law? . . .

200. *Objective Value of the Ideas of Natural Law and Justice.* It is useless to discuss these problems unless one begins by recognizing a meaning in the concepts of natural law and justice as norms of reason, endowed with objective value. True, some claim that men—individuals and collectivities—in their behavior would not let themselves be guided by any ideal principle detached from their passions and their self-interest . . . The statutes and customs making up the positive law would indeed be but the product of the physical or economical superiority of the actual holders of power or, at least, the expression of the balancing of antagonistic forces in a determinate moment of history. To others, natural law and justice do indeed exist as either idea-forces driving humanity, or as an ultimate aid against the established law; but that ideal would be only a "myth" or at least a gratuitous hypothesis. Now, if that is so, everything comes tumbling down at once: Natural law and justice, undoubtedly, and also the norm of a public good prevailing over the individual interest, and the very principle of a subjection of the law that is called positive to a rational method of elaboration. The established law is what it is, nothing more; it is valid by itself, by the power of those who have laid it down. The despotism of the legislator rules and replaces the despotism of the individual.

The vast majority of men, however, ignorant or thoughtful, are communicants of the cult of natural law and justice, and they believe therein as a reality of the philosophical and moral, if not of the peculiarly scientific, order. Unfortunately, save for a uninimity in principle as to the ethical character of the two concepts, disagreement prevails among specialists as to the exact definition of each . . . .

CHAPTER I

The Concept of Natural Law

Section 1. The Traditional Conception

201. *Natural Law as a Norm of Human Conduct.* According to the most generally accepted use of the term in our time, the noun "law" in the expression "natural law" is taken in the sense of a certain rule of conduct with man as its subject and imposed in a categorical fashion upon his activities, and not of a scientific law or a technical rule. . . .

203. *Characteristics of Natural Law: A Norm That Issues from Nature, Universal and Immutable.* On the other hand, as the adjective "natural" indicates without too great ambiguity, the rule of human conduct that is called natural law is deduced from the nature of man as it reveals itself in the basic inclinations of that nature under the control of reason, independently of any formal intervention by any legislator whatsoever, divine or human. Natural law is thus distinguished from another law, which is called "positive" . . . and is supposed to have been established by the will of God or of men. Natural law, furthermore, dominates positive law in the sense that, while positive law may add to natural law or even restrict it, it is prohibited from contradicting it. . . .

From the characteristics of human nature flow the characteristics of natural law. As human nature is identical in all men and does not vary, its precepts have universal and immutable validity. . . .

204. *First Principles and Secondary Precepts.* As to the extent of the "given" of nature and of what must therefore be referred to natural law, views are divided. The traditional school reserves the name natural, with the characteristics of universal-

ity, immutability, and certainty inherent in that quality, to altogether general and necessary "first principles," distinguishing them even from "secondary precepts" or "particular conclusions quite close to the first principles." Other interpretations, of later date, include within natural law not only the first principles, but the more or less close conclusions evolved from the first principles by way of rational argumentation. . . .

The disadvantage of the strict conception evidently is to reduce the concrete content of natural law to rather vague generalities, which gives rise to the objection (an unjust one, incidentally) of useless verbalism; the dangers of the broad conception lie in lending the validity of natural law, that is, absolute authority, to solutions endowed with truth merely relative to the cases. The present tendency is toward the minimum conception. . . .

205. *Subject Matter of Natural Law: The Totality of the Duties of Man* . . . St. Thomas Aquinas classifies "the natural inclinations from which the order of the precepts of natural law flows" as follows: An inclination, common to all substances, toward the conservation of their being according to its proper nature; an inclination, common to men and animals, toward the union of the male and female, the education of the youth, and similar things; an inclination, proper to man, toward the goods conforming to his nature as a rational being, such as the desire to know God and to live in society, which impels him to avoid ignorance, not to do wrong to his neighbor with whom he must maintain relations, and other things of that kind. It is not hard to recognize in that classification the principles corresponding to the totality of the duties of man: Toward himself, toward his family, toward God, toward his neighbor, toward society. . . .

Section 2. Is There a Juridical Natural Law?

207. *The Ambiguity of the Concept of Natural Law* . . . To what sort of regulation is the natural law related? To the regulation

which, aiming at the moral perfection of men, obligates them before their conscience and before God to practice the good and avoid the bad, in short, the moral rule? Or to the regulation of societal origin, laid down by (domestic or international) public authority with a view to the temporal public good (of individuals or states), in short, the legal rule? . . .

208. *Historically, Natural Law Provides Principles of Moral Conduct* . . . What one has always sought of "natural law" is principles of moral conduct, it being understood that man is a social and political being and that morally he has social and political duties. Natural law, the Schoolmen tell us, dictates to man what he must do to arrive at the ultimate end of human life, that is, happiness; it is the rule and measure of peculiarly human actions; its first principle and first precept is that one ought to practice the good and avoid the bad. The traditional teaching is echoed by the "law of nature and of nations" school. According to Grotius, for instance, the law "obliges to what is good and praiseworthy and not merely to what is just, since law, according to the idea we attach to it here, is not confined to the duties of justice but also embraces what makes up the subject matter of the other virtues." Hence this definition: Natural law "consists in certain principles of right reason, which causes us to know that an action is morally honest or dishonest according to its necessary agreement or disagreement with a rational and sociable nature." The connection is clear: Natural law figures among the first notions of moral philosophy or general ethics in the chapter on laws, side by side with the theory of human acts; and the treatises of natural law, where the applications of the rule of natural law to the different matters are set forth and discussed, are nothing else than treatises on special ethics. . . .

210. *Relationships between the Natural Moral Rule and the Legal Rule.* To be sure, natural law in the sense just defined, i.e., as the natural moral rule (at least as to first principles), is not unrelated to law, in the

sense of the rule established by the state. Under the name of "human law" St. Thomas shows us the civil law coming to the aid of natural law "in order by force and fear to compel perverted and ill-disposed men to abstain from evil, at least so that in ceasing to do evil they leave others in peace." On the other hand, the civil laws are called upon to complete natural law, either by way of conclusions derived from the first principles (as in the case of the *jus gentium*) or by way of concrete determination of the first principles (as in the case of the *jus civile* properly so called). For instance, the law of nature prescribes that he who shall commit an offense shall be punished and the civil law defines the kind of penalty. The same analysis is found in the authors of the law of nature school: the role of the civil law is to sanction natural law, in particular in so far as it prescribes what is just. Is it not the first end of the state, and therefore of the law set down by the state, to guarantee "the peaceful enjoyment of one's rights"? It is natural law, moreover, which either on the ground of the necessity of political society (man is a "political animal") or on the ground of the "social contract" (the faith of promises) gives the civil laws their foundation and justifies the subjects' duty of obedience. Finally, everybody admits that civil laws contrary to natural law are bad laws and even that they do not answer to the concept of a law. . . .

212. *Extension of the Concept of Natural Law: "Natural Jurisprudence."* It is true that often the concept of natural law is stretched to include precisely these "useful" things, foreign as such to the category of good and just, which permits assigning a "given" of natural law to the entire civil law, even in those of its dispositions which more or less closely relate to "usefulness to human life." For instance, Grotius suggests a "natural jurisprudence," common to all times and places, detached from anything dependent upon an arbitrary will, a science capable of forming a complete body where one could find treated laws, tributes, judicial

duty, conjectures (or presumptions of will), proofs, presumptions, etc.

That link does indeed bridge the hiatus. Natural law no longer represents—or no longer solely or principally represents—the first principles of morality, of the good, the just; it represents—or equally represents—the first principles of civil legislation in the concern for all values whatsoever with which the latter is charged, that is, not only the moral values but also the properly economic or social values, even if they be of a technical nature and in themselves morally indifferent. . . .

213. *But This Extension Contradicts the Original Concept of Natural Law . . .*

What did natural law mean originally? A rule inscribed in human nature, aiming at the absolute good and just, at honesty. What does the "new style" natural law mean? A quite different concept: a rule invented by man, aiming at things useful to human life in a given social state. No doubt the nature of man is rational and therefore inventive of useful things; it is sociable and therefore concerned about things useful not only to the individual man but also to the society of men. Yet originally it was intended precisely to place in opposition to each other inventive reason and nature, and an express distinction was made between the good and the just, on the one hand, and the useful, on the other. The social was not excluded; on the contrary—but in the social the search continued to be for the absolute good and just and not the contingent useful. That the useful itself, once established, opens up the rule of the good and the just, binding as to the consequences of such establishment, changes nothing in the situation. Thus, prescription and the other rules of security in society remain what they are, to wit, useful and invented solutions, although natural law enjoins us to submit to them—as to every decision made by authority and for the public good. That the useful involves nothing contrary to natural law is obvious but does not justify any confusion. . . .

214. *The Extension Contradicts the Concept of the Legal Rule . . .* It is contradictory

to speak of "natural jurisprudence" because "jurisprudence," down to its most general rules and their aims—not only the useful but also the good and the just—is a matter of prudence, and prudence is a matter of rational appraisal according to the cases and not a matter of inclination of nature . . . Natural law does not dictate any decision to the jurist except negatively, to bring out no precept contrary to moral natural law, and affirmatively, to regulate everything as a function of the possible and realizable public good. . . .

216. *The Dualism of "Natural Law—Positive Law" Replaced by "Morals—Law."* If these views are correct, they yield an important result concerning the statement of the problem here under discussion. One must no longer speak of relationships between natural law and positive law . . . One must speak of relationships between morals, not only natural but also positive, and the civil law, that is to say, the law. This statement does correspond to reality. On the one hand, what makes its appearance throughout natural law is indeed morals. On the other hand, the law has relationships with kinds of values other than the ethical values. . . .

CHAPTER II

The Concept of Justice

Section 1. The Existing Conceptions; Especially, on the Conception of Aristotle and St. Thomas Aquinas

217. *The Modern Conception of Justice as a Specifically Social and Juridical Value.* For one trying to analyze the relationships between natural law and justice, on the one hand, and the law in the sense of the civil law, on the other, the concept of justice, too, calls for clarification. . . .

Reading some legal philosophers, it would seem as if the concept of justice was indissolubly tied to the notions of society and of laws. Consulting only their particular discipline, those authors look at justice only across society and across the laws. Justice to them is the substance, the aim, the ideal of the law, law being understood as positive legal organization. . . .

218. *According to Tradition, Justice Is Primarily a Moral Virtue. . . .* We are here witnessing the same slipping from the moral to the legal plane as in the matter of natural law . . . Before there were organized societies and laws to govern them there was some justice, and today there still exists some justice which is not necessarily that of the laws. In the practice of peoples . . . justice is first a moral virtue, bringing into play the moral perfectioning of the subject without necessarily implying life in political society. The latter may well add specifications or even new orientations, of a properly social character, to the duty of moral justice; it does not bring justice into being, either as its efficient cause or as a condition of its existence. In short, justice is contemporary not with the idea of political society and the civil law but with the idea of the good, of which it constitutes one of the essential categories. . . .

219. *Justice in the Broad Sense of the Good and the Just.* What, then, is the place of justice within the frame of morals, and what is its proper object?

Here one finds several accepted meanings. In the widest sense, justice merges with morality itself: It corresponds to the fulfillment of all duties prescribed by honesty, without distinction of domain or virtue, in the private life of the individual or family and in social life, public or political. . . .

220. *Justice in the Strict Sense of the Virtue Attributing to Everyone His Right.* There is, however, a narrower meaning of justice, yet still a moral one, which limits that virtue to the domain of relations with another. . . .

225. *Justice in the Strict Sense Must Be Defined by "Aequalitas" Rather than by the "Aequum" . . .* The virtue that renders to everyone his right or his dignity deserves to be defined, in the strict sense, not merely by the loose idea of equity (*aequum et bonum*) but by the mathematical idea of equality (*aequalitas*). In this sense, justice equalizes the attitude of the subject to what is the

rigorous right of another individual or collectivity, a right covering and protecting an innate or acquired good, which for its holder is in a certain manner his own, whence it follows that he may exact respect for it if need be by force. If this "his own" is lacking, there is no right that can be exacted, no equality to be realized, and therefore no justice. If there exists "his own," but without any possibility of equalization on account of the basic inability of the debtor, the debt will no longer be one of justice, since it remains outside of the equality postulated by justice. This is not to say that it could not give rise to legal effects, e.g., in the form of the "natural obligation," or even directly to a civil obligation. That is another question, which concerns the determination of the content of the civil law and not the definition of justice.

Section 2. The Three Kinds of Justice

228. *Enumeration and Classification.* Aristotle and St. Thomas . . . divided justice into three kinds, according to the . . . persons concerned.

When these are private persons . . . , the justice which links them is called "commutative." When the persons in question are a collectivity and its members, especially the state and its citizens, justice is called "distributive" as to what is due from the collectivity to its members, and "legal" as to what is due from the members to the collectivity. . . .

231. *In Commutative Justice, Equality Is Determined as of Thing to Thing . . .* The creditor of justice has a right to what belongs to him or is coming to him simply because the thing is his, and it is his regardless of any consideration of his personal quality. Consideration of the person will intervene only where the condition of the person produces a difference in the things, and St. Thomas again takes up the example of the injury: The injury to persons is more or less grave according to the condition of the injured person . . . Contrariwise, the condition of persons becomes altogether irrele-

vant where the question, for instance, is to determine what the user of the thing of another ought to restore or what the buyer [of a thing] ought to pay. . . .

233. *The Subject Matter of Distributive Justice: The Various Kinds of Distributions.* The subject matter of distributive justice consists of the various kinds of distributions which every social body is called upon to effect among its members . . . This means distribution of the social benefits. That in turn means, in the case of the state, participation in the advantages of the public good resulting from the action of the state . . . Then, distribution of the functions and employments that are at the disposal of the body . . . Lastly, allocation of the contributions of every nature that are indispensable to social life, for the body lives only by what its members bring in to it. Now these distributions, active and passive, could not take place except according to a principle of equalization as to the rights and faculties of everyone, which is a rule of justice.

In confronting the society with his claim for his just part in the social benefits, the member claims what is due him as his own in his quality as a member. . . .

234. *Difference between Distributive Justice and Commutative Justice.* However, the position of the member with regard to the social body is not the same as that of one independent individual with regard to another. First, his right is by definition that of a member, that is, of a part in relation to a whole, and therefore his right in distributive justice remains entirely subordinate to the requirements of the good of the body in its entirety. . . .

Furthermore, the right of the member with regard to the body could logically be measured only according to an equality proportional to the "dignity," the rank of the member in the body. Now the ranks in the body are not equal . . . What then is the determining principle of the hierarchy? It is multifarious and also depends upon the diversity of social and political regimes. In modern states, among the criteria of distribu-

tive justice there must be counted, besides merit and services rendered, weakness, meaning not only physical weakness, which has always been entitled to a privilege, but also economic weakness . . . As to justice in imposing burdens, equally governed by the rule of proportionality, the determining principle is that of ability to contribute to what is required, so that the more fortunate will contribute a larger amount than the less fortunate. . . .

235. *Legal Justice: Its General Concept* . . . Conversely to distributive justice, which moves from the society to the members legal (or social) justice goes from the members to the society . . . Legal justice, though, is a *moral* virtue . . . because "it is impossible that a man be good if he is not proportioned to the common good." Is it not the vocation of man to live and perfect himself in and through political society? . . .

237. *What the Individual Owes the Community Organized in the State: "Generality" of Legal Justice* . . . To the community of the individuals associated in the state the individual member owes, besides, the adjustment of his private conduct, the submission of his particular good to the common good of the public . . . It is not enough that he fulfill his civic, political, societal duty toward the state organization. He must also fulfill his social duty, in subordinating all that pertains to him in his personal activity and his property, to the good of the society grouped in the state. . . .

238. *In What Legal or General Justice Remains Special* . . . It happens . . . frequently that legal justice commands or prohibits acts which . . . as such do not fall under any virtue or any vice, and which have moral value exclusively by their reference to the good of the total community. These are, in short, technical values—values of social technique—which their end alone endows with morality. In this case, as in the case of the properly societal duties, legal justice ceases to be general so as to find again a special subject matter, proper to itself, directly ordained for the good of the whole. . . .

CHAPTER III

The "Given" of Natural Law and of Justice in the Elaboration of the Law

* * *

Section 1. Morality and the Temporal Public Good

245. There Could Be No Public Good Against Morals . . . A legal rule positively contrary to morals must be condemned as contrary to the public good. . . .

As concerns justice especially, a conflict with the public good is even less conceivable inasmuch as justice, in the form of legal justice at any rate, is defined by the public good: Justice is what is demanded by or conforms to the public good, always reserving the rights of morality in general. Therefore, all that is laid down by the law in conformity with the public good is at once in conformity with justice. . . .

248. The Law Is Not Bound to Consecrate Every Rule of Morals . . . The public good, which is not compatible with any kind of immoral law, does not necessarily require the intervention of a law in order to compel respect for morals. . . .

251. The Capacity of Morals for "Ordination to the Public Good." The problem of the relations between law and morals finds its definitive answer in the following formulation: The jurist will retain only those of the rules of morals whose consecration or confirmation by the law will in fact under the circumstances be found useful to the public good and practicable with regard to the technical equipment of the jurist. . . .

Section 2. Justice as the Normal Matter of the Legal Rule

252. The Moral Precepts Susceptible of Consecration by the Law. What, then, are the moral precepts that may be ordained for the public good by the intermediary of the laws? Here political prudence comes in, and especially legislative prudence, whose role is precisely that of discerning solutions most adequate to the circumstances of times, places, and cases. Although these solutions are variable in concrete cases, it is not impossible to assign to the work of prudence, if not an inflexible method, at least a marching order of general though provisional value. . . .

. . . The jurist will distinguish among the moral rules governing the relationships among men those implying something due which is capable of exaction: The debt of justice in its three forms, commutative, distributive, and legal, and also the debts that may be called familial . . . As for moral prescriptions other than those of justice, the measure of interest the jurist accords them will depend on the degree of their proximity to justice. . . .

253. Justice as the Precept Most Obviously Fit for Consecration. On several grounds, justice is somehow the natural subject matter of the legal system . . . Legal justice is the virtue most necessary to the public good precisely because its object is the public good (of the state or of the public). It is in legal justice that law and morals meet so closely as almost to merge. . . .

. . . The two justices, commutative and distributive, which refer to the particular good, are . . . subordinate to legal justice, which is qualified to regulate the content thereof, that is to say, the particular right of everyone, according to the requirements of the public good. . . .

254. Exceptional Rectification of the Two Particular Justices on the Ground of Legal Justice. Yet it would be a mistake to believe that the solutions given by commutative and distributive justice on the basis of the individual right alone would always or even frequently call for rectification on the ground of legal justice. Not only is there no necessary opposition between the public good and the particular justices, but such opposition is also relatively rare . . . Nor will any rectification whatever be operative on the ground of the public good except where proof has been made beyond any doubt that the consecration of the right of the individual according to the standard of particular justice either involves positive damage to the public good in the special case or does not permit the attainment of an advantage remotely compensating the evil inherent in any rectification of justice. . . .

256. *Like the Legal Duty, the Duty of Justice Is Capable of Exaction* . . . Morally, by its nature, justice implies the right to repel unjust aggression: This is the case of vindication which may be permissible and sometimes is a virtue, according to the circumstances. Now, similarly, by its nature the legal rule is capable of exaction and proceeds by way of compulsion: What is required by the public good or decided upon in conformity with it calls for being carried out, voluntarily or by force. Thus when the law takes over on its account the moral precept of justice, the compulsion with which it accompanies it does not constitute an innovation. Especially as regards commutative justice, the consecration of a law does nothing but replace the very insufficient (and for the public good deadly) mode of private compulsion with the regulated mode of public compulsion. The change touches only the form of compulsion and not its principle. Contrariwise, the moral duties incapable of exaction are as such repugnant to compulsion, which is foreign to them and even denatures them. . . .

258. *The Law and the Constituent Principles of the Family.* Lastly, among the moral principles whose place is marked in the law, there are to be counted the constituent rules of the family, the rules which define the family as an institution . . . Seen from their inner or intimate side, family relationships belong above all to that part of morals which governs sentiments and acts resulting from sentiments. In the first rank of these sentiments we find love . . . But the law is powerless with respect to the duty of love and even to a degree, the duty of familial piety inasmuch as it involves love. Contrariwise, with regard to the traits by which the family is set apart as an institution and which belong to the institutional part of morals, the powerlessness of the law disappears. It is not impossible for a law to decree that only the

legitimate union, that is, marriage, shall be endowed with legal effects; that this union shall be one and indissoluble, at least in principle; that it shall entail reciprocal duties of cohabitation, faithfulness, aid, and support that parents ought to give their children during their formative period nourishment and education; that children in turn are under the obligation of docility; that the family group shall have a head, the husband and father, charged with authority—and responsibility—toward his wife and children,—all this according to the moral conceptions prevalent in the people under contemplation.

To what extent do the constituent principles of the law of domestic relations approach the type of justice? . . . It is not forbidden to speak of a sort of justice between spouses, which gives them rights that may be exacted from one another, or a sort of justice between parents and children, which makes them creditors (or debtors) of education, nourishment, docility, etc. But this matters little from our point of view. It is enough that the constituent principles of the family evidently concern the "public." Now it may be affirmed beyond doubt: The family concerns the public good at least as much as it concerns justice, as clearly and as closely . . . That is why the law will at once come to the aid of the familial institution, as it comes to the aid of individuals in commutative and distributive justice, and of the state and the public in legal justice.

259. *Yet the Normal Order of Consecration Is Subject to Derogation.* It is granted, again, that these interventions of the law take place not directly in favor of justice, or in favor of the family, but inasmuch as these values—and their legal protection itself—effectively realize the public good in the circumstances, and on the condition also that the intervention should not be technically incapable of realization. Such being the point of view of the jurist, it is possible that the marching order outlined above . . . must undergo certain derogations in practice. Thus some moral rules that would normally require the consecration of the law might

have to go without it, while others which normally would not require it would have to obtain it. . . .

260. *Cases Where the Law Abstains from Consecrating Justice.* It has already been observed, with supporting examples, how commutative justice . . . often enough had to withdraw before more or less urgent considerations of the social order . . . But there is another set where the law foregoes sanctioning commutative justice. Either it refers for the determination of their respective rights to the regulation agreed upon between the interested parties although this may not always conform to natural justice. Or again it leaves the field free to individual activities, where these usually work spontaneously in the direction of justice, or where political prudence or the insufficiency of legal equipment makes it advisable to tolerate them wholly or in part even though they are unjust.

261. *Cases Where the Law Goes Beyond the Framework of Justice.* Also, contrariwise, the law pushes beyond commutative justice, sanctioning moral rules other than the rule of justice . . . Not only fidelity to the pledged word, which is as indispensable to social life as is strict justice, but also, for instance, gratitude and sometimes beneficence and liberality. So-called "social legislation" is full of precepts imposing obligations upon employers to which on the part of the workers no strict right corresponds and which often fall within gratuitous assistance. But these virtues are eminently "social," more social in certain respects than justice. For if justice is the necessary condition of life in society in rendering to each his own, the social virtues, by their disinterested altruistic character, positively tighten the social bond. Hence it will be seen that the law, concerned with concord and fraternity among the members of the group, is led to promulgate statutes "of social solidarity," where the required attitudes become a matter of legal justice by reason of their "ordination" for the public

good. Furthermore, social relations do not exist solely between equals: At their basis is authority. That is why the law prescribes obedience to authorities not only in the state but also in the private groups, in the first place the family. . . .

But the law does not entrench itself in the field of the virtues *ad alterum*. Stepping beyond the circle of justice and the social virtues, it represses some shortcomings in duties toward one's self (e.g., the attempt at suicide, drunkenness, certain alienations of essential rights or liberties), some shortcomings in duties toward God (e.g., blasphemy, sacrilege, perjury) or again acts of cruelty to animals. Why? . . . Because these offenses affect the public, causing trouble or damage in the social environment.

Lastly, beyond justice and even morals, one will have to indicate the innumerable measures of prudence laid down by the law to the end of preventing the violation of the moral precepts it has taken up and sanctioned. Such are the regulations designed to police traffic, industry and labor, and commerce, whose aim it is no doubt to facilitate the activities of traffic, industry, commerce, but also to protect the rights of the persons engaged in those activities against encroachments. Now these preventive measures, though in part ordained for justice, are in themselves means indifferent to justice.

262. *"Just Laws" and Laws Consecrating Justice Are Not Synonymous.* Finally, one will have to guard against confounding just laws and laws which consecrate justice. A law is just when it prescribes what is within its role to prescribe. In this sense, a just law is a law adjusted to its end, the public good, and to its proper means of realization, in short, a law conforming to the legal method . . . Now while ordinarily a just law is a law which consecrates justice, this is not always so. That is all the difference between the lawyer's justice, which is a matter of prudence, and the moralist's justice, which is a matter of truth or science.

20

John Dewey

1859–1952

John Dewey was a practical, rugged Ver-monter, born in Burlington before the Civil War and still hard at writing philosophy ninety years later. John was one of four sons. His father was a grocer with a literary flair; he loved Shakespeare and Milton; he har-bored a theologic distaste for Emerson and Hawthorne. Until John's generation the Deweys were not college ·trained. John's mother's family was eminent; her grand-father was a congressman, her father a squire and an admired lay judge, her brothers had university degrees.

The Dewey boys spent summers on their maternal grandfather's comfortable farm. They tramped the mountains, took canoe and fishing trips, and learned French in Canada. They were not above making money by carrying papers. One of the boys died early. The others were normal, well-adjusted boys.

Public school bored John, but he made good grades and graduated from high school at fifteen. He went to tiny Vermont Uni-versity from which he graduated with a good record in a class of eighteen. He spent three winters teaching public school in Pennsyl-vania and Vermont. He then did graduate work on borrowed money at Johns Hopkins, taking his Doctor's degree in philosophy in 1894. Dewey taught at Minnesota University for a year and at Michigan for five, before he was called to Chicago University where he first came to national prominence.

Chicago University had a special attrac-tion for him; pedagogy was taught in its department of Philosophy and Psychology. Dewey organized "The Laboratory School"

in which educational theories could be tried out. The School enrolled children from faculty families and outstanding professors in several departments took part in estab-lishing its experimental methods and cur-riculum. To raise money for the Laboratory School, Dewey gave a series of talks. These talks were printed under the title *School and Society* (1899) which has been translated into a dozen different languages and is one of Dewey's most influential works. He was a pioneer in "progressive" education, and is still almost the patron saint of many educa-tors. In 1932 the National Educational As-sociation elected Dewey honorary life president. Dewey was crushed when in 1904, without consultation with him, a college of education was set up at Chicago University and his Laboratory School was turned over to it. He resigned with no other job in view, but was immediately snapped up by Colum-bia University where he taught until his retirement.

Edman, later himself a fine teacher of philosophy at Columbia, described Dewey's teaching in his *Philosopher's Holiday*. Though Edman had read and admired Dewey's writings, the first lecture was a shock of dullness and confusion. Dewey had none of the graces of an effective lecturer; he fum-bled with crumpled paper, looked out of the window and seemed to be reporting what happened to come into his head. But when Edman took and studied notes he found that his mind, not Dewey's, had wandered, and that Dewey's lectures had "extraordinary co-herence, texture, and brilliance." Edman found that he was listening to a man think, rather than to a performance; he learned Dewey's lectures could be "arresting educational experiences." In seminars Dewey's greatest talent came to the fore; he initiated inquiry; he did not disseminate doctrine.

Dewey's fame as an educator accounted for much of his extensive foreign travel. He was consulted on educational policy in Japan, China, Soviet Russia, and a number of other countries. He refused the Order of the Rising Sun, the highest Japanese decoration. Sidney Hook says that Dewey's refusal was prompted by his feeling that citizenship in our democratic community is distinction enough for Americans.

Dewey wrote prodigiously. In a day he could write a full chapter of five thousand words or more. He did not revise; when he wanted something else he started from scratch. Hook says that, as a result, some of Dewey's best analyses are unpublished.

Dewey has the reputation of being hard to read. His earlier work (e.g., *How We Think*, published in 1910) was written in a clear and easy style. Some of his later work must be read with great care and concentration. The works following this note are not difficult. The first excerpts come from his *Human Nature and Conduct* (1922) which has gone through many printings. The second is a summary of Dewey's views on jurisprudence which is reprinted in full; it was printed in a collection of essays called *My Philosophy of Law* (1941). Like William James, Dewey was much interested in, and influenced by developments in psychology; Dewey and James are usually thought of as the founders of American "pragmatic" philosophy.

Dewey took an active part in promotion of many liberal and reform movements and organizations. He was a leader in the Teachers Union, from which he withdrew when it fell under political domination. He was active in many attempts to form a Farmer-Labor party. He was a founder of the American Civil Liberties Union. One of his most colorful experiences resulted from his efforts on behalf of Leon Trotsky. Dewey had visited Soviet Russia with a group of educa-

tors in 1928. Soviet education impressed him favorably—except when classrooms were used for dogmatic propaganda. In 1937 Trotsky, who was Lenin's co-founder of the Soviet Union, fled for his life when charged by Stalin's henchmen with plotting Stalin's assassination, and with treason. A group, including Dewey, went to Mexico to give Trotsky a fair trial in the forum of world opinion. This "commission" found that Russian conviction of Trotsky *in absentia* was a frame-up. The experience, however, left Dewey completely disillusioned with communism. After he came back from Mexico, he is quoted in the *Washington Post* of December 19, 1937, as saying, "The great lesson . . . is the complete breakdown of revolutionary Marxism . . . The great question for all American radicals is that they must . . . reconsider . . . means of inquiry about social change and of truly democratic methods of approach to social progress."

Dewey habitually suspected absolutes and wide generalities. In one direction, however, he never waivered. For him no bar to investigation and learning was supportable. In a 1937 speech he said, ". . . if liberalism means anything, it means complete and courageous devotion to freedom of inquiry."

HUMAN NATURE AND CONDUCT *

Part Three

THE PLACE OF INTELLIGENCE IN CONDUCT

V

The Uniqueness of Good

. . . Good consists in the meaning that is experienced to belong to an activity when conflict and entanglement of various incompatible impulses and habits terminate in a unified orderly release in action. This human good, being a fulfilment conditioned upon thought, differs from the pleasures

* Reprinted by permission of Henry Holt & Co., Inc.

which an animal nature . . . hits upon accidentally. Moreover there is a genuine difference between a false good, a spurious satisfaction, and a "true" good, and there is an empirical test for discovering the difference. The unification which ends thought in act may be only a superficial compromise, not a real decision but a postponement of the issue. Many of our so-called decisions are of this nature. Or it may present . . . a victory of a temporarily intense impulse over its rivals, a unity by oppression and suppression, not by coordination. . . .

In quality, the good is never twice alike. It never copies itself . . . For it marks the resolution of a distinctive complication of competing habits and impulses which can never repeat itself. Only with a habit rigid to the point of immobility could exactly the same good recur twice . . . Rigid habits sink below the level of any meaning at all. And since we live in a moving world, they plunge us finally against conditions to which they are not adapted and so terminate in disaster.

To utilitarianism with all its defects belongs the distinction of enforcing in an unforgettable way the fact that moral good, like every good, consists in a satisfaction of the forces of human nature, in welfare, happiness. To Bentham remains . . . the imperishable renown of forcing home to the popular consciousness that "conscience" . . . is too often not intelligence but is veiled caprice, . . . vested class interest. It is truly conscience only as it contributes to relief of misery and promotion of happiness. . . .

An adequate discussion of why utilitarianism with its just insight into the central place of good, and its ardent devotion to rendering morals more intelligent and more equitably human took its onesided course (and thereby provoked an intensified reaction to transcendental and dogmatic morals) would take us far afield into social conditions and the antecedent history of thought. We can deal with only [one] factor, the domination of intellectual interest by economic considerations. The industrial revolution was bound in any case to give a new direction to thought . . . It opened up marvelous possibilities in industry and commerce, and new social conditions conducive to invention, ingenuity, enterprise, constructive energy and an impersonal habit of mind dealing with mechanisms rather than appearances. But new movements do not start in a new and clear field. The context of old institutions and corresponding habits of thought persisted. The new movement was perverted in theory because prior established conditions deflected it in practice. Thus the new industrialism was largely the old feudalism, living in a bank instead of a castle and brandishing the check of credit instead of the sword.

An old theological doctrine of total depravity was continued and carried over in the idea of an inherent laziness of human nature which rendered it averse to useful work, unless bribed by expectations of pleasure, or driven by fears of pains. This being the "incentive" to action, it followed that the office of reason is only to enlighten the search for good or gain by instituting a more exact calculus of profit and loss. Happiness was thus identified with a maximum net gain of pleasures on the basis of analogy with business conducted for pecuniary profit, and directed by means of a science of accounting dealing with quantities of receipts and expenses expressed in definite monetary units. . . .

. . . There exists a difference in kind between business calculation of profit and loss and deliberation upon what purposes to form. . . .

. . . Now business calculation is obviously of the kind where the end is taken for granted and does not enter into deliberation. It resembles the case in which a man has already made his final decision, say to take a walk, and deliberates only upon what walk to take . . . Deliberation is not free but occurs within the limits of a decision reached by some prior deliberation or else fixed by unthinking routine. Suppose, however, that a man's question is not which path to walk upon, but whether to walk or to stay with a friend whom continued confinement has rendered peevish and uninteresting as a companion. The utilitarian theory demands that in the latter case the two alternatives still be of the same kind, alike in quality, that their only difference be a quantitative one, of plus or minus in pleasure. This assumption . . . asserts by implication that there is no genuine doubt or suspense as to the meaning of any impulse or habit. Their meaning is ready-made, fixed: pleasure. The only "problem" or doubt is as to the *amount* of pleasure (or pain) that is involved.

This assumption does violence to fact. The poignancy of situations that evoke reflection lies in the fact that we really do not know the meaning of the tendencies that are pressing for action. We have to search, to experiment. Deliberation is a work of discovery. Conflict is acute; one impulse carries us one way into one situation, and another impulse takes us another way to a radically different objective result. Deliberation is not an attempt to do away with this opposition of quality by reducing it to one of amount. It is an attempt to *uncover* the conflict in its full scope and bearing. . . .

In short, the thing actually at stake in any serious deliberation is not a difference of quantity, but what kind of person one is to become, what sort of self is in the making, what kind of a world is making . . . Deliberation as to whether to be a merchant or a school teacher, a physician or a politician is not a choice of quantities. It is just what it appears to be, a choice of careers which are incompatible with one another, within each of which definitive inclusions and rejections are involved. With the difference in career belongs a difference in the constitution of the self, of habits of thought and feeling as well as of outward action . . . Our minor decisions differ in acuteness and range, but not in principle. . . .

. . . There is something abnormal and in the strict sense impossible in mere means, in, that is, instruments totally dissevered from ends. We may view economic activity in abstraction, but it does not *exist* by itself. Business takes for granted non-business uses to which its results are to be put. . . .

. . . The attempt to assimilate other activities to the model of economic activity (defined as a calculated pursuit of gain) reverses the state of the facts. The "economic man" defined as a creature devoted to an enlightened or calculating pursuit of gain is morally objectionable because the conception of such a being empirically falsifies empirical facts. Love of pecuniary gain is an undoubted and powerful fact. But it and its importance are affairs of social not of psychological nature . . . It cannot be used to define the nature of desire, effort and satisfaction, because it embodies a socially selected type of desire and satisfaction. It affords, like steeple-chasing, or collecting postage stamps, seeking political office, astronomical observation of the heavens, a special case of desire, effort, and happiness. And like them it is subject to examination, criticism and valuation in the light of the place it occupies in the system of developing activities.

The reason that it is so easy and for specific purposes so useful to select economic activities and subject them to separate scientific treatment is because the men who engage in it are men who are also more than business men, whose usual habits may be more or less safely guessed at. As human beings they have desires and occupations which are affected by social custom, expectation and admiration. The uses to which gains will be put, that is the current scheme of activities into which they enter as factors, are passed over only because they are so inevitably present. Support of family, of church, philanthropic benefactions, political influence, automobiling, command of luxuries, freedom of movement, respect from others, are in general terms some of the obvious activities into which economic activity fits. . . .

A certain tragic fate seems to attend all intellectual movements. That of utilitarianism is suggested in the not infrequent criticism that it exaggerated the role of rational thought in human conduct . . . Thus a partially sound criticism is employed to conceal the one factor in utilitarianism from which we ought to learn something; is used to foster an obscurantist doctrine of trusting to impulse, instinct or intuition. Neither the utilitarians nor any one else can exaggerate the proper office of reflection, of intelligence, in conduct. The mistake lay not here but in a false conception of what constitutes reflection, deliberation. The truth that men are not moved by consideration of self-interest, that men are not good judges of where their interests lie and are not moved to act by these judgments, cannot properly be converted into the belief that consideration of consequences is a negligible factor in conduct. So far as it is negligible in fact it evinces the rudimentary character of civilization. We may indeed safely start from the assumption that impulse and habit, not thought, are the primary determinants of conduct. But the conclusion to be drawn from these facts is that the need is therefore the greater for cultivation of thought. The error of utilitarianism is not at this point. It is found in its wrong conception of what thought, deliberation, is and does.

VI

The Nature of Aims

. . . The ends, objectives, of conduct are those foreseen consequences which influence present deliberation and which finally bring it to rest by furnishing an adequate stimulus to overt action. Consequently ends arise and function within action. They are not, as current theories too often imply, things lying beyond activity at which the latter is directed. They are not strictly speaking ends or termini of action at all. They are terminals of deliberation, and so turning points *in* activity . . . The utilitarian sets up pleasure as such an outside-and-beyond, as something necessary to induce action and in which it terminates. Many harsh critics of utilitarianism have however agreed that there is some end in which action terminates, a final goal. They have denied that pleasure is such an outside aim, and put perfection or self-realization in its place. The entire popular notion of "ideals" is infected with this conception of some fixed end beyond activity at which we should aim. . . .

When men believed that fixed ends existed for all normal changes in nature, the conception of similar ends for men was but a special case of a general belief. If the changes in a tree from acorn to full-grown oak were regulated by an end which was somehow immanent or potential in all the less perfect forms, and if change was simply the effort to realize a perfect or complete form, then the acceptance of a like view for human conduct was consonant with the rest of what passed for science. Such a view, consistent and systematic, was foisted by Aristotle upon western culture and endured for two thousand years. When the notion was expelled from natural science by the intellectual revolution of the seventeenth century, logically it should also have disappeared from the theory of human action. But man is not logical . . . He hangs on to what he can in his old beliefs even when he is compelled to surrender their logical basis. So the doctrine of fixed ends-in-themselves at which human acts are—or should be—directed and by which they are regulated if they are regulated at all persisted in morals, and was made the cornerstone of orthodox moral theory. The immediate effect was to dislocate moral from natural science, to divide man's world as it never had been divided in prior culture. . . .

In fact, ends are ends-in-view or aims. They arise out of natural effects or consequences which in the beginning are hit upon, stumbled upon so far as any purpose is concerned. Men *like* some of the consequences and *dislike* others . . . These consequences constitute the meaning and value of an activity as it comes under deliberation. Meantime of course imagination is busy. Old consequences are enhanced, recombined, modified in imagination. Invention operates. Actual consequences, that is effects which have happened in the past, become possible future consequences of acts still to be performed . . . Ends are foreseen consequences which arise in the course of activity and which are employed to give activity added meaning and to direct its further course.

They are in no sense ends *of* action. In being ends of *deliberation* they are redirecting pivots *in* action.

Men shoot and throw. At first this is done as an "instinctive" or natural reaction to some situation. The result when it is observed gives a new meaning to the activity. Henceforth men in throwing and shooting think of it in terms of its outcome; they act intelligently or have an end. Liking the activity in its acquired meaning, they not only "take aim" when they throw instead of throwing at random, but they find or make targets at which to aim. This is the origin and nature of "goals" of action. . . .

Even the most important among all the consequences of an act is not necessarily its aim. Results which are objectively most important may not even be thought of at all; ordinarily a man does not think in connection with exercise of his profession that it will sustain him and his family in existence. The end-thought-of is uniquely important, but it is indispensable to state the respect in which it is important . . . In a temporary annoyance, even if only that caused by the singing of a mosquito, the thought of that which gives relief may engross the mind in spite of consequences much more important, objectively speaking. Moralists have deplored such facts as evidence of levity. But the remedy, if a remedy be needed, is not found in insisting upon the importance of ends in general. It is found in a change of the dispositions which make things either immediately troublesome or tolerable or agreeable.

When ends are regarded as literally ends to action rather than as directive stimuli to present choice they are frozen and isolated. It makes no difference whether the "end" is "natural" good like health or a "moral" good like honesty. Set up as complete and exclusive, as demanding and justifying action as a means to itself, it leads to narrowness; in extreme cases fanaticism, inconsiderateness, arrogance and hypocrisy . . . Moral theorists constantly assume that the continuous course of events can be arrested at the point of a particular object; that men can

plunge with their own desires into the unceasing flow of changes, and seize upon some object as their end irrespective of everything else . . . One reminds one's self that one's end is justice or charity or professional achievement or putting over a deal for a needed public improvement, and further questionings and qualms are stilled.

. . . Common sense revolts against the maxim, conveniently laid off upon Jesuits or other far-away people, that the end justifies the means . . . Overlooking means is only a device for failing to note those ends, or consequences, which, if they were noted would be seen to be so evil that action would be estopped. Certainly nothing can justify or condemn means except ends, results. But we have to include consequences impartially . . . It is wilful folly to fasten upon some single end or consequence which is liked, and permit the view of that to blot from perception all other undesired and undesirable consequences . . . Not *the* end—in the singular—justifies the means; for there is no such thing as the single all-important end. . . .

. . . In general, the identification of the end prominent in conscious desire and effort with *the* end is part of the technique of avoiding a reasonable survey of consequences. The survey is avoided because of a subconscious recognition that it would reveal desire in its true worth and thus preclude action to satisfy it—or at all events give us an uneasy conscience in striving to realize it. Thus the doctrine of the isolated, complete or fixed end limits intelligent examination, encourages insincerity, and puts a pseudo-stamp of moral justification upon success at any price.

Moralistic persons are given to escaping this evil by falling into another pit. They deny that consequences have anything at all to do with the morality of acts. Not ends but motives they say justify or condemn acts. The thing to do, accordingly, is to cultivate certain motives or dispositions, benevolence, purity, love of perfection, loyalty. The denial of consequences thus turns out formal, verbal. In reality a consequence is set up at which to aim, only it is a subjective consequence. "Meaning well" is selected as *the* consequence or end to be cultivated at all hazards, an end which is all-justifying and to which everything else is offered up in sacrifice. The result is a sentimental futile complacency . . . .

Roughly speaking, the course of forming aims is as follows: The beginning is with a wish, an emotional reaction against the present state of things and a hope for something different. Action fails to connect satisfactorily with surrounding conditions. Thrown back upon itself, it projects itself in an imagination of a scene which if it were present would afford satisfaction. This picture is often called an aim, more often an ideal. But in itself it is a fancy which may be only a phantasy, a dream, a castle in the air. In itself it is a romantic embellishment of the present; at its best it is material for poetry or the novel. Its natural home is not in the future but in the dim past or in some distant and supposedly better part of the present world. Every such idealized object is suggested by something actually experienced, as the flight of birds suggests the liberation of human beings from the restrictions of slow locomotion on dull earth. It becomes an aim or end only when it is worked out in terms of concrete conditions available for its realization, that is in terms of "means."

This transformation depends upon study of the conditions which generate or make possible the fact observed to exist already. The fancy of the delight of moving at will through the air became an actuality only after men carefully studied the way in which a bird although heavier than air actually sustains itself in air. A fancy becomes an aim, in short, when some past sequence of known cause-and-effect is projected into the future, and when by assembling its causal conditions we strive to generate a like result . . . The great trouble with what passes for moral ends and ideals is that they do not get beyond the stage of fancy of something agreeable and desirable based upon an emotional wish; very often, at that, not even an original wish, but the wish of some leader which has been conventionalized and transmitted through channels of authority. . . .

VII

The Nature of Principles

. . . A principle is intellectually what a habit is for direct action. As habits set in grooves dominate activity and swerve it from conditions instead of increasing its adaptability, so principles treated as fixed rules instead of as helpful methods take men away from experience. The more complicated the situation, and the less we really know about it, the more insistent is the orthodox type of moral theory upon the prior existence of some fixed and universal principle or law which is to be directly applied and followed. . . .

In fact, situations into which change and the unexpected enter are a challenge to intelligence to create new principles . . . Human history is long. There is a long record of past experimentation in conduct, and there are cumulative verifications which give many principles a well earned prestige. Lightly to disregard them is the height of foolishness. But social situations alter; and it is also foolish not to observe how old principles actually work under new conditions, and not to modify them so that they will be more effectual instruments in judging new cases. Many men are now aware of the harm done in legal matters by assuming the antecedent existence of fixed principles under which every new case may be brought. They recognize that this assumption merely puts an artificial premium on ideas developed under bygone conditions, and that their perpetuation in the present works inequity. Yet the choice is not between throwing away rules previously developed and sticking obstinately by them. The intelligent alternative is to revise, adapt, expand and alter them. The problem is one of continuous, vital readaptation.

. . . Men ought to carry back their aversion to manipulation of particular cases, until they will fit into the procrustean beds of fixed rules, to the point where it is clear that all principles are empirical generalizations from the ways in which previous judgments of conduct have practically worked out. When this fact is apparent, these generalizations will be seen to be not fixed rules for deciding doubtful cases, but instrumentalities for their investigation, methods by which the net value of past experience is rendered available for present scrutiny of new perplexities. Then it will also follow that they are hypotheses to be tested and revised by their further working. . . .

Nothing is more instructive about the genuine value of generalization in conduct than the errors of Kant. He took the doctrine that the essence of reason is complete universality (and hence necessity and immutability), with the seriousness becoming the professor of logic. Applying the doctrine to morality he saw that this conception severed morals from connection with experience. Other moralists had gone that far before his day. But none of them had done what Kant proceeded to do: carry this separation of moral principles and ideals from experience to its logical conclusion. He saw that to exclude from principles all connection with empirical details meant to exclude all reference of any kind to consequences. He then saw with a clearness which does his logic credit that with such exclusion, reason becomes entirely empty: nothing is left except the universality of the universal. He was then confronted by the seemingly insoluble problem of getting moral instruction regarding special cases out of a principle that having forsworn intercourse with experience was barren and empty. His ingenious method was as follows: Formal universality means at least logical identity; it means self-consistency or absence of contradiction. Hence follows the method by which a would-be truly moral agent will proceed in judging the rightness of any proposed act. He will ask: Can its motive be made universal for all cases? How would one like it if by one's act one's motive in that act

were to be erected into a universal law of actual nature? Would one then be willing to make the same choice?

Surely a man would hesitate to steal if by his choice to make stealing the motive of his act he were also to erect it into such a fixed law of nature that henceforth he and everybody else would always steal whenever property was in question. No stealing without property, and with universal stealing also no property; a clear self-contradiction. Looked at in the light of reason every mean, insincere, inconsiderate motive of action shrivels into a private exception which a person wants to take advantage of in his own favor, and which he would be horrified to have others act upon. It violates the great principle of logic that A is A. Kindly, decent acts, on the contrary, extend and multiply themselves in a continuing harmony.

This treatment by Kant evinces deep insight into the office of intelligence and principle in conduct. But it involves flat contradiction of Kant's own original intention to exclude consideration of concrete consequences. It turns out to be a method of recommending a broad impartial view of consequences. Our forecast of consequences is always subject . . . to the bias of impulse and habit. We see what we want to see, we obscure what is unfavorable to a cherished, probably unavowed, wish . . . Deliberation needs every possible help it can get against the twisting, exaggerating and slighting tendency of passion and habit. To form the habit of asking how we should be willing to be treated in a similar case—which is what Kant's maxim amounts to—is to gain an ally for impartial and sincere deliberation and judgment . . . Demand for consistency, for "universality," far from implying a rejection of all consequences, is a demand to survey consequences broadly, to link effect to effect in a chain of continuity. Whatever force works to this end *is* reason . . . What we need are those habits, dispositions which lead to impartial and consistent foresight of consequences. Then our judgments are reasonable; we are then reasonable creatures.

Part Four

CONCLUSION

II

Morals Are Human

Since morals is concerned with conduct, it grows out of specific empirical facts. Almost all influential moral theories, with the exception of the utilitarian, have refused to admit this idea. For Christendom as a whole, morality has been connected with supernatural commands, rewards and penalties. Those who have escaped this superstition have contented themselves with converting the difference between this world and the next into a distinction between the actual and the ideal, what is and what should be. The actual world has not been surrendered to the devil in name, but it is treated as a display of physical forces incapable of generating moral values. Consequently, moral considerations must be introduced from above. . . .

But in fact morals is the most humane of all subjects . . . It is ineradicably empirical, not theological nor metaphysical nor mathematical . . . Human nature exists and operates in an environment . . . Hence physics, chemistry, history, statistics, engineering science, are a part of disciplined moral knowledge so far as they enable us to understand the conditions and agencies through which man lives, and on account of which he forms and executes his plans. Moral science is not something with a separate province. It is physical, biological and historic knowledge placed in a human context where it will illuminate and guide the activities of men.

. . . In a reaction from that error which has made morals fanatic or fantastic, sentimental or authoritative by severing them from actual facts and forces, theorists have gone to the other extreme. They have insisted that natural laws are themselves moral laws, so that it remains, after noting them, only to conform to them. This doctrine of accord with nature has usually marked a transition period . . . When social life is so disturbed that custom and tradition fail to supply their wonted control, men resort to Nature as a norm. They apply to Nature all the eulogistic predicates previously associated with divine law; or natural law is conceived of as the only true divine law. . . .

. . . Human intelligence is thought to mark an artificial interference if it does more than register fixed natural laws as rules of human action . . . All that reason can do is to acknowledge the evolutionary forces, and thereby refrain from retarding the arrival of the happy day of perfect harmony. Meantime justice demands that the weak and ignorant suffer the effect of violation of natural law, while the wise and able reap the rewards of their superiority.

The fundamental defect of such views is that they fail to see the difference made in conditions and energies by perception of them. It is the first business of mind to be "realistic," to see things "as they are" . . . But knowledge of facts does not entail conformity and acquiescence. The contrary is the case. Perception of things as they are is but a stage in the process of making them different. They have already begun to be different in being known, for by that fact they enter into a different context, a context of foresight and judgment of better and worse. . . .

. . . Morality begins at this point of use of knowledge of natural law, a use varying with the active system of dispositions and desires. Intelligent action is not concerned with the bare consequences of the thing known, but with consequences *to be* brought into existence by action conditioned on the knowledge. . . .

III

What is Freedom?

. . . I have no desire to add another to the cheap and easy solutions which exist of the seeming conflict between freedom and organization. It is reasonably obvious that organization may become a hindrance to freedom; it does not take us far to say that the trouble lies not in organization but in over-organization. At the same time, it must be admitted that there is no effective or objective freedom without organization. It is easy to criticize the contract theory of the state which states that individuals surrender some at least of their natural liberties in order to make secure as civil liberties what they retain. Nevertheless there is some truth in the idea of surrender and exchange. A certain natural freedom is possessed by man. That is to say, in some respects harmony exists between a man's energies and his surroundings such that the latter support and execute his purposes. In so far he is free; without such a basic natural support, conscious contrivances of legislation, administration and deliberate human institution of social arrangements cannot take place. In this sense natural freedom is prior to political freedom and is its condition. But we cannot trust wholly to a freedom thus procured. It is at the mercy of accident. Conscious agreements among men must supplement and in some degree supplant freedom of action which is the gift of nature. In order to arrive at these agreements, individuals have to make concessions. They must consent to curtailment of some natural liberties in order that any of them may be rendered secure and enduring. They must, in short, enter into an organization with other human beings so that the activities of others may be permanently counted upon to assure regularity of action and far-reaching scope of plans and courses of action. The procedure is not, in so far, unlike surrendering a portion of one's income in order to buy insurance against future contingencies, and thus to render the future course of life more equably secure. It would be folly to maintain that there is no sacrifice; we can however contend that the sacrifice is a reasonable one, justified by results.

Viewed in this light, the relation of individual freedom to organization is seen to be an experimental affair. It is not capable of being settled by abstract theory. Take the question of labor unions and the closed or open shop. It is folly to fancy that no restrictions and surrenders of prior freedoms and possibilities of future freedoms are in-

volved in the extension of this particular form of organization. But to condemn such organization on the theoretical ground that a restriction of liberty is entailed is to adopt a position which would have been fatal to every advance step in civilization, and to every net gain in effective freedom. Every such question is to be judged not on the basis of antecedent theory but on the basis of concrete consequences . . . It is definitely an affair of specific detail, not of wholesale theory. It is equally amusing to see one man denouncing on grounds of pure theory the coercion of workers by a labor union while he avails himself of the increased power due to corporate action in business and praises the coercion of the political state; and to see another man denouncing the latter as pure tyranny, while lauding the power of industrial labor organizations. The position of one or the other may be justified in particular cases, but justification is due to results in practice not to general theory.

Organization tends, however, to become rigid and to limit freedom. In addition to security and energy in action, novelty, risk, change are ingredients of the freedom which men desire. Variety is more than the spice of life; it is largely of its essence, making a difference between the free and the enslaved. . . .

. . . A world that is at points and times indeterminate enough to call out deliberation and to give play to choice to shape its future is a world in which will is free, not because it is inherently vacillating and unstable, but because deliberation and choice are determining and stabilizing factors. . . .

IV

Morality is Social

. . . At present we not only have no assured means of forming character except crude devices of blame, praise, exhortation and punishment, but the very meaning of the general notions of moral inquiry is matter of doubt and dispute. The reason is that these notions are discussed in isolation from the concrete facts of the interactions of human beings with one another . . . Take for example such a basic conception as that of Right involving the nature of authority in conduct . . . This notion is the last resort of the anti-empirical school in morals. . . .

In effect its adherents argue as follows: "Let us concede that concrete ideas about right and wrong and particular notions of what is obligatory have grown up within experience. But we cannot admit this about the idea of Right, of Obligation itself. Why does moral authority exist at all? . . . Why not follow our own immediate devices if we are so inclined? There is only one answer: We have a moral nature, a conscience, call it what you will. And this nature responds directly in acknowledgment of the supreme authority of the Right over all claims of inclination and habit. We may not act in accordance with this acknowledgment, but we still know that the authority of the moral law, although not its power, is unquestionable. Men may differ indefinitely according to what their experience has been as to just *what* is Right, what its contents are. But they all spontaneously agree in recognizing the supremacy of the claims of whatever is thought of as Right." . . .

Grant the foregoing argument, and all the apparatus of abstract moralism follows in its wake. A remote goal of perfection, ideals that are contrary in a wholesale way to what is actual, a free will of arbitrary choice; all of these conceptions band themselves together with that of a non-empirical authority of Right and a non-empirical conscience which acknowledges it. They constitute its ceremonial or formal train.

Why, indeed, acknowledge the authority of Right? . . . We live in a world where other persons live too. Our acts affect them. They perceive these effects, and react upon us in consequence. Because they are living beings they make demands upon us for certain things from us. They approve and condemn —not in abstract theory but in what they do to us. The answer to the question "Why not put your hand in the fire?" is the answer of fact. If you do your hand will be burnt. The answer to the question why acknowledge the

right is of the same sort. For Right is only an abstract name for the multitude of concrete demands in action which others impress upon us, and of which we are obliged, if we would live, to take some account. Its authority is the exigency of their demands, the efficacy of their insistencies. There may be good ground for the contention that in theory the idea of the right is subordinate to that of the good, being a statement of the course proper to attain good. But in fact it signifies the totality of social pressures exercised upon us to induce us to think and desire in certain ways. Hence the right can in fact become the road to the good only as the elements that compose this unremitting pressure are enlightened, only as social relationships become themselves reasonable.

It will be retorted that all pressure is a non-moral affair partaking of force, not of right; that right must be ideal. Thus we are invited to enter again the circle in which the ideal has no force and social actualities no ideal quality. We refuse the invitation because social pressure is involved in our own lives, as much so as the air we breathe and the ground we walk upon . . . The pressure is not ideal but empirical, yet empirical here means only actual. It calls attention to the fact that considerations of right are claims originating not outside of life, but within it. They are "ideal" in precisely the degree in which we intelligently recognize and act upon them. . . .

Accordingly failure to recognize the authority of right means defect in effective apprehension of the realities of human association, not an arbitrary exercise of free will. This deficiency and perversion in apprehension indicates a defect in education—that is to say, in the operation of actual conditions, in the consequences upon desire and thought of existing interactions and interdependencies . . . The belief in a separate, ideal or transcendental, practically ineffectual Right is a reflex of the inadequacy with which existing institutions perform their educative office—their office in generating observation of social continuities. It is an endeavor to "rationalize" this defect. Like all rationalizations, it operates to divert attention from the real state of affairs. Thus it helps maintain the conditions which created it, standing in the way of effort to make our institutions more humane and equitable. A theoretical acknowledgment of the supreme authority of Right, of moral law, gets twisted into an effectual substitute for acts which would better the customs which now produce vague, dull, halting and evasive observation of actual social ties. . . .

. . . But there are enormous differences of better and worse in the quality of what is social. Ideal morals begin with the perception of these differences. Human interaction and ties are there, are operative in any case. But they can be regulated, employed in an orderly way for good only as we know how to observe them. And they cannot be observed aright, they cannot be understood and utilized, when the mind is left to itself to work without the aid of science. For the natural unaided mind means precisely the habits of belief, thought and desire which have been accidentally generated and confirmed by social institutions or customs. But with all their admixture of accident and reasonableness we have at last reached a point where social conditions create a mind capable of scientific outlook and inquiry. To foster and develop this spirit is the social obligation of the present because it is its urgent need. . . .

. . . Within the flickering inconsequential acts of separate selves dwells a sense of the whole which claims and dignifies them. In its presence we put off mortality and live in the universal. The life of the community in which we live and have our being is the fit symbol of this relationship. The acts in which we express our perception of the ties which bind us to others are its only rites and ceremonies.

MY PHILOSOPHY OF LAW *

When the question of the nature of law is examined in the light of the doctrines of

* Reprinted by permission of the West Publishing Co.

various schools and the controversies between them, it is found to break up into at least three distinct yet related questions. The three issues concern the *source* of law, its *end,* and its *application,* including under this last head questions of the methods by which law is and can be made effective.

The problems involved in the discussions about law that can be called philosophical seem to arise from the need for having some principles which can be employed to justify and/or criticize existing legal rules and practices. This need and motive are perhaps most clearly manifested in those philosophies which made an explicit distinction between what they called positive law on one side and the law of nature on the other hand, the latter being employed as the end positive laws ought to realize and the standard to which they should conform. This particular formulation is at present in vogue only in the school of thought that remains faithful to the general line of ideas formulated in the Middle Ages and that continued to influence continental writers on law through the seventeenth century. But the distinction between what happens to exist at a given time and what might and should be, and the need for such a conception of the latter as will provide "principles" for organizing, justifying, and/or disapproving and reforming some aspects of what exists seem to be back of all movements that fall in the field of legal philosophy.

From this point of view, discussion of the source and the end of law can be brought under a single head, that of the *standard* or criterion by which to evaluate existing legal regulations and practices. The question of what law *is* then reduces itself to a question of what it is believed regulations and practices *should be.* According to traditions that are highly influential, determination of the end and standard is intimately bound up with determination of an *ultimate* source— as is obvious when the Will or Reason of God, or the ultimate and intrinsic Law of Nature, is held to be the source of law. What lies back of this identification of source with end and standard is the belief that unless a source higher and more fixed than that of experience can be found, there is no sure ground for any genuinely philosophic valuation of law as it actually exists. This appeal to a source is not, then, the same as appeal to origin in time, since that last procedure links the matter up with experience, and with all the defects that the classic tradition attaches to whatever is experiential.

These preliminary remarks have a double purpose. On one hand, they are designed to express the belief that there is a genuine and important matter involved in the discussions called "legal philosophy"; the question, namely, of the ground upon which existing legal affairs, including rules of law, the work of legislation, judicial decisions, and administrative practices, can be legitimately and profitably evaluated. The other point is that as matter of fact legal philosophies have reflected and are sure to continue to reflect movements of the period in which they are produced, and hence cannot be separated from what these movements stand for.

This last remark is a sweeping one. To many persons, it will seem to beg all the important questions with which legal philosophy is concerned. However, upon the side of past systems, it signifies that they have to be viewed in connection with actual cultural and social movements of the periods in which they appeared. The view also holds that the real significance of those philosophies is increased when they are viewed as manifestations of efforts put forth practically. For upon an exclusively intellectual basis, the various legal philosophies are in such conflict with one another as to indicate that all alike are attempting the impossible. On the view here suggested, they have all the importance that is possessed by the movements they reflect; their conflicts are proofs of a certain vital genuineness. On the same score, if different contributions to this volume represent incompatible positions, it is because they express different attitudes toward practical questions of what should be done and how best to do it. At all events, what I myself have to say is put forth in this spirit. Fundamentally, a program for action

to be tested in action is set forth, not something that can be judged (beyond assertions of fact and matters of logical consistency) on a purely intellectual basis.

The standpoint taken is that law is through and through a social phenomenon; social in origin, in purpose or end, and in application. Now one cannot utter or write the word "social" without being aware of all the ambiguities and controversies that attend the meaning of the words *society* and *social*. Here what was just said may be objected to on the ground that it tries to explain what is obscure, namely the nature of law, by reference to something still more obscure, namely, society. For the purpose of the present topic, however, it is needful to make only two statements regarding what is denoted by "social." It is postulated that whatever else social means it applies, first, to human *activities,* and secondly to these activities, as forms of behavior, as *inter*-activities. By saying that social facts, or phenomena, are activities, it is meant, negatively, that they are *not* facts of the kind indicated when "fact" is taken to mean something done, finished, and over with; and positively that they are processes, things going *on*. Even in the case of past events, when social facts are under consideration, it is important to recognize that they represent slices of time having a dimension long enough to cover initial conditions and a later stage of issue or outcome, the latter being in its turn an *ongoing*. With reference to law, this position signifies that law must be viewed both as intervening in the complex of other activities, and as itself a social process, not something that can be said to be done or to happen at a certain date. The first part of the foregoing statement means that "law" cannot be set up as if it were a separate entity, but can be discussed only in terms of the social conditions in which it arises and of what it concretely does there. It is this fact which renders the use of the word "law" as a single general term rather dangerous, making it needful to state explicitly that the word is used as a summary term to save repeating legal rules, legislative and administrative activities (as far as the latter influence the course of human activities), judicial decisions, etc.

The second part of the statement involves the conclusion that what is called *application* is not something that happens *after* a rule or law or statute is laid down but is a necessary part of them; such a necessary part indeed that in given cases we can judge what the law *is* as matter of fact only by telling how it operates, and what are its effects in and upon the human activities that are going on. For special purposes, the signification of "applicability" may be restricted much more technically. But from the standpoint that can be called philosophical, application must be taken broadly. A given legal arrangement *is* what it *does,* and what it does lies in the field of modifying and/or maintaining human activities as going concerns. Without application there are scraps of paper or voices in the air but nothing that can be called law.

It might seem as if what is conveyed by saying that social activities are *inter*-activities were already included in the word *"social,"* since social means association. By calling especial attention to this trait, however, we indicate that there is a *de facto,* though not necessarily *de jure* or moral, reciprocity in every fact of social behavior. A *trans*-action does not just go across in a one-way direction, but is a two-way process. There is reaction as well as action. While it is convenient to view some human beings as agents and others as patients (recipients), the distinction is purely relative; there is no receptivity that is not also a re-*action* or response, and there is no agency that does not also involve an element of receptivity. The emphasis upon agreement, contract, consensus, in various political and legal philosophies is in effect a recognition of this aspect of social phenomena, although a rather overidealized expression of it.

Social processes have conditions which are stable and enduring as compared with the multitudes of special actions composing the process. Human beings form habits as surely as they perform special deeds, and habits, when embodied in interactivities, are customs. These customs are, upon the view here taken, the *source* of law. We may use the analogy, or if one prefers, the metaphor, of a river valley, a stream, and banks. The valley in its relation to surrounding country, or as the "lie of the land," is the primary fact. The stream may be compared to the social process, and its various waves, wavelets, eddies, etc., to the special acts which make up a social process. The banks are stable, enduring conditions, which limit and also direct the course taken by the stream, comparable to customs. But the permanence and fixity of the banks, as compared with the elements of the passing stream, is relative, not absolute. Given the lie of the land, the stream is an energy which carves its way from higher to lower levels and thereby, when viewed as a long run (in time as well as in space) process, it forms and reforms its own banks. Social customs, including traditions, institutions, etc., are stable and enduring as compared with special deeds and with the serial arrangement of these acts which forms a process. But they, and therefore the legal regulations which are their precipitated formulations, are only relatively fixed. They undergo, sooner or later, more slowly or more rapidly, the attrition of ongoing processes. For while they constitute the *structure* of the processes that go *on,* they are the structure *of* the processes in the sense that they arise and take shape within the processes, and are not forced upon the processes from without.

Habit and custom introduce factors into the constitution of human activities which were not taken account of by earlier philosophers who called themselves empirical; factors which, when they are taken account of, profoundly modify the demand for an origin and source of law outside of time, and for a standard or norm that is outside of and independent of experience. As for the first point, earlier empirical philosophers in their revolt against universals and principles that were alleged to be immutable and eternal, beyond criticism and beyond alteration, often pulverized experience, and reduced all general and enduring factors in it to the general names they bore. Every habit and every custom is, however, general within certain limits. It arises out of interaction of environing conditions, which change slowly, with needs and interests of human beings which also endure with but slight change throughout considerable periods of time. Limitation of space does not permit an adequate statement of the nature of the connections that exist between habits and rules of law. But it is clear without extended argument that explicit enactment of a custom into law, however the enactment takes place, reinforces and often extends the relatively enduring and stable character of custom, thus modifying its general character.

It is possible that the bearing of the generality of custom and law, as structural conditions of social activities, upon mooted problems of legal philosophical doctrine is not readily apparent. The point is that recognition of this aspect of social phenomena makes it unnecessary to appeal, on *practical* grounds, to an outside source. As a matter of pure metaphysical theory, a person may continue to have a very low opinion of time and of things affected by temporal conditions. But from any practical standpoint, recognition of the relatively slow rate of change on the part of certain constituents of social action is capable of accomplishing every useful, every *practically* needed, office that has led in the past and in other cultural climes to setting up external sources such as the Will or Reason of God, the Law of Nature in medieval theory and in philosophers like Grotius and his successors, the General Will of Rousseau, and the Practical Reason of Kant.

What has been said does not apply to the doctrine that *sovereignty* is the source of law. Sovereignty is used to denote something which is at least of the nature of a social fact, something existing *within* social activities and relations and not outside of them. Unless I am mistaken, the fact that this view which once highly commended itself to students of politics and of jurisprudence no longer exercises any great appeal indicates

why a brief statement about it will suffice. For (unless again I am much mistaken) the view already wears a certain antiquarian air, so that it is hard even in imagination to see why once it had such a vogue. Seen in perspective, this doctrine owed its force to two things. It got away from making law depend upon outside metaphysical sources; it instituted in their place reliance upon conditions and agencies to which some verifiable empirical meaning could be given. In the second place, sovereignty is a *political* term, and the vogue of the doctrine coincided with that immense outburst of legislative activity which took place in the field conventionally labeled "political." The Austinian theory of the source of law may be said to constitute a rationalized approbation of a movement to bring legal rules and arrangements within the scope of deliberate purposive action, at the expense of the comparatively unplanned results of customs interpreted in judicial decisions. The doctrine has lost much of its original appeal because development of the social sciences, viz., of history, anthropology, sociology, and psychology, has tended to make sovereignty at best an expression of the working of a vast multitude of social forces, and at worst a pure abstraction. The sovereignty doctrine of the source of law thus represents a transition from acceptance of "sources" outside of social actions into one within them, but a transition which fastened on only one social factor and froze that one in isolation. When it was discovered that social customs, and to some extent social interests, lord it over any specific set of persons who can be picked out and called "sovereign," the doctrine declined. The growing tendency to interpret political activities in connection with economic factors acted, of course, in the same direction.

So far the topic of end and standard has not received attention. It may be urged that if the account that has been given of the experiential source of law is accepted, it only strengthens the case for an end and standard that lie outside of actual social activities. For, it is argued, the fact that such and such customs and laws have grown up is no sign that they *should* exist; it furnishes no test for their value. In short, we come here upon the large problem of "value in relation to fact," and upon the conclusion, held by many that they are so separate that standards for judging the value of what exists must have *their* source as standards outside of any possible empirical field.

With reference to this issue, recognition of the ongoing character of social facts as continuing activities is of fundamental importance. If what are taken to be social facts are chopped off by being regarded as closed and completely ended, then there is much to be said on theoretical grounds for the view that the standard for evaluating them must lie outside the field of actual existences. But if they are ongoing, they have consequences; and consideration of consequences may provide ground upon which it is decided whether they be maintained intact or be changed.

When it stated that there is much to be said *theoretically* for the view that an outside end and standard are needed if social facts are not taken as going concerns, it is not meant that much can be said in favor of the applicability of such standards to actual social conditions, with which, by definition, they have nothing to do. It is undeniable that different standards, so different as to conflict with one another, have been held and used at different places and times in the past. Their conflict is sufficient evidence that they were not derived from any *a priori* absolute standard. Denial of the possibility of extracting a standard from actual social activities is thus in effect a denial that an absolute standard, even if it exists, ever had any influence or effect. *For what reason is there for thinking that the standards now put forth by those who appeal to a non-empirical absolute end, will have a different fortune from those put forward in the past?*

The usual way of meeting difficulties of this type is to admit that a distinction must be made between *form*, which is absolute, and its contents or filling, which are historical and relative. The admission is fatal to everything which the doctrine of absolute ends was framed to meet. For according to the admission, all concrete valuations must be based upon what is admitted to be experiential and temporal.

On the view here presented, the standard is found in consequences, in the *function* of what goes on socially. If this view were generally held, there would be assurance of introduction on a large scale of the rational factor into concrete evaluations of legal arrangements. For it demands that intelligence, employing the best scientific methods and materials available, be used, to investigate, in terms of the context of actual situations, the consequences of legal rules and of proposed legal decisions and acts of legislation. The present tendency, hardly more as yet than in a state of inception, to discuss legal matters in their concrete social setting, and not in the comparative vacuum of their relations to one another, would get the reinforcement of a consistent legal theory. Moreover, when it is systematically acknowledged in practice that social facts are going concerns and that all legal matters have their place *within* these ongoing concerns, there will be a much stronger likelihood than at present that new knowledge will be acquired of a kind which can be brought to bear upon the never-ending process of improving standards of judgment.

21

Benjamin Nathan Cardozo

1870–1938

The Cardozos were a prosperous and proud family of Sephardic Jews whose ancestors were driven out of Spain and Portugal by the Inquisition. The first American Cardozo was a London merchant who came to this country in 1752.

Benjamin was born in a well-kept New York town house, son of a Tammany-sponsored New York Supreme Court judge. He had a twin sister, three other sisters, and an older brother. His father was charged with political corruption in the Boss Tweed scandals and resigned from the bench in disgrace. His mother died when he was nine. His oldest sister Nell raised the younger children; all of them except Benjamin and Nell died early deaths. His father died when Benjamin was fifteen, leaving his once prosperous family only a small competence.

The Cardozo children did not go to public school; their father engaged a tutor for them. This tutor turned out to be Horatio Alger, writer of best-selling boys' books about poor but honest heroes (who always rose to fame and fortune). Years later Cardozo wrote for Columbia University's alumni records, "He did not do as successful a job for me as he did with the careers of his newsboy heroes." His sheltered childhood did not preserve Cardozo's orthodoxy. But he held fast to his inherited, voting membership in the New York Sephardic congregation and opposed change in its traditional modes of worship. Cardozo had no enthusiasm for Zionism until the rise of the Hitlerian anti-semitism. When Palestine became a hope of refuge for the persecuted, Cardozo joined in supporting the movement to resettle refugees there.

At fifteen Cardozo was one of sixty freshmen who entered the liberal arts college at Columbia University. Columbia then had no dormitories and served mostly New Yorkers living in their own homes. One teacher described Benjamin as "desperately serious." He was too young for college social life and too small for college athletics. He was an avid debater in his own literary society, but would never represent it in public debates with other clubs. He made top marks and his popularity grew. His class elected him vice-president and graduation orator. His graduation speech was a philippic against Communism. Cardozo took a Master's degree at Columbia and then entered Columbia law school. During his second year of law school, the authorities decided to extend the two-year course to three years. Cardozo and many of his classmates rebelled, refused to attend this third year, and got no degrees. Years later he said, "I was anxious to go out into the world and make my living, so I never came back for a third year. It wasn't of much value, for it had not yet been coordinated with other courses of instruction, but represented a lot of extras."

Cardozo as a young lawyer was driven to redeem his family name, disgraced by his father. He worked like a demon in a partnership with his older brother, Albert. The firm prospered, merged with other firms, took in new men, lost elder members. Albert died in 1909, when Benjamin was in his late thirties. By then Cardozo was known as a "walking encyclopedia" of the law, who remembered needed cases by name and citation. He was a "lawyers' lawyer" often retained to help in difficult cases. He was known for candor and honesty. Judge Lehman said of Cardozo, "He tried no sensational cases . . . he would not appeal to the passions or prejudices of a jury . . . He was unfitted for any struggle where scrupulous integrity and fine sense of what is right might be a handicap; but judges felt the persuasive force of his legal arguments, and lawyers and laymen sought his counsel and assistance in the solution of intricate legal problems." His fees were always low. He often took pains with little claims that were important to clients of small means. One biographer describes these days of Cardozo, "Early in the morning he was at his office in lower Broadway. The hurried luncheon of an ever-rapid eater broke into Cardozo's daylong hours of conferences, research, and the writing of briefs. Then back to the Madison Avenue house for the family dinner. Sometimes this was followed by a brief respite at the piano, playing four handed with Nell; or there might be an occasional evening at concert or opera—rarely at the theatre. Work was almost invariably the order of the night as of the day."

In 1913 forty-three-year-old Cardozo ran for the bench. A reform, anti-Tammany victory made Mitchell Mayor of New York and Cardozo a Judge of the New York Supreme Court. His election was close. Perhaps he was given a needed margin by Italian voters who thought he was their countryman. He had served only two months when he was named by the governor to New York's highest court, the Court of Appeals. His temporary appointment was followed by a permanent one, and then he was elected for a regular term. Later he was elected Chief Justice. He served on the Court of Appeals for almost twenty years. His week days were spent in Albany where the court sat; there he led a solitary life. He worked most evenings and rarely accepted social engagements. Weekends he went to New York to be with his sister Nell. His life became more old-maidish as he grew older. He did not smoke

or drink. Once when he turned down a cigarette and the offeror asked if judges have any bad habits, he replied, "None that the people know of." On the court he was patient and gentle. One of his colleagues told of a hearing during which a lawyer kept interrupting Cardozo; Cardozo tapped his desk with a blotter and said, "When the court and counsel wish to speak at the same time, it *does* seem to me that the court should have precedence." "That," said the colleague, "is as angry as I ever saw him."

In the Twenties Nell's health failed more and more each year. She became a possessive sister. The last of the other sisters died in 1922. When Cardozo was not in Albany, he and Nell lived by themselves. In 1929 Nell died and for the rest of his life Cardozo lived alone. He had many friends and well-wishers and could dine out as often as he would, but he seldom accepted invitations. He enjoyed going to his club—an exclusive small dining club with eminent and interesting members. Part of his loneliness was dispelled by vigorous participation in launching the American Law Institute.

Cardozo's jurisprudential writing dates from 1920. Professor Corbin asked him to give the Storr's Lectures at Yale Law School. When he said he had nothing worth saying to law students Corbin asked him to come and tell the students how he decided cases. He agreed and resulting lectures were his most famous work, *The Nature of the Judicial Process,* excerpts from which follow this note. His other best known philosophical works are *The Growth of the Law* (1924) and *Paradoxes of Legal Science* (1928).

Holmes' retirement from the United States Supreme Court in 1932 left a vacancy for which Cardozo was the logical man. Perhaps Senator Borah's influence in his behalf was the proximate cause of President Hoover's decision to offer Cardozo the post—scores of other influential people urged his appointment, and Hoover might have made it without any urging. Cardozo was loath at sixty-two to change his ways and leave his friends. He wrote his cousin, "I am trying to stave off the appointment. Whatever reputation I have built up has been made as a state judge. I don't want to start all over again and build up another. But most of all I don't want to live in utter loneliness." Yet he accepted.

His fear of homesickness was not unfounded. At first his only associates were his brethren on the court—most of whom were his friends. He refused social invitations because he thought them prompted by his place rather than his qualities. But as time passed he made many warm Washington friends. Cardozo's six years on the United States Supreme Court were, perhaps, the court's most trying years—the time when the court had to pass on revolutionary New Deal legislation. Cardozo favored most of this legislation and voted to uphold it; he voted against the constitutionality of extreme measures. He privately abhorred Roosevelt's court-packing plan.

During his third year in Washington, Cardozo suffered a heart attack. He was put to bed for the summer and seemed to improve greatly. In January 1938 a stroke laid him low and he languished for six months before he died.

Cardozo had lived frugally and invested his savings conservatively. He left an estate of more than $300,000, much of which he bequeathed to Columbia University.

Law was not the sole object of Cardozo's interest. He listened to music and read widely. His tastes ranged from the classics to the contemporary. He was sometimes puzzled by moderns like James Joyce, but never damned what he did not understand. His letters, especially the later ones, are a joy to read. Many of them are quoted in the biography by Hellman from which much of the above information comes.

Cardozo's judicial idol was Holmes. He once said to Learned Hand, "What's the use of talking about the rest of us? Holmes is a mountain. All we others flatten out." In 1930 Cardozo, then sixty, visited Holmes who was eighty-nine. After he left Holmes said, "I know I would love him if I knew him better."

THE NATURE OF THE JUDICIAL PROCESS *

LECTURE I

Introduction. The Method of Philosophy

The work of deciding cases goes on every day in hundreds of courts throughout the land. Any judge, one might suppose, would find it easy to describe the process which he had followed a thousand times and more. Nothing could be farther from the truth . . . What is it that I do when I decide a case? To what sources of information do I appeal for guidance? In what proportions do I permit them to contribute to the result? In what proportions ought they to contribute? If a precedent is applicable, when do I refuse to follow it? If no precedent is applicable, how do I reach the rule that will make a precedent for the future? If I am seeking logical consistency, the symmetry of the legal structure, how far shall I seek it? At what point shall the quest be halted by some discrepant custom, by some consideration of the social welfare, by my own or the common standards of justice and morals? Into that strange compound which is brewed daily in the caldron of the courts, all these ingredients enter in varying proportions. I am not concerned to inquire whether judges ought to be allowed to brew such a compound at all. I take judge-made law as one of the existing realities of life . . . The elements have not come together by chance. *Some* principle, however unavowed and inarticulate and subconscious, has regulated the infusion. It may not have been the same principle for all judges at any time, nor the same principle for any judge at all times. But a choice there has been, not a submission to the decree of Fate . . . There will be need to distinguish between the conscious and the subconscious. I do not mean that even those considerations and motives which I shall class under the first head are always in consciousness distinctly, so that they will be

* Reprinted by permission of the Yale University Press.

recognized and named at sight. Not infrequently they hover near the surface. They may, however, with comparative readiness be isolated and tagged . . . There is in each of us a stream of tendency . . . which gives coherence and direction to thought and action. Judges cannot escape that current any more than other mortals. All their lives, forces which they do not recognize and cannot name, have been tugging at them—inherited instincts, traditional beliefs, acquired convictions; and the resultant is an outlook on life, a conception of social needs, a sense in James's phrase of "the total push and pressure of the cosmos," which, when reasons are nicely balanced, must determine where choice shall fall . . . .

. . . Our first inquiry should . . . be: Where does the judge find the law which he embodies in his judgment? There are times when the source is obvious. The rule that fits the case may be supplied by the constitution or by statute. If that is so, the judge looks no farther. The correspondence ascertained, his duty is to obey. The constitution overrides a statute, but a statute, if consistent with the constitution, overrides the law of judges . . . Codes and statutes do not render the judge superfluous, nor his work perfunctory and mechanical. There are gaps to be filled. There are doubts and ambiguities to be cleared. There are hardships and wrongs to be mitigated if not avoided. Interpretation is often spoken of as if it were nothing but the search and the discovery of a meaning which, however obscure and latent, had none the less a real and ascertainable pre-existence in the legislator's mind . . . The ascertainment of intention may be the least of a judge's troubles in ascribing meaning to a statute. "The fact is," says Gray . . . "that the difficulties of so-called interpretation arise when the legislature has had no meaning at all; when the question which is raised on the statute never occurred to it; when what the judges have to do is, not to determine what the legislature did mean on a point which was present to its mind, but to guess what it would have intended on a point not present to its mind, if the point

had been present" . . . Today a great school of continental jurists is pleading for a still wider freedom of adaptation and construction. The statute, they say, is often fragmentary and ill-considered and unjust. The judge as the interpreter for the community of its sense of law and order must supply omissions, correct uncertainties and harmonize results with justice through a method of free decision . . . Courts are to "search for light among the social elements of every kind that are the living force behind the facts they deal with." The power thus put in their hands is great, and subject, like all power, to abuse; but we are not to flinch from granting it. In the long run "there is no guaranty of justice," says Ehrlich, "except the personality of the judge." The same problems of method, the same contrasts between the letter and the spirit, are living problems in our own land and law. Above all in the field of constitutional law, the method of free decision has become, I think, the dominant one today . . . Codes and other statutes may threaten the judicial function with repression and disuse and atrophy. The function flourishes and persists by virtue of the human need to which it steadfastly responds. Justinian's prohibition of any commentary on the product of his codifiers is remembered only for its futility.

I will dwell no further for the moment upon the significance of constitution and statute as sources of the law . . . We reach the land of mystery when constitution and statute are silent, and the judge must look to the common law for the rule that fits the case. . . .

The first thing he does is to compare the case before him with the precedents, whether stored in his mind or hidden in the books. I do not mean that precedents are ultimate sources of the law, supplying the sole equipment that is needed for the legal armory . . . Back of precedents are the basic juridical conceptions which are the postulates of judicial reasoning, and farther back are the habits of life, the institutions of society, in which those conceptions had their origin, and which by a process of interaction, they have modified in turn. None the less, in a system so highly developed as our own, precedents have so covered the ground that they fix the point of departure . . . If they are plain and to the point, there may be need of nothing more. *Stare decisis* is at least the everyday working rule of our law . . . Some judges seldom get beyond that process in any case. Their notion of their duty is to match the colors of the case at hand against the colors of many sample cases spread out upon their desk. The sample nearest in shade supplies the applicable rule. But, of course, no system of living law can be evolved by such a process, and no judge of a high court, worthy of his office, views the function of his place so narrowly. . . .

. . . If we seek the psychological basis of this tendency, we shall find it, I suppose, in habit. Whatever its psychological basis it is one of the living forces of our law. Not all the progeny of principles begotten of a judgment survive, however, to maturity. Those that cannot prove their worth and strength by the test of experience, are sacrificed mercilessly and thrown into the void. The common law does not work from pre-established truths of universal and inflexible validity to conclusions derived from them deductively. Its method is inductive, and it draws its generalizations from particulars. The process has been admirably stated by Munroe Smith: "In their effort to give to the social sense of justice articulate expression in rules and in principles, the method of the law-finding experts has always been experimental. The rules and principles of case law have never been treated as final truths, but as working hypotheses, continually retested in those great laboratories of the law, the courts of justice. Every new case is an experiment; and if the accepted rule which seems applicable yields a result which is felt to be unjust, the rule is reconsidered. It may not be modified at once, for the attempt to do absolute justice in every single case would make the development and maintenance of general rules impossible; but if a rule continues to work injustice, it will eventually be reformulated. The principles themselves are continually retested; for if the rules derived from a principle do not work well, the principle itself must ultimately be reexamined."

The way in which this process of retesting and reformulating works, may be followed in an example. Fifty years ago, I think it would have been stated as a general principle that A may conduct his business as he pleases, even though the purpose is to cause loss to B, unless the act involves the creation of a nuisance. Spite fences were the stock illustration, and the exemption from liability in such cimcumstances was supposed to illustrate not the exception, but the rule. Such a rule may have been an adequate working principle to regulate the relations between individuals or classes in a simple or homogeneous community. With the growing complexity of social relations, its inadequacy was revealed. As particular controversies multiplied and the attempt was made to test them by the old principle it was found that there was something wrong in the results, and this led to a reformulation of the principle itself. Today, most judges are inclined to say that what was once thought to be the exception is the rule, and what was the rule is the exception. A may never do anything in his business for the purpose of injuring another without reasonable and just excuse. There has been a new generalization which, applied to new particulars, yields results more in harmony with past particulars, and, what is still more important, more consistent with the social welfare. This work of modification is gradual. It goes on inch by inch . . . .

We are not likely to underrate the force that has been exerted if we look back upon its work . . . Hardly a rule of today but may be matched by its opposite of yesterday . . . These changes or most of them have been wrought by judges. The men who wrought them used the same tools as the judges of today. The changes, as they were made in this case or that, may not have seemed momentous in the making. The result, however, when the process was prolonged throughout the years, has been not merely to supplement or modify; it has been to revolutionize and transform . . . Doubtless in the last three centuries, some lines, once wavering, have become rigid. We leave more to legislatures today, and less perhaps to judges. Yet even now there is change from decade to decade. The glacier still moves.

In this perpetual flux, the problem which confronts the judge is in reality a twofold one: he must first extract from the precedents the underlying principle, the *ratio decidendi;* he must then determine the path or direction along which the principle is to move and develop, if it is not to wither and die.

The first branch of the problem is the one to which we are accustomed to address ourselves more consciously than to the other. Cases do not unfold their principles for the asking . . . The thing adjudged comes to us oftentimes swathed in obscuring dicta, which must be stripped off and cast aside. Judges differ greatly in their reverence for the illustrations and comments and side-remarks of their predecessors, to make no mention of their own. All agree that there may be dissent when the opinion is filed. Some would seem to hold that there must be none a moment thereafter. Plenary inspiration has then descended upon the work of the majority. No one, of course, avows such a belief, and yet sometimes there is an approach to it in conduct. I own that it is a good deal of a mystery to me how judges, of all persons in the world, should put their faith in dicta. A brief experience on the bench was enough to reveal to me all sorts of cracks and crevices and loopholes in my own opinions when picked up a few months after delivery, and reread with due contrition . . . Let us assume too that the principle . . . has been skillfully extracted and accurately stated. Only half or less than half of the work has yet been done. The problem remains to fix the bounds and the tendencies of development and growth, to set the directive force in motion along the right path at the parting of the ways.

The directive force of a principle may be exerted along the line of logical progression; this I will call the rule of analogy or the method of philosophy; along the line of historical development; this I will call the method of evolution; along the line of the customs of the community; this I will call the method of tradition; along the lines of justice, morals and social welfare, the *mores* of the day; and this I will call the method of sociology.

I have put first among the principles of selection to guide our choice of paths, the rule of analogy or the method of philosophy. In putting it first, I do not mean to rate it as most important. On the contrary, it is often sacrificed to others. I have put it first because it has, I think, a certain presumption in its favor. Given a mass of particulars, a congeries of judgments on related topics, the principle that unifies and rationalizes them has a tendency, and a legitimate one, to project and extend itself to new cases within the limits of its capacity to unify and rationalize. It has the primacy that comes from natural and orderly and logical succession. . . .

. . . Logical consistency does not cease to be a good because it is not the supreme good . . . I am not to mar the symmetry of the legal structure by the introduction of inconsistencies and irrelevancies and artificial exceptions unless for some sufficient reason, which will commonly be some consideration of history or custom or policy or justice. Lacking such a reason, I must be logical, just as I must be impartial, and upon like grounds. It will not do to decide the same question one way between one set of litigants and the opposite way between another . . . Adherence to precedent must . . . be the rule rather than the exception if litigants are to have faith in the even-handed administration of justice in the courts. A sentiment like in kind, though different in degree, is at the root of the tendency of precedent to extend itself along the lines of logical development . . . The judge who moulds the law by the method of philosophy may be satisfying an intellectual craving for symmetry of form and substance. But he is doing something more. He is keeping the law true in its response to a deep-seated and imperious sentiment . . . In default of other tests, the method of philosophy must remain the organon of the courts if chance and favor are to be excluded, and the affairs of men are to be governed with the serene and impartial uniformity which is of the essence of the idea of law. . . .

The directive force of logic does not always exert itself, however, along a single and unobstructed path. One principle or precedent, pushed to the limit of its logic, may point to one conclusion; another principle or precedent followed with like logic, may point with equal certainty to another. In this conflict, we must choose between the two paths, selecting one or other, or perhaps striking out upon a third . . . Let me take as an illustration of such conflict the famous case of *Riggs v. Palmer,* 115 N. Y. 506. That case decided that a legatee who had murdered his testator would not be permitted by a court of equity to enjoy the benefits of the will . . . There was the principle of the binding force of a will disposing of the estate of a testator in conformity with law. That principle, pushed to the limit of its logic, seemed to uphold the title of the murderer. There was the principle that civil courts may not add to the pains and penalties of crimes. That, pushed to the limit of its logic, seemed again to uphold his title. But over against these was another principle, of greater generality, its roots deeply fastened in universal sentiments of justice, the principle that no man should profit from his own inequity or take advantage of his own wrong. The logic of this principle prevailed over the logic of the others . . . One path was followed, another closed, because of the conviction in the judicial mind that the one selected led to justice . . . Consistency was preserved, logic received its tribute, by holding that the legal title passed, but that it was subjected to a constructive trust. A constructive trust is nothing but "the formula through which the conscience of equity finds expression" . . . Such formulas are merely the remedial devices by which a result conceived of as right and just is made to square with principle and with the symmetry of the legal sys-

tem . . . The murderer lost the legacy . . . because the social interest served by refusing to permit the criminal to profit by his crime is greater than that served by the preservation and enforcement of legal rights of ownership . . . We go forward with our logic, with our analogies, with our philosophies, till we reach a certain point. At first, we have no trouble with the paths; they follow the same lines. Then they begin to diverge, and we must make a choice between them. History or custom or social utility or some compelling sentiment of justice or sometimes perhaps a semi-intuitive apprehension of the pervading spirit of our law, must come to the rescue of the anxious judge, and tell him where to go . . . .

LECTURE II

The Methods of History, Tradition and Sociology

The method of philosophy comes in competition, however, with other tendencies which find their outlet in other methods. One of these is the historical method, or the method of evolution. The tendency of a principle to expand itself to the limit of its logic may be counteracted by the tendency to confine itself within the limits of its history. I do not mean that even then the two methods are always in opposition. A classification which treats them as distinct is, doubtless, subject to the reproach that it involves a certain overlapping of the lines and principles of division. Very often, the effect of history is to make the path of logic clear. Growth may be logical whether it is shaped by the principle of consistency with the past or by that of consistency with some preestablished norm, some general conception, some "indwelling, and creative principle." The directive force of the precedent may be found either in the events that made it what it is, or in some principle which enables us to say of it that it is what it ought to be. Development may involve either an investigation of origins or an effort of pure reason. Both methods have their logic. For the moment, however, it will be convenient to identify the method of history with the one, and to confine the method of logic or philosophy to the other. Some conceptions of the law owe their existing form almost exclusively to history. They are not to be understood except as historical growths. In the development of such principles, history is likely to predominate over logic or pure reason. Other conceptions, though they have, of course, a history, have taken form and shape to a larger extent under the influence of reason or of comparative jurisprudence. They are part of the *jus gentium*. In the development of such principles logic is likely to predominate over history. An illustration is the conception of juristic or corporate personality with the long train of consequences which that conception has engendered. Sometimes the subject matter will lend itself as naturally to one method as to another. In such circumstances, considerations of custom or utility will often be present to regulate the choice. A residuum will be left where the personality of the judge, his taste, his training or his bent of mind, may prove the controlling factor. I do not mean that the directive force of history, even where its claims are most assertive, confines the law of the future to uninspired repetition of the law of the present and the past. I mean simply that history, in illuminating the past, illuminates the present, and in illuminating the present, illuminates the future. "If at one time it seemed likely," says Maitland, "that the historical spirit (the spirit which strove to understand the classical jurisprudence of Rome and the Twelve Tables, and the Lex Salica, and law of all ages and climes) was fatalistic and inimical to reform, that time already lies in the past. . . . Nowadays we may see the office of historical research as that of explaining, and therefore lightening, the pressure that the past must exercise upon the present and the present upon the future. Today we study the day before yesterday, in order that yesterday may not paralyze today, and today may not paralyze tomorrow."

Let me speak first of those fields where there can be no progress without history. I think the law of real property supplies the readiest example. No lawgiver meditating a code of laws conceived the system of feudal tenures. History built up the system and the law that went with it. Never by a process of logical deduction from the idea of abstract ownership could we distinguish the incidents of an estate in fee simple from those of an estate for life, or those of an estate for life from those of an estate for years. Upon these points, "a page of history is worth a volume of logic" . . . I do not mean that even in this field, the method of philosophy plays no part at all. Some of the conceptions of the land law, once fixed, are pushed to their logical conclusions with inexorable severity. The point is rather that the conceptions themselves have come to us from without and not from within, that they embody the thought, not so much of the present as of the past, that separated from the past their form and meaning are unintelligible and arbitrary, and hence that their development, in order to be truly logical, must be mindful of their origins. In a measure that is true of most of the conceptions of our law. Metaphysical principles have seldom been their life. . . .

If history and philosophy do not serve to fix the direction of a principle, custom may step in . . . .

Undoubtedly the creative energy of custom in the development of common law is less today than it was in bygone times. Even in bygone times, its energy was very likely exaggerated by Blackstone and his followers. "Today we recognize," in the words of Pound, "that the custom is a custom of judicial decision, not of popular action." It is "doubtful," says Gray, "whether at all stages of legal history, rules laid down by judges have not generated custom, rather than custom generated the rules." In these days, at all events, we look to custom, not so much for the creation of new rules, but for the tests and standards that are to determine how established rules shall be applied. When custom seeks to do more than this, there is a growing tendency in the law to leave development to legislation. Judges do not feel the same need of putting the *imprimatur* of law upon customs of recent growth, knocking for entrance into the legal system, and viewed askance because of some novel aspects of form or feature, as they would if legislatures were not in frequent session, capable of establishing a title that will be unimpeached and unimpeachable. But the power is not lost because it is exercised with caution . . . In the absence of inconsistent statute, new classes of negotiable instruments may be created by mercantile practice. The obligations of public and private corporations may retain the quality of negotiability, despite the presence of a seal, which at common law would destroy it . . . The great inventions that embodied the power of steam and electricity, the railroad and the steamship, the telegraph and the telephone, have built up new customs and new law. Already there is a body of legal literature that deals with the legal problems of the air.

It is, however, not so much in the making of new rules as in the application of old ones that the creative energy of custom most often manifests itself today. General standards of right and duty are established. Custom must determine whether there has been adherence or departure. My partner has the powers that are usual in the trade . . . The master in the discharge of his duty to protect the servant against harm must exercise the degree of care that is commonly exercised in like circumstance by men of ordinary prudence. The triers of the facts in determining whether that standard has been attained, must consult the habits of life, the everyday beliefs and practices, of the men and women about them. Innumerable, also, are the cases where the course of dealing to be followed is defined by the customs, or, more properly speaking, the usages of a particular trade or market or profession. The constant assumption runs throughout the law that the natural and spontaneous evolutions of habit fix the limits of right and wrong. A slight extension of custom identifies it with customary morality, the prevailing standard of right conduct, the *mores* of the time. This

is the point of contact between the method of tradition and the method of sociology. They have their roots in the same soil. Each method maintains the interaction between conduct and order, between life and law. Life casts the moulds of conduct, which will some day become fixed as law. Law preserves the moulds, which have taken form and shape from life.

Three of the directive forces of our law, philosophy, history and custom, have now been seen at work. We have gone far enough to appreciate the complexity of the problem. We see that to determine to be loyal to precedents and to the principles back of precedents, does not carry us far upon the road. Principles are complex bundles. It is well enough to say that we shall be consistent, but consistent with what? Shall it be consistency with the origins of the rule, the course and tendency of development? Shall it be consistency with logic or philosophy or the fundamental conceptions of jurisprudence as disclosed by analysis of our own and foreign systems? All these loyalties are possible. All have sometimes prevailed. How are we to choose between them? Putting that question aside, how do we choose between them? Some concepts of the law have been in a peculiar sense historical growths. In such departments, history will tend to give direction to development. In other departments, certain large and fundamental concepts, which comparative jurisprudence shows to be common to other highly developed systems, loom up above all others. In these we shall give a larger scope to logic and symmetry. A broad field there also is in which rules may, with approximately the same convenience, be settled one way or the other. Here custom tends to assert itself as the controlling force in guiding the choice of paths. Finally, when the social needs demand one settlement rather than another, there are times when we must bend symmetry, ignore history and sacrifice custom in the pursuit of other and larger ends.

From history and philosophy and custom, we pass, therefore, to the force which in our day and generation is becoming the greatest of them all, the power of social justice which finds its outlet and expression in the method of sociology.

The final cause of law is the welfare of society. The rule that misses its aim cannot permanently justify its existence . . . I do not mean, of course, that judges are commissioned to set aside existing rules at pleasure in favor of any other set of rules which they may hold to be expedient or wise. I mean that when they are called upon to say how far existing rules are to be extended or restricted, they must let the welfare of society fix the path, its direction and its distance . . . There may be a paramount public policy, one that will prevail over temporary inconvenience or occasional hardship, not lightly to sacrifice certainty and uniformity and order and coherence. All these elements must be considered. They are to be given such weight as sound judgment dictates. They are constituents of that social welfare which it is our business to discover. In a given instance we may find that they are constituents of preponderating value. In others, we may find that their value is subordinate. We must appraise them as best we can.

. . . Our judges cannot say with Hobbes: "Princes succeed one another, and one judge passeth, another cometh; nay heaven and earth shall pass, but not one tittle of the law of nature shall pass, for it is the eternal law of God. Therefore, all the sentences of . . . judges that have ever been, cannot altogether make a law contrary to natural equity, nor any examples of former judges can warrant an unreasonable sentence or discharge the present judge of the trouble of studying what is equity in the case he is to judge from the principles of his own natural reason." Nearer to the truth for us are the words of an English judge: "Our common law system consists in applying to new combinations of circumstances those rules of law which we derive from legal principles and judicial precedents, and for the sake of attaining uniformity, consistency and certainty, we must apply those rules when they are not plainly unreasonable and inconvenient to all cases which arise; and we are not at liberty to reject them and to abandon all analogy to them in those in which they have not yet been judicially applied, because we think that the rules are not as convenient and reasonable as we ourselves could have devised." This does not mean that there are not gaps, yet unfilled, within which judgment moves untrammeled . . . The method of sociology in filling the gaps, puts its emphasis on the social welfare.

Social welfare is a broad term. I use it to cover many concepts more or less allied. It may mean what is commonly spoken of as public policy, the good of the collective body. In such cases, its demands are often those of mere expediency or prudence. It may mean on the other hand the social gain that is wrought by adherence to the standards of right conduct, which find expression in the *mores* of the community. In such cases, its demands are those of religion or of ethics or of the social sense of justice, whether formulated in creed or system, or immanent in the common mind . . . .

It is true, I think, today in every department of the law that the social value of a rule has become a test of growing power and importance. . . .

All departments of the law have been touched and elevated by this spirit. In some, however, the method of sociology works in harmony with the method of philosophy or of evolution or of tradition. Those, therefore, are the fields where logic and coherence and consistency must still be sought as ends. In others, it seems to displace the methods that compete with it. Those are the fields where the virtues of consistency must yield within those interstitial limits where judicial power moves. In a sense it is true that we are applying the method of sociology when we pursue logic and coherence and consistency as the greater social values. I am concerned for the moment with the fields in which the method is in antagonism to others rather than with those in which their action is in unison. . . .

I speak first of the Constitution, and in particular of the great immunities with which it surrounds the individual. No one shall be deprived of liberty without due process of law. Here is a concept of the greatest generality. Yet it is put before the courts *en bloc*. Liberty is not defined. Its limits are not mapped and charted. How shall they be known? Does liberty mean the same thing for successive generations? May restraints that were arbitrary yesterday be useful and rational and therefore lawful today? May restraints that are arbitrary today become useful and rational and therefore lawful tomorrow? I have no doubt that the answer to these questions must be yes. There were times in our judicial history when the answer might have been no . . . *Laissez faire* was not only a counsel of caution which statesmen would do well to heed. It was a categorical imperative which statesmen, as well as judges, must obey . . . The movement from individualistic liberalism to unsystematic collectivism had brought changes in the social order which carried with them the need of a new formulation of fundamental rights and duties . . . Even as late as 1905, the decision in *Lochner v. N. Y.*, 198 U.S. 45, still spoke in terms untouched by the light of the new spirit. It is the dissenting opinion of Justice Holmes, which men will turn to in the future as the beginning of an era. In the instance, it was the voice of a minority. In principle, it has become the voice of a new dispensation, which has written itself into law. "The Fourteenth Amendment does not enact Mr. Herbert Spencer's *Social Statics*." "A constitution is not intended to embody a particular economic theory, whether of paternalism and the organic relation of the citizen to the state, or of *laissez faire*." "The word liberty in the Fourteenth Amendment is perverted when it is held to prevent the natural outcome of a dominant opinion, unless it can be said that a rational and fair man necessarily would admit that the statute proposed would infringe fundamental principles as they have been understood by the traditions of our people and of our law." That is the conception of liberty which is dominant today. It has its critics even yet, but its dominance

is, I think, assured. No doubt, there will at times be difference of opinion when a conception so delicate is applied to varying conditions. At times, indeed, the conditions themselves are imperfectly disclosed and inadequately known . . . Courts know today that statutes are to be viewed, not in isolation or *in vacuo*, as pronouncements of abstract principles for the guidance of an ideal community, but in the setting and the framework of present-day conditions, as revealed by the labors of economists and students of the social sciences in our own country and abroad. The same fluid and dynamic conception which underlies the modern notion of liberty, as secured to the individual by the constitutional immunity, must also underlie the cognate notion of equality. No state shall deny to any person within its jurisdiction "the equal protection of the laws." Restrictions, viewed narrowly, may seem to foster inequality. The same restrictions, when viewed broadly, may be seen "to be necessary in the long run in order to establish the equality of position between the parties in which liberty of contract begins." . . .

From all this, it results that the content of constitutional immunities is not constant, but varies from age to age . . . Statutes are designed to meet the fugitive exigencies of the hour. Amendment is easy as the exigencies change. In such cases, the meaning, once construed, tends legitimately to stereotype itself in the form first cast. A *constitution* states or ought to state not rules for the passing hour, but principles for an expanding future. In so far as it deviates from that standard, and descends into details and particulars, it loses its flexibility, the scope of interpretation contracts, the meaning hardens. While it is true to its function, it maintains its power of adaptation, its suppleness, its play. . . .

Property, like liberty, though immune under the Constitution from destruction, is not immune from regulation essential for the common good. What that regulation shall be, every generation must work out for itself. The generation which gave us *Munn v. Illinois*, 94 U. S. 113 (1876), and like cases, asserted the right of regulation whenever business was "affected with a public use." The phrase in its application meant little more than if it said, whenever the social need shall be imminent and pressing. Such a formulation of the principle may have been adequate for the exigencies of the time. Today there is a growing tendency in political and juristic thought to probe the principle more deeply and formulate it more broadly. Men are saying today that property, like every other social institution, has a social function to fulfill. Legislation which destroys the institution is one thing. Legislation which holds it true to its function is quite another. That is the dominant theme of a new and forceful school of publicists and jurists on the continent of Europe, in England, and even here . . . It is yet too early to say how far this new conception of function and its obligations will gain a lodgment in our law. Perhaps we shall find in the end that it is little more than *Munn v. Illinois* in the garb of a new philosophy. I do not attempt to predict the extent to which we shall adopt it, or even to assert that we shall adopt it at all. Enough for my purpose at present that new times and new manners may call for new standards and new rules.

The courts, then, are free in marking the limits of the individual's immunities to shape their judgments in accordance with reason and justice. That does not mean that in judging the validity of statutes they are free to substitute their own ideas of reason and justice for those of the men and women whom they serve. Their standard must be an objective one. In such matters, the thing that counts is not what I believe to be right. It is what I may reasonably believe that some other man or normal intellect and conscience might reasonably look upon as right . . . Some fields of the law there are, indeed, where there is freer scope for subjective vision. Of these we shall say more hereafter. The personal element, whatever its scope in other spheres, should have little, if any, sway in determining the limits of legis-

lative power. One department of the government may not force upon another its own standards of propriety. . . .

. . . The utility of an external power restraining the legislative judgment is not to be measured by counting the occasions of its exercise. The great ideals of liberty and equality are preserved against the assaults of opportunism, the expediency of the passing hour, the erosion of small encroachments, the scorn and derision of those who have no patience with general principles, by enshrining them in constitutions, and consecrating to the task of their protection a body of defenders. By conscious or subconscious influence, the presence of this restraining power, aloof in the background but none the less always in reserve, tends to stabilize and rationalize the legislative judgment, to infuse it with the glow of principle, to hold the standard aloft and visible to those who must run the race and keep the faith. I do not mean to deny that there have been times when the possibility of judicial review has worked the other way. Legislatures have sometimes disregarded their own responsibility, and passed it on to the courts. Such dangers must be balanced against those of independence from all restraint, independence on the part of public officers elected for brief terms, without the guiding force of a continuous tradition. On the whole, I believe the latter dangers to be the more formidable of the two . . . The restraining power of the judiciary does not manifest its chief worth in the few cases in which the legislature has gone beyond the lines that mark the limits of discretion. Rather shall we find its chief worth in making vocal and audible the ideals that might otherwise be silenced, in giving them continuity of life and of expression, in guiding and directing choice within the limits where choice ranges. This function should preserve to the courts the power that now belongs to them, if only the power is exercised with insight into social values, and with suppleness of adaptation to changing social needs. . . .

The Method of Sociology. The Judge as a Legislator

... Few rules in our time are so well established that they may not be called upon any day to justify their existence as means adapted to an end. If they do not function they are diseased. If they are diseased, they must not propagate their kind. Sometimes they are cut out and extirpated altogether. Sometimes they are left with the shadow of continued life, but sterilized, truncated, impotent for harm . . . .

... Perhaps it is in the field of procedure that we have witnessed the chief changes; though greater ones must yet be wrought. Indictments and civil pleadings are viewed with indulgent eyes. Rulings upon questions of evidence are held with increasing frequency to come within the discretion of the judge presiding at the trial. Errors are no longer ground for the upsetting of judgments with the ensuing horror of new trials, unless the appellate court is satisfied that they have affected the result. Legislation has sometimes been necessary to free us from the old fetters. Sometimes the conservatism of judges has threatened for an interval to rob the legislation of its efficacy. This danger was disclosed in the attitude of the courts toward the reforms embodied in codes of practice, in the days when they were first enacted. Precedents established in those times exert an unhappy influence even now. None the less, the tendency today is in the direction of a growing liberalism. . . .

This conception of the end of the law as determining the direction of its growth, which was Jhering's great contribution to the theory of jurisprudence, finds its organon, its instrument, in the method of sociology. Not the origin, but the goal, is the main thing . . . This means, of course, that the juristic philosophy of the common law is at bottom the philosophy of pragmatism. Its truth is relative, not absolute. The rule that functions well produces a title deed to recognition. Only in determining how it functions we must not view it too narrowly. We must not sacrifice the general to the particular. We must not throw to the winds the advantages of consistency and uniformity to do justice in the instance. We must keep within those interstitial limits which precedent and custom and the long and silent and almost indefinable practice of other judges through the centuries of the common law have set to judge-made innovations . . . Every judge consulting his own experience must be conscious of times when a free exercise of will, directed of set purpose to the furtherance of the common good, determined the form and tendency of a rule which at that moment took its origin in one creative act. Savigny's conception of law as something realized without struggle or aim or purpose, a process of silent growth, the fruition in life and manners of a people's history and genius, gives a picture incomplete and partial. It is true if we understand it to mean that the judge in shaping the rules of law must heed the *mores* of his day. It is one-sided and therefore false in so far as it implies that the *mores* of the day automatically shape rules which, full grown and ready made, are handed to the judge . . . Law is, indeed, an historical growth, for it is an expression of customary morality which develops silently and unconsciously from one age to another. That is the great truth in Savigny's theory of its origin. But law is also a conscious or purposed growth, for the expression of customary morality will be false unless the mind of the judge is directed to the attainment of the moral end and its embodiment in legal forms. Nothing less than conscious effort will be adequate if the end in view is to prevail. The standards or patterns of utility and morals will be found by the judge in the life of the community. . . .

There has been much debate among foreign jurists whether the norms of right and useful conduct, the patterns of social welfare, are to be found by the judge in conformity with an objective or a subjective standard . . . So far as the distinction has practical significance, the traditions of our jurisprudence commit us to the objective standard. I do not mean, of course, that this ideal of objective vision is ever perfectly attained . . . None the less, the ideal is one to be striven for within the limits of our capacity. This truth, when clearly perceived, tends to unify the judge's function . . . It is the customary morality of right-minded men and women which he is to enforce by his decree. A jurisprudence that is not constantly brought into relation to objective or external standards, incurs the risk of degenerating into what the Germans call "Die Gefuhls jurisprudenz," a jurisprudence of mere sentiment or feeling. . . .

Scholars of distinction have argued for a more subjective standard. "We all agree," says Professor Gray, "that many cases should be decided by the courts on notions of right and wrong and, of course, everyone will agree that a judge is likely to share the notions of right and wrong prevalent in the community in which he lives; but suppose in a case where there is nothing to guide him but notions of right and wrong, that his notions of right and wrong differ from those of the community. Which ought he to follow—his own notions, or the notions of the community? . . . I believe that he should follow his own notions." The hypothesis that Professor Gray offers us, is not likely to be realized in practice. Rare indeed must be the case when, with conflicting notions of right conduct, there will be nothing else to sway the balance. If, however, the case supposed were here, a judge, I think, would err if he were to impose upon the community as a rule of life his own idiosyncrasies of conduct or belief. Let us, suppose, for illustration, a judge who looked upon theatre-going as a sin. Would he be doing right if, in a field where the rule of law was still unsettled, he permitted this conviction, though known to be in conflict with the dominant standard of right conduct, to govern his decision? My own notion is that he would be under a duty to conform to the accepted standards of the community, the *mores* of the times. This does not mean, however, that a judge is powerless to raise the level of prevailing conduct. In one field

or another of activity, practices in opposition to the sentiments and standards of the age may grow up and threaten to intrench themselves if not dislodged. Despite their temporary hold, they do not stand comparison with accepted norms of morals. Indolence or passivity has tolerated what the considerate judgment of the community condemns. In such cases, one of the highest functions of the judge is to establish the true relation between conduct and profession. . . .

The truth, indeed, is, as I have said, that the distinction between the subjective or individual and the objective or general conscience, in the field where the judge is not limited by established rules, is shadowy and evanescent, and tends to become one of words and little more . . . The personal and the general mind and will are inseparably united. The difference, as one theory of judicial duty or the other prevails, involves at most a little change of emphasis, of the method of approach, of the point of view, the angle, from which problems are envisaged. Only dimly and by force of an influence subconscious, or nearly so, will the difference be reflected in the decisions of the courts.

My analysis of the judicial process comes then to this, and little more: logic, and history, custom, and utility, and the accepted standards of right conduct, are the forces which singly or in combination shape the progress of the law. Which of these forces shall dominate in any case, must depend largely upon the comparative importance or value of the social interests that will be thereby promoted or impaired. One of the most fundamental social interests is that law shall be uniform and impartial . . . Therefore in the main there shall be adherence to precedent. There shall be symmetrical development, consistently with history or custom when history or custom has been the motive force, or the chief one, in giving shape to existing rules, and with logic or philosophy when the motive power has been theirs. But symmetrical development may be bought at too high a price . . . The social interest served by symmetry or certainty must then be balanced against the social interest served by equity and fairness or other elements of social welfare. These may enjoin upon the judge the duty of drawing the line at another angle, of staking the path along new courses, of marking a new point of departure from which others who come after him will set out upon their journey.

If you ask how he is to know when one interest outweighs another, I can only answer that he must get his knowledge just as the legislator gets it, from experience and study and reflection; in brief, from life itself . . . Each indeed is legislating within the limits of his competence. No doubt the limits for the judge are narrower. He legislates only between gaps. He fills the open spaces in the law. How far he may go without traveling beyond the walls of the interstices cannot be staked out for him upon a chart. He must learn it for himself as he gains the sense of fitness and proportion that comes with years of habitude in the practice of an art. Even within the gaps, restrictions not easy to define, but felt, however impalpable they may be, by every judge and lawyer, hedge and circumscribe his action. They are established by the traditions of the centuries, by the example of other judges, his predecessors and his colleagues, by the collective judgment of the profession, and by the duty of adherence to the pervading spirit of the law . . . The law which is the resulting product is not found, but made. The process, being legislative, demands the legislator's wisdom.
. . . Today the use of fictions has declined; and the springs of action are disclosed where once they were concealed. Even now, they are not fully known, however, even to those whom they control. Much of the process has been unconscious or nearly so. The ends to which courts have addressed themselves, the reasons and motives that have guided them, have often been vaguely felt, intuitively or almost intuitively apprehended, seldom explicitly avowed . . . That is why there is something of a shock in the discovery that legislative policy has made the compound what it is. . . .

In thus recognizing, as I do, that the power to declare the law carries with it the power, and within limits the duty, to make law when none exists, I do not mean to range myself with the jurists who seem to hold that in reality there is no law except the decisions of the courts. I think the truth is midway between the extremes that are represented at one end by Coke and Hale and Blackstone and at the other by such authors as Austin and Holland and Gray and Jethro Brown. The theory of the older writers was that judges did not legislate at all. A pre-existing rule was there, imbedded, if concealed, in the body of the customary law. All that the judges did, was to throw off the wrappings, and expose the statute to our view. Since the days of Bentham and Austin, no one, it is believed, has accepted this theory without deduction or reserve, though even in modern decisions we find traces of its lingering influence. Today there is rather danger of another though opposite error. From holding that the law is never made by judges, the votaries of the Austinian analysis have been led at times to the conclusion that it is never made by anyone else. Customs, no matter how firmly established, are not law, they say, until adopted by the courts. Even statutes are not law because the courts must fix their meaning. . . .

A definition of law which in effect denies the possibility of law since it denies the possibility of rules of general operation, must contain within itself the seeds of fallacy and error. Analysis is useless if it destroys what it is intended to explain. Law and obedience to law are facts confirmed every day to us all in our experience of life. If the result of a definition is to make them seem to be illusions, so much the worse for the definition; we must enlarge it till it is broad enough to answer to realities . . . Statutes do not cease to be law because the power to fix their meaning in case of doubt or ambiguity has been confided to the courts. One might as well say for like reasons that contracts have no reality as expressions of a contracting will. The quality of law is not withdrawn from all precedents, however well established, because courts sometimes exercise the privilege of over-ruling their own decisions . . . Most of us live our lives in conscious submission to rules of law, yet without necessity of resort to the courts to ascertain our rights and duties. Lawsuits are rare and catastrophic experiences for the vast majority of men, and even when the catastrophe ensues, the controversy relates most often not to the law, but to the facts. In countless litigations, the law is so clear that judges have no discretion. They have the right to legislate within gaps, but often there are no gaps. We shall have a false view of the landscape if we look at the waste spaces only, and refuse to see the acres already sown and fruitful. I think the difficulty has its origin in the failure to distinguish between right and power, between the command embodied in a judgment and the jural principle to which the obedience of the judge is due. Judges have, of course, the power, though not the right, to ignore the mandate of a statute, and render judgment in despite of it. They have the power, though not the right, to travel beyond the walls of the interstices, the bounds set to judicial innovation by precedent and custom. None the less, by that abuse of power, they violate the law. If they violate it willfully, i.e., with guilty and evil mind, they commit a legal wrong, and may be removed or punished even though the judgments which they have rendered stand. . . .

The old Blackstonian theory of pre-existing rules of law which judges found, but did not make, fitted in with a theory still more ancient, the theory of a law of nature . . . For a time, with the rise and dominance of the analytical school of jurists, it seemed discredited and abandoned. Recent juristic thought has given it a new currency, though in a form so profoundly altered that the old theory survives in little more than name. The law of nature is no longer conceived of as something static and eternal. It does not override human or positive law. It is the stuff out of which human or positive law is to be woven, when other sources fail . . . I am not concerned to vindicate the accuracy of the nomenclature by which the dictates

of reason and conscience which the judge is under a duty to obey, are given the name of law before he has embodied them in a judgment and set the *imprimatur* of the law upon them . . . What really matters is this, that the judge is under a duty, within the limits of his power of innovation, to maintain a relation between law and morals, between the precepts of jurisprudence and those of reason and good conscience. I suppose it is true in a certain sense, that this duty was never doubted. One feels at times, however, that it was obscured by the analytical jurists, who, in stressing verbal niceties of definition, made a corresponding sacrifice of emphasis upon the deeper and finer realities of ends and aims and functions. The constant insistence that morality and justice are not law, has tended to breed distrust and contempt of law as something to which morality and justice are not merely alien, but hostile. The new development of "naturrecht" may be pardoned infelicities of phrase, if it introduces us to new felicities of methods and ideals. Not for us the barren logomachy that dwells upon the contrasts between law and justice, and forgets their deeper harmonies. . . .

You may say that there is no assurance that judges will interpret the *mores* of their day more wisely and truly than other men. I am not disposed to deny this but in my view it is quite beside the point. The point is rather that this power of interpretation must be lodged somewhere, and the custom of the constitution has lodged it in the judges. If they are to fulfill their function as judges, it could hardly be lodged elsewhere . . . Insignificant is the power of innovation of any judge, when compared with the bulk and pressure of the rules that hedge him on every side. Innovate, however, to some extent, he must, for with new conditions there must be new rules. All that the method of sociology demands is that within this narrow range of choice, he shall search for social justice. . . .

. . . Our jurisprudence has held fast to Kant's categorical imperative, "Act on a maxim which thou canst will to be law universal." It has refused to sacrifice the larger and more inclusive good to the narrower and smaller. A contract is made. Performance is burdensome and perhaps oppressive. If we were to consider only the individual instance, we might be ready to release the promisor. We look beyond the particular to the universal, and shape our judgment in obedience to the fundamental interest of society that contracts shall be fulfilled. There is a wide gap between the use of the individual sentiment of justice as a substitute for law, and its use as one of the tests and touchstones in construing or extending law . . . The judge, even when he is free, is still not wholly free. He is not to innovate at pleasure. He is not a knight-errant, roaming at will in pursuit of his own ideal of beauty or of goodness. He is to draw his inspiration from consecrated principles. He is not to yield to spasmodic sentiment, to vague and unregulated benevolence. He is to exercise a discretion informed by tradition, methodized by analogy, disciplined by system, and subordinated to "the primordial necessity of order in the social life." Wide enough in all conscience is the field of discretion that remains.

LECTURE IV

Adherence to Precedent. The Subconscious Element in the Judicial Process. Conclusion

The system of law-making by judicial decisions which supply the rule for transactions closed before the decision was announced, would indeed be intolerable in its hardship and oppression if natural law, in the sense in which I have used the term, did not supply the main rule of judgment to the judge when precedent and custom fail or are displaced. Acquiescence in such a method has its basis in the belief that when the law has left the situation uncovered by any pre-existing rule, there is nothing to do except to have some impartial arbiter declare what fair and reasonable men, mindful of the habits of life of the community, and of the standards of justice and fair dealing prev-

alent among them, ought in such circumstances to do, with no rules except those of custom and conscience to regulate their conduct. The feeling is that nine times out of ten, if not oftener, the conduct of right-minded men would not have been different if the rule embodied in the decision had been announced by statute in advance. In the small minority of cases, where ignorance has counted, it is as likely to have affected one side as the other; and since a controversy has arisen and must be determined somehow, there is nothing to do, in default of a rule already made, but to constitute some authority which will make it after the event. Some one must be the loser; it is part of the game of life; we have to pay in countless ways for the absence of prophetic vision. No doubt the ideal system, if it were attainable, would be a code at once so flexible and so minute, as to supply in advance for every conceivable situation the just and fitting rule. But life is too complex to bring the attainment of this ideal within the compass of human powers . . . Hardship must at times result from postponement of the rule of action till a time when action is complete. It is one of the consequences of the limitations of the human intellect and of the denial to legislators and judges of infinite prevision. But the truth is, as I have said, that even when there is ignorance of the rule, the cases are few in which ignorance has determined conduct. Most often the controversy arises about something that would have happened anyhow. An automobile is manufactured with defective wheels. The question is whether the manufacturer owes a duty of inspection to anyone except the buyer. The occupant of the car, injured because of the defect, presses one view upon the court; the manufacturer, another. There is small chance, whichever party prevails, that conduct would have been different if the rule had been known in advance. . . .

. . . I think it is significant that when the hardship is felt to be too great or to be unnecessary, retrospective operation is withheld. Take the cases where a court of final appeal has declared a statute void, and afterwards, reversing itself, declares the statute valid. Intervening transactions have been governed by the first decision. What shall be said of the validity of such transactions when the decision is overruled? Most courts in a spirit of realism have held that the operation of the statute has been suspended in the interval. It may be hard to square such a ruling with abstract dogmas and definitions. When so much else that a court does, is done with retroactive force, why draw the line here? The answer is, I think, that the line is drawn here, because the injustice and oppression of a refusal to draw it would be so great as to be intolerable. We will not help out the man who has trusted to the judgment of some inferior court. In his case, the chance of miscalculation is felt to be a fair risk of the game of life, not different in degree from the risk of any other misconception of right or duty. He knows that he has taken a chance, which caution often might have avoided. The judgment of a court of final appeal is felt to stand upon a different basis. I am not sure that any adequate distinction is to be drawn between a change of ruling in respect of the validity of a statute and a change of ruling in respect of the meaning or operation of a statute, or even in respect of the meaning or operation of a rule of common law. Where the line of division will some day be located, I will make no attempt to say. I feel assured, however, that its location, wherever it shall be, will be governed, not by metaphysical conceptions of the nature of judge-made law, nor by the fetish of some implacable tenet, such as that of the division of governmental powers, but by considerations of convenience, of utility, and of the deepest sentiments of justice.

In these days, there is a good deal of discussion whether the rule of adherence to precedent ought to be abandoned altogether. I would not go so far myself. I think adherence to precedent should be the rule and not the exception . . . The labor of judges would be increased almost to the breaking point if every past decision could be reopened in every case, and one could not lay one's own course of bricks on the secure foundation of the courses laid by others who had gone before him . . . But I am ready to concede that the rule of adherence to precedent . . . ought to be in some degree relaxed. I think that when a rule, after it has been duly tested by experience, has been found to be inconsistent with the sense of justice or with the social welfare, there should be less hesitation in frank avowal and full abandonment . . . There should be greater readiness to abandon an untenable position when the rule to be discarded may not reasonably be supposed to have determined the conduct of the litigants, and particularly when in its origin it was the product of institutions or conditions which have gained a new significance or development with the progress of the years. . . .

Our survey of judicial methods teaches us, I think, the lesson that the whole subject-matter of jurisprudence is more plastic, more malleable, the moulds less definitely cast, the bounds of right and wrong less preordained and constant, than most of us, without the aid of some such analysis, have been accustomed to believe. We like to picture to ourselves the field of the law as accurately mapped and plotted. We draw our little lines, and they are hardly down before we blur them. As in time and space, so here. Divisions are working hypotheses, adopted for convenience. We are tending more and more toward an appreciation of the truth that, after all, there are few rules; there are chiefly standards and degrees. It is a question of degree whether I have been negligent. It is a question of degree whether in the use of my own land, I have created a nuisance which may be abated by my neighbor. It is a question of degree whether the law which takes my property and limits my conduct, impairs my liberty unduly. So also the duty of a judge becomes itself a question of degree, and he is a useful judge or a poor one as he estimates the measure accurately or loosely. He must balance all his ingredients, his philosophy, his logic, his analogies, his history, his customs, his sense of right, and all the rest, and adding a little here and taking out a little there, must determine, as wisely as he can, which weight shall tip the scales. If this seems a weak and inconclusive summary, I am not sure that the fault is mine. I know he is a wise pharmacist who from a recipe so general can compound a fitting remedy. But the like criticism may be made of most attempts to formulate the principles which regulate the practice of an art. W. Jethro Brown reminds us in a recent paper on "Law and Evolution" that "Sir Joshua Reynolds' book on painting, offers little or no guidance to those who wish to become famous painters. Books on literary styles are notoriously lacking, speaking as a rule, in practical utility." After the wearisome process of analysis has been finished, there must be for every judge a new synthesis which he will have to make for himself. The most that he can hope for is that with long thought and study, with years of practice at the bar or on the bench, and with the aid of that inward grace which comes now and again to the elect of any calling, the analysis may help a little to make the synthesis a true one.

In what I have said, I have thrown, perhaps too much, into the background and the shadow the cases where the controversy turns not upon the rule of law, but upon its application to the facts. Those cases, after all, make up the bulk of the business of the courts . . . But they leave jurisprudence where it stood before. As applied to such cases, the judicial process, as was said at the outset of these lectures, is a process of search and comparison, and little else . . . Of the cases that come before the court in which I sit, a majority, I think, could not, with semblance of reason, be decided in any way but one. The law and its application alike are plain. Such cases are predestined, so to speak, to affirmance without opinion. In another and considerable percentage, the rule of law is certain, and the application alone doubtful. A complicated record must be dissected, the narratives of witnesses, more or less incoherent and unintelligible, must be analyzed, to determine whether a given situation comes within one district or

another upon the chart of rights and wrongs. The traveler who knows that a railroad crosses his path must look for approaching trains. That is at least the general rule. In numberless litigations the description of the landscape must be studied to see whether vision has been obstructed, whether something has been done or omitted to put the traveler off his guard. Often these cases and others like them provoke difference of opinion among judges. Jurisprudence remains untouched, however, regardless of the outcome. Finally there remains a percentage, not large indeed, and yet not so small as to be negligible, where a decision one way or the other, will count for the future, will advance or retard, sometimes much, sometimes little, the development of the law. These are the cases where the creative element in the judicial process finds its opportunity and power. It is with these cases that I have chiefly concerned myself in all that I have said to you. In a sense it is true of many of them that they might be decided either way. By that I mean that reasons plausible and fairly persuasive might be found for one conclusion as for another. Here come into play that balancing of judgment, that testing and sorting of considerations of analogy and logic and utility and fairness, which I have been trying to describe. Here it is that the judge assumes the function of a lawgiver. I was much troubled in spirit, in my first years upon the bench, to find how trackless was the ocean on which I had embarked. I sought for certainty. I was oppressed and disheartened when I found that the quest for it was futile. I was trying to reach land, the solid land of fixed and settled rules the paradise of a justice that would declare itself by tokens plainer and more commanding than its pale and glimmering reflections in my own vacillating mind and conscience . . . As the years have gone by, and as I have reflected more and more upon the nature of the judicial process, I have become reconciled to the uncertainty, because I have grown to see it as inevitable . . . .

I have spoken of the forces of which judges avowedly avail to shape the form and content of their judgments. Even these forces are seldom fully in consciousness. They lie so near the surface, however, that their existence and influence are not likely to be disclaimed. But the subject is not exhausted with the recognition of their power. Deep below consciousness are other forces, the likes and the dislikes, the predilections and the prejudices, the complex of instincts and emotions and habits and convictions, which make the man, whether he be litigant or judge . . . There has been a certain lack of candor in much of the discussion of the theme, or rather perhaps in the refusal to discuss it, as if judges must lose respect and confidence by the reminder that they are subject to human limitations . . . The great tides and currents which engulf the rest of men, do not turn aside in their course, and pass the judges by. We like to figure to ourselves the processes of justice as coldly objective and impersonal . . . That is an ideal of objective truth toward which every system of jurisprudence tends. It is an ideal of which great publicists and judges have spoken as of something possible to attain. "The judges of the nation," says Montesquieu, "are only the mouths that pronounce the words of the law, inanimate beings, who can moderate neither its force nor its rigor" . . . At the opposite extreme are the words of the French jurist, Saleilles, in his treatise "De la Personnalite Juridique": "One wills at the beginning the result; one finds the principle afterwards; such is the genesis of all juridical construction. Once accepted, the construction presents itself, doubtless, in the ensemble of legal doctrine, under the opposite aspect. The factors are inverted. The principle appears as an initial cause, from which one has drawn the result which is found deduced from it." I would not put the case thus broadly. So sweeping a statement exaggerates the element of free volition. It ignores the factors of determinism which cabin and confine within narrow bounds the range of unfettered choice. None the less, by its very excess of emphasis, it supplies the needed corrective of an ideal of impossible objectivity. Nearer to the truth,

and midway between these extremes, are the words of a man who was not a jurist, but whose intuitions and perceptions were deep and brilliant—the words of President Roosevelt in his message of December 8, 1908, to the Congress of the United States: "The chief lawmakers in our country may be, and often are, the judges, because they are the final seat of authority. Every time they interpret contract, property, vested rights, due process of law, liberty, they necessarily enact into law parts of a system of social philosophy; and as such interpretation is fundamental they give direction to all law-making. The decisions of the courts on economic and social questions depend upon their economic and social philosophy; and for the peaceful progress of our people during the twentieth century we shall owe most to those judges who hold to a twentieth century economic and social philosophy and not to a long outgrown philosophy, which was itself the product of primitive economic conditions."

. . . Roosevelt, who knew men, had no illusions on this score. He was not positing an ideal. He was not fixing a goal. He was measuring the powers and the endurance of those by whom the race was to be run. My duty as judge may be to objectify in law, not my own aspirations and convictions and philosophies, but the aspirations and convictions and philosophies of the men and women of my time. Hardly shall I do this well if my own sympathies and beliefs and passionate devotions are with a time that is past . . . We may figure the task of the judge, if we please, as the task of a translator, the reading of signs and symbols given from without. None the less, we will not set men to such a task, unless they have absorbed the spirit, and have filled themselves with a love, of the language they must read.

. . . In every court there are likely to be as many estimates of the "Zeitgeist" as there are judges on its bench . . . The spirit of the age, as it is revealed to each of us, is too often only the spirit of the group in which the accidents of birth or education or occupation or fellowship have given us a place . . . The training of the judge, if coupled with what is styled the judicial temperament, will help in some degree to emancipate him from the suggestive power of individual dislikes and prepossessions. It will help to broaden the group to which his subconscious loyalties are due. Never will these loyalties be utterly extinguished while human nature is what it is. We may wonder sometimes how from the play of all these forces of individualism, there can come anything coherent, anything but chaos and the void. Those are the moments in which we exaggerate the elements of difference. In the end there emerges something which has a composite shape and truth and order . . . The eccentricities of judges balance one another. One judge looks at problems from the point of view of history, another from that of philosophy, another from that of social utility, one is a formalist, another a latitudinarian, one is timorous of change, another dissatisfied with the present; out of the attrition of diverse minds there is beaten something which has a constancy and uniformity and average value greater than its component elements. The same thing is true of the work of juries. I do not mean to suggest that the product in either case does not betray the flaws inherent in its origin. The flaws are there as in every human institution. Because they are not only there but visible, we have faith that they will be corrected. There is no assurance that the rule of the majority will be the expression of perfect reason when embodied in constitution or in statute. We ought not to expect more of it when embodied in the judgments of the courts. The tide rises and falls but the sands of error crumble.

The work of a judge is in one sense enduring and in another sense ephemeral. What is good in it endures. What is erroneous is pretty sure to perish. The good remains the foundation on which new structures will be built. The bad will be rejected and cast off in the laboratory of the years. Little by little the old doctrine is undermined. Often the encroachments are so gradual that their significance is at first obscured. Finally we discover that the contour of the landscape has been changed, that the old maps must be cast aside, and the ground charted anew. . . .

. . . I sometimes think that we worry ourselves overmuch about the enduring consequences of our errors. They may work a little confusion for a time. In the end, they will be modified or corrected or their teachings ignored. The future takes care of such things. . . .

The future, gentlemen, is yours. We have been called to do our parts in an ageless process. Long after I am dead and gone, and my little part in it is forgotten, you will be here to do your share, and to carry the torch forward. . . .

22

Roscoe Pound

1870–

Roscoe Pound is best known for his twenty years as Dean at Harvard Law School and his writings on jurisprudence.

He was born and raised in Lincoln, Nebraska. He went to college at Nebraska University, majored and took a Ph.D. degree in botany. His botanical competence got him the post of director of the Nebraska Botanical Survey (a part time position) when he was twenty-two, which he held for eleven years.

Pound took two of the three years' course at Harvard Law School, but took no degree. He went back to Nebraska to practice. Soon he was teaching at Nebraska University Law School. After two years' teaching he was made dean. At thirty-seven he moved on for short periods of teaching at Northwestern and Chicago Universities, arriving at Harvard three years later. He served Harvard Law School for thirty-seven years before retiring and has had several short teaching assignments since. Pound served as a judge on the Nebraska Commission of Appeals for two years in his early thirties. He participated in legislative matters as a Commissioner on Uniform State Laws for the State of Nebraska. He studied administrative processes as a member of President Hoover's Commission on Law Enforcement, which was known as the Wickersham Commission and concerned itself with the then-burning problems of national prohibition.

Dean Pound has written voluminously. The work that follows this note is a short summation of his legal credo which was included in a collection of similar statements

called *My Philosophy of Law* published in 1941.

Pound was married twice, is known for his extraordinary memory, has a reputation for skill in speaking to bar associations, and in joining in legal convivialities. He has been honored by universities and learned societies all over the world. Foreign students who come to this country for graduate law study are more likely to know of his works than of those of any other American lawyer.

MY PHILOSOPHY OF LAW *

I think of law as in one sense a highly specialized form of social control in a developed politically organized society—a social control through the systematic and orderly application of the force of such a society. In this sense it is a regime—the regime which we call the legal order. But that regime operates in a systematic and orderly fashion because of a body of authoritative grounds of or guides to determination which may serve as rules of decision, as rules of or guides to conduct, and as bases of prediction of official action, or may be regarded by the bad man, whose attitude is suggested by Mr. Justice Holmes as a test, as threats of official action which he must take account of before he acts or refrains from action. Moreover, it operates through a judicial process and an administrative process, which also go by the name of law—a development and ap-

* Reprinted by permission of the West Publishing Co.

plication of the authoritative grounds of or guides to determination by employing a received and so authoritative technique by the light of received and so authoritative ideals. The idea of system and order and predictability lies behind every meaning which has been given to the term law—to all of what the analytical jurist calls analogous uses of the term—and every application of the word until the rise in recent times of absolutist ideas which would apply the term to whatever is done by those who wield the powers of a politically organized society simply because, and no matter how, they do it.

When, therefore, one asks himself what is the task of the law, what is the end to which this regime, maintained by politically organized societies, adjusting relations and ordering conduct through a judicial and an administrative process, and carried on by employing a body of recognized or established precepts, applied by an authoritative technique in the light of authoritative ideals —when one asks himself what all this complicated machinery is for, the answer must be that the end, whatever it is, is the end of social control of which law in all three of its meanings is a specialized form. But we cannot neglect that question, difficult of answer and far reaching in the implications of the answer as it may be. For received ideas as to the answer, traditionally established, are an important item in the received grounds of or guides to determination of controversies and are decisive in the choice of starting points for legal reasoning, the interpretation of legal precepts and the application of legal standards.

A prevailing type of philosophical thought today, going upon Kantian epistemology, tells us we cannot answer this question. No doubt we cannot answer it absolutely. But law in all its meanings is a practical matter. If we cannot give an answer which will be absolutely demonstrable to every one and wholly convincing to the philosopher, it does not follow that we may not have a good workable blueprint of what we are trying to do and be able to make a good practical approximation to what we seek to achieve.

There are many practical activities the postulates of which will not bear critical logical examination if we demand of them an absolute correspondence of phenomena to theory, but nevertheless serve their practical purposes very well. If, as is now taught, we live in a curved universe in which there are no planes and straight lines and right angles and perpendiculars, it does not follow that we must give up surveying which does its work satisfactorily on the basis of such postulates. If we cannot make a watertight demonstration of the end to which the legal order is directed in practice, if we cannot attain that end completely, the history of civilization shows we can make a continually closer practical approximation, and that it is because of this practical approximation that the legal order and the body of authoritative grounds of or guides to determination have been able to develop and maintain themselves.

What we are seeking to do and must do in a civilized society is to adjust relations and order conduct in a world in which the goods of existence, the scope for free activity, and the objects on which to exert free activity are limited, and the demands upon those goods and those objects are infinite. To order the activities of men in their endeavor to satisfy their demands so as to enable satisfaction of as much of the whole scheme of demands with the least friction and waste has not merely been what lawmakers and tribunals and jurists have been striving for, it has also been put in one way or another by philosophers as what we ought to be doing. Life in accord with nature or measured by reason (that is, in accord with an ideal in which the perfect man seeks only what as such he ought to have, and renders to others as perfect men what they ought to have) reconciling wills of free men in action by a universal law giving a maximum scope for free activity to each, reconciling of what used to be called instincts in action, bringing about a maximum of happiness, satisfying the wants of each so far as compatible with satisfying the wants of all—these are different ways of putting this practical task which the courts and lawyers have been going about doing in a practical way from the time when the rise of political organization of society led to courts and lawyers as agents of organized social control.

If, as lawyers must, we look at law, in all of its senses, functionally with respect to its end, as that end is at bottom the end of social control, our science of law cannot be self-sufficient. Ethics has to do with another great agency of social control covering much of the ground covered by the legal order and having much to tell us as to what legal precepts ought to be and ought to bring about. Security which the law, in an adjustment of relations, has continually to seek to keep in balance with the individual life, is in special degree called for by the economic order which is the subject of another social science. We cannot ignore it in a science of law, but just as some sought to merge jurisprudence in ethics, there are those who would refer everything in law in all of its senses to economics, with no more warrant. Again, there is the science of politics. Since the legal order is a regime of social control through politically organized society, the science which organizes our knowledge of such societies cannot be ignored, although jurists in the English-speaking world have been wont to give it an exaggerated importance in their interpretation of legal history and their accounts of legal institutions. Sociology has for a time gone off into methodology and is more concerned with demonstrating that it is a separate science, by developing its separate method, than with organizing our knowledge of the phenomena of human association. But the science of society did much for the law a generation ago and can do so again particularly in what has been called social pyschology. History is not to be overlooked. The history of civilization has much to tell us of how law has operated to maintain and further civilization, how it has grown out of civilization, how it has been adapted to new types of civilization, and perhaps how at times it has hindered, as at other times it has furthered, civilization. Finally, there is psychology, with much

to tell us not only about the claims and demands we must be busied to reconcile or adjust, but also about the bases of the conduct we seek to order and the underlying bases of the processes, judicial and administrative, as well as the lawmaking process, by which the legal order is maintained and the precepts by which those processes are to be guided and formulated.

From Roman times, except for analytical jurists in the nineteenth century, philosophy has been recognized as something indispensable for the jurist. In a great part of the history of juristic thought it has been misused to frame ideal systems of legal precepts of supposed universal validity for times, places, and men. But it has a task of the first importance in organizing and criticizing the ideal element in the body of authoritative grounds of and guides to determination. When it seeks to do more than that, and, on the one hand, furnish a universal plan or absolute starting points or charts for all times and places, or on the other hand, to tell us that we can't do anything but observe the unfolding of an idea by its intrinsic power or the orbit of development according to fixed laws, as beyond our control as the revolutions of the planets, or that we are inevitably caught in a mess of irreducible antinomies so that we can do no more than let things work themselves out, the lawyer has learned to cease to follow the philosopher and to go on upon the basis of experience developed by reason and reason tested by experience. The philosophical jurisprudence of the seventeenth and eighteenth centuries held that everything in the science of law could be achieved by a sheer exercise of reason. Philosophy was the one necessary instrument of the jurist. The metaphysical jurisprudence of the nineteenth century held that philosophy could demonstrate the idea that was realizing itself in legal development or the orbit of legal evolution, but after showing us these necessary paths from which there was no escape, it could not help us. Much of philosophy of law today is equally assured that we cannot do much toward making law in all its senses achieve its end better. These give-it-up philosophies and the juristic skepticism to which they lead, or which they aid and abet, may serve for philosophies of law. They will not be of help as philosophical jurisprudence.

In the nineteenth century jurists were concerned chiefly with three problems: the nature of law, the interpretation of legal history, and the relation of law and morals.

As to the nature of law, as I see it our difficulties lie in the different meanings for which we have been using the one word. In the languages of Continental Europe the word we translate as law has a meaning for which we have no word in English and conveys an idea very hard for us to understand, which can only be indicated by some such awkward phrase as right-plus-law or what-is-right-backed-by-law. But if we read critically the books in our own tongue we soon perceive that 'law' may mean any one of the three things I indicated at the outset and that some address themselves to the nature of the legal order, some to the nature of the body of authoritative grounds of or guides to decision, and some to the process of adjudication or the process of administration, and assume that a theory of the one will of course do for the other two. Moreover, the oldest of the meanings as employed by jurists, namely, the body of authoritative guides to decision, usually thought of down to Kant and very generally since as a body of rules of conduct, is composite. Instead of being, as Bentham took it to be, an aggregate of laws, that is, of rules in the strict sense, such as the provisions of a penal code, it is made up of precepts, an authoritative technique of developing and applying the precepts, and a body of received ideals as to the end or purpose of the legal order, and hence to what legal precepts ought to be and how they ought to be applied. These received ideals are just as authoritative as the traditionally received precepts and are often much more obstinate and manifestly are longer lived than the rules which were all that the analytical jurist could see in the last century.

But this is not all. The precept element in law in the second sense has no less than four constituents: rules in the strict sense, principles, precepts defining conceptions, and precepts prescribing standards. If all of these could be called rules in a wider sense, yet conceptions and standards, which play very important roles in the administration of justice, are not rules in any sense. Indeed, much harm has been done in American constitutional law by trying to reduce the standard of due process of law to a body of rules analogous to rules of property.

By rules I mean precepts attaching a definite detailed legal consequence to a definite detailed state of facts or situation of fact. Such rules were the staple of ancient codes and are found today chiefly in criminal law, in commercial law, and in the law of property.

By principles I mean authoritative starting points for legal reasoning. They do not attach any definite detailed consequence to any definite, much less detailed, state or situation of fact. They furnish a basis for reasoning when a situation not governed by a precise rule comes up for consideration as to what provision should be made for it. By legal conceptions I mean authoritatively defined categories into which cases may be put with the result that certain rules and principles and standards become applicable. Such things as trust, sale, bailment, will occur to one at once in this connection. Legal standards are defined measures of conduct, to be applied according to the circumstances of each case, entailing liability to respond for resulting injury in case the limits of the standard are departed from. There is no definite state of facts provided for and no definite detailed consequence is prescribed. Examples are the standard of due care, the standard of fair conduct of a fiduciary, the standard of reasonable facilities imposed on a public utility.

When it is pereceived how much we have been seeking to embrace in the one word "law," it will be seen why so much of the discussion as to the nature of law in the last century was so futile.

With the passing of the era of history,

for such was the nineteenth century, the interpretation of legal history is no longer taken to be the key to the science of law, and economics and psychology have arisen to furnish universal solvents instead. As to the relation of law and morals, we have again to contend with difficulties due to the use of one word with more than one meaning in a connection in which the context will not distinguish, because the writer does not. When we write of the relation of law and morals we may mean the relation of the legal order to a received body of ethical custom in a time and place or to an organized body of principles as to what conduct ought to be, not actually obtaining anywhere, but arrived at by speculation instead of by observation. Or we may mean the relation of the body of received grounds of or guides to decision to either or both of what are put under the name "morals." Or we may mean the relation of the judicial or of the administrative process or of both to either or both of the things for which the word 'morals' has been used. It is not unlikely that we may try to reason about the relation of the three to the two as if there were one idea on each side as there is one word. What we can say is that if for convenience we think of the body of received ethical custom as morality and the body of speculative principles as morals, ₌ach of these, as well as law in each of its senses, is an agency of social control. Partly their spheres overlap and in the common area they reinforce or ought to reinforce each other. Partly they deal with matters exclusively in their own domain, where nevertheless they may and do influence each other. But beyond this general statement one cannot go without distinguishing the different meanings of each word.

Today, in my judgment, the most important problem which confronts the jurist is the theory of interests. A legal system attains the ends of the legal order (1) by recognizing certain interests, individual, public, and social; (2) by defining the limits within which these interests shall be recognized legally and given effect through legal precepts; and (3) by endeavoring to secure the interests so recognized within the defined limits. I should define an interest, for the present purpose, as a demand or desire which human beings either individually or in groups or in associations or in relations, seek to satisfy, of which, therefore, the ordering of human relations must take account. This needs to be put psychologically, but we must avoid the controverted questions of group psychology. It is not group demands or desires, but the strivings of men in (or perhaps one should say through) groups and associations and relations to satisfy certain demands or desires. The legal order or the law does not create these interests. There is this much truth in the old idea of a state of nature and theory of natural rights, namely, that interests in this sense would exist if there were no legal order but were some other form of social control, and no body of authoritative guides to conduct or decision. Conflicts or competition between interests arise because of the competition of individuals with each other, the competition of groups or societies of men with each other, and the competition of individuals with such groups or societies, in the endeavor to satisfy human wants. The law, then, does not create these interests. But it classifies them and recognizes a larger or smaller number. Also it defines the extent to which it will give effect to these interests which it recognizes. It may do this in view of other interests. These other interests may be directly recognized and limited or secured, for example, by creating a legal right enforceable by action at law, or by a legal power such as the power of the wife to pledge the husband's credit for necessaries, so that the limits of the right or power must be fixed. For example, the right of reputation is limited by the privilege of confidential communication, and the power of the wife is limited to cases of living apart without her fault. Or the extent to which it will give effect to recognized interests may be limited in view of other interests which get only indirect recognition through limitations imposed on expressly recognized interests. For example, at common law the interest of the child is indirectly recognized by limiting the father's privilege of correction. Or the extent to which legally recognized interests are given effect may be limited in view of the possibilities of effectively securing them through the legal order. Next, the legal order devises means for securing interests when recognized and within the defined limits.

Hence in determining the scope and subject matter of the legal system we have to consider five things: (1) we must take an inventory of the interests which press for recognition and must generalize them and classify them; (2) we must select and determine the interests which the law should recognize and seek to secure; (3) we must fix the limits of securing the interests so selected—this, for example, is the whole problem in the secondary boycott cases; (4) we must consider the means by which the law may secure interests when recognized and delimited, that is, we must take account of the limitations upon effective legal action which may preclude complete recognition or complete securing of interests which otherwise we seek to secure, as, for example, in the case of the rights of husband and wife to consortium as against each other; (5) in order to do these things we must work out principles of valuation of interests. The chief importance of these principles is in determining what interests to recognize, or, in other words, in selection of interests to be recognized. But we must use these principles also in fixing the limits of securing recognized interests, and fixing upon the means of securing interests, and in judging of the weight to be accorded in any given case to the practical limitations upon effective legal action.

We are told nowadays that it is impossible to find a measure of values. But some such measure will be used as different ones have been used in different stages of legal development in the past. Moreover, a practical one, as pointed out above has long been used and has worked reasonably well. It is when courts and lawmakers have departed from this to follow philosophical theories not based on scientifically developed experience that difficulties have arisen. The practitioner of the last generation was distinctly ahead of the jurists if we judge his practice and their theories by the direction which the law has been taking in the last three decades. Bringing to bear upon these problems scientific scrutiny of experience in finding how to deal effectively with concrete cases, being cautious about generalizations and universal formulas, useful as they are when enough concrete observation is behind them, if not a method of jurisprudence, is the method of Anglo-American law and has been the method which has enabled that system of law to go round the world. If we are inclined to scoff at the practitioner, let us remember the warning of William James that the worst enemies of a subject are the professors thereof.

Index

References are to pages. Symbols L and R refer to left and right hand columns of the page.